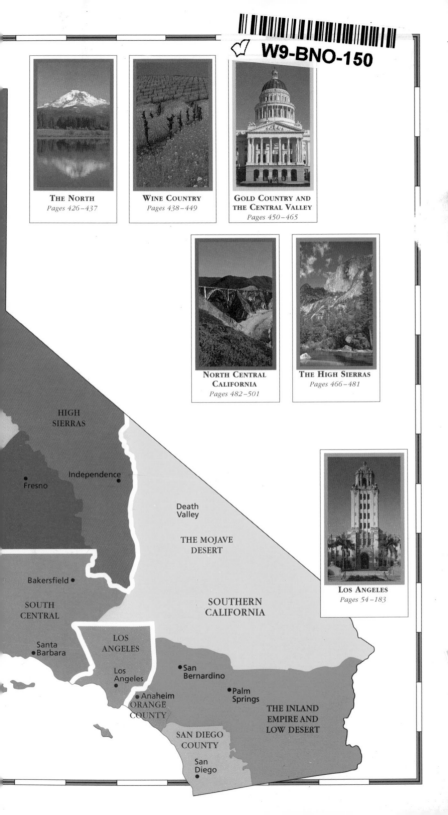

W9-BNO-150

THE NORTH
Pages 426–437

WINE COUNTRY
Pages 438–449

GOLD COUNTRY AND THE CENTRAL VALLEY
Pages 450–465

NORTH CENTRAL CALIFORNIA
Pages 482–501

THE HIGH SIERRAS
Pages 466–481

LOS ANGELES
Pages 54–183

HIGH
SIERRAS

Independence

Fresno

Death
Valley

THE MOJAVE
DESERT

Bakersfield

SOUTH
CENTRAL

SOUTHERN
CALIFORNIA

Santa
Barbara

LOS
ANGELES

Los
Angeles

San
Bernardino

Anaheim
ORANGE
COUNTY

Palm
Springs

THE INLAND
EMPIRE AND
LOW DESERT

SAN DIEGO
COUNTY

San
Diego

EYEWITNESS TRAVEL GUIDES

CALIFORNIA

EYEWITNESS TRAVEL GUIDES

CALIFORNIA

DK PUBLISHING

LONDON • NEW YORK • MUNICH
MELBOURNE • DELHI

Produced by Duncan Baird Publishers, London, England
MANAGING EDITOR Louise Bostock Lang MANAGING ART EDITOR
Clare Sullivan EDITORS Slaney Begley, Joanne Levêque, Zoë Ross
EDITORIAL ASSISTANT Leo Hollis DESIGNERS Christine Keilty, Susan
Knight, Jill Mumford, Alison Verity US EDITOR Mary Sutherland

MAIN CONTRIBUTORS Jamie Jensen, Barry Parr,
Ellen Payne, J Kingston Pierce, Rebecca Poole Forée, Nigel
Tisdall, John Wilcock, Stanley Young

PHOTOGRAPHERS
Max Alexander, Peter Anderson, John Heseltine, Dave King,
Neil Lukas, Andrew McKinney, Neil Setchfield

PICTURE RESEARCH Lindsay Hunt

ILLUSTRATORS
Arcana Studios, Joanna Cameron, Stephen Conlin, Dean
Entwhistle, Nick Lipscombe, Lee Peters, Robbie Polley, Kevin
Robinson, John Woodcock

Reproduced by Colourscan (Singapore)
Printed and bound by South China Printing Co. Ltd., China

First American Edition, 1997
03 04 05 10 9 8 7 6

Published in the United States by
DK Publishing, Inc., 375 Hudson Street,
New York, New York 10014

Reprinted with revisions 1999, 2000, 2001, 2002, 2003
Copyright © 1997, 2003 Dorling Kindersley Limited, London
A Penguin Company

PUBLISHED IN GREAT BRITAIN BY DORLING KINDERSLEY LTD.

A CATALOGING IN PUBLICATION RECORD IS AVAILABLE FROM THE
LIBRARY OF CONGRESS.

ISBN 0-7894-9429-9

See our complete product line at
www.dk.com

CONTENTS

Volleyball on Pismo Beach

LOS ANGELES

Half Dome in Yosemite National Park

State Capitol
building in
Sacramento

HOW TO USE THIS GUIDE

THIS GUIDE helps you to get the most from your stay in California. *Introducing California* maps the whole state and sets it in its historical and cultural context. The ten regional chapters, plus *Los Angeles* and *San Francisco and the Bay Area*, describe important sights with maps, pictures, and illustrations, as well as introductory features on subjects of regional interest.

Suggestions on restaurants, accommodations, shopping, and entertainment are in *Travelers' Needs*. The *Survival Guide* has tips on getting around the state. LA, San Francisco, and San Diego have their own *Practical Information* sections.

LOS ANGELES AND SAN FRANCISCO AND THE BAY AREA

The centers of the two major cities have been divided into a number of sightseeing areas. Each area has its own chapter that opens with a list of the sights described. All the sights are numbered and plotted on an *Area Map*. Information on each sight is easy to locate within the chapter as it follows the numerical order on the map.

Sights at a Glance lists the chapter's sights by category: Historic Streets and Buildings, Shops, Modern Architecture, etc.

A locator map shows where you are in relation to other areas of the city center.

All pages relating to Los Angeles have lilac thumb tabs. San Francisco pages have grass-green thumb tabs.

1 Area Map
For easy reference, the sights are numbered and located on a map. The sights are also shown on the Los Angeles Street Finder *(see pp172–83) or the* San Francisco Street Finder *(see pp384–93).*

2 Street-by-Street Map
This gives a bird's-eye view of the heart of each sightseeing area.

A suggested route for a walk covers the more interesting streets in the area.

Stars indicate sights that no visitor should miss.

3 Detailed Information on Each Sight
All the sights in Los Angeles and in San Francisco and the Bay Area are described individually. Addresses and practical information are provided. The key to the symbols used in the information block is shown on the back flap.

Story boxes explore specific subjects in more detail.

1 Introduction
The landscape, history, and character of each region is described here, showing how the area has developed over the centuries and what it offers to the visitor today.

NORTHERN CALIFORNIA AND SOUTHERN CALIFORNIA
Apart from San Francisco and the Bay Area and Los Angeles, California has been divided into two regions (Northern and Southern California), each of which has five separate area chapters. The most interesting towns and places to visit are numbered on a *Pictorial Map* at the beginning of each chapter.

Each area of California can be identified quickly by its own color coding, which is shown on the inside front cover.

2 Pictorial Map
This shows the main road network and gives an illustrated overview of the whole area. All entries are numbered, and there are also useful tips on getting around the region.

3 Detailed Information
All the important towns and other places to visit are described individually. They are listed in order, following the numbering on the Pictorial Map. *Within each entry, information is given on the most important sights. A map reference refers the reader to the road map inside the back cover.*

For all the top sights, a visitors' checklist provides the practical information you need to plan your visit.

4 California's Top Sights
These are given two or more full pages. Historic buildings are dissected to reveal their interiors; museums and galleries have color-coded floor plans to help you locate the most interesting exhibits; national parks and forests have maps showing facilities and trails.

INTRODUCING
CALIFORNIA

Putting California on the Map

CALIFORNIA IS THE THIRD largest state in the US (after Texas and Alaska) and, with over 30 million people, the most populous. Situated on the Pacific Coast, it is 800 miles (1,300 km) long and 250 miles (400 km) wide, covering an area of 158,710 sq miles (411,060 sq km). The state has two major cities: San Francisco and Los Angeles. Most visitors arrive via the airports in one of these cities; the main cities and towns are linked with each other and with other states by an extensive rail (Amtrak) and road system.

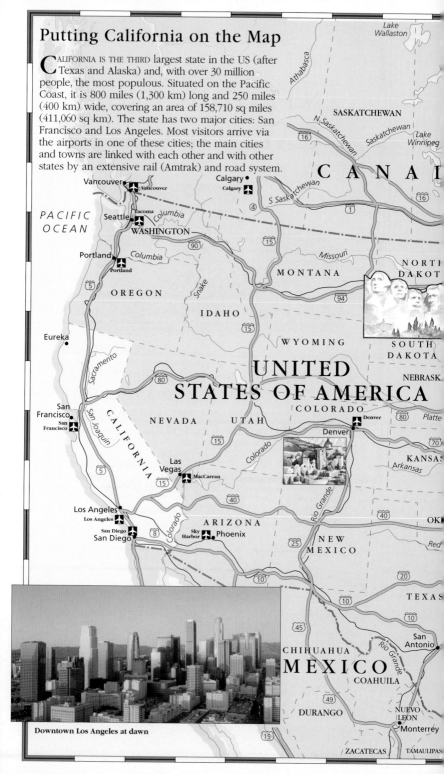

Downtown Los Angeles at dawn

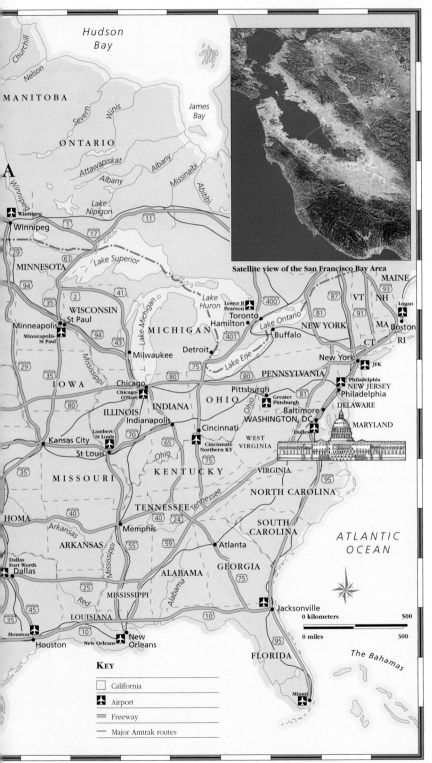

A

Hudson Bay

Churchill

Nelson

MANITOBA

ONTARIO

Severn

Winis

Attawapiskat

Albany

Albany

Missinaibi

Abitibi

James Bay

Lake Nipigon

Winnipeg

Winnipeg

(11)

(1)

(17)

(29)

(61)

MINNESOTA

Lake Superior

(94)

(35)

(2)

(41)

WISCONSIN

St Paul

Minneapolis

Minneapolis-St Paul

(94)

(43)

Lake Michigan

MICHIGAN

Lake Huron

Milwaukee

Detroit

Lake Erie

(401)

Hamilton

Toronto

Lester B Pearson

(400)

Lake Ontario

Buffalo

(81)

(87)

VT NH

MAINE

(93)

Logan

NEW YORK

MA Boston

CT RI

(91)

Mississippi

(29)

(35)

IOWA

Chicago

Chicago-O'Hare

(80)

ILLINOIS

INDIANA

Indianapolis

OHIO

Ohio

Pittsburgh

(80)

New York

JFK

(81)

PENNSYLVANIA

Philadelphia

NEW JERSEY

Philadelphia

DELAWARE

(75)

(80)

Greater Pittsburgh

Baltimore

WASHINGTON, DC

Dulles

MARYLAND

Kansas City

Lambert St Louis

St Louis

(70)

(65)

Cincinnati

Cincinnati Northern KY

(75)

WEST VIRGINIA

MISSOURI

Ohio

KENTUCKY

VIRGINIA

(95)

(35)

NORTH CAROLINA

Tennessee

TENNESSEE

(40)

(24)

SOUTH CAROLINA

HOMA

(40)

Arkansas

Memphis

(55)

(59)

Atlanta

ATLANTIC OCEAN

ARKANSAS

Mississippi

Dallas Fort Worth

Dallas

(25)

ALABAMA

GEORGIA

(75)

Alabama

Red

(45)

MISSISSIPPI

(10)

LOUISIANA

Jacksonville

(35)

Houston

Houston

(10)

New Orleans

New Orleans

(95)

FLORIDA

The Bahamas

Satellite view of the San Francisco Bay Area

0 kilometers   500

0 miles   300

Miami

KEY

☐ California

✈ Airport

▬ Freeway

— Major Amtrak routes

A PORTRAIT OF CALIFORNIA

IMPRESSIVE FOR BOTH ITS SIZE *and its sway over modern culture, California symbolizes the United States' diversity and sense of prosperity. Here can be found towering forests, deserts within half a day's drive of ocean beaches, and two of the world's foremost cities, San Francisco and Los Angeles.*

State seal

Perceptions of California vary so greatly that some now joke that there are two states. The first is geographic: California is the third-largest state in the Union (after Alaska and Texas), containing its largest county, San Bernardino, which covers 20,155 sq miles (52,200 sq km) – larger than Vermont and New Hampshire combined. This California has 840 miles (1,350 km) of coastline and measures 365 miles (587 km) at its widest point. It claims the second highest peak in the country (Mount Whitney) and its lowest expanse of dry land (Death Valley). More than 1,500 plant species grow here that cannot be found anywhere else on earth. Roughly one in every eight Americans is a Californian, making this the most populous of the 50 states, represented by the largest congressional delegation.

And that other California? It is a realm of romance, formed by flickering celluloid images. Think "California" and pictures are immediately conjured up of bikini-clad beachcombers, middle-class suburban families in ranch houses, and film stars emerging from limousines into hordes of autograph-seekers. These stereotypes are perpetuated by the entertainment and tourism media.

Hollywood is only partly to blame for this blurring of fact and fiction. It goes back to Spanish legends of an exotic outpost called California, flung

Sun-worshipers on Manhattan Beach, Los Angeles

◁ Roller coaster at Knott's Berry Farm, Orange County

Joshua Tree National Park

out at the edge of the sea. Most of the world, though, knew nothing of this spot until the Gold Rush of 1849. Tales of the riches to be found encouraged thousands of would-be Croesuses to invade the region. Whether they found their fortunes or not, prospectors spread the same message: California was not as colorful or seductive as they had been told. It was even more so.

SOCIETY AND POLITICS

If the US as a whole is a melting pot of people, California is an ethnic microcosm. It receives the highest number of immigrants (more than 200,000 annually), and the racial makeup is the most diverse in the nation. The percentage of whites and African-Americans is lower than the national average, but the Asian residency is more than triple the national level. Hispanics account for more than a quarter of all Californians – three times the US average. Walk through any of the four most-populated cities

(LA, San Diego, San Jose, and San Francisco), and you receive an immediate taste of this ethnic cocktail. It is still more potent during Mexican *Cinco de Mayo* (May 5) festivities, Chinese New Year bashes, and other multicultural events held around the state.

Racial prejudice has plagued the state since its early days. Abolitionists prevented California's 1849 constitutional convention from barring the entry of blacks into this land, but in the 1870s nativist orators such as Denis Kearney endorsed violence against Chinese immigrants, said to be "stealing" white jobs. Sadly, overcrowding is reigniting racial tensions today, with overpopulation having a negative effect on law enforcement and education. It is raising the already high student–teacher ratios in California's schools, which have been short of funding since property taxes, a source of revenue for state and local governments, were cut and capped in 1978.

Surfer

But the most inevitable result of population growth has been an altered balance between rural and urban sectors. More people means that more land is needed for housing. The

Golden Gate Bridge, San Francisco

Red Rock Canyon in the Mojave Desert

value of California's agricultural goods still outranks that of all other states, but its farmland has declined steadily since the 1950s. Lumber workers have also had a hard time, because of conservation measures and a continuing

California oranges

shrinkage of the state's forests. The fastest-expanding job markets now are in service industries and high technology, which suggest a more metropolitan than pastoral future. Visitors usually come to California to see one of two cities: San Francisco or Los Angeles. In the north and south of the state respectively, these cities define the opposing sides of its character: San Francisco is older and more compact. Although California in general is recognized for its eccentricities and is still the birthplace of new trends, San Francisco is particularly proud of its nonconformity and open-mindedness. It was here that the "Big Four" railroad barons built their millionaire's mansions, but the city has since evolved into a pro-labor hotbed, with a history of activism (the Bay Area was a hub of the anti-Vietnam War movement). It also

has one of the world's largest concentrations of gays and lesbians, with a substantial gay vote.

In contrast to San Francisco, LA is a sprawling city without a real focal point. The car rules, demanding a network of freeways that have hemmed in some of the city's historical buildings and which grind to smoggy standstills during rush hours. The façades of wealth, fame, and glamour leave LA as a dimensionless creation of bright lights and conservative politics.

Wild poppies in Antelope Valley

This is not to say that the north is entirely Democrat (left wing) and the south, Republican (right wing). Hollywood is a chief sponsor of liberal causes, and there are pockets of antigovernment rebels in the northeast. But the conflicting power that the two cities exert on state government in Sacramento

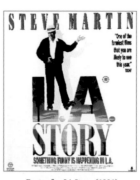
Poster for *LA Story* (1991)

and the state's representatives in Washington, DC explains why California may appear a little schizophrenic.

CULTURE AND LEISURE

High- and low-brow art enjoy comparable support here. For most people, the state's contributions to culture are the many blockbusters made by Hollywood movie studios or televised sitcoms shot on LA sound stages. This is art in unashamed pursuit of the almighty dollar, complete with tabloid scandals and giant movie billboards blotting out the Los Angeles sun. But another creativity reveals itself through the state's history of landscape painting, portraiture, and 20th-century avant-garde art. Modern artists John

McLaughlin and Elmer Bischoff, and ceramists Peter Voulkos and Robert Arneson have all made international reputations. So have a few pioneers of photographic art, such as Imogen Cunningham and Ansel Adams. British artist David Hockney lived here for many years, capturing the state's sun-soaked image on canvas. California is also home to some of the world's finest art museums, including LACMA, the Oakland Museum, the San Francisco MOMA, and the two J Paul Getty Museums. Victorian architecture in the Bay Area has always been a major tourist attraction, as have the many historic buildings across the state designed by Californians such as Willis Polk and Bernard Maybeck. Visiting designers Frank Lloyd Wright and Daniel Burnham have left their

Al Pacino receiving an Academy Award in 1993

Napa Valley Train in Wine Country

El Capitán in Yosemite National Park

mark here, too. Recent influential architects include residents Frank Gehry and Joe Esherick.

The state has seen many writers over the years, including Nobel prize-winner John Steinbeck and Beat authors Jack Kerouac and Allen Ginsburg. The tradition continues with Armistead Maupin *(Tales of the City)*, detective novelist Sue Grafton, and Amy Tan *(The Joy Luck Club)*, among others. Music also plays a major role, whether the work of the cities' orchestras or rock musicians. This is where the Beach Boys, Janis Joplin, the Grateful Dead, and Red Hot Chili Peppers launched their careers.

Californians love to eat out, and chefs Wolfgang Puck and Alice Waters have made their name promoting "California cuisine" – a blend of local ingredients and Asian techniques. This, combined with a selection of local world-class wines, is proof that Californians take care of their palates. Yet residents

are also body-conscious, aware that they live among the "beautiful people" who come here with dreams of film stardom. So they become slaves to the gym or take up a sport. On any weekend, in various parts of the state, you will see cyclists, surfers, in-line skaters, even white-water rafters. Californians are eager supporters of professional baseball and football, but they like to be active themselves. Luckily, surrounded by some of the nation's most beautiful countryside and the gentlest climate, they don't have to go far to enjoy a satisfying outdoor experience.

Padres baseball stadium in San Diego

California's Landscape and Geology

CALIFORNIA'S DRAMATIC LANDSCAPE includes the highest point in the US, Mount Whitney in the High Sierras, and the lowest, Death Valley in the southern deserts. Millions of years ago, subduction of the Pacific Ocean floor beneath the North American Plate created the Coastal Range, the Central Valley, and the granitic rocks of the Sierra Nevada Mountains. Later, the granites were uplifted and tilted westward. The meeting of tectonic plates, now a lateral movement along the San Andreas Fault, is still changing the shape of California.

The Coastal Range along *the Pacific Coast was created around 25 million years ago, when fragments of the ocean floor and oceanic islands were pushed up by plate movements.*

HOW THE WEST WAS MADE

Over a period of 150 million years, ending about 15 million years ago, the movement of the Pacific Plate and North American Plate formed the western margin of California.

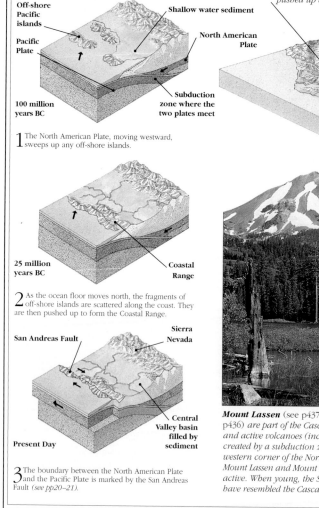

Off-shore Pacific islands

Shallow water sediment

Pacific Plate

North American Plate

100 million years BC

Subduction zone where the two plates meet

1 The North American Plate, moving westward, sweeps up any off-shore islands.

25 million years BC

Coastal Range

2 As the ocean floor moves north, the fragments of off-shore islands are scattered along the coast. They are then pushed up to form the Coastal Range.

San Andreas Fault

Sierra Nevada

Present Day

Central Valley basin filled by sediment

3 The boundary between the North American Plate and the Pacific Plate is marked by the San Andreas Fault (see pp20–21).

MOUNT SHASTA
14,162 ft (4,317 m)

Mount Lassen (see p437) *and Mount Shasta* (see p436) *are part of the Cascades, a range of extinct and active volcanoes (including Mount St. Helens) created by a subduction zone beneath the north-western corner of the North American Plate. Both Mount Lassen and Mount Shasta are still considered active. When young, the Sierra Nevada range must have resembled the Cascades.*

Lemon trees *flourish in central California. The highly fertile surface sediments of the flat Central Valley come from erosion of the surrounding mountains. The sediments have accumulated over the last few hundred thousand years.*

Mount Whitney *(see p479) in the High Sierras is the highest point in the continental United States, rising to 14,494 ft (4,418 m). The process that raised the Sierra Nevada Mountains began more than 50 million years ago, but peaked a few million years ago.*

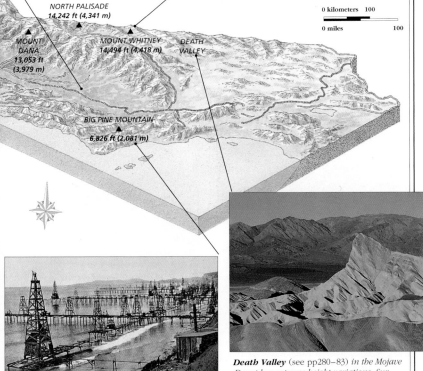

NORTH PALISADE
14,242 ft (4,341 m)

MOUNT
DANA
13,053 ft
(3,979 m)

MOUNT WHITNEY
14,494 ft (4,418 m)

DEATH
VALLEY

BIG PINE MOUNTAIN
6,826 ft (2,081 m)

0 kilometers 100

0 miles 100

Oil wells *sprang up at a frantic pace when oil was discovered in California. The drilling was so intense that the extraction of oil and gas deflated the land. Part of Los Angeles County subsided 28 ft (8.5 m) before oil companies were required to pump sea water down the wells to replace the extracted fuels.*

Death Valley *(see pp280–83) in the Mojave Desert has extreme height variations. Surrounded by some of the highest mountains on the continent, the valley floor lies 280 ft (85 m) below sea level. Death Valley was formed less than 15 million years ago when the North American Plate began to stretch due to the northwest drag created by the Pacific Plate.*

California's Earthquakes

THE SAN ANDREAS FAULT extends almost the full length of California, some 600 miles (965 km) from the Gulf of California northwest to Cape Mendocino. It is not the only fault in California but is the line of most activity. Each year, on average, the Pacific Plate moves 1–1.6 inches (2.5–4 cm) to the northwest. Earthquakes occur when this movement is resisted. Stresses build up and eventually they are released, causing an earthquake. Many of California's major earthquakes have occurred in the northern section of the fault. The terrible fire of 1906 that destroyed San Francisco was caused by an earthquake estimated at 7.8 on the Richter Scale. More recently, the earthquake of October 1989, south of San Francisco, killed 62 people and caused at least $6 billion worth of damage *(see p489)*. In 1994, the Northridge quake, magnitude R6.7, rocked Los Angeles and was felt in Las Vegas, Nevada. Scientists now predict that the next major earthquake, the "Big One," will hit Southern California.

The San Andreas Fault *is one of the few sites on earth where an active plate boundary occurs on land.*

Hayward Fault

1989 earthquake epicenter

1989 earthquake hypocenter

The 1906 earthquake *confounded contemporary geologists and led to the "elastic rebound" theory of earthquake formation, which is still in use today.*

The 1989 earthquake *struck the Santa Cruz Mountains in central California.*

TIMELINE

1750	1800	1850	1900	1950

1769 Members of Portolá's expedition are first Europeans to experience an earthquake in California

1865 San Francisco hit by its first major earthquake on October 9 and another on October 23

1872 Town of Lone Pine is destroyed and Sierra Nevada Mountains rise 13 ft (4m)

1952 Kern County (R7.7)

1940 Imperial Valley (R7.1)

1992 Yucca Valley outside LA (R7.4)

1989 Loma Prieta (R7.1) strikes San Francisco area

Don Gaspar de Portolá

1857 Fort Tejon (R8) is followed by smaller earth tremors in Bay Area

1906 San Francisco earthquake (R7.8) causes a devastating three-day fire that leaves 3,000 dead and 250,000 homeless

1994 Northridge (R6.7). At least 56 people killed, more than 7,000 injured, and 20,000 made homeless. Anaheim Stadium and several Los Angeles freeways are badly damaged

The 1994 earthquake *caused havoc in the Los Angeles area. Collapsed overpasses closed the Santa Monica Freeway and Interstate 5 near Valencia. Fires caused damage in the San Fernando Valley and in Malibu and Venice.*

Seismically safe housing *is designed to withstand the stresses caused by the ground shaking during an earthquake. Every time a strong earthquake occurs, scientists carefully measure how various structural designs respond to earthquake motion.*

The movement of plates is most pronounced along the San Andreas Fault Zone. Friction sometimes causes the fault to "stick."

Garlock Fault

Elsinore Fault

Los Angeles

Santa Barbara

San Diego

San Andreas Fault

S (secondary) waves travel through solid parts of the crust.

North American Plate

PACIFIC PLATE MEETS NORTH AMERICAN PLATE

The San Andreas Fault is a major fracture in the earth's crust. It is the result of friction where two plates meet – the Pacific Plate (consisting of most of the Pacific Ocean and the California coastline) and the North American Plate.

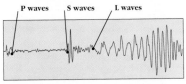

P waves   S waves   L waves

Pacific Plate   Hypocenter

P (primary) waves travel through the earth's core.

It is possible *to calculate the magnitude of an earthquake from a seismograph recording. Printouts show the intensity of earthquake vibrations graphically. The magnitude of the earthquake is registered on the Richter Scale (R).*

Earthquake energy vibrations *move through the earth's crust in waves. There are three types of wave: P or primary waves, S or secondary waves, and L or surface waves. The waves change as energy moves from the hypocenter to the earth's surface. Surface waves cause most of the damage associated with earthquakes.*

Literary California

AS JOURNALIST Carey McWilliams remarked in 1946, "What America is, California is, with accents, in italics." The chance to study the nation in microcosm has been especially appealing to authors. Many, such as Robert Louis Stevenson (1850–94), have simply passed through. He arrived in Monterey in 1879 and later based scenes in *Treasure Island* on the surrounding coastline. But California has not lacked for resident wordsmiths. This, after all, is where Henry Miller (1891–1980) blended erotic and verbal inventiveness and William Saroyan (1908–81) found his eccentric rural characters. Nobel prize-winning playwright Eugene O'Neill (1888–1953) produced some of his best work at Tao House in the Ramon Valley *(see p410)*. California is also where several successful contemporary writers, such as Amy Tan (born in 1952), now chase their muse.

Mask used in plays at Tao House

Robert Louis Stevenson, author of *Treasure Island*

THE PIONEERS

MUCH OF the very early writing about California was unsophisticated, satisfying readers who simply wanted a taste of the frontier environment. But the Gold Rush *(see pp44–5)* created a market for prose that captured the poignancy, romance, and raw humor of life in the West. Bay Area literary journals such as *The Golden Era* and *The Overland Monthly* nurtured many local fiction writers. These included Bret Harte (1836–1902), the author of *The Luck of Roaring Camp,* essayist Henry George (1839–97), and bards ranging from Joaquin Miller (1837–1913) to Ina Coolbrith (the nation's first poet laureate in 1915).

The literary journals also provided an apprenticeship for San Franciscan writer Samuel Clemens (1835–1910). His 1865 publication of the Gold Country yarn, "The Celebrated Jumping Frog of Calaveras County," introduced him to a national readership as Mark Twain.

Writer Samuel Clemens, alias Mark Twain

THE SOCIAL CRITICS

AMBROSE BIERCE (1842–1914) ranked among the first of many California writers who used their art to advocate wide-ranging political and social reforms. During the late 19th century, Bierce filled his *San Francisco Examiner* column with tirades against hypocrites and bureaucrats. His poisonous articles helped to trim the overweening influence of the vast Southern Pacific Railroad Company *(see pp46–7)*.

Frank Norris (1870–1902) attacked America's greed in his novel, *McTeague* (1899). In *The Octopus,* Norris also lashed out at the Southern Pacific, this time for its monopolistic mistreatment of ranchers in the San Joaquin Valley.

Back from the Klondike Gold Rush (setting for *The Call of the Wild*), working-

class author Jack London alternated between writing adventure novels and stories – such as *The Iron Heel* – that showed his faith in Marxism.

Upton Sinclair (1878–1968) had already published *The Jungle,* his exposé of the Chicago stockyards, when he moved to California after World War I. But it was in Pasadena that he wrote most of his novels, campaigning against poverty and inequality.

Social injustice was a frequent theme for Salinas-born novelist John Steinbeck (1902–68). *Tortilla Flat* (1935), about a band of Mexican-American outcasts, was his first success. It was *The Grapes of Wrath* (1939), however, that brought him the prestigious Pulitzer Prize for

Jack London at his Sonoma Valley ranch

Steinbeck on the Californian coast

Literature. Steinbeck's book so powerfully portrayed the miseries endured by migratory laborers that it was banned from public libraries in some parts of the state.

THE CRIME WRITERS

THREE CALIFORNIA writers established the American school of private-eye fiction. The first of these was Dashiell Hammett (1884–1961), a tubercular former Pinkerton Agency detective and San Francisco resident. He began writing for *Black Mask* and other "pulp" crime-fiction magazines in the 1920s. He then went on to produce five novels, including *The Maltese Falcon* (1930). Hammett's work boasted a grim realism not found in either British whodunits or more venal tales by pulp writers lacking his investigative credentials.

Raymond Chandler (1888–1959) was less intimate with urban "mean streets," but was a more lyrical storyteller.

Poster for the film adaptation of Hammett's *The Maltese Falcon*

Chandler was an oil company executive in Los Angeles until he was sacked for drunkenness. He went on to create the quintessential American detective – Philip Marlowe, star of seven novels, the best being *Farewell, My Lovely* and *The Long Goodbye*. But it was Ross Macdonald (né Kenneth Millar) who finally rounded off his genre's rough edges and confirmed LA as its ideal setting. Macdonald was also the most prolific of this trio. He wrote 19 novels about sleuth Lew Archer, including *The Underground Man*.

Beat writers and friends, Jack Kerouac and Neal Cassady

THE BEATS

PROTEST AGAINST the political conservatism of President Eisenhower's America and against the conventions of society and art combined to produce San Francisco's "Beat Movement" of the 1950s. The Beats (or "Beatniks," as *San Francisco Chronicle* columnist Herb Caen labeled them) were led by the writers Allen Ginsberg (1926–97), Jack Kerouac (1922–69), and William Burroughs (1914–97). They extolled poetry made up of random word usages, produced stream-of-consciousness, drug-assisted narratives, and shunned social, literary, and sexual restraints.

The Beatniks' rebellion officially began in December, 1955, when Ginsberg gave a public reading of his poem "Howl," which was more like a shouting. Despite protests that "Howl" was obscene, it was subsequently published by San Franciscan Lawrence Ferlinghetti, poet and owner of City Lights *(see p330)*, the first paperbacks-only bookshop in the United States.

Two years later, Kerouac's novel *On the Road* spread the Beats' bohemian ethic nationwide. The most influential of the Beat writers, Kerouac also wrote *Desolation Angels* and *The Dharma Bums*, both novels set in California. By 1960 the Beat movement was waning, but not before it had paved the way for that decade's hippie movement.

THE MODERNS

TODAY, MOST best-seller lists feature at least one novel by a California author. The state has many distinctive young voices, such as Ethan Canin (*The Palace Thief*, 1988), Michael Chabon (*The Wonder Boys*, 1995), and Ron Hansen (*Mariette in Ecstasy*, 1991). More established authors, such as Joan Didion (*A Book of Common Prayer*, 1977), Amy Tan (*The Joy Luck Club*, 1989, *The Bonesetter's Daughter*, 2001), and Alice Walker (*The Color Purple*, 1985), are still shining as brightly as ever. There are also many genre writers in California, including James Ellroy (*LA Confidential*, 1990), Dean Koontz (*Sole Survivor*, 2000), and Sue Grafton (*P is for Peril*, 2001), all adding new depth to detective fiction.

Novelist Amy Tan

Art in California

IN THE WAKE of the Gold Rush *(see pp44–5)*, California became both a magnet and a breeding ground for artists. They generally eschewed native folk traditions, however, in favor of European aesthetics that, while making the most of this new land and its people, were not dramatically changed by it. Only after World War II did Californians – including painter Richard Diebenkorn and photographer Imogen Cunningham – shed subservience to Old World art movements in order to develop distinctive visual trends, which then spread internationally. Since the 1950s, Los Angeles has challenged San Francisco's cultural primacy, and California art has become a highly valued investment.

Figure on a Porch (1959) by Richard Diebenkorn

PAINTERS

CALIFORNIA'S mountain and desert landscapes and dramatic ocean shores dominated painters' attention here during the late 19th century. Thomas Hill (1829–1908) was born in England and trained in Paris. He moved to California in 1861 and began to produce epic natural panoramas, especially of the stunning Yosemite Valley *(see pp472–5)*. His work not only attracted new visitors to the West Coast but also helped win Yosemite its national park status in 1890. Even more popular was William Keith (1838–1911), a Scotsman who spent 50 years portraying the state's virgin

wilderness. At that time, cities and people may have seemed comparatively pale inspirations. Yet Gilded Age California *(see pp46–7)* could not now be fully understood without such talents as William Hahn (1829–87), a German immigrant who captured life in nascent San Francisco; Grace Carpenter Hudson (1865–1937), renowned for her portraits of coastal natives; and William A Coulter (1849–1936), who recorded maritime scenes.

As early as 1900, the state's two halves displayed stylistically disparate growth. In the north, Xavier Martinez (1869–1943) and his fellow Tonalists filled canvases with the familiar hazy light and gray-brown hues of their

environment. In the south, Guy Rose (1867–1925) led an Impressionist school that used the region's vibrant colors and brighter light to produce Monet-like effects.

Prohibition-era Los Angeles flirted with the Synchromist style of Stanton Macdonald-Wright (1890–1973). San Francisco was enchanted by Cubist Realists such as Otis Oldfield (1890–1969). Another popular artist there was the great Mexican muralist Diego Rivera, who in 1940 composed *Panamerican Mind*, an enormous fresco that can be seen at the City College.

Modernism flowered fully in California after World War II. It was at that time that David Park (1911–60), Richard Diebenkorn (born in 1922), and other members of the Bay Area Figurative School began to blend Expressionism with realistic imagery. In Southern California, Hard-Edge Abstractionists such as Helen Lundeberg and John McLaughlin (1898–1976) drew critical acclaim with their large-scale geometric shapes.

What is remarkable about contemporary California painters is not simply the worldwide recognition that they have earned, but their stylistic breadth. They range from Pop Artist Ed Ruscha (born in 1937) and urban landscapist Wayne Thiebaud (born in 1920), to cutting-edge British émigré David Hockney (born in 1937) and Arthur Carraway (born in 1927), whose work celebrates his African-American heritage.

Afternoon in Piedmont (Elsie at the Window) by Xavier Martinez

Two Callas by Imogen Cunningham

PHOTOGRAPHERS

MANY EARLY California photographs were either portraits or straightforward documentary scenes done by surveyors. Some photographers, however, such as Eadweard James Muybridge (1830–1904), found photography no less powerful than painting in depicting nature. Others preferred to focus on human subjects. Allegorical nudes and other images by Anne Brigman (1869–1950) found fans even in New York City. Arnold Genthe (1869–1942) studied the Bay Area's Asian community, producing (with writer Will Irwin) a 1913 volume called *Pictures of Old Chinatown*.

In 1932 an Oakland group called "f/64" mounted a major exhibition at the MH de Young Memorial Museum in San Francisco *(see pp362–3)*. Members of f/64, among them Ansel Adams (1902–84), Imogen Cunningham (1883–1976), and Edward Weston (1886–1958), believed photography should emphasize realism. This approach was riveting when used in close-ups of plants, or as Dorothea Lange (1895–1965) applied it in her portraits of Californians during the Great Depression.

The range of approaches now includes the snapshot aesthetics of Judy Dater (born in 1941) and photographs of Weimaraner dogs by William Wegman (born in 1942).

SCULPTORS

GERMAN-BORN Rupert Schmid (1864–1932) arrived in San Francisco in the 1880s. He soon became famous for figurative works employing western themes, such as *California Venus* (1895), his life-size female nude adorned with California poppies. More important still was Douglas Tilden (1860–1935), a sculptor from Chico who created impressive civic monuments. Arthur Putnam (1873–1930) also won notoriety with his sensual representations of wild animals.

Schmid's *California Venus*

Californians have been expanding the parallel fields of sculpture and ceramics since the early part of this century. Peter Voulkos (born in 1924) experimented in large-scale fired clay sculptures. Robert Arneson (born in 1930) abandoned more traditional vessel aesthetics to pursue startling and amusing Pop Art ceramics, while Bruce Beasley (born in 1939) and Michael Heizer (born in 1944) have created pieces that take on different dimensions depending on the weather.

ART PATRONAGE IN CALIFORNIA

Private and public patronage have been essential to the vitality of California culture since the late 19th century. Had it not been for railroad baron Henry Huntington's money and interest in art treasures, there would be no Huntington Library, Art Galleries, and Botanical Gardens in Pasadena *(see pp154–7)*. The public would not have access to that institution's collection of 18th-century British art, including Thomas Gainsborough's *The Blue Boy* (c.1770) and many other masterpieces. Multimillionaire J Paul Getty brought together the world-famous collection of Greek and Roman antiquities housed in the J Paul Getty Villa in Malibu *(see p82)* and the painting, sculpture, and decorative arts collection occupying the new J Paul Getty Center in Brentwood *(see pp78–9)*. Another multimillionaire, Norton Simon, amassed the renowned selection of Goyas, Picassos, Rembrandts, and Van Goghs now on public display in the Norton Simon Museum *(see pp152–3)*.

Public financing, too, has enriched the state's art offerings. In the 1930s, the New Deal paid artists to paint the frescoes in San Francisco's Coit Tower *(see p321)* and embellish public structures throughout the state. More recently, city funds have been used to make Los Angeles one of the most important centers of mural art in the world.

Henry Huntington

Architecture in California

CALIFORNIA'S ARCHITECTURAL history began with the arrival of the Europeans in the 18th century (*see pp42–3*). Many of the Spanish missions of the late 18th and early 19th centuries were adaptations of Mexican baroque architecture, and the Spanish-Mexican influence continued to dominate California buildings until the middle of the 19th century. Later, the population influx caused by the Gold Rush led to this Hispanic vernacular merging with styles imported by settlers from the eastern United States and Europe. Architects such as Henry Cleaveland, S & J Newsom, and Bernard Maybeck were all influential in creating the state's unique Victorian style.

Hale House in Heritage Square, Los Angeles

MISSION

Franciscan missionaries, arriving in California from Mexico, established a chain of 21 missions from San Diego to Sonoma as centers from which to colonize the state. They were all designed to be within a day's journey of their nearest neighbors. These provincial versions of Mexican churches and their communal buildings were designed by friars and built of adobe bricks and wood by unskilled Native American laborers. Over the years their crude constructions decayed and were shaken by earthquakes, but many have been carefully restored in the 20th century. Distinctive features include massive walls covered with white lime cement, small window openings, rounded gables, and tiered bell towers.

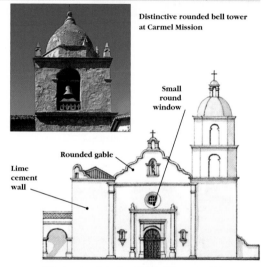

Distinctive rounded bell tower at Carmel Mission

Small round window

Rounded gable

Lime cement wall

Mission San Luis Rey *(1811–51) was the 18th mission to be established and was so architecturally impressive that it was often referred to as a "palace."*

MONTEREY

In the 1850s and 1860s, East Coast settlers flooded into the newly declared 31st state, bringing with them styles that were already going out of fashion on the East Coast, such as Greek Revival. Monterey, the state capital under Mexican rule, gave its name to an architecture that is, in essence, a wooden Greek temple wrapped around a Mexican adobe. Features include two-story wooden porticoes supported by slim square posts, wood shingle roofs, and a chaste symmetry of plan and elevation.

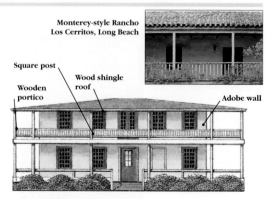

Monterey-style Rancho Los Cerritos, Long Beach

Square post

Wood shingle roof

Wooden portico

Adobe wall

Larkin House *(1837), built by Thomas Larkin, was the first Monterey-style house, with its two stories of adobe brick.*

VICTORIAN

Three major styles emerged in California during the Victorian era: Italianate, most popular in San Francisco *(see pp290–91)*, Queen Anne, and Eastlake. The two latter styles achieved a pinnacle of exuberance in California during the 19th century when they were brought to the state by migrants from the East Coast. The restrained Eastlake style, with its geometrically patterned façades and ornamentation, was often combined with the more extravagant Queen Anne style, notable for its gables, turrets, wraparound porches, and splendidly confused anthology of classical details.

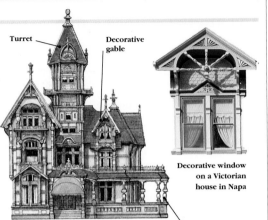

Turret • Decorative gable

Decorative window on a Victorian house in Napa

Carson Mansion *in Eureka (1886) was built by S & J Newsom, who were masters of the Queen Anne style. Now a private club, the house may be California's ultimate Victorian folly.*

Wraparound porch

ARTS AND CRAFTS

Pioneered by William Morris and Charles Voysey in England, the Arts and Crafts movement flourished briefly in California in the early 20th century. Also known as Craftsman style, its leading proponents included Bernard Maybeck and Charles and Henry Greene. Its emphasis is on simplicity and refinement on the outside and in the handcrafted interiors.

Characteristic beamed roof at Gamble House, Pasadena

Clapboard wall • Shady porch

The First Church of Christ Science *in Berkeley (1907) is the finest example of Bernard Maybeck's Arts and Crafts designs.*

MISSION REVIVAL

The Spanish-Mexican style was dormant during the second half of the 19th century. Decorative or pared-down versions were then enthusiastically revived in the early 20th century. The style is distinguishable by its rounded arches, harmonious proportions, and absence of ornamentation.

Red-tiled roof at the Beverly Hills Hotel

White stucco wall • Red-tiled roof • Rounded arch

The Women's Club *(1913) in La Jolla was designed by Irving Gill, a pioneer of modernism who used poured concrete and stucco to create elegant versions of the Mission style.*

Twentieth-Century California Architecture

IN THE EARLY 20TH CENTURY an architecture distinctive to California emerged, after a brief return to the state's Hispanic roots and an Art Deco style imported from Europe. This California style borrowed post-and-beam construction and wide porches from traditional Japanese buildings. Later, during the postwar building boom of the 1950s, the whole country was influenced by Cliff May's California ranch house, with its fusion of indoor and outdoor living. In more recent years, many architects, such as Craig Ellwood and Frank Gehry, have helped to make LA a center of modern architectural innovation *(see pp68–9)*.

San Francisco Museum of Modern Art (1995)

SPANISH COLONIAL

ORNATE VERSIONS of traditional Spanish architecture were first given wide currency by the Panama-California Exposition in San Diego in 1915 *(see pp246–7)*, where many buildings were decorated in this style. Simplified versions became the popular style for houses and public buildings throughout the 1920s. Distinguishing features included ornamental wood, stone, and ironwork, used to set off expanses of white stucco, red pantiled roofs, and lush gardens.

George Washington Smith, the Montecito-based architect, was a master of the style, creating abstracted Andalusian-style villages, such as **Ostoff House** (1924) in San Marino and Casa del Herrero (1925), a private house in Montecito. Another striking example of this style is William Mooser's **Santa Barbara County Courthouse** (1929), with its hand-painted ceilings, murals, and sunken gardens.

STREAMLINE MODERNE

ART DECO made a brief appearance in California at the end of the 1920s, with jazzy reliefs and tile façades. It was superseded by Streamline Moderne, where sleek, rounded forms are animated by ribs, canopies, and reliefs. Its inspirations were machine-age imagery. The style is best seen in movie theaters, such as the **Academy Cathedral** (1939) in Inglewood and the **Paramount Theater** in Oakland (Miller & Pflueger, 1931).

PWA MODERNE

THIS MOVEMENT was named after the Public Works Administration, established in the 1930s to fund public buildings. It is a marriage of Beaux-Arts formality and the simplicity of Modernism. It is notable for its stone façades, pilasters, and carved ornamentation. A good example is the **Monterey County Courthouse** (1937) in Salinas.

CONTEMPORARY

A DIVERSITY of approaches by leading architects has resulted in some striking contemporary buildings. Among the notable achievements of recent years are the ground-hugging, barnlike structures of **Sea Ranch**. This ecologically friendly vacation-home community on the Northern California coast began as a cluster of condominiums by Moore Lyndon Turnbull Whittaker in 1965. In sharp contrast is the **Salk Institute**, in La Jolla (Louis Kahn, 1959–65). State-of-the-art laboratories of poured concrete flank a bare travertine-paved plaza; a symbolic meeting place that links the continent and the ocean.

The **San Francisco Museum of Modern Art** (1995) by Swiss architect Mario Botta is both a civic symbol and an indoor plaza. A cylindrical skylight reaches up from stacked, top-lit galleries clad in precast panels of plain and angled bricks, to light an expansive foyer.

POST-MODERNISM

REACTING to the impersonality of corporate towers, architects such as Michael Graves, Venturi Scott-Brown,

George Washington Smith's Casa del Herrero in Montecito (1925)

and Robert Stern popularized a more decorative approach to Modernism in the 1970s. Buildings such as **The Library** (1984) by Robert Stern in San Juan Capistrano make playful use of historical elements (columns, pediments, and pergolas) while employing colorful palettes.

Jon Jerde scrambles colors and architectural references with even greater abandon in his popular shopping centers, most notably **Horton Plaza** (1989) in San Diego. This multilevel outdoor shopping mall with domes and tilework echoes local Spanish-style buildings.

Programmatic Donut Hole in La Puente, east of Los Angeles

PROGRAMMATIC BUILDINGS

THE AUTOMOBILE began to reshape California as early as the 1920s, and there was fierce competition to attract the attention of passing motorists on the commercial strips that linked scattered communities. An exuberant roadside architecture developed, in which travelers were invited to sleep in wigwam motels or have their shoes repaired inside a huge shoe (Doschander's Shoe Repair Shop, Bakersfield, 1947). Most of these fantasies have been demolished, but a few remain in outlying areas, notably the drive-thru **Donut Hole** (1958) in La Puente and the **Tail o' the Pup** hot dog stand (1946) in West Hollywood.

Post-Modern Horton Plaza

FRANK LLOYD WRIGHT

Born in Wisconsin, Frank Lloyd Wright (1867–1959) lived in California in the 1920s and designed buildings in the state throughout his career. He began with **Hollyhock House** (1917–20) in Hollywood, and ended with the **Marin County Civic Center** in San Rafael, north of San Francisco, completed in 1972. Other notable buildings are the old VC Morris store (1949), now the **Union Square Frank Lloyd Wright Building** in San Francisco, and several LA "textile block" houses, inspired by Mayan temples.

Frank Lloyd Wright's Hollyhock House in Hollywood

Multicultural California

San Francisco's Chinatown

Girl in Native American dress

ALIFORNIA IS the most ethnically diverse state in the Union. In the 19th century, the discovery of gold, silver, and oil each brought an influx of migrants of many nationalities to California; the landscape and climate still attract farmers, fishermen, and vintners from all over the world. By the mid-21st century, many believe California will be a hybrid of cultures, with no clear ethnic majority. The concentration of races varies statewide: a greater number of Hispanics reside in the south, while the Silicon Valley and northern farmlands have attracted Asians and Europeans. Most ethnic communities still celebrate their cultures with festivals *(see pp32–5)*.

Japanese sign

Mexican street musicians in Los Angeles

entire areas of cities. Although many of the younger Chinese have now moved to middle-class areas, the Chinatowns of LA and San Francisco still attract tourists to their traditional shops and restaurants.

THE NATIVE AMERICANS

CALIFORNIA has more resident Native Americans than any other state. The indigenous population grew in the 1960s when they gained more political rights. A few Native Americans still live on reservations, but the majority have opted for integration throughout the state.

THE HISPANIC-AMERICANS

YOU CANNOT go far in California without becoming aware of the state's Hispanic heritage. Spanish explorers who arrived in the 17th and 18th centuries *(see pp42–3)* established many of today's cities. As early as the 1940s the state was home to the largest population of Mexicans outside their own country. Political and economic troubles in Central and South America have continued to fuel Hispanic immigration. Today, almost every city has Mexican influences in its architecture, cuisine, and art. The Hispanics are also responsible for some of the brightest fiestas, including the extravagant *Cinco de Mayo* (May 5) *(see p32)*.

THE CHINESE

CHINESE IMMIGRANTS first arrived in California during the Gold Rush *(see pp44–5)*. A further influx escaped the economic problems of their homeland in the 1860s to work as cheap labor building the transcontinental railroad *(see pp46–7)*. Following its completion, they remained in California, setting up laundries and other businesses, but were met with racial violence by activists claiming they were stealing "white jobs." In the 1880s Congress severely limited Chinese immigration, a law that was not repealed until 1943.

Such antipathy resulted in ghettolike Chinese communities, which dominated

THE AFRICAN-AMERICANS

AFRICAN-AMERICANS have been present in California since the days of Mexican rule. It was the increase in heavy industry during World War II, however, that led to the largest influx from the poorer southern states.

Rotchev House at Fort Ross

In the years that followed, low social standing and racism resulted in the growth of urban ghettos. Racial problems still persist, but many African-Americans are beginning to make their mark in government, entertainment, and business. Cities like Oakland *(see pp406–9)* continue to celebrate traditional festivals.

THE JAPANESE

T HE JAPANESE arrived in California in the early 20th century. The majority of them were farmers who literally sowed the seeds of the state's agricultural industry. During World War II, however, Japanese-Americans were considered a risk to national security and were interned for the duration of the war. The succeeding generation has overridden these events, and Japanese businesses have continued to grow since the 1980s property boom.

THE ITALIANS

I TALIANS, predominantly fishermen, arrived in California in the late 19th century. and settled in North Beach, San Francisco *(see pp330–33)*. The climate and soil also tempted Italian vintners, who founded what is now a highly respected wine industry.

THE RUSSIANS

F UR TRAPPERS from Russia and Alaska were among the first European settlers in California, arriving in the early 1800s. For a short time, they established a successful settlement at Fort Ross *(see p444)*, and today there is a Russian population of some 25,000 in and around San Francisco.

THE IRISH

F EWER PEOPLE of Irish descent reside on the West Coast than on the East Coast, and there are no distinct Irish districts in California. The Irish have largely integrated into a multicultural way of life, but their presence is still felt in the many Irish city bars, and particularly during the statewide parades on St. Patrick's Day *(see p32)*.

Santa Monica English pub sign

THE MELTING POT

O VER THE LAST few decades there has been a steady rise in immigrants from Asia. Long Beach has the largest population of Cambodians outside Cambodia, and the district is known as "Little Phnom Penh." Wars in Korea and Vietnam brought natives of these countries to the liberal atmosphere of California in the 1950s and 1970s. Made to settle in the poorer areas of inner cities, they have now turned many of these into thriving communities. Fresno *(see p500)* has the second largest Hmong population outside Laos in the world.

The technological opportunities of Silicon Valley *(see p412)* have continued to attract Indians and Pakistanis to the region since the 1970s. Santa Monica is home to a large British contingent, complete with "authentic" pubs *(see pp72–3)*. The town of Solvang *(see p209)* was founded by immigrants from Denmark in 1911 and retains its Danish heritage. California also has the second largest Jewish community in the US, two-thirds of whom live in LA.

Danish windmill in Solvang

CALIFORNIA
THROUGH THE YEAR

CALIFORNIA generally enjoys a moderate climate *(see pp36–7)*, which explains how residents can schedule annual events without concern for the weather. The size of the state, however, means that a range of activities can be pursued in different locations: winter can be spent skiing in the north or soaking up the sun in the warmer south. Californians love to celebrate, and the calendar is full of parades and festivals. Many are related to the state's agricultural heritage; others have been inspired by its social history, such as the Gold Rush, or its ethnic diversity. There are also cultural events, including jazz and film festivals, and national sports fixtures.

Runners in the Los Angeles Marathon

SPRING

THERE'S A CLEAR sense of reemergence in spring, when wildflowers carpet California's coastal headlands, gray whales swim north with their newborn offspring, and people start searching frantically for the sunglasses they tucked away the previous October. *Cinco de Mayo* (May 5) celebrations in Los Angeles and San Francisco, Hollywood's glamorous Academy Awards ceremony, baseball games, and San Francisco's Bay-to-Breakers run are all familiar elements of the season.

MARCH

Return of the Swallows *(Mar 19)*, San Juan Capistrano. Crowds gather to see the birds fly back to the mission gardens from their winter homes in Argentina *(see pp230–31)*.

Los Angeles Marathon *(first Sun)*.
Snowfest *(first two weeks)*, Tahoe City. The winter carnival features ski competitions, a "polar bear" (cold water) swim and live music.
St. Patrick's Day Parade *(Sun nearest Mar 17)*, San Francisco. A parade down Market Street is usually followed by Irish coffee in the city's Irish bars.

St. Patrick's Day shamrock

Swallows returning to Mission San Juan Capistrano

Redwood Coast Dixieland Jazz Festival *(end Mar)*, Eureka. Some of the world's finest Dixieland bands gather for this annual event.

APRIL

Academy Awards Ceremony *(Mar)*, Los Angeles. Hollywood's finest gather to honor the year's top films and actors.
Major League Baseball *(Apr–Sep)*. The San Francisco Giants, LA Dodgers, Anaheim Angels, Oakland Athletics, and San Diego Padres compete.
Toyota Grand Prix *(mid-Apr)*, Long Beach. The biggest street race in the US.
Agua Cahuilla Indian Heritage Festival *(mid-Apr)*, Palm Springs. Festivities honor the Native Americans who discovered the local hot springs.
Cherry Blossom Festival *(mid-Apr)*, San Francisco. Japanese dancing and martial arts displays are all part of this traditional annual event *(see p342)*.
Anniversary of the 1906 Earthquake *(Apr 18)*, San Francisco. Survivors and history buffs gather around Lotta's Fountain, at Kearny and Market Streets, to remember the earthquake.
San Francisco International Film Festival *(mid-Apr–early May)*. Independent films from around the world.
Red Bluff Round-Up Rodeo *(third weekend)*. The largest two-day rodeo in the US.

MAY

Raisin Festival *(early May)*, Selma. A parade, art competitions and the Raisin Queen.
Cinco de Mayo *(May 5)*, LA and San Francisco. The state's largest Mexican celebrations feature folk dancing and mariachi music.
Bay-to-Breakers *(third weekend)*, San Francisco. The world's largest fun run is 7.5-miles (12.5-km) from the Embarcadero to Ocean Beach.
Calaveras County Fair *(mid-May)*, Angels Camp. The famous frog jumping contest *(see p463)* and a rodeo.
Mainly Mozart Festival *(end May–early Jun)*, San Diego. Leading orchestras perform Mozart masterpieces.
Carnaval *(last weekend)*, San Francisco. The Mission District turns Latin American, with salsa and reggae bands.
Sacramento Jazz Jubilee *(last weekend)*.

Mexican dancer at the *Cinco de Mayo* festival in Los Angeles

SUMMER

A T NO OTHER time of year are the clichés of California so evident. Beaches are crowded with tanned, muscled bodies and daredevil surfers, and colorfully dressed gays and lesbians parade through San Francisco streets in June. Tourists flood into the state, attending its many outdoor music events, Wild West celebrations (such as Old Miners' Days in Big Bear Lake), and the renowned annual Gilroy Garlic Festival.

Lesbian and Gay Pride parade in San Francisco

JUNE

Lesbian and Gay Pride Day *(Sun in late Jun)*, San Francisco. The largest gay parade proceeds down Market Street.
Lumber Jubilee *(end Jun)*, Tuolumne. Logging competitions recall the history of California's lumber industry.
Monterey Blues Festival *(end Jun)*. Star blues performers draw crowds annually.
Juneteenth *(end Jun)*, Oakland. An African-American cultural celebration, featuring jazz and gospel music.

JULY

International Surf Festival *(whole month)*. Body boarding and surfing events take place at various beaches.
Fourth of July Fireworks Particularly good displays are at Disneyland and on Santa Monica Pier.
Mammoth Lakes Jazz Jubilee *(first weekend after Jul 4)*. Some dozen world-class jazz bands perform.
Obon Festival *(mid-Jul)*, San Jose. Taiko drummers and dancers join in this Japanese-American party.
Carmel Bach Festival *(mid-Jul–early Aug)*. Bach concerts and classes.
Gilroy Garlic Festival *(end Jul)*. This food festival serves garlic in all kinds of dishes.
San Francisco Marathon *(mid-Jul)*.
Old Miners' Days *(end Jul–mid-Aug)*, Big Bear Lake. The Gold Rush is recalled with a

chili cook-off and a liars' contest.
Festival of the Arts *(Jul–Aug)*, Laguna Beach.

AUGUST

Native American Powwow *(early Aug)*, Costa Mesa. A celebration of Native American food and culture.
Old Spanish Days Fiesta *(early Aug)*, Santa Barbara. Spanish markets, a carnival, and dancing.
Nisei Week *(early Aug)*, Japanese festival in LA's Little Tokyo.
Pebble Beach Concours d'Elegance *(mid-Aug)*. Classic automobile show.
California State Fair *(mid-Aug–early Sep)*, Sacramento. Everything from star-studded entertainment to pig races.
Bigfoot Days *(end Aug)*, Willow Creek. A parade and an ice cream social at this homage to Northern California's legendary hermit.

Native American dancers at the Costa Mesa Powwow

Mexican Independence Day parade in Santa Monica

AUTUMN

IN THE HIGH SIERRAS, leaves of deciduous trees turn stunning shades of red and yellow. The Napa Valley wineries *(see pp446–7)* invite visitors to help celebrate their grape harvests with wine tastings and live music. All over the state, Oktoberfests serve up foamy mugs of beer and the "oom-pah-pah" of German bands, while rodeos dramatize California's frontier past.

SEPTEMBER

Pro Football *(Sep–Dec)*. The San Francisco '49ers, Oakland Raiders, and San Diego Chargers take to the field.
Los Angeles County Fair *(whole month)*, Pomona. This vast county fair includes horse races.
Oktoberfest *(early Sep–end Oct)*, Torrance. The largest German beer festival in Southern California.
Mexican Independence Day *(Sep 16)*. Mexican dancing, music and food in Santa Monica, Calexico, and Santa Maria.
Monterey Jazz Festival *(third weekend)*. The world's oldest continuously held annual jazz festival.
Danish Days *(end Sep)*, Solvang. Danish food stands and parades *(see p209)*.
San Francisco Blues Festival *(last weekend)*. Two-day event at Fort Mason.

Football

OCTOBER

Sonoma County Harvest Fair *(early Oct)*, Santa Rosa. A grape stomp and a 6-mile (10-km) run are highlights of this annual fair.
US National Gold Panning Championship *(early Oct)*, Coloma. The 1849 Gold Rush is remembered with a gold panning competition.
Mountain Man Rendezvous *(early Oct)*, Bridgeport. Shooting contests and a barbecue re-create an 1840s get-together of mountain guides and trappers.
Black Cowboy Heritage Invitational Parade and Festival *(early Oct)*, Oakland. Commemorating the part African-Americans played in settling the American West.
Columbus Day Parade *(Sun nearest Oct 12)*, San Francisco. Bands and floats proceed down Columbus Avenue to Fisherman's Wharf.
San Francisco Jazz Festival *(end Oct–early Nov)*. All-star jazz performances throughout the city.
Pumpkin Festival *(mid-Oct)*, Half Moon Bay. The World Heavyweight Pumpkin Championship, pumpkin carving, and pumpkin dishes are served in every edible variety.
International Festival of Masks *(last Sun)*, Los Angeles. Originally part of Halloween, this mask parade now celebrates LA's ethnic diversity.

Halloween *(Oct 31)*, San Francisco. Costumed residents parade through the city streets.
Grand National Rodeo *(end Oct–early Nov)*, Daly City. Lassoing mustangs and a livestock exposition are part of this traditional event.
Butterflies *(end Oct–mid Mar)*, Pacific Grove. Thousands of monarch butterflies migrate here annually *(see p494)*.

Costumed participants in Pasadena's Doo Dah Parade

NOVEMBER

Dia de los Muertos/Day of the Dead *(Nov 1)*. Festivities in LA's El Pueblo and San Francisco's Mission District highlight this Mexican religious festival, when the souls of the dead are said to visit their surviving relatives *(see p122)*.
Death Valley '49ers Encampment *(mid-Nov)*. Fiddlers' competitions, cowboy poetry, and gold panning are all featured.
Doo Dah Parade *(mid-Nov)*, Pasadena. Costumed merchants parody the approaching holiday and current events.

Mexican musicians at the *Dia de los Muertos* festival

Gray whale approaching a boat off Baja California

PUBLIC HOLIDAYS

New Year's Day (Jan 1)
Martin Luther King Jr Day (3rd Mon in Jan)
Presidents' Day (3rd Mon in Feb)
Memorial Day (last Mon in May)
Independence Day (Jul 4)
Labor Day (1st Mon in Sep)
Veterans' Day (Nov 11)
Thanksgiving (4th Thu in Nov)
Christmas Day (Dec 25)

WINTER

CALIFORNIANS LOVE bright lights, and this is most apparent at Christmas, when every building and public square seems to be draped in twinkling bulbs. Churches resound with carols, and film stars take part in seasonal parades. As Lake Tahoe's ski season gets under way, highways jam up with avid skiers traveling north.

DECEMBER

Hollywood Christmas Parade *(first Thu after Thanksgiving)*, Los Angeles. Hollywood and Sunset Boulevards are crowded with this celebrity-heavy extravaganza, held since 1931.
Russian Heritage Christmas Celebration *(weekends, whole month)*, Guerneville. Costumes, food, and music recall the area's early 19th-century Russian influences.

Christmas decorations in Carmel Plaza

International Tamale Festival *(early Dec)*, Indio. Mexican dancing accompanies the *tamale* (spicy corn husk rolls) gluttony.
Whale-watching *(end Dec–Apr)*. California gray whales, migrating south annually from the Bering Strait to Baja, can be sighted along the coast or from whale-watching boats out of many coastal cities *(see p580)*.

Float at the Tournament of Roses Parade in Pasadena

JANUARY

Bald Eagles *(Jan–Feb)*, Mount Shasta. Bird-watchers come to see bald eagles that nest here *(see pp420–21)*.
Tournament of Roses Parade *(Jan 1)*, Pasadena. A pageant, followed by the Rose Bowl intercollegiate football game *(see p151)*.
Palm Springs International Film Festival *(early–mid Jan)*. Screenings and awards.
Gold Discovery Day *(Jan 24)*, Coloma. Gold-panning demonstrations take place on the anniversary of the first gold discovery *(see p459)*.

AT&T Pebble Beach Pro-Am Golf Tournament *(end Jan–early Feb)*. Pros and celebrities play golf together.

FEBRUARY

Dickens Festival *(early Feb)*, Riverside. Writer Charles Dickens' life is celebrated in a re-creation of a mid-19th-century London marketplace.
Napa Valley International Mustard Festival *(mid-Feb)*, Calistoga. Hundreds of mustards are available for tasting.
Riverside County Fair and National Date Festival *(mid–late Feb)*, Indio. Date dishes and camel and ostrich races *(see p249)*.
Chinese New Year Festival *(mid-Feb–early Mar)*, San Francisco. The nation's largest Chinese New Year festival includes a Golden Dragon parade through the Financial District and Chinatown.

Chinese New Year celebrations in San Francisco

The Climate of California

APART FROM the extremes of the North and the deserts, the state's climate is neither oppressive in summer nor too cold in winter. The Northern Coastal Range is temperate, although wet in the winter. To the east, rain turns to snow on the Sierra Nevada Mountains. Central California and the Central Valley have a Mediterranean climate. The weather becomes drier and warmer toward the south with soaring temperatures in the desert during the summer.

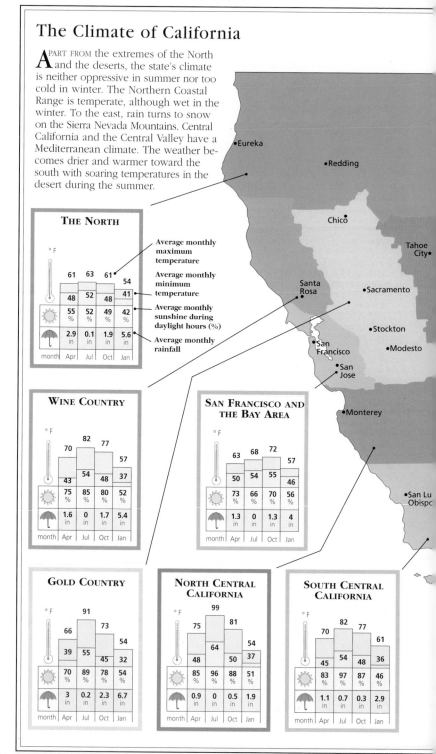

THE NORTH

°F

	Apr	Jul	Oct	Jan
max	61	63	61	54
min	48	52	48	41
sun %	55	52	49	42
rain in	2.9	0.1	1.9	5.6

Average monthly maximum temperature

Average monthly minimum temperature

Average monthly sunshine during daylight hours (%)

Average monthly rainfall

WINE COUNTRY

°F

month	Apr	Jul	Oct	Jan
max	70	82	77	57
min	43	54	48	37
sun %	75	85	80	52
rain in	1.6	0	1.7	5.4

SAN FRANCISCO AND THE BAY AREA

°F

month	Apr	Jul	Oct	Jan
max	63	68	72	57
min	50	54	55	46
sun %	73	66	70	56
rain in	1.3	0	1.3	4

GOLD COUNTRY

°F

month	Apr	Jul	Oct	Jan
max	66	91	73	54
min	39	55	45	32
sun %	70	89	78	54
rain in	3	0.2	2.3	6.7

NORTH CENTRAL CALIFORNIA

°F

month	Apr	Jul	Oct	Jan
max	75	99	81	54
min	48	64	50	37
sun %	85	96	88	51
rain in	0.9	0	0.5	1.9

SOUTH CENTRAL CALIFORNIA

°F

month	Apr	Jul	Oct	Jan
max	70	82	77	61
min	45	54	48	36
sun %	83	97	87	46
rain in	1.1	0.7	0.3	2.9

Eureka

Redding

Chico

Tahoe City

Santa Rosa

Sacramento

Stockton

San Francisco

Modesto

San Jose

Monterey

San Luis Obispo

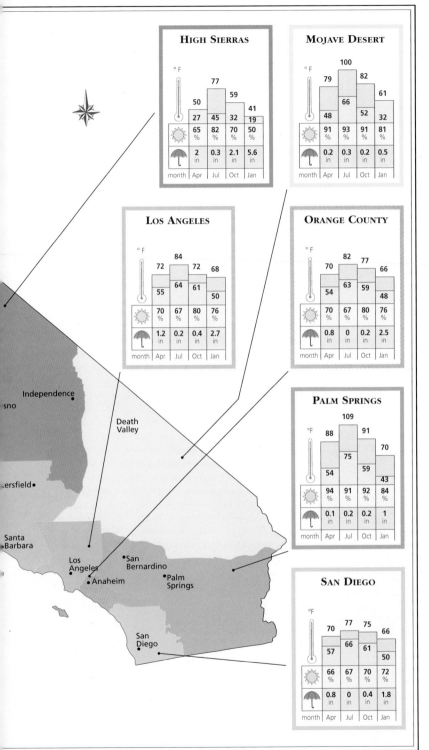

HIGH SIERRAS

°F

month	Apr	Jul	Oct	Jan
	50	77	59	41
	27	45	32	19
☀	65 %	82 %	70 %	50 %
☂	2 in	0.3 in	2.1 in	5.6 in

MOJAVE DESERT

°F

month	Apr	Jul	Oct	Jan
	79	100	82	61
	48	66	52	32
☀	91 %	93 %	91 %	81 %
☂	0.2 in	0.3 in	0.2 in	0.5 in

LOS ANGELES

°F

month	Apr	Jul	Oct	Jan
	72	84	72	68
	55	64	61	50
☀	70 %	67 %	80 %	76 %
☂	1.2 in	0.2 in	0.4 in	2.7 in

ORANGE COUNTY

°F

month	Apr	Jul	Oct	Jan
	70	82	77	66
	54	63	59	48
☀	70 %	67 %	80 %	76 %
☂	0.8 in	0 in	0.2 in	2.5 in

PALM SPRINGS

°F

month	Apr	Jul	Oct	Jan
	88	109	91	70
	54	75	59	43
☀	94 %	91 %	92 %	84 %
☂	0.1 in	0.2 in	0.2 in	1 in

SAN DIEGO

°F

month	Apr	Jul	Oct	Jan
	70	77	75	66
	57	66	61	50
☀	66 %	67 %	70 %	72 %
☂	0.8 in	0 in	0.4 in	1.8 in

Independence

sno

Death Valley

ersfield

Santa Barbara

Los Angeles

San Bernardino

Anaheim

Palm Springs

San Diego

THE HISTORY OF CALIFORNIA

A N EARLY 16th-century chivalric Spanish novel, *Las Sergas de Esplanadían (The Exploits of Esplanadían)*, first gave the name *California* to a mythical island, plump with natural wealth and ruled by Calafía, a pagan queen. By 1542, when the Portuguese navigator Juan Rodríguez Cabrillo (João Rodrigues Cabrilho) sailed north from Mexico on Spain's behalf and discovered what he believed to be an island, the name California was already familiar enough for him to use it in his journal. Two centuries would pass, however, before Spain made a real claim on the land, sending Father Junípero Serra in 1769 to establish Franciscan missions along the length of California.

State seal

THE GOLD RUSH

Still, the territory remained remote until 1848; the same year that Mexico ceded California to the US, gold was found in the Sierra Nevada foothills. By 1849, hordes of fortune seekers had arrived in Northern California.

The Gold Rush, followed by silver finds in the western Sierras and the completion of the transcontinental railroad in 1869, brought prosperity to the whole state. But the changes caused social rifts: whites charged Chinese immigrants with "stealing" their jobs, and by the beginning of the 20th century, economic divisions left over from the time of plenty had helped to create powerful labor unions.

20TH-CENTURY CALIFORNIA

San Francisco's earthquake in 1906 convinced many that California's heyday was over. However, during the next 90 years, Hollywood drew international attention with its movie-making. Oil wells serviced the needs of increasingly car-dependent residents, and by 1937 orange groves had become a symbol of the state's fertile future. When the UN charter was signed in San Francisco in 1945, it was clear that California, once considered at the edge of civilization, was finally a player at center stage.

Early map of the United States, showing California as an island

◁ **Mural at the Santa Barbara County Courthouse showing Cabrillo's landing in California**

Early California

IT IS ESTIMATED that, at the time of European discovery, between 100,000 and 275,000 natives lived in California. They were not warlike, nor did they have much in the way of government. Only on the Colorado River did they practice agriculture; most relied on hunting, fishing, or the gathering of staples such as acorns for food. Their religion and medical beliefs were bound together in the person of a shaman, said to be in direct communication with the spirit world. They congregated in villages of 100 to 150 inhabitants generally living in conical or dome-shaped dwellings. Social classes were almost nonexistent, but there were great language divisions between different tribes.

Early basketry

Tcholovoni People
Various tribes, including these Tcholovoni people, settled in small villages on the shores of San Francisco Bay.

Money Box
Natives of Northern California used dentalium shells for money, held in ornately carved boxes.

Jewelry
This necklace, made of abalone and clamshells, is thought to be one of the earliest artifacts of Native California life.

Gift baskets, such as this Miwok example, were often decorated with beads.

Quail feathers and geometric dancers decorate this basket of the Yokut people.

Eel trapper

BASKETRY
Basket-weaving was the primary native activity. They used a wide range of materials, which were twined or coiled into imaginative or symbolic designs. Baskets were used in all walks of life, including hunting, storage, cooking, and eating.

Headdresses
This headpiece, made out of black and white magpie feathers, derives from the native Miwok people.

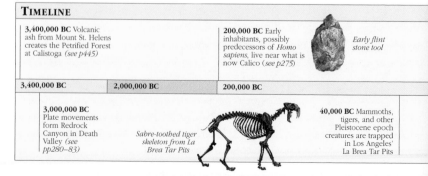

TIMELINE

3,400,000 BC Volcanic ash from Mount St. Helens creates the Petrified Forest at Calistoga *(see p445)*

200,000 BC Early inhabitants, possibly predecessors of *Homo sapiens*, live near what is now Calico *(see p275)*

Early flint stone tool

3,400,000 BC	2,000,000 BC	200,000 BC

3,000,000 BC Plate movements form Redrock Canyon in Death Valley *(see pp280–83)*

Sabre-toothed tiger skeleton from La Brea Tar Pits

40,000 BC Mammoths, tigers, and other Pleistocene epoch creatures are trapped in Los Angeles' La Brea Tar Pits

Kule Loklo People
These early Bay Area inhabitants were depicted by Anton Refregier in his mural in the foyer of the Rincon Center (see p307).

WHERE TO SEE EARLY CALIFORNIA

The George C Page Museum of La Brea Discoveries *(see p114)* includes fossil reconstructions of creatures recovered from the nearby tar pits. The Chumash Painted Cave State Historic Park *(p209)* has rare pictographs executed by the Chumash people. LA's Southwest Museum *(p149)* and the California Academy of Sciences in San Francisco *(pp360–61)* both feature Native American artifacts.

***Painted caves** dating back thousands of years have been carefully preserved in the Chumash Painted Cave State Historic Park in Southern California.*

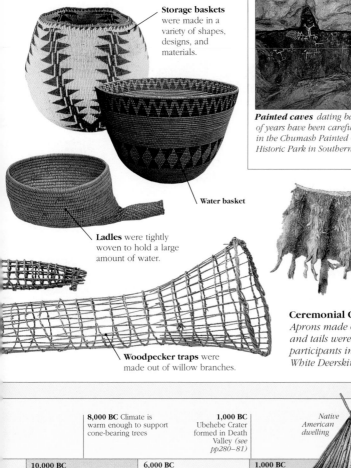

Storage baskets were made in a variety of shapes, designs, and materials.

Water basket

Ladles were tightly woven to hold a large amount of water.

Woodpecker traps were made out of willow branches.

Ceremonial Costumes
Aprons made of animal skins and tails were worn by participants in the traditional White Deerskin Dance.

8,000 BC Climate is warm enough to support cone-bearing trees

1,000 BC Ubehebe Crater formed in Death Valley *(see pp280–81)*

Native American dwelling

| 10,000 BC | 6,000 BC | 1,000 BC | | AD 100 |

10,000–8,000 BC Pleistocene epoch (Ice Age) ends. First Indians settle in California area

6,000 BC Climate is warm enough to support deciduous trees

AD 100 Devil's Golf Course in Death Valley formed by an evaporated lake *(see pp280–81)*

The Colonial Period

ALTHOUGH THE SPANISH "discovered" California in 1542, they did not colonize the area until the 18th century. Their rule was enforced through a trio of institutions – the mission (church), the *presidio* (fort), and the *pueblo* (town). Of these, the mission was the most influential. Beginning at San Diego in 1769, Franciscan friars founded 21 missions at approximately 30-mile (48-km) intervals

Mission statue

along *El Camino Real* ("the Royal Road"). Missionaries wanted to bring religion to the "benighted Indian," but they also used natives as cheap labor. European colonists committed a more serious crime by spreading diseases that would reduce the native population to about 16,000 by 1900.

- San Francisco de Solano (1823)
- San Rafael Arcangel (1817)
- San Francisco de Asis (1776)
  - San Jose (1797)
  - Santa Clara de Asis (1777)

Santa Cruz (1791)
- San Juan Bautista (1797)

- Nuestra Señora de la Soledad (1791
San Carlos Borromeo de Carmelo (1770)
- San Antonio de Padua (1771)

El Camino Real

- San Miguel Arcangel (1797)

- San Luis Obispo de Tolos (1772)
- La Purisma Concepcion (1787)

- Santa Ines (1804)
- Santa Barbara (1786

San Buenaventura (1782) •

Sir Francis Drake
The English navigator landed in California in 1579 to make repairs to his ship, the Golden Hind. *He named the land "Nova Albion" and claimed it for Queen Elizabeth I.*

Father Junípero Serra
Originally from the Spanish island of Majorca, Father Junípero Serra led the Franciscan expedition to establish a chain of missions in California.

Jedediah Smith
In 1828, a fur-trapper, Jedediah "Strong" Smith, was the first white man to reach California overland across the Sierra Nevada Mountains, from the eastern United States.

TIMELINE

1524 Hernán Cortés, Spanish conqueror of Mexico, encourages King Charles V to seize control of the "California Islands"	**1579** English privateer Francis Drake anchors his *Golden Hind* near Point Reyes (see pp396–7)	
1500	**1600**	**1650**
1542 Juan Rodríguez Cabrillo (João Rodrigues Cabrilho) sails north from Mexico to San Diego harbor, making him the official discoverer of California	**1595** Portuguese navigator Sebastián Rodríguez Cermeño discovers Monterey Bay	**1602** Spanish merchant-adventurer Sebastián Vizcaíno sails up the California coast, naming landmarks as he goes – including San Diego, Santa Barbara, Point Concepcíon, and Carmel

Juan Rodríguez Cabrillo

Mission San Gabriel Arcángel
Ferdinand Deppe's 1832 work is thought to be the first painting of a mission. It depicts the central role of the mission in the community, surrounded by Native American dwellings.

WHERE TO SEE COLONIAL CALIFORNIA

Restored living quarters are displayed at the Santa Barbara Mission Museum.

Mission-era artifacts can be found at San Francisco's Mission Dolores (see p351), the Oakland Museum of California (pp408–409), the Mission San Carlos Borromeo in Carmel (pp496–7), and the Mission Santa Barbara (pp212–13). Most of the 21 missions offer public tours.

US Victory
On July 9, 1846, 70 US sailors and marines marched ashore at San Francisco (then Yerba Buena) and claimed it for the US.

Mission Artifacts
The Franciscan friars brought many items from Spain and Mexico to California. As well as decorative objects, some, such as these prayer bells, had practical purposes.

• San Fernando Rey de España (1797)

 • San Gabriel Arcangel (1771)

  • San Juan Capistranol (1776)

• San Luís rey de Francia (1798)

• San Diego de Alcalá (1769)

EL CAMINO REAL

The 21 missions along El Camino Real, from San Diego to Sonoma, were planned so that each was one day's journey on horseback from the next.

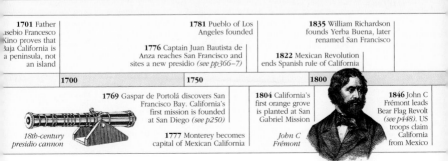

1701 Father ...sebio Francesco Kino proves that Baja California is a peninsula, not an island

1776 Captain Juan Bautista de Anza reaches San Francisco and sites a new presidio (see pp366–7)

1781 Pueblo of Los Angeles founded

1822 Mexican Revolution ends Spanish rule of California

1835 William Richardson founds Yerba Buena, later renamed San Francisco

1700

1750

1800

18th-century presidio cannon

1769 Gaspar de Portolá discovers San Francisco Bay. California's first mission is founded at San Diego (see p250)

1777 Monterey becomes capital of Mexican California

1804 California's first orange grove is planted at San Gabriel Mission

John C Frémont

1846 John C Frémont leads Bear Flag Revolt (see p448). US troops claim California from Mexico

The Rush For Riches

Forty-Niners
Gold prospectors from all over the US traveled to California in 1849, hence their name. They carried tools, weapons, and food provisions on their journey.

IN 1848 newspaperman Sam Brannan brandished nuggets that had been found in the Sacramento Valley, shouting "Gold! Gold! Gold from the American River!" Most of the prospectors who thereafter stampeded California's Mother Lode did not find fortune. But the gold-seeking hordes changed the area forever – especially San Francisco. Between 1848 and 1850, the town's population shot from 812 to 25,000. Food and property prices skyrocketed and crime thrived. In 1859, after the Gold Rush had ended, silver ore (the Comstock Lode) was exposed on the eastern Sierras, and Northern California boomed again.

Nugget of Californian gold

Pickaxes were used to loosen hard rock ready for the sluice.

Barbary Coast Saloon
Gambling and prostitution were rife in San Francisco's Barbary Coast region, and men were often pressed into naval service.

State Capital
Once little more than farmland, Sacramento grew into a bustling city within two years of the Gold Rush. It became the state capital in 1854.

The sluice was a long trough with wooden bars. As water was flushed along, gold particles were trapped behind the bars.

TIMELINE

1848 California is annexed by the US. Gold discovered at Sutter's Mill *(see p459)*

Sign from the Flying Cloud clipper ship

1854 Sacramento becomes California state capital

1849 Almost 800 ships leave New York, full of men bound for the gold fields

| 1848 | 1850 | 1852 | 1854 |

1850 California becomes 31st state of the Union

1851 San Francisco vigilante movement hangs several lawbreakers. Clipper ship *Flying Cloud* sails from New York to San Francisco in a record 89 days

1853 Levi Strauss lands in the Bay Area and begins selling his canvas trousers *(see p333)*

John Sutter (1802–1880)

Count Agoston Haraszthy
The Hungarian was the first vintner to plant European grape-vine cuttings in California.

Hydraulic mining blasted away rock with water to uncover gold underneath.

WHERE TO SEE THE ERA OF RICHES

Many of the settlements that were once thronged with gold miners have since disintegrated into ghost towns, such as Bodie *(p478)* and Calico *(p275)*. But you can still get a feel for the times at Columbia State Historic Park *(pp464–5)*, a restored Mother Lode town. The Wells Fargo History Museum in San Francisco *(p304)* has mementos of the Gold Rush. The Jackson Square Historical District *(p304)* was once part of the Barbary Coast.

Old schoolhouse at Calico ghost town

Comstock Lode Silver
Between 1859 and the mid-1880s, 400 million dollars worth of silver was extracted from mines in the High Sierras.

Gold panning involved swirling dirt and water around a flat-bottomed pan until only gold residue remained.

Emperor Norton
Self-proclaimed Emperor of the United States and Protector of Mexico, the eccentric Joshua Norton printed his own currency and gave advice to Sacramento legislators.

GOLD MINING TECHNIQUES

As the rush for gold increased, ways of extracting the ore became more sophisticated. What began as an adventure became a highly developed industry.

1855 Vigilante justice is enforced in Los Angeles	**1856** Street-murder of newspaper publisher James King of William sparks San Francisco's second vigilante uprising; William T Sherman leads militia campaign to restrain them		**1859** Prospector James Finney discovers silver deposits, the Comstock Lode	**1860** Bankrupt grain merchant Joshua Norton declares himself Norton I, Emperor of the United States until his death in 1880
1856		1858		1860
San Francisco vigilante medal	**1857** Agoston Haraszthy, father of California's wine industry, founds the Buena Vista estate in the Sonoma Valley *(see p449)*			**1861** California swears allegiance to the Union. The first oil well is drilled *Humboldt County oil well*

The Gilded Age

F OR CALIFORNIA'S *nouveaux riches*, the smartest address during the late 19th century was on Nob Hill in San Francisco *(see p320)*, where grand mansions were built. This was a time of ostentation but also of expansion, thanks to train connections with the East and South. California oranges could now be exported easily to New York markets; taking the return trip were European immigrants and others hoping for a better life on the West Coast. Land prices increased in LA County, and by 1900 San Francisco's population exceeded 300,000.

Gold pocket watch

Victorian Décor
Windows in the Winchester Mystery House (see pp414–15) are typically ornate.

Transcontinental Railroad
On May 12, 1869, the final spike was driven for the new railroad, linking the East and West Coasts.

Bathroom, with original bath tub and tiles

Front parlor

Dining room

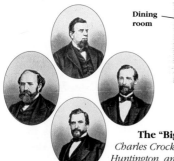

The "Big Four"
Charles Crocker, Leland Stanford, Collis Huntington, and Mark Hopkins made millions investing in the transcontinental railroad.

TIMELINE

1863 Construction begins on the Central Pacific Railroad

1871 Racial violence in LA leaves about 20 Chinese dead

1873–5 Orange planting begins in Riverside

1876 Southern Pacific Railroad reaches Los Angeles

California oranges

1884 Sarah Winchester embarks on her 38-year house-building project in San Jose *(see pp414–15)*

1870   1875   1880

1869 Transcontinental railroad is completed

1873 Andrew Hallidie tests San Francisco's first cable car

San Francisco's first cable car

1877 San Franciscans torch Chinese stores and laundries to protest against cheap labor

1882 US Congress passes the Chinese Exclusion Act, limiting Chinese immigration

Sutro Baths
The largest swimming pool in San Francisco stood from 1896 until the 1960s.

Yosemite National Park
Made a national park in 1890, Yosemite also became California's first tourist attraction and a popular image for advertisers.

WHERE TO SEE GILDED AGE CALIFORNIA

Public tours are held at the Haas-Lilienthal House *(see p338)* and the first cable car is on display at the Cable Car Barn *(p321)*, both in San Francisco. The "golden spike" from the transcontinental railroad is displayed, along with Big Four mementos, at the Stanford University Art Museum *(p411)*. Train buffs will also enjoy the California State Railroad Museum in Sacramento *(p457)*.

The California State Railroad Museum is a celebration of rail travel on the West Coast.

The living room was originally the master bedroom.

Porch

Hall, with Victorian corner sofa

Chinese Immigrants
The "coolies" who helped build the transcontinental railroad stayed and set up businesses, such as laundries and restaurants, but were met with racism.

HAAS-LILIENTHAL HOUSE

Grocer William Haas built this elaborate Queen Anne-style house in 1886, one of many in San Francisco. Today it is a museum, and shows how a wealthy family would have lived at the end of the 19th century *(see p338)*.

1890 Yosemite wins national park status *(see pp472–5)*

Stanford University seal

1893 San Andreas Fault discovered by University of California geologist Andrew Lawson

1896 Comstock tunnel builder Adolph Sutro opens the world's largest indoor saltwater swimming center in San Francisco

1885   **1890**   **1895**

1888 Hotel del Coronado opens in San Diego *(see p245)*

1891 Stanford University opens *(see p411)*; future president Herbert Hoover is in the first graduating class

1894 West Coast's first world's fair is held in San Francisco's Golden Gate Park

1897 San Francisco merchants prosper by outfitting gold miners traveling to Canada's Klondike River

The Rise of Hollywood

IN 1887, KANSAS PROHIBITIONIST Harvey Henderson Wilcox wanted to call his farm and the LA suburb surrounding it "Figwood," after his chief crop. His wife chose instead a name she had overheard on a train: "Hollywood." By the 1920s, the film industry was making the town famous and offering Americans entertainment to help them escape the reality of World War I, Prohibition, and later, the Great Depression. Silent film stars such as Mary Pickford and Charlie Chaplin were succeeded by icons of a more glamorous Hollywood, such as Mae West and Errol Flynn. Wall Street bankers were quick to realize their potential and invested heavily in the film industry.

Oscar statuette

Panama Canal
Two world fairs celebrated the completion of the canal in 1915.

Clara Bow, dubbed the "It" girl, was one of Hollywood's first sex symbols.

San Francisco Earthquake and Fire
After the 1906 disaster, many buildings had to be demolished.

Actors were chosen for their looks and often had little stage experience.

Los Angeles Aqueduct
The vast aqueduct was built at a cost of $24.5 million to irrigate the arid south with melted snow from the High Sierras.

HOLLYWOOD'S SILENT ERA
The movie industry grew rapidly and soon large corporate studios emerged. *Mantrap* (1927) was one of hundreds o silent movies made each month.

TIMELINE

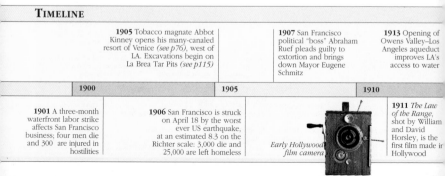

1901 A three-month waterfront labor strike affects San Francisco business; four men die and 300 are injured in hostilities

1900

1905 Tobacco magnate Abbot Kinney opens his many-canaled resort of Venice *(see p76)*, west of LA. Excavations begin on La Brea Tar Pits *(see p115)*

1906 San Francisco is struck on April 18 by the worst ever US earthquake, at an estimated 8.3 on the Richter scale: 3,000 die and 25,000 are left homeless

1905

1907 San Francisco political "boss" Abraham Ruef pleads guilty to extortion and brings down Mayor Eugene Schmitz

Early Hollywood film camera

1910

1913 Opening of Owens Valley–Los Angeles aqueduct improves LA's access to water

1911 *The Law of the Range*, shot by William and David Horsley, is the first film made in Hollywood

Prohibition *(1920–33)*
Los Angeles became a popular port of entry for smugglers bringing illegal alcohol into the United States from Mexico during the nationwide ban.

WHERE TO SEE CLASSIC HOLLYWOOD

The likenesses of numerous movie stars are displayed at the Hollywood Wax Museum *(p105)*. The Hollywood Studio Museum *(p108)*, once Cecil B De Mille's offices, now exhibits movie mementos. Some 200 stars have cemented their fame in front of Mann's Chinese Theatre *(p106)*.

MAY THIS CEMENT OUR FRIENDSHIP Joan Crawford 9-14-29

***Mann's Chinese Theatre** has hand-prints, footprints, and autographs of film stars cemented in its forecourt.*

***Paramount Studios** are the only studios now located in Hollywood and still attract would-be stars* (p109).

Studios operated like factories, filming different movies on adjacent sets.

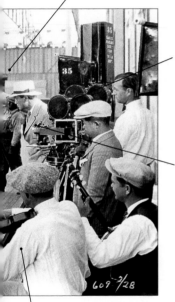

Cameramen used 35 mm cameras, operating at 24 frames per second.

Directors also found fame and fortune in the new industry.

Orchestras were often hired to play in the background of a scene during filming to create the right mood for the actors.

Aimee Semple McPherson
In 1923 the controversial evangelist and spiritualist opened her Angelus Temple in LA where she held regular spiritual revivalist meetings.

1916 The Lockheed brothers start building airplanes in Santa Barbara

WR Hearst

1924 LA eclipses San Francisco as the most important port on the West Coast

1929 Stock exchange crash causes national Depression. Actor Douglas Fairbanks, Sr. hosts the first Academy Awards presentation

1915   **1920**   **1925**

1915 San Francisco and San Diego both hold Panama-Pacific Expositions

1917 The US enters World War I

1919 WR Hearst begins construction of his magnificent castle at San Simeon *(see pp202–205)*

Norma Talmadge

1927 Actress Norma Talmadge is the first star to cement her foot-prints at Mann's Chinese Theatre *(see p106)*

1928 Cartoonist Walt Disney creates character of Mickey Mouse

The California Dream

MOVIES AND THE NEW MEDIUM of television made California *the* symbol of America's postwar resurgence – suddenly everybody wanted the prosperous middle-class existence they believed was common here. The airplane industry, ship-yards, and agriculture had burgeoned during the war, and a sense of prosperity lasted through the 1950s. Suburbs sprang up to meet the needs of returning soldiers, while new highways were laid to make them accessible. Yet at the same time, state schools lacked funds, African- and Mexican-Americans faced discrimination and violence, and Hollywood found itself attacked by politicians as a hotbed of Marxist Communism.

Olympic Games 1932
Los Angeles won the bid to hold the 1932 games and built Exposition Park for the event (see pp160–61).

Kitchen units became more practical, with Formica counters.

Longshoreman's Strike
On July 5, 1934, police opened fire on dockers striking for better conditions, killing two.

Household appliances became more widely available, easing domestic duties.

Hoover Dam
In 1936 Hoover Dam was built on the Colorado River to supply electricity.

TIMELINE

1932 LA hosts its first Olympic Games	**1934** Alcatraz Island becomes a maximum security penitentiary (*see pp28–9*)	**1936** Hoover Dam begins supplying Southern California with much-needed electricity	**1940** Los Angeles opens its first freeway – Arroyo Seco Parkway		**1942** Japanese Americans sent to relocation camps for "war security reason" (*see p479*)
1930		**1935**		**1940**	
1933 Prohibition ends. "Sunny Jim" Rolph, a popular San Francisco mayor turned California governor, shocks supporters by praising a lynch mob in San Jose	*"Sunny Jim" Rolph*	**1937** The Golden Gate Bridge opens	**1939** San Francisco's third world's fair, the Golden Gate Exposition, is held on Treasure Island	**1941** Japan attacks US fleet at Pearl Harbor	**1943** California becomes nation's leading agricultural state

Golden Gate Bridge
On May 28, 1937, an official convoy of black limousines were the first vehicles to cross the bridge, which links San Francisco with Marin County.

WHERE TO SEE THE CALIFORNIA DREAM

LA's Petersen Automotive Museum celebrates California's love affair with the car *(see p114)*. At the Treasure Island Museum in San Francisco, memorabilia from the Golden Gate International Exposition is displayed *(p396)*. A trip to the Sleeping Beauty Castle in Disneyland is the ultimate California Dream experience *(p223)*.

The Petersen Automotive Museum
displays many classic models. This 1959 Cadillac epitomizes California cars.

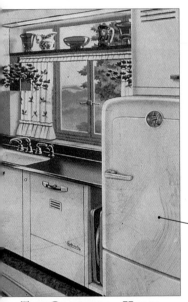

Land of Plenty
California's agricultural industry boomed in the 1940s, and its farmland was the most productive in the US.

Large refrigerators, stocked with food, were a symbol of the California "good life."

THE CALIFORNIA HOME

Eduardo Paolozzi's image is a pastiche of California's white, middle-class lifestyle in the 1950s. Nuclear families, ranch houses, and outdoor living were all part of the "dream."

San Francisco Giant
Willie Mays was part of the first team to bring professional baseball to California in 1958.

1945 End of World War II. International delegates meet at San Francisco April 25–June 25 to found the United Nations

1955 Disneyland opens in Anaheim. Actor James Dean, 24, dies in a car accident near Paso Robles

James Dean

1945	1950	1955

United Nations flag

1953 Beginning of Cold War is a boost to California defense industry

1958 New York Giants baseball team moves to San Francisco, finally bringing Major League baseball to the West Coast

California Today

SINCE 1962, when California surpassed New York as the most populous state in the Union, it has become the focus of many of the country's most significant issues. UC Berkeley was home to America's Free Speech Movement during the 1960s, and Haight Ashbury in San Francisco was the mecca for the "hippie" movement. Silicon Valley leads high-tech development in the US, and California benefits commercially from its proximity to the Far East. However, the state is still at risk from earthquakes; San Francisco has a high proportion of the country's AIDS cases; and racial tension, especially in LA, has led to riots.

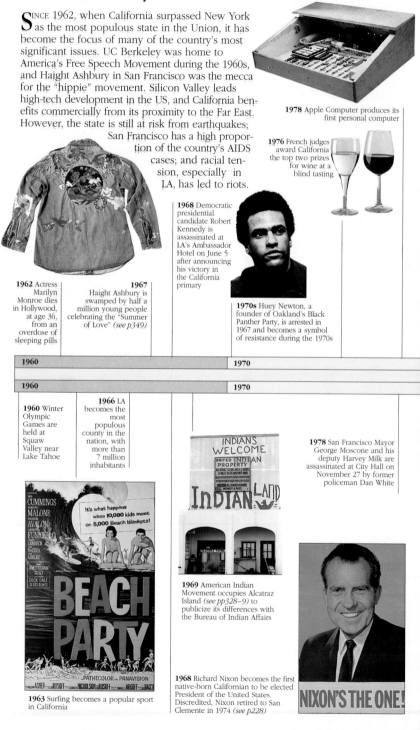

1978 Apple Computer produces its first personal computer

1976 French judges award California the top two prizes for wine at a blind tasting

1968 Democratic presidential candidate Robert Kennedy is assassinated at LA's Ambassador Hotel on June 5 after announcing his victory in the California primary

1962 Actress Marilyn Monroe dies in Hollywood, at age 36, from an overdose of sleeping pills

1967 Haight Ashbury is swamped by half a million young people celebrating the "Summer of Love" *(see p349)*

1970s Huey Newton, a founder of Oakland's Black Panther Party, is arrested in 1967 and becomes a symbol of resistance during the 1970s

1960 | 1970

1960 | 1970

1960 Winter Olympic Games are held at Squaw Valley near Lake Tahoe

1966 LA becomes the most populous county in the nation, with more than 7 million inhabitants

1978 San Francisco Mayor George Moscone and his deputy Harvey Milk are assassinated at City Hall on November 27 by former policeman Dan White

INDIANS WELCOME
UNITED INDIAN PROPERTY
InDIAN LAND

1969 American Indian Movement occupies Alcatraz Island *(see pp328–9)* to publicize its differences with the Bureau of Indian Affairs

BOB CUMMINGS
DOROTHY MALONE
FRANKIE AVALON
ANNETTE FUNICELLO

BEACH PARTY

1963 Surfing becomes a popular sport in California

1968 Richard Nixon becomes the first native-born Californian to be elected President of the United States. Discredited, Nixon retired to San Clemente in 1974 *(see p228)*

NIXON'S THE ONE!

1991 AIDS becomes San Francisco's number one killer of men

1989 The Bay Area endures its second worst earthquake, measuring 7.1 on the Richter Scale; 67 people die, another 1,800 are left homeless

1991 Fires in the Oakland hills kill 26 people and destroy 3,000 homes

1996 After 15 years as the speaker of the California Assembly, Democrat Willie Brown is sworn in as San Francisco's first black mayor

1981 Ronald Reagan, one-time film actor and former California governor, is sworn in as President of the United States

1990

1990

1995 The America's Cup yacht race, in which five countries compete, is held in San Diego from January to May

1987 Film director Steven Spielberg starts his own studio, Dreamworks

1984 LA hosts its second Olympic Games

1992 Riots in LA follow the acquittal of four white police officers who were videotaped beating a black motorist, Rodney King

1994 An earthquake measuring 6.8 on the Richter scale strikes LA, killing more than 60 people, injuring 9,000, and destroying freeways

LOS ANGELES

Los Angeles at a Glance

GREATER LOS ANGELES is made up of 80 different towns, with a total population of more than 8.5 million and covering more than 460 sq miles (1,200 sq km). In this book, LA has been divided into six areas. Downtown is a cultural melting pot, juxtaposing Hispanic El Pueblo, China-town, Little Tokyo, and the Business District. The glamour of the movies is just one aspect of Hollywood and West Hollywood, which today is a vibrant area of museums and galleries. Beverly Hills, Bel Air, and Westwood are still the playgrounds of the stars. Beaches and ports in the coastal regions of Santa Monica Bay, Palos Verdes, and Long Beach show the importance of the sea to Angelenos. Around Downtown covers some of the outlying districts of the city, including Pasadena.

AROUND DOWNTOWN
(See pp136–61)

BEVERLY HILLS, BEL AIR, AND WESTWOOD
(See pp84–95)

SANTA MONICA BAY
(See pp70–83)

Sunset Boulevard (see pp98–103) *is one of the most famous roads in the world. Lined with clubs and hotels, the section known as Sunset Strip is the center of LA's nightlife.*

0 kilometers 5

0 miles 5

The J Paul Getty Museum at the Getty Center (see pp78–81) *is situated on a hill and has stunning views across Los Angeles and the Santa Monica Mountains. Included in its world-class collection is Joseph Nollekens' marble statue of Venus (1773).*

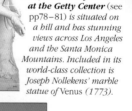

LACMA (see pp110–13) *has been located in Hollywood's Hancock Park since 1965. The six museum buildings house a remarkable collection of European, American, Asian, Middle Eastern, and Japanese art.*

At Universal Studios (see pp142–5), just north of Hollywood, visitors can see working film sets on the Studio Tour. A series of thrilling rides, based on the studios' movies, includes Jurassic Park – The Ride.

The Huntington Library, Art Collections, and Botanical Gardens (see pp154–7) in Pasadena have a wealth of treasures. The North Vista is one of the gardens' loveliest views.

OLLYWOOD
AND WEST
OLLYWOOD
e pp96–115)

DOWNTOWN
LOS ANGELES
(See pp116–25)

AROUND DOWNTOWN
(See pp136–61)

El Pueblo (see pp122–3), in the heart of Downtown Los Angeles, is the site of the city's first settlement. The area's Mexican population throngs its churches, plaza, and colorful markets, especially at festival time.

The Queen Mary (see pp130–31), one of the most famous liners in the world, is now permanently docked in Long Beach. The ship is still in use as a tourist attraction and luxury hotel. Many of its Art Deco features remain intact.

LONG BEACH AND
PALOS VERDES
(See pp126–35)

The Shape of Los Angeles

THE CITY OF LOS ANGELES sits in a broad, flat basin, facing the Pacific Ocean and enclosed by mountains. The San Gabriel Mountains and the Traverse Range come from the north, meeting the Santa Ana Mountains east of the city. The Santa Monica Mountains and the Hollywood Hills in the northwest split the basin, dividing the city center from the San Fernando Valley in the north. The shoreline varies from the rocky cliffs of Palos Verdes to the sands of Santa Monica Bay. Downtown, with the impressive skyscrapers of the Business District, sits in the center of the basin. Hollywood, Beverly Hills, and Santa Monica lie to the west.

Hollywood (see pp96–115) *is the birthplace of the modern film industry. Its famous sign* (see p141) *stands out like a beacon above Tinseltown.*

The San Fernando Valley *(see p140)*, the city's great suburban sprawl, is home to the Mission San Fernando Rey de España.

SAN GABRIEL MOUNTAINS

SANTA SUSANA MOUNTAINS

BURBANK

SAN FERNANDO VALLEY

HOLLYWOOD H

Mulholland Drive

Sunset Boulevard

SANTA MONICA MOUNTAINS

Malibu *(see pp82–3)* is an area of fine surfing beaches, wildlife havens, and private beach colonies nestled below rugged mountains.

Santa Monica (see pp72–5), *perched on palm-lined bluffs overlooking beautiful beaches, boasts stunning views. It is LA's oldest, largest beach resort, with all the traditional seaside attractions, such as a pier and amusement park. Santa Monica is also known for its excellent restaurants, boutiques, exciting nightlife, and vibrant arts scene.*

Beverly Hills (see pp84–93) *is home to the rich and famous of Los Angeles. Their lifestyle is epitomized by the exclusive shops that line Rodeo Drive.*

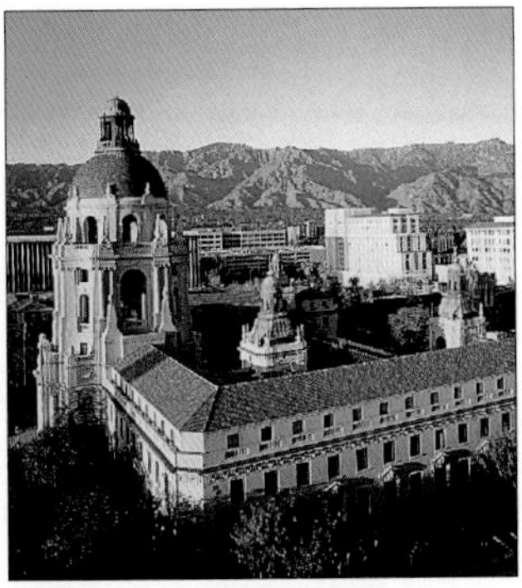

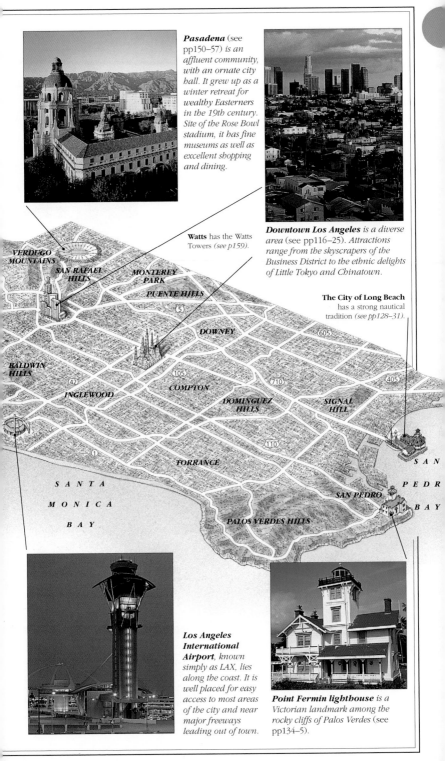

Pasadena (see pp150–57) *is an affluent community, with an ornate city hall. It grew up as a winter retreat for wealthy Easterners in the 19th century. Site of the Rose Bowl stadium, it has fine museums as well as excellent shopping and dining.*

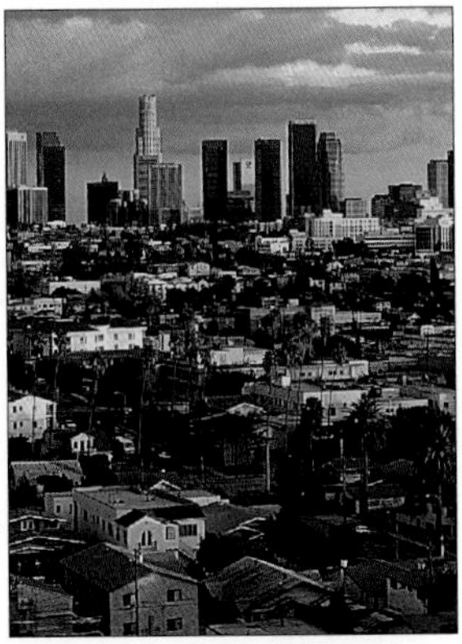

Downtown Los Angeles *is a diverse area* (see pp116–25). *Attractions range from the skyscrapers of the Business District to the ethnic delights of Little Tokyo and Chinatown.*

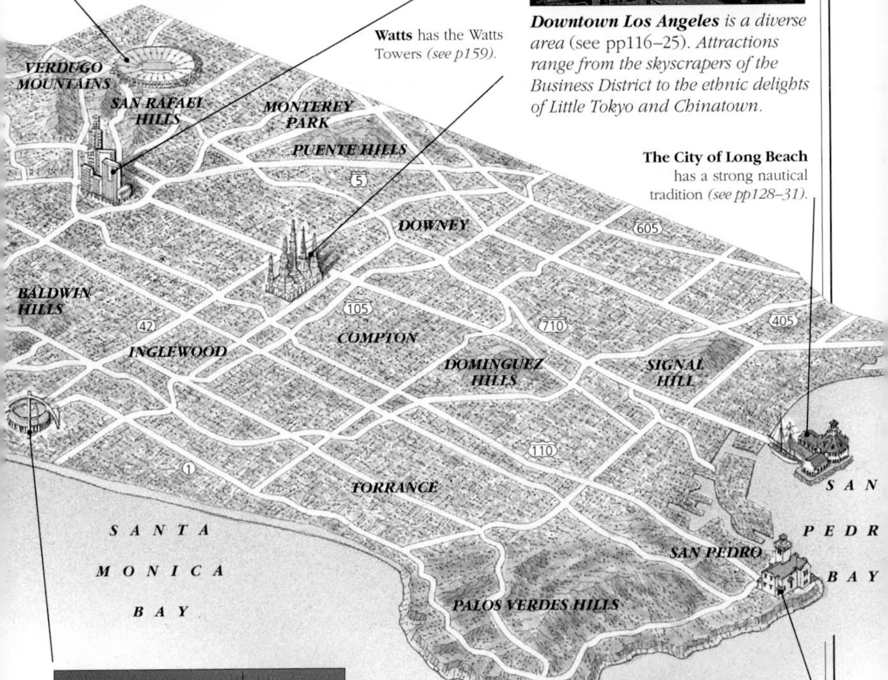
VERDUGO MOUNTAINS
SAN RAFAEL HILLS
MONTEREY PARK
PUENTE HILLS
5
DOWNEY
605
BALDWIN HILLS
105
42
INGLEWOOD
COMPTON
710
405
DOMINGUEZ HILLS
SIGNAL HILL
110
1
TORRANCE
SAN PEDRO BAY
SANTA MONICA BAY
SAN PEDRO
PALOS VERDES HILLS

Watts has the Watts Towers *(see p159).*

The City of Long Beach has a strong nautical tradition *(see pp128–31).*

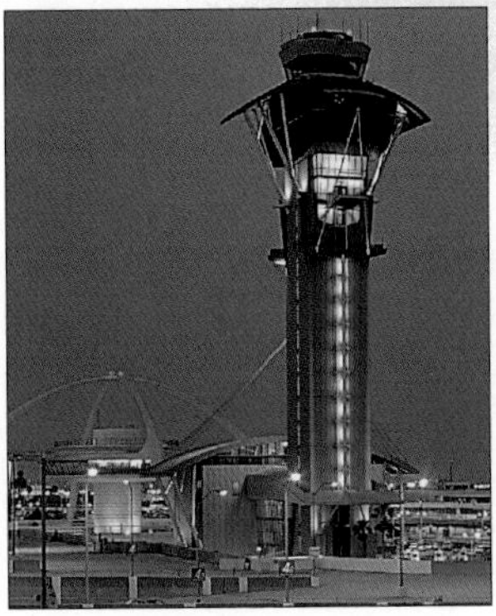

Los Angeles International Airport*, known simply as LAX, lies along the coast. It is well placed for easy access to most areas of the city and near major freeways leading out of town.*

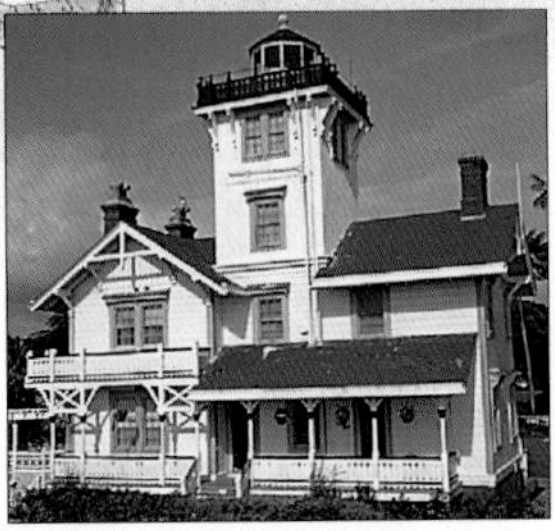

Point Fermin lighthouse *is a Victorian landmark among the rocky cliffs of Palos Verdes* (see pp134–5).

North Los Angeles Coastline

EACH YEAR MORE than 30 million people visit the beaches around Los Angeles, making them the most popular destination on the West Coast. The Malibu headland, from Point Dume to Malibu Lagoon, alternates between rocky shorelines and beaches. Farther along, the shoreline becomes a long sandy strand leading to the renowned beaches at Santa Monica and Venice. Inland, the terrain of the Santa Monica Mountains is rugged and largely unspoiled, with plenty of hiking trails leading to panoramic views of the Pacific Ocean. The waters off the Malibu Pier, Leo Carillo, and Topanga state beaches are considered to be the best for surfing.

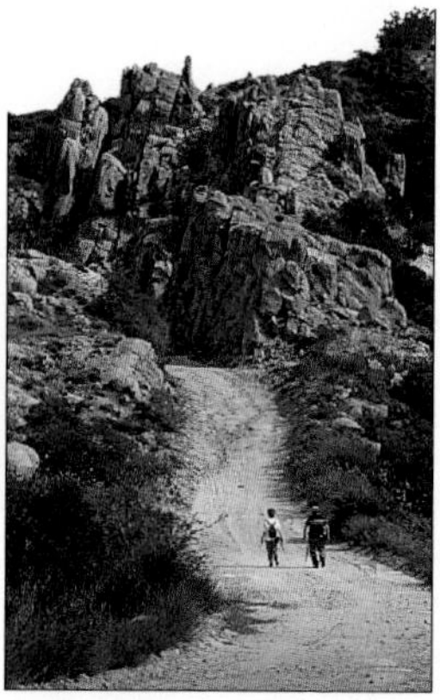

***Castro Crest** is characterized by large areas of exposed reddish purple sandstone and oak woodland. The park's hiking trails offer magnificent views inland of the Santa Susana mountains and, offshore, the Channel Islands.*

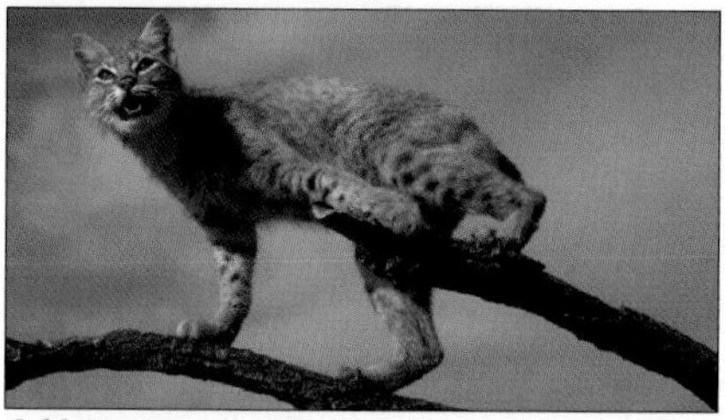

***Cold Creek Canyon Preserve** was set up in 1970 to protect the rich diversity of fauna and flora found in the Santa Monica Mountains, including the bobcat, the Pacific tree frog, and the stream orchid.*

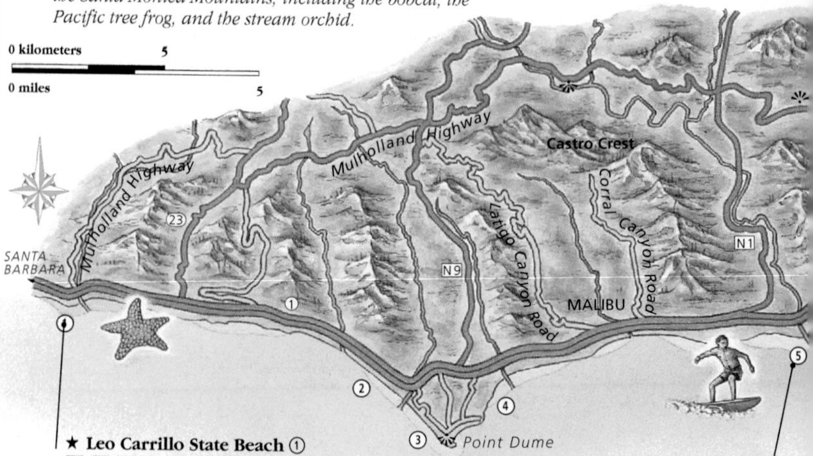

★ Leo Carrillo State Beach ①

🏄 🌊 🏊 ⛑ ♿ 🚻 ⛺ 🐚

At low tide it is possible to explore the wide variety of life in the rock pools around Sequit Point.

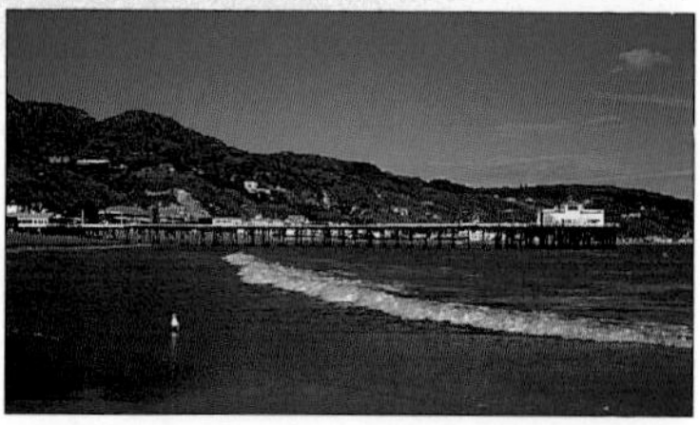

★ Surfrider County Beach ⑤

🏄 🏊 ⛑ ♿ 🚻

One of California's finest surfing beaches, Surfrider has featured in many surfing films. Malibu Pier is a good place from which to watch the action.

Zuma County Beach ②
The white sands of Malibu's largest beach are very popular during the summer. There is good surfing and swimming, but be careful of the hazardous rip tides.

Point Dume County Beach ③
Surf fishing, diving, sunbathing, and exploring the rock pools beneath Point Dume are all popular activities on this sandy sheltered beach.

Paradise Cove ④
This privately owned cove was featured in the TV series *The Rockford Files*. The pier is a good place for surf fishing, and the beach is ideal for sunbathing and swimming.

Topanga State Beach ⑥
This narrow sandy beach is popular with windsurfers. It is divided in two by the mouth of Topanga Creek.

LOCATOR MAP

KEY

▬	Freeway
▬	Major road
▬	Minor road
▭	River
❖	Viewpoint

Marina del Rey Harbor ⑩
This is one of the world's largest artificial harbors *(see p76)*. The quaint Fisherman's Village, next to Basin H, has shops, cafés, and restaurants.

★ Venice City Beach ⑨
Backed by picturesque Venice *(see p76)*, Venice City Beach offers an eclectic mix of street performers, skaters, and body builders, working out on Muscle Beach.

★ Will Rogers State Beach ⑦
Named after the Hollywood actor *(see p77)*, this is a good beach for body surfing.

★ Santa Monica State Beach ⑧
This is one of Santa Monica's *(see pp72–5)* most popular beaches. The group of houses at the western end of the beach are known collectively as "the Gold Coast."

South Los Angeles Coastline

The coast between Dockweiler State Beach and Torrance County Beach boasts shallow waters and wide stretches of sand, which are ideal for families. The two main communities, Manhattan Beach and Redondo Beach, have some of the cleanest waters off LA. Farther down the coast, the rocky bluffs of the Palos Verdes Peninsula shelter coves with rock pools teeming with marine life. Beyond Worldport LA, the coastline turns into a vista of white sand and rolling waves bordering Long Beach, the second largest city in LA County. Belmont Shores is popular with anglers. Windsurfers, sea kayakers, and jet-skiers frequent Alamitos Bay, home to the man-made canals and islands of Naples.

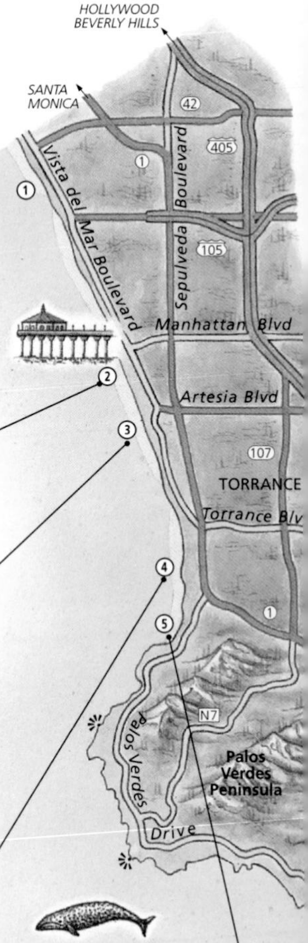

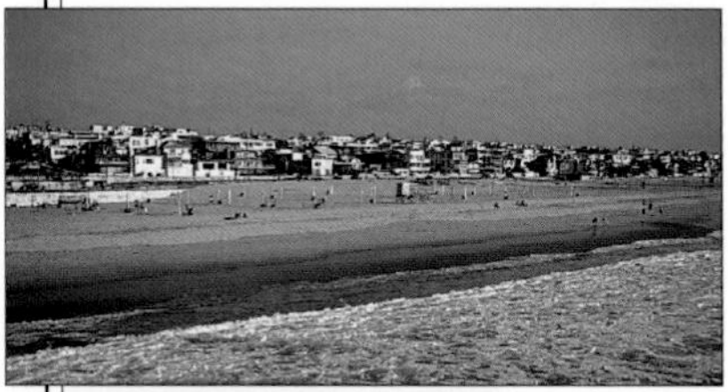

★ Manhattan State Beach ②

🏄 🌊 🏊 🛟 ♿ 🚻

Backed by the coastal cycle path, this long wide beach is good for swimming, surfing, and fishing.

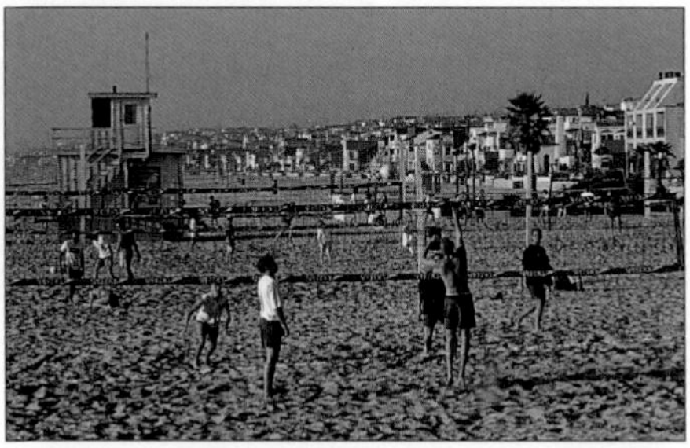

★ Hermosa City Beach ③

🏄 🌊 🏊 🛟 ♿ 🚻

This family beach is ideal for all types of beach sports, as well as being popular with anglers who fish the surf for perch.

★ Torrance County Beach ⑤

🏄 🌊 🏊 🛟 ♿ 🚻

Popular with surfers, swimmers, anglers, and divers alike, this beach marks the end of the Santa Monica Bay coastal cycle path *(see p168).*

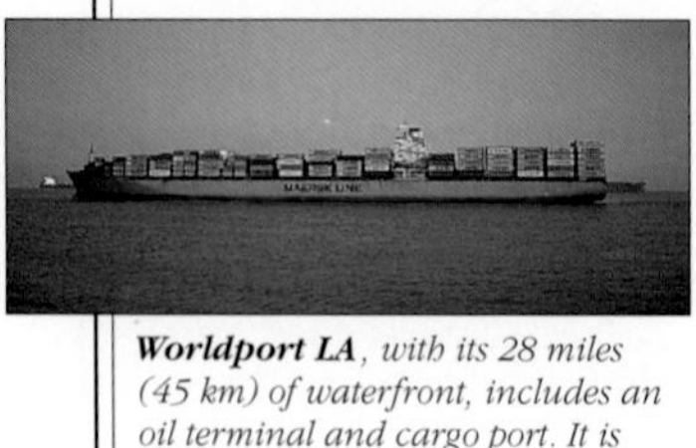

***Worldport LA**, with its 28 miles (45 km) of waterfront, includes an oil terminal and cargo port. It is also home to the country's second largest fishing fleet.*

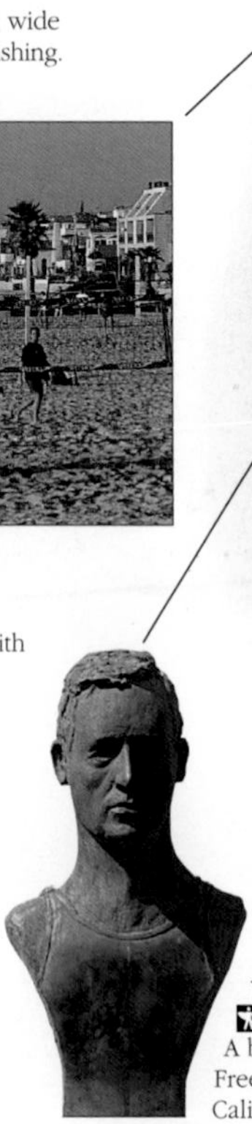

★ Redondo State Beach ④

🏄 🌊 🏊 🛟 ♿ 🚻

A bronze bust commemorates George Freeth, who introduced surfing to California in 1907 at Redondo Beach.

Dockweiler State Beach ①

The north end of Dockweiler, beyond the harbor entrance, includes a nesting area for the rare California least tern.

Cabrillo Beach ⑥

Split in two by the breakwater, Cabrillo has a fishing pier on the ocean side and a protected stretch of sand within San Pedro Bay.

Long Beach City Beach ⑦

At the western end of Long Beach Strand, as it is also known, stands the old, clapboard lifeguard headquarters, now a lifeguard museum.

Belmont Shores ⑧

Belmont Pier, situated at the northern end of the beach, is used by anglers fishing for halibut, bonito, and perch. It is also a roosting site for the endangered California brown pelican. The beach stretches south as far as the mouth of the San Gabriel River.

LOCATOR MAP

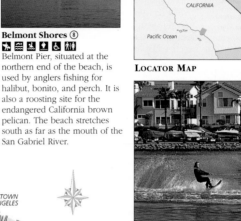

Alamitos Bay ⑨

Windsurfing, waterskiing, and swimming are all popular activities in the protected waters of the bay.

Worldport LA

KEY

▬	Freeway
▬	Major road
▬	Minor road
▭	River
☀	Viewpoint

Palos Verdes Peninsula rises 1,300 ft (400 m) above the rocky shoreline, which is home to many wading birds. Steep trails connect the shore to the clifftop with its panoramic views.

The Movies in Los Angeles

WHEN PEOPLE refer to Los Angeles as an "industry town," they invariably mean the movie industry. Its great fantasy factories employ more than 60,000 people and pump about $4 billion into the LA economy every year. Hollywood Boulevard has sadly lost much of its glamour over the years; some film companies have decamped to cheaper movie-making places. But the air of Hollywood as a dream-maker, a place where a secretary named Ava Gardner or college football player John Wayne could be "discovered" and go on to earn million-dollar salaries, still persists.

Hollywood street sign

Film crews *shooting location scenes for various Hollywood movies are a regular sight on Los Angeles' streets.*

The Griffith Observatory (see p146) *was the setting for the teenage school trip and dramatic car race at the climax of the legendary film* Rebel Without A Cause *(1955). The film catapulted James Dean to stardom, but he was to die in a car crash later the same year.*

WRITERS IN HOLLYWOOD

Hollywood novels have been a literary feature since the 1930s. Some writers, such as Nathaneal West and F Scott Fitzgerald, worked in Hollywood, only to turn against the town and publish novels that exposed its shallow and often cruel sides. West's *The Day of the Locust* (1939) is still considered the classic literary put-down of the film industry. Fitzgerald's posthumous *The Last Tycoon* (1941) sentimentalizes the career of Irving Thalberg, one of the most influential producers during Hollywood's "Golden Age." More recent is James Ellroy's *LA Confidential* (1997), a retro, atmospheric story of corruption and redemption in 1950s Los Angeles.

The Last Action Hero, *Arnold Schwarzenegger's 1993 blockbuster, filled this LA street with the excitement of controlled explosions, car chases, and stuntmen flying through the air.*

LA LOCATIONS

As well as utilizing the man-made sets erected on the backlots of the major studios in the 1940s and 1950s, film directors now regularly turn to the local landmarks of Los Angeles as locations for their films, often disguising them as other towns and cities. As a consequence, many of these places have become familiar to moviegoers all over the world.

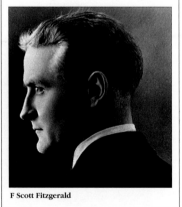

F Scott Fitzgerald

Million-dollar contracts *have been a feature of Hollywood since Charlie Chaplin's eight-picture deal in 1917. Two-time Oscar winner Tom Hanks now demands as much as $20 million a picture – 100 times as much as the salary of the US President. Also in the eight-figure category are Robin Williams, Julia Roberts, and Harrison Ford. Studio executives justify these salaries by saying that big stars bring in a large enough audience to recoup the high production costs.*

Julia Roberts   **Harrison Ford**

The Venice district (see p76) *saw actress Sarah Jessica Parker dancing around Steve Martin, in his 1991 hit film* LA Story. *The colorful buildings and characters of the area make it a popular film location.*

TOP GROSSING FILMS

Critics gush over *Citizen Kane* (1941) and *Casablanca* (1943) is the most popular Hollywood love story ever made. Yet neither of these films appears on trade paper *Variety*'s list of the American film industry's top ten moneymakers:

1. *Titanic* (1997)
2. *Star Wars* (1977)
3. *Harry Potter and the Philosopher's Stone* (2001)
4. *Phantom Menace* (1999)
5. *E.T., the Extra Terrestrial* (1982)
6. *Jurassic Park* (1993)
7. *Forrest Gump* (1994)
8. *The Lion King* (1994)
9. *Return of the Jedi* (1983)
10. *The Fellowship of the Ring* (2001)

The only films made before 1960 on the top 50 list are *Gone With the Wind* (1939), at No. 40, and *Snow White and the Seven Dwarfs* (1937), at No. 45.

Santa Monica Pier (see p74) *should be familiar to fans of the gangster film* The Sting *(1973), starring actors Robert Redford and Paul Newman.*

Stargazing *is enjoyed by both visitors and locals in LA's many glamorous venues. Good opportunities to spot actors, directors, and film executives can be found at Wolfgang Puck's trendy Spagos (see p550) and the Polo Lounge at the Beverly Hills Hotel (see p508).*

Film poster for *E.T., the Extra Terrestrial*

Los Angeles's Best: Museums and Galleries

THE MUSEUMS of LA reflect the great diversity of the city. Collections ranging from natural history to Native American artifacts and from cowboy heritage to the history of the Holocaust educate and inspire the visitor. The city also contains many museums of art. Some of these display the private collections of the wealthy, such as Norton Simon, J Paul Getty, and Henry and Arabella Huntington, and feature internationally acclaimed Old Masters, Impressionist paintings, and European and Asian works of art. "Museum Row" on Wilshire Boulevard is home to five museums, including the renowned LACMA.

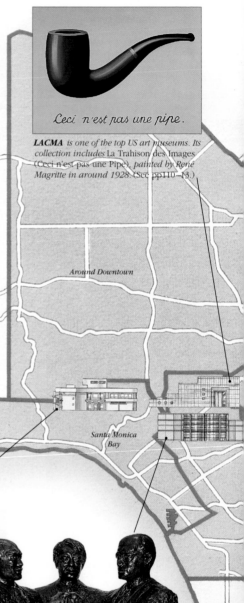

Ceci n'est pas une pipe.

LACMA *is one of the top US art museums. Its collection includes* La Trahison des Images *(Ceci n'est pas une Pipe), painted by René Magritte in around 1928. (See pp110–13.)*

Around Downtown

Santa Monica Bay

J Paul Getty Museum *has recently relocated most of its holdings to the Getty Center in the Santa Monica Mountains.* La Promenade *(1870) by Pierre-Auguste Renoir is just one of the extraordinary paintings in this collection. (See pp78–81.)*

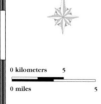

The Museum of Tolerance *aims to promote understanding between peoples. This sculpture of President Sadat of Egypt, with President Carter of the United States and Prime Minister Begin of Israel, illustrates that aim. (See p89.)*

0 kilometers   5

0 miles   5

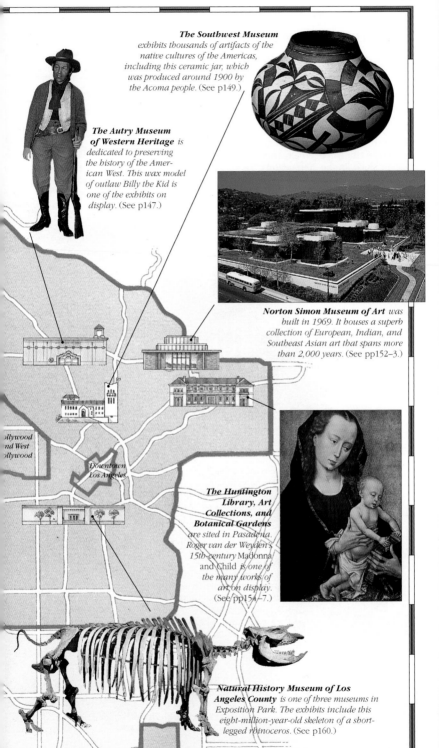

The Southwest Museum exhibits thousands of artifacts of the native cultures of the Americas, including this ceramic jar, which was produced around 1900 by the Acoma people. (See p149.)

The Autry Museum of Western Heritage is dedicated to preserving the history of the American West. This wax model of outlaw Billy the Kid is one of the exhibits on display. (See p147.)

Norton Simon Museum of Art was built in 1969. It houses a superb collection of European, Indian, and Southeast Asian art that spans more than 2,000 years. (See pp152–3.)

ollywood nd West ollywood

Downtown Los Angeles

The Huntington Library, Art Collections, and Botanical Gardens are sited in Pasadena. Roger van der Weyden's 15th-century Madonna and Child is one of the many works of art on display. (See pp154–7.)

Natural History Museum of Los Angeles County is one of three museums in Exposition Park. The exhibits include this eight-million-year-old skeleton of a short-legged rhinoceros. (See p160.)

Contemporary Architecture in Los Angeles

For more than a century after it was founded in 1781, LA remained a small town of modest adobe buildings. It was not until the late 19th century that settlers from the East and Midwest introduced the Victorian styles of building they had grown up with. When the transcontinental railroad reached LA in 1887 there was a building boom, and the city has been expanding ever since. In the 20th century, LA's finest contributions to architecture have been the inventive reworkings of past styles. In recent years, architects have remodeled dilapidated commercial buildings to create lively, fashionable structures.

Kate Mantilini's *(1985)*
This building-within-a-building restaurant is typical of LA's avant-garde deconstructivism (see p544).

2 Rodeo *(1990)*
This pastiche of European architecture, including a replica of Rome's Spanish Steps, is part of the famous shopping district (see p90). The parking lot has Victorian-style streetlamps and a cobblestone surface.

Around Downtown

Beverly Hills, Bel Air and Westwood

Santa Monica Bay

Eames House *(1949)*
This steel-framed house and studio were designed by Charles and Ray Eames as one of 36 projects commissioned by Arts & Architecture *magazine.*

TBWA Chiat/Day Advertising Agency *(1991)*
Frank Gehry, the leading LA architect, designed this striking building (see p74).

Disney Studio Office Building *(1991)*
Michael Graves' Post-Modern Disney building in Burbank includes a classically inspired pediment supported by 19-ft (5.7-m) statues of the Seven Dwarfs. Inside, chairs incorporate Mickey Mouse in their design (see pp140–41).

Ennis House *(1924)*
The base, plan, and textured interiors of this house are typical of Frank Lloyd Wright's "textile block" houses.

Gamble House
(1908)
This is the finest example of Charles and Henry Greene's turn-of-the-century Arts and Crafts bungalows. Its expansive eaves, outdoor sleeping porches, and elegant interior are characteristic of the brothers' style (see p150).

Hollywood and West Hollywood

Downtown Los Angeles

Union Station *(1939)*
The last of the great American railroad terminals, the vaulted concourse, arches, waiting room, and patios combine Mission Revival and Streamline Moderne styles (see p124).

Eastern Columbia Building *(1930)*
This Art Deco building, designed by Claude Beelman, is one of the most impressive of its kind in LA.

In-line skaters on Venice Beach boardwalk

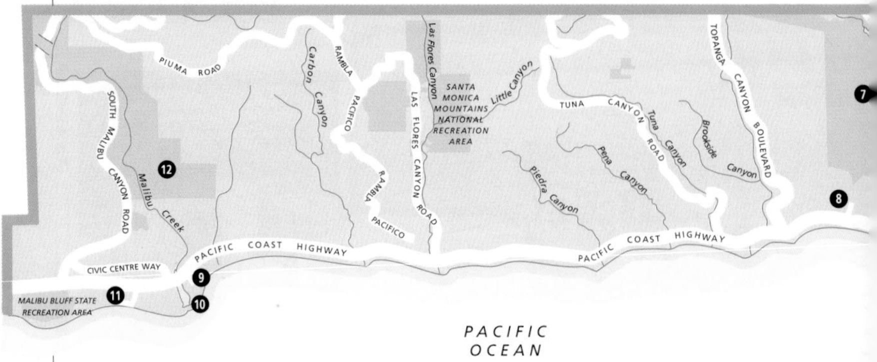
PIUMA ROAD
SOUTH MALIBU CANYON ROAD
Malibu Creek
12
Carbon Canyon
RAMBLA PACIFICO
Las Flores Canyon
LAS FLORES CANYON ROAD
SANTA MONICA MOUNTAINS NATIONAL RECREATION AREA
Little Canyon
TUNA CANYON ROAD
Tuna Canyon
Pena Canyon
Piedra Canyon
Brookside Canyon
TOPANGA CANYON BOULEVARD
7
8
PACIFIC COAST HIGHWAY
CIVIC CENTRE WAY
9
10
11
MALIBU BLUFF STATE RECREATION AREA
PACIFIC OCEAN

Sights at a Glance

Districts
Malibu Colony 11
Marina del Rey 3
Santa Monica pp72–5 1
Venice 2

Museums
Adamson House and Malibu Lagoon Museum 9
J Paul Getty Museum at the Getty Center pp78–81 5
The Getty Villa 8
Museum of Flying 4

Parks and Beaches
Malibu Creek State Park 12
Malibu Lagoon State Beach 10
Topanga State Park 7
Will Rogers State Historic Park 6

Key

Street-by-Street map
See pp72–3

0 kilometers 2

0 miles 2

SANTA MONICA BAY

WITH ITS WARM SUN, cool sea breezes, miles of sandy beaches, excellent surf, and world-class museums, Santa Monica Bay epitomizes the best of California. The area was inhabited by the Chumash and Tongva/Gabrielino peoples for 2,500 years before the arrival in 1542 of the Spanish explorer Juan Cabrillo *(see p42)*. In the early 19th century, Santa Monica Bay was divided into several land grants, including Rancho San Vicente y Santa Monica and Rancho Topanga Malibu Sequit. In 1875, Nevada senator John Percival Jones bought control of the former, hoping the port of Los Angeles would be built there. Thankfully, that honor went to

Swimmer in Venice Beach

San Pedro *(see pp134–5)* and the beach resorts of Santa Monica and Venice were developed in its place. These areas have remained two of the most attractive and lively parts of Los Angeles.

Farther along the coast, the Rancho Topanga Malibu Sequit was bought in 1887 by Frederick and May Rindge. The Rindge family fought with the state for many years to keep their property secluded. Eventually failing, they sold much of Malibu to the rich and famous. Large areas of Santa Monica Bay have remained undeveloped, however. The vast Topanga and Malibu Creek state parks help to improve Los Angeles's air quality and offer miles of hiking trails.

GETTING THERE

Santa Monica lies at the end of the Santa Monica Freeway (I-10) and is linked to Malibu by the Pacific Coast Highway. Santa Monica and Venice are well served by the Santa Monica Blue Bus Company. Possibly the best way to see the area is by renting a bicycle and taking the coastal cycle path *(see p168)*.

Street-by-Street: Santa Monica ❶

Street entertainer

SANTA MONICA'S fresh sea breezes, mild climate (on average, the sun shines here 328 days a year), and pedestrian-friendly streets make it one of the best places in LA to go for a stroll. The city is perched on a high yellow cliff overlooking Santa Monica Bay and miles of broad, sandy beach. Running along the cliff edge is palm-shaded Palisades Park, a narrow, 26-acre (10-ha) garden offering spectacular views, especially at sunset. A stairway leads down to Santa Monica's famous beach and pier. A few blocks inland from the hotel-lined seafront is Third Street Promenade – a great place to sit outside a café or restaurant and people-watch.

View from Palisades Park
The cliff top park offers panoramic views of Santa Monica Bay. Looking northward, you can see all the way to Malibu.

★ Third Street Promenade
Metal and topiary fountains, shaped like dinosaurs, decorate these three lively blocks. This is one of the best outdoor shopping areas in LA.

SANTA MONICA BLVD

WILSHIRE BOULEVARD

ARIZONA AVENUE

Hotels line the beach.

★ Palisades Park
This narrow strip of parkland, planted with mature palm trees, is a good place to walk, jog, or sit on a bench and admire the view. In the evening, many people come here to watch the sun go down.

STAR SIGHTS

★ Palisades Park

★ Santa Monica Pier

★ Third Street Promenade

KEY

— — — Suggested route

0 meters	200
0 yards	200

Santa Monica Place
This lively shopping mall was designed by architect Frank Gehry in 1979. The first-floor food hall offers a variety of reasonably priced meals. The stores on the upper two levels range from chain stores to individual boutiques.

LOCATOR MAP

★ Santa Monica Pier
Since 1908, Angelenos and visitors alike have flocked to this landmark pier. With its long boardwalk, arcades, and fishing areas, it still has plenty to offer. A new amusement area, Pacific Park, has a Ferris wheel, roller coaster, and bumper cars.

Tourist information

Beach
Following the success of the television series Baywatch, *Santa Monica's beach is famous throughout the world.*

Exploring Santa Monica

Statue in Bergamot Station gallery

SANTA MONICA has been the star of LA's coast-line since the 1890s, when trolleys linked it to the city, and beach parties became the rage. In the early days, it lived a dual life as a sleepy coast town and the head-quarters for offshore gambling ships. In the 1920s and 1930s, movie stars such as Cary Grant and Mary Pickford bought land here, creating "the Gold Coast." The beach and pier are still major attractions, but the city is now also famous for its restau-rants *(see p548)*. With the cleanest air in LA, Santa Monica offers many outdoor shopping areas and an active arts scene. Bergamot Station and the Edge-mar complex on Main Street have a range of galleries.

Frank Gehry's innovative design for the TBWA Chiat/Day Advertising Agency

Around Santa Monica

Grassy parks dot the city's landscape, with none quite as beautiful or revered as **Palisades Park** on the bluff overlooking the ocean. Stretching 1.5 miles (2.5 km) along the cliff's edge, this narrow, well-manicured park is one of the best spots to watch the sun go down. For the quintessential California experience, take a walk or jog along the paths, with the ocean as a backdrop and the towering palms overhead. The landscaping is beautiful, with semitropical trees and plants. At the northern end, the aptly named Inspiration Point has great views of the bay, stretching from Malibu to Palos Verdes.

Inland, between Wilshire Boulevard and Broadway, is **Third Street Promenade**. Once a decaying shopping street, this boulevard has undergone a major face-lift and is now one of the live-liest places in Los Angeles. Its three pedestrian blocks are lined with shops, coffee houses, restaurants, bookstores,

and theaters. At night the mood is especially festive. Street perform-ers entertain passers-by with music, dance, puppet shows, and magic tricks. Nearby, on Arizona Avenue, a farmers' market on Saturdays and Wed-nesdays is one of the best in the city.

Santa Monica's other important shop-ping area is **Main Street**, which runs south toward Venice *(see p76)*. At the turn of the 20th century, Main Street was the commercial district for Pacific Ocean Park, an amusement park, baths, and pier. By the early 1970s, however, the majority of the neigh-borhood's attractions had been demolished, and Main Street itself had become a slum.

Today, this revital-ized street abounds with a wide range of

shops, superb restaurants, and first-rate art galleries.

There are many examples of public art displayed along Main Street. Sculptor Paul Conrad's *Chain Reaction* (1991) is a stainless-steel and copper-link chain statement against nuclear war. It stands next to the Civic Auditorium. *Ocean Park Pier* (1976), a mural by Jane Golden and Barbara Stoll, is situated at the junction with Ocean Park Boulevard and depicts the Pacific Ocean Park in the early 1900s.

A lovely example of Spanish Colonial architecture remains at the northwest corner of Main Street and Pier Avenue. Nearby, the TWBA Chiat/Day Advertising Agency building, designed in 1991 by Frank Gehry and shaped like a giant pair of binoculars, dominates the street *(see p68)*.

🎡 Santa Monica Pier

Colorado & Ocean aves. **(** *(310) 458-8900; 260-8744 Pacific Park information.* 🔘 *daily.* **Carousel** 🔘 *May–Sep: 10am–5pm Tue–Sun; Oct– Apr: 10am–5pm Sat & Sun.* 🈺

This popular 1908 landmark is the West Coast's oldest amusement pier. All the attrac-tions are here, such as popcorn, cotton-candy, bumper cars, and an amusement arcade. At the western end, Pacific Park has a roller coaster and a Ferris wheel rising 11 stories high. Nearby, the 1922 Looff Carousel, similar to that in Santa Cruz *(see p490)*, with 44 handcrafted horses, was featured in George Roy Hill's

Chain Reaction by Paul Conrad

Beach apartments along the front of Palisades Park

1973 film *The Sting (see p65).* You can fish without a permit from the pier's lower deck. On Thursday evenings during the summer, there is free dancing and live music *(see p163).*

🏛 Bergamot Station
2525 Michigan Ave. **[** *(310) 829-5854.* **◻** *10am–5:00pm Tue–Sat.* **●** *Sundays and public hols.*
Bergamot Station is a 5.5-acre (2-ha) arts complex that stands on the site of an abandoned Red Line trolley station. The crude buildings are constructed from aluminum siding, with an added touch of high-tech styling. More than 20 galleries showcase the latest works in contemporary and radical art, including painting, sculpture, photography, furniture, and glass, as well as collectibles and African art. Bergamot Station also houses a number of artists' studios.

Victorian façade of the California Heritage Museum

there are changing exhibitions on topics such as surfing *(see pp188–9),* the Hollywood Western, quilts, and Monterey Rancho-style furniture.

🏛 Santa Monica Museum of Art
Building G-1, Bergamot Station. **[** *(310) 586-6488.* **◻** *11am–6pm Tue–Sat, 10am–5pm Sun.* **●** *Jan 1, Jul 4, Thanksgiving, Dec 25.* **🔲**
The Santa Monica Museum of Art is dedicated to both contemporary and modern art. Its main aim is to publicize the work of living artists, particularly those involved in performance and multimedia art. In May 1998 the museum re-opened after moving to its exciting new, 930 sq m (10,000 sq ft) home. It is located in the large arts complex, Bergamot Station, along with over 20 other galleries. Although the museum does not have any permanent collections, a wide range of artists' work is represented in the individual exhibitions. The new site also houses a museum book shop.

VISITORS' CHECKLIST

Road map inset A. 🚗 *90,000.* ✈ *LAX 8 miles (13 km) SE of Santa Monica.* 🚌 *4th St & Colorado Blvd.* 🛈 *Palisades Park, 1400 Ocean Ave (310-393-7593).* 🎉 *Santa Monica Festival (Apr).*

Cuban political poster on display in Bergamot Station

🏛 California Heritage Museum
2612 Main St. **[** *(310) 392-8537.* **◻** *For specific exhibits only. Call for information.* **●** *Jan 1, Jul 4, Thanksgiving, Dec 25.* 📷 ♿
The Queen Anne museum building was built in 1894 by architect Sumner P Hunt as the home of Roy Jones, son of the founder of Santa Monica *(see p71).* On the first floor, the rooms depict the lifestyle of various periods in Southern California history: a Victorian dining room, an Arts and Crafts living room, and a 1930s kitchen. Upstairs,

RAYMOND CHANDLER
Novelist and screenwriter Raymond Chandler (1888–1959) set several of his works wholly or partly in Santa Monica, a city that he loathed and that he thinly disguised as sleazy Bay City in *Farewell, My Lovely.* There was some truth in Chandler's portrayal of Santa Monica. Corruption and vice in the 1920s and 1930s are well documented. Illegal gambling ships were anchored offshore, including the *Rex,* 5 miles (8 km) out in Santa Monica Bay, called the *Royal Crown* in *Farewell, My Lovely.*

Chandler's novels *Farewell, My Lovely, The Big Sleep, The High Window, The Little Sister,* and *The Long Goodbye* were made into films that portrayed the shadowy side of LA. With an elegant, dark style, he wrote vivid dialogue in the voice of the common man. His character Philip Marlowe was the definitive detective. A loner with a hard-boiled veneer often hiding a soft heart, Marlowe uttered tough one-liners, played by the rules, and usually didn't get the girl.

Film poster for *The Big Sleep* (1946)

Venice ❷

Road map inset A. 🛈 *2904 Washington Blvd, Suite 100 (310 396-7016). www.venice.net*

SINCE ITS INCEPTION, Venice has attracted a bohemian society, from the rowdy crowd who frequented its dance hall and bathhouse in the 1910s to beatniks in the 1950s. Today, the town has a large population of artists, whose studios line the streets.

The community was founded in 1900 by tobacco magnate Abbot Kinney as a US version of Venice, Italy. Hoping to spark a cultural renaissance in southern California, he built a system of canals and imported gondolas and gondoliers to punt along the waterways. Unfortunately, Kinney did not take the tides into consideration when designing Venice, and the area was constantly dogged by sewage problems.

Today, only a few of the original 7 miles (11 km) of canals remain, the rest having been filled in during 1927. The traffic circle at Windward Avenue was the main lagoon, and Grand Boulevard, which runs southeast from there, was the Grand Canal. The best place to see the remaining canals is on Dell Avenue, where old bridges, boats, and ducks grace the waterways.

Over the years, the circus atmosphere of Venice Beach has never faltered. On the boardwalk during weekends, semiclad men and women whiz past on bicycles and skates, while a zany array of street performers, like chainsaw jugglers and one-man bands, captivates the crowds. . Muscle Beach, where Arnold Schwarzenegger used to work out, still attracts body builders.

While Venice Beach is safe to explore on foot by day, it is best avoided at night.

Yachts in the harbor at Marina del Rey

Marina del Rey ❸

Road map inset A. 🛈 *4111 Via Marina (310 821-0555).*

COVERING AN AREA of just 1.3 sq miles (3.4 sq km), approximately half of which is water, Marina del Rey has the world's largest artificial small-craft harbor. Those attracted to this town tend to be young and single or with families, and enjoy outdoor activities such as skating, cycling, and water sports. Everything from paddle boats to yachts can be rented, or you can charter boats for deep-sea fishing or a luxury cruise.

Fisherman's Village, on Fiji Way, resembles a New England fishing town. It has a variety of shops, restaurants, and cafés, many of which offer beautiful views of the harbor.

Museum of Flying ❹

2772 Donald Douglas Loop N, Santa Monica. **Road map** inset A. ☎ *(310) 392-8822.* ⏰ *10am–5pm Wed–Sun.* ⬤ *Jan 1, Jul 4, Thanksgiving, Dec 25.* 📷 ♿ ✒

THE FIRST AIRPLANE to fly around the world, the 1924 *New Orleans*, is on display at this fascinating museum of aviation history. Other highlights of the collection of 40 aircraft are P-51 Mustangs and Spitfires, the victorious fighter planes of World War II. Interactive exhibits explain the complexities of aircraft design, and there are workshops for children, who can take part in a variety of related activities. Some of the vintage aircraft remain airworthy, and visitors

Man-made canal in Venice

can watch them take off from and land at the adjacent Santa Monica Airport. Classic aviation films are also shown.

Yellow Peril Boeing Stearman at the Museum of Flying

J Paul Getty Center ❺

See pp78–81.

Will Rogers State Historic Park ❻

1501 Will Rogers State Park Blvd, Pacific Palisades. **Road map** inset A. 📞 *(310) 454-8212.* ⏰ *8am–sunset daily.* 🌑 *Jan 1, Thanksgiving, Dec 25.* ♿ 🅿 *lawn area.* 📷

WILL ROGERS (1879–1935) started life as a cowboy and went on to become a film star, radio commentator, and newspaper columnist. Called the "Cowboy Philosopher," he was famous for his homespun humor and shrewd comments on current events, usually made while performing rope tricks. His show business career lasted from 1905 until his death. When his widow, Betty, died in 1944, she deeded the house and the surrounding 186 acres (75 ha) of land to the state. Her will stipulated that nothing in the house be changed and that polo matches be held on weekends (Rogers was an avid polo player).

Hiking trails lead up from the ranch, many of them originally cut by Rogers. The lawn just east of the house is an ideal setting for a picnic. Tours of the house include the living room, where Rogers used to practice his roping skills.

THE WILDLIFE OF SANTA MONICA BAY

Among the marine mammals that inhabit the waters of Santa Monica Bay are harbor seals, California sea lions, and bottlenosed dolphins. From December to February gray whales can be seen migrating from Alaska to Baja California to calve. One of the best places in Los Angeles for whale-spotting is Point Dume. In the mountains, the range of wildlife is exceptional. The rare mountain lion can reach a size of 7 ft (2 m) in length and tends to live in the rockier, more remote areas. Its cousin the bobcat is smaller, with tufts of hair on the ends of its ears. Coyotes come out at dusk, often preying on the pets of people living in the hills. The bold, intelligent raccoon raids camp sites even when people are present. Mule deer, desert cottontail, and striped skunk also abound. Birds seen here include golden eagles and red-tailed hawks.

Raccoon (Procyon lotor)

Topanga State Park ❼

20825 Entrada Rd, Topanga. **Road map** inset A. 📞 *(310) 455-2465 & (805) 488-8147 for fire conditions in summer & autumn.* ⏰ *8am–sunset daily.* 🅿 ♿

TOPANGA STATE PARK stretches from the Pacific Palisades to the San Fernando Valley *(see p140)*. Topanga is thought to be an Indian term meaning "the place where the mountains meet the sea." The area was inhabited by the Tongva/ Gabrielino and Chumash Indians 5,000 years ago. Today, its groves of sycamore and oak trees attract people seeking an alternative way of life.

The marked entrance to the 10,000-acre (4,000-ha) park lies just north of Topanga village, off Hwy 27 on Entrada Road. Most of the land falls within the LA city boundary, making it the largest city park in the US. As such, it vastly improves the region's air quality and provides ample space for hiking and riding.

As you ascend the Santa Monica Mountains, canyons, cliffs, and meadows give way to vistas of the ocean and the San Fernando Valley. Four trails begin from the park's headquarters at Trippet Ranch: a 1-mile (1.6-km) self-guided nature trail; the Dead Horse Trail; Musch Ranch Trail (which leads to a camp site); and East Topanga Fire Road, which connects with Eagle Junction. The 2.5-mile (4-km) Eagle Rock/Eagle Spring Trail from Eagle Junction is one of the most popular.

Bicycles are allowed on the park's dirt fire roads, and horses on all but one of the trails.

Hiking trails crossing the Santa Monica Mountains in Topanga State Park

J Paul Getty Museum at the Getty Center ❺

THE GETTY CENTER, which opened in December 1997, holds a commanding physical and cultural position in the city. It is situated amid the wild beauty of the Santa Monica Mountains, in the Sepulveda Pass, next to the San Diego Freeway (I-405). The complex houses not only the museum but also the Getty's research, conservation, and education institutes, dedicated to art and cultural heritage. Getty made his fortune in the oil business and became an ardent collector of art. He wanted his collection, which focuses on European art from the Renaissance to Post-Impressionism, to be open to the public without charge. Greek and Roman antiquities are displayed at the Getty Villa in Malibu (see p82).

LOCATOR MAP

▦ Illustrated area

☐ Research, conservation, education, administration, restaurant, café, and auditorium buildings

🚉 Tram station

★ **Irises** (1889)
This work was painted by Vincent Van Gogh while he was in the asylum at St-Rémy. Its graphic style reveals the influence of artists such as Paul Gauguin (1848–1903) and the Japanese print-maker Hokusai (1760–1849).

East Pavilion

Hispano-Moresque Deep Dish
This elaborately decorated earthenware dish was made in Valencia, Spain, in the mid-15th century. The use of lustrous colors was a specialty of Moorish potters at that time.

North Pavilion

Courtyard

Entrance

STAR PAINTINGS

★ **Wheatstacks, Snow Effect, Morning by Claude Monet**

★ **The Abduction of Europa by Rembrandt**

★ **Irises by Vincent Van Gogh**

Cabinet on Stand
Attributed to the French master craftsman A-C Boulle, this 17th-century cabinet was made to celebrate the victories of Louis XIV.

South Pavilion

West Pavilion

South Promontory

Korean Man
(c.1617)
This drawing in black and red chalk is by the Flemish artist Peter Paul Rubens. He used the red chalk to highlight the fine detail of the subject's face.

★ Wheatstacks, Snow Effect, Morning (1891)
This is one in a series of works by Monet that shows the same landscape at different times of the day and year.

Temporary exhibitions
and the museum café are housed in this building.

★ The Abduction of Europa (1632)
One of Rembrandt's few landscapes, this depicts the Roman god Jupiter, disguised as a bull, kidnapping Europa, princess of Tyre.

GUIDE TO THE GETTY CENTER
From below, the Getty Center may look like a fortress, but once on top, the scale is intimate, with fountains, walkways, courtyards, and niches. An electric tram brings visitors from the parking lot to the complex. The museum has a tall, airy foyer that opens onto a central courtyard. From here radiate five two-story pavilions, which contain the art collections. The Conceptualist artist Robert Irwin has created a central garden to the west of the museum. Across the main plaza from the tram station there is a café and restaurant. Another café and a bookstore are located within the museum.

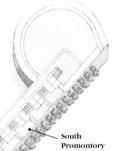

Exploring the Getty Museum

J PAUL GETTY (1892–1976) amassed a remarkable collection of European painting, sculpture, and decorative arts, focusing on pre-20th-century artistic movements. Getty was a bold collector who enjoyed the pursuit of an object almost more than the possession of it. Since his death, the Getty Trust has strengthened the museum's holdings by purchasing works of the highest quality to complement the existing collection. New departments in related areas such as drawings and manuscripts have also been added. Since the move to the Getty Center in 1997, the museum can now display twice as much of its collection as at the Getty Villa *(see p82).*

Man with a Hoe, painted between 1860 and 1862 by Jean-François Millet

EUROPEAN PAINTINGS AND SCULPTURE

T HE MUSEUM boasts a superb collection of European paintings, dating from the 13th century to the late 19th century. Italian works from the Renaissance and Baroque periods include *The Adoration of the Magi* (c.1495–1505) by Andrea Mantegna and *View of the Dogana, Venice* (1744) by Canaletto. Rembrandt's *The Abduction of Europa* (1632) is a highlight from the Flemish and Dutch collections, which also include an oil sketch by Peter Paul Rubens (1577–1640) and a portrait by Anthony Van Dyck (1599–1641).

Of the French artworks on display, *The Race of the Riderless Horses* (1817) is an important painting by the Romantic painter Théodore Géricault. In *Still Life with Apples* (1900) by Paul Cézanne, the artist's preoccupation with gradations of light and color reveals the progression in the late 19th century from the old, realistic style of painting, to a more modern, abstract approach. This painting, along with

Claude Monet's *Wheatstacks, Snow Effect, Morning (see p79),* and Vincent Van Gogh's *Irises (see p78),* has helped to elevate the museum's collection of Impressionists and Post-Impressionists.

European sculptures in the Getty date from the 16th century to the end of the 19th century. Pier Jacopo Antico's *Bust of Marcus Aurelius* (c.1520) was created at the end of the High Renaissance in Italy. The elongated body favored by the Mannerists can be seen in Benvenuto Cellini's *Satyr* (c.1542). Fine examples of Baroque sculpture are *Pluto Abducting Proserpine* (c.1693–1710) by François Girardon and Gian Lorenzo Bernini's *Boy with a Dragon* (c.1614). Neo-Classical works include three statues by Joseph Nollekens: *Venus, Juno,* and *Minerva* (1773).

DRAWINGS

T HE PURCHASE in 1981 of Rembrandt's red chalk study of *Nude Woman with a Snake* (c.1637) marked the beginning of the museum's drawings collection. Today, the collection contains more than 400 works in a wide range of media, spanning the 15th to the late 19th century. *The Stag Beetle* (1505) by Albrecht Dürer is an exquisitely detailed illustration in watercolor and gouache. By contrast, Leonardo da Vinci's *Three Sketches of a Child with a Lamb* (c.1503–6) is a looser pen-and-ink study.

Peter Paul Rubens' *Korean Man (see p79)* is one of several portrait drawings. The *Self-Portrait* (c.1857–8) by Edgar Degas, executed in oil on paper and showing the young artist on the threshold of his extraordinary career, is another.

PHOTOGRAPHS

T HE MUSEUM launched its photographic department in 1984 with the purchase of several major private collections, including those of Bruno Bischofberger, Arnold Crane, and Samuel Wagstaff. The holdings focus on European and American photography up to the 1950s. Exceptionally rich in works from the early 1840s, the collection features

Columbia River, Oregon (1867) by Carleton E Watkins

many of the pioneers of photography. In daguerreotypes, the identity of the sitter was often more important than that of the maker. The museum has one portrait of Louis-Jacques-Mande Daguerre himself, taken in 1848 by Charles R Meade.

Englishman William Henry Fox Talbot (1800–1877) was the first to make prints from negatives. A lovely example of his work is *Oak Tree* (c.1845). Other early practitioners on exhibition include Hyppolyte Bayard (1801–87), portraitist Julia Margaret Cameron (1815–79), war photographer Roger Fenton (1819–69), Gustave Le Gray (1820–82), and Nadar (1820–1910).

Among the important early 20th-century artists represented are Edward Weston (1886–1958), who created beautiful still lifes, and Walker Evans (1903–75), who was a pivotal influence in American documentary photography.

Renaissance chalcedony, or agate, glass bowl, made in Venice, Italy, in around 1500

APPLIED ARTS

APPLIED ARTS in the museum encompass pre-1650 European pieces and works from southern Europe from 1650 to 1900. They have been chosen to complement the Getty's extensive holdings of French decorative arts.

Highlights include glass and earthenware from Italy and Spain; metalwork from France, Germany, and Italy; and highly decorated furniture. An extravagantly inlaid display cabinet from Augsburg in Germany (c.1620–30) falls into this last category. All four of the piece's sides open to reveal numerous drawers and compartments for collectibles.

Sèvres porcelain basket, dating from the mid-18th century

DECORATIVE ARTS

DECORATIVE ARTS were Getty's first love as a collector, after he rented a New York penthouse furnished with 18th-century French and English antiques. Originally, his collection focused on furnishings from the reign of Louis XIV to the Napoleonic era (1643–1815), encompassing the Regency, Rococo, and Empire periods.

The age of Louis XIV saw the development of French furniture reach great artistic heights, where appearances mattered more than function. The premier craftsman during that time was André-Charles Boulle (1642–1732), who was noted for his complex veneers and marquetry. The museum has several pieces attributed to Boulle from the French royal household. Two coffers on stands (c.1680–85), made for the Grand Dauphin, son of Louis XIV, probably held jewelry and valuable objects.

Several of the tapestries in the collection have remained in excellent condition, with their colors still vibrant. They include one woven by Jean de la Croix (active 1662–1712) for Louis XIV. The holdings also include ceramics, silver and gilded objects such as chandeliers and wall lights.

In recent years, pieces from Germany, Italy, and northern Europe have been added. A Neo-Classical rolltop desk (c.1785), made by the German David Roentgen, has a weight-operated, concealed writing stand. This type of elaborate mechanical feature was Roentgen's trademark.

MANUSCRIPTS

THE MUSEUM began collecting illuminated manuscripts in 1983 with the purchase of the Ludwig Collection of 144 works, which emphasized German and Central European texts. Tracing the development of illumination from the 6th to the 16th century, the collection today has masterpieces from the Byzantine, Ottoman, Romanesque, Gothic, and Renaissance periods.

Illuminated manuscripts were written and decorated entirely by hand. Initially, most were produced in monasteries, which were then the center of European intellectual life. Later, in the 12th century, they were also produced in the growing number of universities. Most books contained religious material, but some also preserved the philosophy, history, literature, law, and science of Western civilization. Kings, nobles, and church leaders commissioned these richly painted books, some of which were decorated with jewels and precious metals.

The manuscripts are exhibited on a rotating basis during the year. Highlights include an Ottoman Gospel lectionary from either Reichenau or St. Gall (950–75); an English Gothic Apocalypse (c.1250); two Byzantine Gospel books; *The Visions of Tondal* (1474), in the Flemish holdings; and the *Hours of Simon de Varie*, illuminated by French artist Jean Fouquet in 1455.

Portrait of St. John (c.1120–40) from the German Abbey of Helmarshausen's Gospel book

The Getty Villa ⑧

17985 Pacific Coast Hwy. 🄲 *(310) 440-7300.* ⬤ *until late 2003.*

THE J PAUL GETTY VILLA, built in the hills above Santa Monica Bay in the 1960s and 70s, will be the new home of the Antiquities collection of the Getty Center *(see pp78-81)*. Getty's vision – of a museum where his collection of antiquities could be displayed in a place where such art might originally have been seen – will finally come to fruition. The museum will display ancient art on both floors of the building.

The Villa is a re-creation of the Villa dei Papiri, the country estate of a Roman consul. The gardens of the villa are planted with seeds and bulbs imported from Italy. The Main Peristyle Garden is spectacular, with its large pool bordered by bronze statuary. The buildings combine authentic Roman detailing with modern technology.

Getty's original home on this property, and the site of the first Getty Museum, holds a library, seminar rooms, and offices for scholars. The Ranch House, as Getty called it, will house the Antiquities Conservation Department of the Getty Museum.

Decorative façade and grounds of Adamson House

Adamson House and Malibu Lagoon Museum ⑨

23200 Pacific Coast Hwy. **Road map** inset A. 🄲 *(310) 456-8432.* ☐ *11am–3pm Wed–Sat.* ⬤ *Jan1, Jul 4, Thanksgiving, Dec 25.* 🈺 🈁 📷 *last tour 2pm.*

ADAMSON HOUSE was built in 1929 for husband and wife Merritt and Rhoda Adamson. Rhoda was the daughter of Frederick and May Rindge, the last owners of the Rancho Malibu Spanish land grant. Until 1928, the family owned 24 miles (39 km) of Malibu coastline.

Intricate tile detail in Adamson House

Situated on the beach, the idyllic house and its 6 acres (2.5 ha) of gardens overlook Malibu Pier and Malibu Lagoon. The house was designed by Stiles Clements. The Spanish Colonial style building is covered with vivid tiles from the Malibu Potteries – a ceramics firm that was started by May Rindge and owned by the family. These tiles, each one individually designed, are featured throughout the house and grounds. The floors, walls, doorways, and fountains are all intricately decorated. The house's original 1920s furnishings are also on display.

Located in the converted garage of Adamson House is the Malibu Lagoon Museum, which is devoted to the history of Malibu. Artifacts, documents, and photographs tell the story not only of the Rindge family but also of the early Chumash population and José Tapia, who in 1802 became Malibu's first Spanish landowner.

Malibu Lagoon State Beach ⑩

Road map inset A. 🄲 *(818) 880-0367.* ☐ *8am–sunset daily.* 🈺 🈁

THE CHUMASH people built Humaliwo, their largest village, on the shores of this lagoon. By the 16th century, about 1,000 people had their home here, making it one of the most populated Native American villages north of what is now Mexico.

The estuary supports a wide range of marine life and is an important feeding ground for up to 200 species of migratory and native birds. To the east of

The Getty Villa's Main Peristyle Garden

Exclusive beach houses in Malibu Colony

the lagoon, the 35-acre (14-ha) Surfrider County Beach is devoted to surfers; swimming is prohibited. With its rare point break, Malibu is one of the finest surfing spots in southern California. The area closest to the pier is thought to have the best waves for longboarding in the world. Volleyball courts are also located on the beach.

View across Malibu Lagoon to the Santa Monica Mountains

Malibu Colony ⓫

Road map inset A. 🚌 ℹ️ *23805 Stuart Ranch Rd, Suite 100 (310-456-5737).*

Iⁿ 1928, to raise money for an ongoing battle to keep Malibu in the family, May Rindge sold this section of shoreline to film stars such as Bing Crosby, Gary Cooper and Barbara Stanwyck. Today, the colony is a private, gated compound, still favored by people working within the entertainment industry. There is no public access to the beach, but stars can often be spotted in the Malibu Colony Plaza, which is located near the entrance.

Malibu Creek State Park ⓬

Road map inset A. 📞 *(818) 880-0367, (818) 880-0350, or (800) 444-7275 for campsite reservations.* 🔓 *daily.* 🖼️ ♿ 📷

Tʜɪs 10,000-acre (4,000-ha) park was inhabited by the Chumash Indians until the mid-19th century. A varied landscape of forests, meadows, and rocky outcrops create the illusion of a vast wilderness, miles from civilization.

Some 2,000 acres (800 ha) of the park were once owned by 20th Century Fox, which made it a favorite location for movie-making *(see pp64–5).*

M*A*S*H (1970), *Butch Cassidy and the Sundance Kid* (1969), and *Planet of the Apes* (1968) were all filmed here. The state bought the land back from the film company in 1974.

The information center is close to the parking lot and has exhibits on the area's history, flora, and fauna. The stunning Gorge Trail starts from the center of the park and leads to a rock pool, which was used as a pseudo-tropical location to film the movies *South Pacific* (1958) and *Tarzan* (1959).

Off Crags Road, the marshy Century Lake harbors catfish, bass, bluefish, red-winged blackbirds, buffleheads, coots, and mallards. In spring the meadows are a riot of colorful wildflowers. Groves of live and valley oaks, redwood, and dogwood trees are scattered throughout the park.

Within the park there are 20 trails for hiking, cycling, or horseback riding; a nature center; and many picnic areas.

Malibu Creek State Park, near Castro Crest *(see p60)*

BEVERLY HILLS, BEL AIR, AND WESTWOOD

BEVERLY HILLS is a city, independent of Los Angeles and with its own laws and regulations. Since the early 1920s it has been the entertainment industry's favorite residential address. Beverly Hills' Golden Triangle is the West Coast's answer to New

City limits sign

York's Madison Avenue, with its array of restaurants, shops, and coffee bars. South of Bel Air's shady canyons, youthful Westwood brims with UCLA students. In the business-minded Century City, high-rises crowd the skyline. Together, these areas are known as the Westside.

SIGHTS AT A GLANCE

Historic Buildings
Beverly Hills Civic Center ❶
Beverly Hills Hotel ❽
Hotel Bel-Air ⓫

Parks and Gardens
Greystone Park and Mansion ❼
Virginia Robinson Gardens ❾

Shopping Areas
Century City ❻
Rodeo Drive p90 ❸
2 Rodeo ❹

Tours
Tour of the Stars' Homes
pp92–3 ❿

Museums
Museum of Television and
Radio ❷
Museum of Tolerance ❺

Universities
UCLA and Westwood
Village ⓬

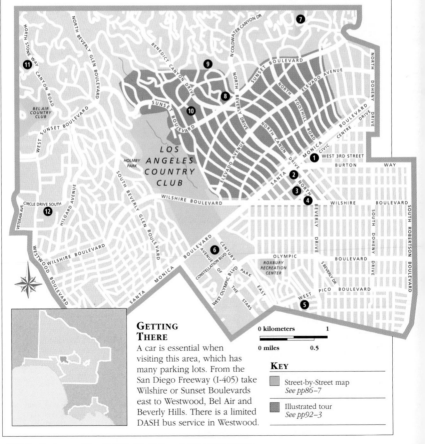

GETTING THERE

A car is essential when visiting this area, which has many parking lots. From the San Diego Freeway (I-405) take Wilshire or Sunset Boulevards east to Westwood, Bel Air and Beverly Hills. There is a limited DASH bus service in Westwood.

0 kilometers 1

0 miles 0.5

KEY

Street-by-Street map
See pp86–7

Illustrated tour
See pp92–3

◁ **Distinctive tower of Beverly Hills City Hall, part of the Civic Center**

Street-by-Street: The Golden Triangle

T HE AREA BORDERED by Santa Monica
Boulevard, Wilshire Boulevard, and
North Crescent Drive, known as the
"Golden Triangle," is the business district
of Beverly Hills. The shops, restaurants,
and art galleries lining the streets are
some of the most luxurious in the world.
Cutting through the middle is Rodeo
Drive, where many international designer
boutiques are to be found. On Wilshire
Boulevard, the cream of American department stores offer a heady mix of style and
opulence. To the north are the beautifully
manicured Beverly Gardens, the elegant
Civic Center with its landmark City Hall,
and the recently opened Museum of
Television and Radio.

★ **Museum of Television
and Radio**
*The latest addition to the
Golden Triangle, this
museum gives a
comprehensive
history of broad-
casting* ❷

The Electric Fountain was built
in 1930. The statue on the top is of
a Native American praying for rain.
Scenes from California history are
depicted on the base frieze.

SANTA MONICA BOULEVARD

LITTLE SANTA MONICA BOULEVARD

NORTH CAMDEN DRIVE

NORTH BEDFORD DRIVE

NORTH ROXBURY DRIVE

BRIGHTON WAY

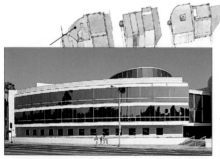

Saks Fifth Avenue is
one of the four major
department stores along
Wilshire Boulevard.

The Creative Artists Agency was built
in 1989 by architect IM Pei. Its curving
mirrored glass and marble walls anchor
Santa Monica and Wilshire Boulevards.

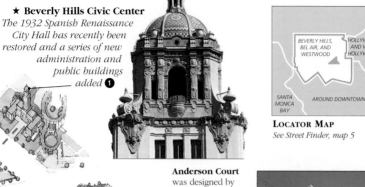

★ **Beverly Hills Civic Center**
The 1932 Spanish Renaissance City Hall has recently been restored and a series of new administration and public buildings added ❶

LOCATOR MAP
See Street Finder, map 5

Anderson Court
was designed by Frank Lloyd Wright in 1953.

2 Rodeo
When built in 1990, this center included the first new street in Beverly Hills since the city established independence from LA in 1914 ❹

The MGM Building was built in the 1920s by Louis B Mayer. The white and gold Art Deco structure was the headquarters of the newly formed Metro-Goldwyn-Mayer film studios.

The Beverly Theater, a Moorish-style building built in 1925, was the site of many film premieres in the 1920s and 1930s. It is now the Israeli Discount Bank.

0 meters	100
0 yards	100

KEY

- - - Suggested route

Rodeo Drive
The three blocks of Rodeo Drive are one of the most famous shopping areas in the world ❸

The Regent Beverly Wilshire Hotel first opened in 1928. In 1970 a second wing was added to the original Beaux-Arts building. A private, cobblestone street links the two wings *(see p508)*.

STAR SIGHTS

★ **Beverly Hills Civic Center**

★ **Museum of Television and Radio**

Beverly Hills Civic Center with City Hall in the background

Beverly Hills Civic Center ❶

455 N Rexford Drive. **Map** 5 F3.
📞 (310) 285-1000. ⏰ 7:30am–
5:30pm Mon–Thu; 8am–5pm Fri.
🔵 public hols. ♿

THE SPANISH COLONIAL City Hall, with its majestic tower capped by a tiled cupola, was designed in 1932 by local firm Koerner and Gage. Over the years it has become a symbol of the elegant, European-inspired city of Beverly Hills.

In 1990, architect Charles Moore linked the building to a new Civic Center by a series of diagonal landscaped and pedestrianized courtyards. On the upper levels, balconies and arcaded corridors continue the Spanish Colonial theme. The sympathetic modern addition houses a beautiful public library as well as the local fire and police stations.

Billboards are banned in the area, and a height restriction of three stories or 45 ft (14 m) is imposed on any new buildings, leaving City Hall to dominate the skyline.

Museum of Television and Radio ❷

465 N Beverly Drive. **Map** 5 F3.
📞 (310) 786-1000. ⏰ noon–5pm
Wed–Sun (until 9pm Thu). 🔵 public
hols. 🏷 ♿ 🎫
🌐 www.mtr.org

VISITORS TO the Museum of Television and Radio may watch and listen to news and a collection of entertainment and sports programs from the earliest days of radio and television to the present.

Pop music fans can see footage of the early Beatles or a young Elvis Presley making his television debut. Sports fans can relive classic Olympic competitions.

Visitors can select up to four extracts from the library's computerized catalogue at any one time. These are then played on small private consoles. The museum also has a 150-seat theater, which hosts major exhibitions, seminars, and screenings on specialized subjects and selected actors or directors.

The collection of more than 75,000 television and radio programs includes such timeless classics as *I Love Lucy* (see p145) and *The Honeymooners*. Favorite television and radio commercials, encompassing the industry's advertising history, are also available.

The holdings duplicate those of New York's highly successful Museum of Television and Radio, which was created in 1975 by the late William S. Paley, when he was the head of CBS Television.

Rodeo Drive ❸

See p90.

2 Rodeo ❹

Map 5 F3. ℹ️ 268 N. Rodeo Drive
(310-247-7040).
🌐 www.2rodeo.com

DEVELOPED IN 1990 on the corner of Rodeo Drive (see p90) and Wilshire Boulevard, 2 Rodeo is one of the most expensive retail centers ever made. It looks like a film set of a European street, complete with a public square and Victorian-style streetlamps. Exclusive shops such as Cole Haan and Charles Jourdan

Lucille Ball, the most popular television star during the 1950s

Spanish Steps leading to 2 Rodeo

line Via Rodeo, the cobbled lane that bisects the center. Via Rodeo meanders to the Spanish Steps, which descend to Wilshire Boulevard.

Museum of Tolerance ❺

9786 W Pico Blvd. **Map** 5 F5.
📞 *(310) 553-8403.* ⏰ *11.30am–4pm Mon–Thu, 11.30am–1pm Fri (Apr–Oct: 11.30am–3pm), 11am–5pm Sun.* ⬤ *Jan 1, Thanksgiving, Dec 25, and all major Jewish holidays.* 📷 ♿
🌐 *www.wiesenthal.com/mot*

THIS MUSEUM is dedicated to the promotion of respect and understanding among all people. Its two primary areas of focus are the history of racism and prejudice in the United States and the European Holocaust experience, examined in both historical and contemporary contexts.

The museum tour begins in the Tolerancenter, where visitors are challenged to confront racism and bigotry through interactive exhibits. "The Other America" is a computerized wall map that locates and gives information on more than 250 known racist groups in the US. A 16-screen video wall depicts the 1960s civil rights struggle in America. Interactive video monitors ask visitors for their personal profiles and then challenge them on questions of responsible citizenship and

social justice. They also offer footage of the LA riots of 1992 (*see p53*), with follow-up interviews. One of the most hard-hitting exhibits is the 15-ft (4.5-m) "Whisper Gallery," in which visitors hear racial and sexual taunts.

At the beginning of the Holocaust section, each visitor is given the details and photograph of a child whose life was in some way altered by that period.

Throughout the tour, the child's history is updated and, at the end, his or her fate is revealed. During the tour, visitors become a witness to events in Nazi Germany. Wax models in an outdoor café scene, set in prewar Berlin, seem to discuss the impending Nazi takeover of Germany. In a re-creation of the Wannsee Conference, the Third Reich leaders decide on the "The Final Solution of the Jewish Question." Videotaped interviews with concentration camp survivors shown in the "Hall of Testimony" tell of their harrowing experiences. Artifacts on display include Anne Frank's original letters and memorabilia from the camps.

The upper floors of the museum house special exhibits, films, and lectures. There is also a multimedia learning center with interactive computers containing additional information on World War II topics. Some of the exhibits may not be suitable for children under the age of ten.

History of racial prejudice at the Museum of Tolerance

Century City ❻

Map 5 D5. ℹ️ *2049 Century Park E, Suite 2600, Century City, 90067 (310-553-2222).*

THIS SITE used to be part of 20th Century Fox's backlot. It was sold in 1961 to the developers of Century City, who designed a high-rise complex of offices, stores, and homes on the 180 acres (73 ha).

Today lawyers, agents, and production companies fill the office blocks. Despite this, the area has never developed a community feel and at night the streets are empty.

The Century City Shopping Center, however, is a notable success. This outdoor complex has more than 120 stores, some 20 restaurants, and a 14-screen theater.

Century City Shopping Center

Greystone Park and Mansion ❼

905 Loma Vista Drive. **Map** 5 F1.
📞 *(310) 550-4654.* **Park** ⏰ *10am–5pm daily.* ⬤ *Jan 1, Dec 25.* ♿ *terrace & lower grounds.*

IN 1928 Edward L Doheny, an oil millionaire, built this 55-room mock-Tudor manor house for his son. Just three weeks after moving in with his family, Doheny's son was found dead in his bedroom with a male secretary, an apparent murder-suicide. His wife and children soon moved out, and since then the mansion has often been vacant.

Now owned by the city of Beverly Hills, Greystone is used in films, music videos, and commercials. The house is closed to the public, but visitors can walk or picnic in the beautiful 18-acre (7-ha) terraced gardens, which offer views across Los Angeles.

Rodeo Drive ❸

THE NAME RODEO DRIVE is derived from *El Rancho Rodeo de las Aguas* ("the ranch of the gathering of waters"), the name of an early Spanish land grant that included Beverly Hills. Today, Rodeo Drive is one of the most celebrated and exclusive shopping streets in the world, with Italian designer boutiques, the best of French fashion, world-class jewelers, and some of the leading LA retailers. For those who enjoy celebrity-spotting, Rodeo Drive is a prime area.

Rodeo Drive's *wide sidewalks, bordered by trees, help create a pleasant shopping environment.*

• 421

Barakat *sells fine jewelry and also has an impressive collection of pre-Columbian and ancient Greek artifacts. Barakat is located in the group of shops known as the Rodeo Collection, under an atrium, at No. 421.*

BRIGHTON WAY

Gucci, *at No. 347, is a leading Italian boutique. Best known for its leather accessories and colorful scarves, it also produces furnishings, such as this cushion.*

D R I V E

• 347

HERMES

R O D E O

• 317

Hammacher Schlemmer & Co.
Established 1848

VAN CLEEF & ARPELS

DAYTON WAY

Lalique, *at No. 317, is famous for its Art Deco and Art Nouveau glassware. The shop's frosted lamps are typical of Lalique's style.*

Fred Hayman Beverly Hills, *at No. 273, is a fashion boutique with a fireplace and bar.*

0 meters   50
0 yards   50

• 273

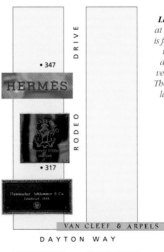

• 230

TIFFANY & CO

Christian Dior, *at No. 230, is one of the leading names in French haute couture. The founder of the house was responsible for the 1950s "New Look."*

The landmark Beverly Hills Hotel

Beverly Hills Hotel ⑧

9641 Sunset Blvd. **Map** 5 D2. ☎ (310) 276-2251, (800) 283-8885. ◯ daily. ♿ See **Where to Stay** p508.

Dubbed "the Pink Palace," this extravagant Mission Revival-style hotel was built in 1912 by developer Burton E Green, to attract people to Beverly Hills. The hotel's 21 secluded bungalows, set in 12 acres (5 ha) of landscaped gardens, have been romantic hideaways for film stars such as Marilyn Monroe, Clark Gable, Richard Burton, and Elizabeth Taylor.

Recently, the Beverly Hills Hotel has undergone a $100 million program of renovations, reviving the style of Hollywood's heyday. Its legendary pool and cabanas have remained one of the places to be seen and heard in Los Angeles, and its famous restaurants, The Polo Lounge and Polo Grill, are once more at the center of the movie industry's deal-making.

Virginia Robinson Gardens ⑨

1008 Elden Way. **Map** 5 D1. ☎ (310) 276-5367. ◯ Tue–Fri. ● public hols. 📷 ♿ ☑ obligatory 10am & 1pm Tue–Thu, 10am Fri. Advance reservations required.

In 1908 department-store heir Harry Robinson and his wife, Virginia, bought a plot of land in Beverly Hills. Three years later they completed the city's first house here and planted 6 acres (2.5 ha) of landscaped gardens set amid terraces, ponds, and fountains.

Bequeathed to LA County, the gardens were opened to the public in 1982. One of the most impressive sights is the 2.5-acre (1-ha) palm forest, where you can see the largest king palms outside Australia.

The organized tour includes part of the house, which still has its original furnishings.

Tour of the Stars' Homes ⑩

See pp92–3.

Hotel Bel-Air ⑪

701 Stone Canyon Rd. **Map** 4 A1. ☎ (310) 472-1211. ◯ daily. ♿ See **Where to Stay** p508 ☒ www.hotelbelair.com

Considered one of the best hotels in the US, Hotel Bel-Air is located in a heavily wooded canyon, giving it an air of privacy and tranquillity. The 1920s Mission Revival-style buildings are set in 11 acres (4.5 ha) of beautiful gardens, interspersed with fountains and intimate courtyards.

Among the trees and shrubs rarely seen in Southern California are coastal redwoods, white-flowering bird of paradise trees, and a floss silk tree – the largest of its kind outside its native South America. The gardens are fragrant with roses, gardenias, jasmine, and orange blossoms. In fact, the Bel-Air is so perfect that one guest stayed for 40 years.

Pool at Hotel Bel-Air, surrounded by attractive gardens

Tour of the Stars' Homes ⑩

Security guard sign

In Los Angeles image is everything, and Beverly Hills has long been the symbol of success for those in the entertainment industry. When, in 1920, Mary Pickford and Douglas Fairbanks built their mansion, Pickfair, at the top of Summit Drive, everyone else followed – and stayed. Sunset Boulevard divides the haves from the have-nots: people who live south of it may be rich, but it is those who live to the north of the road who are considered to be the super-rich. Houses come in almost every architectural style. Some are ostentatious, others are surprisingly modest.

Jimmy Stewart's former home at No. 918 Roxbury Drive ⑬

South of Sunset

Start at No. 714 Palm Drive, the elegant home of Faye Dunaway ①, who starred with Warren Beatty in *Bonnie and Clyde* (1967). Continue south and turn right on Elevado Avenue. The former home of Rita Hayworth ② is situated on the corner at No. 512 Palm Drive.

At Maple Drive, turn right. No. 720 is the white and green New England-style home of the late George Burns and Gracie Allen ③. Continue north and just before Sunset Boulevard make a sharp left onto Lomitas Avenue. Go two blocks and turn left onto Foothill Road. On the corner, at No. 701, is the unassuming house of Carroll Baker ④. This blonde-haired beauty made her debut in *Giant* (1956) with James Dean. At one time she was being groomed to be the next Marilyn Monroe.

Turn right onto Elevado Avenue, take the next right onto Alpine Drive, left onto Lomitas Avenue, and left at Crescent Drive. Doris Day's modest house ⑤ is barely visible at No. 713, hidden behind a tall hedge and gate.

Turn right on Carmelita Avenue and right again at Cañon Drive. The pretty house ⑥ where Robert Wagner and Natalie Wood once lived can be seen through the low wall at No. 603. Continue north to the junction with Elevado Avenue. Just across the road, at No. 707 Cañon Drive, lush palm trees in the front mark the beginning of Kirk Douglas's walled and gated property ⑦.

Turn left onto Elevado Avenue. As you cross Rodeo Drive, look to your right. The lovely home of the late Gene Kelly ⑧ is at No. 725 Rodeo Drive. This renowned Hollywood icon performed in such classics as *An American in Paris* (1951) and *Singing in the Rain* (1952).

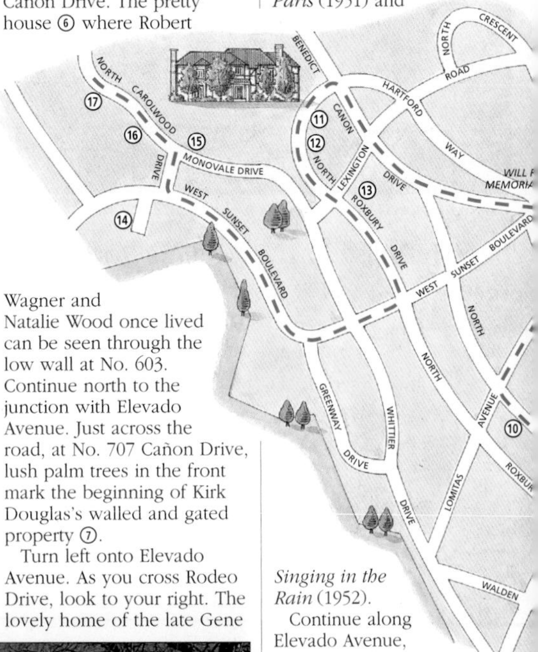

Continue along Elevado Avenue, then turn right on Bedford Drive. The comedian and actor Steve Martin ⑨ has a home at No. 721. A modern block structure, it has no front windows and can be only partially glimpsed behind a bougainvillea hedge. Lana Turner's scandal-ridden house ⑩ at No. 730, on the

Key

– – – Tour route

Faye Dunaway's house at No. 714 Palm Drive ①

Jayne Mansfield's Pink Palace at No. 10100 Sunset Boulevard ⑭

LOCATOR MAP
See Street Finder, map 5

His former neighbors at No. 1000 Roxbury Drive were Lucille Ball and Desi Arnaz ⑫. Their successful show *I Love Lucy (see pp88 and 145)* reruns daily on television. Nearby, at No. 918, is the mock-Tudor former home of the much-respected Jimmy Stewart ⑬.

At Sunset Boulevard, turn right. Jayne Mansfield's Pink Palace ⑭ is at No. 10100, on the southwest corner of Sunset Boulevard and Carolwood Drive. When Mansfield moved in, she put in a heart-shaped pool with the inscription "I love you Jaynie" written on the bottom.

Turn right onto North Carolwood Drive. Just to the right, at No. 144 Monovale Drive ⑮, is one of rock-and-roll king Elvis Presley's former homes. Only the tennis courts can be seen from the street.

Continue along Carolwood Drive. Barbra Streisand ⑯ lives at No. 301 on a heavily guarded estate. The actress won an academy award in 1969 for her role as Fanny Brice in the musical *Funny Girl*. The late Walt Disney, who captured the imagination of the world with his cartoon characters, used to live just north of here at No. 355 Carolwood Drive ⑰. His house is on a bend, behind a gate.

Walt Disney's mailbox ⑰

North of Sunset
Cross Sunset Boulevard, taking the street farthest to the left, which is now Benedict Canyon Drive. On the corner is the Beverly Hills Hotel, *(see p91)*, long a celebrity rumor mill. The private bungalows behind its pink façade saw many a romantic tryst, including, it is said, those between Marilyn Monroe and John and Robert Kennedy.

At Roxbury Drive, turn left and curve south with the road. At No. 1002 is the late Jack Benny's traditional-looking brick house ⑪, which he occasionally used in his shows.

corner of Bedford Drive and Lomitas Avenue, was where her gangster-lover Johnny Stompanato was stabbed to death with a kitchen knife by her daughter, Cheryl Crane.

Turn right onto Lomitas Avenue, then make a sharp left on Cañon Drive.

TIPS FOR DRIVERS

Tour length: 5 miles (8 km).
Warning: Film stars' homes or former homes are private residences. Do not attempt to trespass or you may be arrested.

University of California Los Angeles, Westwood Village @

A LARGE UNIVERSITY with a first-rate reputation, UCLA has a wide range of academic departments and professional schools, including the respected UCLA Hospital. Sited on 419 acres (170 ha), with more than 35,000 students, it is a city within a city. The original campus was designed in 1925 to resemble the Romanesque towns of southern Europe. The first four buildings followed this theme, but as the university expanded more modern architecture was favored. The disappointing mix of bland structures that resulted is redeemed by the beautiful landscaped grounds.

Romanesque-style façade of UCLA's Royce Hall

Exploring UCLA and Westwood Village

Since it was first developed in 1928, Westwood Village has been one of the most successful shopping districts in Southern California. For years, the pleasant streets south of UCLA were the most popular weekend destination in the city. People still enjoy the pedestrian-friendly avenues, the productions at the Geffen Playhouse *(see p164)*, and the large number of theaters that often preview the latest films. However, cheap modernization of some of the storefronts has disrupted the overall cohesiveness of the village's Spanish Colonial design.

Detail of ceiling in Royce Hall

🏛 Royce Quadrangle

Dickson Plaza. **(** (310) 825-2101. ◻ *daily.*
The four buildings that make up the Royce Quadrangle are the oldest on UCLA's campus in Westwood. Built of red brick in the Italian Romanesque style, Royce, Kinsey, and Haines halls, and Powell

Library far surpass the other buildings at UCLA in beauty. The best of them all is Royce Hall, which is based on the basilica of San Ambrogio in Milan, Italy. Its auditorium hosts professional music, dance, and theater shows throughout the year. Next door, Powell Library's grand rotunda was modeled on San Sepolcro in Bologna, Italy.

🏛 UCLA at the Armand Hammer Museum of Art and Cultural Center

10899 Wilshire Blvd. **(** (310) 443-7000. ◻ *11am–7pm Tue, Wed, Fri, Sat; 11am–9pm Thu; 11am–5pm Sun.* ● *Jul 4, Thanksgiving, Dec 25.* 🎟 *free 6–9pm Thu.* ♿ 🎁 *www.hammer.ucla.edu*
The museum presents selections from the collection of businessman Armand Hammer (1899–1990). Works are largely Impressionist or Post-Impressionist by artists such as Mary Cassatt (1845–1926), Claude Monet (1840–1926), Camille Pissarro (1830–1903), John Singer Sargent (1856–1925), and

Vincent Van Gogh (1853–90). Exhibits from the Armand Hammer Daumier and Contemporaries Collection are also shown on a rotating basis and include paintings, sculptures, and lithographs by Daumier and his contemporaries. Displays are also drawn from the UCLA Grunwald Center for the Graphic Arts, which holds more than 35,000 works on paper dating from the Renaissance to the present day.

🌷 Franklin D Murphy Sculpture Garden

((310) 443-7041. ◻ *daily.*
This is the largest sculpture garden on the West Coast with more than 70 20th-century sculptures. The highlights

UCLA AND WESTWOOD VILLAGE

KEY

🚌	Bus terminal
ℹ	Tourist information
🅿	Parking

Entrance to UCLA at the Armand Hammer Museum of Art

Automne (Autumn, 1948) by Henri Laurens

VISITORS' CHECKLIST

Map 4 A3. 🚌 20, 21, 22.
UCLA Campus 🛈 *Visitor Information (310 825-4321).*
Westwood Village
🛈 *10779 W Pico Blvd, Westside (310 475-8806).*

include Henry Moore's *Two-Piece Reclining Figure, No. 3* (1961) and Jacques Lipchitz's *Baigneuse* (*Bather*, 1923–5).

🌺 Mildred E Mathias Botanical Garden

📞 *(310) 825-1260.* ⏰ *8am–5pm Mon–Fri, 8am–4pm Sat & Sun.* ⛔ *public hols.* ♿

Tucked away in a small shady canyon, this serene garden contains almost 4,000 rare and native species. Divided into 13 thematic sections, the gardens feature both subtropical and tropical plants. The trees are spectacular and include some outstanding Australian eucalyptus and some large specimens of dawn redwoods.

🏛 Fowler Museum of Cultural History

📞 *(310) 825-4361.* ⏰ *noon–5pm Wed–Sun (until 8pm Thu).* ⛔ *public hols.* 🎫 *free Thu.*

This university museum is committed to enriching the community's understanding of other cultures. Its exhibitions focus on the prehistoric, historic, and contemporary societies of Africa, Asia, the Americas, and Oceania. The collection of 750,000 artifacts makes it one of the nation's leading university museums.

🏛 Westwood Memorial Park

1218 Glendon Ave. 📞 *(310) 474-1579.* ⏰ *8am–5pm daily.* ♿

Off the beaten track, this small cemetery is located behind the Avco Center theaters and parking lot. The tranquil grounds are now the final resting place for celebrities such as Dean Martin, Peter Lorre, Buddy Rich, Natalie Wood, and Marilyn Monroe. For several decades after her death, Monroe's second husband, Joe DiMaggio, used to have six red roses placed on her tomb every week.

Tranquil Westwood Memorial Park, shaded by trees

MARILYN MONROE

Born Norma Jean Baker in the charity ward of Los Angeles General Hospital, Marilyn Monroe (1926–62) was placed in foster care by her mother when she was two weeks old. Her first marriage, at the age of 16, lasted four years, before she gave it up to pursue her dream of being an actress. In 1950, her career took off with *The Asphalt Jungle* and *All About Eve*. With films such as *The Seven-Year Itch* (1955) and *Some Like It Hot* (1959), she became the biggest sex symbol Hollywood has ever seen. In the latter part of her life, she struggled to escape the narrow confines of her on-screen persona.

Marilyn Monroe's memorial plaque

0 meters 500

0 yards 500

HOLLYWOOD AND WEST HOLLYWOOD

I N 1887, Harvey Henderson Wilcox and his wife, Daeida, set up a Christian community, free of saloons and gambling, in a Los Angeles suburb and called it Hollywood. It is ironic that the movie business with all its decadence came to replace their Utopia. The takeover started in 1913, when Cecil B De Mille filmed *The Squaw Man* in a rented barn at the corner of Vine and Selma.

Hollywood's Walk of Fame

For the next several decades the studios were based here, generating wealth and glamour. In recent years the area fell into decline, and today only a handful of landmarks recall its Golden Age. Sunset Boulevard has now become the focal point for nightlife in Los Angeles. West Hollywood, with its large gay community, is also a lively area for dining and shopping.

SIGHTS AT A GLANCE

Museums

Craft and Folk Art Museum **17**
George C Page Museum of La Brea Discoveries **10**
Hollywood Studio Museum **7**
Los Angeles County Museum of Art pp110–13 **12**
Petersen Automotive Museum **14**

Historic Streets and Buildings

Hollywood Bowl **6**
Miracle Mile **13**
Paramount Studios **10**
Roosevelt Hotel **1**
Walk of Fame **4**

Cemeteries

Hollywood Memorial Park **9**

Cinemas and Theaters

El Capitan Theater **3**
Mann's Chinese Theatre **2**
Pantages Theater **8**
The Improv **15**
Wiltern Theater **18**

Shops and Markets

Farmers Market **11**
Frederick's of Hollywood **5**

See pp101–3

See pp104–5

See pp98–100

0 kilometers 2

0 miles 1

KEY

Illustrated areas

M Metro Red Line station

GETTING THERE

The Metro Red Line currently runs from Downtown's Union Station to Wilshire Boulevard at Western Avenue. Bus services from Downtown include: No. 1 (along Hollywood Boulevard), No. 2 (Sunset Boulevard), No. 4 (Santa Monica Boulevard), No. 10 (Melrose Avenue), and Nos. 20, 21, and 22 (Wilshire Boulevard). Freeway 101 runs through Hollywood from Downtown and on to Ventura.

◁ **Mann's Chinese Theatre, a lavish remnant of Hollywood's Golden Age**

A View of Sunset Boulevard: Sunset Strip

SUNSET BOULEVARD curves west for 26 miles (42 km) from downtown LA to the Pacific Coast Highway. Sunset has been associated with the movies since the 1920s, when it was a dirt track linking the burgeoning film studios in Hollywood with the hillside homes of the screen stars. Today, much of the boulevard is still lined with the mansions of the rich and famous (see pp92–3). Sunset Strip is the liveliest and most historically rich stretch, filled with restaurants, luxury hotels, and nightclubs. The 1.5-mile (2.4-km) section was first paved in the mid-1930s. Its lack of local government made it a magnet for gambling and bootlegging. Famous nightclubs included the Trocadero, Ciro's, and the Mocambo – where young Margarita Cansino met studio boss Harry Cohen, who renamed her Rita Hayworth. Sunset Strip is still the center of LA's nightlife today.

Sunset Strip and the Santa Monica Mountains from Crescent Heights

Rainbow Bar & Grill
The walls of this restaurant, at No. 9015, are lined with wine casks and gold records. Formerly the Villa Nova, Vincente Minnelli proposed to Judy Garland here and, eight years later in 1953, Marilyn Monroe met Joe DiMaggio here on a blind date.

The Original Spago
Wolfgang Puck, who is regarded by many as the founder of Californian cuisine, had his first LA restaurant at No. 8795. During the 1970s and 1980s Oscar night parties were held here, hosted by the legendary Hollywood agent Irving "Swifty" Lazar.

The Roxy
This trendy nightclub, at No. 9009, occupies the site of the old Club Largo.

The Viper Room, at No. 8852, is a popular live music club (see p164), part-owned by the actor Johnny Depp. In October 1993 young film star River Phoenix, having taken a lethal cocktail of drugs, collapsed and died on the sidewalk outside.

CLARK ST

LARRABEE ST

HORN AVE

HOLLOWAY

HAMMOND ST

HILLDALE AVE

SAN VICENTE BLVD

Hyatt Hotel
Visiting rock stars regularly stay at this hotel, at No. 8401 (see p513). Jim Morrison stayed here when he played with The Doors at the nearby Whisky A Go Go.

Argyle Hotel
This hotel is an Art Deco high-rise. In Hollywood's heyday it was an apartment complex and home to Jean Harlow, Clark Gable, and other luminaries. (See p513.)

Cajun Bistro (The Source) at No. 8301 is where Woody Allen rants about LA in his film *Annie Hall* (1977).

The Comedy Store
This is a world-famous spot for stand-up comedy, often enjoying television coverage. It stands on the site of the 1940s nightclub, Ciro's.

0 meters 100
0 yards 100

The Mondrian Hotel, at No. 8440, is decorated with stripes in primary colors, as a tribute to artist Piet Mondrian. *(See p513.)*

N LA CIENEGA BLVD

OLIVE DRIVE

Sunset Plaza
This area is lined with chic stores and cafés. It is a good section to explore on foot.

The House of Blues
This tin-roofed blues bar, at No. 8430, has been transported from Clarksdale, Mississippi. It is part-owned by the actor Dan Ackroyd, who co-starred with John Belushi in the 1980 cult movie The Blues Brothers *(see p164).*

Hollywood Athletic Club
Film stars of the 1930s and 1940s exercised here. Flash Gordon *star Buster Crabbe trained in the swimming pool before winning a gold medal at the 1932 Olympics.*

Cinerama Dome
The distinctive dome of No. 6360 was the first wide-screen movie theater on the West Coast.

The Cat and Fiddle
This British-style pub, at No. 6530, is built around an attractive Mediterranean-style patio. British beers are served along with pub food, such as bangers and mash. There is a dartboard inside.

TIME CAPSULE

In 1954 the Los Angeles Chamber of Commerce decided to preserve the history of Hollywood with a time capsule. A copy of Bing Crosby's hit record "White Christmas," released that year, a script of the most successful film made to date, *Gone With the Wind,* and various contemporary radio and television tapes were deposited under the sidewalk at the famous intersection between Sunset Boulevard and Vine Street. The time capsule is planned for retrieval 50 years after it was planted, in 2004.

Singer Bing Crosby

A sidewalk plaque marking the site notes that the legend of Hollywood was born here in 1913 with the making of the first feature-length film, *The Squaw Man,* by Cecil B De Mille and Jesse Lasky. The actual location of their barn studio, now preserved on North Highland Avenue (*see p108*), was farther up the block at No. 1521 Vine Street. Hollywood had also been incorporated as a town ten years earlier and numerous short films had been made here during that decade.

Poster of *Gone With the Wind* (1939)

A View of Sunset Boulevard: Old Studio District

DURING THE FIRST HALF of the 20th century, this 2-mile (3-km) stretch of Sunset Boulevard was the center of Hollywood's film industry. Major studios, including 20th Century Fox, RKO, Warner Bros., Paramount, and United Artists, were all in the vicinity, and the streets were filled with directors, actors, and would-be film stars. In the area known as Gower Gulch, low-budget outfits churned out Westerns by the score. There are still some studios here, but most have relocated. Of the major studios, only Paramount *(see p109)*, on Melrose Avenue to the south, remains.

Sunset Boulevard during its heyday in the 1940s

A & M Records
These mock-Tudor buildings, stretching from the southeast corner of Sunset Boulevard down La Brea Avenue, were constructed by Charlie Chaplin as homes for workers at his studio.

Crossroads of the World
Hollywood's first shopping mall, built in 1936, is located at No. 6621. Designed to resemble an ocean liner, with a globe-topped tower on its prow, it has now been converted into offices.

Hollywood High School
A long list of famous alumni have attended Hollywood High School, at No. 6800, including Lana Turner. The actress was first discovered in 1936 by director Mervyn LeRoy, sipping a soda in the now-defunct Top Hat Malt Shop. Its site, opposite the school, is now occupied by a garage.

The Roxbury Club, behind the big billboard to the west of the Chateau Marmont hotel, is currently popular with the stars of teenage TV shows. It stands on the site of the Players Club, owned in the 1940s by movie director Preston Sturges.

Chateau Marmont
The hotel at No. 8221 (see p513) was modeled on a Loire Valley château. When it opened in 1929, it attracted actors such as Errol Flynn and Greta Garbo. Among today's regulars are Christopher Walken and Winona Ryder.

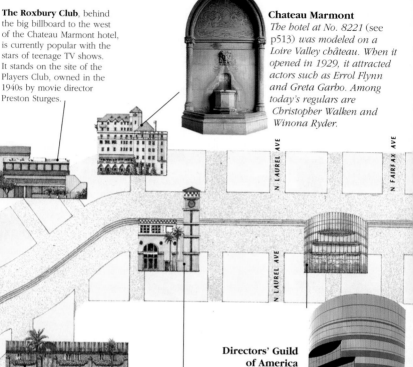

N LAUREL AVE

N FAIRFAX AVE

N LAUREL AVE

Directors' Guild of America
This is one of the many offices on Sunset Boulevard connected with the entertainment industry.

The Trocadero nightclub, at No. 8610, had Nat "King" Cole as its pianist in its heyday. Only three steps remain of the old building.

Schwab's
The former drugstore was a popular meeting place for film stars and columnists. A Virgin Megastore now occupies the site. Across Crescent Heights was the legendary Garden of Allah apartment complex whose residents included Scott Fitzgerald and Dorothy Parker.

BILLBOARDS

The most visible pieces of art along Sunset Strip are the huge, hand-painted billboards, produced by some of Hollywood's finest artists and designers to advertise new films, records, and personalities. They are often three-dimensional, a technique introduced in 1953 when Las Vegas's Sahara Hotel rented a billboard, erected a real swimming pool, and filled it with swimsuited models. During the 1960s the billboards were dominated by the music industry, with advertising space along Sunset Strip even being written into some rock stars' contracts. LA's well-known antipathy toward smoking now shows up in anti-smoking ads, which mimic the Marlboro cowboy style, on the massive boards outside the Chateau Marmont.
Marlboro and tequila billboards on Sunset Strip

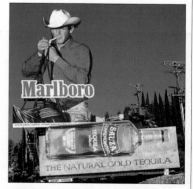

Hollywood Palladium
Norman Chandler, of the Los Angeles Times *dynasty, built this theater at No. 6215. It was opened by Lana Turner in 1940, when Frank Sinatra gave a concert. Big bands and musical stars still perform here.*

CBS Studios
No. 6121 was inherited from Columbia Pictures. It in turn succeeded the Nestor Film Co., which rented the site in 1911 for $40 a month.

Gower Gulch
Now a shopping mall, in the 1930s and 1940s would-be actors gathered here each morning hoping for $10-a-day jobs at the small studios shooting low-budget Westerns.

0 meters 100
0 yards 100

Warner Bros. Studio
The first talkie, Al Jolson's The Jazz Singer *(1927), was made here at No. 5858. The following year the studio moved to Burbank (see p141). The building now houses local radio stations.*

WARNER BROS. SUPREME TRIUMPH
AL JOLSON
in
The JAZZ SINGER

Sunset Boulevard Theater
Showman Earl Carroll's Vanities Theater originally occupied this site at No. 6220 in the 1940s. It had the world's largest revolving stage, which held 60 dancers.

A View of Hollywood Boulevard

First National Bank detail

HOLLYWOOD BOULEVARD is one of the most famous streets in the world, and its name is still redolent with glamour. Visitors wishing to recapture a Golden Age of film, however, may be disappointed, although a renewal plan has been under way for the last few years. Mann's Chinese Theatre and its autograph patio live up to expectations, as does the Walk of Fame. World premieres of Disney films at the El Capitan Theater often feature a live revue by the Magic Kingdom's favorite characters. Other attractions include the Hollywood Wax Museum, the Hollywood Guinness World of Records, Ripley's Believe It or Not!®, and the Hollywood Entertainment Museum.

LOCATOR MAP
See Street Finder map 2

★ **Mann's Chinese Theatre**
Stars' autographs are set in the concrete courtyard ❷

The Hollywood Galaxy houses a six-screen movie complex and the Hollywood Entertainment Museum, which has film, television, radio, and recording memorabilia.

HOLLYWOOD BOULEVARD NORTH SIDE ➤➤➤➤➤➤➤➤➤➤➤➤➤➤➤➤➤➤➤➤➤➤➤➤➤➤➤➤➤➤

★ **Walk of Fame**
Marilyn Monroe's star is embedded in the sidewalk at No. 6776 Hollywood Boulevard. The camera symbol below her name indicates her career as a film actress ❹

MARILYN MONROE

Hollywood Guinness World of Records uses models, videos, and special effects to bring record-breaking achievements alive. It is housed in the area's first movie theater.

Ripley's Believe It or Not!® is a museum devoted to the bizarre. The building, topped by a model *Tyrannosaurus rex*, contains more than 300 exhibits, such as shrunken heads and two-headed calves.

HOLLYWOOD BOULEVARD SOUTH SIDE ➤➤➤➤➤➤➤➤➤➤➤➤➤➤➤➤➤➤➤➤➤➤➤➤➤➤➤➤➤➤

KEY

▶▶▶▶▶▶ North Side walking east

◀◀◀◀◀◀ South Side walking west

N ORANGE DR *N ORCHID AVE* *N HIGHLAND AVE*

N ORANGE DR *N HIGHLAND AVE*

STAR SIGHTS

★ **Mann's Chinese Theatre**

★ **Walk of Fame**

First National Bank marks the junction with Highland Avenue. Its tiered façade is decorated with stone reliefs of historical figures such as Christopher Columbus and Nicolaus Copernicus.

The Hollywood Wax Museum has life-size models of film stars, musicians, and public figures. Clint Eastwood, Marilyn Monroe, Madonna, Michael Jackson, Dolly Parton, and Ronald Reagan are among those on display. There is also a wax tableau based on Leonardo da Vinci's painting *The Last Supper* (1497).

meters   200

yards   200

El Capitan Theater
Neon lights welcome filmgoers to this beautifully restored Art Deco theater. Movies can be seen in old-fashioned comfort, but with state-of-the art sound ❸

The Masonic Hall now displays interactive exhibitions of Disney shows.

Clarion Hotel Hollywood Roosevelt
An image of the actor Charlie Chaplin (1889–1977) decorates the wall of this 1920s hotel ❶

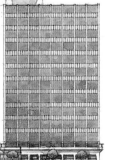

Sid Grauman's famous Chinese Theatre (now Mann's)

Clarion Hotel Hollywood Roosevelt ❶

7000 Hollywood Blvd. **Map** 2 B4.
[(323) 466-7000.] See **Where to Stay** *p510*.

N AMED AFTER US president Theodore Roosevelt, this hotel was opened in 1927 by joint owners Louis B Mayer, Mary Pickford, Marcus Loewe, Douglas Fairbanks, Sr., and Joseph Schenk. Marilyn Monroe, Ernest Hemingway, and Clark Gable were all visitors and, on May 16, 1929, the first Academy Awards banquet was held in the Roosevelt's Blossom Room.

Renovations in 1986 revealed a Spanish Colonial design. The following year the pool was decorated by David Hockney *(see p24)*. The Hollywood Historical Review exhibition, documents the area's history.

Clarion Hotel Hollywood Roosevelt, locale for the first Academy Awards

Mann's Chinese Theatre ❷

6925 Hollywood Blvd. **Map** 2 B4.
[(323) 461-3331. [(323) 464-8111.] daily. 🖼 ♿

O NE OF THE most famous sights in Hollywood has not changed much since it opened in 1927 with the gala premiere of Cecil B De Mille's *King of Kings*. The exterior is an ornate medley of Chinese temples, pagodas, lions, and dragons, reflecting the keen sense of showmanship of the theater's creator, Sid Grauman.

Besides the spectacle of the movie premiere, Grauman also thought up one of the longest-running publicity stunts in Hollywood history: inviting movie stars to impress their handprints, footprints, and autographs in the cement courtyard of his theater. There are many versions of how this custom began. One tells of silent screen star Norma Talmadge accidentally stepping in the wet cement at the gala opening *(see p49)*. Another is that the French stonemason, Jean Klossner, put his hand in the wet cement for posterity. Whatever the precedent, Sid Grauman liked the idea and invited Norma Talmadge to legitimately leave her mark, along with Mary Pickford and Douglas Fairbanks, Sr., on May 17, 1927.

Anyone can visit the courtyard, but only filmgoers can see the extravagant interior of the theater. Make sure the film is playing in the main auditorium and not in one of the additions in the east wing.

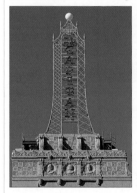

Steel tower of El Capitan Theater

El Capitan Theater ❸

6838 Hollywood Blvd. **Map** 2 B4.
[(323) 467-7674.] daily. 🖼

B UILT IN 1926 as a theater, El Capitan was later converted to a movie house. It was the venue for many premieres, such as Orson Welles's *Citizen Kane* (1941). In 1942 El Capitan was refurbished, and its interior was covered up. It was renamed the Hollywood Paramount.

Disney and Pacific Theaters bought El Capitan in 1991 and restored it to its former glory. Luckily, the original Art Deco interior was found virtually intact. Today, many Disney feature animations open here, such as *The Lion King* (1994) and *A Bug's Life* (1999).

Walk of Fame ❹

Map 2 B4. 🏛 *6541 Hollywood Blvd*
(323) 461-2804. 📱 *(323) 469-8311.*

PERHAPS THE ONLY pavement in the city to be cleaned six times a week, the Walk of Fame is set with more than 2,000 polished marble stars. Since February 1960, celebrities from the worlds of film, radio, television, theater, and music have been immortalized on Hollywood Boulevard and Vine Street. Stardom does not come easily, however: each personality has to be sponsored and approved by the Chamber of Commerce, and pay a $7,500 installation fee. Among the most famous are Charlie Chaplin (No. 6751), and Alfred Hitchcock (No. 6506).

Frederick's of Hollywood ❺

6608 Hollywood Blvd. **Map** 2 C4.
📞 *(323) 466-8506.* 🕐 *10am–9pm Mon–Fri, Sat; 10am–7pm Fri; 11am–6pm Sun.* ● *Jan 1, Thanksgiving, Dec 25.* ♿

FREDERICK MELLINGER launched his now world-famous mail-order business in 1946, selling provocative lingerie. He believed that "fashions may change, but sex appeal is always in style." This purple and pink Art Deco building is Frederick's flagship store. As well as selling underwear, it

Garish exterior of Frederick's of Hollywood

houses a Celebrity Lingerie Hall of Fame, which includes the bra worn by Marilyn Monroe in *Let's Make Love* (1960), Tony Curtis's black lace bra from the classic *Some Like It Hot* (1959), and Madonna's infamous black bustier.

Hollywood Bowl ❻

2301 N Highland Ave. **Map** 2 B3.
📞 *(323) 850-2000.* 🕐 *late Jun–mid-Sep.* ● *Labor Day.* 🅿 ♿
Box office 🕐 *10am–9pm Mon–Sat; noon–6pm Sun.* ● *Labor Day.*
Edmund D Edelman Hollywood Bowl Museum 📞 *(323) 850-2058.*
🕐 *Jul–mid-Sep: 10am–8:30pm Tue–Sat; mid-Sep–Jun: 10am–4:30pm Tue–Sat.* ● *public hols.*

SITUATED IN a natural amphitheater that was once revered by the Cahuenga Pass Gabrielino Indians, the Bowl has now become sacred to Angelenos. Since 1922 it has been the summer home of the LA Philharmonic *(see p121)*. Even though the acoustics are not perfect, the atmosphere cannot be beaten.

Thousands gather on warm evenings to picnic – often in high style – under the stars and listen to the orchestra. There are 13 picnic areas on the 60-acre (24-ha) site. Jazz, country, folk, and pop concerts are also performed during the season.

The most popular events at the Bowl are the concert with fireworks on the Fourth of July, the Easter Sunrise Service, and a Tchaikovsky Spectacular with cannons, fireworks, and a military band.

Much altered over the years, the shell-shaped stage was originally designed in 1929 by Lloyd Wright, son of architect Frank Lloyd Wright. Rumor has it that the materials for the building were taken from the set of Douglas Fairbanks, Sr.'s movie *Robin Hood* (1922). There is seating for 18,000 people at the Bowl, including the privately owned and much sought-after boxes at the front.

The Edmund D. Edelman Hollywood Bowl Museum explores the rich history of the Bowl, through videos, old programs and posters, and memorabilia of the artists who have come here, from violinist Jascha Heifetz to The Beatles. Film excerpts shot at the Bowl include William Wellman's *A Star is Born* (1937).

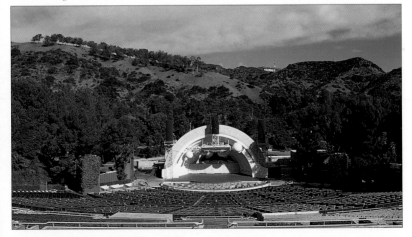

Hollywood Bowl, nestling in the Hollywood Hills

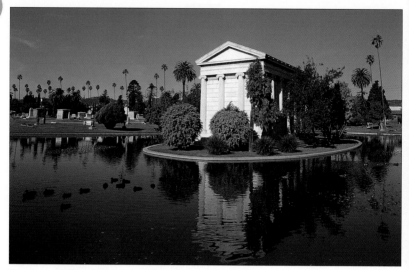

Mausoleum of William A Clark, Jr. in Hollywood Memorial Park

Hollywood Studio Museum ❼

2100 N Highland Ave. **Map** 2 B3.
(*(323) 874-2276.* ☐ *10am–4pm Sat; noon–4pm Sun. Weekdays by appt.* ⬚ ♿ ⬚

In 1913, Cecil B De Mille and the Jesse L Lasky Feature Play Company rented this barn, then located on Vine Street, just north of Sunset Boulevard. That year De Mille used the building to make *The Squaw Man*, the first feature-length movie produced in Hollywood. In 1935 the company was renamed Paramount Pictures.

The barn was moved to its present site, in the Hollywood Bowl parking lot *(see p107)*, in 1983. Thirteen years later a fire prompted a major renovation. Today the barn is a museum, displaying props, costumes, photographs, and other memorabilia from the early days of filmmaking.

Pantages Theater ❽

6233 Hollywood Blvd. **Map** 2 C4.
(*(323) 468-1700.* ☐ *daily.* ⬚ ♿

To attend a show at the Pantages is to experience the glory days of the 1930s movie palaces. Built in 1929, the marble and bronze Art Deco theater catered to the comfort of its audience, with a spacious foyer and luxurious lounges. It opened in 1930 with *The Floradora Girl*, starring Marion Davies, the mistress of WR Hearst *(see p204)*. Between 1949 and 1959 the Academy Awards Ceremony was also held here.

Splendidly renovated in the 1980s, today Pantages is used to stage Broadway musicals. Only show ticket holders are allowed into the breathtaking interior, with its magnificent chandeliers, vaulted ceilings, and columns decorated with geometric patterns.

Elegant Art Deco façade of the Pantages Theater

Hollywood Memorial Park ❾

6000 Santa Monica Blvd. **Map** 8 C1.
(*(323) 469-1181.* ☐ *8am–5pm Mon–Fri; 10am–3pm Sun.* ⬤ *public hols.* ♿

A map of this cemetery is available at the front office and reads like an early history of film. Tyrone Power has a white memorial overlooking a pond on the eastern side. Next to him, the mausoleum of Marion Davies bears her family name of Douras. Cecil B De Mille, Nelson Eddy, and many others from Hollywood's heyday are also buried in this area. Douglas Fairbanks, Sr.'s grave has a reflecting pool and monument, reputed to have been paid for by his ex-wife, the silent film star Mary Pickford. Inside the gloomy Cathedral Mausoleum is the tomb of Rudolph Valentino, still the cemetery's biggest attraction. Every year, on August 23, a "Lady in Black" pays her respects to the actor on the anniversary of his death.

The back of Paramount Studios forms the southern wall of the cemetery, and Columbia used to be to the north. Columbia boss Harry Cohn is said to have picked his plot so that he could keep an eye on his studio.

Paramount Studios ⑩

5555 Melrose Ave. **Map** 8 C1.
📞 *(323) 956-5000.* 🕐 *9am–2pm Mon–Fri.* ⬤ *Jan 1, Easter Sun, Thanksgiving, Dec 25.* 📷 ♿ 🎬
Visitors' Center and Ticket Window *860 N Gower St.* 📞 *(323) 956-5575.* 🕐 *8:30am–4pm Mon–Fri.* ⬤ *Jan 1, Easter Sun, Thanksgiving, Dec 25.*

T HE LAST MAJOR STUDIO still located in Hollywood, Paramount was also the first in operation. Cecil B. De Mille, Jesse Lasky, and Samuel Goldwyn joined forces with Adolph Zukor in 1914 to form what became known as the directors' studio. The roster of stars was equally impressive: Gloria Swanson, Rudolph Valentino, Mae West, Marlene Dietrich, Gary Cooper, and Bing Crosby all signed with Paramount.

Aspiring actors still hug the wrought-iron gates at Bronson Avenue and Marathon Street. Seeking luck, they quote Norma Desmond's final line in *Sunset Boulevard*: "I'm ready for my close-up, Mr. De Mille."

Classics such as *The Ten Commandments*, *The War of the Worlds*, *The Greatest Show on Earth*, and the *Godfather Parts I, II,* and *III* were all made in Paramount's 63 acres (25 ha) of backlot and sound stages. A two-hour tour of the studio provides details of its history and gives visitors a behind-the-scenes view of films and television shows currently in production *(see p165)*.

MELROSE AVENUE

Once a bland avenue, Melrose burst onto the Los Angeles street scene in the mid-1980s with quirky shops and good restaurants. The prime area stretches for 16 blocks between La Brea and Fairfax avenues, providing a rare opportunity to walk and shop outdoors in the city. From Fifties to punk to classic, the clothing, shoe, and accessory boutiques offer a wide range of styles and goods and stay open until late *(see pp166–7)*. The same can also be said of the avenue's many restaurants, which represent the diverse ethnic flavors of Los Angeles. Mexican and Thai are two of the

Colorful shop window on Melrose Avenue

favorite cuisines, but pasta and pizza dominate the street, as they do the rest of the city.

At the western end of Melrose, at San Vincente Boulevard, is the huge 600-ft (183-m) high blue-glass Pacific Design Center, known to the locals as the Blue Whale. Designed by César Pelli in 1975, this showcase for interior designers and architects is the largest on the West Coast. Although it caters mainly to trade, the center also welcomes the general public. Admission charges and purchasing policies may vary between individual showrooms.

Farmers Market ⑪

6333 W 3rd St. **Map** 7 D3. 📞 *(323) 933-9211.* 🕐 *9am–6:30pm Mon–Sat; 10am–5pm Sun.* ⬤ *Jan 1, Easter Sun, Memorial Day, Jul 4, Labor Day, Thanksgiving, Dec 25.* ♿

I N 1934, during the Great Depression *(see p49)*, a group of farmers began selling their produce directly to the public in a field then at the edge of town. Since then, Farmers Market has been a favorite meeting place for Angelenos. There are stalls selling fresh flowers, meats,

Clock tower at entrance to Farmers Market

cheeses, fruit, vegetables, and breads. There are also more than 100 shops that sell everything from antiques to T-shirts and garden supplies. Among the best of the numerous cafés and restaurants are Bob's Donuts, where some of the finest doughnuts in town can be sampled; Kokomo Café, which fills up quickly with a fashionable crowd, hungry for strawberry pancakes or black bean-filled omelettes *(see p546)*; and The Gumbo Pot, where the traditional Cajun food is spicy and the *beignets* (dough fritters) are sweet *(see p546)*.

Poster for Paramount's *The War of the Worlds* **(1953)**

Los Angeles County Museum of Art ⑫

THE LARGEST ENCYCLOPEDIC ART MUSEUM west of Chicago, the Los Angeles County Museum of Art (LACMA) has one of the finest collections in the country. Founded in 1910, the museum moved to its present site in prestigious Hancock Park in 1965. The six-building complex offers a wide selection of European and American art. LACMA West, across the street, holds Latin American art and a Children's Gallery. Also impressive are the museum's Asian and Middle Eastern works and its group of pre-Columbian artifacts. To display its Japanese art, including the Shin'enkan and Bushell collections, LACMA added the spectacular Pavilion for Japanese Art in 1988.

★ **In the Woods at Giverny**
This work of 1887, subtitled "Blanche Hoschedé at her easel with Suzanne Hoschedé reading," depicts the daughters of Monet's mistress.

★ **Mother about to Wash her Sleepy Child** *(1880)*
Mary Cassatt was a leading American Impressionist artist, who promoted that movement avidly in the United States. Nearly one third of the works that she produced are domestic scenes, such as this intimate portrait.

Flower Day *(1925)*
Diego Rivera depicts various religious influences in Mexico. This and other Latin American artworks are displayed in the new LACMA West.

Third level

Second level

Entrance

Plaza level

Lower level

AHMANSON BUILDING

STAR EXHIBITS

★ **In the Woods at Giverny by Claude Monet**

★ **Mother about to Wash her Sleepy Child by Mary Cassatt**

★ **Mulholland Drive by David Hockney**

MUSEUM GUIDE

European and American works of art are displayed in the Ahmanson and Hammer buildings. The limestone, terra-cotta and glass-brick Anderson Building, completed in 1986 by Hardy Holzman Pfeiffer, holds the museum's 20th-century art collection. The Sculpture Garden has bronzes by Auguste Rodin. The Pavilion for Japanese Art, designed by architectural maverick Bruce Goff, combines Japanese elements with 1950s American styling. The Plaza Café is located in the Bing Center. LACMA West is across the street.

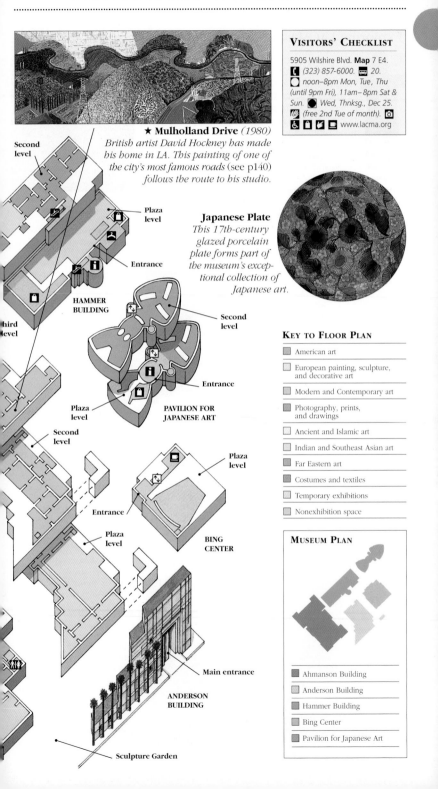

★ Mulholland Drive *(1980)*
British artist David Hockney has made his home in LA. This painting of one of the city's most famous roads (see p140) follows the route to his studio.

VISITORS' CHECKLIST

5905 Wilshire Blvd. **Map** 7 E4.
(323) 857-6000. 20.
noon–8pm Mon, Tue, Thu
(until 9pm Fri), 11am–8pm Sat &
Sun. Wed, Thnksg., Dec 25.
(free 2nd Tue of month).
www.lacma.org

Japanese Plate
This 17th-century glazed porcelain plate forms part of the museum's exceptional collection of Japanese art.

Second level

Plaza level

Entrance

HAMMER BUILDING

Second level

Third level

Entrance

Plaza level

PAVILION FOR JAPANESE ART

Second level

Plaza level

Entrance

Plaza level

BING CENTER

Main entrance

ANDERSON BUILDING

Sculpture Garden

KEY TO FLOOR PLAN

- American art
- European painting, sculpture, and decorative art
- Modern and Contemporary art
- Photography, prints, and drawings
- Ancient and Islamic art
- Indian and Southeast Asian art
- Far Eastern art
- Costumes and textiles
- Temporary exhibitions
- Nonexhibition space

MUSEUM PLAN

- Ahmanson Building
- Anderson Building
- Hammer Building
- Bing Center
- Pavilion for Japanese Art

Exploring LACMA

A TOUR OF LACMA offers a comprehensive survey of the history of art throughout the world. The museum has more than 250,000 objects that represent many cultures, dating from prehistoric to modern and contemporary periods. Ancient art treasures encompass pre-Columbian finds as well as the largest Islamic art collection in the western United States. Decorative arts, which include European and American pieces from medieval times to the present, are exhibited alongside paintings and sculpture from the same period. The museum also has a superb collection of costumes and textiles. A program of world-class traveling exhibitions complements the permanent collection.

Standing Warrior

Magdalen with the Smoking Flame (c.1640) by Georges de la Tour

AMERICAN ART

THE COLLECTION of paintings traces the history of American art from the 1700s to the 1940s. Dating from the Colonial period are John Singleton Copley's *Portrait of a Lady* (1771) and Benjamin West's *Cymon and Iphigenia* (1773).

In the mid-1800s American artists such as Edwin Church (1826–1900), Winslow Homer (1836–1910), and Thomas Moran (1837–1926) turned from portrait painting and Classical subjects to landscapes of the New World. Notable Impressionist works include Mary Cassatt's *Mother about to Wash Her Sleepy Child (see p110)* and Childe Hassam's *Avenue of the Allies* (1918). *Flower Day (see p110)* by Diego Rivera forms part of the Latin American collection.

Decorative arts range from Chippendale and Federal-style furniture to lamps by Louis Comfort Tiffany (1848–1933).

Monument to Balzac, sculpted in the 1890s by Auguste Rodin

EUROPEAN PAINTING, SCULPTURE, AND DECORATIVE ARTS

THE COLLECTION of European works of art spans the 12th to early 20th centuries, beginning with medieval religious objects. Fine portraits by Lucas Cranach (1472–1553) and Hans Holbein (1497–1543) represent the Northern Renaissance.

Religious paintings by Fra Bartolommeo (1472–1517) and Titian (c.1490–1576) date from the Italian Renaissance.

One of the European collection's strengths is its 17th-century Dutch and Flemish canvases. Rembrandt's *The Raising of Lazarus* (c.1630) and Anthony Van Dyck's *Andromeda Chained to the Rock* (1637–8) are among the highlights. Works displayed from the French and Italian schools include Georges de la Tour's *Magdalen with the Smoking Flame*, painted around 1640, and Guido Reni's *Portrait of Cardinal Roberto Ubaldino*, which dates from before 1625. The French collections from the 18th and 19th centuries are also impressive, with works by Eugène Delacroix (1798–1863) and Camille Corot (1796–1875). The sculpture collection concentrates mostly on 19th-century French artists, with more than 40 works by Auguste Rodin (1840–1917).

Impressionist and Post-Impressionist works are hung in the Hammer Building. Two of the highlights are *In the Woods at Giverny* by Claude Monet *(see p110)* and Edgar Degas' *The Bellelli Sisters* (1862–4). Others include paintings by Pierre Auguste Renoir (1841–1919), Vincent Van Gogh (1853–90), and Paul Cézanne (1839–1906).

Among the finest decorative arts pieces are a Venetian enameled and gilded blue glass ewer, dating from about 1500, and a mid-16th-century Limoges plaque that depicts Psyche and Cupid.

The Cotton Pickers (1876) by Winslow Homer

MODERN AND CONTEMPORARY ART

HOUSED IN the Anderson Building, the 20th-century collection has examples of every significant movement of modern art. The third level presents works dating from 1900 to 1970, including Pablo Picasso's *Portrait of Sebastian Juñer Vidal* (1903) and René Magritte's *La Trahison des Images (see p66)*. *Mulholland Drive* by David Hockney *(see p111)* is also hung here, due to its size. German Expressionists are well represented, with works from both *Die Brücke* (The Bridge) and *Der Blaue Reiter* (The Blue Rider) groups.

Post-1970 paintings, sculptures, and installations are displayed on the second level.

PHOTOGRAPHY, PRINTS, AND DRAWINGS

THE MUSEUM'S outstanding photography holdings give a rare overview of the medium. Exhibits range from early 19th-century daguerreotypes and albumen prints to abstract mixed media images. A large group of works by Edward Weston (1886–1958) is filled with texture and sensuality.

LACMA's holdings of prints and drawings includes the Robert Gore Rifkind Collection of German Expressionist works. Erich Heckel's woodcut, *Standing Child* (1910), is just one of its outstanding prints.

ANCIENT AND ISLAMIC ART

THE ANCIENT ART of Egypt, western Asia, Iran, Greece, and Rome is displayed on the second level of the Ahmanson Galley. There are massive carved stone panels from a 9th-century BC Assyrian palace; a rare Egyptian bronze from the 25th Dynasty; and delicate Iranian figures, some dating from 3,000 BC. The Islamic art collection spans almost 1,400 years. Its Iranian and Turkish holdings are particularly strong.

Carved stone objects and ceramic vessels and statues from Central America and Peru comprise the pre-Columbian holdings. *Standing Warrior* (100 BC–AD 300), a Mexican effigy, is the largest known work of its kind.

INDIAN AND SOUTHEAST ASIAN ART

WITH MORE than 5,000 works dating from the 3rd century BC, the museum has one of the most comprehensive collections outside Asia. It is especially strong in Indian arts, from splendid sculpture to intricate watercolors on cloth and paper. There are manuscripts and *thankas* (paintings on cloth) from Tibet and Nepal, and stone and bronze sculptures from Indonesia, Thailand, Sri Lanka, Cambodia, and Burma.

Pair of Officials (618–907), from the Tang dynasty, China

FAR EASTERN ART

THIS SECTION includes ceramics, sculpture, screens, and scrolls from China, Japan, and Korea. The highlight, however, is the Shin'enkan Collection in the Pavilion for Japanese Art. The collection's 200 screens and scroll paintings from the Edo period (1615–1868) are considered the most outstanding in the Western world. Masterpieces include Ito Jakuchu's 18th-century hanging scroll, *Rooster, Hen and Hydrangea*, and Suzuki Kiitsu's 19th-century *Seashells and Plums*. The Bushell Collection of *netsukes* (carved toggles used to secure a small container), ceramics, sculpture, and woodblock prints is also impressive.

COSTUMES AND TEXTILES

AN ENCYCLOPEDIA of clothing and textiles, the collection boasts some 55,000 artifacts that represent more than 300 of the world's cultures. The oldest pieces are embroidered Peruvian burial shrouds that date from 100 BC and an Egyptian Coptic tunic from the 5th century AD. One of the most important pieces is the early 16th-century Iranian "Ardebil" carpet, named after a shrine in northwest Iran for which it was commissioned. A French noblewoman's gown, made from silk, gold, and silver, is one of only two complete 17th-century dresses in the US.

***Dunes, Oceano* (1936) by Edward Weston**

Miracle Mile ⑬

Wilshire Blvd between La Brea &
Fairfax Aves. **Map** 7 D4. ⓘ 685
S Figueroa St (213-689-8822), 6541
Hollywood Blvd (213-689-8822).

IN 1920, developer AW Ross
bought 18 acres (7.2 ha) of
land along Wilshire Boulevard
and built a shopping district
aimed at the wealthy families
living in nearby Hancock Park.
With its Art Deco and Streamline Moderne buildings, wide
sidewalks and streets built for
cars rather than carriages, it
earned the nickname "Miracle
Mile." The suburban department stores were designed
with parking lots, a convenience that attracted hordes of
shoppers from the city. It was
the start of LA's decentralization.

Today, this stretch of boulevard is a shadow of its former
self, dotted with grocery stores
catering to various ethnic communities. At the eastern end, a
few Streamline Moderne relics
survive, such as the small gold-
and-black building at No. 5209,
a smaller version of the razed
Richfield Tower in Downtown.

Fortunately, the western end
of the Miracle Mile has fared
somewhat better. Anchoring
the corner of Fairfax Avenue,
the May Company building has
a gold and mosaic cylinder that
resembles a large perfume
bottle. With its five museums,
including LACMA (see pp110–
13), the area has now become
Museum Row.

1932 Duesenberg Model J roadster at the Petersen Automotive Museum

Petersen Automotive Museum ⑭

6060 Wilshire Blvd. **Map** 7 D4.
☎ (323) 930-2277. ◷ 10am–6pm
Tue–Sun. ● Jan 1, Thanksgiving,
Dec 25. 🖼 ♿ ✔

DIORAMAS and temporary
exhibitions illustrate the
evolution of the United States'
car culture (see pp190–91). On
the first floor there are highly
detailed displays featuring cars
such as the 1911 American
Underslung "Stuck in the Mud"
and Earl Cooper's 1915 "White
Squadron" Stutz Racer. A 1922
Ford Model-T is shown in a
scene from a Laurel and Hardy
film, and a trio of beautiful
vintage cars appear in a 1920s
street setting.

Other displays include a
1920s garage; a 1930s car
showroom, whose opulence
defied the Depression; and a
1950s drive-in restaurant.
A 1930s billboard shows how
advertising was used to boost
the popularity of the car.

Upstairs, five galleries showcase everything from hot rods
and motorcycles to vintage
classics and cars of the stars.
Vehicles that fall into the last
category are Rita Hayworth's
1953 Cadillac and Clark Gable's
Mercedes Benz.

The Improv ⑮

8162 Melrose Ave. **Map** 8 B2.
☎ (323) 651-2583. ◷ 8pm
Mon–Thu; 8.30pm & 10.30pm Sat &
Sun. 🖼 ♿

WHEN IT OPENED in 1975,
the Improv immediately
became one of the finest
comedy clubs in town, and
today it is known throughout
the world. Famous names such
as Jay Leno, Richard Lewis,
and Damon Wayans appear
regularly, and Drew Carey

performs most Thursdays
with costars from the Drew
Carey Show. The club is also
a great place to see talented
newcomers, many of whom
have glittering careers ahead.

Food can be bought in the
showroom itself or in the
restaurant, Hell's Kitchen,
which specialises in Italian
food, and a minimum of two
drinks per head can be
ordered at the bar.

Given the club's popularity,
it is best to book a table a day
or two in advance.

Popular comedian Drew Carey
performing at the Improv club

George C Page Museum of La Brea Discoveries ⑯

5801 Wilshire Blvd. **Map** 7 E4.
☎ (323) 934-7243. ◷ 9.30am–5pm
daily. ● Jan 1, Thanksgiving, July 4,
Dec 25. 🖼 free first Tue of month.
♿ ✔ 📷

OPENED IN 1976, the George
C Page Museum has a
collection of over one million
fossils that were discovered
at the La Brea Tar Pits. These
include more than 200 types
of mammals, birds, reptiles,

Gold tower of the May Company
building on Wilshire Boulevard

LA BREA TAR PITS

The tar in the La Brea Pits was formed some 42,000 years ago by oil rising to the earth's surface and gelling. Animals entering the pits to drink the water became stuck in the tar and died. Their bones were then fossilized.

For centuries the tar was used by Gabrielino Indians to waterproof baskets and boats. Later, Mexican and Spanish settlers tarred their roofs with it. In 1906 geologists discovered the largest collection of fossils from the Pleistocene Epoch ever found in one place, and the pits began to attract greater attention. The land was deeded to the county in 1916.

Models at the La Brea Tar Pits depicting how animals were trapped

plants, and insects. Some of the pieces date back nearly 42,000 years. Among the highlights are mastodons, saber-toothed tigers, American lions, and an imperial mammoth. The display of more than 400 wolf skulls shows just how much variation can occur within a single species.

The only human skeleton to have been found in the pits is that of "La Brea Woman." A hologram changes her from a skeleton to a fully fleshed person and back again.

Pit 91 has produced most of the fossils. During the summer, visitors on the viewing station can watch paleontologists at work. Inside the museum, a glass-walled laboratory allows observation of the ongoing cleaning, identification, and cataloging of the fossils.

Craft and Folk Art Museum ⓱

5814 Wilshire Blvd. **Map** 7 E4.
📞 (323) 937-4230. ⏱ 11am–5pm Tue–Sun. ⬤ Jan 1, Thanksgiving, Dec 25. 🎟 ✔

THE MUSEUM'S COLLECTION has more than 3,000 folk art and craft objects from around the world, ranging from 19th-century American quilts to contemporary furniture, to African masks. Those interested in design will enjoy the regular exhibitions on subjects such as toys, glassware, and textiles.

The extensive collection of Mexican artworks includes a fine selection of the Linares family's papier-mâché pieces.

A series of exhibitions is held throughout the year, and every

October the museum runs the International Festival of Masks in nearby Hancock Park.

African mask at the Craft Museum

Wiltern Theater ⓲

3790 Wilshire Blvd. **Map** 9 D4.
📞 (213) 380-5005. ⏱ performances only. 🎟 ♿ ✔

BUILT AS A movie theater in 1931, the Wiltern Theater was restored in 1985 and is a center for the performing arts. Its Art Deco tower and wings are faced with turquoise-glazed terra-cotta, and its main entrance is marked by a sun-burst canopy. The sun motif continues in the auditorium, where rays of low-relief skyscrapers decorate the interior ceiling.

To see inside the Wiltern Theater visitors must buy a ticket to a show.

Mammoth skeleton at the George C Page Museum

DOWNTOWN LOS ANGELES

CONSIDERED A BACKWATER a little over a hundred years ago, Los Angeles has confounded its critics by becoming a powerful worldwide influence. The city's Spanish roots are here, at El Pueblo, where the Avila Adobe and Old Plaza Church stand as reminders of Mexican frontier days, when *rancheros* and their *señoras* strolled through the streets. To the north of El Pueblo is Chinatown, with its numerous Asian shops and restaurants. To the south, Little Tokyo is the heart of the largest Japanese-American community in North America. Downtown's business district is centered on Bunker Hill, once a wealthy neighborhood where the city's Victorian elite lived. Today, confident office towers such as the First Interstate World Center and the Wells Fargo Center dominate the Downtown landscape. The district is also home to the Museum of Contemporary Art (MOCA) and the Music Center for the performing arts.

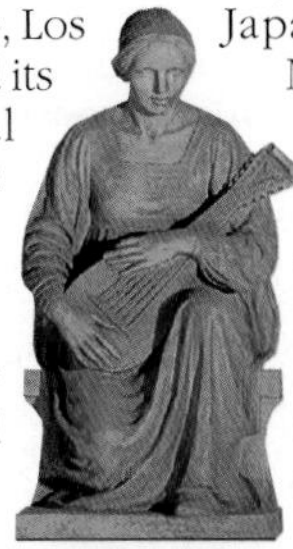

Detail from the Fine Arts Building on West 7th Street

SIGHTS AT A GLANCE

Historic Districts and Buildings

Angels Flight 2
Bradbury Building 4
Chinatown 8
El Pueblo pp122–3 7
Grand Central Market 3
Little Tokyo 13
Los Angeles Central Library 1
Los Angeles City Hall 11
Union Station 9

Museums and Galleries

Geffen Contemporary at MOCA 12
Japanese American National Museum 14
Los Angeles Children's Museum 10
Museum of Contemporary Art 5

Arts Complex

Music Center 6

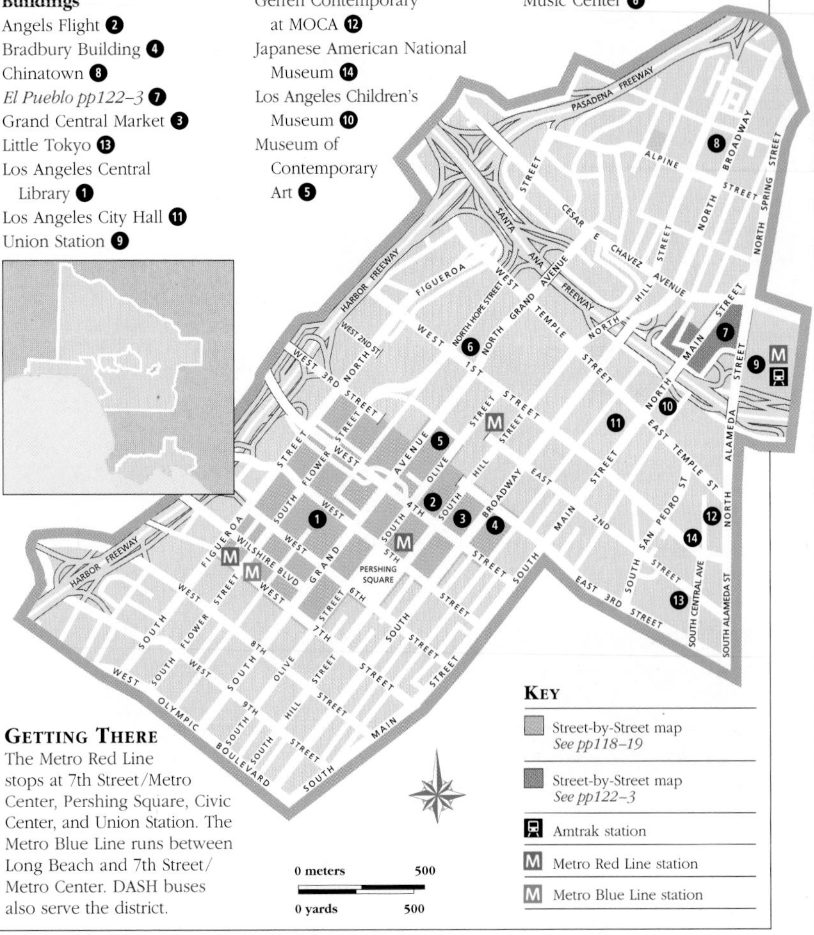
PASADENA FREEWAY
ALPINE
BROADWAY
NORTH SPRING STREET
STREET
NORTH
CESAR E CHAVEZ AVENUE
SANTA ANA FREEWAY
HILL STREET
HARBOR FREEWAY
FIGUEROA
NORTH HOPE STREET
WEST
GRAND AVENUE
TEMPLE STREET
NORTH MAIN STREET
WEST 2ND ST
NORTH
1ST STREET
WEST 3RD STREET
NORTH ALAMEDA STREET
EAST TEMPLE ST
SOUTH FLOWER STREET
OLIVE
SOUTH HILL STREET
BROADWAY
EAST 2ND STREET
SAN PEDRO ST
MAIN STREET
WEST 4TH STREET
WILSHIRE BLVD
WEST 5TH STREET
PERSHING SQUARE
6TH STREET
EAST 3RD STREET
SOUTH CENTRAL AVE
SOUTH ALAMEDA ST
WEST 7TH STREET
WEST 8TH STREET
OLYMPIC BOULEVARD
9TH STREET
SOUTH MAIN
0 meters 500
0 yards 500

KEY

Street-by-Street map *See pp118–19*

Street-by-Street map *See pp122–3*

Amtrak station

[M] Metro Red Line station

[M] Metro Blue Line station

GETTING THERE

The Metro Red Line stops at 7th Street/Metro Center, Pershing Square, Civic Center, and Union Station. The Metro Blue Line runs between Long Beach and 7th Street/Metro Center. DASH buses also serve the district.

◁ **Wells Fargo Center, slicing the Downtown skyline**

Street-by-Street: Business District

Stone carving on Biltmore Hotel

THE 20TH CENTURY saw LA expand west toward the ocean, temporarily relegating Downtown to a minor role in the city. All that has changed. Today a revitalized business district has developed around Flower Street, and the sidewalk are once more filled with tourists and Angelenos alike. California's banking industry has its headquarters here, housed in striking skyscrapers such as the Wells Fargo Center. The revival has continued eastward across Downtown, where the jewelry, toy, food, and garment wholesale industries are flourishing. A commitment to the arts has also borne fruit. The Museum of Contemporary Art (MOCA), Music Center, and Los Angeles Central Library have together encouraged a thriving cultural environment that has drawn people back to the city's center.

The Westin Bonaventure Hotel has external elevators with views of the business district for guests ascending to the cocktail lounge *(see p510)*.

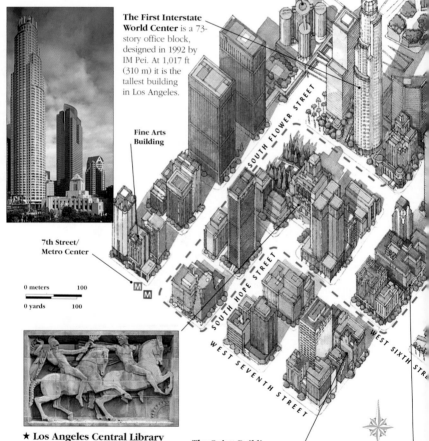

The First Interstate World Center is a 73-story office block, designed in 1992 by IM Pei. At 1,017 ft (310 m) it is the tallest building in Los Angeles.

Fine Arts Building

7th Street/ Metro Center

0 meters   100
0 yards   100

SOUTH FLOWER STREET

SOUTH HOPE STREET

WEST SIXTH STREET

WEST SEVENTH STREET

★ **Los Angeles Central Library**
The newly expanded Beaux-Arts library is decorated with carvings and inscriptions on the theme "the Light of Learning" ❶

The Oviatt Building (1925) is a marvelous example of Art Deco styling. René Lalique made some of the glass.

The Biltmore Hotel has been one of LA's most luxurious hotels since 1923 *(see p509)*.

★ Museum of Contemporary Art
Located off California Plaza, MOCA's sandstone building was greeted with acclaim when it opened in 1986. The collection gives an exciting overview of post-1940 art **5**

LOCATOR MAP
See Street Finder, map 11

The Wells Fargo Center, the LA branch of this California company *(see p304)*, has a museum and sculpture court, with works by artists such as Jean Dubuffet.

Angels Flight
The funicular (now closed) runs from South Hill Street to California Plaza **2**

★ Bradbury Building
The atrium of this unassuming Victorian office block is one of the finest of its kind in the US **4**

KEY

– – – Suggested route

Pershing Square Metro station

Grand Central Market
This indoor market lies at the heart of the old theater district **3**

Pershing Square was designated the city's first public park in 1866. The now-concreted square is still a popular meeting place and has been landscaped with trees, benches, and statuary.

STAR SIGHTS

★ Bradbury Building

★ Los Angeles Central Library

★ Museum of Contemporary Art

Façade of the Los Angeles Central Library

Los Angeles Central Library ❶

630 W 5th St. **Map** 11 D4. *(213)
228-7000.* ☐ *10am–8pm
Mon–Thu; 10am–6pm Fri, Sat;
1–5pm Sun.* ● *public hols.* &
Ⓦ *www.lapl.org*

BUILT IN 1926, this civic
treasure was struck by an
arson attack in 1986. It was
closed for seven years while a
$213.9 million renovation
program was carried out.
Sympathetic to the
original architecture, the
improvements have
doubled the library's
capacity to more than
2.1 million books.

The original building
combines Beaux-Arts
grandeur with Byzan-
tine, Egyptian, and
Roman architectural
elements, inscriptions,
and sculpture on the
theme "the Light of
Learning." The murals
in the rotunda, painted
by Dean Cornwell
(1892–1960), depict the
history of California and
are well worth seeing.

**Statue on the
library wall**

The attention given to detail
in the new Tom Bradley wing
is impressive. One example is
the three atrium chandeliers,
created by Therman Statom to
represent the natural, ethereal,
and technological worlds.

The Central Library's garden
is situated by the Flower Street
entrance. Weary sightseers
will appreciate its fountains,
sculptures, shaded benches,
and restaurant.

A varied program of arts
events takes place within the
library, including prose and
poetry readings, lectures,
concerts, and plays.

Angels Flight ❷

Between Grand, Hill, 3rd & 4th Sts.
Map 11 D4. *(213) 626-1901.*
Closed for the foreseeable future.

BILLED AS the "shortest railway in the world," Angels
Flight transported riders the
315 ft (96 m) between Hill
Street and Bunker Hill for
almost 70 years. Built in
1901, the funicular quickly
became a familiar and
much-loved method of
travel. But, by 1969,
Bunker Hill had sadly
degenerated and was
considered an eyesore.
The city dismantled
Angels Flight, but
promised to reinstall
the funicular once the
area had been redevel-
oped. In 1996, some
27 years later, the
city finally fulfilled
that vow.

Grand Central Market ❸

317 S Broadway. **Map** 11 E4.
(213) 624-2378. ☐ *9am–6pm
daily.* ● *Jan 1, Thanksgiving,
Dec 25.* &

ANGELENOS have been coming to this vibrant indoor
bazaar since 1917. Today,
more than 40 stallholders
operate inside the marketplace. Neatly arranged mounds
of bargain-priced fresh fruits
and vegetables line the many
produce stands, and friendly
stallholders frequently offer
free samples of fruit.

Almost all the signs are in
English and Spanish. The
market's predominantly Latin
American clientele come here
to buy exotic products from
their home countries, such as
fresh Nogales cacti and beans
from El Salvador. The seafood
stands are filled with an array
of fish caught in the waters
off Southern California. Goat
heads and tripe are offered
alongside the more familiar
cuts of meat at the butcher
stalls. Herb stands offer a range
of homeopathic alternatives for
minor ills. Amid all this bustle,
fragrant aromas of powdered
chilies, herbs, and spicy foods
waft through the air.

Among the many cafés and
food stands in the market is
China Café, which has been
serving its popular chow mein
since the 1930s. At Chapalita
Tortilleria, visitors can enjoy
watching the rickety assembly-
line machine turn *masa* (corn
flour dough) into tortillas and
then partake of the free samples on the counter. Mexican
stalls, such as Ana Maria, sell
tacos and burritos, which are
filled with all kinds of meat
and seafood.

Venturing from the market
onto Broadway, you will find
yourself on the main shopping street of Los Angeles'
Hispanic community. Before
World War II, this was the
movie district, with extravagant theaters and fashionable
shops. Today, most of the
theaters have either closed
down or are being used for
religious meetings conducted
in Spanish. The street has a
great deal of energy – the feel
is that of Mexico City or Lima,
Peru – but tourists should be
wary of pickpockets.

China Café in the market

Atrium of the Bradbury Building

Bradbury Building ❹

304 S Broadway. **Map** 11 E4.
((213) 626-1893. ◐ 9am–5pm
daily. ♿ from 3rd St.

T HE BRADBURY BUILDING was
designed by architectural
draftsman George Herbert
Wyman in 1893. It is one of
the few surviving Victorian
structures in LA. Although the
red façade is simple, the atrium
is outstanding, with its lace-
work of wrought-iron railings,
oak paneling, glazed brick
walls, two open-cage elevators,
and a glass roof. It is the only
office building in LA to be
designated a National Historic
Landmark. Visitors may get a
feeling of *déjà vu* – the building is a popular film location,
with Ridley Scott's *Blade
Runner* (1982) just one of the
movies shot here.

Museum of Contemporary Art ❺

250 S Grand Ave. **Map** 11 D4.
((213) 621-2766. ◐ 11am–5pm
Tue–Sun (until 8pm Thu). ● Jan 1,
July 4, Thanksgiving, Dec 25. 🎫 free
5–8pm Thu. ♿
W www.moca.org

R ATED BY the American
Institute of Architects as
one of the best works of
architecture in the US, this
museum's building is as

interesting as its collection. It
is an intriguing combination of
pyramids, cylinders, and
cubes, designed in 1986 by
Japanese architect Arata
Isozaki. Its warm native
sandstone walls, which sit on
a red granite foundation, are in
pleasing contrast to the cool
tones of the district's
surrounding skyscrapers.
   The gallery area lies off the
sunken entrance courtyard
and is reached via a sweeping
staircase. Four of the seven
galleries are naturally lit from
pyramid-shaped skylights that
punctuate the roofline.
   Founded in 1979, the Museum of Contemporary Art has
quickly amassed a respected
selection of post-1940 work
from artists such as Piet Mondrian, Jackson Pollock, Louise
Nevelson, and Julian
Schnabel. Added weight
is given by the Panza
Collection of 80 works
of Pop Art and Abstract
Expressionism by
artists such
as Robert
Rauschen-
berg, Mark
Rothko, and Claes
Oldenburg. In 1995,
MOCA acquired the
2,100-print Freidus
Collection of photo-
graphs, which traces
the development of
documentary photo-
graphy in the United
States from the 1940s
through the 1980s. The
collection includes works by
Diane Arbus and Robert Frank.
   MOCA stands at the northern
end of the 11-acre (4.5-ha)

**Coca-Cola Plan
(1958) by Robert
Rauschenberg**

California Plaza. This vast
development funded the creation of MOCA, donating 1.5
percent of its budget, as stipulated by LA law, to public art.
The spectacular fountain at
the center of the plaza repeats
its synchronized program
every 20 minutes. The finale
drops a 10,000-gal (45,500-
litre) wave that washes over
the fountain edge.

Music Center ❻

135 N Grand Ave. **Map** 11 E3.
((213) 972-7211. 🎫 ♿ **Dorothy
Chandler Pavilion** box office
◐ 10am–6pm Mon–Sat. **Mark
Taper Forum & Ahmanson Theater**
box offices ◐ noon–8pm Tue–Sun.
W www.musiccenter.org

T HIS PERFORMING arts
complex is situated
at the northern end of
Bunker Hill. The
Dorothy Chandler Pavil-
ion is named after the
wife of the former
publisher of the
*Los Angeles
Times.* It
is host to the annual
Academy Awards cere-
mony, the home of the
LA Music Center Opera,
the LA Master Chorale,
and, from autumn to
spring, the LA Philhar-
monic. The Ahmanson
Theater has moveable
walls to adjust the
auditorium size, and it stages
Broadway plays. The Mark
Taper Forum presents first-
class plays such as Tony
Kushner's *Angels in America.*

Music Center plaza and fountain leading to the Mark Taper Forum

Street-by-Street: El Pueblo ❼

Statue of LA's founder, Felipe de Neve

E L PUEBLO DE LA REINA DE LOS ANGELES, the oldest part of the city, was founded in 1781 by Felipe de Neve, the Spanish governor of California. Today, El Pueblo is a State Historic Monument. The shops along Olvera Street sell colorful Mexican dresses, leather *baraches* (sandals), *piñatas* (clay or paper-mâché animals), and snacks like *churros*, a Spanish-Mexican fried bread. During its festivals El Pueblo is ablaze with color and sound. The Blessing of the Animals, *Cinco de Mayo* (May 5), the Mexican Independence Day fiesta (September 13–15), and the candlelight procession of *Las Posadas* (December 16–24) are celebrated with passion *(see pp32–5)*.

★ **Old Plaza Church**
The Annunciation *(1981)*, a mosaic by Isabel Piczek, is on the façade of the city's oldest church.

Site of the first cemetery in Los Angeles.

Pico House
California's last Mexican governor, Pío Pico, constructed the three-story Pico House in 1870. The Italianate building was for many years the area's finest hotel.

Plaza
A wrought-iron bandstand is set in the middle of the plaza. Nearby is a list of the first 44 settlers and a statue of Felipe de Neve.

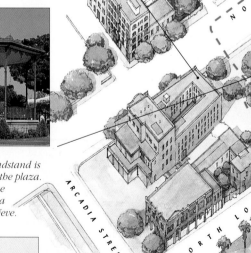

NORTH MA

NORTH

NORTH LOS ANGEL

ARCADIA STREET

Firehouse

STAR SIGHTS
★ Avila Adobe
★ Old Plaza Church

KEY

– – – – Suggested route

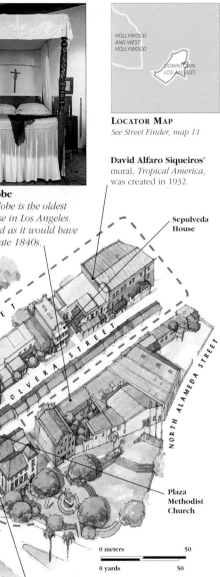

LOCATOR MAP
See Street Finder, map 11

David Alfaro Siqueiros'
mural, *Tropical America*,
was created in 1932.

Avila Adobe
*he Avila Adobe is the oldest
xisting house in Los Angeles.
is furnished as it would have
een in the late 1840s.*

**Sepulveda
House**

**Plaza
Methodist
Church**

0 meters   50

0 yards   50

Olvera Street
*This pedestrian
street was preserved
in the 1930s as a
Mexican market-
place following
a campaign by
local civic leader
Christine Sterling.*

Chinatown ❽

Map 11 F2. 🛈 *977 N Broadway,
Suite E (213 617-0396).*

THE CHINESE first came to
California during the Gold
Rush *(see pp44–5)* to work in
the mines and build the railroads. Confronted by prejudice,
they developed tightknit communities. LA's first Chinatown
was established in 1870 on
the present-day site of Union
Station *(see p124)*. It was relocated about 900 yds (820 m)
northward in the mid-1930s.
Today it is the home of over
12,000 people, who live and
work in this colorful district.

The ornate East Gate on
North Broadway leads into
Gin Ling Way and the New
Chinatown Central Plaza. This
pedestrian precinct is lined
with brightly painted buildings
that have exaggerated pagoda-
style roofs. Here, import shops
sell everything from exquisite
jade jewelry and antiques to
inexpensive trinkets.

In the surrounding streets,
the buildings are more bland,
but tantalizing restaurants offer
all manner of Chinese food,
from dim sum (filled, steamed,
or grilled dumplings, *see p540*)
to spicy Szechuan dishes.

Although on a smaller scale
than the celebrations in San
Francisco *(see p35)*, LA has its
own Chinese New Year Parade
in early February. The festivities include dragon and lion
dancers, who snake through
the district's streets accompanied by drums, cymbals, floats,
and firecrackers.

**Restaurant in Chinatown, topped
by a pagoda**

Unique blending of architectural styles on Union Station's façade

Union Station ⑨

800 N Alameda St. **Map** 11 F3.
☎ (213) 683-6979; (800) 872-7245.
⏰ 24 hours daily. ♿

DATING FROM 1939, this grand
railroad passenger terminal
was the last of its kind to be
built in the United States. The
exterior is a successful merging
of Spanish Mission, Moorish,
and Streamline Moderne styles
(see pp26–8). The tiles edging
the interior walls, the inlaid
marble designs of the floors,
and the filigree work over the
windows and doorways all
use Spanish motifs.

The vast concourse, with its
52-ft (15.8-m) high roof, will
be familiar to any fan of 1940s
films – stars were frequently
photographed here arriving in
Los Angeles. In recent years it
has been the location for several movies, including Sydney
Pollack's The Way We Were
(1973) and Barry Levinson's

Bugsy (1991). Today the station
is quieter, but there are still
daily departures to Chicago,
Seattle, and San Diego.

Los Angeles Children's Museum ⑩

Currently closed for renovation and
relocation. Will reopen in new location
in 2004.
🌐 www.lacm.org

THIS IMAGINATIVE and stimulating museum is guided
by the principle that children
learn best by doing. Opened
in 1979, it quickly became a
popular family destination.

Some 20 hands-on activities
are linked by a series of
ramps. Called the "discovery
maze," the system was
designed by architect Frank
Gehry. One of the favorite
exhibits is the Videozone.

This brings out the performer
in children as they sing,
dance, and tell stories on
video. In Sticky City, large,
brightly colored foam-and-
Velcro blocks cling to each
other, the walls, and even
the participants as they
build skyscrapers, mountains,
and tunnels.

Children between 2 and
12 years old enjoy role-
playing as the driver of a
bus in the City Streets exhibit.
In the Cave of the Dinosaurs,
young visitors can experience
primitive life in their own
cave, complete with realistic
dinosaur sounds.

All children must be
accompanied by an adult.

Los Angeles City Hall ⑪

200 N Spring St. **Map** 11 E4. ☎ (213)
485-2121. ⏰ 8am–5pm Mon–Fri.
● public hols. ♿ from Main St.
📷 advance reservations required.

UNTIL 1957, this 28-story
structure was the tallest in
Downtown – all others were
limited to 12 floors. When it
was built in 1928, sand from
every California county and
water from each of the state's
21 missions was added to the
City Hall's mortar.

Today City Hall is dwarfed
by surrounding skyscrapers,
but its distinctive tower is still
one of Los Angeles's most

Entrance to Los Angeles Children's Museum

familiar landmarks. Among its many film and television roles it has been the location for the *Daily Planet*, Clark Kent's place of work in the television series *Superman*.

Inside, the rotunda has a beautiful inlaid-tile dome and excellent acoustics. The dome is decorated with eight figures showing the building's major concerns: education, health, law, art, service, government, protection, and trust.

Organized groups who take the 45-minute tour of the City Hall can ascend to an observation area in the tower, which has been restored after damage by the 1994 Northridge earthquake *(see p53)*. From here there are panoramic views across the city.

Rotunda of LA City Hall

Geffen Contemporary at MOCA **⑫**

152 N Central Ave. **Map** 11 F4. **[** (213) 621-2766. **○** 11am–5pm Tue–Sun (until 8pm Thu). **●** Jan 1, Thanksgiving, Dec 25. **[图] [法]**

I N 1983, this old police garage was used as a temporary exhibition space until MOCA's California Plaza facilities were completed *(see p121)*. Frank Gehry's renovations were so successful that the warehouse became a permanent fixture of the Los Angeles art scene. Exhibitions change regularly and often include highlights from MOCA's collection.

Little Tokyo **⑬**

Map 11 E4. **[i]** *244 S San Pedro St. (213 628-2725).*

L YING BETWEEN First, Third, Los Angeles, and Alameda streets, Little Tokyo has more than 200,000 visitors who throng its Japanese markets, shops, restaurants, and temples.

The first Japanese settled here in 1884. Today, the heart of the area is the Japanese American Cultural and Community Center at No. 244 South San Pedro Street, from which cultural activities and festivals such as Nisei Week *(see p33)* are organized. The center's fan-shaped Japan America Theater is often a venue for performers from Japan, such as the Grand Kabuki.

The Japanese Village Plaza at No. 335 East Second Street has been built in the style of a rural Japanese village, with blue roof tiles, exposed wood frames, and paths landscaped with pools and rocks. A traditional fire watchtower marks the plaza's First Street entrance. Stores include Enbun Market, one of Little Tokyo's oldest businesses, and the Mikawaya Candy Store. Off San Pedro Street, Onizuka Street offers more upscale shops.

Central Avenue entrance to the Japanese American Museum

Japanese American National Museum **⑭**

369 E 1st St. **Map** 11 F4. **[** (213) 625-0414. **○** 10am–5pm Tue–Sun (until 8pm Thu). **●** Jan 1, Thanksgiving, Dec 25. **[图] [法] [✓]** **[W]** www.janm.org

T HE FORMER Nishi Hongwanji Buddhist Temple is now a museum. In 1925, architect Edgar Cline designed a building with a dual personality. The First Street entrance has an unremarkable brick façade, but the ceremonial entrance, on Central Avenue, mixes oriental and Egyptian motifs. The concrete canopy is modeled after the gateway to a Kyoto temple, and the brick pilasters have Egyptian-style capitals made of terra-cotta.

The museum is committed to preserving the history of Japanese-Americans in the US and has the largest collection of Japanese-American memorabilia in the world. Because most Japanese-Americans' property was lost when they were interned during World War II, the collection has simple, everyday items, such as newspapers, luggage, and clothing. An archive of camp records is available alongside camp mementos that include crafts and furniture.

Temporary exhibitions cover subjects such as the "Issei Pioneers," "America's Concentration Camps," and "Japanese-American Soldiers." A series of workshops is also offered.

Onizuka Street in Little Tokyo, looking toward Los Angeles City Hall

The *Queen Mary*, Long Beach's most famous hotel

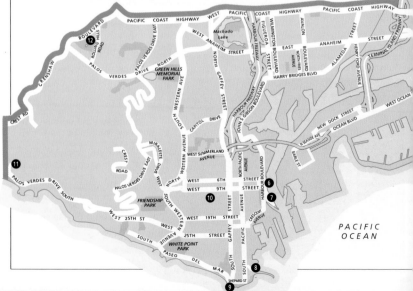

LONG BEACH AND PALOS VERDES

T HE OCEAN is the unifying force of this disparate region, where waves crash against the cliffs of the Palos Verdes Peninsula and tankers head for the busy ports of Los Angeles and Long Beach. The peninsula, a magnificent stretch of coastline, is an affluent area, with mansions and stables set amid the rolling

Statue in Ports O'Call Village

hills. On its southeastern side, working-class San Pedro is home to the Port of Los Angeles as well as generations of fishermen. The big city in the area – the fifth-largest in the state – is Long Beach. Aptly named for its 5.5-mile (9-km) expanse of white sand, this community has long attracted those who love the ocean. Its most famous landmark is the ocean liner *Queen Mary*.

SIGHTS AT A GLANCE

Historic Ships
Queen Mary pp130–31 **5**

Districts
Long Beach **1**
Naples **4**
Ports O'Call Village **7**
San Pedro **10**

Historic Buildings
Rancho Los Alamitos **3**
Rancho Los Cerritos **2**

Modern Architecture
Wayfarers Chapel **11**

Parks and Gardens
Point Fermin Park **9**
South Coast Botanic Garden **12**

Museums
Cabrillo Marine Aquarium **8**
Los Angeles Maritime Museum **6**

GETTING THERE
The Metro Blue Line connects Long Beach to downtown Los Angeles. The busy port is well served by freeways that link it to the rest of the city. A free shuttle bus, the Runabout, makes frequent journeys between downtown Long Beach, Shoreline Village, the *Queen Mary*, and the Catalina Island terminus *(see pp232–3)*. Cyclists can take the Oceanside Bike Path *(see p168)* from Long Beach to Naples.

0 kilometers 2

0 miles 2

KEY

Street-by-Street map
See pp128–9

M Metro Blue Line station

Street-by-Street: Long Beach ●

Shoreline Village sign

WITH PALM TREES and the ocean as a backdrop, downtown Long Beach is a mixture of carefully restored buildings and modern glass high-rises. At its heart, Pine Avenue still retains the early mid-western charm that gave the city its nickname of "Iowa by the Sea." The trendy atmosphere attracts locals, who come to relax, enjoy a cup of espresso, and sample some of the best food in the area. Nearby, Long Beach Convention and Entertainment Center was once the site of the Pike Amusement Park, famous for its roller coaster. Now the Terrace Theater's respected music and dance programs draw the crowds. Along the ocean, the shops and restaurants in Shoreline Village offer views of the *Queen Mary*.

Farmers and Merchants Bank Tower
When erected in 1922, this terra-cotta building was Long Beach's first skyscraper. Its hall is a fine example of period styling.

Transit Mall Metro station

Long Beach Municipal Auditorium Mural
This 1938 mural of a day at the beach was originally housed in the Municipal Auditorium. It was moved in 1979 when that building was demolished to make way for the Terrace Theater.

The Promenade is the site of Long Beach's farmer's market. Every Friday the street is filled with stands selling fruit, vegetables, and crafts.

The 1929 Mediterranean-style Ocean Center Building was the start of the Pike Amusement Park's Walk of a Thousand Lights.

KEY

– – – Suggested route

STAR SIGHTS

★ **Pine Avenue**

★ **Shoreline Village**

★ **Pine Avenue**
The center of downtown Long Beach, Pine Avenue is lined with stores, cafés, and restaurants. Some of these businesses are housed in historic buildings, such as the 1903 Masonic Temple at No. 230.

1st Street Metro station

AROUND DOWNTOWN

LONG BEACH AND PALOS VERDES

LOCATOR MAP

Convention and Entertainment Center
This newly expanded complex includes the Terrace Theater, the home of Long Beach's symphony orchestra and opera company.

The Breakers (1925), an elegant former hotel, now houses senior citizens.

Planet Ocean (1992)
Recognized as the world's largest mural, artist Wyland's Planet Ocean *covers the 116,000-sq-ft (11,000-sq-m) surface of Long Beach Arena with life-size sea creatures.*

The Hyatt Regency Hotel
adjoins the Convention Center *(see p511).*

★ Shoreline Village
This waterfront complex of restaurants and shops boasts a 1906 Looff merry-go-round. Shoreline Village is a good place to view the Queen Mary *(see pp130–31).*

The tall ship *Californian*
is docked at Shoreline Village. Both short and long cruises are available.

0 meters	200
0 yards	200

Rancho Los Cerritos ❷

4600 Virginia Rd. **[** (562) 570-1755. **◻** 1–5pm Wed–Sun. **●** Jan 1, Easter Sun, Thanksgiving, Dec 25. **&** ☑ Sat & Sun only.

Rancho los cerritos was once part of a 300,000-acre (121,400-ha) land grant, given between 1784 and 1790 to Spanish soldier Manuel Nieto. Mission San Gabriel reclaimed nearly half of the property. The rest was left to Nieto's children on his death in 1804. In 1834 it was split into five ranches.

In 1844 Los Cerritos was bought by John Temple, who built the adobe ranch house. Following droughts in the early 1860s he decided to sell to the firm Flint, Bixby & Co.

Over the years, most of the ranch was sold, but the house and surrounding 5 acres (2 ha) of land remained in the Bixby family until it was bought by the City of Long Beach in 1955.

Today, Rancho Los Cerritos is run as a museum, focusing on those who lived here from 1840 to 1940. The Monterey-style house (see p26) is furnished to reflect the late 1870s.

Rancho Los Alamitos ❸

6400 Bixby Hill Rd. **[** (562) 431-3541. **◻** 1–5pm Wed–Sun. **●** Jan 1, Easter Sun, Thanksgiving, Dec 25. **Donation**. **&** ☑

Rancho los alamitos stands on a mesa inhabited since AD 500. In 1790 it formed part of the Manuel Nieto land grant.

Cactus Garden on the grounds of Rancho Los Alamitos

The house was built in 1806, making it one of Southern California's oldest dwellings. It changed hands frequently during the 19th century, until

Queen Mary ❺

Pier J, 1126 Queens Hwy. **Road map** inset A. **[** (562) 435-3511. **◻** 10am–6pm daily. 🅿 **&** ☑ See **Where to Stay** p511 and **Where to Eat** p547. **W** www.queenmary.com

Named after the wife of British King George V, this liner set new standards in ocean travel with its maiden voyage of May 27, 1936. The jewel in the crown of the Cunard White Star Line, the Queen Mary made weekly trips between Southampton, England, and New York City.

Although the second- and third-class quarters may look small next to the grandeur of

Royal Jubilee Week, 1935 by AR Thomson, above the bar in the Observation Lounge

the first-class rooms, they were considered to be chic and spacious for their time.

On its five-day voyages, the liner carried an average of 3,000 passengers and crew members. They used the two swimming pools, two chapels, synagogue, gymnasium, ballroom, and children's playrooms. Anyone who was anyone sailed on the Queen Mary, from royalty to Hollywood stars.

From 1939 to 1946, the liner was converted into a troopship

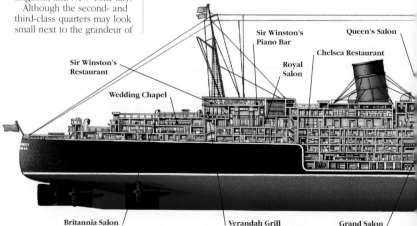

Sir Winston's Piano Bar

Queen's Salon

Chelsea Restaurant

Sir Winston's Restaurant

Royal Salon

Wedding Chapel

Britannia Salon

Verandah Grill

Grand Salon

it was bought by the Bixby family in 1881. In 1906 Fred and Florence Bixby moved into the property and began to shape the house and garden.

The ranch was given to the City of Long Beach in 1968, to be developed as a historic and educational facility. Inside, the house is furnished as it was in the 1920s and 1930s. The elegant grounds are a rare example of a pioneer garden.

Naples ❹

Road map inset A. 🚌 *Long Beach.* ℹ *One World Trade Center, Suite 300 (562 436-3645).* **Gondola Getaway** *5437 E Ocean Blvd (562 433-9595).*

I N 1903, developer Arthur Parson began creating his own version of the city of Naples in Italy, complete with winding streets and waterways spanned by small bridges (even though the original does not have canals and gondolas).

Taking heed of the mistakes made by Abbot Kinney in Venice *(see p76)*, Arthur Parson designed his canals so that the Pacific Ocean's tidal flows would keep them clean.

Finished in the late 1920s, this most charming of Long Beach neighborhoods is actually three islands in the middle of Alamitos Bay. An eclectic architectural mix of shingled, Mission Revival, Victorian, and Arts and Crafts houses *(see pp26–9)* line the

Canal in residential Naples, with boats moored alongside the private jettys

Italian-named streets. The Rivo Alto Canal, the largest in the network, surrounds the Colonnade Park, which is in the center of Naples. For a full exploration of the islands, meander through the streets on foot. Alternatively, book Gondola Getaway two weeks in advance for a cruise on an authentic Venetian gondola.

---

called the *Grey Ghost*, carrying more than 800,000 soldiers during its wartime career. At the end of the war, it transported more than 22,000 war brides and children to the US during "Operation Diaper."

In 1967, after 1,001 transatlantic crossings, the liner was bought by the City of Long Beach. It was permanently docked for use as a hotel and tourist attraction.

Detail inside the ship's Grand Salon

Today, visitors can view part of the original Engine Room, examples of the different travel accommodations, and an exhibition on the war years. Many of the original Art Deco features, created by more than 30 artists, still decorate the interior. Open to the public for dining, the Grand Salon and Observation Lounge are fine examples of period styling.

Dual set of brass steering wheels in the *Queen Mary*'s wheelhouse

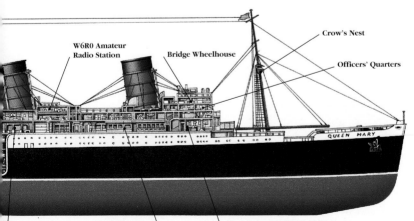

Crow's Nest

W6R0 Amateur Radio Station

Bridge Wheelhouse

Officers' Quarters

QUEEN MARY

Promenade Café and Bar

Piccadilly Circus

Observation Lounge

Relaxing on Redondo Beach, LA *(see p62)* ▷

Los Angeles Maritime Museum **6**

Berth 84, 6th St, San Pedro. **Road map** inset A. **[** *(310) 548-7618.* **○** *10am–4:30pm Tue–Sun.* **●** *Thanksgiving, Dec 25.* **Donation.** **と**

HOUSED in a restored ferry terminal building, the Los Angeles Maritime Museum contains an array of nautical paintings and memorabilia. A wooden figurehead of British Queen Victoria is just one of the museum's artifacts. An extensive model ship collection includes an 18-ft (5.5-m) scale model of the *Titanic.* Begun in 1971 by a 14-year-old boy, it took five years to complete. Also on display is the bow and bridge of US Navy cruiser USS *Los Angeles.* Early 20th-century Monterey fishing boats *(see p493)* can be seen in the museum's dock.

Figurehead of Queen Victoria

Ports O'Call Village **7**

Berth 77, San Pedro. **Road map** inset A. **[** *(310) 732-7696.* **○** *11am–7pm Sun–Thu; 11am–8pm Fri & Sat.*

PORTS O'CALL VILLAGE is a pastiche of many different seaports from all around the world. Building styles range

Street scene in the picturesque Ports O'Call Village

from a 19th-century New England fishing village, to a Mediterranean harbor, to a Mexican town.

The village's 75 shops and 15 restaurants are linked by cobblestone walkways. Street entertainers frequent this popular area during the summer. A number of fisheries supply freshly caught fish, which can be cooked and served to you on the premises. From the dockside boardwalk visitors can watch the huge cargo ships and cruise liners sail by. Daily harbor cruises tour the inner harbor, coastguard station, marina, freighter operations, and scrap yards. Tours to Catalina Island *(see pp232–3)* and winter whale-watching tours are also available.

Cabrillo Marine Aquarium **8**

3720 Stephen White Drive, San Pedro. **Road map** inset A. **[** *(310) 548-7562.* **○** *noon–5pm Tue–Fri; 10am–5pm Sat & Sun.* **●** *Thanksgiving, Dec 25.* **🅿** *for parking only.* **と** **🚗** **W** *www.cabrilloaq.org*

DESIGNED BY architect Frank Gehry and surrounded by a geometric chain-link fence, the Cabrillo Marine Aquarium houses one of the largest collections of Southern California marine life. Sharks, moray eels, and rays thrill thousands of visitors each year. The exhibition hall includes interpretive displays that explain the typical plants and animals of the region. It is divided into three environments – rocky shores, beaches and mudflats, and open ocean.

An outdoor rock pool tank contains sea cucumbers, sea anemones, starfish, and sea urchins that visitors are permitted to touch. This small museum also boasts 14,150 gallons (64,400 liters) of circulating sea water, as well as a tidal tank that allows viewers to see below a wave. Another exhibit shows how human activities have altered Los Angeles Harbor.

The beautifully maintained clapboard Point Fermin Lighthouse

Point Fermin Park **9**

Gaffey St & Paseo del Mar, San Pedro. **Road map** inset A. **[** *(310) 548-7756 (310 832-4444 for whale-watching tours Dec–Apr).* **○** *daily.*

THIS TRANQUIL 37-acre (15-ha) park sits on a bluff overlooking the Pacific Ocean. Between January and March, migrating gray whales can be spotted offshore and, on a clear day, there are views of Catalina Island. The charming Eastlake-style lighthouse dates from 1874. Its bricks and lumber were shipped around Cape Horn. The lighthouse originally used oil lamps that emitted approximately 2,100 candlepower. They were replaced by an electric lamp in 1925.

San Pedro **10**

Road map inset A. **✈** *LAX, 15 miles (24 km) NW of San Pedro.* **🚌** *MTA.* **ℹ** *390 W 7th St (310 832-7272).*

FAMOUS FOR THE Worldport LA, blue-collar pride, and a tradition of family fishermen, San Pedro ("San Peedro" to the locals) has a strong Eastern European and Mediterranean flavor. The harbor is the nation's busiest import-export site and an important link with the Pacific Rim. The houses are tiny compared to those in Palos Verdes, but this is a very important center of industry.

Korean Friendship Bell in Angels Gate Park, San Pedro

In Angels Gate Park, at the end of Gaffey Street, there is a Korean Friendship Bell, given to the United States in 1976 by South Korea.

Steps leading to the hilltop Wayfarers Chapel

Wayfarers Chapel ❶

5755 Palos Verdes Drive S, Rancho Palos Verdes. **Road map** inset A.
📞 (310) 377-1650. 🕐 *call ahead (frequently booked for weddings)*.
Gardens 🕐 *daily*. ♿
🌐 www.wayfarerschapel.org

THIS GLASS and redwood-framed chapel sits on a hilltop above the ocean. From the street below, all that can be seen is a thin stone and concrete tower rising from the greenery.

When the architect Lloyd Wright (son of Frank Lloyd Wright) designed the chapel in 1949, he tried to create a natural place of worship, surrounding it by trees. Today, its charm makes it a popular site for weddings.

The chapel is sponsored by the Swedenborgian church, which follows the teaching of Emanuel Swedenborg, the 18th-century Swedish theologian and mystic.

South Coast Botanic Garden ❷

26300 S Crenshaw Blvd, Palos Verdes.
Road map inset A. 📞 (310) 544-6815. 🕐 9am–5pm daily.
⬤ Dec 25 . 🖼 ♿ ✍

THIS 87-ACRE (35-ha) garden was created on top of some 3,175,000 tons of waste that were dumped here from 1956 to 1960. Prior to that, the area was the location of a mine for algae-rich diatomaceous earth. Today, gas formed underground as a result of the waste decomposing is collected and used to generate electricity.

The garden is a study in land reclamation, with an emphasis on drought-resistant landscaping. Specimens from all the continents except Antarctica are planted within the grounds.

In the Herb Garden plants are divided into three main categories: fragrant, medicinal, and culinary. The Rose Garden has more than 1,600 roses, including old-fashioned and miniature roses, floribundas, hybrid teas, and grandifloras.

One of the most innovative areas is the Garden for the Senses. Here, plants are chosen for their extraordinary qualities of color, smell, or touch. Some of the flowerbeds are raised, making them more accessible.

Children's Garden in the South Coast Botanic Garden

AROUND DOWNTOWN

FROM THE FREEWAYS, *it is hard to appreciate the many treasures that lie within Los Angeles's sprawl. But a short drive beyond the central sights to nearby areas can be surprisingly rewarding. Upscale Pasadena, with its delightful Old Town, also has the excellent Norton Simon Museum as well as the Huntington Library, Art Collections, and Botanical Gardens.*

Northeast of Downtown are the Heritage Square Museum with its historic buildings, Lummis House, and the Southwest Museum, one of the finest collections of Native American artifacts in the country. Just north of Hollywood, hilly Griffith Park offers precious open spaces for picnicking, hiking, and horseback riding as well as the Los Angeles Zoo, Griffith Observatory and Autry Museum of Western Heritage.

Nearby, Universal Studios offers tours of its backlots as well as theme park rides. Universal is one of four major studios based in Burbank, which has replaced Hollywood as the head-quarters for the film and television industries. Farther north in the broad, flat San Fernando Valley, Mission San Fernando Rey de España provides a historical insight into California's origins.

South of Downtown, the Natural History Museum of Los Angeles County and the California Museum of Science and Industry are among the top attractions at Exposition Park, along with the stately buildings of the University of Southern California.

For sheer scenic delight and outstanding views over the city and San Fernando Valley, twisting mountainous Mulholland Drive is hard to beat.

Tranquil Japanese Garden at the Huntington Botanical Gardens

◁ **Monument to astronomers outside the Griffith Observatory**

Exploring Around Downtown

T HE OUTLYING AREAS of Los
Angeles contain a vast range
of museums, galleries, historic
buildings, and parks. A little
forward planning is necessary,
however, to make the best use
of time. The Heritage Square and
Southwest museums are easily
visited on the way to Pasadena.
While Universal Studios needs a
day to itself, other studio tours in
Burbank can be combined with
a trip to Griffith Park (a good
spot to see the Hollywood sign)
or to Mission San Fernando Rey
de España. Get an early morning
start at the Flower Market before
tackling the three museums at
Exposition Park, or take a trip
east to see the Watts Towers in
between museum visits.

SIGHTS AT A GLANCE

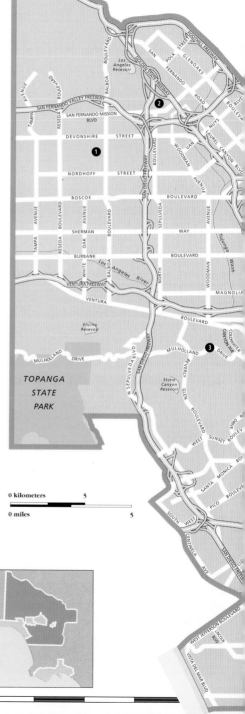

0 kilometers   5

0 miles   5

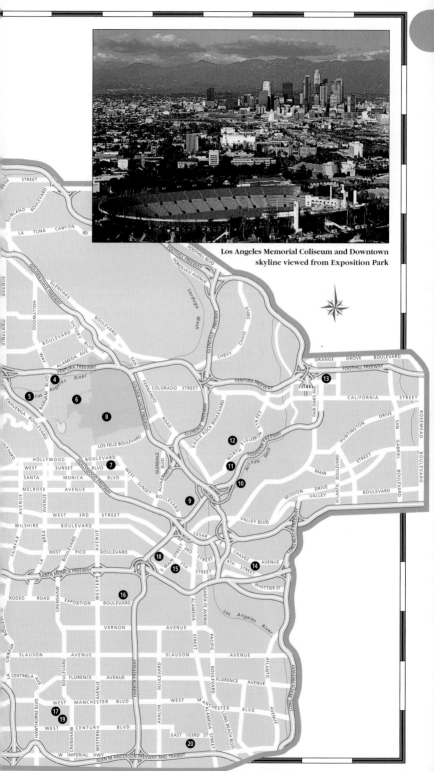

Los Angeles Memorial Coliseum and Downtown skyline viewed from Exposition Park

View of San Fernando Valley from Mulholland Drive

San Fernando Valley ❶

Road map inset A. 🚉 *Burbank-Glendale-Pasadena, 20 miles (32 km) SE of San Fernando.* 🚌 *MTA.* ℹ️ *519 S Brand Blvd, San Fernando (818 361-1184).*

T HE CITY OF LOS ANGELES is split into two distinct halves by the Santa Monica Mountains *(see pp58–9)*. To the north, the San Fernando Valley spreads out in a seemingly endless vista of neat houses, freeways, and shopping malls, such as the Sherman Oaks Galleria *(see p166)*. Residents south of the mountains tend to dismiss "the Valley," as they call it, as it is more smoggy and noticeably hotter in the summer.

In the 19th century, the San Fernando Valley was made up of ranches, orange groves, and nonirrigated farms. With the completion of the LA Aqueduct in 1913 *(see pp192–3)*, the city was insured a plentiful water supply. As a result, the Valley quickly developed into a mass of suburbs. Today, more than a million people live in this area of Los Angeles, which encompasses only 177 sq miles (460 sq km).

On January 17, 1994, San Fernando Valley was at the epicenter of a devastating earthquake, which measured 6.8 on the Richter Scale *(see pp20–21)*. The area had also been badly damaged by the February 1971 earthquake.

Mission San Fernando Rey de España ❷

15151 San Fernando Mission Blvd, Mission Hills. **Road map** inset A. 📞 *(818) 361-0186.* ⏰ *9am–5pm daily.* ⛔ *Thanksgiving, Dec 25.* ♿ *grounds only.* 📷

O NE OF THE 21 Franciscan missions in California *(see pp42–3)*, San Fernando Rey de España was founded in 1797 and named after King Ferdinand III of Spain. The present church is an exact replica of the original, which was completely destroyed in the 1971 earthquake. The *convento* (living quarters) has a 21-arch portico, and is the largest mission building still standing in California. A tour of the complex offers an insight into the early days of Spanish rule, when the monks and Native Americans worked together to make the mission self-sufficent.

Mission altar detail

Mulholland Drive ❸

Off Hwys 1 & 27, from Hollywood Fwy to Leo Carrillo State Beach. **Map** *1 C2.* ℹ️ *Malibu Chamber of Commerce, 23805 Stuart Ranch Rd, Ste 100 (310 456-9025).*

M ULHOLLAND DRIVE, one of the most famous roads in Los Angeles, runs for nearly 50 miles (80 km) from north Hollywood to the Malibu coast *(see pp60–61)*. As it winds along the ridge of the Santa Monica Mountains, the route has spectacular views across the city, San Fernando Valley, and some of LA's most exclusive houses. Its spirit was captured in David Hockney's painting of the area, which hangs in LACMA *(see p111)*.

The road was named after William Mulholland *(see p192)*. Although better known for his work on the LA Aqueduct, he oversaw the completion of Mulholland Drive in 1924.

Burbank ❹

Road map inset A. 🚉 *Burbank-Glendale-Pasadena.* 🚌 *MTA.* ℹ️ *200 W Magnolia Burbank (818 346-3111). See* **Entertainment in Los Angeles** *pp164–5.* 🌐 *www.burbankchamber.com*

S INCE 1915, when Universal Studios moved near here *(see pp142–5)*, Burbank has been competing with Hollywood as the true center of the Los Angeles film industry. Today there are four major studios in the area: Universal, Disney, NBC, and Warner Bros.

The Disney studios are

Mission San Fernando Rey de España in the Mission Hills

Warner Bros Studios in Burbank

closed to the public, but the building, designed by Michael Graves, can be seen from Alameda Avenue. Its fanciful façade incorporates the Seven Dwarfs as pillars supporting the pediment *(see p69)*.

Next door, at NBC, *The Tonight Show* and many other television programs are recorded before a live studio audience. Visitors are offered a 70-minute tour of the wardrobe area, production studios, and *The Tonight Show* set.

Nearby, at the Warner Bros lot, a 2-hour-plus VIP Tour includes the backlot, sound stages, craft, and technical areas. Visitors may view the sets of *The West Wing* and other television series, subject to availability.

Universal Studios **❺**

See pp142 – 5.

Hollywood Sign **❻**

Mt Cahuenga, above Hollywood.
ℹ️ *Hollywood Visitors Information Center, 6541 Hollywood Blvd (213 689-8822).*

THE HOLLYWOOD SIGN is an internationally recognized symbol of the movie business. Set high up in the Hollywood Hills, it is now a protected historic site. It is visible for miles from many parts of Los Angeles, but it is not possible for the public to reach the sign itself as there is no legitimate trail leading up to the 45-ft (13-m) tall letters.

Erected in 1923, it originally advertised the Hollywoodland housing development of the former *LA Times* publisher Harry Chandler *(see p121)*. The "land" was removed in 1949. Nearly 30 years later, donors pledged $27,000 per letter for a new sign. It has been the scene of one suicide – that of

disappointed would-be actress Peg Entwhistle, who jumped off the "H" in 1932 – and numerous prank spellings, such as "Hollyweed," acknowledging the more lenient marijuana laws of the 1970s, "UCLA" during a football game, and "Perotwood" for the 1992 presidential election.

Hollyhock House **❼**

4808 Hollywood Blvd. 📞 *(323) 661-2364.* ⬤ *until 2003 for renovations.* Ⓦ *www.galinsky.com/buildings/hollyhock*

AMERICAN ARCHITECT Frank Lloyd Wright *(see p29)* designed a number of houses in LA. Hollyhock House was the first and remains one of the best known. An excellent example of Wright's infatuation with pre-Columbian styles, the hilltop house resembles a Mayan temple. The house is undergoing complete renovation until 2003.

It was completed in 1921 for oil heiress Aline Barnsdall, who asked that her favorite flower, the hollyhock, be used as a decorative motif throughout the building. A band of stylized hollyhocks, fashioned in concrete, therefore adorns the exterior of the house. The flowers also feature as ornamentation inside, such as on the dining room chairs and other Wright-designed furnishings. The adjacent 11-acre Barnsdall Park, donated by Aline Barnsdall, is now a public art park with galleries.

Hollywood Sign, high above Los Angeles in the Hollywood Hills

Universal Studios [5]

Universal Studios Logo

CARL LAEMMLE bought a chicken ranch on this site in 1915 and moved his film studio here from Hollywood. He charged visitors 25 cents to see films being made, and guests could also buy fresh eggs. With the advent of the "talkies" in 1927, the sets needed quiet and the visits stopped. In 1964, Universal Studios Hollywood was launched as a behind-the-scenes tram ride. The Studio Tour through Universal's 415 acres brings visitors face-to-face with soundstages and movie sets. Here, everything is, or looks like, a film set. The attractions, from the Rugrats to the latest virtual-reality thrill ride, create a world of magic and Hollywood glamor.

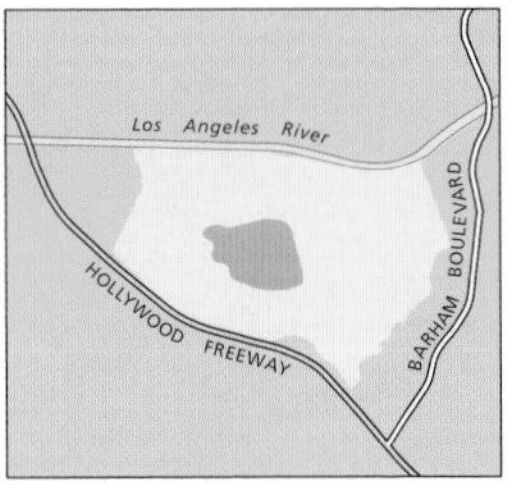

LOCATOR MAP

☐ Universal Studios

The Studio Tour takes in over 500 sets and façades on the backlot

TACKLING THE PARK

Spread over 415 acres (168 ha) Universal Studios Hollywood is the world's largest working movie and television studio and theme park. The complex is divided into three areas: the Entertainment Center, Studio Center, and the studio lots.

As soon as you walk through the gate, visitors stroll through the Streets of the World, which are actual working sets depicting anything from a 1950s America to a European village. The Studio Tour, boarded from the Entertainment Center, is the only way of seeing Universal's main television and movie stages, sets, and movie stars. The Entertainment Center is also the place to catch such shows as the Rugrats Magic Adventure and other spectacular shows. A futuristic escalator, the Starway, links the upper and lower portions of the studio lots. The lower level is where the major thrill rides, such as Jurassic Park and the E.T. Adventure can be found. Universal CityWalk connects the working studios, the theme park, and various cinemas, and offers more than 60 different entertainment venues.

STUDIO TOUR

THE ORIGINAL Universal Studios attraction, this classic Studio Tour gives visitors an up-close and personal view of the past, present, and future of Hollywood movie-making. Guests ride through Universal's soundstages and sets in trams, each outfitted with state-of-the-art audio and video systems. Celebrity hosts, such as actor Jason Alexander and director Ron Howard, narrate and explain the inner workings of the real Hollywood. If they are lucky, visitors may also see a film being made on one of the working soundstages. Passengers experience an earthquake, encounter King Kong and Jaws, and survive a collapsing bridge, flash flood, and avalanche. The tour also passes the Bates Motel, used in Hitchcock's *Psycho* (1960).

A favorite part of the tour is the "Before They Were Stars" montage and the special weather-effects demonstrations. The 35 different soundstages, various movie and TV sets, props, cameras, lights, and lots of action give guests a first-hand look into filmland's realities and illusions. Special installations of 'The Mummy," "Earthquake –

SET LOCATIONS ON THE BACKLOT

Guests on the Studio Tour will see these working sets for hundreds of movies and TV productions, many of which are instantly recognizable. Each tram has an LCD flat screen, audio system, and DVD player to put a frame of reference to every set visited.

1. Courthouse Square: most frequently used set (***Back to the Future*** film series, ***To Kill a Mockingbird***, ***Batman & Robin***).
2. Psycho House/Bates Motel: most famous set (***Psycho*** original and the remake of the same movie).
3. Court of Miracles: most historic set (***Frankenstein*** and ***Dracula***).
4. Denver Street: 7/8 scale to make actors in Westerns look larger than life (***Winchester '73, Babe***).
5. Falls Lake with Backdrop: most flexible set (***Apollo 13, Charlie's Angels, O Brother Where Art Thou***).

UNIVERSAL STUDIOS HOLLYWOOD TICKETS AND PASSES

General Admission: Tickets are either Adult or Child (3-11). Parking is extra.
1. Hollywood CityPass: Admission to Universal Studios and six other themed Hollywood sights. Valid for 30 days.
2. Celebrity Annual Pass: Unlimited park access for one year (contains 30 blackout days).
3. VIP: Admission, private tram, personalized tours, front-of-line privileges, and reserved seats for all shows.
4. Star Package: Accommodations, admission to Universal Studios, a live TV taping, and lunch or dinner.
5. Southern California Value Pass: Admission to Universal Studios and Sea World San Diego. Valid for 14 days.
For more information, call 1-800-UNIVERSAL (1-800-864-8377) or visit the website.

The Big One," "King Kong," and "Jaws Lake" let visitors experience the live action of each working set.

The Tour brings a pleasant sense of deja-vu to every guest because they have vicariously visited many of the film locations through the magic of movies. In spite of all the virtual-reality, thrill-action rides and state-of-the-art attractions, the Studio Tour is really what Universal Studios Hollywood is all about.

UNIVERSAL CITYWALK

In 1993, AMERICAN architect Jon Jerde designed a festive assortment of façades for the shops and restaurants that make up CityWalk's promenade. Now, with the addition of more than 30 new attractions, including bars, nightclubs, and theaters Universal's CityWalk is being hailed as the entertainment mecca of Southern California. Designed to appeal to guests' sense of whimsy, a giant neon-lit baseball player swings his bat above a sports store. To enter an ice-cream store, visitors must walk under an upside-down pink convertible that has crashed through a Hollywood Freeway sign. Jillian's Hi-Life Lanes, a multimedia rock 'n' roll bowling alley gives guests a chance to work off some extra energy; Howl at the Moon, a duelling piano bar, encourages audience partici-pation; and the festive Cafe TuTu Tango offers tapas and a decor that mimics an artist's loft, complete with paint-brushes on the tables,

An upside-down car hangs above the entrance to a CityWalk store

artworks in progress, and spontaneous performances by dancers and musicians.

The three-storey IMAX 3D theater shows the latest venture into knock-your-socks-off film, and the NASCAR virtual racecar experience can be an antidote to the newest retail shops, name-brand outlets, and restaurants. This spectacular venture into California fantasy and entertainment is still one of the prime areas where you can buy Hollywood souvenirs and memorabilia.

Bright lights, big buildings, and prime entertainment in CityWalk

TOP 5 ATTRACTIONS

★ **Animal Planet Live!**

★ **Studio Tour**

★ **Universal CityWalk**

★ **Terminator 2 3-D**

★ **Jurassic Park**

Rides and Special Effects

THRILL RIDES are what theme parks do best. Not only does Universal offer some of the most spectacular rides but, coupled with the special effects at this working studio, some of the best in the business. The newest ride is Nickelodeon's *Splash!* with wild water buckets and a huge water rocket while an updated ride, complete with more horrifying monsters, is the Terminator 2: 3D. Visitors can also see King Kong on the world's largest sound-stage and may get the rare chance to get a sneak peek at some of the films currently in production, such as Jurassic Park III. Each attraction here is a thrill ride in itself, where the excitement of movies comes alive.

Filming at the Studios

adventures and spectacular stunts are projected onto the world's largest 3D screen.

A star of Animal Planet Live! shows a talented paw

ENTERTAINMENT CENTER

THE ENTERTAINMENT CENTER has dozens of themed souvenir shops and restau-rants. The spectacular shows in this area of the park give visitors an insight into the stunts and special effects used to make a film.

Animal Planet Live!
Animal stars, multi-media effects, human co-stars, and unique sketches from TV's Animal Planet Network offer warm, family entertainment.

Terminator 2: 3D
This new show has been hailed as the world's most advanced film-based attrac-tion. Arnold Schwarzenegger and the rest of the original cast from *Terminator 2: Judgment Day* (19xx) star in this sequel and continues the science-fiction epic in startling 3D. Interactive virtual

WaterWorld – A Live Sea War Spectacular
The audience is part of the action and right in the middle of this thrilling, high-tech show, which packs pyrotechnics – a giant fireball that rises 50 feet (15 m) in the air – battle scenes, extraordinary stunts, and wild jet-skiing into 16 minutes of daredevil action.

The Wild Wild Wild West Stunt Show
This 15-minute slapstick show stars some of Hollywood's finest stuntmen and horses. The performance is packed with explosions, gunfights, horseplay, and saloon brawls. The ultimate showdown is superbly destructive.

Back to the Future – The Ride
Housed in the world's tallest Omnimax theater, guests accompany Doc Brown in eight-seat DeLorean time-travel simulator cars. They pursue the diabolical Biff from the 1980s movie trilogy as they try to save the Universe. Hurtling through the space-time continuum, from the Ice Age to the year 2015, the car free-falls through a volcanic tunnel, cascades down glacial cliffs, and almost ends up as dinner for some prehistoric monsters. This ambitious ride uses sophisticated sound, film outtakes, and hydraulics to simulate the wild chase.

Rugrats and kids make magic!

Nickelodeon Blast Zone: Rugrats Magic Adventure
This huge interactive play-ground is based around Nickelodeon's most popular children's TV shows and features a spectacular Rugrats Magic Adventure show.

Young children will love the magic and the music in

Terrifying the audience at the Terminator 2: 3D show

this new show. Angelica takes center stage and transforms a backyard magic show into an all-out extravaganza. Siblings Chuckie, Tommy, Phil, and Lil join in for a lot of awesome mischief and fun.

Blues Brothers Show

This 20-minute live music stage show celebrates the antics and blues songs of the Blues Brothers. There's plenty of audience participation, with dancing, sing-alongs, and some outrageous humor.

STUDIO CENTER

T HE STARWAY, which links the upper and lower portions of Universal's working lots, offers some spectacular views. The Studio Center on the lower lot has three super-thrilling rides and several other attractions that reveal the secrets of some of the studio's most successful films and television series. There are, of course, lots of photo opportunities around each corner, from the giant 24-foot (7-m) hanging shark to Universal's mascot Woody Woodpecker. You might also meet Charlie Chaplin, Frankenstein, Dracula, the Mummy, or Marilyn Monroe.

The E.T. Adventure

Drawing on the most popular movie of all time, endearing E.T. takes everyone on a starbound bicycle ride through the night sky as he tries to escape from the police and government scientists on his way home to the "Green Planet." At the end of the ride, E.T. says the name of each guest. The storyline and set are well known, and the magic of E.T. captures everyone's heart and imagination.

Backdraft

In a re-creation of the final scene from the fire-fighting film *Backdraft* (1992), the audience can literally feel the heat of the film's blazing warehouse inferno. Beforehand, a technician explains how the scenes were created and controlled. The temperature rises when the firestorm explodes, causing ret-hot ashes to rain down and overhead pipes to burst, leaving the audience scared and thrilled. The experience may be too frightening for young children.

The World of Cinemagic

The mysteries of special effects are explained in this fascinating look at film technology. In the *Back to the Future* (19xx) section, audience members re-create a scene in Doc Brown's DeLorean car. The Magic of Alfred Hitchcock show lets guests in on moviedom's scariest cinematic sorcery with scenes from *Psycho* (1960). With scenes from *The Nutty Professor* (19xx), the new Sound Effects Stage show allows guests to re-create their favorite funny moments, using the secrets of Hollywood's special effects.

Gameworks

This state-of-the-art video arcade with the latest virtual reality games allows grown-ups and kids to pay and play to their hearts content.

Jurassic Park–The Ride roars to life

Jurassic Park sign

Lucy – A Tribute

This exhibit displays memorabilia of the Queen of Comedy, Lucille Ball, one of the world's favorite stage and television stars. This tribute includes the "I Love Lucy" set and the den of her Beverly Hills home, which have been meticulously re-created. There's even an interactive game for trivia buffs to test their Lucy knowledge.

Jurassic Park – The Ride

Based on one of the most successful films of all time, Jurassic Park – The Ride takes visitors on a 5.5-minute trip through 6 acres (2.5 ha) of exotic prehistsoric wilderness. Steven Spielberg's epic movie leaps and roars to life with the most sophisticated state-of-the-art computer and robotic technology ever designed. Guests are hurled into the steamy world of Jurassic Park, where huge five-storey dinosaurs swoop to within inches of riders' faces, and a terrifying *Tyrannosaurus rex* with a mouthful of razorsharp teeth considers each rider part of his dinner. The ride ends with an 84-ft (25-m) drop into complete darkness.

King Kong, beloved of filmgoers, on Universal's Studio Tour

Griffith Park ❽

Merry-go-round horse

G RIFFITH PARK is a 4,000-acre (1,600-ha) wilderness of rugged hills, forested valleys, and green meadows in the center of LA. The land was donated to the city in 1896 by Colonel Griffith J Griffith, a Welshman who emigrated to the United States in 1865 and made his money speculating in mining and property. Today, people come to Griffith Park to escape from the city crowds, visit the sights, picnic, hike, or go horseback riding. The park is safe during the day, but it should be avoided at night.

Griffith Observatory on Mount Hollywood

Exploring Griffith Park

The ranger station, located on Crystal Springs Drive, has maps of the park showing its numerous picnic areas and miles of hiking trails and bridle paths. There are two public 18-hole golf courses on the eastern side of the park and tennis courts on Riverside Drive and in Vermont Canyon.

In the hills just off Griffith Park Drive is a 1926 merry-go-round. Adults and children can still ride on its 66 carved horses and listen to its giant band organ. Across the street, an informal Sunday gathering of drummers has been meeting since the 1960s.

Fern Dell, at the Western Avenue entrance, is a beautiful shady glen with a flowing stream and small waterfalls.

⛪ Griffith Observatory

2800 Observatory Rd.
⛪ *(323) 664-1181.* 🎫 *Planetarium.*
W www.griffithobs.org
Currently closed for renovation.
Situated on Mount Hollywood, Griffith Observatory commands stunning views of the Los Angeles basin below. The Art Deco observatory is divided into three main areas: the Hall of Science museum, the Planetarium theater, and the telescopes.

In the Main Rotunda of the Hall of Science, the Foucault Pendulum demonstrates the speed of the earth's rotation. Above the pendulum are murals on a scientific theme, painted by Hugo Ballin in 1934. Characters from Classical mythology are depicted on the domed ceiling. Below this, eight rectangular panels show important scientific concepts and figures through the ages.

Visitors are taken on a journey through space and time, as some 9,000 stars, moons, and planets are projected onto the ceiling. On the roof, the 12-in (30-cm) Zeiss Telescope is open to the public on clear nights.

🏛 Travel Town

5200 Zoo Drive. **⛪** *(323) 662-5874 & (323) 662-9678 for train ride.* 🕐 *10am–4pm Mon–Fri; Sat & Sun 10am–5pm.* ● *Dec 25.*
The spirit of the rails comes alive at this outdoor collection of vintage trains and cars. Children and adults can climb aboard freight cars and railroad carriages, or ride on a small train.

East of Travel Town, on Zoo Drive, miniature steam trains take people on rides during weekends.

Steam locomotive from 1922, one of 16 steam trains in Travel Town

🎭 Greek Theatre

2700 N Vermont Ave. **⛪** *(323) 665-1927.* 🕐 *Open for engagements only.* 🎫 *for concerts.*
W wwwgreektheatrela.com
Styled after an ancient Greek amphitheater, this open-air music venue has excellent acoustics. On summer nights, over 6,000 people can sit under the stars and enjoy performances by leading popular and classical musicians. Bring a sweater as evenings can be chilly.

Flamingos at Los Angeles Zoo

🦋 Los Angeles Zoo

5333 Zoo Drive. ☎ *(323) 644-6400.* ◯ *10am–5pm daily.* ⬤ *Dec 25.* 📷 W *www.lazoo.org*

This 113-acre (46-ha) hilly compound has more than 1,200 mammals, reptiles, and birds living in simulations of their natural habitats. All the favorite animals are here, from lions and gorillas to sharks and snakes.

Many newborn creatures can be seen in the Animal Nursery, including some from the zoo's respected breeding program for rare and endangered species. The Koala House is dimly lit to encourage the nocturnal creatures to be active. Adventure Island focuses on southwestern animals and habitats. There are several animal shows that are aimed toward a young audience. Be prepared to walk long distances, or use the Safari Shuttle bus.

VISITORS' CHECKLIST

Map 3 F2. 🚌 96. ◯ *6am–10pm daily.* 🛈 *4730 Crystal Springs Drive.* ☎ *(213) 485-5027.* 📷 ♿ 🚻 🎁 🍴 🛒

🏛 Autry Museum of Western Heritage

4700 Western Heritage Way (opposite the zoo). ☎ *(323) 667-2000.* ◯ *10am–5pm Tue–Sun (until 8pm Thu).* ⬤ *Thanksgiving, Dec 25.* 📷 *(free second Tue of month).* W *www.autry-museum.org*

The Autry Museum of Western Heritage explores the many cultures that have shaped the American West. Artworks by such artists as Albert Bierstadt and Frederic Remington *(see pp24–5)* depict a romantic view of life in the region. Tools, firearms, tribal clothing, and religious figurines are some of the artifacts that show the diversity of the people who have lived here. In the museum's Discovery Center, children can play in a replica of a 19th-century Mexican-American ranch from Arizona. Founded by the film star Gene Autry, "the singing cowboy," the museum also houses a superb collection of movie and television memorabilia.

Deerskin Sioux dress

🦋 Bird Sanctuary

Vermont Canyon Rd (just N of Greek Theater). ☎ *(323) 913-4688.* ◯ *10am–5pm daily.*

Many trees and bushes have been planted in this secluded canyon to encourage local birds to nest here. Although you may not see too many birds, you will definitely hear their song. Depending on the season, water may be running in the stream, adding to the serenity of the area.

GRIFFITH PARK

Autry Museum of Western Heritage ③
Bird Sanctuary ⑤
Fern Dell ⑧
Greek Theater ⑥
Griffith Observatory ⑦
Los Angeles Zoo ②
Merry-go-round ④
Travel Town ①

0 kilometers | 1
0 miles | 0.5

KEY

🛈 Tourist information

Dodger Stadium ❾

1000 Elysian Park Ave (at Stadium Way). **Map** 11 F1. 📞 *(323) 224-1400.* 🔲 *for special events only.*
🖼️ ♿

THIS BASEBALL STADIUM seats 56,000 spectators. Built in 1962 for the Brooklyn team, which had moved to LA in 1958, the stadium has a cantilevered design that guarantees every seat an unobstructed view of the field.

From the stadium there are equally impressive panoramas of the city. To the south is Downtown LA, to the north and east are the San Gabriel Mountains. Around the arena are 300 acres (120 ha) of landscaped grounds, planted with more than 3,000 trees such as California rosewood, acacia, and eucalyptus.

Queen Anne-style Hale House at Heritage Square Museum

Heritage Square Museum ❿

3800 Homer St, Los Angeles. 📞 *(626) 449-0193.* 🔲 *12–4pm Sat & Sun.*
🖼️ ♿ 📷

MOST VICTORIAN buildings in Los Angeles were demolished during redevelopments, but some were saved by the Cultural Heritage Board and moved to this location. Dating from 1865 to 1914, they include a train depot, a church, and a carriage barn. Hale House, a Queen Anne-style building *(see p27)*, has been restored in authentic colors.

Restored interior of the 19th-century Lummis House

Lummis House ⓫

200 East Ave 43, Los Angeles. 📞 *(323) 222-0546.* 🔲 *noon–4pm Fri–Sun.* **Donation.** ♿ 📷

ALSO KNOWN AS "El Alisal," Spanish for "Place of the Sycamore," this house was the home of Charles Fletcher Lummis (1859–1928), who built it out of concrete and rocks from the local riverbed. The structure's various design elements – Native American, Mission Revival, and Arts and Crafts – reveal the dominant influences of Lummis's life. Constructed between 1898 and 1910, mostly by his own hands, the design reveals a creative, independent thinker.

Lummis was a newspaper editor, writer, photographer, artist, and historian. In 1885 he walked across the United States, from Ohio to LA, where he settled. He played a central role in the city's cultural life, editing the *LA Times*. As a co-founder of the California Landmark Club, he campaigned successfully for the preservation of the state's missions *(see pp42–3)*. His collection of Native American artifacts was the basis of the holdings at the Southwest Museum.

Today, Lummis House is the headquarters of the Historical Society of Southern California. Although few of Lummis's belongings remain in the house, there are some Native American artifacts. The built-in furnishings include a splendid Art Nouveau fireplace.

The garden was originally planted with vegetables and fruit trees. It was redesigned in 1985 and now grows drought-tolerant and native Southern California plant species.

THE DODGERS

The Dodgers came originally from Brooklyn, New York. They used to train by dodging the streetcars that traveled down that borough's streets, thus earning their name. Since moving to Los Angeles in 1958, they have become one of the most successful baseball teams in the United States. In 1955, they won the first of five world championships. Today, going to the Dodger Stadium is a rite of spring for Los Angeles fans.

Over the years the team has had a number of outstanding players, such as Sandy Koufax and Roy Campanella. In 1947, the Dodgers made headlines when they signed Pasadena-born Jackie Robinson, the first African-American to play in the major leagues.

Japanese star pitcher Hideo Nomo joined the Dodgers team in 1995, and created a sensation in his first season. During the playoffs, crowds brought Tokyo to a standstill as Nomo prepared to pitch on the other side of the Pacific Ocean.

Part of the victorious 1959 world championship team

Mission Revival-style Southwest Museum

Southwest Museum ⑫

234 Museum Drive, Los Angeles.
【 (323) 221-2164. ☐ 10am–5pm
Tue–Sun. ● Jan 1, Easter Sun,
Thanksgiving, Dec 25. 🎫 🎟
W www.southwestmuseum.org

WITH ONE of the nation's leading collections of Native American art and artifacts, the Southwest Museum was the brainchild of Charles Fletcher Lummis. During his cross-country trek in the late 19th century, Lummis spent a long time in the Southwest and became one of the first whites to appreciate the history and culture of Native Americans. Lummis donated many of his personal holdings to start the collection.

The museum displays tribal objects from prehistoric times to the present day. Exhibits come from South America to Alaska. They are organized by their place of origin: the Plains, the Northwest Coast, the Southwest, and California. The last two regions are the most strongly represented, but there is an excellent overview of Native American heritage. The 11,000 baskets in the collection are particularly

Sequoyah Indian relief

impressive. Tepees, workshops, and storytelling help to involve children at the museum. The Mission Revival building *(see p27)* is set on top of Mount Washington, with views of Downtown Los Angeles to the south. It has a seven-story tower and is surrounded by a garden planted with indigenous species.

GALLERY GUIDE
The galleries are situated on two floors, with the main entrance on the upper level. Artifacts from the Northwest Coast, California, and the Plains are displayed on this level, as are temporary exhibitions. The downstairs galleries are dedicated to the museum's collection of baskets and its holdings from the Southwest. The shop is also located here. Adjacent to the museum is the Braun Research Library, dedicated to the Native and Hispanic peoples of the Americas.

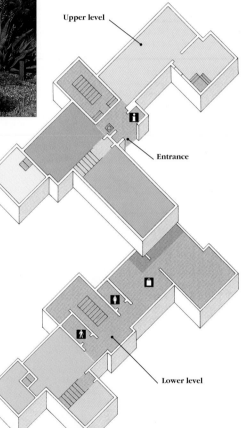

Upper level

Entrance

Lower level

KEY TO FLOOR PLAN

☐	The Northwest Coast
☐	The Southwest
☐	The Plains
☐	California
☐	Basketry study
☐	Temporary exhibitions
☐	Nonexhibition space

Pasadena ⓭

WITH THE COMPLETION of the Santa Fe Railroad in 1887, wealthy people from the East Coast began to spend the winter in the warmth and sunshine of Southern California. Many settled in Pasadena and were soon joined by artists and bohemians, who were also seeking the sun. This mix of creativity and wealth has resulted in a city with a splendid cultural legacy. The highlights of the area include the Huntington Library, Art Collections, and Botanical Gardens (*see pp154–7*), and the outstanding collection of Old Masters and Impressionist paintings at the Norton Simon Museum (*see pp152–3*).

Rose Bowl statue

Exploring Pasadena

Just east of the Norton Simon Museum is **Old Pasadena**, once a decaying section of town. A dozen blocks of commercial buildings dating from the 1880s and 1890s have been restored and are now filled with stores, restaurants, and movies. The mixture of Victorian, Spanish Colonial, and Art Deco architecture adds to the area's pleasant environment. The stately Beaux-Arts **Civic Center**, on Union Street at Garfield Avenue, was designed by Edward Bennett in the early 1920s. It includes the city hall, police station, post office, library, and civic auditorium. The neighborhood northeast of the Gamble House has many examples of Arts and Crafts architecture (*see p27*), most notably along tree-lined **Prospect Boulevard**.

Tiffany lamp in the Gamble House

🏟 Rose Bowl

1001 Rose Bowl Drive. ▐ (626) 577-3100. ⏰ 7:30am–5:30pm Mon–Fri. ● every other Fri & public hols (except Jan 1). 🎫

Sited in a wealthy neighborhood, the stadium seats more than 100,000 people. It was built in 1922 for the annual Rose Bowl football game, which matches college teams from the Midwest and the West Coast.

The first collegiate game played here was delayed for more than an hour when the visiting team was stuck in traffic, a fate that befalls many visitors today.

This is the home of UCLA's football team, the Bruins. Numerous Super Bowl games have also been played here as well as the World Cup Championships in 1994 and the 1984 Summer Olympics soccer competitions. There is also a flea market here every month.

Pasadena's city hall in the Beaux-Arts Civic Center

🏟 Gamble House

4 Westmoreland Place. ▐ (626) 793-3334. ⏰ noon–3pm Thu–Sun. ● public hols. 🎫 🎦 obligatory.

A masterpiece of the era, this wooden house epitomizes the Arts and Crafts movement, which stressed simplicity of design with superior craftsmanship. The dwelling was built in 1908 for David Gamble, of the Procter and Gamble Company. It is considered the crowning achievement of brothers Charles and Henry Greene, Boston-trained architects who visited Pasadena in 1893 and never left (*see p27*).

The Gamble House was tailor-made for LA's climate. Its wide terraces and open sleeping porches, influenced by Japanese architecture, facilitate indoor-outdoor living, and broad overhanging eaves shade the house. At certain times of day, the sun illuminates the stained-glass front door, a dazzling sight.

🏛 Pacific-Asia Museum

46 N Los Robles Ave. ▐ (626) 449-2742. ⏰ 10am–5pm Wed–Sun. ● public hols. 🎫

Built in 1924 to a traditional northern Chinese design, the Pacific-Asia Museum houses a collection of Far Eastern art founded by Grace Nicholson. Changing exhibitions on the arts of Asia and the Pacific Basin supplement the permanent collection. The museum's lovely courtyard garden is one of only two authentic Chinese gardens in the United States.

A packed Rose Bowl during a football game

♣ LA State and County Arboretum

301 N Baldwin Ave, Arcadia. *(626) 821-3222.* ○ *9am–4:30pm daily.* ● *Dec 25.* 🎫 ♿ ✓

Situated on 127 acres (51 ha) east of Pasadena, the arboretum has more than 30,000 plant species displayed according to their geographical origin. The park includes a herb garden, a waterfall, lily ponds, and a tropical jungle. It was used as the backdrop for all of Johnny Weissmuller's *Tarzan* films (1932–48) and

Tropical landscaping in the LA Arboretum

for some parts of Humphrey Bogart's *African Queen* (1951). Among the historical buildings in the grounds are Gabrielino Native American *wickiups* (huts), the reconstructed 1839 Hugo Reid adobe, and the picturesque Queen Anne cottage.

🏛 Kidspace Museum

390 S El Molino Ave. *(626) 449-9143.* ○ *mid-Jun–Aug: 1–5pm Sun–Thu, 10am–5pm Fri–Sat; Sep–mid-Jun: 1–5pm Tues–Fri & Sun; 10am–5pm Sat.* ● *public hols.* 🎫

Children from 2 to 10 years old can dress up and play at this stimulating museum. They can try on real firemen's uniforms at the Fire Station, or dress up as one of many characters in the Back Stage exhibit. Other attractions include TV Studio, Computer Room, and the popular Critter Caverns, with its tree house and live animals.

THE ROSE PARADE

In 1890 the Pasadena Valley Hunt Club decided to hold the first Tournament of Roses to celebrate – and advertise – the region's balmy winters. Little did they know that their quaint parade of horse-drawn carriages draped with rose garlands would turn into a world-famous extravaganza. Today, many of the floats have moving parts and sometimes feature people doing stunts.

Rose Parade float

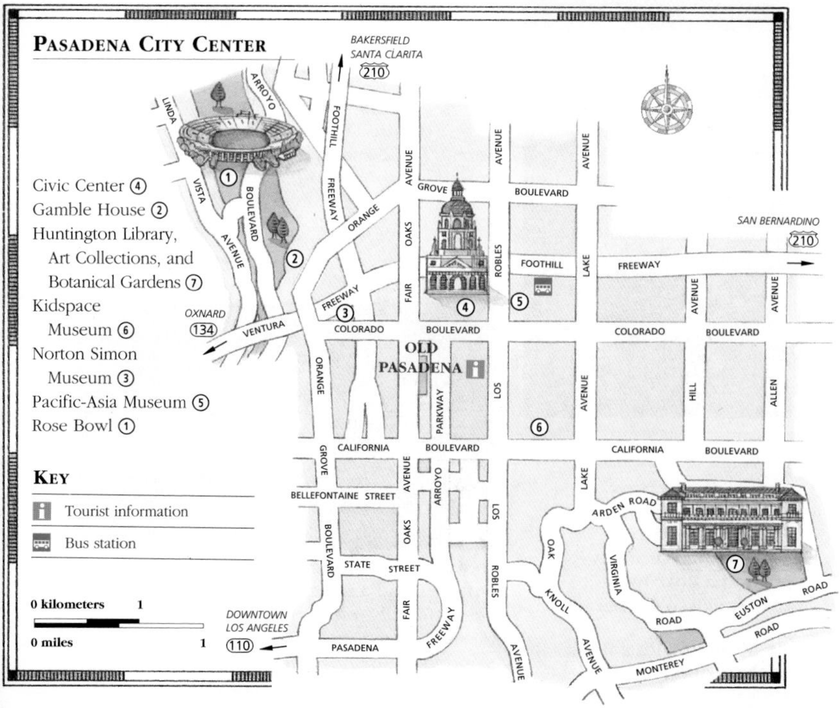

PASADENA CITY CENTER

Civic Center ④
Gamble House ②
Huntington Library, Art Collections, and Botanical Gardens ⑦
Kidspace Museum ⑥
Norton Simon Museum ③
Pacific-Asia Museum ⑤
Rose Bowl ①

KEY

ℹ Tourist information

🚌 Bus station

0 kilometers   1
0 miles   1

Norton Simon Museum

NORTON SIMON (1907–93) was a businessman who combined running his multinational corporation with forming an internationally acclaimed collection of works of art. From the 1950s to the 1970s, he amassed, with the genius of a connoisseur, masterpieces spanning more than 2,000 years of Western and Asian art. Within the European holdings, the Old Masters and Impressionist paintings are especially strong. Renaissance, Post-Impressionism, German Expressionism, and the modern period are also well represented. Sculptures from India and Southeast Asia are among the finest outside the region and offer an insight into the complex roles art and religion play in these cultures.

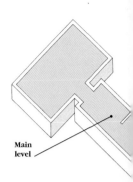

Main level

Sculpture Garden

Lower level

★ **Woman with a Book** *(1932)*
Pablo Picasso, one of the great artistic forces of the 20th century, was a major influence on both the Cubist and Surrealist movements. His mistress Marie-Thérèse Walter, was the subject of a number of his paintings in the 1930s.

Self-Portrait *(c.1636–8)*
Rembrandt painted nearly 100 self-portraits during his lifetime. This one shows the artist in his early thirties.

★ **Still Life with Lemons, Oranges and a Rose** *(1633)*
The Spanish painter Francisco Zurbarán excelled at contemplative still lifes. Many of his works were exported to the Spanish Americas, where they influenced colonial painters.

STAR PAINTINGS

★ **Still Life with Lemons, Oranges and a Rose by Francisco Zurbarán**

★ **Woman with a Book by Pablo Picasso**

Saints Paul and Frediano *(c.1483)*
This is one of a pair of religious panels executed by Florentine artist Filippino Lippi. It shows the influence of Lippi's more famous father, Fra Filippo Lippi, and his other mentor, Botticelli.

GALLERY GUIDE

The museum's galleries are on two floors, linked by a spiral staircase. European paintings, prints, sculpture, and tapestries, dating from the Renaissance to the 20th century, are on display on the main level. The museum bookstore is also on this level. The lower galleries showcase the Norton Simon's impressive collection of Indian and Southeast Asian works, as well as displaying special and touring exhibitions.

The buildings and gardens underwent an extensive renovation program, which was completed in October of 1999. The outdoor space was transformed into an enormous sculpture garden with a natural pond in the center, inspired by the artworks of Claude Monet.

Spiral staircase

Main entrance

The Little Fourteen-Year-Old Dancer
(1878–81)
This bronze is one of more than 100 works by Edgar Degas in the museum. It features one of the artist's favorite subjects, the ballet.

Buddha Enthroned
This bronze was made in Kashmir in India in the 8th century. It is inlaid with silver and copper.

Spiral staircase

Huntington Library, Art Collections, and Botanical Gardens

Detail from garden urn

Visitors and scholars alike are united in their love of the Huntington. The Beaux-Arts mansion was built between 1909 and 1911 for Henry Huntington (1850–1927), who made his fortune building a network of interurban trams in Los Angeles. In 1913 he married his uncle's widow, Arabella. Together they amassed one of the most important libraries and collections of 18th-century British art in the world. The key elements of the gardens were planted during Huntington's lifetime.

Mausoleum
Designed by the architect John Russell Pope, this building in the form of a Greek temple is made of Colorado yule marble.

Main entrance

Camellia Garden

Orange Grove

Breakfast in Bed *(1897)*
The Virginia Steele Scott Gallery is devoted to American art, including one of Mary Cassatt's most successful Impressionist paintings of a mother and child. The artist used this theme many times in her work (see p110).

Camellia Garden

Ikebana House

Herb Garden

Japanese House

Zen Garden

STAR FEATURES

★ **The Blue Boy by Thomas Gainsborough**

★ **Gutenberg Bible**

★ **Japanese Garden**

★ **Japanese Garden**
Designed as a place for quiet contemplation, the traditional Japanese garden always includes water, both flowing and still, crossed by small curved bridges, known as moon bridges.

★ **Gutenberg Bible**
This Bible was printed on vellum around 1450–55 by Johannes Gutenberg in Mainz, Germany. It is the oldest printed book in the Huntington Library.

VISITORS' CHECKLIST

1151 Oxford Rd. ☎ (626) 405-2100. ⏰ Jun–Aug: 10:30am–4:30pm Tue–Sun; Sep–May: noon–4:30pm Tue–Fri; 10:30am–4:30pm Sat & Sun. ● public hols. 🖼 ◎ ♿ 🚻 🎁 ✍ 💻

Jungle Garden
The palms, ferns, gingers, and other plants in this garden are all typical of a tropical rainforest. Orchids and bromeliads can be seen growing high up in the trees.

Shakespeare Garden

Conservatory

Palm Garden

Desert Garden

Lily Ponds

★ **The Blue Boy** *(c.1770)*
Thomas Gainsborough's portrait of Jonathan Buttall, a merchant's son, is one of the most famous paintings in the Huntington Art Gallery.

Subtropical Garden

Australian Garden

Rose Garden

North Vista
Backed by the San Gabriel Mountains, the vista re-creates the feel of a 17th-century European garden, complete with an Italian Baroque fountain at one end.

Exploring the Huntington

I N 1919 Henry and Arabella Huntington put their home and gardens into a trust, creating a nonprofit research institution. Today, the Huntington plays a dual role as an educational facility and cultural center, serving scholars and the general public. The institution comprises one of the world's great research libraries, an outstanding art collection, and more than 130 acres (50 ha) of botanical gardens. The Huntington is only open to the public for a few hours each day, so plan your visit in advance.

***Diana Huntress* (1782) by Jean-Antoine Houdon**

HUNTINGTON LIBRARY

B UILT in 1920, the library specializes in British and American history and literature. It attracts nearly 2,000 scholars every year. The general public can view key items and other changing exhibits in the Library Exhibition Hall.

Among the 600,000 books and three million manuscripts are a copy of the *Magna Carta* and the Ellesmere manuscript of Chaucer's *Canterbury Tales*, dating from around 1410. The vast holding of books printed before 1501 includes a Gutenberg Bible (c.1455) – one of only 12 surviving copies printed on vellum in the world.

There are also first editions and manuscripts by noted British and American authors, including Mark Twain, Charles Dickens, and Lord Tennyson, and early editions of Shakespeare's plays. Letters written by George Washington, Benjamin Franklin, and Abraham Lincoln are part of the collection on the Revolutionary and Civil Wars.

Pilgrim from *The Canterbury Tales*

ARABELLA D HUNTINGTON MEMORIAL COLLECTION

T HE WEST WING of the main library building houses a small group of Renaissance paintings, the most important of which is the *Madonna and Child (see p67)* by Flemish artist Roger van der Weyden (c.1400–1464). The wing also displays French furniture,

Sèvres porcelain, and most of the Huntington's collection of French sculpture. *Portrait of a Lady* (1777) by Jean-Antoine Houdon is considered one of the sculptor's finest busts.

HUNTINGTON ART GALLERY

T HE HUNTINGTONS' mansion now houses the majority of the art collection, including British and French art from the 18th and early 19th century. The most famous works are a group of full-length portraits in the Main Gallery. They include Thomas Gainsborough's *The Blue Boy* (c.1770), *Pinkie* (1794) by Thomas Lawrence, and *Mrs Siddons as the Tragic Muse* (1784) by Joshua Reynolds. Also in the Main Gallery is the *View on the Stour near Dedham* (1822) by John Constable. Other British paintings are displayed throughout the building.

The Large Library Room contains some outstanding 18th-century furnishings, which

include two Savonnerie carpets made for Louis XIV, and five Beauvais tapestries.

The Small Library houses a collection of Renaissance bronzes. *Nessus and Deianira* by Italian sculptor Giovanni da Bologna (1529–1608) is a fine example of his work. In the North Passage is a collection of 15th- to 19th-century British silver. It includes John Flaxman's silver-gilt *Shield of Achilles* (1821).

European artists influential to British painting are also on show. Flemish artist Anthony Van Dyck (1559–1642) was admired by 18th-century British portraitists. While at the English court of Charles I, he produced *Anne Killigrew, Mrs Kirke* (c.1638), which hangs at the head of the stairs. There are also works by Canaletto, who had a profound effect on British landscape painting.

French furniture in the Large Library Room

VIRGINIA STEELE SCOTT GALLERY OF AMERICAN ART

OPENED IN 1984, this collection displays American art from the 1740s to the 1930s.

During the colonial period, artists such as Benjamin West (1738–1820) and Gilbert Stuart (1755–1828) were admirers of British portraitists. It was only prior to the Civil War that an American style of painting emerged. Following two visits to Ecuador, Frederic Edwin Church captured the vastness of that country in *Chimborazo* (1864). Another 19th-century highlight is Mary Cassatt's *Breakfast in Bed* (1897).

The Dorothy Collins Brown Wing houses furniture designed by the American architects, brothers Charles and Henry Greene *(see p27)*.

Desert Garden

BOTANICAL GARDENS

IN 1904, Henry Huntington hired landscape gardener William Hertrich to develop the grounds, which now contain 15 principal gardens.

The 12-acre (5-ha) Desert Garden has more than 4,000 drought-tolerant species from around the world. In the Rose Garden, a walkway traces the history of the species over 1,000 years, with 2,000 varieties. The oldest are found in the Shakespeare Garden.

One of the most popular areas is the Japanese Garden, with a moon bridge, Zen Garden, and Japanese plants.

HUNTINGTON ART GALLERY

Ground floor

First floor

1 Large Library Room
2 Large Drawing Room
3 Small Drawing Room
4 Dining Room
5 North Passage
6 Main Gallery
7 Hall
8 Small Library

9 Quinn Room
10 Southeast Room
11 Wedgwood Room
12 The Adele S Browning Memorial Collection
13 The Moseley Collection
14 Southwest Room
15 Temporary exhibitions

ARABELLA D HUNTINGTON MEMORIAL COLLECTION

1 Sèvres Porcelain Room
2 French Furniture Room
3 French Sculpture Room
4 Renaissance Paintings Room
5 Temporary exhibitions

HUNTINGTON LIBRARY

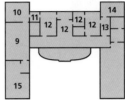

1 Medieval Manuscripts and Early Printing
2 English and American Literature
3 American History

Ground floor

VIRGINIA STEELE SCOTT GALLERY OF AMERICAN ART

1 Permanent Collection
2 Dorothy Collins Brown Wing

3 Print Room (closed to the public)
4 Temporary exhibitions

Ground floor

Cowboy boot stand at El Mercado

El Mercado ⑭

3425 E 1st St. 🄲 *(323) 268-3451.*
🄾 *10am–8pm Mon–Fri; 9am–9pm
Sat & Sun.* ♿

E AST LOS ANGELES is the heart of the Mexican-American community *(see p30),* and this marketplace caters to the locals. Its three levels bustle with taco vendors, *mariachis* (Mexican street musicians), and families out for a good meal. Unlike Olvera Street *(see p123),* El Mercado is not designed as a tourist spot. The greatest attraction here is the authentic Mexican food and regional music.

On the main floor stands offer everything from chilies to snack food. A *tortillaria* sells fresh, hot tortillas; bakeries display traditional Mexican breads and pastries, and delicatessens have meats you may never have seen before. To hear the *mariachis,* go to the mezzanine level, which is also where the cafeteria-style restaurants are located.

Brightly colored Mexican clothing, furniture, and crafts fill the shops in the basement, along with the sounds of Latin American salsa music.

THE LAKERS AND BASKETBALL

Basketball originated in Springfield, Massachusetts in 1891 as a team sport that could be played indoors during the harsh winters. LA's winter may be warm, but people still love the fast-paced, high-scoring game. The city's team, the Lakers, has a huge following.

Such illustrious players as Magic Johnson, Wilt Chamberlain, Kareem Abdul-Jabbar, Shaquile O'Neal, and Kobe Bryant have helped make the team one of the most successful in the National Basketball Association (NBA). The Lakers started out in Minnesota; in 1960 they came to LA; they won the NBA Championship four times in the 1980s, and now play in the new state-of-the-art Staples Center.

Magic Johnson

Flower Market ⑮

752 Maple Ave. 🄲 *(213) 627-2482.*
🄾 *8am–noon Mon–Sat.* ♿

I N THE EARLY HOURS of the morning, before sunrise, the city's florists flock to this two-block long area to buy fresh flowers and plants wholesale for their own clients. Warehouses lined with tables and stands are laden with brightly colored blossoms that contrast sharply with the gray surrounding buildings. An enormous range of flowers is offered, so that California varieties compete with plants from Columbia, New Zealand, France, and Holland.

Anyone can take advantage of the inexpensive prices (great bargains are available after 8 am). However, it is best to arrive early because supplies sell out quickly.

Exposition Park and University of Southern California ⑯

See pp160–61.

Great Western Forum ⑰

3900 Manchester Blvd, Inglewood.
Road map inset A. 🄲 *(310) 673-1300.* 🄾 *for events only.* 🎫 *for events.* ♿ **Box Office** 🄾 *10am–6pm daily.*

T HE GREAT WESTERN FORUM is one of LA's most famous concert and sports arenas. Seating 17,000, the Forum also hosts local sports contests, graduation ceremonies, Hollywood parties, and media events.

Great Western Forum in Inglewood

Staples Center ⑱

1111 S Figueroa St. **Map** 9 C5.
📞 *(877) 305-1111.* 🕐 *for events.*
♿ *for events.*
🌐 *www.staplescenterla.com*

HOME TO THREE PROFESSIONAL ball clubs, the LA Lakers, the LA Clippers (basketball), and the LA Kings (ice hockey), this stadium has revitalized downtown LA for sports fans. It also boasts the Disney Concert Hall for the LA Philharmonic, the US Figure Skating Championships, major rock star concerts, WWF wrestling, Hollywood awards events, and graduation ceremonies.

Hollywood Park Racetrack ⑲

1050 S Prairie Ave, Inglewood. **Road map** inset A. 📞 *(310) 419-1500.*
🕐 *1–5pm Wed–Fri; 12:30–5pm Sat & Sun.* ♿ 👍

FROM APRIL to July racing enthusiasts, Hollywood stars, and tourists come to Hollywood Park to bet on the thoroughbreds. This is an elegant, nostalgic racetrack, beautifully landscaped with lagoons and lush trees. A large computer-operated screen relays the action from the obscured back straight, as well as showing instant replays, photo finishes, and race statistics. In the North Park, the children's play area includes a merry-go-round.

Landscaped racetrack at Hollywood Park in Inglewood

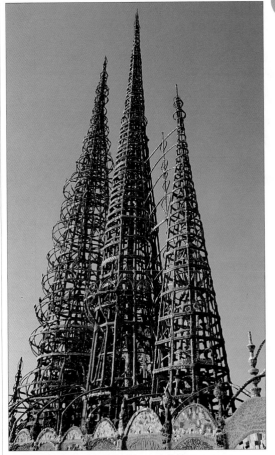

Watts Towers, covered in shells, china, and glass

Watts Towers ⑳

1765 E 107th St, Watts. **Road map** inset A. 📞 *(213) 847-4646.*
🕐 *10am–4pm Tue–Sat; noon–4pm Sun.* ♿ *Towers only.* 👍 *Arts Center only.* 📷

WATTS TOWERS is a masterpiece of folk art that embodies the perseverance and vision of Simon Rodia, an immigrant from Naples, Italy. Between 1921 and 1954, the tile-worker sculpted steel rods, pipes, and whatever else he could find into a huge skeletal framework. The highest tower reaches 100 ft (30 m). Rodia adorned the cemented surface with fragments of seashell, tile, china, and glass. He never gave a reason for building the towers and, upon finishing, he deeded the land to a neighbor and left Los Angeles.

Despite several attempts to have Watts Towers razed, it is now a State Historic Site and has undergone extensive renovation. It stands as a symbol of hope in this area that, in 1965, was the site of the worst riots in Los Angeles.

Adjacent to the monument is the Watts Towers Arts Center. This complex displays temporary exhibitions of work by African-American artists in the community and hosts workshops for artists of all ages.

South Central LA, which includes Watts, is a high-crime neighborhood. Visitors should not stay in the area after dark. Take common-sense precautions, and do not stray from the towers or the Center.

Exposition Park and University of Southern California ⓰

Tommy Trojan statue

EXPOSITION PARK began life in the 1880s as an area of open-air markets, carnivals, and horse-racing. By the end of the century, the district was rife with drinking, gambling, and prostitution. When Judge William Miller Bowen's nearby Sunday school pupils began skipping church to enjoy local temptations, he pushed for the transformation of the area into a cultural landmark that today includes three museums. The Exposition Park Rose Garden in their midst contains more than 19,000 rose bushes. Across the street, the University of Southern California (USC) covers 152 acres (62 ha) and is attended by almost 28,000 students. Founded in 1880, it is the oldest and largest private university in the western United States.

Bovard Administration Building

🏛 Doheny Memorial Library

Corner of Hoover Blvd and Childs Way. ☎ *(213) 740-4039.* ☐ *daily.*
A majestic building with Italian Romanesque, Egyptian, and Moorish design influences, USC's main reference library was built in 1932 in memory of Edward L Doheny Jr, a trustee of the university. The building benefits from a monumental marble staircase at the entrance, and ornate stone and woodwork throughout. The main hall is illuminated by stained-glass windows.

🏛 Natural History Museum of Los Angeles County

900 Exposition Blvd. ☎ *(213) 763-3466.* ☐ *10am–5pm Tue–Sun.* ● *Jan 1, Thanksgiving, Dec 25.* 🎟 *free first Tue of every month.*
This is the third largest natural history and cultural museum in the US. From dinosaur fossils to gems, a wide variety of specimens and artifacts are on display. The Schreiber Hall of Birds, a Pueblo cliff dwelling, the Insect Zoo, and a hands-on Discovery Center are other attractions. The Page Museum *(see pp114–15)* at the La Brea Tar Pits is also part of the Natural History Museum.

Natural History Museum in Exposition Park

🏛 Bovard Administration Building

Hahn Plaza. ☐ *daily.*
This Italian Romanesque structure was named after USC's fourth president, George Bovard. The former bell tower has eight sculpted figures of great men, including John Wesley, Abraham Lincoln, Theodore Roosevelt, Cicero, and Plato. The restored Gothic Norris Auditorium seats 1,600 people. *Tommy Trojan*, a statue of a Trojan warrior and the university's symbol, stands outside the main entrance. It was sculpted in 1930 by Roger Nobel Burnham.

SIGHTS AT A GLANCE

Aerospace Museum ⑦
Bovard Administration Building ①
California Afro-American Museum ⑧
California Science Center ⑨
Doheny Memorial Library ③
Fisher Gallery ⑤
Los Angeles Memorial Coliseum ⑩
Mudd Memorial Hall ④
Natural History Museum of Los Angeles County ⑥
Tommy Trojan ②

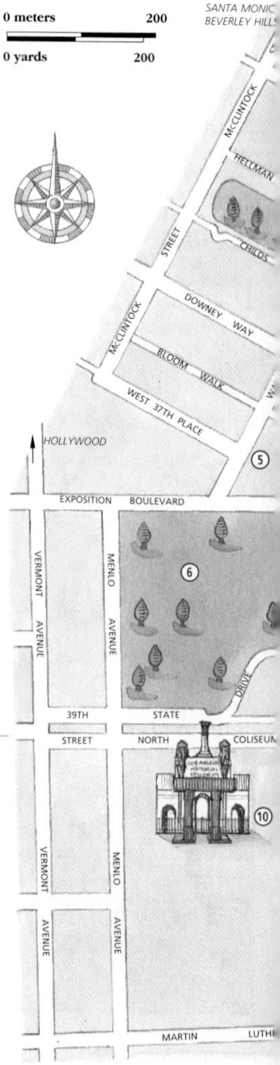
0 meters 200
0 yards 200
SANTA MONIC
BEVERLEY HILL
MCCLINTOCK
HELLMAN
STREET
CHILDS
DOWNEY WAY
MCCLINTOCK
BLOOM WALK
WEST 37TH PLACE
HOLLYWOOD
EXPOSITION BOULEVARD
VERMONT AVENUE
MENLO AVENUE
DRIVE
39TH STREET
STATE
NORTH
COLISEU
MARTIN
LUTH

Los Angeles Memorial Coliseum

🏟 Los Angeles Memorial Coliseum

3939 S Figueroa St. **📞** *(213) 748-6136.* **🕐** *for events and tours.* **♿** **🎫** *10:30am, noon, 1:30pm Tue, Thu & Sat; call ahead (213 765-6347).*

Host to the 1932 and 1984 Olympic Games, the Coliseum has also been the site of professional and USC football games, rock concerts, Pope John Paul II's Mass in 1987 and John F Kennedy's acceptance speech as the Democratic candidate at the Democratic National Convention in 1960. A 40-minute walking tour of the press conference room, locker rooms, and press boxes gives a history of the stadium.

🏛 California Science Center

700 State Drive. **📞** *(213) 724-3623.* **🕐** *10am–5pm daily.* **●** *Jan 1, Thanksgiving, Dec 25.* **🎫**
w www.casciencectr.org

One of the largest of its kind in the United States, the California Museum of Science and Industry aims to make science accessible to people of all ages. The World of Life exhibit in the Kinsey Hall of Health explores how living things function, with Body Works, a 50-ft (15-m) long transparent human figure with illuminated organs, as its centerpiece. The Creative World area shows how people create what they need, following an idea from inception to production. The IMAX Theater, also at the museum has a five-story-high screen with Surround Sound. It presents nature-related movies on such subjects as volcanoes, Africa, and outer space. Aerospace Museum, designed by Frank Gehry, has an F-104 Starfighter jet bolted to its façade. The building features all kinds of winged craft, from a Wright Brothers' glider to a Gemini 11 space capsule.

🏛 Fisher Gallery

Bloom Walk. **📞** *(213) 740-4561.* **🕐** *noon–5pm Tue–Fri; 11am–3pm Sat.* **●** *public hols.*

Named after the gallery's benefactor, Mrs. Walter Harrison Fisher, the collection includes 19th-century French and American landscapes as well as works by the Dutch artist Peter Paul Rubens.

VISITORS' CHECKLIST

Road map inset A. **🚌** *DASH Shuttle C from Business District.* **🚌** *81.* **Exposition Park** **📞** *individual sights.* **University of Southern California** **📞** *(213) 740-5371.* **♿**

🏛 California Afro-American Museum

600 State Drive. **📞** *(213) 744-7432.* **🕐** *10am–5pm Tue–Sun.* **●** *Jan 1, Thanksgiving, Dec 25.*

This museum is a record of Afro-American achievements in the arts, sciences, politics, religion, and sports. The permanent art collection includes works by artists such as Martin Pierré, Betye Saar, Noah Purifoy, and the 19th-century landscape painter Robert Duncanson. Frequent temporary exhibitions are held in the sculpture court at the entrance to the building.

🏟 Mudd Memorial Hall

Corner of Trousdale Parkway and Exposition Blvd. **🕐** *daily.*

The philosophy department's hall was modeled after a medieval monastery in Tuscany. Its bell tower is 146 ft (44 m) high and was used in the 1939 film *The Hunchback of Notre Dame*. Statues of great philosophers are detailed on the exterior, with the Cynic Diogenes placed over the entrance. The Hoose Library of Philosophy has more than 60,000 volumes and is considered to be one of the best in the country.

Italianate façade of the Mudd Memorial Hall

ENTERTAINMENT IN LOS ANGELES

Hollywood
movie sign

As the center of the film industry, Los Angeles has
dominated the world
stage during much of the 20th
century. It is therefore not surprising that the city sees itself
as the Entertainment Capital of
the World. LA's large and successful artistic community
ensures that there is always plenty to
do in the city, although only small areas
tend to be lively after dark.

LA also has a huge number of
theaters, which range from
1930s movie palaces to state-
of-the-art multiplexes. Stage
productions are also plentiful
and diverse. The city has a well-
respected symphony orchestra
and opera company, which in the
summer give outdoor concerts in
places such as the Hollywood Bowl (see
p107). Jazz and blues bars and clubs
are centered on Sunset Boulevard.

**LA listings
publications**

INFORMATION

Various publications can
help sift through the city's
embarrassment of entertainment riches. The *LA Weekly* –
a free paper available at bars,
clubs, and corner markets
across the city – has the most
comprehensive entertainment
and arts listings. It is aimed at
the younger generation and
outshines the *Los Angeles View*.
The *New Times* is a well-
produced magazine and the
Sunday Los Angeles Times
"Calendar" section is another
reliable source for information.
 The monthly publications
include *Los Angeles Magazine*,
which lists all the main events
in the city and also has reliable
restaurant reviews. *Buzz*
magazine's recommendations,
"Buzz Bets," may appeal to a
younger readership. More
general information, aimed at
tourists, is provided in the
monthly *Where Magazine*.
 Listings for gay and lesbian
readers include *Planet Homo*,
The Edge, and *LA Girl Guide*.

The main branch of the **Los
Angeles Convention and
Visitors' Bureau** is in Downtown, and it offers multilingual
assistance. Their
visitors' guide,
*Destination Los
Angeles*, gives list-
ings of restaurants,
hotels, shops, and
attractions. There is
also a 24-hour
events hotline. The
city's two other main
information centers
are the **Hollywood
Visitors' Information
Center** and the **Beverly Hills
Visitors' Bureau**.

BUYING TICKETS

The simplest source of
tickets to concerts, plays,
and sports events in LA is
Ticketmaster. You can order
the tickets by telephone using
a credit card, or visit one of
their centers in
Music Plus or
Tower Records
stores, or
Robinsons-May
department stores.
If you want to
avoid their service
charges, try calling
the venues direct.
Other agencies
include **Tickets
LA**, **Telecharge**,
and **Good Time
Tickets**. Theater
productions and
times are available
by calling
Theater LA's
information line.

DISCOUNT TICKETS

A good source of discount
tickets is **Theater LA**. It
supplies information on, and
sells, cheap tickets only on
the day of performance.
Tickets LA also offers half-
price tickets to some events.
Bookings must be made by
credit card, and tickets can be
collected at the venue.
 If you are willing to gamble
on availability a few hours
before the show starts, then
you can try telephoning the
box office direct. Many places
offer last minute "rush"
discounts on unsold seats for
performances.
 Students who hold a valid
ISIC card *(see p590)* may be
able to get discounts to some
concerts and plays. The best
spots to try are those affiliated
with Los Angeles's universities, such as UCLA's Geffen
Playhouse *(see p164)*.

LACMA *(see pp110–13)*, a venue for free concerts

Hollywood Bowl, one of LA's premier concert venues *(see p107)*

FREE EVENTS

MOST OF THE AREAS within Los Angeles have local festivals, particularly in the summer, which feature food, live music, arts, and crafts. Contact the **LA Cultural Affairs Department** for details. On Thursday nights in the summer, Santa Monica Pier has concerts featuring a variety of music styles *(see pp74–5)*.

Also in the summer, the LA Philharmonic allows visitors to listen to its midday concert rehearsals at the Hollywood Bowl *(see p107)*.

Some of Los Angeles's museums do not charge entrance fees. They include the California Museum of Science and Industry *(see p161)*, Travel Town in Griffith Park *(see p146)*, and the J Paul Getty Museum *(see pp78–81)*. Los Angeles County Museum of Art *(see pp110–13)* hosts concerts of jazz and chamber music on Fridays and Sundays in the museum plaza.

Detail on a LA theater

FACILITIES FOR THE DISABLED

AS ELSEWHERE in California *(see p590)*, almost all clubs, movies, and theaters in LA are wheelchair accessible and will provide special seating. Most establishments also have parking and toilets designed to facilitate the needs of people with disabilities.

A brochure published by the **Los Angeles County Commission on Disabilities** lists the services provided by both public- and private-sector agencies. It also includes information on transportation and recreational facilities as well as equipment for sale or rent.

A few local organizations provide services for persons with disabilities, such as the **Westside Center for Independent Living**.

Los Angeles's public transportation organization, the Metropolitan Transit Authority *(see pp168–9)*, operates a fleet of buses equipped with automatic wheelchair lifts. The **800** number (for LA only) can help arrange local transportation for those with special needs.

Art Deco façade of Hollywood's Pantages Theater *(see p108)*

DIRECTORY

USEFUL NUMBERS

Beverly Hills Visitors' Bureau
239 S Beverly Dr,
Beverly Hills, CA 90212.
(310) 248-1015.

Hollywood Visitors' Information Center
Janes House Square,
6541 Hollywood Blvd,
Hollywood, CA 90028.
(213) 689-8822.

LA Cultural Affairs Department
433 S Spring St, 10th Fl,
Los Angeles, CA 90012.
(213) 485-2433.

Los Angeles Convention and Visitors' Bureau
685 S Figueroa St,
Los Angeles, CA 90017.
(213) 689-8822.

TICKET AGENCIES

Good Time Tickets
(323) 464-7383.

Telecharge
(800) 432-7250.

Theatre LA
(213) 688-2787.
www.theatrela.org

Ticketmaster
(213) 381-2000.

Tickets LA
(323) 655-8587.

FACILITIES FOR THE DISABLED

MTA
(800) 266-6883
or *(213) 922-2000*

Los Angeles County Commission on Disabilities
500 W Temple St, Room 383,
Los Angeles,
CA 90012.
(213) 974-1053
or *(213) 974-1707 TDD.*

Westside Center for Independent Living
12901 Venice Blvd,
Los Angeles,
CA 90066.
(310) 390-3611.

Entertainment Venues

AS BEFITS A CITY OF ITS SIZE AND REPUTATION, Los Angeles has a vast range of entertainment spots. The Music Center in Downtown Los Angeles *(see p121)* is home to the LA Philharmonic, the LA Opera, and two award-winning theaters. Hollywood and West Hollywood are filled with historic movie houses, theaters, and celebrity-owned nightclubs such as the Viper Room *(see p98)*. By day, visitors can join a live television studio audience or see a game at one of the city's major sports arenas.

Hollywood Galaxy *(see p104)* on Hollywood Boulevard

MOVIES

MOST VISITORS don't spend a lot of time seeing movies in LA, even though all the current releases and countless classics are always being shown. The movie palaces themselves, however, draw the crowds, with Mann's Chinese and El Capitan theaters *(see 106)* on Hollywood Boulevard being the best known. Multiplexes, such as those in **Universal City** and the **Beverly Center**, offer state-of-the-art entertainment. And for a real nostalgia trip, visit **Silent Movie**, which runs classics from the 1920s.

THEATER

WITH MORE THAN 1,000 professional plays put on in LA each year, there is bound to be something for everyone. Downtown's Music Center *(see p121)* houses two important theaters – the Ahmanson Theater and the Mark Taper Forum. Pantages *(see p108)* in Hollywood and the **Shubert Theater** in Century City are the leading spots for touring Broadway musicals. Housed in beautiful Mediterranean-style theaters, the **Pasadena**

Playhouse and the **Geffen Playhouse** both put on new works as well as old favorites. More alternative productions are usually performed at the city's smaller spaces, such as the **Actors' Gang Workshop** or **Theater/Theater**.

OPERA, DANCE, AND CLASSICAL MUSIC

THE LA PHILHARMONIC, which winters at the Dorothy Chandler Pavilion *(see p121)* and summers alfresco at the Hollywood Bowl *(see p107)*, is a first-rate orchestra. The **LA Opera** also performs at the Pavilion between September and June. Chamber groups perform at various places throughout the city. The **UCLA Center for the Performing Arts** features prominent international artists. The **Joffrey Ballet** has its second home at the Music Center of Los Angeles on Wilshire Blvd.

ROCK, JAZZ, AND BLUES

NAKED AMBITION and unbridled youth fuel the rock clubs that line Sunset Strip *(see pp98–100)*. The venerable

Whiskey a Go Go and **Roxy** compete with relative newcomers such as the **Viper Room** and the **Key Club**. LA's jazz scene is exemplified by cozy joints such as the **Baked Potato** and **Catalina Bar & Grill**. Dan Ackroyd's **The House of Blues** is just one place that also serves food *(see p549)*. The biggest names perform at LA's arenas, including the Greek Theater *(see p146)* and **Universal Amphitheater** *(see p143)*.

CLUBS

WHETHER IT'S 1970s funk-pop at the **Crush Bar**, hip-house at **Catch One**, or hipster big beats at **The Garage**, the LA club scene runs all types of dance music. With its large gay population, West Hollywood has a lot of discos. One current favorite is **Axis**. If you want to see celebrities, try **Bar Marmont**. Fashion changes quickly, though, so consult the local listings. The over-21 law is enforced, so make sure you have ID. Comedy clubs include **The Comedy Store** on Sunset Boulevard *(see p99)*.

Club sign on Sunset Boulevard

STUDIO TOURS AND TV SHOWS

MANY OF LA'S television and film studios offer behind-the-scenes tours as well as tickets to tapings of popular shows. In the high-tech studios of **CBS-TV**, soap operas such as *The Bold and the Beautiful* and game shows that include *The Price is Right* are taped before live audiences. For

Paramount Studios' famous gates *(see p109)*

tickets, write about six weeks before your trip, specifying the date and show you wish to see. Audience members must speak and understand English.

In Burbank *(see pp140–41)*, **NBC-TV** offers tickets to shows and a tour of the studios. Next door, the **Warner Bros** tour is probably the truest look at modern-day film-making.

Visitors on the Paramount Studios tour *(see p109)* must be at least eight years old.

OUTDOOR ACTIVITIES

L OS ANGELES'S BEACHES are a great natural resource and offer surfing, swimming, and volleyball. Topanga State Park *(see p77)* and Griffith Park

(see pp146–7) offer miles of hiking trails. Spectator sports include baseball at Dodger Stadium *(see p148)*, basketball, and ice hockey at the Great

Western Forum *(see pp158–9)*, horse racing at the Hollywood Park Racetrack *(see p159)*, and polo at Will Rogers State Historic Park *(see p77)*.

Surfers at Manhattan Beach *(see p62)*

DIRECTORY

CINEMAS

Cineplex Odeon Beverly Center Cinemas
8522 Beverly Blvd.
Map 6 C2.
((310) 652-7760.

Cineplex Odeon Universal City Cinemas
Universal City, CA 91608.
((818) 508-0588.

Mann's Village Westwood
961 Broxton Ave.
Map 4 A4.
((310) 208-4575.

Pacific Cinerama Dome
6360 W Sunset Blvd.
Map 2 C5.
((323) 466-3401.

Silent Movie
611 N Fairfax Ave.
Map 7 D1.
((323) 655-2520.

THEATERS

Actors' Gang Workshop
6209 Santa Monica Blvd.
Map 8 B1.
((323) 465-0566.

Geffen Playhouse
10886 Le Conte Ave.
Map 4 A4.
((310) 208-5454.

Pasadena Playhouse
39 S El Molino Ave,
Pasadena, CA 91101.
((626) 356-7529.

Shubert Theater
2020 Avenue of the Stars.
Map 5 D4.
((800) 233-3123.

Theater/Theater
1713 N Cahuenga Blvd.
Map 2 C4.
((323) 871-0210.

OPERA, DANCE, AND CLASSICAL MUSIC

Alex Theater
216 N Brand Blvd,
Glendale, CA 91206.
((818) 243-2539.

Ford Amphitheatre
2580 E Cahuenga Blvd.
Map 2 B3.
((323) 461-3673.

LA Civic Light Opera
((323) 468-1704.

Joffrey Ballet
((323) 563-3739.

LA Opera
135 N Grand Ave.
Map 11 E3.
((213) 972-8001.

UCLA Center for the Performing Arts
405 Hilgard Ave.
Map 4 A4.
((310) 825-2101.

ROCK, JAZZ, AND BLUES

Baked Potato
3787 Cahuenga Blvd W,
Studio City, CA 91105.
((818) 980-1615.

BB Kings' Blues Club
1000 Universal Center Drive, CA 91608.
((818) 622-5464.

Catalina Bar and Grill
1640 N Cahuenga Blvd.
Map 2 C4.
((323) 466-2210.

House of Blues
8430 W Sunset Blvd.
Map 1 A5.
((323) 848-5100.

Key Club
9041 W Sunset Blvd.
Map 6 A1.
((310) 274-5800.

The Roxy
9009 W Sunset Blvd.
Map 6 A1.
((310) 276-2222.

Universal Amphitheater
Universal City, CA 91608.
((818) 622-4440.

Viper Room
8852 W Sunset Blvd.
Map 6 B1.
((310) 358-1880.

Whiskey a Go Go
8901 W Sunset Blvd.
Map 6 B1.
((310) 652-4202.

CLUBS

Axis
652 N La Peer Drive.
Map 6 A2.
((323) 460-2531.

Bar Marmont
8171 W Sunset Blvd.
Map 1 B5.
((323) 650-0575.

Catch One
4067 W Pico Blvd,
Los Angeles, CA 90035.
((323) 734-8849.

Crush Bar
1743 N Cahuenga Blvd.
Map 2 C4.
((323) 461-9017.

The Garage
4519 Santa Monica Blvd.
Map 9 F1.
((323) 662-6166.

STUDIO TOURS AND TV SHOWS

CBS-TV
7800 Beverly Blvd.
Map 7 D2.
((323) 575-2624.

NBC-TV
3000 W Alameda Ave,
Burbank,
CA 91523.
((818) 840-3538.
((818) 840-3537.

Warner Bros
4000 Warner Blvd,
Burbank, CA 91522.
((818) 954-1744.

SHOPPING IN LOS ANGELES

WHATEVER MONEY CAN BUY can be found in Los Angeles, from Cartier necklaces to everyday items. While indoor shopping malls are the norm for much of the United States, LA's temperate climate allows for a range of pleasant outdoor alternatives. Melrose Avenue *(see p109)* and Santa Monica's Third Street Promenade *(see p74)* are both young, lively areas, while **LA shopper** upscale Rodeo Drive *(see p90)* is probably the most famous. The best areas for the latest in fashion and home décor are Robertson Boulevard between Melrose Avenue and Burton Way, and Beverly Boulevard at Martel Avenue. Perhaps the most pleasant area in which to spend your money, is Old Pasadena *(see p150)*, which has a range of unique shops in restored late 19th-century buildings.

Interior of the Westside Pavilion, just south of Westwood Village

SHOPPING CENTERS AND MALLS

LOS ANGELES does have its share of shopping centers, several of which outclass most American malls. The **Beverly Center** has an excellent selection of more than 170 stores. In a sophisticated outdoor setting, the Century City Shopping Center *(see p89)* has more than 120 shops. Nearby, the **Westside Pavilion** has an excellent array of children's shops. A more intimate space, Santa Monica Place *(see p73)*, is at the southern end of the Third Street Promenade. In the San Fernando Valley, the **Sherman Oaks Galleria** spawned Frank Zappa's "Valley Girl" of the 1980s.

DEPARTMENT STORES

EVERY SHOPPING MALL has at least one department store, all of which stock a vast range of goods. The favorites are **Bloomingdales** and **Macy's**.

Where Wilshire Boulevard runs through Beverly Hills' Golden Triangle *(see pp86–7)* is called Department Store Row. Among its four big-name retailers are **Barneys New York** and **Saks Fifth Avenue**. **Nordstrom**'s shoe department is legendary, as are its January and June half-price sales.

CLOTHES

FASHION STYLES are casual in LA, but couture clothes are available in Beverly Hills. **Todd Oldham** and **Tyler Traffi-cante** are two of the hottest women's fashion labels in town. **American Rag** features new and second-hand clothes and shoes for men, women, and children. **Maxfield** and **Fred Segal** are aimed at the well-heeled client who loves exciting and stylish clothes. **Friends** produces dresses and jeans that appeal to girls, while Melrose's **Betsey Johnson** maintains her fun attitude toward women's clothing. **Bernini** and **Mark Michaels** have some of the best fashion for men. For a casual LA look, visit **Urban Outfitters** in Santa Monica. And if you have left home without your bikini, visit **Canyon Beachwear**.

Shop logo on Melrose Avenue

ART, BOOKS, MUSIC, AND ANTIQUES

RESIDENTS OF THIS CITY buy more books than in any city in the country. Some of the favorite independent bookshops are **Book Soup**, **Dutton's**, and **Midnight Special Bookstore**. Many large chains, such as **Barnes and Noble** and **Borders**, may also have coffee bars.

Antiques shops are centered around Melrose Place, near Melrose Avenue, while some of the city's leading art galleries are located at Bergamot Station *(see p75)*. Other galleries include **LA Louver** and **G Ray Hawkins**. There are plenty of record stores located throughout the city. The two stores with the most extensive collections are **Tower Records** and the **Virgin Megastore**, both of which are on West Sunset Boulevard.

Upscale shops on Rodeo Drive *(see p90)*

SPECIALTY SHOPS

Hollywood memorabilia is on sale throughout the city. Two of the best shops, however, are **Fantasies Come True** and **Larry Edmund's Cinema Bookshop**. A strong selection of Latin American arts and crafts, popular in Los Angeles, are at **The Folk Tree**. The award for the shop with the most gadgets and toys, aimed at the executive who has everything, goes to Rodeo Drive's Hammacher Schlemmer *(see p90)*.

FOOD AND WINE

California has been blessed with excellent produce. Both Grand Central Market *(see p120)* and Farmers Market *(see p109)* are overflowing with a wide range of fresh fruit and vegetables. Considered one of the finest reasons to live in LA, **Trader Joe's** sells an array of gourmet foods and wines. The **Whole Foods Market** does the same for its health-conscious customers. **The Wine Merchant**'s cellars in Beverly Hills are superb.

Colorful stalls of produce in Grand Central Market *(see p120)*

DIRECTORY

SHOPPING CENTERS AND MALLS

Beverly Center
8500 Beverly Blvd.
Map 6 C2.
℡ *(310) 854-0070.*

Sherman Oaks Galleria
15301 Ventura Blvd,
Sherman Oaks, CA 91403.
℡ *(818) 382-4100.*

Westside Pavilion
10800 W Pico Blvd,
Los Angeles, CA 90064.
℡ *(310) 474-6255.*

DEPARTMENT STORES

Barneys New York
9570 Wilshire Blvd.
Map 5 F4.
℡ *(310) 276-4400.*

Bloomingdales
Beverly Center,
8500 Beverly Blvd.
Map 6 C2.
℡ *(310) 360-2700.*

Macy's
Beverly Center,
8500 Beverly Blvd.
Map 6 C2.
℡ *(310) 854-6655.*

Nordstrom
Westside Pavilion, 10830
W Pico Blvd, CA 90064.
℡ *(310) 470-6155.*

Saks Fifth Avenue
9600 Wilshire Blvd.
Map 5 E4.
℡ *(310) 275-4211.*

CLOTHES

American Rag
150 S La Brea Ave.
Map 7 F2.
℡ *(323) 935-3154.*

Bernini
Beverly Center,
8500 Beverly Blvd.
Map 6 C2.
℡ *(310) 855-1786.*

Betsey Johnson
Fashion Square Mall.
Sherman Oaks,
CA 91403
℡ *(818) 986-9810.*

Canyon Beachwear
Beverly Center,
8500 Beverly Blvd.
Map 6 C2.
℡ *(310) 652-7848.*

Fred Segal
8118 Melrose Ave.
Map 7 D1.
℡ *(323) 651-1935.*

Friends
Beverly Center, 8500
Beverly Blvd.
Map 6 C2.
℡ *(310) 657-6025.*

Mark Michaels
4672 Admiralty Way,
Marina del Rey,
CA 90292.
℡ *(310) 822-1707.*

Maxfield
8825 Melrose Ave.
Map 6 B2.
℡ *(310) 274-8800.*

Todd Oldham
7386 Beverly Blvd.
Map 7 E2.
℡ *(323) 936-6045.*

Tyler Trafficante
2001 Saturn St, Monterey
Park, 91755 **Map** 7 F2.
℡ *(323) 869-9299.*

Urban Outfitters
1440 Third St Promenade,
Santa Monica,
CA 90401.
℡ *(310) 394-1404.*

ART, BOOKS, MUSIC, AND ANTIQUES

Barnes and Noble
1201 Third St Promenade,
Santa Monica,
CA 90401.
℡ *(310) 260-9110.*

Book Soup
8818 W Sunset Blvd.
Map 1 A5.
℡ *(310) 659-3110.*

Borders
1360 Westwood Blvd.
Map 4 A5.
℡ *(310) 475-3444.*

Dutton's
11975 San Vicente Blvd,
Brentwood, CA 90049.
℡ *(310) 476-6263.*

G Ray Hawkins
908 Colorado Ave,
Santa Monica,
CA 90401.
℡ *(310) 394-5558.*

LA Louver
45 N Venice Blvd,
Venice, CA 90291.
℡ *(310) 822-4955.*

Midnight Special Bookstore
1318 Third St Promenade,
Santa Monica, CA 90401.
℡ *(310) 393-2923.*

Tower Records
8801 W Sunset Blvd.
Map 1 A5.
℡ *(310) 657-7300.*

Virgin Megastore
8000 W Sunset Blvd.
Map 1 B5.
℡ *(323) 650-8666.*

SPECIALTY SHOPS

Fantasies Come True
8012 Melrose Ave.
Map 7 D1.
℡ *(323) 655-2636.*

The Folk Tree
199 S Fair Oaks Ave,
Pasadena,
CA 91105.
℡ *(626) 793-4828.*

Larry Edmund's Cinema Bookshop
6644 Hollywood Blvd.
Map 2 B4.
℡ *(323) 463-3273.*

FOOD AND WINE

Trader Joe's
7304 Santa Monica Blvd.
Map 7 F1.
℡ *(323) 851-9772.*

Whole Foods Market
239 N Crescent Drive.
Map 5 F4.
℡ *(310) 274-3360.*

The Wine Merchant
9701 S Santa Monica Blvd.
Map 5 E4.
℡ *(310) 278-7322.*

GETTING AROUND LOS ANGELES

THE SPRAWLING 467 sq miles (1,200 sq km) of Los Angeles may seem daunting to navigate. A network of freeways *(see pp170–71)* provides an accessible, if sometimes crowded, means of traveling in the area. The only time-effective method of touring the city is by car, although the public transportation system works well in Downtown

Taxi in Beverly Hills

Los Angeles and Hollywood. Taxis must usually be ordered by telephone. Taxis run from the airport, but can be expensive. Buses are often crowded and slow, but they run on most of the main streets in the city. LA's growing subway system, the Metro, is very useful when exploring the business district. Some neighborhoods are best seen on foot.

Driving toward downtown Los Angeles on the freeway

DRIVING

PLANNING IS THE KEY to making driving in Los Angeles less overwhelming. First, refer to the map on pages 170–71 to see which freeway changes or exit you will need. Second, avoid rush hour on the freeways. The peak times are from Monday to Friday, 8am to 9:30am and 4pm to 6:30pm. Some freeways are busy regardless of the hour, and it can be less stressful to take one of the city's major streets. When parking, read the posted signs for limitations and carry plenty of quarters for the parking meters. At night it is safer to valet park.

WALKING

EVEN THOUGH the city is very spread out, some districts are pedestrian-friendly. Third Street Promenade and the

beach and Main Street in Santa Monica *(see pp72–5)* are all nice areas for walking. Other areas include: the business district in Downtown Los Angeles *(see pp118–19)*, Old Pasadena *(see p150)*, Melrose Avenue *(see p109)*, the Golden Triangle in Beverly Hills *(see pp86–7)*, and Long Beach's Pine Avenue *(see p128)*. Do not walk at night unless the street is well lit and populated.

CYCLING

THE COASTAL BIKE path that runs for 25 miles (40 km) beside Santa Monica Bay is the best place to cycle. Other popular areas are Griffith Park and the Oceanside Bike Path in Long Beach. Bicycles are not allowed on the freeways. The **LA Department of Transportation** provides detailed route maps. Bikes are available from **Sea Mist Skate Rentals** (Santa Monica Pier), the pizza stands (Santa Monica Beach, and **Marina Bikes** (Redondo Beach).

BUSES AND SUBWAY

GREATER LA is served by the **Metropolitan Transportation Authority (MTA)**. Bus stops display an MTA sign. Buses run on main thoroughfares: Wilshire Boulevard to Santa Monica Beach, Nos. 20 and 320; to Westwood and UCLA, No. 21; Santa Monica Boulevard to the beach, No. 4; Sunset Boulevard to Pacific Palisades, No. 2.

The **DASH** shuttle provides travel within small areas, such as Downtown LA and Hollywood, for a quarter. The **Santa Monica Blue Bus Co.** and **Long Beach Transit** service those communities.

The Metro Red Line starts at Union Station and runs to Universal City and North Hollywood. The Blue Line operates between Downtown Los Angeles and Long Beach. Running from Norwalk to Redondo Beach, the Green Line is useful for the airport.

Take a shuttle bus from LAX to Aviation/I-105 station.

Cycling through Venice on the coastal bike path

Train at Pershing Square station on the Metro Red Line

Last travel times are: Red Line 5am– 9pm Monday to Friday, 5am– 7pm at weekends; Blue Line 5am–11:30pm; Green Line 4am–11pm. The subway is closed on public holidays except for New Year's Day.

Bus tickets can be bought at most grocery stores. Metro tickets are available at the stations.

OTHER WAYS TO GET AROUND

SOMEONE ELSE CAN always do the driving. Two reliable taxi companies are **LA Best Transportation** and the **Independent Cab Co**. Rent a limousine for a luxurious alternative from **Limousine Connection** and **Entertainment Limos**.

Private bus lines such as **LA Tours** and **Starline Tours** offer package tours. **Grave Line Tours** shows visitors the scenes of famous scandals and deaths from a Cadillac hearse. **Casablanca Tours** and **Beyond the Glitz** offer in-depth looks at Hollywood and cultural tours of LA. **LA Nighthawks** arranges a luxurious night out in the city.

DIRECTORY

CYCLING

Marina Bike Rentals
505 N Harbor Dr,
Redondo Beach, CA 90277
(*(310) 318-2453.*

LA Department of Transportation
221 N Figueroa St, Los Angeles,
CA 90012. **Map** 11 D3.
(*(213) 580-1199.*

Sea Mist Skate Rentals
1619 Ocean Front Walk,
Santa Monica, CA 90401.
(*(310) 395-7076.*

PUBLIC TRANSPORTATION

DASH
(*(800) 266-6883.*

Long Beach Transit
(*(800) 266-6883.*

Metropolitan Transportation Authority (MTA)
(*(800) 266-6883.*

Santa Monica Blue Bus Co.
(*(800) 266-6883.*

TAXIS

Independent Cab Co.
(*(213) 385-8294.*

LA Best Transportation
(*(323) 962-4949.*

LIMOUSINES

Limousine Connection
(*(800) 266-5466.*

Entertainment Limos
(*(818) 997-3856.*

TOURS

Casablanca Tours
(*(323) 461-0156.*

Grave Line Tours
(*(323) 469-4149.*

LA Nighthawks
(*(310) 392-1500.*

LA Tours
(*(323) 460-6490.*

Beyond the Glitz Tours
(*(323) 658-7920.*

Starline Tours
(*(323) 463-3333.*

LA's METRO NETWORK

North Hollywood
Universal City
Hollywood/Highland
Hollywood/Vine
Hollywood/Western
Vermont/Sunset
Vermont/Santa Monica/ LA City College
Vermont/Beverly
Pasadena
7th Street/Metro Center
Pershing Square
Wilshire/Western
Wilshire/Normandie
Wilshire/Vermont
Westlake/MacArthur Park
Pico
Grand
San Pedro
Washington
Vernon
Slauson
Florence
Firestone
Kenneth Hahn/ 103rd St
Tom Bradley/ Civic Center
Union Station
Aviation/I-105
Hawthorne/I-105
Imperial/Wilmington
Long Beach/I-105
Lakewood/I-105
Mariposa/Nash
El Segundo/Nash
Douglas/Rosecrans
Marine/Redondo
Crenshaw Fwy/I-105
Vermont/I-105
Harbor Fwy/I-105
Avalon/I-105
Compton
Artesia
Del Amo
I-605/I-105
Wardlow
Willow
Pacific Coast Hwy
Anaheim
Pacific
Transit Mall
5th Street
1st Street

KEY
— Metro Red Line
— Metro Blue Line
···· Metro Blue Line (future)
— Metro Green Line

Los Angeles Freeway Route Planner

A CAR IS ESSENTIAL in Los Angeles and is the quickest way of getting around this vast city. All freeways are numbered but most also have names, such as the Golden State Freeway (I-5). Plan your trip carefully: freeway exits are marked by street name and direction rather than by area. It is advisable not to use the freeways during rush hour (8–9:30am and 4–6:30pm). For more details on getting around LA see pages 168–9.

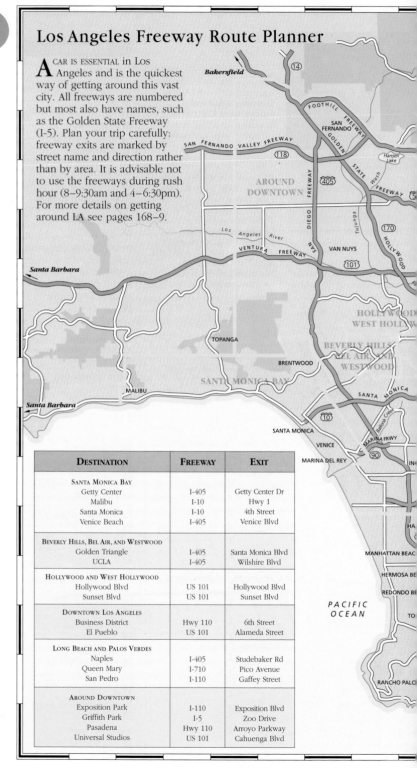

DESTINATION	FREEWAY	EXIT
SANTA MONICA BAY		
Getty Center	I-405	Getty Center Dr
Malibu	I-10	Hwy 1
Santa Monica	I-10	4th Street
Venice Beach	I-405	Venice Blvd
BEVERLY HILLS, BEL AIR, AND WESTWOOD		
Golden Triangle	I-405	Santa Monica Blvd
UCLA	I-405	Wilshire Blvd
HOLLYWOOD AND WEST HOLLYWOOD		
Hollywood Blvd	US 101	Hollywood Blvd
Sunset Blvd	US 101	Sunset Blvd
DOWNTOWN LOS ANGELES		
Business District	Hwy 110	6th Street
El Pueblo	US 101	Alameda Street
LONG BEACH AND PALOS VERDES		
Naples	I-405	Studebaker Rd
Queen Mary	I-710	Pico Avenue
San Pedro	I-110	Gaffey Street
AROUND DOWNTOWN		
Exposition Park	I-110	Exposition Blvd
Griffith Park	I-5	Zoo Drive
Pasadena	Hwy 110	Arroyo Parkway
Universal Studios	US 101	Cahuenga Blvd

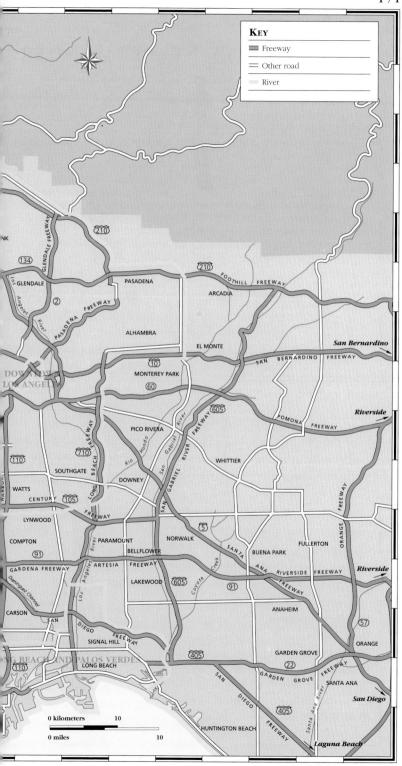

KEY

■ Freeway

═ Other road

░ River

GLENDALE FREEWAY

(210)

(134)

Los Angeles River

GLENDALE

(2)

PASADENA FREEWAY

PASADENA

(210) FOOTHILL FREEWAY

ARCADIA

ALHAMBRA

EL MONTE

San Bernardino

(10) SAN BERNARDINO FREEWAY

MONTEREY PARK

DOWNTOWN LOS ANGELES

(60)

(605)

POMONA FREEWAY

Riverside

PICO RIVERA

Rio Hondo

San Gabriel River

SAN GABRIEL RIVER FREEWAY

WHITTIER

LONG BEACH FREEWAY

(710)

(110)

SOUTHGATE

DOWNEY

WATTS

CENTURY (105)

FREEWAY

LYNWOOD

(5)

ORANGE FREEWAY

COMPTON

PARAMOUNT

NORWALK

SANTA

BUENA PARK

FULLERTON

(91)

Los Angeles River

Dominguez Channel

GARDENA FREEWAY

BELLFLOWER

ARTESIA FREEWAY

Coyote Creek

ANA RIVERSIDE FREEWAY

Riverside

LAKEWOOD (605)

(91)

ANAHEIM

(57)

CARSON

SAN DIEGO FREEWAY

SIGNAL HILL

(405)

GARDEN GROVE

(22)

ORANGE

GARDEN GROVE FREEWAY

SANTA ANA

San Diego

(110)

LONG BEACH AND PALOS VERDES

LONG BEACH

SAN DIEGO FREEWAY

(405)

Santa Ana River

0 kilometers   10

0 miles   10

HUNTINGTON BEACH

Laguna Beach

Los Angeles Street Finder

The key map below shows the areas of LA covered in the *Street Finder*. It includes the city districts of Beverly Hills, Bel Air and Westwood, Hollywood and West Hollywood, and Downtown Los Angeles. All places of interest in these areas are marked on the maps in addition to useful information, such as railroad stations, metro stops, bus terminals, and emergency services. A *Freeway Route Planner* can be found on pages 170–71. The map references given with sights described in the LA section of the guide refer to the maps on the following pages. Map references are also given for entertainment venues *(see p165)*, shops *(see p167)*, hotels *(see pp508–13)* and restaurants *(see pp544–50)* in LA. Road map references refer to the map inside the back cover. The symbols used for sights and other features on the *Street Finder* maps are listed in the key below.

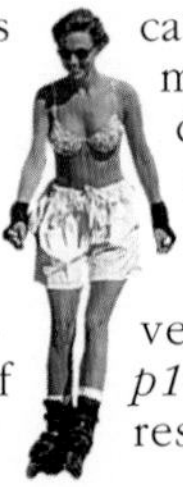

In-line skater at Venice Beach

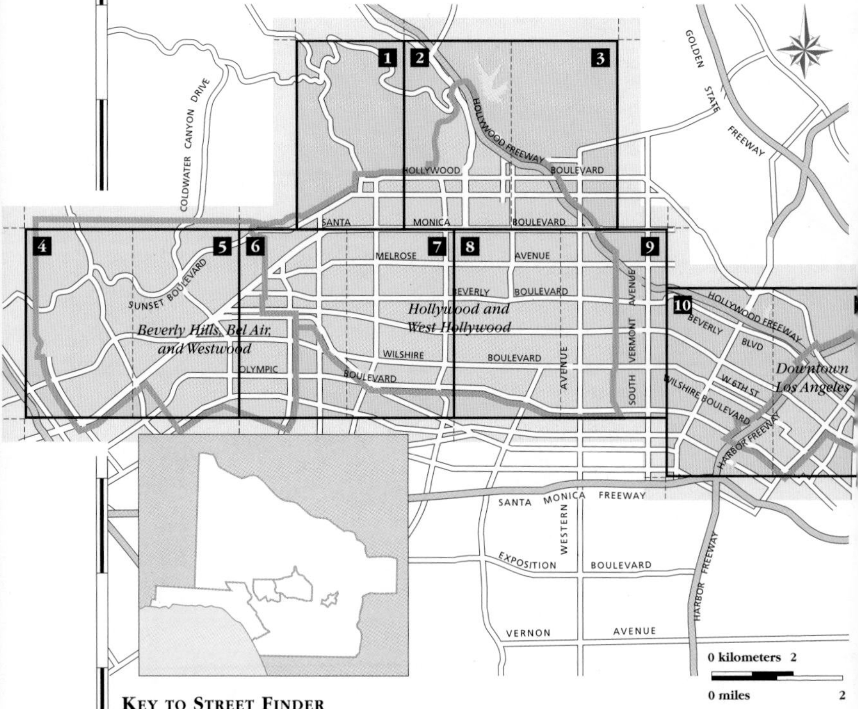

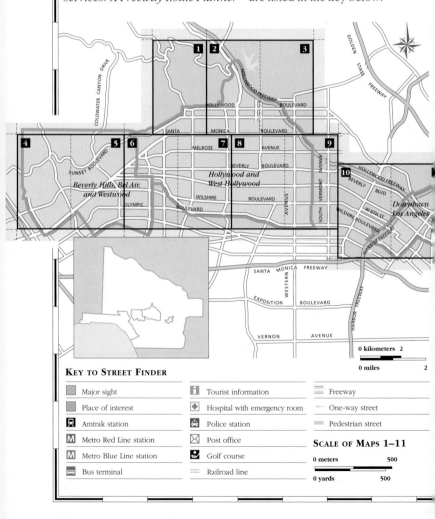

Key to Street Finder

- Major sight
- Place of interest
- Amtrak station
- Metro Red Line station
- Metro Blue Line station
- Bus terminal
- Tourist information
- Hospital with emergency room
- Police station
- Post office
- Golf course
- Railroad line
- Freeway
- One-way street
- Pedestrian street

Scale of Maps 1–11

0 meters 500

0 yards 500

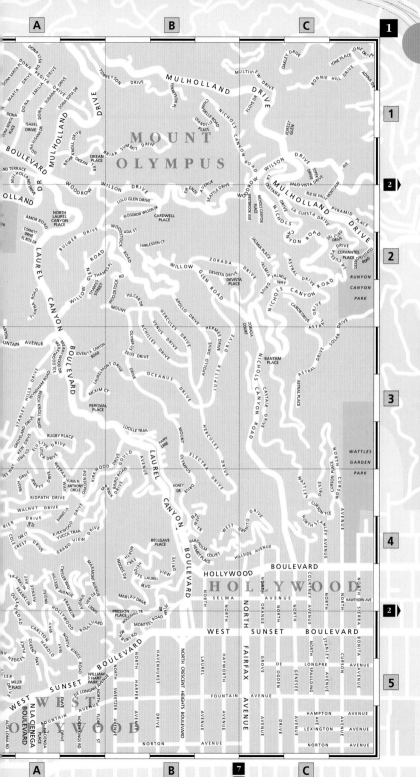

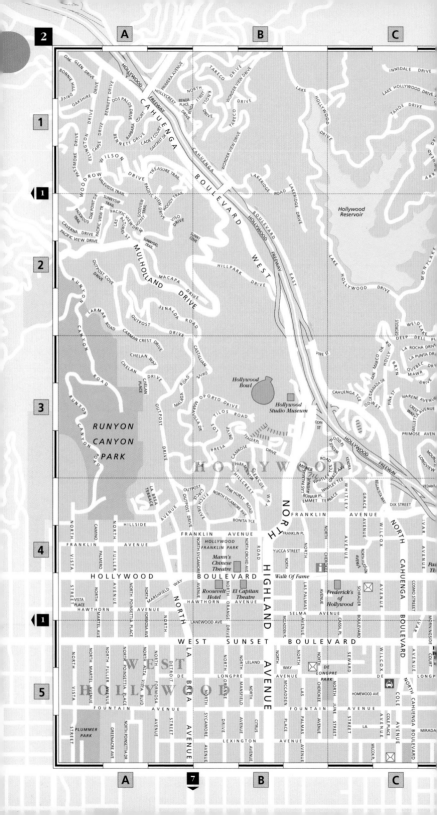

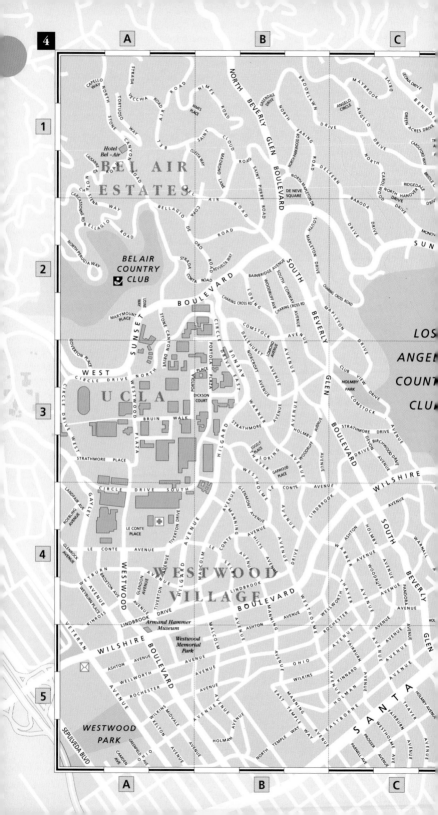

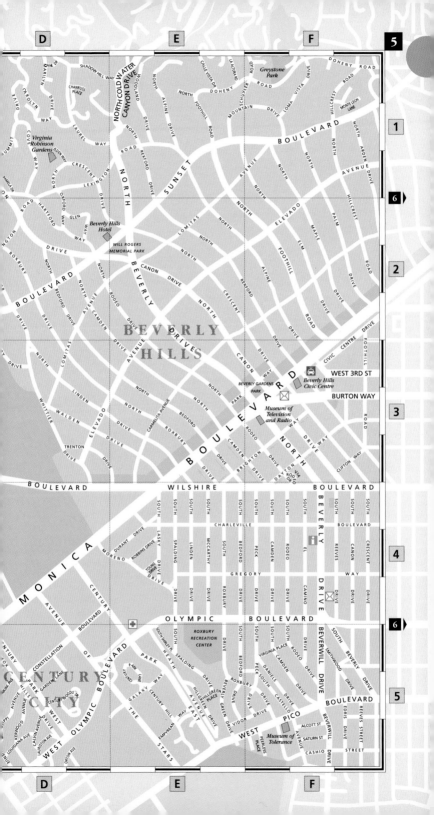

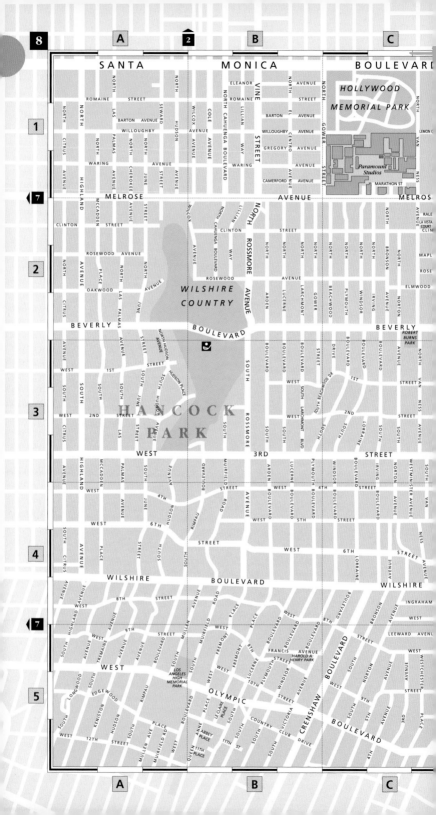

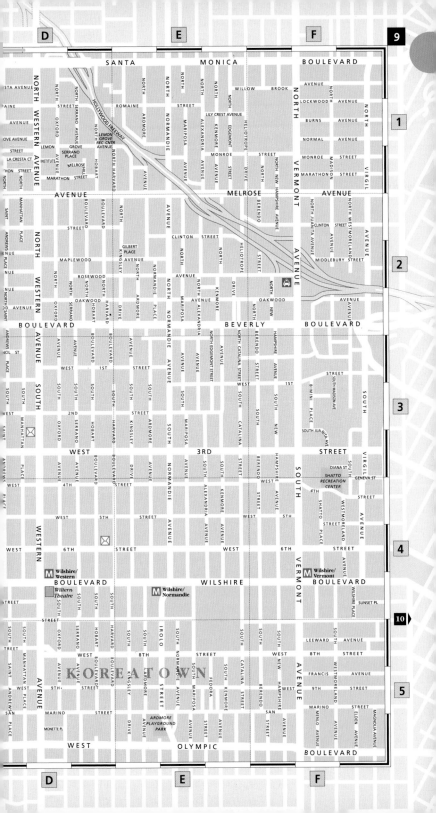

SOUTHERN
CALIFORNIA

Southern California at a Glance

SOUTHERN CALIFORNIA is a region of startling contrasts. Scorching deserts give way to snowcapped mountains, with views of the coast. It is possible to surf in the morning, ski in the afternoon, and play golf in the evening. From San Simeon to San Diego, the coast is lined with resorts, reflecting a shoreline that ranges from rugged bluffs to golden sands. Attractions along the way include historic missions, the charming cities of Santa Barbara and San Diego, and the theme parks of Orange County. Farther inland are two of the most startling desert areas in the United States: Death Valley National Park and the Joshua Tree National Park.

Santa Barbara Mission (see *pp212–13*) *is the most visited mission in the state and is the only one in the chain of missions to have remained in continuous use since it was founded in 1786. The church façade is in Classical style, a theme continued inside the building.*

SOUTH CENTRAL
CALIFORNIA
(See pp194–215)

LOS ANGELE
(See pp54–18

ORANGE COU
(See pp216–3

***Hearst Castle*™** (see *pp202–205*), *on the south central coast, was built by publishing tycoon William R Hearst. In the 1930s and '40s he invited Hollywood stars and royalty here and entertained them lavishly. The Neptune Pool is particularly stunning.*

0 kilometers   50

0 miles   50

Mission San Juan Capistrano (see *pp230–31*) *in southern Orange County is known as the "Jewel of the Missions." Founded in 1776, its main buildings have been beautifully restored and feature historical exhibits.*

Death Valley National Park (see pp280–83) *in the Mojave Desert encompasses one of the hottest places on earth and the lowest point in the Western Hemisphere. Within Death Valley, which is 140 miles (225 km) long, lie dry lake beds, sand dunes, and small outposts built around springs. Despite the harsh conditions, the area is rich in flora and fauna. Sights of historical interest in the park include Scotty's Castle.*

THE MOJAVE DESERT
(See pp270–83)

Joshua Tree National Park (see pp268–9) *in the Low Desert is famed for its distinctive trees. Within easy reach of the city of Palm Springs, it offers breathtaking views of the stark desert landscape with its remarkable rock formations.*

THE INLAND EMPIRE AND LOW DESERT
(See pp258–69)

SAN DIEGO COUNTY
(See pp234–57)

Balboa Park (see pp246–9) *in San Diego was the site of the Panama–Pacific Exposition of 1915. The park is now home to many museums, such as the San Diego Museum of Man, housed in the landmark California Building. The famous San Diego Zoo lies just to the north of Balboa Park.*

Surfing and Beach Culture

Bust of Duke
Kahanamoku

IF SOUTHERN CALIFORNIANS worship at the altars of youth, health, and beauty, then their churches are the beaches. Here, unbelievably beautiful men and women parade their surgically enhanced bodies beneath the ever-present sun. Favorite sports include skating and volleyball, but the ability to look good on a surfboard is the ultimate cool. Surfing was originally practiced by the Hawaiian nobility as a religious ceremony. It was introduced to California by Hawaiian George Freeth in 1907 *(see p62)* and popularized in the 1920s in Waikiki by Olympic swimmer Duke Kahanamoku. In 1961 the Beach Boys released "Surfin" and the sport took off around the world. Today surf culture is part of the mainstream consciousness. The loose-fitting clothes favored by surfers are reproduced on the catwalk, and surfing slang is used by many who have never been near the beach.

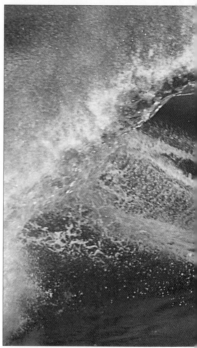

The Beach Boys sang of the joys of surfing despite the fact that none of the group could surf.

Films such as Gidget *(1959),* Ride the Wild Surf *(1964), and* Beach Blanket Bingo *(1965), as well as the documentary* Endless Summer, *helped to establish the cultural allure of surfing. Lengthy beach parties in the style of these films were highly popular during the 1960s.*

WHERE TO LEARN TO SURF

Beginners are advised to start by body surfing without a board. Boogie boarding, with a half-length board, is also far easier to master than surfing. Beaches with waves that break parallel to the beach (a surf break) are the most suitable. The best beaches on which to learn to boogie board include Santa Monica *(see p61)*, Carpinteria *(p199)*, and Del Mar *(p239)*. Beginners should avoid famous surfing beaches, such as Surfrider *(p60)*, San Clemente *(p220)*, and Huntington *(p220)*, as conditions can overwhelm the inexperienced.

Boys with boogie boards weighing up the surf

Lifeguards are stationed on most county and state beaches in California during the summer. Their distinctive gray huts have been made famous throughout the world by the television series Baywatch. *Always follow their instructions on the beach, and ask if you are in doubt about the tidal conditions.*

A "tube" is a cylindrical passage formed when a wave breaks and the crest curls over.

SURFING HIGHLIGHTS

One exhilarating surfing experience is to "beat the tube." The surfer rides beneath the crest, regulating his speed and position to stay just ahead of the falling wave. If he goes too fast he comes out of the wave; too slowly and he gets knocked off. The wave loses momentum as it nears the shore. At this point the surfer will shoot out of the tube, remaining upright.

By changing position a surfer can alter the speed and direction in which he or she is traveling. Crouching lowers the center of gravity and increases stability.

OTHER BEACH ACTIVITIES

Southern California's spectacular beaches are used by a wide variety of sports enthusiasts. Although the beaches are most popular in summer, activities are enjoyed year-round by hardy souls. Sailing is popular, with thousands of yachts of all sizes harbored in a string of marinas along the coast. Windsurfing and kite flying also take advantage of the prevailing onshore winds. Sea kayakers often explore the rocky coasts of the Channel Islands *(see p214)* and the mainland. Volleyball, once limited to friendly matches, is now a major professional sport with competitions held along the Southern California coast each summer.

Modern surfboards are made out of light, man-made materials, such as fiberglass, allowing surfers to reach much higher speeds. Their bright colors make them easy to see in the water.

The first boards came from Hawaii and were called coffin lids because of their distinctive shape. Made out of wood, they were heavy and unwieldy. Early surfboards can be seen at the Lighthouse Surfing Museum in Santa Cruz (see p491).

Friendly volleyball game in Santa Monica

California Car Culture

California license plate

IT IS DIFFICULT TO understand Southern California without considering the influence of the car. The introduction of the freeway system in LA in 1940 *(see p50)* spawned an entirely new culture centered around the automobile. Owning a car became integral to the California identity, and the open desert road came to symbolize the freedom of the state. Customizing automobiles also made the car an art object. Drive-in movies led to the convenience of drive-in banks and fast-food restaurants. But there was a price to pay: smog, the result of car exhaust and sunlight, has become a fact of life in LA. Today, cars have cleaner exhausts, but LA has to cope with some 8 million cars on its increasingly "gridlocked" streets.

Los Angeles' freeways, begun in the 1950s, have expanded into a complex network, linking the city with the rest of the state.

Ford Thunderbird emblem

The canvas top could be lowered for sunny weather or raised in rain.

Chrome trimmed the backup lights.

Chrome sidepanel strip

BIRTHPLACE OF THE MOTORCYCLE GANG

In the 1950s especially, California was home to rival gangs of "outlaw bikers." The most famous, the Hell's Angels, began with a group of World War II veterans in San Bernardino in 1948. Their notorious reputation was immortalized in the 1953 film *The Wild One* with Marlon Brando. Today, the Hell's Angels have around 1,000 members worldwide, who continue to symbolize defiance of authority.

Marlon Brando

Japanese cars, such as those imported through Worldport LA (see p62), continue to be hot competition for American-made automobiles.

This car advertisement for Pontiac dates from 1950. As automobiles became more of a status symbol, manufacturers competed for customers with increasingly bright ads.

WHERE TO SEE CALIFORNIA CAR CULTURE

Californians are very proud of their car culture and history; most towns have a parade or car show featuring vintage, classic, and customized automobiles. For information, inquire at the local visitors' center *(see p589)*. One of the largest automobile shows is held in early April at the LA County Fairgrounds in Pomona. Other meetings include the Muscle Car Show in Bakersfield *(see p215)*, West Coast Kustom Cars in Paso Robles *(see pp200–201)*, and the Graffiti USA Festival and Cruise in Modesto. California also hosts several famous motor races, such as the Long Beach Toyota Grand Prix in April *(p32)* and the Savemart 300 Nascar Winston Cup Race in Sonoma *(pp448–9)*. There are several world-class automobile museums in the state, including the Petersen Automotive Museum *(p114)* in Los Angeles and the Behring Auto Museum near San Jose *(pp412–13)*.

Tucker Torpedo, one of the cars on display at the Petersen Automotive Museum in LA

Chrome door lights were turned on from inside.

The wraparound windshield imitated aircraft designs.

PINK CADILLAC

With its glamorous design and convertible roof, the 1959 pink Cadillac suited California's image and climate perfectly. However, the car's two-ton weight meant that its steering was heavy, and it soon gave way to more efficient designs.

Chrome bumpers protected the front of the car.

White sidewall tires were a popular option because of their expensive look.

The Model T Ford (affectionately known as the Tin Lizzie) first appeared in 1908. In 1913, Henry Ford introduced the assembly line and cars could be bought for as little as $500. This photograph of a 1924 beachside traffic jam shows that it took only a few years for Californians to become dependent on the car.

Recreational vehicles (RVs) became popular in the 1960s. Californians could now take to the open road and explore the state's wilderness without leaving any home comforts behind.

Deserts and Water Networks

MUCH OF SOUTHERN CALIFORNIA is desert, and before 1913, migrants to this area depended on wells for their water. The population grew extremely quickly and it soon became necessary to engineer what is now one of the most elaborate water networks on earth. This network has turned parts of what was once inhospitable desert into productive land, and made possible the desert resort of Palm Springs and the huge populations of the Southern Californian cities. However, the South's high rate of water consumption places a great demand on the region's major sources of water: the Colorado River and the Sierra Nevada Mountains.

The Sacramento/San Joaquin River Delta supplies water to the farms of the south. At peak times, pumping causes the river to flow in reverse, bringing salt water from San Francisco Bay.

Owens Lake (see p479) lies between the Sierra Nevada Mountains and the Mojave Desert, in Owens Valley. The Los Angeles Aqueduct diverted water from Owens River to LA and the 100-sq mile (260-sq km) lake gradually dried up.

BAKERSFIELD

SAN LUIS OBISPO

SANTA BARBARA

SAN GA
MOUNT

LOS ANGELES

The Los Angeles Aqueduct made the San Fernando Valley fertile (see p140). Land speculators made their fortunes when the aqueduct was completed in 1914.

WILLIAM MULHOLLAND

As head of the Los Angeles city water department, William Mulholland (1855–1935) *(see p140)* and his colleague Fred Eaton designed an aqueduct and a series of tunnels to lead from Owens Valley to LA. Completed in 1914, it cost more than $24 million. By 1929 the supplies were no longer sufficient, and they had to divert water from Mono Basin and the Colorado River, 400 miles (645 km) away.

0 kilometers   75

0 miles   75

KEY

	Populated areas
	Rivers
	Dry rivers
	Canals
	Aqueducts

LOCATOR MAP

☐ *Southern California*

Death Valley *(see pp280–83) is so hot, the valley floor shimmers. The tiny amount of rain that falls provides nourishment for the 900 different plant species that live within Death Valley National Park.*

Palm Springs *(see pp264–5) is located at the edge of the Low Desert, where clouds are seldom seen. However, water from the nearby mountains and underground springs keep this lush vacation oasis green.*

Parker Dam

Joshua Tree National Monument *(see pp268–9)* is in the Low Desert. Joshua trees, which are adapted to a dry climate, thrive here and are home to 25 species of birds.

The All American Canal brings water from the Colorado River to irrigate the Imperial Valley, which provides the US with year-round lettuce, melons, tomatoes, and peas.

SOUTHERN CALIFORNIA'S WATER NETWORK

Southern California has two main sources of water: ice-melt from the Sierra Nevada Mountains in the north, brought to LA via the LA Aqueduct, and the Colorado River to the southeast. The Colorado River Aqueduct system carries water 672 miles (1,080 km) from the Parker Dam via 395 miles (635 km) of pipes. Imperial Valley has a network of canals, making it fertile. The same canals irrigate the desert resort of Palm Springs.

The Salton Sea *was formed in 1905 when a break in the Imperial Valley's irrigation system allowed flood waters into the Salton Basin.*

SOUTH CENTRAL CALIFORNIA

OUTH CENTRAL CALIFORNIA *is a land of lonely passes and wooded streams. Broad sandy beaches stretch for miles along the gentle coast with empty, tawny hills as their only backdrop. It is a region of small and friendly towns, scattered farms and vineyards nestled in scenic valleys. Farther inland is Los Padres National Forest, where mountain lions roam freely, and eagles and condors soar overhead.*

The region's Spanish heritage is highly visible, and no more so than in Santa Barbara. Here the area's most important garrison and the legendary structure that came to be known as "Queen of the Missions" *(see pp212–13)* can be found. The city's red tile Mission Revival-style architecture *(see p27)* has been imitated throughout the State.

Following the breakup of the wealthy missions during the 1830s, the land was divided into a handful of sprawling ranches, then the 1849 Gold Rush brought an influx of Easterners to California. The newcomers subdivided the large estates and set up small farming communities. They touted the land throughout the world as a "semitropical paradise," where the first season's crops would pay for the cost of the land.

In the early part of the 20th century the Central Coast was a popular vacation destination, drawing thousands of people each summer to seaside towns such as Pismo and Avila Beach. Farther north, at San Simeon, millionaire William Randolph Hearst built his own personal playground, the fabulous private museum now known as Hearst Castle™.

Today, South Central California provides a wealth of activities, from horse-drawn wine-tasting tours in the scenic Santa Ynez valley to relaxation on empty beaches. The more active can try kayaking on the Kern River near Bakersfield. Offshore, the Channel Islands offer a unique view of the area's ecosystems and an opportunity to see the annual passage of the magnificent gray whales. The east of the region is dominated by the Los Padres National Forest, an area of breathtaking beauty with miles of hiking trails and drives through mountain scenery. Here, too, are signs of the Chumash Indians who once lived in thriving communities along the coast. Their enigmatic petroglyphs remain as silent reminders of their presence throughout these hills.

Seasonal produce on display in Morro Bay

◁ **Fishing off the pier at Pismo Beach**

Exploring South Central California

South Central California's beaches and coastal plains are backed by low rolling hills covered with groves of oak. Beyond this, the Los Padres National Forest has hundreds of miles of mountainous hiking trails. Just north of Santa Barbara, the gentle countryside around Santa Ynez has proved perfect for growing vines. Along the coast of San Luis Obispo County, the seaside towns of Morro Bay and Pismo Beach are known for their fishing and clamming. In the northwest, Hearst Castle is one of California's most popular tourist attractions.

Mission San Miguel Arcángel's campanario

Sights at a Glance

- Atascadero 5
- Bakersfield 20
- Cambria 3
- Channel Islands National Park 16
- Chumash Painted Cave State Historic Park 13
- *Hearst Castle pp202–5* 2
- Lompoc Valley 9
- Los Padres National Forest 19
- Mission San Miguel Arcángel 1
- Mission Santa Inés 12
- Morro Bay 6
- Ojai 18
- Paso Robles 4
- Pismo Beach 8
- Ronald Reagan Presidential Library 17
- San Luis Obispo 7
- *Santa Barbara pp210–13* 14
- Solvang 11
- Ventura 15

Tour

Santa Ynez Valley Wineries *p208* 10

See Also

- ***Where to Stay*** pp514–15
- ***Where to Eat*** pp551–3

Key

- Freeway
- Major road
- Minor road
- Scenic route
- River
- Viewpoint

Rugged mountains in the vast Los Padres National Forest

GETTING AROUND

I-101 and Hwy 1 follow the coast, passing through all the major sights. Amtrak runs a daily service, the Coast Starlight, from Los Angeles to San Francisco, stopping at Santa Barbara and San Luis Obispo. Greyhound buses also stop at these cities. There are roads through the Los Padres National Forest to Bakersfield, but the most common route to that city is I-5 from Los Angeles. Trips to the Channel Islands National Park leave from Ventura.

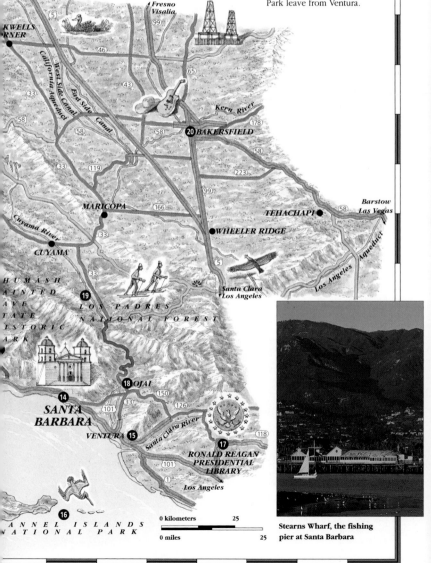

Stearns Wharf, the fishing pier at Santa Barbara

California Coastline: South Central

THE SOUTH CENTRAL COAST offers miles of accessible, broad, sandy beaches and some of the best surfing in the state. The water here is cooler than the ocean off the Los Angeles to San Diego coast, but these beaches offer privacy and solitude for swimming, sunbathing, and picnicking. The rugged mountain backdrop appears so close you can almost smell the pine and chaparral. Several South Central beaches are within state parks and have hiking and nature trails that climb upward, offering spectacular views of the unspoiled coast below.

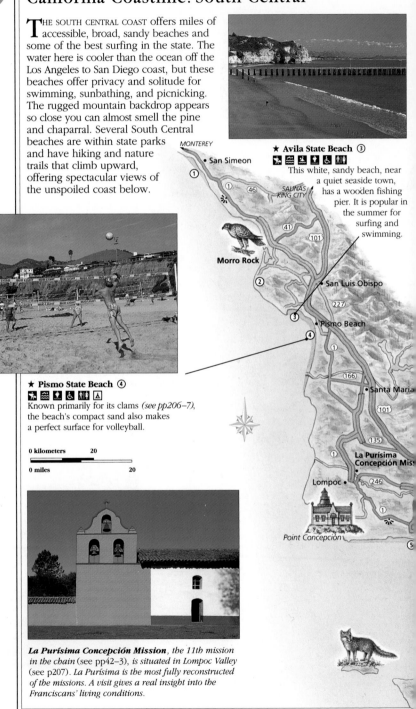

★ **Avila State Beach** ③

This white, sandy beach, near a quiet seaside town, has a wooden fishing pier. It is popular in the summer for surfing and swimming.

★ **Pismo State Beach** ④

Known primarily for its clams *(see pp206–7)*, the beach's compact sand also makes a perfect surface for volleyball.

0 kilometers   20

0 miles   20

MONTEREY

• San Simeon

SALINAS
KING CITY

Morro Rock

• San Luis Obispo

• Pismo Beach

• Santa Maria

La Purísima
Concepción Mis!

Lompoc •

Point Concepción

La Purísima Concepción Mission, the 11th mission in the chain *(see pp42–3), is situated in Lompoc Valley (see p207). La Purísima is the most fully reconstructed of the missions. A visit gives a real insight into the Franciscans' living conditions.*

Morro Rock *is one of South Central California's most endearing landmarks. Used as a navigation point by the first Spanish explorers, it is best seen at sunrise or sunset* (see p206).

LOCATOR MAP

William R Hearst Memorial State Beach ①

Situated below Hearst Castle™ *(see pp202–5)*, this sheltered, crescent-shaped beach is a good spot for a picnic. Boats can be chartered from the pier for deep-sea fishing trips.

Montana de Oro State Park ②

The rocky beach is backed by 8,000 acres (3,250 ha) of park. Hiking trails wind through the hills and, in winter, monarch butterflies can be seen in the eucalyptus trees *(see p209)*.

★ East Beach ⑦

This sandy beach stretches for 1.5 miles (2.5 km) from Stearns Wharf, Santa Barbara's fishing pier. Children will enjoy the playground and paddling pool.

Gaviota State Park ⑤

This 5.5-mile (9-km) beach, in a sheltered cove, has a playground and fishing pier. It adjoins 2,800 acres (1,100 ha) of parkland with hiking trails.

El Capitan State Beach ⑥

El Capitan is a good place for spotting wildlife, both in the rock pools along the beach and in the woods behind. Gray whales pass close to the shore during the winter *(see p580)*.

Carpinteria State Beach ⑧

Backed by the Santa Ynez Mountains, this sheltered beach is one of the safest and most pleasant places to swim in Southern California.

Point Mugu State Park ⑩

At the western end of the Santa Monica Mountains, the park is crisscrossed with hiking trails. Dolphins and California sea lions are often seen offshore.

Leo Carrillo State Beach North ⑪

This stretch of Leo Carrillo State Beach *(see p60)*, which extends across the LA County border, is one of the classic spots for surfing in California.

★ San Buenaventura State Beach ⑨

Close to the center of Ventura *(see p214)*, this broad beach is sheltered by the harbor breakwater, making it a good area for swimming.

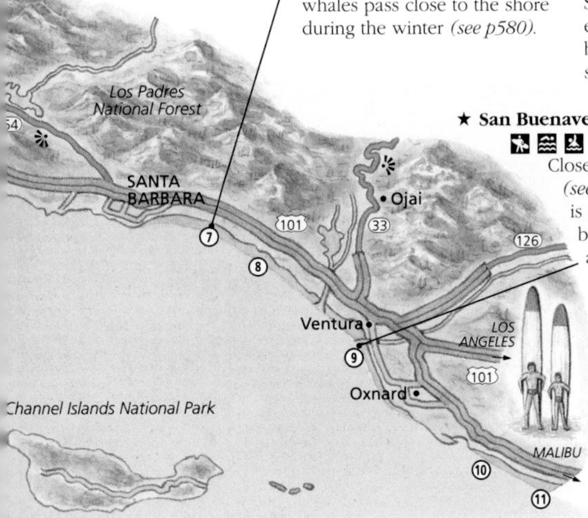

Los Padres National Forest

SANTA BARBARA

Ojai

101 33 126

7

8

Ventura

9

Oxnard

101

LOS ANGELES

MALIBU

10

11

Channel Islands National Park

KEY

▬▬	Freeway
▬▬	Major road
▬▬	Minor road
▭▭	River
✲	Viewpoint

Arched colonnade at the Mission San Miguel Arcángel

Mission San Miguel Arcángel ❶

801 Mission St, San Miguel.
Road map B5. 🛈 (805) 467-3256.
🕐 8:30am–4:30pm daily. ⚫ Jan 1,
Easter, Thanksgiving, Dec 25. 🚻

T HE 16TH MISSION in the
Californian chain (see
pp42–3) was founded
in 1797 by Father
Fermín de Lasuén, the
successor to Father
Junípero Serra (see p42).
Nine years later the original
church was destroyed by fire
and the present building,
which is still in use as
a parish church, was
completed in 1819.

The six rooms in the
mission's museum are
furnished as they would
have been in the early 19th
century. The first contains a
16th-century carved wooden
statue depicting the mission's
patron saint, St. Michael the
Archangel, vanquishing the
devil. The wall decorations in
the church were painted by
Native Americans in 1822–3,
under the direction of Esteban
Munras of Monterey.

In addition to growing grain
and raising cattle, the padres
made their own sacramental
wine. Today the surrounding
hills shelter over 30 wineries.

Following secularization in
1834, the mission was used as
a warehouse and bar. In 1928
it was returned to the padres,
and restoration was begun.
Today it functions as a retreat
center and Franciscan novitiate.

Hearst Castle™ ❷

See pp202–205.

Cambria ❸

Road map B5. 🏠 5,000. 🚌
🛈 767 Main St. 🛈 (805) 927-3624.

S ITUATED BETWEEN rugged seashore and pine-clad hills,
Cambria began as a mercury
mining settlement in 1866.
Later it became a center for
dairy farming and lumber
production, and today it is a
popular location for artists
and craftspeople.

The town is divided into two
distinct districts: East Village,
a charming colony of Arts
and Crafts houses (see p27),
and West Village, which is
more modern. Main Street,
which joins the two, is lined
with specialty shops, art
galleries, and restaurants as
well as Lull House, Cambria's
oldest residence.

Among the houses
on Hillcrest Drive, just
north of Main Street,
is Nit Wit Ridge. It
was built by local
contractor Art Beal,
who was known as
"Captain Nit Wit." This
whimsical abode was
fashioned over
six decades, start-
ing in the 1930s,
out of salvaged
material, from sea
shells to old tires.

**Statue of St. Michael
the Archangel**

To the north of the town, on
Moonstone Drive, at the edge

of the ocean, is the beautiful
Leffingwell Landing, which
offers excellent views of the
crashing surf and occasionally
the sea lions, whales, and
otters out at sea. At low tide it
is also possible to climb down
to the rock pools at the bottom
of the cliffs. The area is also
well equipped for picnickers.

Paso Robles ❹

Road map B5. 🏠 21,000. 🚌
🛈 1225 Park St. 🛈 (805) 238 - 0506.

P ASO ROBLES, or "Pass of the
Oaks," was once part of
the 26,000-acre (10,500-ha) El
Paso de Robles ranch. In 1857,
a sulfurous hot spring, long
used by Indians for its curative
powers, was transformed into
a health resort. With the arrival
of the Southern Pacific railroad
to the area in 1886, the town
quickly developed and was
incorporated three years later.

Today, Paso Robles is ringed
with horse ranches, vineyards,
wineries, and more than 5,000
acres (2,000 ha) of almond
orchards that bloom in early
spring. The hot springs have
now been capped – they were
polluting the Salinas River –
but the town still has much to
offer. On Vine Street, between
12th and 20th streets, are several restored buildings from the
1890s, including **Call-Booth
House Gallery**. Here works
by mainly local artists are displayed in a Victorian setting.

Some of Paso Robles' many
restaurants are also located in

Nit Wit Ridge in Cambria, made out of junk

Wine festival at the Arciero Winery in Paso Robles

19th-century buildings: Berardi & Sons was once the home of the town's daily newspaper; McLee's Steak House, with its huge stained-glass windows, was formerly a church; and Touch of Paso occupies a former post house on the Overland Stage Company route.

The Paso Robles Inn and Gardens, at 1003 Spring Street, stands on the site of the 1860 Hot Springs Hotel. The latter was replaced in 1891 with a three-story redbrick hotel designed by Stanford White. This building in turn was burned down in a fire in 1940. Visitors to the town may wander through the current hotel's landscaped gardens.

Two important events on Paso Robles' calendar are the California Mid-State Fair – a large agricultural and livestock fair in early August with a reputation for top entertainment – and the Wine Festival in May, during which visitors can sample wines from more than 20 vineyards in the surrounding area.

ENVIRONS: Situated 17 miles (27 km) northwest of Paso Robles, off County Road G14, **Lake Naciemento** is a local recreational spot. Set in a picturesque valley amid pine and oak trees, the lake offers fishing (bass and catfish are often caught here), camping, water sports, and picnicking.

At the second junction of Hwy 46 and Hwy 41, 24 miles (39 km) east of Paso Robles, is the **James Dean Monument**. Set around a tree of heaven, it is a memorial to the film actor who died here, at the age of 24, when he crashed his silver Porsche 550 Spider on September 30, 1955. A metal plaque gives details of James Dean's short life.

🏛 Call-Booth House Gallery
1315 Vine St. 📞 (805) 238-5473. ⬜ Wed–Sun. ⬤ public hols. 📷

Atascadero ❺

Road map B5. 🏠 25,300.
🚆 San Luis Obispo. 🚌 Dial-A-Ride (805 466-7433). 📧 ℹ 6550 El Camino Real (805 466-2044).

ATASCADERO, which means "muddy place" in Spanish, was founded in 1913 by the publisher Edward G Lewis, who bought the 23,000-acre (9,300-ha) ranch to build his ideal town. Lewis's headquarters were in an attractive Italian Renaissance-style building, constructed in 1914 for almost half a million dollars. Since then it has been used as a boy's school and a veterans' memorial. Today it houses the City Administration Building. The **Atascadero Historical Society Museum**, situated in the first floor rotunda, houses hundreds of photographs that were taken by Lewis's official photographer. The museum also contains artifacts that belonged to early settlers in the area. The building is set in the lovely Sunken Gardens Park, surrounded by fountains and statuary.

Unfortunately, Lewis went bankrupt before Atascadero was finished. The town continued to grow steadily from the 1950s, however, as more people were attracted by its rural atmosphere. It was incorporated in 1979.

Today's visitors frequent the town's antique shops, stylish boutiques, and its weekly farmers' market. There is a week-long Colony Days celebration in October, when the town remembers its early history with a parade and other festivities.

Just south of the town, off Hwy 41, Atascadero Park and Lake has pleasant walks and offers fishing, picnic areas, and a children's playground. Next door, the 3-acre (1-ha) **Charles Paddock Zoo** houses more than 100 animal species, including monkeys, meerkats, grizzly bears, a pair of tigers, and a jaguar.

🏛 Atascadero Historical Society Museum
6500 Palma Ave. 📞 (805) 466-8341. ⬜ 1–4pm Mon–Sat. ⬤ public hols. **Donation**.

✳ Charles Paddock Zoo
9100 Morro Rd, Atascadero. 📞 (805) 461-5080. ⬜ daily. ⬤ Thanksgiving, Dec 25. 📷

Ducks swimming on Atascadero Lake

Hearst Castle™ ❷

Tile detail

Ⓗ EARST CASTLE™ perches on a hill above the village of San Simeon. The private playground and museum of media tycoon William Randolph Hearst is today one of California's top tourist attractions. Its three guest houses are superb buildings in their own right, but the highlight of the tour is the twin-towered Casa Grande. Designed by the Paris-trained architect Julia Morgan and built in stages from 1922 to 1947, its 115 rooms hold many artworks and epitomize the glamour of the 1930s and 1940s.

Façade
Casa Grande's poured concrete façade is in the Mediterranean Revival style. It is embellished with ancient architectural fragments.

Theater
The walls of Hearst's private cinema are lined with damask. Lamps held by gilded caryatids light the 50 seats.

★ Billiard Room
This room features a French early 16th-century millefleurs tapestry.

TIMELINE

	1920	1930	1940	1950
1865 George Hearst buys 48,000 acres (19,425 ha) of land near San Simeon	**1921** Casa del Mar completed **1924** Casa del Sol completed		*16th-century wooden chest, depicting Christ Meeting St. Peter on the lid* **1951** Hearst dies	**1958** Hearst Castle™ opens to public
1919 WR Hearst inherits family fortune. Plans a house on "Camp Hill"	**1922** Work begins on Casa Grande	**1928** Hearst moves into Casa Grande **1935** Neptune Pool completed	**1947** Hearst has heart attack and leaves San Simeon	*Classical Greek amphora dating from 3rd century AD*

★ **Gothic Study**
When in San Simeon, Hearst ran his empire from the Gothic Study. He kept his books behind grilles.

VISITORS' CHECKLIST

750 Hearst Castle Rd. **Road map** B5. [(805) 927-2020; 800-444-4445. ⟶ to San Simeon ◯ 8am–4pm daily. ● Jan 1, Thanksgiving, Dec 25. 🖉 📷 ♿ call ahead. 🚻 🎫 obligatory. W www.hearstcastle.org

Celestial Suite
The two Celestial Suite bedrooms are located high up in the north and south towers. They are linked by a spacious sitting room.

★ **Assembly Room**
A 16th-century French fireplace dominates the Assembly Room. Italian choir stalls line the walls, which are hung with Flemish tapestries.

Main entrance

★ **Refectory**
Tapestries, choir stalls, and colorful banners cover the walls of the massive dining hall. Its long tables are decorated with silver candlesticks and serving dishes.

STAR FEATURES

★ **Assembly Room**

★ **Billiard Room**

★ **Gothic Study**

★ **Refectory**

Exploring Hearst Castle™

Statue of Victory

Visitors to Hearst Castle™ must take one of four guided tours, all of which start from the Visitors' Center. Tour One is recommended for first-time visitors. It includes the ground floor of Casa Grande, one of the guest houses, both pools, and part of the gardens. Other tours cover the upper floors of the main house. During the spring and autumn, evening tours of the estate feature actors or "guests" in 1930s costume.

Hearst's private movie theater. Here, up to 50 guests would watch film premieres. The screen could be removed, revealing a small stage, where famous actors and actresses would sometimes put on plays.

The exquisite heated indoor Roman Pool, entirely covered in mosaics of hammered gold and Venetian glass, was a popular choice for romantic assignations, despite Hearst's disapproval of such activities.

The house was continually being renovated or rebuilt in accordance with Hearst's ever-changing ideas. One supporting wall was moved at great cost to make room for a bowling alley that was never built. With scores of bedrooms and bathrooms, two pools, and a theater, Casa Grande was a gilded playhouse for the many visitors who came here.

Gold and glass décor of the Roman Pool

CASA GRANDE: THE BIG HOUSE

LA CASA GRANDE is built from reinforced concrete to withstand California's earthquakes. However, it has been designed to look like a masonry cathedral in the Mediterranean Revival style.

Houseguests stayed in one of 22 bedrooms, surrounded by works from the magnate's eclectic art collection. Hearst himself lived in the third-floor Gothic Suite. His bedroom was decorated with a 14th-century Spanish ceiling and a renowned *Madonna and Child* from the School of Duccio di Buoninsegna (c.1255–1318). A sitting room with ocean views linked it to Marion Davies' bedroom.

Across the hall, the Gothic Study housed Hearst's most prized books and manuscripts. It was from this room that he directed his media empire.

The Assembly Room, on the ground floor, was designed around a massive 16th-century French fireplace. It came from the d'Anglure family's Château

des Jours in Burgundy. The high-ceilinged Refectory Room, next door, features a medieval dining table, cathedral seats, and flagstones from Siena. Guests at Hearst Castle™ were required to attend their late evening meals here.

The Billiard Room, with its Spanish Gothic ceiling, showcases an early 16th-century millefleurs tapestry of a stag hunt. Adjoining this room is

THE GROUNDS AND NEPTUNE POOL

HEARST TRANSFORMED the barren California hillside into a veritable Garden of Eden. Fan palms 15 ft (4.5 m) high, fully-grown Italian cypresses, and enormous 200-year-old oaks were hauled up the dirt road at great expense.

Massive loads of topsoil were brought up to create flowerbeds for the 127 acres (51 ha) of gardens. Five greenhouses supplied colorful plants

WILLIAM RANDOLPH HEARST

The son of a multimillionaire, WR Hearst (1863–1951) was an ebullient personality who made his own fortune in magazine and newspaper publishing. He married Millicent Willson, an entertainer from New York, in 1903. On his mother's death in 1919, Hearst inherited the San Simeon property. He began to build the castle and grounds as a tribute to his mother. On moving in, he installed his mistress, actress Marion Davies. The couple entertained royally at San Simeon over the next 20 years. When Hearst suffered problems with his heart in 1947, he moved to a house in Beverly Hills, where he died in 1951.

Portrait of WR Hearst, age 31

throughout the year. To hide a water tank on the adjoining hill, 6,000 Monterey pines were planted in holes blasted out of the rock. An additional 4,000 fruit trees were planted on the estate, providing an abundance of fresh fruit.

Ancient and modern statues were collected to adorn the terraces. Among the finest are four statues of Sekhmet, the Egyptian goddess of war. The oldest works at San Simeon, they date from 1350–1200 BC.

The *pièce de résistance* of the grounds is the 104-ft (32-m) long Neptune Pool. Made in white marble, it is flanked by colonnades and the façade of a reproduction Greek temple. The latter is made from ancient columns and decorated with authentic friezes. The statues around the pool were carved in the 1920s by Charles-George Cassou, a Parisian sculptor.

A great lover of the outdoors, Hearst had a 1-mile (1.6-km) long covered bridlepath built, so that he could ride in all weathers. Two tennis courts were also constructed on top of the indoor Roman Pool.

Hearst had a private zoo on "Camp Hill." The remains of enclosures can still be seen where lions, bears, elephants, pumas, and leopards were once kept. Giraffes, ostriches, zebras, and even a baby elephant were free to wander the grounds.

JULIA MORGAN

Julia Morgan, the architect of San Simeon, was 47 when she began her 30-year collaboration with Hearst. One of the first women graduates of engineering at the University of California, Berkeley, Morgan was the first woman to receive a certificate in architecture from the Ecole Nationale et Spéciale des Beaux-Arts in Paris. She was a multitalented architect and artist – she designed almost every aspect of Hearst Castle™, from tiles and windows to swim-

Julia Morgan (1872–1957)

ming pools and fountains – and a rigorous supervisor of the project's many contractors and artisans. Her relationship with Hearst was based on mutual respect but was often tempestuous. After spending long hours together finalizing a plan, Hearst would often telegraph Morgan with changes.

Tiered façade of Casa del Sol

THE GUEST HOUSES

UNTIL THE MID-1920s, when Casa Grande became ready for occupancy, Hearst lived in the 19-room Casa del Mar, the largest of the three guest houses. He enjoyed his years in the smaller house, but on viewing the completed Casa Grande admitted, "If I had known it would be so big, I would have made the little buildings bigger." The "little buildings," however, are mansions in their own right.

Casa del Sol is built on three levels and has 18 rooms. It features views of the sunset and has a broad terrace with a tall fountain topped with a cast bronze copy of *David* by Donatello. The smallest of the houses, Casa del Monte, faces the hills and has ten rooms.

Neptune Pool, flanked by colonnades and a reproduction Greek temple façade

Fishing boats encircling Morro Rock in Morro Bay

Morro Bay ❻

Road map B5. 🏔 *10,000.* 🚌 *Dial-A-Ride (805 772-2744).* 🚐 ℹ️ *880 Main St (805 772-4467).*

THIS SEASIDE PORT was founded in 1870 to ship produce from the area's cattle-ranching and dairy-farming businesses. Today, tourism has become the town's main industry, and the waterfront is lined with galleries, shops, an aquarium, and seafood restaurants. Whale-watching trips, bay cruises, and a commercial fishing fleet also operate from here. A redwood stairway, celebrating the town's 100th birthday, descends from a stone pelican at clifftop level down to the Embarcadero where a giant chessboard sports redwood pieces up to 33 inches (84 cm) tall. The view from Black Hill Lookout is worth the hike from the parking lot to the top of the mountain.

The bay's principal feature is Morro Rock, a dome-shaped 576-ft (175-m) high volcanic peak – one of nine in the area. Named "El Moro" by Juan Cabrillo in 1542, who thought it resembled a Moor's turban, it was connected to the mainland by a causeway in 1933. Between 1880 and 1969 it was used as a quarry, and a million ton of rock were blasted away to construct breakwaters up and down the coast.

Today, Morro Rock is a wildlife preserve housing nests of peregrine falcons. You can drive to Coleman Park at the rock's base, which is a highly popular fishing spot.

San Luis Obispo ❼

Road map B5. 🏔 *43,000.* ✈️ *San Luis Obispo.* 🚐 🚌 ℹ️ *1037 Mill St, (805 541-8000).*

THIS SMALL CITY, situated in a valley in the Santa Lucia Mountains, developed around the **San Luis Obispo Mission de Tolosa**. The mission was founded on September 1, 1772, by Father Junípero Serra *(see p42).* Fifth in the chain of 21 missions built by the Franciscan Order, and one of the wealthiest, it is still in use as a parish church. Beside the church, the mission's museum displays Chumash Indian artifacts, such as baskets, vessels, and jewelry; the padre's bed; and the mission's original altar.

In front of the church is Mission Plaza, a landscaped public square bisected by a tree-lined creek. During the 1860s, bullfights and bear-baiting took place in the park; today it is the site of many of the city's less bloody events.

Just west of the plaza, at 800 Palm Street, is the Ah Louis Store. Founded in 1874 by a Chinese cook and railroad laborer *(see pp46–7),* Ah Louis became the center of a then thriving Chinatown, and served as a post office, bank, and general store. It is still owned by the Louis family, but it is now a gift shop.

🏛 **San Luis Obispo Mission de Tolosa**
751 Palm St. 📞 *(805) 781-8220.* 🕐 *9am–4pm daily.* ⬤ *Jan 1, Easter, Thanksgiving, Dec 25.*

Pismo Beach ❽

Road map B5. 🏔 *8,700.* ✈️ *San Luis Obispo.* 🚐 *San Luis Obispo.* 🚌 ℹ️ *581 Dolliver St (805 773-4382).*

PISMO BEACH is famous for the Pismo clam. At the turn of the century up to 40,000 clams were harvested per day. In 1911 harvesters were limited to 200 clams per person; now,

Pismo Beach, backed by rolling hills

with a license, they may pick only ten. A clam festival is held in Pismo Beach every autumn.

The town's beach *(see p198)* stretches south for 8 miles (13 km) to the Santa Maria River. It offers campsites, boating, fishing, and picnic facilities. The sand is firmly compacted, so cars are allowed onto the beach via ramps at Grand Avenue in Grover Beach and Pier Avenue in Oceano.

Extensive sand dunes shelter birdlife, sagebrush, wildflowers, verbena, and other seashore plants along with the occasional foxes, rabbits and coyotes. Shell mounds in the dunes, especially near Arroyo Grande Creek, identify sites where Chumash Indians once lived.

During the 1930s and 1940s the dunes were the center of a cult of artists, nudists, and mystics. Filmmakers have also been drawn to these sands, which have been compared to the Sahara Desert. One of the many movies made here is *The Sheik* (1921) starring silent screen idol Rudolph Valentino *(see p108)*.

Lompoc Valley ❾

Road map B5. ✈ *Santa Barbara.* 🚌 *Lompoc.* 🛈 *111 S I St, Lompoc (805 736-4567).*

Lompoc valley is one of the world's major producers of flower seed. The hills and flower fields surrounding the valley are a blaze of color between late spring and midsummer. Among the varieties grown are marigolds, sweet peas, asters, lobelia, larkspur,

DUNE ECOLOGY

Coastal dunes are the product of wind and, surprisingly, plants. Just above the high-tide line, dry sand is stabilized by sea lettuce. Behind it, beach grass and silver lupine trap more sand, creating small hummocks held in place by the plants' roots. Lupine compost mixes with the sand to produce soil, allowing other plants, such as dune buckwheat and haplopapus, to move in and overcome the lupine itself. Eventually, ice plant, verbena, and morning glory take root in the sandy soil. The plants provide food and protection for a broad range of insects and animals, from sand wasps and beetles to Jerusalem crickets and tiny mice. Most beach wildlife depends on the dew that drops from these plants into the sand below. If part of the fragile plant cover is destroyed by storms, high winds, or people, sand is dispersed farther inland, and a new dune is formed.

Ice plant growing among the coastal sand dunes

nasturtiums, and cornflowers. A map of the flower fields in the area is distributed by the town of Lompoc's Chamber of Commerce. The Civic Center Plaza, between Ocean Avenue and C Street, has a display garden in which all the many flowers are identified.

La Purísima Concepción Mission, 3 miles (5 km) northeast of the town, was the 11th mission to be founded in California. It was declared a State Historic Park during the 1930s. The early 19th-century buildings have now been sympathetically reconstructed, and the complex and grounds provide a real insight into the missionary way of life.

Visitors to the mission are able to view the priests' living quarters, furnished with authentic pieces, in the elegant residence building. The simple, narrow church is decorated with colorful stencilwork. In the adjacent workshops, cloth, candles, leather goods, and furniture were at one time produced for the mission.

La Purísima's gardens have been faithfully restored. The varieties of fruit, vegetables, and herbs that are grown here were all common in the 19th century. Visitors can also view the system that provided the mission with water.

🏠 **La Purísima Concepción Mission**
2295 Purísima Rd, Lompoc. 📞 *(805) 733-3713.* 🕐 *9am–5pm daily.* ⬤ *Jan 1, Thanksgiving, Dec 25.* 🖼

La Purísima Concepción Mission in Lompoc Valley

Tour of the Santa Ynez Valley Wineries ⑩

Local wine

SANTA YNEZ VALLEY is one of the newest and most distinctive wine regions in the state. The area is prone to coastal fog, which produces microclimates according to shifts in altitude and distance from the sea. The area also has a longer growing season than Northern California. These unique conditions, coupled with varied soils, produce a selection of classic grape varieties.

Tips for Drivers

Tour length: *30 miles (48 km).*
Stopping-off points: *Los Olivos Café* (*see p551*) *is a pleasant place to stop for lunch. You can buy picnic fare or a packed basket at the café's deli. The wineries all have picnic areas where you can enjoy a local wine with your meal.*

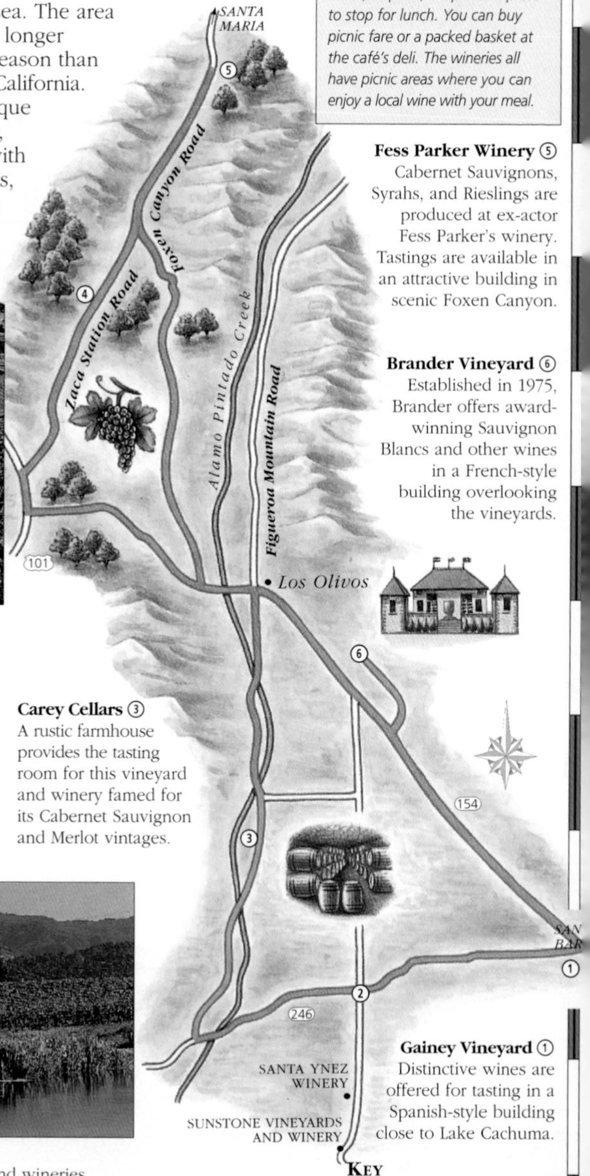

Fess Parker Winery ⑤
Cabernet Sauvignons, Syrahs, and Rieslings are produced at ex-actor Fess Parker's winery. Tastings are available in an attractive building in scenic Foxen Canyon.

Brander Vineyard ⑥
Established in 1975, Brander offers award-winning Sauvignon Blancs and other wines in a French-style building overlooking the vineyards.

Firestone Vineyard ④
The largest producer in the region presents distinctive Rieslings, Chardonnays, and Merlots in a large tasting room adjoining the winery.

Carey Cellars ③
A rustic farmhouse provides the tasting room for this vineyard and winery famed for its Cabernet Sauvignon and Merlot vintages.

Santa Ynez ②
Among the vineyards and wineries surrounding this town are the Santa Ynez Winery and the Sunstone Vineyards and Winery.

Gainey Vineyard ①
Distinctive wines are offered for tasting in a Spanish-style building close to Lake Cachuma.

0 kilometers 2
0 miles 2

Key
Tour route
Other roads

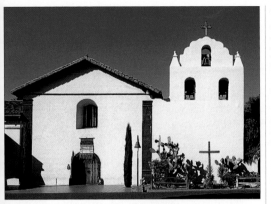

Mission Santa Inés church façade and campanile

Solvang ⑪

Road map C5. 👥 5,000. 🚌
ℹ 1511-A Mission Drive (805 688-6144).

THIS SCANDINAVIAN-STYLE town was established in 1911 by a group of Danish educators. They paid $360,000 for 9,000 acres (3,650 ha) of mustard and bean fields on which to build a Danish colony and school. The original schoolhouse, a two-story frame structure on Alisal Road, is no longer standing, having been replaced by the Bit o' Denmark Restaurant. Solvang's Bethnania Lutheran church, built in 1928 to a traditional Danish design, has a model sailing ship hanging from its ceiling. Visitors can tour the town in a horse-drawn streetcar, the *honen* (hen), and see windmills, chimneys with artificial storks, and gas streetlights. Beer gardens serve *aebleskiver* (a type of Danish pastry), during the town's Danish Days festival in September (*see p34*).

Mission Santa Inés ⑫

1760 Mission Drive, Solvang. Road map C5. 📞 (805) 688-4815. 🕐 daily. 🌙 Easter, Thanksgiving, Dec 25. ♿

FOUNDED ON September 17, 1804, Santa Inés was the 19th in the chain of California missions (*see pp42–3*). In 1812 an earthquake destroyed the larger part of the church. It was rebuilt with 5-ft (1.5-m) thick walls and rededicated five years later. Before secularization in 1834 the mission was prosperous, with a herd of 12,000 cattle; afterward, it fell into disrepair and most of the Native Americans left. In 1843, the mission became the site of the state's first seminary. Restoration work began after World War II, including the campanile (financed by WR Hearst, *see p204*) and the church sanctuary. The mission also has a small museum, with period furnishings, parchment books, the vestments worn by early priests, and original murals by Native Americans. There is a landscaped garden.

Statue of the Madonna

Chumash Painted Cave State Historic Park ⑬

Painted Cave Road. 📞 (805) 968-1033. 🚌 from Santa Barbara. Parking limited to 2 vehicles.

IN THE Santa Ynez Mountains, 8 miles (13 km) to the northwest of Santa Barbara, are a number of remote and scattered caves with Chumash drawings or pictographs. The most famous example is a 20 by 40 ft (6 by 12 m) cave just off Hwy 154. Inside, an egg-shaped cavity, covered in small ocher scratchings, is protected by a metal screen.

Some caves have primitive drawings that resemble lizards, snakes, and scorpions, executed in red, black, or white paint. Tribes are known to have traded different pigments with each other. Some experts believe the drawings are symbolic of the Chumash religion; others think they are random, with no significant meaning.

Native American paintings in the Chumash caves

MONARCH BUTTERFLIES

Each year millions of monarch butterflies migrate from the western US and Canada to winter in Southern and Central California and Mexico. Starting their journey in October and November, the butterflies cover up to 80 miles (130 km) a day at speeds approaching 30 mph (50 km/h). Along the central coast, they usually settle in eucalyptus groves. After the mating season in January and February, the butterflies attempt the journey back to their summer habitat. In season they can often be seen around Montana de Oro State Park (*see p199*), Pismo Beach, and Ventura.

Monarch butterfly

Street-by-Street: Santa Barbara ⓮

SANTA BARBARA is a Southern Californian rarity: a city with a single architectural style. Following a devastating earthquake in 1925, the center was rebuilt according to strict rules that dictated Mediterranean-style architecture. The city was founded as a Spanish garrison in 1782 – four years before Santa Barbara Mission *(see pp212–13)*. During the 19th century Santa Barbara was a quiet pueblo, home to only a few hundred families and a center for the nearby cattle ranches. Remarkably, about a dozen adobes from that era have survived. Today, Santa Barbara is a quiet administrative center with a large student population, which lends an informal feel to the city.

Fountain outside the County Courthouse

To Santa Barbara Mission

★ Museum of Art
This outstanding regional art collection includes Asian art, antiquities, American art, prints, drawings, and photography. In the 19th-century French section is Jules Bastien-Lepage's The Ripened Wheat (1884).

★ County Courthouse
The 1929 Spanish Colonial-style courthouse is still in use. It is decorated with Tunisian tiles and wrought-iron metalwork. Murals by DS Groesbeck in the Assembly Room depict California history (see p38). There are panoramic views from the clock tower.

KEY

— — — Suggested route

STAR SIGHTS

★ County Courthouse

★ Museum of Art

★ Presidio

Paseo Nuevo
This colorful outdoor shopping and dining center complements an older arcade on the opposite side of State Street.

★ **Presidio**
Santa Barbara's Presidio was built in 1782 by the Spanish. It was the last in a chain of four fortresses erected along the California coast.

The Cañedo Adobe once housed soldiers and families from the Presidio.

El Cuartel is the Presidio's family living quarters.

Lobero Theater
This graceful 1924 building stands on the site of the city's original theater, which was built in 1873 by Jose Lobero, an Italian musician.

STREET

SANTA BARBARA STREET

STREET

NON PERDIDO STREET

DE LA GUERRA STREET

STATE STREET

ORTEGA STREET

To East Beach

Historical Museum
The Historical Society's collections are housed in two adobe buildings. Among the many artifacts is a statue of the 4th-century martyr St. Barbara.

0 meters	100
0 yards	100

Santa Barbara Mission

Lₐᵦₑₗₑ𝒹 ᴛʜᴇ "Queen of the Missions," Santa Barbara is the most visited mission in the state. Founded in 1786 on the feast day of St. Barbara, it was the tenth mission built by the Spanish *(see pp42–3)*. After the third adobe church on the site was destroyed by an earth-quake in 1812, the present structure took shape and was completed in 1833. Its twin towers and mix of Roman, Moorish, and Spanish styles served as the main inspiration for what came to be known as Mission Style *(see p26)*. The mission was again hit by an earthquake in 1925, damaging the towers and façade of the church. These sections were repaired but, because of a chemical reaction between the alkalies and aggregates in the cement, the entire front had to be rebuilt in 1953, following the original design. Santa Barbara is the only California mission to have been in continuous use since it was founded.

Franciscan monk

Central Fountain
Palm trees tower above a central fountain in the Sacred Gardens.

A missionary's bedroom has been furnished as it would have been in the early 1800s.

Entrance

Arcaded Corridor
An open corridor fronts the museum rooms. Originally the living quarters, these now display a rich collection of mission artifacts.

Kitchen
The kitchen has been restored to show the typical cooking facil-ities of the early 1800s. Most of the food eaten was produced on the mission, which had fields and livestock.

STAR FEATURES
★ Church
★ Main Façade
★ Sacred Gardens

★ **Sacred Gardens**
The beautifully landscaped Sacred Gardens were once a working area for Native Americans to learn Western trades. Workshops and some living quarters were located in the surrounding buildings.

VISITORS' CHECKLIST

2201 Laguna St. 📞 *(805) 682-4713.* 🚌 *22.* 🕐 *9am–5pm daily.* **Donation.** ✝ *7:30am Mon–Fri; 4pm Sat; 7:30am, 9am, 10:30am, noon Sun.* 📷 ♿ 🚻

★ **Church**
The narrow church has a Neo-Classical interior. Imitation marble columns and detailing have been painted on the walls and doorways. The reredos has a painted canvas backdrop and carved wooden statues.

The side chapel, next to the altar, is dedicated to the Blessed Sacrament.

The width of the nave was determined by the height of the trees used as cross beams.

The cemetery garden contains the graves of some 4,000 Native Americans as well as friars.

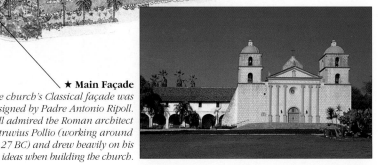

★ **Main Façade**
The church's Classical façade was designed by Padre Antonio Ripoll. Ripoll admired the Roman architect Vitruvius Pollio (working around 27 BC) and drew heavily on his ideas when building the church.

San Buenaventura Mission's church in Ventura

Ventura ⓯

Road map C5. 🏢 102,000. 🚌 ℹ️
89C S California St. 📞 (805) 648-2075.

ALL THAT REMAINS of the **San Buenaventura Mission**, founded in 1782 and completed in 1809, is a church with a courtyard garden and tiled fountain. A museum at the mission details the buildings of the original complex.

Two mid-19th-century adobe houses survive in the city. The tiny **Ortega Adobe** reveals the harsh living conditions many experienced at that time. In contrast, the Monterey-style *(see p26)* **Olivas Adobe** is a two-story ranch hacienda, furnished in period style, with rose and herb gardens.

Today Ventura is largely an agricultural center. Ventura Harbor Village has 30 stores, restaurants, a merry-go-round, and a community theater. Harbor and whale-watching cruises, as well as boats to the Channel Islands National Park depart from here.

On a hillside at the northern end of town, the **City Hall** (1913) has a copper-covered dome and marble exterior.

🏛 **San Buenaventura Mission**
211 E Main St. 📞 (805) 643-4318.
◯ daily. ● Jan 1, Easter, Thanksgiving, Dec 25.
🏛 **Ortega Adobe**
100 W Main St. 📞 (805) 658-4726.
◯ daily. ● Jan 1, Easter Sun, Labor Day, Thanksgiving, Dec 25.
🏛 **Olivas Adobe**
4200 Olivas Park Drive. 📞 (805) 648-5823. **Grounds** ◯ daily.
House ◯ Sat & Sun. ● Jan 1, Easter, Thanksgiving, Dec 25.

Channel Islands National Park ⓰

Road map C6. 🚉 Ventura. 🚌
Visitors' Center 📞 (805) 658-5730.
◯ daily. ⛴ Island Packers, 1867 Spinnaker Drive (805 642-1393).

THE ISLANDS of Santa Barbara, Anacapa, San Miguel, Santa Cruz, and Santa Rosa together make up the Channel Islands National Park, a series of volcanic islands unpopulated by humans. Access to the islands is strictly monitored by park rangers, who issue landing permits from the Visitors' Center. Camping is allowed on all the islands, but visitors must make reservations at least two weeks in advance. They must also bring all their own food and water supplies, because there are none available on any of the five islands.

Depending on the island and the time of year, lucky visitors may spot dolphins, gray whales, and California brown pelicans on the passage across the Santa Barbara Channel. Wildlife on the small, picturesque islands is plentiful and includes cormorants, sea lions, elephant seals, and gulls.

Day trips to Anacapa, the nearest island to the mainland, offer an insight into this unique coastal ecosystem. Even more can be learned, however, by taking one of the various guided walks, conducted by park rangers, on all the islands. Visitors must stay on the designated trails, and pets are not allowed.

The rock pools on all of the islands are rich in marine life, and the kelp forests surrounding the islands provide shelter for more than 1,000 plant and animal species.

The islands' many sea caves make sea-kayaking a unique and exciting experience. The snorkeling and scuba diving in this area are also considered to be among the best on the entire Pacific Coast.

California brown pelican

Ronald Reagan Presidential Library ⓱

40 Presidential Drive, Simi Valley.
Road map C5. 📞 (800) 410-8354.
◯ 10am–5pm daily. ● Jan 1, Thanksgiving, Dec 25. 🚫 ♿
🔳 www.reagan.utex.edu

PRESIDENT REAGAN'S papers are all archived in this Mission Revival-style structure. The library features a permanent exhibition documenting the life of Reagan and his wife, Nancy. There are also temporary exhibitions of gifts, costumes, works of art, and other objects related to his eight-year tenure in the White House. A full-size replica of the Oval Office is correct in every detail, and a large piece of the Berlin Wall, with its original graffiti, can be seen on the patio against the panoramic backdrop of the nearby Simi Hills and the Santa Susana Mountains.

Reconstruction of the Oval Office at the Reagan Presidential Library

Mission Revival arcade on Main Street, Ojai

Ojai ⑱

Road map C5. 🏔 8,000. 🚌 🚇 🛈
150 W Ojai Ave. 📞 (805) 646-8126.

FOUNDED IN 1874, this town was originally called Nordhoff after the author Charles Nordhoff, who wrote a book promoting California in the 1870s. In 1917 the town was renamed Ojai, a Chumash Indian word for moon, a reference to the crescent-shaped valley where the town lies.

Ojai's Mission Revival arched arcade was funded by Edward J Libby, a glass-manufacturing millionaire, and was designed in 1917 by Richard Requa. Its tower was modeled on a campanile in Havana, Cuba. The arcade fronts two blocks of shops on the main street.

Another attraction is Barts Corner bookshop at No. 302 West Matilija Street. Here, 25,000 volumes are displayed, many of them outdoors. Late-night readers can browse and then pay for their finds through a slot in the door.

Spiritual groups have been going on retreats in the Ojai Valley since the 1920s. Today several New Age and religious organizations are based here.

Los Padres National Forest ⑲

Road map C5. 🚌 Santa Barbara.
Visitors' Center 🕐 8:30am–4:30pm
Mon–Fri. 📞 (805) 683-6711.

LOS PADRES National Forest covers almost 2 million acres (810,000 ha) of terrain that varies from desert to pine-clad mountains with peaks as high as 9,000 ft (2,700 m). Black bears, foxes, deer, and mountain lions are among the animals found here. Birds include golden eagles and giant condors. The latter are North America's largest birds with a wingspan of 9 ft (3 m).

Coastal redwood trees grow on the lower slopes, and the higher elevations are thick with firs, bristling with pine cones. Temperatures in the summer can be scorching, and there is very little, if any, rain here between May and October.

The forest is crisscrossed by hundreds of miles of hiking trails for experienced hikers, but there are few roads. Hwy 33 and Hwy 150 are two exceptions. Hwy 154 crosses one corner as it runs between Santa Ynez (see p208) and Santa Barbara (see pp210–13). On the way, it passes over the spectacular Cold Spring Arch Bridge.

Scattered within Los Padres National Forest are 88 camp sites. Activities include fishing, horseback riding, and, on Mount Pinos, skiing.

Bakersfield ⑳

Road map C5. 🏔 384,000. 🚌 🛈
1325 P St. 📞 (661) 325-5051.

BAKERSFIELD WAS NAMED after Colonel Thomas Baker, a settler who planted a field of alfalfa here. The shrub fed the animals of early travelers who rested here before crossing the Tehachapi Mountains, the "border" that divides Northern and Southern California.

Many consider the town to be the final stop on I-5 from San Francisco before the ascent up Grapevine Canyon to LA. However, it can also be reached from Santa Maria or Ojai along minor roads through the Los Padres National Forest.

Bakersfield's modern history began with the discovery of gold in the 1850s and several oil strikes in the following decades. Many people from Mediterranean countries settled on the fertile land, bringing agriculture to the area.

Today it is among the fastest growing cities in California, but still manages to retain a rural feel and is a recognized center for country music. There are also fine restaurants, antique shops, and the **Kern County Museum**, a 16-acre (6.5-ha) outdoor museum.

Bisecting Bakersfield, Kern River is renowned for its white-water rafting and kayaking (see p578). Lake Isabella, 40 miles (65 km) east of the city, is a center for water sports.

🏛 **Kern County Museum**
3801 Chester Ave. 📞 (805) 852-5000. 🕐 daily. 🌑 Jan 1, Thanksgiving, Dec 24, 25, 31. 🗟

Cold Spring Arch Bridge, Los Padres National Forest

ORANGE COUNTY

A CENTURY AGO *Orange County lived up to its name. This dry, sunny land, which stretches from the Santa Ana Mountains to the beautiful Pacific coastline, was indeed scattered with orange orchards and farms. Today, the region is a mass of freeways and suburban housing. Visitors to the county can explore a wide range of museums, sites of historical interest, and entertainment complexes.*

In the mid-1950s, the roads leading to the county's theme parks still passed through extensive orange groves. At that time, Disneyland was attracting its first enthusiastic crowds, and a local boy called Richard Nixon had become Vice President of the US. Today, orange groves have given way to urban development and fruit crate labels have become collectors' items. More than two million people live here, enjoying perennial sunshine and a high standard of living.

The coastline of Orange County is lined with wide, sandy beaches and a succession of legendary surfing haunts, marinas, and artists' enclaves. In the affluent coastal towns, few visitors can resist the temptation to seek out a clifftop bar and watch the sun set.

Inland lies a variety of cultural sights. Mission San Juan Capistrano, founded in 1776, is a reminder of the days of the Spanish Franciscan settlers. The Bowers Museum of Cultural Art in Santa Ana houses superb examples of the art of indigenous peoples from all around the world. At Yorba Linda, the impressive Richard Nixon Library and Birthplace commemorates the life of Orange County's most famous son.

Orange County is the entertainment capital of California. For visitors seeking family fun and roller-coaster thrills, there are the homey Knott's Berry Farm, America's oldest theme park, and the fantasy kingdom of Disneyland, which is, as the saying goes, "the most famous people-trap ever built by a mouse."

Reflecting Pool at the Richard Nixon Library and Birthplace

◁ **Log Ride at Knott's Berry Farm theme park**

Exploring Orange County

MUCH OF ORANGE COUNTY's 798-sq mile (2,050-sq km) area is covered with sprawling urban communities linked by ever-busy freeways. Anaheim, home of Disneyland, is its second largest city, after Santa Ana. The popular Knott's Berry Farm theme park lies a few miles northwest at Buena Park, and together these cities form the tourist capital of the county. Most of the coastline is built-up, but its communities have more variety and character than those around the theme parks. Inland, open spaces can be found where the county's eastern region encompasses part of the vast Cleveland National Forest and the Santa Ana Mountains.

BUENA PARK

Los Angeles

RICHARD NIXON LIBRARY AND BIRTHPLACE

YORBA

Long Beach

LA PALMA AVE

ANAHEIM

KNOTT'S BERRY FARM & ❷
SOAK CITY USA

DISNEYLAND RESORT ❶   ❹ CRYSTAL CATHEDRAL
GARDEN GROVE BLVD

❺

BOWERS MUSEUM OF CULTURAL ART

SANTA ANA

HARBOR BLVD

MAIN STREET

HUNTINGTON BEACH

❻

DISCOVERY MUSEUM

San Diego

IRV

Santa Ana River

NEWPORT BEACH

Catalina Island's Two Harbors

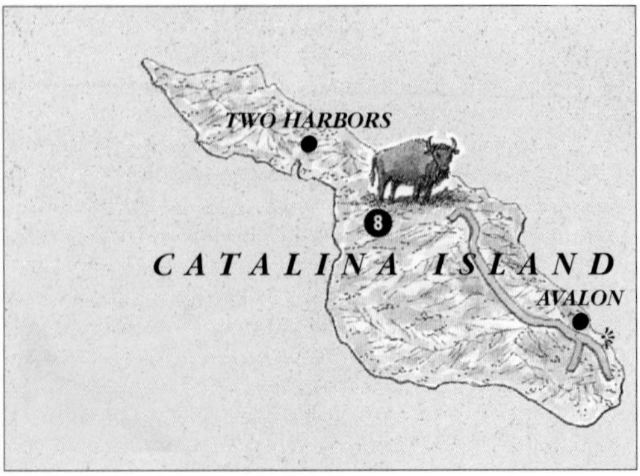

TWO HARBORS

❽

CATALINA ISLAND

AVALON

0 kilometers   5

0 miles   5

KEY

	Freeway
	Major road
	Minor road
	River
☀	Viewpoint

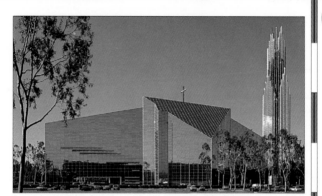

Enormous Crystal Cathedral at Garden Grove, south of Anaheim

SIGHTS AT A GLANCE

Bowers Museum of
  Cultural Art **5**
Catalina Island pp232–3 **8**
Crystal Cathedral **4**
Discovery Museum **6**
Disneyland Resort pp222–5 **1**

*Knott's Berry Farm and Soak
  City pp226–7* **2**
*Mission San Juan Capistrano
  pp230–31* **7**
Richard Nixon Library and
  Birthplace **3**

SEE ALSO

• **Where to Stay** pp516–17

• **Where to Eat** pp553–5

GETTING AROUND

Interstate-5 is a major north–south artery, which links Los Angeles and San Diego. New express toll lanes now operate in an effort to eliminate traffic jams. The more scenic Hwy 1, the Pacific Coastal Highway, unites the coastal resorts. Amtrak *(see p600)* and Metrolink commuter trains run south from Los Angeles. Stops include San Juan Capistrano and Anaheim. Most bus routes are designed to meet the needs of local commuters, but shuttle vans and tour buses offer quick connections to the theme parks and to Los Angeles. Ferries to Catalina Island run daily in summer, but travelers should check schedules in winter. Crossings from the mainland to Avalon or Two Harbors take 1–2 hours.

Orange County Coastline

THE BEACHES AND RESORTS that make up Orange County's coast are Southern California at its most classic. The northern shoreline is flat and low-lying. South of the Balboa Peninsula, the coast features scenic cliffs and sheltered coves. Million-dollar homes, luxury marinas, constant sports activity, and a fashionable lifestyle reflect the wealth and vitality of its communities.

The Balboa Pavilion
opened in 1905 as a terminal for the Pacific Electric Red Car Line from LA. Stars of the Big Band era, such as Count Basie, played here in the 1930s and 1940s. Today the wooden pavilion is a restaurant and center for sightseeing cruises around Newport Harbor.

★ **Huntington State Beach** ③

A premier Californian "surf city." Huntington Beach has a surfing museum, international competitions, and waters full of surfers whose exploits can be watched from the long pier.

Upper Newport Bay Ecological Preserve *is a 750-acre (300-ha) wedge of coastal wetland providing a refuge for wildlife and migratory birds. Facilities in the bay include a bike path, fishing, and guided tours on foot and by kayak.*

KEY

▦	Freeway
▬	Major road
▭	Minor road
▱	River
☀	Viewpoint

Seal Beach ①

This is a quiet, 1-mile (1.6-km) long beach with level sand and some surfers. The wooden pier is popular with anglers. A walk along its 1,865-ft (570-m) length offers views northward to the high-rise buildings of Long Beach *(see pp128–9)*.

Bolsa Chica State Beach ②

The name Bolsa Chica means "little pocket" in Spanish. Flat, wilderness sands, oil extractors, and the protected wetlands of the 300-acre (120-ha) Bolsa Chica Ecological Reserve give this beach a unique atmosphere.

Newport Beach ④

Famous for its million-dollar homes and lifestyles to match, Newport Beach boasts a 3-mile (5-km) stretch of wide sand and two piers. Fresh fish, caught by the historic Dory fishing fleet, is sold beside Newport Pier at the northern end of the beach.

Aliso Beach ⑦

At the mouth of Aliso Creek lies this small, sandy beach. The 620-ft (190-m) long concrete pier is used by anglers. At the southern end of the beach is a marine life refuge with beds of giant kelp offshore.

Doheny State Beach ⑧

This sandy beach and marine life refuge is close to the mouth of San Juan Creek. The beach attracts a typically Southern Californian mix of swimmers, surfers, bird-watchers, anglers, cyclists, and campers.

San Clemente State Beach ⑨

The hillside community of San Clemente has a narrow, sandy beach at its foot. Near the railroad station there is a municipal pier. Farther south, the 100-acre (40-ha) State Beach has landscaped facilities including picnic areas and a camp site.

★ **Corona del Mar State Beach** ⑤

Overlooked by cliffs lined with stylish houses and land-scaped viewpoints, this is a family beach with good swimming, sandy coves, and rock pools to explore.

LOCATOR MAP

NEVADA

CALIFORNIA

Pacific Ocean

0 kilometers 5

0 miles 5

LOS ANGELES

73   405

Upper Newport Bay Ecological Reserve

133

• Corona del Mar

Balboa Pavilion

5

Laguna Beach

⑥

⑦
South Laguna •

Crown Valley Parkway

San Juan Capistrano •

5

①

Dana Point   ⑧

5

San Clemente •

⑨   SAN DIEGO

★ **Laguna Beach** ⑥

With its clifftop promenades, small, sheltered beaches, and artistic community, Laguna courts the atmosphere of the Mediterranean Riviera. The ideal spot for a cocktail at sunset, Laguna is famous for its summer arts festival, the Pageant of the Masters *(see p33)*.

Dana Point *headland is named after the author Richard Dana, whose 1840 book* Two Years Before the Mast *chronicled the early days of California. A replica of the contemporary brig,* Pilgrim, *is moored in the harbor.*

Disneyland® Resort ❶

DISNEY'S "MAGIC KINGDOM" in Anaheim is not only the top tourist attraction in California, it is part of the American Dream. Now encompassing the original Disneyland Park, Disney's California Adventure, Downtown Disney, plus three enormous hotels, the Resort has become the model for theme parks around the globe. Visitors to "The Happiest Place on Earth" find fantasy, thrill rides, glittering shows, and shopping in a brightly orchestrated land of lines, fireworks, and Mickey Mouse, which is as American as apple pie.

Exploring the Resort

Spread over 85 acres (34 ha), the original Disneyland Park is divided into eight theme areas, known as "lands." Transportation around the park is provided by the Disneyland Railroad and monorail. Disney's California Adventure Park has three theme areas *(see p225)*. Smaller in area than Disneyland Park, Disney's California Adventure is easily covered by walking. This newest venture into nostalgia Disney-style is more suited to the interests and tastes of teenagers and young adults, as the rides and attractions may be too intense for toddlers. In the heart of the Resort, between the two theme parks, lies Downtown Disney. This lively area is full of restaurants, shops, and innovative entertainment venues.

It takes at least three days to make the best of a visit, now that the Resort has grown so large. A joint ticket *(see p223)* can be bought for all the theme parks; it provides access to all the rides and shows, and includes a park map, and a schedule of the day's events. Both parks stay open late in the evening during the peak seasons; and the **Fireworks Show** in Disneyland and in Downtown Disney are well worth losing a little sleep for.

MAIN STREET USA

THIS SPOTLESSLY clean, colorful street lined with turn-of-the-century buildings welcomes visitors to Disneyland. The circular **Central Plaza** is where the daily "Parade of the Stars," takes place, featuring cheerfully waving Disney characters and scenes from many of Disney's most famous movies. This is only one of the places where guests can meet and talk with many of the famous Disney cartoon characters. If you're lucky, you can find ample opportunities here for photographs and videos.

City Hall offers maps, dining and entertainment schedules, and general information about the park, while the **Main Street Cinema** screens early Disney silent films. Main Street itself has a large selection of attractions, shops, and places to eat.

TOMORROWLAND

VISIONS OF THE FUTURE inspire the attractions here, and sights change regularly to keep one step ahead of real-life technology and still retain a sense of fantasy. One of the first attractions in 1955 was **Autopia**, now completely redesigned and updated to take guests into a parallel universe from a car's point of view. The track winds through Tomorrowland and Fantasyland.

Star Tours

Designed in collaboration with the *Star Wars* genius George Lucas, the use of flight-simulator technology makes this one of the most realistic rides in the park. Visitors board a Star-Speeder space-ship and are taken on a wild ride through outer space strewn with star-ships, comets, and asteroids.

Space Mountain

A hands-down Disneyland favorite and updated for the Millennium, this attraction provides a high speed roller-coaster ride, 118 ft (36 m) above ground. Conducted almost entirely in darkness, the ride has sudden meteoric flashes, celestial showers, and space-age music. Not suitable for very young children.

MICKEY'S TOONTOWN

THE COLORFUL architecture of cartoons comes to life in this three-dimensional cartoon world, Mickey Mouse's hometown. All of

---

TOP 5 ATTRACTIONS

★ **Pirates of the Caribbean**

★ **Haunted Mansion**

★ **Space Mountain**

★ **Matterhorn Bobsleds**

★ **Star Tours**

SHOPPING

The Disneyland shops, particularly those along Main Street, USA, are often busy late in the day, especially at closing time. If you can, it is worth making your purchases earlier in the day and then collecting them later from the Redemption Center. Although many of the goods on sale in the theme park bear the faces of Disney characters, each of the eight lands adds its own variations to what is on offer to buy. In Adventureland, for example, you can buy Indiana Jones-style clothing and Native American Crafts are on sale in Frontierland. The Disney Gallery in New Orleans Square sells limited-edition lithographs by the Disney cartoonists. The largest of all the shops within the Magic Kingdom is the Emporium in Main Street.

Fairytale facade of Sleeping Beauty Castle in Fantasyland

Disney's favorite animated characters reside here. This is the part of the park where visitors are most likely to find Mickey, Goofy, and other well-known cartoon characters strolling around, having their pictures taken with guests.

The most popular celebrity residences are Mickey's house and Minnie's cottage, where subtle touches typify Disney's legendary attention to detail. Most of the attractions in this area are geared toward kids from age three up. **Chip 'n Dale Treehouse**, a mini-roller coaster, **Goofy's Bounce House**, and a floating bumper-boat ride offer gentle excitement for this younger set.

Roger Rabbit's Car Toon Spin is Toontown's largest and most popular attraction. It's spinning cars provide a madcap taxi drive through a surreal cartoon world fraught with near misses.

FANTASYLAND

DOMINATED BY the pink and gold towers of **Sleeping Beauty Castle** and a replica of the **Matterhorn**, Fantasyland is a shrine to children's dreams and adult nostalgia. Nursery heroes such as Peter Pan, Dumbo, and Snow White provide the themes for gentle fairytale rides in vehicles that range from flying galleons

canal boats and the Mad Hatter's giant spinning teacups. There are almost twice as many attractions to enjoy here as in most of the other lands, and the constant crowds illustrate the enduring appeal of this area.

Matterhorn Bobsleds

This historic attraction and major park landmark has been providing "icy" roller-coaster rides since 1959. A copy of the famous peak near Zermatt in Switzerland, the Matterhorn Mountain towers 147 ft (45 m) above the park. Bobsleds carrying four passengers climb to the mountain's snow-capped summit, then drop into a steep, high-speed descent, zooming in and out of the hollow peak, passing glacier caves and waterfalls as they go. At the end of the trip, riders in the front seats are splashed as the sleds careen into a lake.

It's a Small World

This show offers a Utopian vision of global harmony and the famous song, repeated throughout the ride. Colorful boats transport passengers through the attraction, which features nearly 300 singing-and-dancing Audio-Animatronics dolls, all in intricate national costumes.

TICKETS AND TIPS

A basic one-day ticket to Disneyland or Disney's California Adventure covers admission and most of the rides and attractions. Parking is extra, as are certain shows, food, and arcades. Multi-day tickets for three to four days and Annual Passports allow unlimited admission and access to rides and attractions. Fastpass lets guests obtain a voucher with a computer-assigned boarding time for specific attractions or rides. This eliminates waiting in long lines. You can also save time at the front gate by buying your tickets in advance.at any Disney store or online at www.disney.com. To help you plan your day, there is updated information on showtimes, waiting times and ride closures at the information board at the end of Main St, opposite the Plaza Pavillion.

Mark Twain Riverboat navigating the Rivers of America

FRONTIERLAND

THIS AREA IS INSPIRED by the adventurous days of the Wild West. Skirt-lifting song and dance take place on the **Golden Horseshoe Jamboree** stage. Every weekend at night the spectacular **Fantasmic!** show, complete with fireworks, sound effects, and live performers light up the skies above Frontierland. The **Mark Twain River-boat** offers visitors a 15-minute cruise on a paddle-wheel boat. While it crosses the Rivers of America, look out for the plastic moose and deer inhabiting the forests along the shore and on Tom Sawyer Island.

Thrill-seekers love the **Big Mountain Thunder Railroad** roller-coaster ride. Open ore trucks set off from the 1880s mining town of Big Thunder without a driver. The runaway train then speeds through the cavernous interior of Big Thunder Mountain, narrowly escaping boulders and waterfalls. Remember that this ride has height and age restrictions.

CRITTER COUNTRY

BUILT IN A RUSTIC style, based on the rugged American Northwest, Critter Country is a 4-acre (1.6-ha) area next to Frontierland. Home of Splash Mountain, one of the most popular attractions in Disneyland, and a quiet restaurant, the Hungry Bear.

Splash Mountain
This is a winding, watery ride in hollowed-out logs. Brer Rabbit and Brer Fox are among the furry, singing characters from the 1946 film *Song of the South*, who inhabit the mountain through which the ride passes. The ride culminates in a plummet down a steep waterfall. As on the Matterhorn ride, people in the front seats will get wet.

Davy Crockett's Explorer Canoes
Groups can take to the water and row downriver frontier-style. Guides provide lessons and ensure safety.

Teddi Barra's Swingin' Arcade
In keeping with the spirit of Critter Country, this is a frontier-style gallery of electronic games.

NEW ORLEANS SQUARE

THIS CHARMING town square is modeled on the French Quarter in New Orleans, as it was in that city's heyday in the 19th century. The buildings have wrought-iron balconies and house interesting French-style shops.

Haunted Mansion
Some of the visitors to this attraction, which promises 999 "ghosts and ghouls," are now so familiar with its introductory commentary that they join in as they descend into its spooky world of mischievous spirits and grave-diggers. The ethereal

---

DOWNTOWN DISNEY

Located between the entrances to Disneyland park and Disney's California Adventure, Downtown Disney® is a garden paradise, offering guests some 300,000 sq.ft. of innovative restaurants, shops, and entertainment venues. The fact that this area has no admission fee makes Downtown Disney® one of the more popular – but crowded – spaces. A 12-screen AMC Theatre®, ESPN Zone™, and a LEGO Imagination Center® are the top attractions here. The snack shops, top-notch restaurants, plus a vast range of retail and specialty shops and a travel center, create a total Disney experience.

figures, including a talking woman's head in a crystal ball, are extremely realistic.

Pirates of the Caribbean

This show provides a floating ride through a yo-ho-ho world of ruffians and wenches who have been empowered with the gifts of song, dance, and heavy drinking by Audio-Animatronics. This technique, which brings models to life using electronic impulses to control their sounds and actions, was perfected at Disneyland.

The Disney Gallery

Visitors interested in the art behind the world of Disney should visit this gallery, located above the entrance to Pirates of the Caribbean. Some of the original artwork and designs for Disney's elaborate projects are on display here.

ADVENTURELAND

THE EXOTIC ATMOSPHERE in Adventureland offers dark, humid waterways lined with tropical plants. This is the smallest, but perhaps the most adventuresome, "land" in the park. **The Enchanted Tiki Room** showcases mechanical singing birds in a zany, musical romp through the tropics.

Indiana Jones™ Adventure Inspired by the 1982 film trilogy, passengers set off on a jeep-style drive through the Temple of the Forbidden Eye.

Theatrical props and scenery, a realistic soundtrack, sensational film images, and the physical sensation of a roller coaster make this the ultimate experience created by Disneyland to date.

Jungle Cruise

This safari-style boat ride through a jungle forest full of rampant apes and bloodthirsty headhunter is narrated by a real-life captain, who tells his captive audience terrible but amusing jokes during the ride through steamy waterways.

Tarzan™'s Treehouse

A climb-up, climb-through experience, starring Tarzan and Jane, with an interactive and musical play area at the base of the tree.

Disney's California Adventure

THE NEWEST STAR in Anaheim is Disney's California Adventure, adjacent to Disneyland and built on 55 acres (22 ha) of the old parking lot. Disney's California Adventure is divided into three primary "lands," each offering themed experiences that celebrate the California dream. The emphasis here is on adults and older teens, but there are still plenty of rides and attractions that appeal to all ages. Together with the original Disneyland Park, Disney's California Adventure adds to the Disney legend.

HOLLYWOOD PICTURES BACKLOT

THE BACKLOT OFFERS a tongue-in-cheek view of the motion picture industry. There are two blocks of facades and fakery, giving the visitor a Disney-eye view of the Hollywood. The **Hyperion Theater** features staged live musical shows, and at Jim Henson's **Muppet*Vision 3-D** you can see Miss Piggy and Kermit and all the lovable Muppet characters in a salute to movie making.

GOLDEN STATE

A tribute to the state's topography and agriculture, the rock-carved Grizzly Peak stands as the landmark icon of California Adventure. The centerpiece ride is **Soarin' Over California**, a simulated hang-glider ride that portrays the beauties of California's varied landscape on a huge wrap-around screen. There is no narrative, but guests can feel the wind currents and smell the scent of orange blossoms as they soar 40 feet (12 m) aloft. **Bountiful Valley** features healthy snacks and a 3-D film starring Flik from *A Bug's Life*. Smell-o-Vision and touchy-feelies make this a completely buggy experience for all.

PARADISE PIER

Considerably lower key than the thrill rides in the original park, Paradise Pier is the place where roller coasters, Ferris wheels, and parachute rides rule. **California Screamin'**, the giant **Sun Wheel**, **Boardwalk Games,** and **King Triton's Carousel** are reminiscent of seaside recreation parks of years ago.

Grizzly River Run is California Adventure's signature attraction

Knott's Berry Farm and Soak City USA ❷

Statues of cowboys on a Ghost Town bench

KNOTT'S BERRY FARM has grown from a 1920s boysenberry farm to a 21st-century multi-day entertainment complex. America's first theme park offers more than 165 different rides and attractions, but its main charm lies in its emphasis on authenticity. The Old West Ghost Town at the heart of the park has original ghost town buildings and artifacts. Located in Buena Vista in Orange County, a half-hour drive from LA, Knott's offers six themed areas, dozens of live-action stages, thrill rides, shopping and dining, and a full-fledged resort.

STAR FEATURES

★ Old West Ghost Town

★ Camp Snoopy

★ Soak City USA

GHOSTRIDER
Built in 1998, this mega-woodie has risen to the top of the "best coaster ride" list. The initial drop of 108 ft (33 m) at speeds approaching 60 mph (97km/h), the 2.5-minute ride is a must for every visitor to the Old Ghost Town.

OLD WEST GHOST TOWN

THIS 1880S GOLDRUSH TOWN has authentic century-old buildings lining its streets. An 1880 steam train, the **Ghost Town & Calico Railroad**, circles the park, and a genuine **Overland Trails stagecoach** takes passengers on a trip into the past.

The **Gold Trails Hotel and Mercantile**, a restored Kansas school-house, and the **Western Trails Museum** are chock full of Wild West memorabilia and artifacts. Visitors can pan for gold at the **Old Farm Mine** or join a line-dance at **Calico Square**. The **Ghost Rider Log Ride** floats visitors through a real 1880s sawmill before plunging down a 42-foot (13-m) waterfall. At the heart of Ghost Town, the spectacular 4533-ft- (1382-m)-long **GhostRider** wooden roller coaster towers over the park.

Largest wooden coaster in the United States at 118 ft (36 m) high

4,533-ft (1,382-m) long track

An 1880 steam engine transports visitors around the park

CAMP SNOOPY

INSPIRED BY THE MAJESTIC High Sierra, Camp Snoopy's six-acre (2.4-ha) wonderland is an interactive participatory children's paradise. There are 30 kid-tested attractions and pint-sized rides, hosted by the beloved Peanuts characters Snoopy, Lucy, and Charlie Brown. Children under 12 delight in the **Timberline Twister** roller coaster, the Red Baron's airplanes, and an old-fashioned Ferris wheel, where parents and kids can soar over the park for some wonderful views. The **Charlie Brown Speed-way** appeals to little stock-car

enthusiasts and their parents. There's a barnyard for petting baby animals, a swinging bridge competition, rushing waterfalls, and lively musical shows – all themed to the Peanuts comic strip.

Kids get behind the wheel at the Charlie Brown Speedway

FIESTA VILLAGE

CELEBRATING CALIFORNIA'S Spanish legacy, Fiesta Village offers a collection of south-of-the-border adventures and high-energy thrills. **Casa Arcada** challenges the whole family to the latest video technology, while a ride on the world's oldest **Dentzel Carousel** is a nostalgic treat. Two large roller coasters, the **Jaguar** and **Montezooma's Revenge** provide the thrills. End your day with a sizzling fireworks and laser display at **Reflection Lake**.

Replica of Philadelphia's Independence Hall

INDIAN TRAILS

INTRICATE ARTS AND CRAFTS of Native Americans from the Pacific Northwest, Great Plains, Southwest, and Far West are showcased in this area. Totem poles and tipis from the Blackfoot, Nez Perce, and Arapaho tribes seen throughout Indian Trails were built to convey the beauty and diversity of Native American culture. Through participatory learning adventures and exquisite artworks, visitors will understand how the people lived, and how their beliefs, climate, and environment influenced their daily lives.

THE BOARDWALK

A CONTINUOUS BEACH PARTY is the theme here, where everything centers around Southern California's seaside culture. Beachside concessions and the most radical thrill rides rule: **Supreme Scream** simulates a rocket launch while the **Perilous Plunge** is not for the faint of heart. Then, relax and take in a big-stage show at the **Charles M. Schultz Theater**.

WILD WATER WILDERNESS

EXPERIENCE THE MAGIC of the 1900s river wilderness with a raging white-water river, soaring geysers, and a giant waterfall – **Bigfoot Rapids** will fulfill your wildest dreams. The multi-sensory **Mystery Lodge** celebrates Native American culture, complete with an Indian storyteller, music, and dance.

The **Ranger Station** has a resident naturalist who makes friends with Sasquatch, the California High Sierra creature also known as Bigfoot.

SOAK CITY USA

SOUTHERN CALIFORNIA'S newest water adventure park has 21 awesome water rides – all themed to the 1950s and 1960s surfing culture.

Adjacent to Knott's main park, and separately gated, Soak City USA serves up 13 water-logged acres (5.3 ha),

replete with tube and body slides, surfing pipelines, a six-lane super slide, and **Tidal Wave Bay**, a special pool with gentle to moderate wave action. **Gremmie Lagoon** is a wet kid's playground with hands-on fun.

All rides have age and height requirements. There are plenty of places to snack and buy souvenirs; men's and women's changing rooms and lockers are also available.

RADISSON RESORT, KNOTT'S BERRY FARM

UNDER THIS UMBRELLA are Southern California's three finest entertainment venues: Knott's Berry Farm Theme Park, Soak City USA, and the Radisson Resort. Guests in the 321-room hotel can stay in Snoopy-themed suites and take advantage of the pools, sports facilities, fitness center, and children's activity area. First-rate restaurants, such as Cucina! Cucina! Italian Cafe add to the festive atmosphere. There are, of course, special rates for frequent guests, value-added packages.

Spectacular water rides at Soak City USA

House in which Richard Nixon was born

Richard Nixon Library and Birthplace ❸

Road map D6. 18001 Yorba Linda Blvd. 📞 *(714) 993-5075.* 🚌 *to Fullerton.* ⏰ *10am–5pm Mon–Sat; 11am–5pm Sun.* ⭘ *Thanksgiving, Dec 25.* 📷 ♿ 🎥
🌐 www.nixonlibrary.org

THE LIFE AND achievements of the Republican politician Richard Nixon, president of the United States from 1969 to 1974, are celebrated in this museum and archive. In the immaculately landscaped grounds is the simple wooden house where the former president was born in 1913. Nearby are a Reflecting Pool and the graves of Nixon and his wife, Pat, marked by matching black granite tombstones.

In the museum, a walk-through exhibit provides a chronological account of Nixon's rise and fall, emphasizing his role as a peacemaker and international statesman. The Foreign Affairs gallery has a reconstruction of a Chinese pavilion housing an exhibit on Nixon's 1972 state visit to China. There is also a replica of St. Basil's Cathedral in Moscow, with a display on Nixon's trip to the Soviet Union that same year.

Don't miss the World Leaders' Room, where statues of famous politicians are surrounded by some of the many gifts that Nixon received while in office, such as a 6th-century BC statue of the goddess Isis from Anwar Sadat of Egypt, a Sonia Delaunay painting from Georges Pompidou of France, and a malachite jewelry box from Leonid Brezhnev of the Soviet Union.

Historic items exhibited in other galleries include a three-billion-year-old lump of rock from the moon, a 12-ft (3.5-m) section of the Berlin Wall, and dresses worn by the First Lady. Visitors are able to eavesdrop on the infamous "Watergate Tapes," which led to Nixon's resignation. In the Presidential Forum, a touch-screen exhibit using archive footage allows visitors to put questions to the late president. In additional galleries changing exhibitions are held. These cover popular aspects of US presidential history, such as the visits paid to the White House by such pop stars as Elvis Presley.

Crystal Cathedral ❹

12141 Lewis St, Garden Grove. 📞 *(714) 971-4013.* 🚌 *45 N.* ⏰ *Mon–Sat.* ♿ 🎥 🎫 *9:30am, 11am, 6:00pm Sun.* 🌐 www.crystalcathedral.org

CONSTRUCTED from an elaborate maze of white steel trusses covered with more than 10,000 panes of silvered glass, the Crystal Cathedral is a shimmering monument to the television-led evangelism that enthralls millions of Americans today. The cathedral, which can comfortably hold almost 3,000 worshipers, is the pulpit from which its founder, Dr. Robert H Schuller, broadcasts his famous "Hour of Power" service live on Sundays.

Everything about this unique cathedral is large – music is provided by one of the biggest pipe organs in the world, and there is a 15-ft (4.6-m) wide color video screen. A huge glass door opens during the

Vast interior of the Crystal Cathedral in Garden Grove

Sunday services, to enable the drive-in congregation outside to listen to the service without leaving their cars. The memorial cemetery has a capacity of 10,000.

Designed in 1980 by Philip Johnson, the star-shaped cathedral is both a spiritual shrine and an architectural wonder. Beside the building is a 236-ft (72-m) steeple, added in 1990 and adorned with polished stainless-steel prisms.

The cathedral represents the culmination of a lengthy evangelical crusade that began in 1955 when the indefatigable Dr. Schuller started preaching in a nearby drive-in theater. Today he has many followers in the US, Canada, and Australia.

Worshipers come from afar to attend pageants performed at Christmas and Easter, featuring people dressed as angels flying from the ceiling.

There are free tours of the cathedral and to the adjacent Southern California Community Church, the drive-in church that preceded it. The original drive-in theater where it all began is still standing nearby.

Bowers Museum of Cultural Art **5**

2002 N Main St, Santa Ana. **Road map** D6. **(** (714) 567-3600. **■** to Anaheim. **🚌** 45 S. **◯** 10am–4pm Tue–Sun. **●** Jan 1, Jul 4, Thanksgiving, Dec 25. **📷 ♿ ✓**

T HE BOWERS has long been considered to be Orange County's leading art museum. Its serene Mission-style buildings house rich permanent collections and high-profile temporary exhibitions. There is a stylish California café *(see p554)* and a shop packed with ethnic crafts and art books.

The museum was founded in 1932. Its world-class display of African masks, collected by Paul and Ruth Tishman and now on long-term loan from the Disney Corporation, is reason enough for a pilgrimage. Other galleries, with exhibitions of treasures from the pre-colonial cultures of Southeast Asia, Oceania, Mexico, and Native America, reflect the

Entrance arch leading to the Bowers Museum of Cultural Art

Bower Museum's commitment to the art of indigenous peoples. Fascinating examples of their crafts illustrate both the religious beliefs and the daily lives of these people.

The upstairs galleries, decorated with 1930s murals and plaster work, cover the mission and rancho periods of California and Orange County history *(see pp42–3)*. One block away, a former bank has been converted into the companion **Kidseum**, where children are encouraged to take part in arts-related activities and can try on masks and costumes from all around the world.

Mayan statuette (AD 800– 950), Bowers Museum

🏛 Kidseum

1802 N Main St, Santa Ana. **(** (714) 480-1520. **◯** 10am–4pm Sat & Sun only. **📷 ♿**

Discovery Museum of Orange County **6**

3101 W Harvard St, Santa Ana. **Road map** D6. **(** (714) 540-0404. **■** to Anaheim. **🚌** 45 S. **◯** 1–5pm Wed–Fri; 11am–3pm Sun. **●** Jan 1, Easter Sun, Thanksgiving, Dec 25. **📷 ♿ ✓**

V ICTORIAN TIMES in Orange County are brought to life in this curious three-story mansion, built in 1898 by a civil engineer, Hiram Clay Kellogg. Fascinated by ships,

Kellogg incorporated several nautical design features into his Santa Ana residence. The oval, cabinlike dining room has an oak and walnut floor, laid in strips to resemble a ship's deck. Some of the drawers in the built-in wooden cabinets can also be opened from the kitchen, on the other side of the wall. Clusters of fruit are painted on the ceiling, and the room is overlooked by an elegant circular staircase with a mastlike central pillar.

The mansion now houses an exciting and child-friendly museum, which is also of historic and architectural interest to adults. Young visitors are given the opportunity to dress up in genuine antique clothing and experience life as it was at the turn of the century.

Upstairs, rooms are furnished with antique school desks, dolls' houses, and period games. In the master bedroom, now the textile room, a treadle sewing machine and spinning wheel are on display. Downstairs, children are invited to investigate mysterious instruments, including a stereoscope and a hand-crank telephone. Visitors can also explore the old-fashioned kitchen, which is equipped with icebox and butter churn.

Next door stands an 1899 ranch house, carriage barn, and water tower. There is also an orchard of orange trees – now a rare sight in the county.

Implements for orange cultivation at the Discovery Museum

Mission San Juan Capistrano ❼

Statue of St. John of Capistran

THIS BEAUTIFUL "Jewel of the Missions" was founded in 1776, and its chapel is the only surviving building in California in which the famous Father Junípero Serra (see p42) preached. One of the largest and most prosperous in the whole chain, the mission was crowned by a Great Stone Church, completed in 1806. Six years later this was destroyed by an earthquake, leaving a ruined shell set amid a rambling complex of adobe and brick buildings. A restoration program, ornamental gardens, and many historical exhibits now enable visitors to imagine the mission's former glory.

★ Padres' Living Quarters
The fathers of Mission San Juan Capistrano lived in sparsely furnished rooms and slept on hard plank beds. Visitors enjoyed more comfortable accommodation.

The kitchens have corner ovens and displays of utensils.

A domed hut, built from wooden poles, resembles the traditional dwellings of Native American villages at the time of the mission.

Sacred Garden Bells
The original four bells from the Great Stone Church now hang in the wall of a small garden. The larger pair date from 1796.

STAR FEATURES

★ **Courtyard Gardens**

★ **Padres' Living Quarters**

★ **Serra's Chapel**

Junípero Serra
A statue of Father Serra and a Native American boy stands in a corner of the gardens.

VISITORS' CHECKLIST

Camino Capistrano & Ortega
Hwy. **Road map** D6. **(** (949)
234-1300. **(** 8:30am–5pm
daily. **(** Good Fri pm, Thanksgiving, Dec 25. **(** **(** **(** **(**
(**(** Swallow Festival (March).

★ **Courtyard Gardens**
*This courtyard was at the heart of mission
life. Surrounded by cloisters, it still has a
fountain at its center and is today graced
by mature trees and beautiful gardens.*

The Bodega, or
warehouse, where tallow,
grains, woolens, and
hides were stored.

Cloisters
*Covered walkways with
arches frame the mission's
central courtyard. With their
tiled walls, the cloisters provide a cool, shaded place in
which to stroll or sit and
contemplate the gardens.*

★ **Serra's
Chapel**
*Built from cherry
wood and covered
with gold leaf, the 300-
year-old altar in the
mission's chapel was
brought from Barcelona,
Spain, in 1906.*

Ruins are all that remain of
the cruciform Great Stone
Church, which is currently
undergoing restoration.

SWALLOWS AT THE MISSION

Every spring thousands of migrating swallows return to San
Juan Capistrano from South America. Their annual arrival is
celebrated with a festival held on March 19, St. Joseph's
Day *(see p32).* The birds have been
nesting in the tiled roofs and adobe walls
of the mission for more than two
centuries. They use mud pellets to build
enclosed nests, in which four or five
eggs are incubated. When the autumn
comes, the swallows fly south again.

Migratory swallow at the mission

Catalina Island ❽

Just 21 miles (50 km) from the mainland, Catalina Island is the most accessible of California's Channel Islands. It was named Santa Catalina by the Spanish explorer Sebastián Vizcaíno when he landed here in 1602 on the feast day of St. Catherine of Alexandria. Much of the island's mountainous landscape remains unspoiled, and it has long been a favorite weekend and vacation destination.

Catalina's main town is the virtually traffic-free port of Avalon. The biggest buildings were constructed by the chewing-gum millionaire William Wrigley Jr., who bought the island in 1919. Today most of Catalina's 76 sq miles (200 sq km) are owned by the Santa Catalina Island Conservancy, which preserves the island's natural beauty.

Two Harbors
This low-lying isthmus backe by two bays is a popular anchorage for yachts. Facilit include a camp site, diving center, and general store.

West End •

Airport-in-the-Sky and Nature Center

Two Harbors •

Empire Landing Road

Catalina Harbor

Little Harbor Road

BIG SPRINGS CANYON

El Rancho Escondido is a ranch on which prize-winning horses are raised. It can be visited on guided tours of the island.

Little Harbor •

El Rancho Escondido

BLA JA MOU

Middle Canyon Trail

BULLRUSH CANYON

Little Harbor
This out-of-the way spot located on the island's west shore has a sheltered cove with a beach and a scenic harbor. There are also several hiking trails and a good camp site.

Black Jack Mountain, which rises to 2,006 ft (610 m), is the second-highest mountain on Catalina Island and was mined in the 1920s for lead, zinc, and silver.

CATALINA WILDLIFE

Over the centuries, Catalina has become a sanctuary for plants and animals that have died out on the mainland. Rare ironwood and mahogany trees and the highly poisonous wild tomato are among eight endemic plants surviving on the island. Distinctive animal subspecies have also evolved, such as the small gray Catalina fox and the beechey ground squirrel. Some animals brought to the island by early settlers have now turned wild, including goats, pigs, and deer. Catalina even has a population of bison, ferried over in 1924 for a film shoot and never rounded up.

One of the island's wild bison

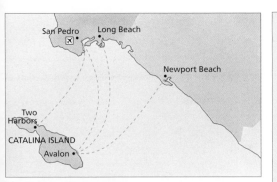

VISITORS' CHECKLIST

Road map C6. 🏘 *3,000.* ☒
Island Express Helicopter Service
*(310 510-2525) from San Pedro &
Long Beach to Avalon.* 🚢 **Catalina
Express** *(310 519-1212) from San
Pedro to Avalon or Two Harbors &
from Long Beach to Avalon;*
Catalina Cruises *(800 228-2546)
from Long Beach to Avalon;*
Catalina Passenger Service *(949
673-5245) from Newport Beach
to Avalon.* 🛈 *1 Green Pleasure
Pier (310 510-1520).* 🎭 *Catalina
Arts Festival (late Sep).*

★ Avalon Casino
*Guided tours can be taken of
this 1929 Art Deco jewel, once
a famous spot for big bands
and now lovingly restored.*

KEY

═══	Minor road
═══	Road in poor condition
- - -	Trail
〜	River
☒	Airport
🚢	Ferry service
🛈	Tourist information
🌿	Viewpoint

```
0 kilometers          5
0 miles        2
```

Avalon Museum is on
the casino's lower floor.
This historical museum
shows how the island has
been variously used for
ranching, mining, tourism,
and as a film location.

**Lovers Cove
Marine Reserve**
is visited by glass-
bottomed boats that
reveal the colorful
marine life existing
around Catalina.

★ Avalon Bay
*About 3,000 people live in Avalon, which
has a pier and souvenir shops. Locals travel
around in golf carts, which visitors can rent.*

Seal Rocks are included on
sightseeing cruises, which visit
this part of the island to admire
colonies of migratory sea lions.

**★ Wrigley
Memorial &
Botanical Gardens**
*This 38-acre (15-ha)
park honoring
William Wrigley, Jr.
has an imposing
memorial and a
collection of plants
endemic to Catalina.*

STAR SIGHTS

★ **Avalon Bay**

★ **Avalon Casino**

★ **Wrigley Memorial &
Botanical Gardens**

SAN DIEGO COUNTY

I N SAN DIEGO IN 1769, *the Spanish friar Junípero Serra laid down the first link in the chain of 21 missions that underpins the modern state of California (see pp42–3). Blessed with a near-perfect climate and a magnificent natural harbor, his settlement has now become the sixth largest city in America. San Diego County has much to offer visitors, with its Pacific coastline, inland forests, and extensive state parks.*

San Diego's character has always been determined by the sea. In the 19th century, gold prospectors, hide dealers, and whalers sailed into San Diego Bay. The United States Navy arrived in 1904, starting an enthusiastic courtship that has made San Diego the largest military establishment in the world. Aircraft carriers are a common sight in the bay, but so are cruise ships, fishing boats, yachts, and pleasure craft. San Diego is a city of sports and leisure – three times host to the Americas Cup, home of the Padres baseball team and the Chargers football team. There are plenty of opportunities for surfing, sailing, golf, and water sports.

First-time visitors are always surprised by the sense of space and how much there is to enjoy. Most have heard of San Diego Zoo and the Sea World marine park, but few realize that San Diego is a fast-growing city, with shimmering new skyscrapers soaring beside the waterfront. Culturally, San Diego is rapidly gaining prestige, as the many museums and arts venues of Balboa Park flourish.

North of the city the rugged Pacific Coast is lined with affluent beachside communities and wildlife preserves. Inland lie small towns, surrounded by peaceful countryside and fertile farmland. Deep forests and several state parks make the interior of San Diego County a paradise for hikers and campers escaping the frantic pace of city life. To the east, the region becomes increasingly mountainous, giving way to desert landscapes. And to the south, just a short trolley ride away from San Diego, is the bustling Mexican border town of Tijuana.

Bazaar del Mundo in San Diego Old Town

◁ **Marina in San Diego Bay, with the skyscrapers of Downtown in the background**

Exploring San Diego County

COVERING MORE than 4,000 sq miles (10,350 sq km), San Diego County has a coastline of rocky cliffs, sandy beaches and wetlands, and a spacious, mountainous hinterland. The Anza-Borrego Desert *(see pp266–7)* forms a natural boundary to the east. San Diego city lies close to the border with Mexico, exploiting a large bay protected by two peninsulas. Stunning beaches and plentiful opportunities for leisure activities are the main attractions along the Pacific shoreline. A drive inland takes the visitor to the tranquillity of the Cleveland National Forest and the wilderness of state parks, such as Palomar Mountain and Cuyamaca Rancho.

Cuyamaca Rancho State Park landscape

SEE ALSO

- *Where to Stay* pp517–19
- *Where to Eat* pp555–7

Shelter Island yacht harbor in San Diego Bay

San Mateo Creek

Santa Margarita River

Rivers

Los Angeles

15

5

MISSION SAN LUIS REY

8

78

San Diego Aqueduct

ESCONDIDO

5

S6 Lak Hodg

Second San Diego Aqueduct

ENCINITAS

S21

San Dieguito River

I

52

LA JOLLA 5

5

MISSION BAY 4 3 SEA WORLD

MIS SAN DE A

SAN DIEGO 1

CHULA VISTA NATURE CENTER

75 13

TIJUANA

0 kilometers   5

0 miles   5

SIGHTS AT A GLANCE

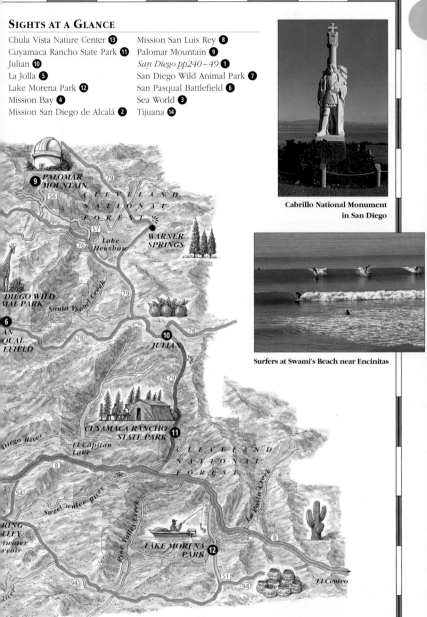

Cabrillo National Monument in San Diego

Surfers at Swami's Beach near Encinitas

KEY

Freeway

Major road

Minor road

Scenic route

River

Viewpoint

GETTING AROUND

The main transportation routes run from north to south – the coastal I-5 and Amtrak railway line both provide a fast connection with Los Angeles via the Orange County coast *(see p220)*. The scenic Coaster train route serves stations between San Diego and Oceanside. A car is essential for exploring the county's inland areas. Within San Diego itself, public transportation is a viable option for the visitor *(see p256)*. The city has a comprehensive bus network, and the two lines of the efficient San Diego Trolley system extend east to El Cajon and south to the Mexican border.

San Diego County Coastline

STRETCHING FROM Orange County to the Mexican border, the coastline of San Diego County has 70 miles (112 km) of lovely sandy beaches, cliffs, coves, and seaside resorts. The beach culture is sophisticated, and the sports activity is frenzied. Peace can be found at Batiquitos Lagoon, Torrey Pines State Preserve, and the Chula Vista Nature Center *(see p254)*, which are all sanctuaries for coastal wildlife. At Carlsbad, Legoland California is a 128-acre family theme park for youngsters aged 2–12, with a castle, miniature brick cities, and driving school.

Sign at entrance to Swami's Beach

Batiquitos Lagoon *lies between South Carlsbad and Leucadia State Beaches. A project is under way to clean up the lagoon and create a wildlife preserve with a nature trail and visitors' center. The lagoon has a large bird population and a rich variety of saltwater plants.*

The Del Mar Racetrack *was made famous in the 1930s by the singer Bing Crosby and other Hollywood stars. Its annual meetings remain a high point of the social calendar. San Diego's County Fair takes place at the adjacent fairground every June, and the racing season runs from late July to mid-September.*

Torrey Pines State Preserve *and Santa Rosa Island (see p214) are the only two places in the world where the Torrey Pine, or Pinus torreyana, survives. A remnant of pre-Ice Age forests, this tree is well adapted to this area's dry, sandy environment.*

KEY

▰	Freeway
▬	Major road
▭	Minor road
⇌	River
☆	Viewpoint

0 kilometers   5

0 miles   5

★ **San Onofre State Beach** ①
🚶 🏖 🎣 🚻 🛝 ⚠ 📷
Although close to the coastal San Onofre nuclear power plant and the vast Camp Pendleton military base, this beach is worth visiting to see serious California surfers in action.

Swami's ③
🚶 🏖 🎣 🚻
This surfing beach is named after the founder of the Self-Realization Fellowship Temple, which overlooks the shore.

Cardiff State Beach ④
🚶 🏖 🎣 ♿ 🚻 ⚠ 📷
On the south side of Encinitas, Cardiff offers swimming, surfing, and fine white sand, as well as oceanfront dining on Restaurant Row at its north end.

Torrey Pines State Beach ⑥
🚶 🏖 🎣 🚻 📷
This beach is popular for picnics and swimming. Just to the south is the Torrey Pines State Preserve, where several cliff-top hiking trails among the pine trees offer views over the ocean.

Mission Beach ⑨
🚶 🏖 🎣 🚻 ♿ 🚻
This is the liveliest beach in San Diego with plenty of opportunity for people-watching, plus the fairground attractions of Belmont Park *(see p251).*

Ocean Beach ⑩
🚶 🏖 🎣 🚻 ♿ 🚻
Ocean Beach's T-shaped pier, popular with pelicans, has good views of the coastline.

Silver Strand Beach ⑫
🚶 🏖 🎣 🚻 ♿ 🚻 ⚠ 📷
This long, thin beach is sandwiched between areas of land reserved for naval training. It takes its name from the silvery shells in its sand.

SAN CLEMENTE

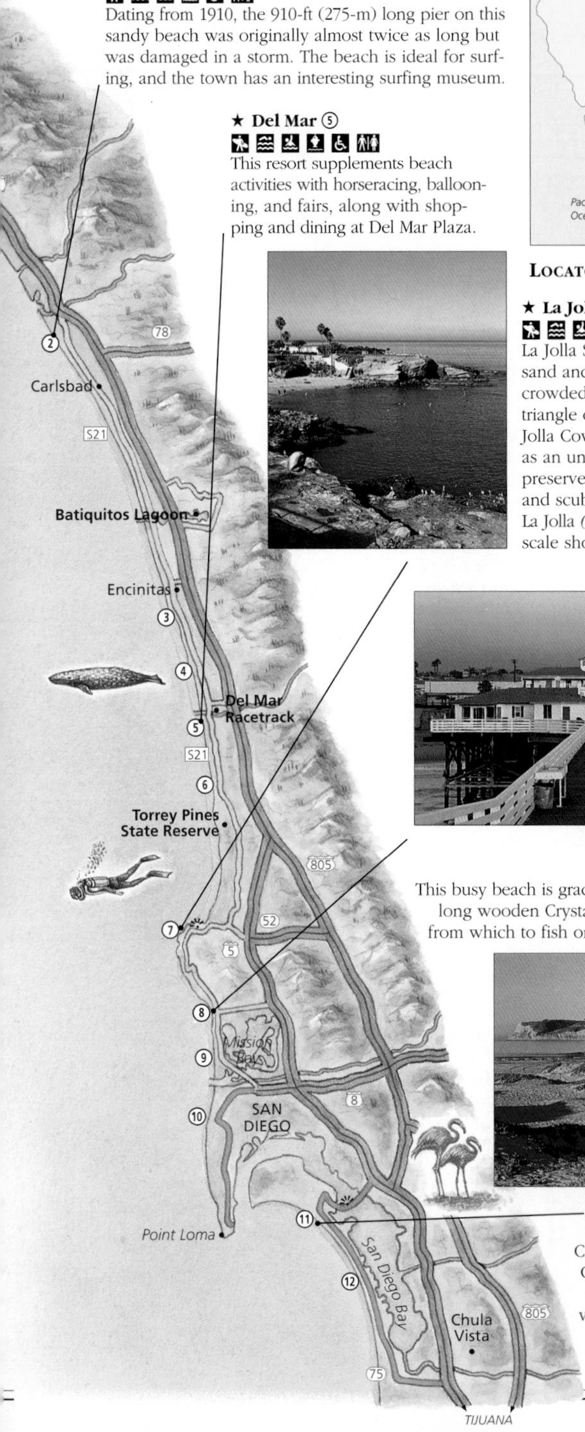

2
78
Carlsbad
S21
Batiquitos Lagoon
Encinitas
3
4
Del Mar Racetrack
5
S21
6
Torrey Pines State Reserve
805
7
52
5
8
Mission Bay
9
SAN DIEGO
8
10
11
Point Loma
San Diego Bay
12
Chula Vista
805
75
TIJUANA

★ Oceanside 2

🏄 🌊 🏊 🛟 ♿ 🚻

Dating from 1910, the 910-ft (275-m) long pier on this sandy beach was originally almost twice as long but was damaged in a storm. The beach is ideal for surfing, and the town has an interesting surfing museum.

★ Del Mar 5

🏄 🌊 🏊 🛟 ♿ 🚻

This resort supplements beach activities with horseracing, ballooning, and fairs, along with shopping and dining at Del Mar Plaza.

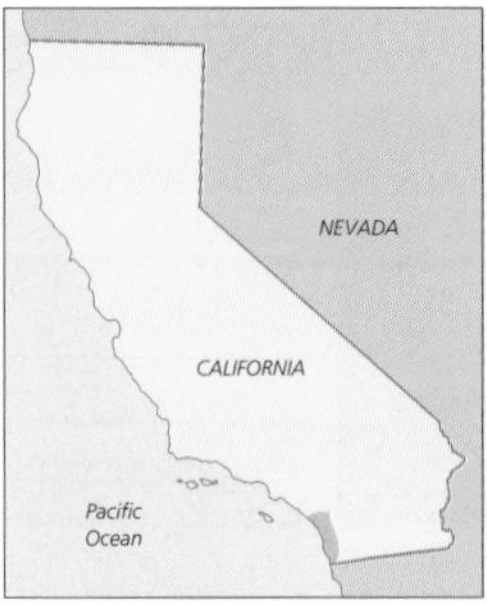

NEVADA
CALIFORNIA
Pacific Ocean

Locator Map

★ La Jolla 7

🏄 🌊 🏊 ♿ 🚻

La Jolla Shores has excellent sand and activities but can be crowded in the summer. A triangle of offshore water by La Jolla Cove has been designated as an underwater ecological preserve, open for snorkeling and scuba-diving. The town of La Jolla *(see p251)* has many upscale shops and restaurants.

★ Pacific Beach 8

🏄 🌊 🏊 🛟 ♿ 🚻

This busy beach is graced by the 400-ft (120-m) long wooden Crystal Pier. It is a good place from which to fish or watch surfers in action.

★ Coronado Beach 11

🏄 🌊 🏊 🛟 ♿ 🚻

Crowned by the Hotel del Coronado *(see p245)* and offering wide sands and views across the bay, this is one of San Diego's most romantic beaches.

San Diego ❶

SHAPED LIKE A HOOK and protected by the peninsula of Coronado (see p245), the 22 sq miles (57 sq km) of San Diego Bay form a natural deep-water harbor around which the second largest city in California has grown. Discovered in 1542 by the Portuguese explorer Juan Rodríguez Cabrillo (João Rodrigues Cabrilho),

Tiles in Santa Fe Depot

colonization did not follow until 1769. In that year, the founding father of the mission chain, Junípero Serra, arrived in the region as part of a military expedition to secure Alta California (the part of California north of the Baja Peninsula) for Spain. Its commanders built a presidio and mission near the San Diego River, an area now known as Old Town (see pp244–5).

Shops in Seaport Village

Exploring Downtown San Diego

The growth of modern San Diego began in the 1870s, when Alonzo Horton, a San Francisco businessman, began to develop the town's water-front areas. He laid down the grid of streets of the Gaslamp Quarter (see pp242–3), which, along with the Horton Plaza shopping center, has become the centerpiece of San Diego's rejuvenated Downtown district. Historically, the city's main street is Broadway, punctuated at its western end by the **Santa Fe Depot**. The towers and brightly tiled interior of this Spanish Colonial-style railroad station date from 1915. It was built to impress visitors to the Panama-Pacific Exposition in Balboa Park (see pp246–7).

Since the 1980s, Downtown San Diego has become the site of an ongoing architectural competition. Close to the Santa Fe Depot, one of the city's tallest buildings, the **America Plaza**, is home to the Museum of Contemporary Art. On the

waterfront, the galleon-like **San Diego Convention Center**, which opened in 1989, overlooks San Diego Bay.

The promenades and piers of the **Embarcadero** water-front pathway provide an introduction to San Diego's role as a major commercial and military port. At the northern end are the Maritime Museum's historic ships. A short stroll south is **Broadway Pier**, where visitors can join a harbor excursion. **Seaport Village**, a shopping and dining complex, has views across to the aircraft carriers of the **North Island United States Naval Air Station**.

🚻 Horton Plaza

Broadway, G St, 1st & 4th Aves.
📞 (619) 239-8180. ⏰ daily.
🚫 Thanksgiving, Dec 25.
This innovatively designed shopping center, built in 1985, has acted as a catalyst in the regeneration of Downtown San Diego. The plaza is painted in a festive array of pastel shades and built on interlocking levels lined with 140 shops, department stores, and cafés. Visitors can enjoy some evening shopping, close to the restaurants of the Gaslamp Quarter.

Three of the colorful levels in the Horton Plaza shopping center

SAN DIEGO

🏛 Maritime Museum

1492 North Harbor Drive. 【 *(619) 234-9153.* ◯ *9am–8pm daily.* 🈂

The lofty masts of the *Star of India*, an 1863 merchantman, dominate this museum of historic vessels. Beside it is the beautiful San Francisco Bay passenger ferry, the *Berkeley*, dating from 1898. The luxurious steam yacht *Medea*, which was built in 1904, is moored alongside.

🏛 Museum of Contemporary Art

1001 Kettner Blvd. 【 *(619) 234-1001.* ◯ *Tue–Sun.* ● *Jan 1, Dec 25.* 🈂

This two-story museum, which opened in 1993, is the Downtown counterpart of the museum of the same name in La Jolla *(see p251)*. The four galleries display changing exhibitions of new work by living artists, as well as selections from the museum's large permanent collection. There is also a very well-stocked bookstore.

🏨 Villa Montezuma

20 Ave and K St. 【 *(619) 239-2211.* ◯ *10am–4:30pm Fri, Sat & Sun.* ● *Jan 1, Dec 24 pm, Dec 25.* 🈂 🈸

This lavish Victorian mansion was built in 1887 for Jesse Shepard, an author, musician, and spiritualist from England. The remarkably well-preserved Queen Anne-style interior gives visitors an insight into life in old San Diego.

Stained glass in Villa Montezuma

🏛 Children's Museum

200 W Island Ave. 【 *(619) 233-5437.* ◯ *10am–4pm Tue–Sat.* ● *Jan 1, Thanksgiving, Dec 25.* 🈂

A former warehouse has been transformed into a spacious museum devoted to entertaining and educating children. The emphasis is on activity and discovery; facilities include a dressing-up stage, an art zone, virtual reality games, and a bus called *The Bookstop*.

KEY

🈂	Military zone
✈	Airport
🚉	Railroad station
🚊	Trolley station
—	Trolley line
🚌	Bus station
⚓	Ferry terminal
🛈	Tourist information

Taking part in one of the many activities at the Children's Museum

A Walk through the Gaslamp Quarter

DURING THE BOOM YEARS of the 1880s, the 16 blocks of the San Diego's Gaslamp Quarter became known as the "Stingaree." It was an area notorious for prostitution, gambling, and drinking, where naïve customers could easily be "stung" by confidence tricksters. In spite of police clampdowns in the following decades and the growth of a close-knit Asian community, its streets remained in decline until the 1970s, when moves were made to revive its fortunes and protect its wealth of historic buildings. In 1980, the area was designated a National Historic District. As a result, the Gaslamp Quarter has recently emerged as the new heart of San Diego. It is now renowned as a

One of the quarter's gaslamps place to shop, dine, and dance. Visitors can also admire the period buildings, ranging from a pie bakery and a hardware store to ornate office blocks and grand Victorian hotels. The district is particularly attractive at night, when it is illuminated by graceful gaslamps that line its pavements.

VISITORS' CHECKLIST

Broadway & 4th–6th Aves. **Road map** D6. ▭ 1. ▮ Bayside. ℹ 410 Island Ave (619 233-4692). ◙ ♿ ▯ ♓ ▢

Old City Hall
This 1874 Italianate office building once housed the entire city government.

The Lincoln Hotel at No. 536 was built in 1913. Its architecture is influenced by Chinese style.

The Backesto Building office block at No. 614 dates from 1873.

FIFTH AVENUE WEST SIDE ≫≫≫≫≫≫≫≫≫≫≫≫≫

★ **Louis Bank of Commerce**
Constructed in 1888, this was the first granite building in the city and housed the Bank of Commerce for just five years. It has also served as an oyster bar and a brothel.

The Marston Building
This retail outlet on the corner of 5th Avenue and F Street dates from 1881. It was built by civic leader George Marston as a department store. The structure was remodeled in 1903 following fire damage.

FIFTH AVENUE EAST SIDE ≫≫≫≫≫≫≫≫≫≫≫≫≫≫≫≫≫≫≫≫≫≫≫≫≫≫

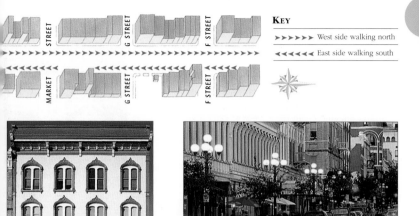

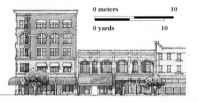

The Gaslamp Quarter at night
In the evening the streets of the Gaslamp Quarter bustle with people eating and drinking in its many restaurants and bars, or simply strolling around.

Llewelyn Building
Dating from 1877, this structure housed a shoe store until 1906 and then a succession of hotels.

0 meters 10

0 yards 10

★ Yuma Building
Completed in 1882, this commercial property was one of the first brick buildings in Downtown. In 1915, the Yuma Building housed the first brothel to be closed down during a police raid of the red-light district.

STAR SIGHTS

★ Louis Bank

★ Yuma Building

Wyatt Earp
Lawman Wyatt Earp ran three gambling halls in the district during the 1880s. In order to distance themselves from the "Stingaree," the area's more respectable businesses moved north of Market Street.

Beyond Downtown

FOUR MILES (6.5 km) north of the present Downtown lies the area now known as Old Town. Here, visitors can see San Diego's earliest buildings, many of which have been restored to their original state, and explore the fascinating Junípero Serra Museum. To the west of Old Town, the coast runs south to the end of the Point Loma Peninsula. From here, visitors have magnificent views of the Pacific Ocean and the city's waterfront across the bay. South of Point Loma, Coronado, with its numerous luxury hotels and popular sandy beaches, enjoys a privileged location at the end of a low-lying peninsula thrusting into San Diego Bay.

Victorian house in Heritage Park

Interior of Mason Street School in Old Town

Exploring Old Town

Until the 1870s the city of San Diego was centered around the presidio, the site of the original Spanish military outpost, in an area now known as Old Town. Today more than 20 historic buildings from this period have been restored or re-created to form the Old Town San Diego State Historic Park. At its center lies the grassy Plaza where parades and fiestas once took place. The **Robinson-Rose Building** at the western end of the Plaza now serves as the park's headquarters and visitors' center.

Other buildings of historical interest include the **Colorado House** and **Mason Street School**, which dates from 1866. Mexican themes are evoked in the vibrant **Bazaar del Mundo** shopping center (see p256) in the north corner of the Plaza.

Old Town San Diego spreads far beyond the official limits of the park. Constructed in 1856, **Whaley House** at No. 2482 San Diego Avenue was the first two-story brick building in California and once functioned as a courthouse.

🏛 Junípero Serra Museum

2727 Presidio Drive. **(** (858) 297-3258. **◯** Tue–Sun. **●** Thanksgiving, Dec 25. 🈶

Crowning Presidio Park, the whitewashed Junípero Serra Museum was built in 1929 in the Mission Revival style (see p27) and is named after the founder of California's mission chain. Overlooking the San Diego River, the park occupies the site of the presidio fort and mission, which were built by the Spanish in 1769. The ruins of the presidio are still being explored by a team of archaeologists, and some of their finds, from fine china to cannonballs, can be seen in the museum. Its displays cover San Diego's early days and the city's successive Native American, Spanish, Mexican, and American residents. Of particular interest is a didactic painting *La Madre Santísima de la Luz*, painted in Mexico by Luís Mena (c.1760), depicting Native Americans kneeling before the Virgin Mary. The painting is a rare surviving artifact from the time of the first mission, which moved to San Diego de Alcalá in 1774 (see p250). Exhibits upstairs describe the first Spanish expedition to California, daily life in the presidio, and the changing face of San Diego.

🏚 Heritage Park

2455 Heritage Park Row. **(** (858) 565-3600. **◯** daily. **●** Thanksgiving, Dec 25.

On the east side of Old Town, Heritage Park is a collection of immaculately restored Victorian buildings, rescued from various corners of the city.

Junípero Serra Museum in Old Town San Diego

🛏 Casa de Estudillo

4001 Mason St. 🔲 (619) 220-5422. ◐ 10am–5pm daily. ● Jan 1, Thanksgiving, Dec 25. **Donation**.

Of the original adobe and wooden buildings that visitors can now admire in Old Town San Diego State Historic Park, this is one of the oldest and the most impressive. It was constructed by the commander of the presidio, José Mariá de Estudillo, in 1829. The house has 13 rooms built around an internal courtyard and has been refurnished in the style of the late Spanish period.

🛏 Seeley Stable

Calhoun & Mason Sts. 🔲 (619) 220-5427. ◐ daily. ● Jan 1, Thanksgiving, Dec 25. **Donation**.

The museum housed in this reconstructed stable displays a collection of horse-drawn carriages and stagecoaches, as well as some interesting Wild West memorabilia.

Exploring Point Loma

The 144-acre (58-ha) **Cabrillo National Monument** park straddles the southern part of the Point Loma Peninsula. The monument was named after the Portuguese explorer Juan Rodríguez Cabrillo (also known as João Rodrigues Cabrilho) *(see p42)*, the first European to step ashore in California in 1542. His statue appropriately overlooks the ships passing in and out of San Diego Bay.

Between late December and the end of February the nearby Whale Overlook is a popular place from which to watch enormous gray whales undertaking their annual southward migration. Visitors can also follow the 2-mile (3-km) Bayside Trail around the Point, with the aid of a highly informative leaflet, and visit rock pools on its western shore.

🏛 Cabrillo National Monument Visitor Center

1800 Cabrillo Memorial Drive. 🔲 (619) 557-5450. ◐ daily. 🎥 🗹

Close to the Cabrillo National Monument park entrance, this excellent visitors' center has a small museum. A film recounts Juan Rodríguez Cabrillo's 800-mile (1,300-km) voyage along the California coast.

Old Point Loma Lighthouse

🛏 Old Point Loma Lighthouse

1800 Cabrillo Memorial Drive. 🔲 (619) 557-5450. ◐ 9am–5.15pm daily. 🎥 ♿ 🗹

The lighthouse, a short walk south from the Cabrillo statue, sent its first beams into the night in 1855 and operated for 36 years. Although its tower is usually closed to the public, the lower rooms re-create the lighthouse keepers' living quarters as they were in 1890s.

Exploring Coronado

The city of Coronado, at the head of a 4,100-acre (1,650-ha) peninsula in the middle of San Diego Bay, is moneyed and self-confident. Businessman Elisha Babcock Jr. bought the land in 1885 and set out to develop a world-class resort. Coronado now boasts San Diego's most exclusive homes, boutiques, hotels, and restaurants. Its Pacific shore is lined by a stunning beach *(see p239)*, which is dominated at its southern end by the landmark Hotel del Coronado.

⛴ Coronado Ferry

1050 N Harbor Drive. 🔲 (619) 234-4111. ◐ daily. 🗹

Until the opening of the spectacular San Diego–Coronado Bay Bridge in 1969, the ferry provided the area's principal link with the mainland, a service that has now been revived for the benefit of both tourists and locals.

The 15-minute trip between the Broadway Pier on the Embarcadero and the Ferry Landing Marketplace is breathtaking at dusk when the setting sun illuminates the skyscrapers of Downtown. From the Ferry Landing, visitors can take a bus or walk along Orange Avenue to the Pacific shore.

🛏 Hotel del Coronado

1500 Orange Ave, Coronado. 🔲 (619) 435-6611; (800) 468-3533. ◐ daily. 🎥 ♿ 🗹

Opened in 1888, the "Del" *(see p517)* is a lovingly preserved grand Victorian seaside hotel. It was built using both architects and labor from the railroads – a heritage that is most obvious in the domed ceiling of the Crown Room, which is built from sugar pine without a single nail. The list of illustrious guests who have stayed here reads like a Who's Who of 20th-century United States history – presidents from Franklin D Roosevelt to Bill Clinton, film stars from Marilyn Monroe to the *Baywatch* belles. The hotel has been the setting for several films, including *Some Like It Hot*, the 1959 classic starring Marilyn Monroe, Jack Lemmon, and Tony Curtis. "Del" devotees can take a 35-minute audio tour.

Impressive turrets and gables of the exclusive Hotel del Coronado

Balboa Park and San Diego Zoo

Statue of El Cid in Balboa Park

NAMED AFTER the Spanish explorer who first set eyes on the Pacific Ocean in 1513, Balboa Park was founded in 1868. Its beauty owes much to the dedicated horticulturalist Kate Sessions who, in 1892, promised to plant trees throughout its 1,200 acres (485 ha) in exchange for renting space for a nursery. In 1915 the park was the site of the city's Panama-Pacific Exposition *(see p339)*, a world's fair celebrating the opening of the Panama Canal. Several of the Spanish Colonial-style pavilions built in that year survive along El Prado (the park's main street), and the animals gathered for the exhibition formed the nucleus from which San Diego Zoo has grown *(see p249)*. Twenty years later the organizers of the California-Pacific International Exposition added more exhibition spaces around Pan-American Plaza. All these buildings now form a rich concentration of museums and performance venues.

Plaza de Panama
This plaza in the center of the El Prado thoroughfare was at the heart of the Panama-Pacific Exposition.

Skyfari

★ San Diego Museum of Man
This historical museum is housed in the 1915 California Building. Designed in Spanish Colonial style, its façade is decorated with statues representing famous Californians.

Old Globe Theater

El Prado

San Diego Automotive Museum

Aerospace Museum
This A-12 Blackbird, built in 1962, stands beside a museum devoted to the history of flight.

STAR SIGHTS

★ **California Building/San Diego Museum of Man**

★ **San Diego Museum of Art**

★ **San Diego Zoo**

Pan-American Plaza

Spreckels Organ Pavilion

Tour bus

0 meters		100
0 yards		100

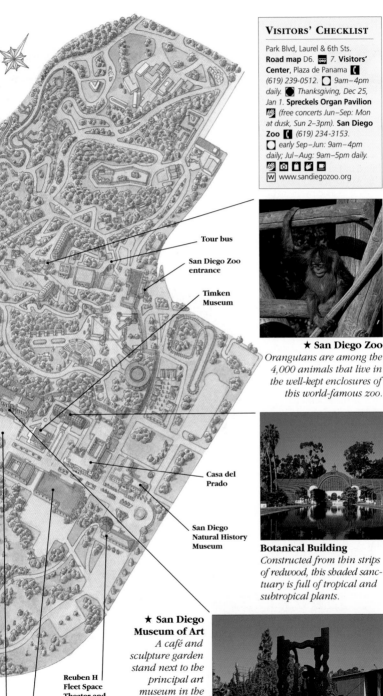

VISITORS' CHECKLIST

Park Blvd, Laurel & 6th Sts.
Road map D6. 🚌 7. **Visitors' Center**, Plaza de Panama 🛈
(619) 239-0512. 🕒 9am–4pm daily. ● Thanksgiving, Dec 25, Jan 1. **Spreckels Organ Pavilion** 🎵 (free concerts Jun–Sep: Mon at dusk, Sun 2–3pm). **San Diego Zoo** 🛈 (619) 234-3153.
🕒 early Sep–Jun: 9am–4pm daily; Jul–Aug: 9am–5pm daily.
🎵 📷 🛈 🍴 🛍 🚻
Ⓦ www.sandiegozoo.org

Tour bus

San Diego Zoo entrance

Timken Museum

★ **San Diego Zoo**
Orangutans are among the 4,000 animals that live in the well-kept enclosures of this world-famous zoo.

Casa del Prado

San Diego Natural History Museum

Botanical Building
Constructed from thin strips of redwood, this shaded sanctuary is full of tropical and subtropical plants.

★ **San Diego Museum of Art**
A café and sculpture garden stand next to the principal art museum in the park. Both North American and European works are exhibited.

Reuben H Fleet Space Theater and Science Center

Casa de Balboa

a de ama

Exploring Balboa Park and San Diego Zoo

Topiary elephant at zoo entrance

BALBOA PARK, located at the heart of San Diego, is one of the city's most popular attractions. On the weekend, its pleasant, lush grounds and traffic-free promenades are crowded with strollers, joggers, cyclists, and street artists. In between museum tours, visitors can picnic in one of the shady picnic groves or play ball games on the grassy lawns. Just to the north of the museums and recreation grounds of Balboa Park lies San Diego Zoo, where 800 species from all over the world are housed in enclosures designed to resemble as closely as possible their natural habitat.

Sunday afternoon street entertainers in Balboa Park

🏛 San Diego Museum of Man

1350 El Prado. ☎ (619) 239-2001. ◯ 10am–5pm Fri–Wed (9pm Thu). ● Jan 1, Thanksgiving, Dec 25. 📷

The landmark pavilion of the Panama-Pacific Exposition of 1915 (see p246), also known as the California Building, houses an anthropological museum about the early history of mankind. Exhibits arranged over two floors cover topics such as the cultures of ancient Egypt and the Mayans, and Native American crafts.

🏛 San Diego Museum of Art

1450 El Prado. ☎ (619) 232-7931. ◯ Tue–Sun. ● Jan 1, Thanksgiving, Dec 25. 📷

This museum's large, varied art collection is boosted by a program of special exhibitions. European and American art from 1850 to the 20th century is shown in the first-floor galleries, along with exhibits from southern Asia, Japan, and China. The displays on the second floor feature work from 1300 to 1850, including *Coronation of the Virgin* (1508), by Luca Signorelli.

Portrait of a Gentleman (1634) by Frans Hals in the Timken Museum

🏛 Timken Museum of Art

1500 El Prado. ☎ (619) 239-5548. ◯ Tue–Sun. ● Jan 1, 4 Jul, Thanksgiving, Dec 25.

Opened in 1965, the Timken exhibits a few exquisite works in an inviting space. On display are works by European masters such as Frans Hals (1581/5–1666), François Boucher (1703–70), and Paul Cézanne (1839–1906). The Timken also has works by 19th-century American artists, including *The Yosemite Fall* (1864) by Albert Bierstadt, and a collection of Russian icons.

🏛 Museum of Photographic Arts

1649 El Prado. ☎ (619) 238-7559. ◯ daily. ● Dec 25. 📷

This museum is located on the main floor of the ornate Casa de Balboa. It specializes in high-quality traveling exhibitions that demonstrate the art and power of photography. There is also an interesting and well-stocked bookstore.

🏛 Museum of San Diego History

1649 El Prado. ☎ (619) 232-6203. ◯ 10am–4.30pm Tue–Sun. ● Jan 1, Thanksgiving, Dec 24 & 25. 📷

As well as a large number of fascinating old photographs and books about the city, the museum has excellent exhibitions about cars, quilts, and the quest for a city water supply. "Out of Our Vaults" is an exhibition of new material taken from the museum's research archives, and never before seen by the public.

🏛 Reuben H Fleet Space Theater and Science Center

El Prado, Plaza de Panama & Park Blvd. ☎ (619) 238-1233. ◯ daily. 📷 call ahead for OMNIMAX® show times.

The big attraction here is the vast dome of the OMNIMAX cinema in the Space Theater, where impressive films about the world around us are projected onto an enormous tilting screen. Laser and planetarium shows are also staged.

The complex is open in the evenings and has a Science Center with hands-on exhibits that demonstrate the laws of science. There is also a café, and a shop selling books and intriguing games and puzzles.

Ornate Colonial-style façade of the San Diego Museum of Art

🏛 San Diego Natural History Museum

1788 El Prado, Balboa Park. ▮ (619) 232-3821. ◻ daily. ● Jan 1, Thanksgiving, Dec 25. 🎟 free first Tue of month.
W www.sdnhm.org

The museum's ground floor displays traveling exhibits on themes such as whales and insects. There is also a Hall of Mineralogy, which is built to resemble a mine. The galleries on the lower level explore Southern California's ecological zones of desert, shore, and ocean, highlighting topics such as the mountain lion and off-shore kelp beds.

🏛 San Diego Aerospace Museum

2001 Pan American Plaza. ▮ (619) 234-8291. ◻ daily. ● Jan 1, Thanksgiving, Dec 25. 🎟
W www.aerospacemuseum.org

San Diego has long been a city of pioneering aviation. The *Spirit of St. Louis*, in which pilot Charles Lindbergh made the first nonstop solo transatlantic flight in 1927, was built here. A model of the plane takes pride of place among a collection of more than 60 original and full-scale reconstructions of aircraft. Exhibits range from a batwing glider to a Vietnam War helicopter.

A 1948 Tucker Torpedo from the Automotive Museum's collection

🏛 San Diego Automotive Museum

2080 Pan American Plaza. ▮ (619) 231-2886. ◻ daily. ● Jan 1, Thanksgiving, Dec 25. 🎟

Dream cars and motorcycles from both the United States and Europe shine on in this unashamedly nostalgic museum. Because most of the cars are privately owned, the collection is constantly changing, but gleaming paintwork, aesthetic curves, and whitewall tires are guaranteed.

SAN DIEGO ZOO

San Diego Zoo is one of the best-known zoos in the world, famous both for its conservation programs and as a highly educational source of family entertainment. With some 4,000 animals dispersed over 100 acres (40 ha), the best introduction is to take the 35-minute narrated bus tour that covers most of the zoo. The aerial Skyfari ride, which offers a trip across the south of the park in gondola cars 180 ft (55 m) up, is also rewarding. After these, visitors can track down their favorites in the animal world by following the paths and moving walkways. There is also a Children's Zoo, and in summer the zoo is open for nocturnal exploration.

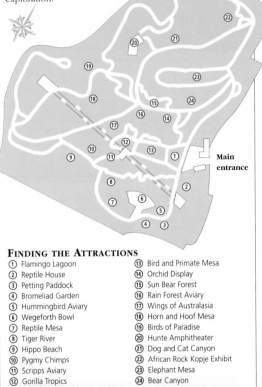

FINDING THE ATTRACTIONS

1. Flamingo Lagoon
2. Reptile House
3. Petting Paddock
4. Bromeliad Garden
5. Hummingbird Aviary
6. Wegeforth Bowl
7. Reptile Mesa
8. Tiger River
9. Hippo Beach
10. Pygmy Chimps
11. Scripps Aviary
12. Gorilla Tropics
13. Bird and Primate Mesa
14. Orchid Display
15. Sun Bear Forest
16. Rain Forest Aviary
17. Wings of Australasia
18. Horn and Hoof Mesa
19. Birds of Paradise
20. Hunte Amphitheater
21. Dog and Cat Canyon
22. African Rock Kopje Exhibit
23. Elephant Mesa
24. Bear Canyon

Sichuan takin calf resting in San Diego Zoo

Interior of the church at the Mission San Diego de Alcalá

Mission San Diego de Alcalá ②

10818 San Diego Mission Rd, San Diego. **Road map** D6. ((619) 283-7319. 20, 13. daily. Jan 1, Thanksgiving, Dec 25. **Donation.** 7am & 5:30pm daily.

Originally located at what is now the Junípero Serra Museum in Presidio Park (see p244), San Diego's mission was moved to Mission Valley in 1774. The land surrounding the new site was more fertile and had a larger population of potential Native American converts. The name Diego refers to St. Didacus, who was born in Alcalá, Spain, in 1400.

The first mission in the California chain (see pp42–3) is today engulfed by freeways and urban development, but its harmonious buildings and gardens retain an atmosphere of peace. Early this century, the complex was restored to its appearance of 1813. The church retains some original materials, such as the timbers over its doorways, the floor tiles, and the adobe bricks in the baptistry.

In the garden stands the Campanario (bell tower), and a statue representing St. Francis. A small museum honors the state's first Christian martyr, Padre Luís Jayme, who was murdered when a gang made up of 600 Native Americans attacked the newly established mission in 1775.

Statuette at San Diego de Alcalá

Sea World ③

500 Sea World Drive. **Road map** D6. ((619) 226-3901. 9. daily. W www.seaworld.com

In this state famous for its theme parks, the great lure of San Diego's Sea World is the chance to get close to the creatures that inhabit our oceans. Steadily expanded since its opening in 1964, this marine park now covers 150 acres (60 ha) of Mission Bay and can provide its visitors with entertainment for a full day.

A good starting point is the five-minute ride up the Skytower, a 320-ft (98-m) column with panoramic views. Another interesting aerial perspective is offered by the 100-ft (30-m) high Bayside Skyride in the park's northwest corner, where gondola cars take passengers in a 0.5-mile (1-km) loop over the waters of Mission Bay.

The stars of Sea World are its performing whales and dolphins. It is advisable to call in advance in order to plan a visit around their shows. One performance reveals the intelligence of dolphins and pilot whales, while another demonstrates the virtuosity of killer whales. Among the many other attractions in the park are pools with sharks, otters, and turtles and freshwater aquariums, as well as opportunities to feed killer whales and seals and touch rays and starfish. Close to the Skytower is Shamu's Happy Harbor, an aquatic adventure park for children.

There is also a more serious side to Sea World – its staff are devoted to animal rescue and rehabilitation and take in an average of one sick or abandoned animal per day. The park also runs education and conservation programs.

Mission Bay ④

Road map D6. from Downtown San Diego. **Visitors' Center** ((619) 276-8200. daily.

Mission Bay Park is an area of 4,600 acres (1,850 ha) entirely given over to public recreational use. San Diegans come here to keep fit and relax in the well-tended parkland.

Killer whales performing acrobatic feats for the crowds at Sea World

Sailing on the peaceful waters of Mission Bay

The area was once a marsh, but systematic dredging and landscaping, begun in the 1930s, transformed it. The San Diego River has been corralled into a channel to the south, creating a pleasant world of beaches, water-sports centers, and islands. Although the main attraction in Mission Bay is Sea World, visitors can also enjoy kite-flying, volleyball, golf, and cycling. Along the 27-mile (43-km) shoreline, swimming, fishing, and sailing take place in designated areas.

In the southwest corner of the bay is Mission Beach (see p238), one of the most lively beaches in San Diego County. Lovers of traditional seaside amusements will enjoy the beachfront **Belmont Park**. Its restored wooden Giant Dipper dates from 1925.

🎢 **Belmont Park**
3146 Mission Blvd. 📞 (858) 488-0668. ◯ daily.

La Jolla ❺

Road map D6. 🏠 32,000. 🚌 from San Diego. ℹ 1055 Wall St, Suite 110 (858 454-1444).

THE ORIGIN of the name La Jolla (which is pronounced "La Hoya") is the subject of an on-going debate – while some people believe it to come from the Spanish la joya, meaning "jewel," others claim it was inspired by a Native American word, with the same pronunciation, which means "cave." Located 4 miles (6 km) north of San Diego's Mission Bay, La Jolla is an elegant, upscale coastal resort set amid beautiful cliffs and coves (see p239). Its pretty streets are lined with gourmet chocolatiers, designer clothes shops, and top-name jewelers. San Diegans and tourists alike come to enjoy the many art galleries and the chic restaurants promising a "Mediterranean" view.

A companion to the gallery in Downtown San Diego (see p241), La Jolla's **Museum of Contemporary Art** occupies a prime oceanfront location. It displays works from its permanent collection of post-1950 art and houses a bookstore, café, and sculpture garden.

The town is also home to the University of California at San Diego and to the famous **Salk Institute for Biological Studies**, founded in 1960 by Dr. Jonas Salk, who developed the polio vaccine.

Overlooking Scripps Beach is the Scripps Institution of Oceanography, where the magnificent **Birch Aquarium at Scripps** is housed. The aquarium provides an insight into the fascinating world of oceanography, through permanent exhibits, interactive displays, and even a simulated deep-sea dive. In the adjacent aquarium, visitors can observe sea life from the waters of the north Pacific as well as from the tropics, including a balletic Alaskan giant octopus.

🏛 **Museum of Contemporary Art**
700 Prospect St. 📞 (858) 454-3541. ◯ Tue–Sun. ● Jan 1, Dec 25. ♿

🏫 **Salk Institute for Biological Studies**
10010 N Torrey Pines Rd. 📞 (858) 453-4100. ◯ Mon–Fri. ● public hols. ♿ call ahead.

🐠 **Birch Aquarium at Scripps**
2300 Expedition Way. 📞 (619) 534-3474. ◯ daily. ● Thanksgiving, Dec 25. ♿

Beautiful rocky shoreline of La Jolla Cove

Memorial plaque at the battlefield site in San Pasqual Valley

San Pasqual Battlefield **6**

Road map D6. *(760) 489-0076.* ☐ *Sat & Sun, public hols.* ● *Jan 1, Thanksgiving, Dec 25.*

IN 1846, during the war between the United States and Mexico *(see p43)*, the San Pasqual Valley was the scene of a costly victory for the US Army over the rebel Californios (Mexican settlers in California). Handicapped by wet gunpowder, exhaustion, and cold, 22 of the 100 soldiers fighting under General Kearny were killed by the Californio lancers and 16 were wounded.

There is a **Visitors' Center**, run by volunteers, in which a film about the battle is shown.

Every December, local history enthusiasts in replica 19th-century military uniforms re-enact the events of the battle.

ℹ Visitors' Center
15808 San Pasqual Valley Rd. *(760) 737-2201.* ☐ *May–Sep: daily; Oct–Apr: Sat & Sun.* ● *public hols.*

San Diego Wild Animal Park **7**

Hwy 78. *(760) 480-0100.* 🚌 *Escondido.* ☐ *daily.* 🏪 ♿ ✉

A RURAL COUNTERPART to San Diego Zoo *(see p249)*, this wildlife park displays an encyclopedic variety of birds and mammals in its 1,800 acres (730 ha) of carefully landscaped grounds. Opened in 1972, the park was conceived as a breeding sanctuary for the world's endangered species and has remained at the forefront of the conservation race. As well as caring for its 3,200 residents, the park exchanges animals with zoological institutions around the world, with the ultimate goal of releasing endangered species back into the wild. Among the program's success stories is that of the California condor, a species once close to extinction. Many condors successfully reared in the park have been returned to their natural habitat.

A good way to begin a visit is to take the Wgasa Bush Line Monorail. This 50-minute, five-mile guided ride around the large park passes the principal

animal enclosures and provides a useful orientation. Another fascinating journey is along the 2-mile (3-km) Kilimanjaro Safari Walk, offering superb views of re-created African and Asian landscapes.

For many visitors, the big animals, such as elephants, lions, and rhinos, are the stars. However, the park's various simulated natural environments, such as the Australian Rainforest and the Hidden Jungle, are also engrossing, and the Petting Kraal is very popular with children. Before visiting the Wild Animal Park, it is worth calling ahead to find out the times of daily events.

Anyone who likes to see wildlife in close-up can join a Photo Caravan, which takes small groups on tours inside the park's enclosures in an open-topped truck. Call ahead for reservations.

Nairobi Village is a 17-acre (7-ha) area, where the park's amphitheaters and most of its facilities are to be found. Its many shops sell Africa-related books and souvenirs.

Mission San Luis Rey **8**

Hwy 76 (Mission Ave), Rancho del Oro Drive, San Luis Rey. *(760) 757-3651.* 🚌 *from San Diego.* ☐ *daily.* **Donation.**

ONE OF THE LARGEST and most prosperous estates in the California mission chain *(see p42)*, San Luis Rey de Francia

Animals roaming around freely in the San Diego Wild Animal Park

Façade of Mission San Luis Rey

was founded by the Spanish priest Padre Fermín Lasuén in 1798. The mission was named after the canonized 13th-century French king, Louis IX, and owed much of its success to the cooperation of the local Luiseño Indians. More than 3,000 Native Americans lived and worked in Mission San Luis Rey. They kept sheep and cattle and cultivated crops such as grain and fruit.

The majority of the mission's remaining buildings benefited from a long period of restoration in the early 20th century. Visitors are guided first into a **museum** outlining the history of the mission and the surrounding area. Of the vestments and religious artifacts on display, several have survived only because, after the church was secularized in 1833, some of its treasures were hidden by the Christian Native Americans. Their families returned the artifacts to the mission only when it was designated a Franciscan monastery in 1893.

A statue in the church

The church at San Luis Rey has a cruciform shape as at San Juan Capistrano *(see p231),* but it was the only one in the chain with a domed wooden ceiling. The wooden pulpit is original, and the painted designs are based on surviving stencils. The mission still functions as a church and retreat, and in its grounds are a partly restored laundry area, a large cemetery, and California's oldest pepper tree, brought from Peru in 1830.

🏛 Museum

Eastern Cloister. ☐ *daily.* ⬤ *Jan 1, Thanksgiving, Dec 25.* 🈂 ♿

Palomar Mountain ❾

Road map D6. 🚌 *from Julian.*

Rising to 6,200 ft (1,900 m) and thickly forested, Palomar Mountain offers visitors breathtaking views over north San Diego County from the long, winding road that climbs its slopes. The Palomar Mountain State Park encompasses 1,600 acres (645 ha) of the mountain's scenic landscape. It has good hiking trails and also provides facilities for activities, such as camping, hiking, and trout fishing.

At the summit of Palomar Mountain is the surreal-looking white dome of the **Palomar Observatory**. Operated by the California Institute of Technology, this internationally renowned observatory first opened in 1948. It houses a computer-controlled Hale telescope with a 200-inch (510-cm) mirror capable of studying areas of the universe that are more than a billion light years away. From 1948 to 1956, the observatory's Oschin telescope was used to photograph the entire night sky. A second survey began in 1983 and is still in progress today. The images it produces will be compared to the earlier ones to reveal the changes that have taken place since the 1950s and thus provide vital data for researchers.

The Observatory is open daily from 9am to 4pm. Visitors are not permitted to look through the 540-ton telescope. However, an exhibition area and photo gallery explain how it functions.

🏛 Palomar Observatory

35899 Canfield Rd, Palomar Mountain. ⬤ *Dec 24 & 25.* 📞 *(760) 742-2119.*

Dome of the Palomar Observatory at sunset

Julian ⑩

Road map D6. 🚶 *2,000.* 🚌 *from San Diego.* ℹ️ *2129 Main St (760 765-1857).*

W HEN SAN DIEGANS want to go for a pleasant drive or spend a romantic weekend in the "back country," they often head for the mountain town of Julian. Gold was discovered here in 1870, and the restored 19th-century wooden buildings that line the main street help to re-create the atmosphere of those pioneer days.

Today tourists rather than gold-diggers flock here. In autumn, the "Apple Days" of October attract hundreds of visitors, who come to taste Julian's famous apple pie and buy rustic souvenirs in the quaint gift shops. The delightfully cluttered **Julian Pioneer Museum** is packed with curiosities and photographs evoking the town's history. Visitors can also venture inside an original gold mine at the **Eagle and High Peak Mines**.

For visitors wishing to stay overnight, there is plenty of homey bed-and-breakfast accommodation both in and around the town *(see p518).*

🏛 **Julian Pioneer Museum**
2811 Washington St. ☏ *(760) 765-0227.* 🕐 *Apr–Nov: Tue–Sun; Dec–March: Sat, Sun & public hols.* 🚫
⛏ **Eagle and High Peak Mines**
C St. ☏ *(760) 765-0036.* 🕐 *daily, but call ahead.* ● *Jan 1, Easter Sun, Thanksgiving, Dec 25.* 🚫

Apple pie store sign in Julian

Cuyamaca Rancho State Park ⑪

Road map D6. 🚌 ℹ️ *(760) 765-0755.* 🕐 *daily.*

O NLY AN HOUR's drive east of San Diego, Cuyamaca Rancho State Park is a place to get away from it all. Almost half of its 25,000 acres (10,100 ha) are an officially designated wilderness that is home to skunks, bobcats, coyotes, mule deer, and mountain lions.

In addition to horseback riding, camping, and mountain biking facilities, there are 130 miles (210 km) of hiking trails in the park. The Cuyamaca Peak Trail is an arduous but rewarding ascent by paved fire road. From the summit, hikers can enjoy fine views over the forested hills of northern San Diego County as far as Palomar Mountain *(see p253).*

Information on other trails and facilities is available from the **Park Headquarters**, located on Highway 79. Also at the Park Headquarters is a **museum** that pays homage to Cuyamaca Rancho's first inhabitants, the Kumeya'ay Indians.

At the northern end of the park lie the ruins of the Stonewall Gold Mine. Once a 500-strong prospectors' town, it produced more than two million dollars' worth of gold in the 1880s.

ℹ️ **Park Headquarters and Museum**
12551 Hwy 79. ☏ *(760) 765-0755.* 🕐 *daily.* ● *public hols.*

Shores of Lake Morena

Lake Morena Park ⑫

Road map D6. 🚌 *from San Diego.* ☏ *(619) 478-5473.*

T HIS LUSH, oak-shaded park surrounding a large fishing lake forms an oasis in the dry southeastern corner of San Diego County. The park covers 3,250 acres (1,300 ha) of land ranging from flat terrain to low scrub-covered hills.

The extensive waters of Lake Morena are well stocked with bass, bluegill, crappie, and catfish. For those who come to fish or simply enjoy a peaceful afternoon on the lake, rental boats are available.

Chula Vista Nature Center ⑬

Road map D6. ☏ *(619) 409-5900.* 🚌 *E St, Bay.* 🕐 *Jun–Aug: daily; Sep–May: Tue–Sun.* ● *Jan 1, Easter Sun, Thanksgiving & following day, Dec 24, 25 & 31.* 🚫 🚹

T HIS REMARKABLE conservation project beside San Diego Bay was established in 1988 to provide refuge for the wildlife of California's coastal wetlands. A free bus takes visitors to the Nature Center from a parking lot located by I-5.

Here visitors can learn about the fragile environment of the 316 acres (130 ha) of protected land. From the Nature Center, several hiking trails lead to the bay shore. Birds that can be seen all year round include herons, ospreys, and kestrels. The refuge is also a nesting site for endangered species, such as the California least tern.

Horseback riding in the Cuyamaca Rancho State Park

Tijuana ⑭

Carved wooden Mexican bird

Few visitors to San Diego can resist a brief trip south into Baja California. The international border crossing at Tijuana is the busiest in the world, and the contrast between the American and Mexican ways of life is marked. Thousands of Americans, who come to Tijuana every year to enjoy its inexpensive shopping and exuberant nightlife, often affectionately refer to the city as "TJ."

LOCATOR MAP

— International border

— San Diego Trolley line

▨ Mexico

Exploring Tijuana

The border city of Tijuana is hardly representative of the fabled Mexico of Mayan art and Spanish colonial architecture, but it is interesting as a hybrid frontier town devoted to extracting dollars from its wealthy neighbor.

The city's futuristic **Centro Cultural Tijuana** was built on the banks of the Tijuana River in 1982. This cultural center has an OMNIMAX theater, where films about Mexico are shown on an enormous tilting screen. Changing exhibitions on various Mexican themes are also held here. The open-air **Mexitlán** rooftop exhibition re-creates the country's architectural treasures in miniature.

Most visitors come to shop and party – Tijuana has long been popular with young Americans taking advantage of laws permitting anyone over 18 to drink alcohol.

The best shopping is in the quiet bazaars situated to the sides of the lively Avenida Revolución. Painted pottery, leather boots, silver jewelry,

Bottles of liqueur on sale in a street bazaar in Tijuana

and tequila are some favorite buys. Tourists are encouraged to barter with the merchants.

English-speaking staff at the **Tijuana Tourist Office** can provide maps and free advice on visiting the city.

🏛 **Centro Cultural Tijuana**
Paseo de los Héroes. 📞 (011-52-66) 84-11-11. ◻ daily. 🈂

🏛 **Mexitlán**
Ave Ocampo, Calles 2–3. 📞 (011-52-66) 38-41-01. ◻ Wed– Sun. 🈂

🛈 **Tijuana Tourist Office**
Ave Revolución y Calle. 📞 (011-52-66) 88-05-55. ◻ daily.

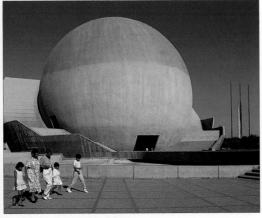

Façade of the Centro Cultural Tijuana

PRACTICAL INFORMATION

S AN DIEGO is an easy city to get to know, with a clean, efficient public transit system and a welcoming attitude toward visitors. The regeneration of the city's heart is evident in the growing number of shops, restaurants, and nightspots around Horton Plaza (see p240) and the Gaslamp Quarter (see pp242–3). A variety of public transportation penetrates this Downtown area, where there

Jessop's Clock
in Horton Plaza

are all the shops and entertainment spots you would expect in a vibrant California city. There are also regular connections to Old Town, Balboa Park, Coronado, and the Mexican border, while the best way to enjoy the waterfront of the Embarcadero (see p240) is on foot. Tourist information is available from excellent visitors' centers located in Horton Plaza, and Balboa Park, as well as in Coronado.

Passengers boarding a San
Diego bus

GETTING AROUND

T HE TWO LINES of the **San Diego Trolley**, the city's streetcar system, link Old Town, El Cajon, and San Ysidro on the Mexican border with the city center. Trolleys run every 15 minutes during the day and operate until around 1am. A comprehensive bus network runs throughout the city. The **San Diego–Coronado Bay Ferry** offers a regular service to the Coronado Peninsula (see p245). Maps, timetables, and special one- or four-day Day Tripper passes, valid for unlimited travel on any bus, trolley, or ferry, can be obtained

from the **Transit Store**. **Old Town Trolley Tours** offer regular guided tours visiting all the principal sights.

The city's **Amtrak** station is housed in the beautiful Santa Fe Depot in Downtown. **San Diego International Airport** is located 3 miles (5 km) northwest of Downtown. Buses, taxis, and rental cars are all available from the airport.

The **Balboa Park Tram** provides free rides around the cultural park (see pp246–7). In the vast Mission Bay aquatic playground (see pp250–1), the **Harbor Hopper** water taxi takes visitors to points of interest around the shoreline.

San Diego is also a bicycle-friendly city, well served with bike paths and bike rental shops. There is a gentle route from Mission Beach to La Jolla (see p251), offering fine ocean views. Bikes can be carried on trolleys and buses for a small fee. If you prefer to let someone else do the work, you can hail bicycle taxis in Downtown.

It is generally safe to walk around the areas to the north and west of Downtown, even at night. However, the areas to the south of Downtown and particularly, to the east of the Gaslamp Quarter are best avoided after dark.

Mexican-style shopping in the
Bazaar del Mundo

SHOPPING

I F YOU INTEND to visit Tijuana (see p255), avoid doing too much shopping before you go, since bargain goods are the main reason for crossing the border. The Bazaar del Mundo in Old Town San Diego (see p244) also has plenty of Mexican crafts and souvenirs.

Horton Plaza is the city's most colorful shopping center and can meet most tourists' needs, while the Paladion next door sells couture clothing. The oceanfront Seaport Village complex (see p240) is a good place to buy souvenirs and gifts to take home. Farther up the coast, Prospect Street in

A San Diego Trolley, offering a fast, frequent service to the Mexican border

Attractive shopping area of Seaport Village, on the waterfront

La Jolla has a selection of elegant stores. Del Mar and Carlsbad also have a good mix of boutiques, antique shops, and art galleries.

There are several factory outlet centers in San Diego County, where outlet stores sell well-known brand-name goods at considerably reduced prices *(see p583)*. The San Diego Factory Outlet Center, located just before the Mexican border crossing in San Ysidro, is one of the largest and best in the region, with more than 30 factory outlet stores. Ask at the information desk in the large parking lot for a sheet of discount tokens, which allow you to obtain further reductions of up to 15 percent in many of the shops.

Here, as throughout the state, major credit cards are accepted, and the hours of most shops are 10am–6pm Monday to Saturday, with some stores open on Sundays as well. A local sales tax of 8.5 percent applies to all purchases. This is automatically added to the advertised price of the goods when you pay for them.

ENTERTAINMENT

S AN DIEGO HAS a reputation for its cultural energy and has its own symphony orchestra, opera, and repertory theater companies. Listings of all the current cultural events can be found in the *San Diego Union-Tribune* and a range of complimentary tourist magazines. *The Reader*, available free in cafés, bars, and bookstores, is a good weekly source for finding out about poetry readings, live music, and the

alternative arts. Tickets for all these events can be bought from the **Times Arts Tix** office in Horton Plaza.

The Gaslamp Quarter *(see pp242–3)* is the best area to go to for good restaurants and nightclubs. The nearby Lyceum and Spreckels theaters have regular stage performances. In Balboa Park, the Old Globe Theater *(see p246)* stages award-winning shows and is one part of a three-stage performing arts complex.

Like most Californians, San Diegans are also avid sports fans – the Chargers football team and the Padres baseball team each has a stadium in Mission Valley. If, however, you prefer participating in sports to watching them, Mission Bay *(see pp250–1)* offers a wide range of water sports, as well as beach games such as volleyball. San Diego County also benefits from 83 excellent golf courses – ask at hotels or at local visitors' centers for more information.

San Diego's own baseball team, the Padres

THE INLAND EMPIRE AND LOW DESERT

T HE INLAND EMPIRE AND LOW DESERT *landscape is one of the most varied in California. The countryside changes from pine forests, cooled by gentle breezes, to searing desert. The contrast can be startling: passengers taking the Palm Springs Aerial Tramway make the transition between these two ecosystems in 14 minutes.*

The Anza-Borrego Desert State Park was the forbidding entry point to California for tens of thousands of hardy miners and settlers coming overland in the 1850s. Thirty years later communities in the northwest of the region, known as the Inland Empire, were transformed from a small collection of health resorts into the heart of a veritable economic empire based on the navel orange. The thick-skinned seedless Brazilian fruit, which traveled well, came to represent the sweet and healthy promise of California for millions of Americans. Many of the Victorian mansions built by citrus millionaires are still standing in the towns of Redlands and Riverside, but most of the fragrant orange groves have disappeared under asphalt and urban sprawl. Today Riverside is practically a suburb of Los Angeles.

At the heart of this region is Palm Springs, a favorite weekend retreat for Angelenos seeking relaxation and the desert sun. Just under two hours drive from LA, it has luxurious hotels, verdant golf courses, 600 tennis courts, and more than 10,000 swimming pools.

Lying to the east of Palm Springs is the Joshua Tree National Park. This is a land of hot, dry days, chilly nights, tumbleweed, and creosote bushes. The stark and silent beauty of the rocky landscape evokes images of desperados, hardy pioneers in covered wagons, and leather-clad high plains drifters – visions of the Wild West of so many novels and films.

When the desert becomes too hot, travelers can escape to one of the mountain resorts. The Rim of the World Tour is a spectacular drive in the heart of the San Bernardino Mountains.

Western film set in Pioneertown, near Yucca Valley

◁ Joshua tree silhouetted against the barren desert landscape

Exploring the Inland Empire and Low Desert

Tʜᴇ ɪɴʟᴀɴᴅ ᴇᴍᴘɪʀᴇ is a region of vast scenic and
climatic contrasts. In the northwest is the San
Bernardino National Forest, with its cool mountain
air and breathtaking views.
Farther south lies the
sun-baked Coachella
Valley, ending in the
steamy Salton Sea. Palm
Springs, the largest of
the desert resorts, is
flanked by the stark
Joshua Tree National
Park and the alpine
community of
Idyllwild. The
forbidding Anza-
Borrego Desert
State Park, in
the southwest
of the region, is
the gateway to San
Diego County.

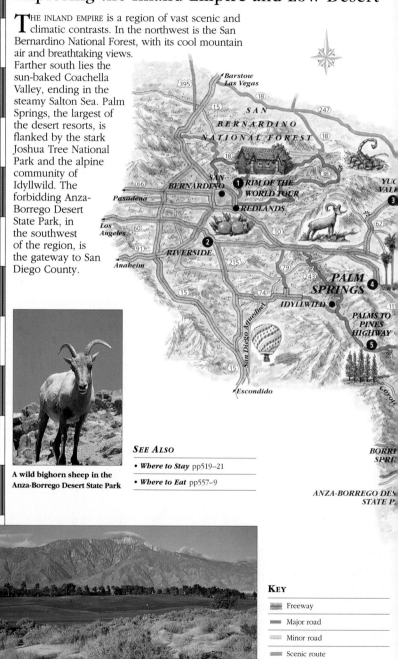

A wild bighorn sheep in the
Anza-Borrego Desert State Park

Sᴇᴇ Aʟsᴏ

• *Where to Stay* pp519–21

• *Where to Eat* pp557–9

View across Desert Dunes golf course, near Palm Springs

Kᴇʏ

	Freeway
	Major road
	Minor road
	Scenic route
	River
☼	Viewpoint

SIGHTS AT A GLANCE

Wind turbines in the Coachella Valley

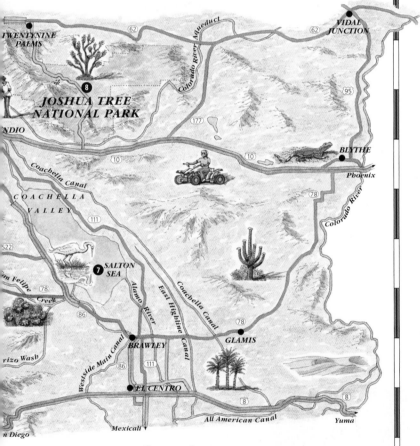

GETTING AROUND

The safest way to explore the desert areas is by car. The I-10 crosses the Inland Empire and Low Desert from east to west. Palm Springs, 107 miles (170 km) southeast of LA and 120 miles (190 km) northeast of San Diego, has a Greyhound bus terminal, an airport, and is a good base for exploring the region. Buses regularly go to and from the Amtrak station in nearby Indio.

0 kilometers   20

0 miles   20

Rim of the World Tour ❶

Elf at Santa's Village

FROM SAN BERNARDINO this invigorating drive winds across the forested San Bernardino Mountains, offering spectacular views of the desert beyond. The altitude provides for distinct seasons, with warm, pine-scented air in the summer and brisk, cool days in the winter, when the snow-covered mountain trails are perfect for cross-country skiing. The tour passes through the resorts beside Lake Arrowhead and Big Bear Lake, both favorite destinations for those wanting to escape the heat and smog of LA. In Redlands visitors are offered a sense of the area's heady Victorian past, and yet another pleasure: the sweet smell of orange groves.

San Bernardino Mountain landscape

Big Bear Lake ③
A popular resort area, Big Bear Lake offers a range of sports including fishing, sailing, swimming, and, in the winter, skiing. Its two commercial centers are Big Bear City, to the east, and Big Bear Village, to the south.

Heaps Park Arboretum ④
A 1,230-yd (1,130-m) nature trail winds through this wooded hillside, planted with native and other trees. Species include dogwoods, Jeffrey pine, ponderosa pine, black oaks, live oaks, and white fir.

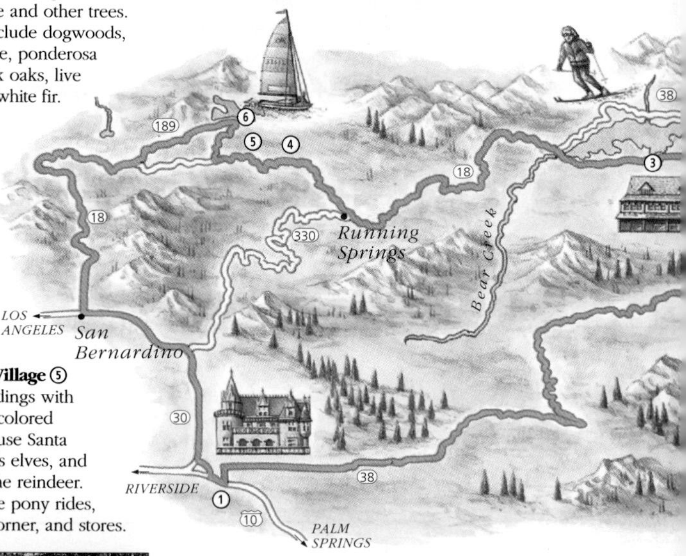
38
189
6
5
4
18
3
18
330
Running Springs
Bear Creek
LOS ANGELES
San Bernardino
30
RIVERSIDE
1
38
10
PALM SPRINGS

Santa's Village ⑤
Log buildings with brightly colored roofs house Santa Claus, his elves, and Rudolf the reindeer. There are pony rides, a pets' corner, and stores.

Lake Arrowhead ⑥
Lake Arrowhead Village, on the south shore, offers shops, restaurants and accommodations in both hotels and log cabins. Trips up the lake aboard the *Arrowhead Queen* also begin here. The north shore is almost exclusively residential.

Redlands ①
This town is famous for its Victorian mansions, built at the end of the 19th century by those who made their fortunes growing navel oranges *(see p46)*. Among the finest are Kimberly Crest House and Gardens, the Morey Mansion, and the Edwards Mansion.

Onyx Summit ②
At 8,443 ft (2,573 m), Onyx Summit is the highest point on the aim of the World Tour. From a viewpoint near the top there are stunning views across the mountainous San Bernardino National Forest to the desert.

kilometers   10

miles   5

.EY

▬ Tour route

═ Other roads

Ornate Mission Inn in Riverside

Riverside ②

Road map D6. 🏚 250,000. 🚌 🛈
7920 Limonite Ave (909 681-9242).

SOME OF THE MOST elegant architecture in Southern California is to be found in Riverside. During the late 19th century, the town was the center of California's citrus industry and by 1905 it had the highest per capita income in the United States. One of the two original orange trees responsible for this great success was planted in 1875 by Eliza and Luther Tihbetts (see p46). It is still thriving in a small park at the intersection of Magnolia and Arlington avenues.

Riverside's **Mission Inn**, built in 1880 as a 12-room adobe house, was expanded early in the 20th century into a 234-room hotel (see p521). Architecturally, the hotel is a mixture of Mission Revival, Moorish, and oriental styles, with flying buttresses, spiral staircases, and gargoyles. The **Riverside Municipal Museum** features exhibits on the town's history and Native American culture.

Riverside is also known for its two major car races. The California 500 is held in early September, and the Winston Western 500 runs in January.

🏨 **Mission Inn**
3649 Mission Inn Ave. ☎ (909) 784-0300. ◻ 9.30am–4pm daily.
🏛 **Riverside Municipal Museum**
3720 Orange St. ☎ (909) 826-5273. ◻ daily.

Pot at Hi-Desert Nature Museum

Yucca Valley ③

Road map D5. 🏚 44,000. 🚌
🛈 56711 Twenty-nine Palms Hwy (760 365-6323).

YUCCA VALLEY is a small town located just north of the Joshua Tree National Park (see pp268–9). On a hillside, the **Desert Christ Park** has 30 statues depicting the life of Jesus, sculpted by Antone Martin in the 1950s. The town's **Hi-Desert Nature Museum** has various exhibits on the region's geology, crafts, flora, and fauna. **Pioneertown**, 4 miles (6 km) northwest of Yucca Valley, is a hamlet built in 1947 as a Western film set.

🌿 **Desert Christ Park**
End of Mohawk Trail. ☎ (760) 365-6323. ◻ daily.
🏛 **Hi-Desert Museum**
58116 Twenty-nine Palms Hwy. ☎ (760) 369-7212. ◻ Tue–Sun.
● public hols.

Statue of Christ at the Antone Martin Memorial Park

Palm Springs ④

Popcorn in Ruddy's

THE COACHELLA VALLEY has been inhabited for 10,000 years, but it was only in 1853 that a government survey party came across a grove of palm trees surrounding a mineral pool bubbling up out of the desert sand. The area's first hotel was constructed in 1886, and by the turn of the century the city of Palm Springs was a thriving health spa. In the 1920s and 1930s the area become a fashionable winter resort, colonized by the rich and famous.

Exploring Palm Springs

The postwar building boom *(see p50)* brought rapid hotel and residential development to Palm Springs. Drawn by the city's growing popularity, developers later began opening up the empty desert lands eastward along the Coachella Valley. From 1967 to 1981, the resort cities of Cathedral City, Rancho Mirage, Palm Desert, Indian Wells, and La Quinta shot up between Palm Springs and the date-growing center of Indio, 22 miles (35 km) away. Desert Hot Springs, a spa just northeast of Palm Springs, also became a popular vacation destination. The extraordinary proliferation of luxury golf courses – there are more than 80 in the region – dates from this period *(see p267)*.

Today Palm Springs remains the largest of the desert cities. Its population doubles each winter, when visitors come to enjoy its healthy, relaxing, outdoor lifestyle. First-class accommodations, such as the Marriott and Givenchy hotels, abound *(see pp521)*. Many celebrities still live here, and several companies offer guided tours that point out their houses.

The two main shopping streets in downtown Palm Springs are Palm Canyon and Indian Canyon drives. Each is lined with outdoor restaurants, exclusive boutiques, and art galleries. In the city center, the pedestrian Desert Fashion Plaza houses two department stores and several smaller luxury shops.

The city's unique sense of desert chic is maintained in discreet ways. Street lights, for example, are hidden within palm leaves and bushes to lend the area a subtle glow.

Old Shredded Wheat advertisement from Ruddy's in Village Green

🚂 Village Green Heritage Center

221 S Palm Canyon Drive. 📞 *(760) 323-8297.* ⏰ *Oct–May: Wed–Sun.* ● *public hols.* 🎫

This quiet enclave, in the heart of Palm Springs' shopping district, contains four historical buildings. Palm Springs' first white resident, John Guthrie McCallum, built the McCallum Adobe in 1884. Originally it stood near the Indian village of Agua Caliente, the site of the natural hot springs that inspired the town's name. The house was moved to its present location during the 1950s.

The Cornelia White House (1893) is built partly out of railroad ties. It is furnished with antiques dating from Palm Springs' pioneer era.

The heritage of the area's Cahuilla people is related through artifacts and photographs in the Agua Caliente Cultural Museum. There is also a collection of antique baskets that were handcrafted by local Native American weavers.

Also in the Village Green Heritage Center is Ruddy's 1930s General Store Museum. Once the town's only druggist, Ruddy's is an immaculate and well-stocked replica of a Depression-era shop. Authentically packaged goods range from licorice and shoelaces to flour and patent medicines.

🏊 Oasis Water Resort

1500 Gene Autry Trail. 📞 *(760) 327-4664.* ⏰ *Mar–early Sep: daily; Sep–Oct: Sat & Sun.* ● *public hols.* 🎫

This state-of-the-art water park covers 21 acres (8.5 ha). It boasts 13 waterslides, including an exciting 70-ft (20-m) free-fall slide and a 600-ft (180-m) artificial "river" for riding inflated inner tubes. There are special slides and pools for young children. California's largest wave-action pool creates 4-ft (1.2-m) high artificial waves suitable for surfing and boogie boarding. Surfboards and inner tubes can be rented from the park on either an hourly or a daily basis.

The Oasis Water Resort also includes a hotel, a rock climbing center, heated spas, a health club, and an assortment of fine restaurants.

Children emerging from a Scorpion free-fall slide at the Oasis Water Resort

Palm Springs Aerial Tramway ascending to the Mountain Station

Palm Springs Aerial Tramway

Tramway Rd. (760) 325-1391.
daily.
www.pstramway.com

The Aerial Tramway's two Swiss-built cars, each holding 80 passengers, are one of Palm Springs' most popular attractions. The trams depart from Valley Station, situated 6 miles (10 km) northwest of Palm Springs. The 2.5-mile (4-km) trip at an angle of 50° takes 14 minutes and ascends 5,900 ft (1,790 m) over spectacular scenery to the Mountain Station in the Mount San Jacinto Wilderness State Park.

Passengers travel through five distinct ecosystems, ranging from desert to alpine forest, which is akin to traveling from Mexico to Alaska. The temperature changes dramatically during the journey. The heat of the valley floor sometimes differs as much as 50° F (10° C) from the icy temperature at the peak, so make sure you carry extra clothing.

At the top there are 54 miles (85 km) of hiking trails, one of which leads to Idyllwild (see p266). A Nordic ski center is open in the winter for cross-country skiing. There are also campsites, a ranger station, picnic areas, and 20-minute mule-pack rides on the slopes.

Observation decks perched on the edge of the 8,500-ft (2,600-m) high lookout offer views of the Coachella Valley, Palm Springs, and the San Bernardino Mountains. On a very clear day, it is possible to see for 50 miles (80 km) to the Salton Sea (see p267).

Both stations have gift shops, cocktail lounges, and snack bars. The Mountain Station also has a cafeteria.

Palm Springs Desert Museum

101 Museum Drive. (760) 325-7186. Tue–Sun. public hols. free first Fri of month.
www.psmuseum.org

The Palm Springs Desert Museum focuses on art, natural science, and the performing arts. Paintings in the museum's galleries date from the 19th century to the present day. Native American artifacts and local natural history exhibits are also on display. A stunning array of modern sculpture adorns the patios and gardens.

The adjoining Annenberg Theater is a 450-seat center for the performing arts, which features both local and touring dance, drama, and orchestral companies. The lush gardens are enhanced by fountains and demonstrate that the desert need not be a barren place.

Two trails lead out from the museum and enable visitors to explore the flora and fauna of this desert region. The 2-mile (3-km) Museum Trail climbs 800 ft (244 m) up into the Mount San Jacinto State Park. It joins the Lykken Trail at Desert Riders Overlook (a viewpoint from which to look out across Palm Springs and the Coachella Valley). The

VISITORS' CHECKLIST

Road map D6. 42,000.
Palm Springs Regional Airport, 1 mile (1.5 km) NE of Downtown. Indio. 3111 N Indian Ave. 2500 N Whitewater Drive. (800) 347-7746, (760) 778-8418. Palm Springs International Film Festival (early–mid-Jan).

Lykken Trail then continues for another 4 miles (6 km) to the mouth of the Tahquitz Canyon (see p266).

Sculpture garden in the Palm Springs Desert Museum

PALM TREES

Only one palm variety in Palm Springs is native to California, the desert fan palm (*Washingtonia filifera*), which crowds the secluded mountain oases. Unlike other palm varieties, the dead fronds do not drop off the trunk but droop down to form a "skirt" that provides a shelter for wildlife.

Date palms (*Phoenix dactylifera*) were introduced from Algeria in 1890 as an experiment. Today, the Coachella Valley supplies 90 percent of the dates consumed in the US. A mature date palm can produce up to 300 lb (135 kg) of dates a year. An annual ten-day National Date Festival in Indio features a cornucopia of dried and fresh dates (see p35).

Date palm grove in the Coachella Valley

🏵 Indian Canyons

S Palm Canyon Drive. ☎ (760) 325-5673. ⏰ 9.30am–5pm daily. ♿

Approximately 5 miles (8 km) south of Palm Springs are four spectacular natural palm oases, set in stark, rocky gorges and surrounded by barren hills. Clustered along small streams fed by mountain springs, Murray, Tahquitz, Andreas, and Palm canyons are located on the land of the Agua Caliente Cahuilla people. Rock art and other traces of the area's early inhabitants can still be seen.

The 15-mile (24-km) long Palm Canyon is the largest of the gorges and contains more wild palms in one place than anywhere else in the world. A trading post near the parking lot offers refreshments, and from here it is a short but steep walk down to the main trail. Picnic tables have been set out beside a trickling stream in the shade of the 82-ft (25-m) high desert fan palms (see p265).

Desert fan palm oasis in the Indian Canyons

🏵 Living Desert Wildlife and Botanical Park

47900 Portola Ave. ☎ (760) 346-5694. ⏰ daily. ● Dec 25. ♿
🌐 www.livingdesert.org

The well-designed Living Desert Wildlife and Botanical Park offers a comprehensive view of North America's desert regions. The park covers 1,200 acres (485 ha), but most of its major attractions can be seen in half a day. Broad paths and paved walkways pass through interpretive botanical displays covering North America's 10 desert areas, which describe some of the 130 animal species that inhabit them.

Flowering ocotillo in the Living Desert Wildlife and Botanical Park

Of special interest are golden eagles, mountain lions, a large selection of nocturnal creatures, and the new cheetah exhibit. Roadrunners (desert birds that run rather than fly) roam free in their natural setting. On winter days, walking through the park is a pleasure. A guided tram tour is recommended in hotter weather.

Palms to Pines Highway ❺

Road map D6. 🛈 72–990 Hwy 111, Palm Desert (760 862-9984).

ONE OF THE MOST interesting drives in Southern California begins at the junction of Hwy 111 and Hwy 74 in Palm Desert. As you climb Hwy 74, you gradually leave behind the desert ecosystem with its palms, creosote, and desert ironwood trees and move into mountain scenery, made up of pines, juniper, and mountain mahogany. The view from Santa Rosa Summit, just under 5,000 ft (1,500 m) high, is spectacular. Continue northwest on Hwy 74 to Mountain Center and the lush meadows of Garner Valley.

At Mountain Center, take Hwy 243 to the picturesque alpine village of Idyllwild, with its many restaurants, lodges, and camp sites. The renowned Idyllwild School of Music and the Arts holds regular classical music concerts during the summer. More active visitors can follow one of the many surrounding hiking trails, for which maps are available at the Ranger Station. One 8-mile (13-km) trek leads to the Mountain Station of the Palm Springs Aerial Tramway (see p265). This provides the quickest way back to the desert floor. Mule-pack rides are available in the summer, and during the winter months there is cross-country skiing.

Anza-Borrego Desert State Park ❻

Road map D6. 🚌 Escondido. **Visitors' Center** ☎ (760) 767-4205. ⏰ Jun–Sep: Sat & Sun; Oct–May: daily. 🌐 www.anzaborregostatepark.org

STARTING WITH the Gold Rush of 1849 (see pp44–5), the Southern Emigrant Trail, the only all-weather land route into California, brought tens of thousands of miners and early settlers through the Anza-Borrego Desert. Today, this former overland gateway is a

Picturesque mountain town of Idyllwild

Badlands in the Anza-Borrego Desert State Park

remote and pristine park, offering a rare insight into a unique desert environment.

The desert's well-equipped visitors' center is in Borrego Springs. This is the only significant town in the otherwise undeveloped park. Nearby, the leisurely 1.5-mile (2.5-km) Palm Canyon Nature Trail leads to an oasis where the endangered bighorn sheep can occasionally be seen.

The Box Canyon Historical Monument is 31 miles (50 km) southwest of the visitors' center on County Road S2. Here you can view the old road once used by those miners who braved the desert climate on their way to the goldfields, which lay 500 miles (800 km) to the north.

The Anza-Borrego Desert is inhospitable for most of the year. Between March and May, however, following the winter rains, the burning land bursts into life. Cacti and desert flowers such as brittle-bush, desert poppies, and dune primroses produce a riot of color.

The desert's geology is as fascinating as its ecosystem. Over the millennia, a network of earthquake faults lifted and tilted the ground. Winter rains then carved through the shattered landscape, leaving multicolored "layer-cake" bluffs, steep ravines, and jagged canyons such as the famous Borrego and Carizzo Badlands.

Much of the Anza-Borrego State Park, including its well-kept camp sites, is easily accessible via 100 miles (160 km) of surfaced and scenic highways. However, four-wheel drive vehicles are recommended for use on the park's 500 miles (800 km) of unsurfaced roads.

Drivers of standard vehicles should contact the visitors' center in advance to check on current road conditions.

Salton Sea **7**

Road map E6. 🚗 *Mecca.*
🚌 *Indio.* **Visitors' Center** 📞 *(760) 393-3052.* ⬜ *Nov–Mar: daily; Apr & May: call ahead.*

THE SALTON SEA was created by accident in 1905 when the Colorado River flooded and flowed into a newly dug irrigation canal leading to the Imperial Valley. It took a team of engineers two years to stem the flow. By then, however, a 35-mile (55-km) inland sea had formed in the Salton Sink, 230 ft (70 m) below sea level.

Despite rising salinity and selenium levels, and algae blooms that turn the water a brownish color during the summer, there are still saltwater game fish in this inland sea, with 10-lb (4.5-kg) orangemouth corvina being caught regularly.

Windsurfing, water-skiing, and boating are also popular activities here. The northeastern shore of the sea has the best spots for swimming, particularly the stretch of water off Mecca Beach.

The sea's adjoining marshlands are a refuge for a wide variety of migrating birds, such as geese, ducks, blue herons, and egrets. On the east side of the Salton Sea there are hiking trails and camp sites set within the State Recreation Area. There is also a visitors' center and a small playground.

DESERT GOLF

Thanks to irrigation with water supplied from underground sources, Palm Springs is now known as the golf capital of the United States. There are more than 80 courses in the region, most of which belong to private clubs or are attached to resorts or hotel complexes. Some courses are rugged, while others are more lush. Among the professional golf events held in the area each year are the Bob Hope Desert Classic in January and the Dinah Shore Tournament at the end of March. A few courses are open to the public, including the Desert Dunes course, noted for adding the desert terrain to its challenging layout. In the summer it is best to tee off early in the morning. November and December offer better value and cooler weather. Most courses are closed in October for reseeding.

Tahquitz Creek Palm Springs Golf Resort

Joshua Tree National Park ❽

National park sign

The JOSHUA TREE NATIONAL PARK was established in 1936 to preserve the groves of the unusual, spiny-leaved Joshua tree. The species was named in 1851 by early Mormon travelers, who saw in the twisted branches the upraised arms of the biblical Joshua. This large member of the yucca family is unique to the area and can grow up to 30 ft (9 m) tall, sometimes living for 1,000 years. The 630,800-acre (255,300-ha) park offers uncommon vistas of the stark Californian desert, with its astounding formations of pink and gray rocks and boulders. A climber's paradise, Joshua Tree is also a fascinating area for hikers, who can discover lost mines, palm oases, and in the spring, a wealth of desert flowers. The Visitors' Center provides the latest weather report.

Joshua Trees
Large groves of Joshua trees thrive in the higher, wetter, and somewhat cooler desert areas of the park's western half.

Hidden Valley
The gigantic boulders here formed natural corrals, making this a legendary hideout for cattle rustlers in the days of the Wild West.

Key's View gives a sweeping view of the stunning valley, desert, and mountain terrain from its summit.

Lost Horse Mine
A 2-mile (3.2-km) trail leads to this historic gold mine, which was discovered by a cowboy searching for his lost horse. More than $270,000 in gold was extracted during the mine's first decade of operation.

KEY

▬▬	Freeway
▬▬	Major road
▬▬	Minor road
▭▭	Unsurfaced road
▪▪▪	Hiking trail
—	National Park boundary
🚶	Ranger station
🅂	Fee station
Ⓐ	Campsite
🅿	Picnic area
✲	Viewpoint

DESERT WILDLIFE

Despite the harshness of the arid desert environment, a variety of animals thrives here. In many cases, they have adapted to cope with lack of water. The kangaroo rat gets both its food and water from seeds alone, while its very large hind feet enable it to travel over the hot sand. Powerful legs, rather than wings, also serve the roadrunner, which gets its moisture from insects and small prey. The jackrabbit is born with a full coat of muted fur to camouflage it from large predators such as the coyote, bobcat, and eagle.

Coyote, wily denizen of the desert

VISITORS' CHECKLIST

Road map D5. 🚌 *Desert Stage Lines from Palm Springs to Twentynine Palms.* 🏢 **Oasis Visitors' Center** *74485 National Park Drive, Twentynine Palms.* 📞 *(760) 367-5500.* 🕐 *daily.* ⬤ *Dec 25.* 🌐 *www.nps.gov/jotr*

| 0 kilometers | 10 |
| 0 miles | 10 |

The arid wilderness of the Colorado Desert *(see p193)* occupies the park's eastern half. This inhospitable region is difficult to reach.

PINTO MOUNTAINS

COXCOMB MOUNTAINS

PINTO BASIN

lla us den

Pinto Basin Road

HEXIE MOUNTAINS

NWOOD INS

Cottonwood 🚶 📷
Cottonwood Spring △

Lost Palms Oasis

EAGLE MOUNTAINS

LM RINGS   (10)   BLYTHE

Lost Palms Oasis
A 4-mile (6.4-km) trail leads through attractive desert scenery to the largest group of palms in the park. It is one of the few areas where water occurs naturally near the surface.

Cottonwood Spring is a man-made oasis of palms and cottonwood trees that attracts desert birds. There is a visitors' center nearby.

Cholla Cactus Garden
A dense concentration of cholla cacti are the focal point of a short nature trail featuring desert flora and fauna. But beware – the cactus's fluffy fingers are really sharp spines.

THE MOJAVE DESERT

THE MOJAVE DESERT *is the state's greatest secret, all too often missed by travelers who zoom through it on the interstate highway. The desert is a harsh environment – Death Valley is one of the hottest places in the United States. But this dry region supports a surprising amount of plant life and for a few weeks each year, when the wildflowers appear amid the arid rocks, it becomes hauntingly beautiful.*

The Mojave Desert was a year-round overland gateway to California for much of the 19th century. Trappers, traders, and early settlers traveled hundreds of miles along the Old Spanish Trail from Santa Fe in New Mexico to Los Angeles. Passing through the towns of Barstow and Tecopa, the journey across the vast desert was both demanding and dangerous.

In the 1870s, gold, silver, borax, and various other precious minerals were discovered in the region, attracting large numbers of miners. Instant cities such as Calico sprang up, but when the mines became exhausted, many of the settlements were abandoned. In 1883 commercial mining became more viable when the Santa Fe Railroad was completed. Towns located along the route prospered, and the human population of the Mojave Desert increased.

In the early 20th century a new breed of desert lovers emerged. Jack Mitchell settled in the empty expanses of the East Mojave Desert in the 1930s and turned the spectacular Mitchell Caverns into a popular tourist destination. Death Valley Scotty was another desert enthusiast. He spent much of his life in a castle built in the 1920s by his friend, Albert Johnson, near the hottest and lowest point in the western hemisphere. Death Valley National Park now attracts thousands of visitors each year, who come to explore the area's wealth of historical landmarks and impressive natural sights.

The main draw of the Mojave Desert region today, however, is Nevada's Las Vegas, a five-hour drive from Los Angeles. This center of entertainment and gambling is proof that people are still trying to strike it rich in the desert.

Death Valley's Moorish-style Scotty's Castle

◁ **Desert shrubs in Death Valley**

Exploring the Mojave Desert

MOST OF THE MOJAVE DESERT is at an altitude of over 2,000 ft (600 m). It has cold winters and baking hot summers. Many of the region's rivers and lakes are seasonal and are dry during the summer. The desert is home to an array of plant species and a range of animals, from tortoises to foxes, which have evolved to survive in this climate. Barstow, the largest town in the Mojave region, caters to travelers to and from Las Vegas. The northern Mojave is dominated by the Death Valley National Park. To the east lie the resorts of Lake Havasu.

Premises of a 19th-century ore smelter in Calico Ghost Town

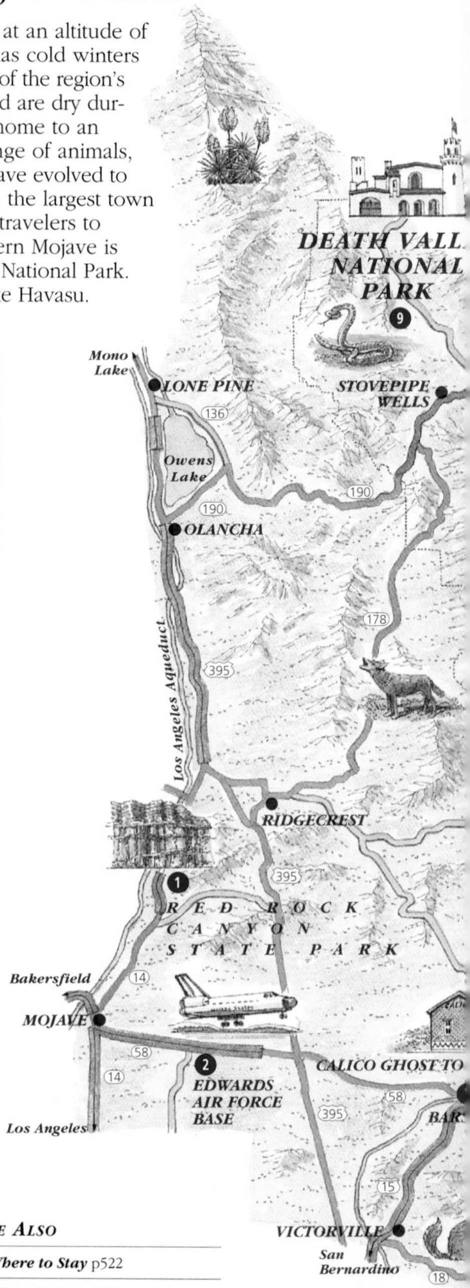
DEATH VALL
NATIONAL PARK
9
Mono Lake
LONE PINE
STOVEPIPE WELLS
136
Owens Lake
190
190
OLANCHA
178
Los Angeles Aqueduct
395
RIDGECREST
395
1
RED ROCK CANYON STATE PARK
Bakersfield
14
MOJAVE
58
14
2
EDWARDS AIR FORCE BASE
CALICO GHOST TO
58
395
BAR
Los Angeles
15
VICTORVILLE
San Bernardino
18

SIGHTS AT A GLANCE

Barstow 3
Calico Ghost Town 4
Death Valley National Park pp280–83 9
Edwards Air Force Base 2
Kelso Dunes 5
Lake Havasu 7
Las Vegas 8
Mitchell Caverns 6
Red Rock Canyon State Park 1

KEY

- Freeway
- Major road
- Minor road
- Scenic route
- River
- Viewpoint

SEE ALSO

• ***Where to Stay*** p522

• ***Where to Eat*** p559

0 kilometers 25

0 miles 25

Sand dunes north of Furnace Creek in the Death Valley National Park

GETTING AROUND

I-15 crosses the region. It links San Diego to Las Vegas, Nevada, via San Bernardino. This route follows the northern border of the East Mojave National Preserve, and I-40 skirts its southern border. The main south-north route across the desert is Hwy 127, from which Hwy 190 branches out, crossing the Death Valley National Park from southeast to southwest. In the west, US Hwy 395 leads south to LA. For safety reasons, it is vital that visitors to the desert obey posted signs and do not stray from main roads. Always carry water, a jack, a usable spare tire, a cell phone, and stay close to your vehicle if you break down. There is no public access to the area's clearly marked military zones *(see p274)*.

FURNACE
CREEK
190

DEATH
VALLEY
JUNCTION

178

TECOPA

Amargosa River

127

BAKER

15

15

MOJAVE
NATIONAL
PRESERVE

8 LAS VEGAS

95

5 6
KELSO   MITCHELL
DUNES   CAVERNS

40

ve River

40

HOMER

Colorado River

Arizona

7
LAKE
HAVASU

95

Palm Springs

Joshua Tree
National Monument

Stunning colors of Red Rock Canyon

Red Rock Canyon State Park ➊

Road map D5. 🚌 *from Mojave, Ridgecrest.* **Visitors' Center** 📞 *(661) 942-0662.* ◯ *Feb–May & Oct–Nov: Fri–Sun.*

ALTERNATE LAYERS of white clay, red sandstone, pink volcanic rocks, and brown lava are spectacularly combined in Red Rock Canyon. This beautiful state park is situated in the El Paso Mountains, which lie at the southern end of the Sierra Nevada Mountains. Like the High Sierras *(see p468)*, Red Rock Canyon is the product of plate movements that pushed up the bedrock approximately 3 million years ago. The western side of the canyon slopes gently upward in stark contrast to the high, abrupt cliffs on its eastern side, which have been carved and crenellated by water and wind.

Three major desert ecozones overlap here, providing a wealth of plant and animal life. Eagles, hawks, and falcons nest in the cliffs. Coyotes, kit foxes, bobcats, and various reptiles, such as the desert iguana, are common. The landscape has been used as the backdrop for countless Westerns, advertisements, and science-fiction films, making it oddly familiar to many visitors.

Edwards Air Force Base ➋

Road map D5. 📞 *(661) 258-3446.* 🚌 *from Mojave, Rosamond.* ◯ *Mon–Fri.* ⬤ *public hols.* ♿ ⬛ *by appointment only.*

WHILE IT IS famous around the world as the site of the West Coast space shuttle landings, Edwards Air Force Base has been steeped in the history of America in flight since 1933. The 65-sq-mile (168-sq-km) flat expanse of Rogers Dry Lake provides an enormous natural runway that is perfect for emergency landings. The area's year-round fine and clear weather adds to its suitability for aircraft testing and the training of test pilots. It was here that the very first jet-propelled aircraft was tested in 1942. Here, too, Captain Chuck Yeager became the first to break the sound barrier on October 14, 1947, in a Bell XS-1 rocket plane. Fifty pilots still graduate each year from the Test Pilot School.

Edwards is also home to the NASA Dryden Flight Research Center. Free guided tours of the space Aeronautics Center are available by reservation. Tours include a video on the history of aeronautics research and a visit to a hangar housing current aircraft.

Space shuttle Atlantis landing at Edwards Air Force Base

Barstow ➌

Road map D5. 🏠 *22,000.* 🚌 📍 *831 Barstow Rd (760 252-6000).*

DURING THE 19th century, this was a small settlement that served farmers as well as emigrants and miners on the Old Spanish Trail *(see p271)*. In 1886 the new Barstow–San Bernardino rail line opened, linking Kansas City with the Pacific Coast. Barstow's original railroad station, the Casa del Desierto, has recently been restored.

THE MILITARY IN THE MOJAVE

The United States government has set aside vast areas of the Mojave Desert for military use. All such areas are strictly off-limits to civilians. During World War II, the Desert Training Center covered 17,500 sq miles (45,300 sq km) and was used by General Patton to train his forces. Today, smaller military preserves include the China Lake Weapons Center, northeast of Mojave, which is used for live bombing and artillery testing. North of Barstow, the Fort Irwin National Training Center (NTC), which covers more than 1,000 sq miles (2,600 sq km), is an important US Army installation. The NTC has a population of 12,000, including civilian workers. Its desert terrain was used to prepare troops for the Gulf War in 1990–91, and is one of the main US training areas for tanks and weapons.

T-38 Talon high-altitude jet trainer at Edwards Air Force Base

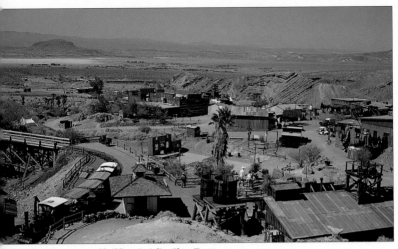

Restored and reconstructed buildings in Calico Ghost Town

From 1937 to the late 1950s, Barstow was an important town along Route 66, the only surfaced road from Chicago to the West Coast. The town is best known today as being the midway point on I-15 between Los Angeles and Las Vegas. To the 41 million people who make this journey each year, it is a convenient stopping-off point. But many also come here in search of the precious minerals and gemstones to be found in the surrounding desert.

The **California Desert Information Center**, in Barstow, has informative indoor displays on the Mojave Desert's flora and fauna. Maps of the area and hotel and restaurant information are available, and the center has a bookstore.

California Desert Information Center
831 Barstow Rd, Barstow. ((760) 252-6060. ☐ 11am–4pm Tue–Sat. ● Jan 1, Dec 25.

Calico Ghost Town ④

Road map D5. ((760) 254-2122.
🚌 Barstow. ☐ 9am–5pm daily.
● Dec 25. 📷 ♿ ✓

CALICO GHOST TOWN, 11 miles (18 km) east of Barstow, is a late-19th-century mining town, which is part-authentic and part-reconstruction. Silver was found in the Calico Mountains on March 26, 1881, and soon hundreds of miners arrived. Some of the veins they struck were so rich that they produced 25 lb (11 kg) of silver per ton. Two years later, borax was discovered 3 miles (5 km) east of Calico, and the town's prosperity seemed assured. During the 1880s, Calico boasted a population of 1,200 – and 22 saloons – but after the price of silver fell

A flint tool from the Early Man Site

and the equally valuable borax gave out, the miners left. By 1907, Calico was a ghost town. Walter Knott, founder of Knott's Berry Farm (see p226), began the restoration process in the 1950s. Calico's isolation and desert setting reinforce the sense of a rough old mining town. Many of the original buildings remain, and visitors can take a ride in a mine train or explore tunnels in Maggie Mine, one of the most famous silver mines on the West Coast. Shows and tours are also held, including mock "shoot-outs" staged on the main street, and walking tours given each day by the town's resident historian.

ENVIRONS: About 10 miles (16 km) west of Calico lies the **Calico Early Man Site**. At this archaeological site, thousands of 100,000-year-old stone tools have been discovered. They were made by North America's earliest-known inhabitants, who once lived in this area on the shores of a great lake. The renowned archaeologist and paleontologist Dr. Louis Leakey was director of the site, consisting of several pits, from 1964 until his death in 1972.

Calico Early Man Site
Off I-15 & Minneola Rd. ((760) 252-6000. ☐ Wed–Sun. ● Jan 1, Jul 4, Dec 25. **Donation**.

Casa del Desierto, Barstow's historic railroad station

Mesquite mud flats in Death Valley National Park (see pp280–83) ▷

Kelso Dunes ❺

Road map E5. 🚍 *Baker.* 🛈 *Mojave National Preserve (760) 733-4040.*

K ELSO DUNES tower more than 700 ft (210 m) above the desert floor. Situated in the Mojave National Preserve, the dunes are formed from grains of golden rose quartz that have been blown from the Mojave River basin, 35 miles (56 km) to the west. Known as the "singing" dunes, they occasionally emit buzzing and rumbling sounds. These are thought to be caused by the upper layers of sand sliding down the face of the dune, producing vibrations that are then amplified by the underlying sand.

The desert floor with the Kelso Dunes in the background

Mitchell Caverns ❻

🛈 *(760) 928-2586.* 🚍 *from Barstow.* ⏱ *Sep–Jun: daily.* 📷 ✦ *(Sat & Sun in summer only).*

M ITCHELL CAVERNS are a spectacular collection of caves along the eastern slope of the Providence Mountains. The caverns were formed 12–

The original London Bridge, now located in Lake Havasu City

15 million years ago, when acidic rainwater began to carve through layers of ancient limestone. Arrowheads and pottery shards have been found here, left behind by the Chemehuevi people. Until the 1860s, the Native Americans had stored food and held religious ceremonies in the caves for nearly 500 years. Opened as a tourist attraction in the 1930s by silver miner Jack Mitchell, the caverns are now owned and run by California State Parks.

Inside, the chambers feature three types of cave formation: flow stones (delicate curtain shapes); drip stones (stalagmites and stalactites); and erratics (ribbons, shields and "staghorn coral"). In one room, the rare combination of a cave shield, flowstone column, and coral pipes can be seen. Sturdy walking shoes are recommended for the two-hour tour, which includes El Pakiva (The Sacred Pools), one of the most famous chambers. A nearby 1-mile (1.6-km) trail up Crystal Spring Canyon climbs into the Providence Mountains and offers views of the desert.

Lake Havasu ❼

Road map E5. 🚍 *Las Vegas.* 🛈 *(520) 855-4115.*

L AKE HAVASU is a 46-mile (74-km) long reservoir, which was created in 1938 when the Colorado River was blocked by the Parker Dam *(see p193).* Lake Havasu City, a resort town on the border between California and Arizona, was developed by the millionaire Robert McCulloch in the 1960s. McCulloch imported the historic London Bridge stone-by-stone to the newly created development. The bridge spans a channel dredged especially for it and overlooks English-style shops and restaurants on a nearby plot of land known as English Village.

The lake itself lies within a National Wildlife Refuge, which is frequented by bird-watchers and anglers. There are many camp sites and marinas that offer houseboats, boats, and water-sports equipment for rent. Several short boat tours around the lake are available. A daily three-hour excursion to Topock Gorge, at the northern end of Lake Havasu, offers a more leisurely introduction to this rugged desert setting.

ENVIRONS: Off Hwy 95, 20 miles (32 km) south of Lake Havasu City, lies the Colorado River Indian Reservation. Here, visitors can admire a collection of giant prehistoric figures, carved out of the rocks that form the desert floor. In both human and animal form, it is not known whether the mysterious figures were made for religious or artistic reasons.

Impressive cave formations in Mitchell Caverns

Las Vegas

L AS VEGAS IS in Nevada, 37 miles (60 km) from the California border. With the construction of the Hoover Dam in the 1930s, it grew into a major city. Gambling was legalized in Nevada in 1931. In 1945 the Flamingo Hotel and Casino were built on the outskirts on what is known as "The Strip." Similar places soon sprang up, and Las Vegas became a 24-hour oasis of gambling and entertainment.

One of the city's many neon signs

Las Vegas "Strip" at dusk

Exploring Las Vegas

Today, Las Vegas is changing its image to appeal to families as well as gamblers. The city offers a wide variety of entertainment for all tastes and budgets in some of the most affordable and largest hotel and convention complexes in the world. Las Vegas is now a city of nearly one million permanent residents, with its own museums and other cultural institutions. But it is the 30 million tourists who visit Las Vegas each year who continue to fuel the amazing development of

this metropolis. Despite the neon lights, swimming pools, and hotels, the blazing sun and cloudless skies serve as a constant reminder that Las Vegas is surrounded by desert.

Hotels in Las Vegas provide more than just food and lodging. They are architectural marvels that offer some of the best sightseeing and entertainment in town. The Treasure Island Hotel and Casino stages mock sea battles between the British Navy and pirates. Next door is the Mirage Hotel and Casino with its massive aquariums, tropical rainforest, white tigers, and rumbling "volcano." The Luxor, built on the same scale as the pyramids of Egypt, houses the largest atrium in the world, complete with animatronic camels, Egyptian decor and high-tech laser shows. At night, the Luxor shoots the world's brightest beam of light into the sky from its pinnacle. The nearby MGM Grand offers a theme park called "The Emerald City of Oz," always a great favorite with children.

Stratosphere Tower

2000 Las Vegas Blvd S. ((702) 380-7777.

At 1,149 ft (350 m), Stratosphere Tower is the tallest freestanding observation tower in the United States. At the top there is an incomparable view of Las Vegas (best seen at night), a revolving restaurant and cocktail lounge, three wedding chapels, and two thrilling rides. The world's highest roller coaster leaves from 909 ft (275 m) up and runs for 865 ft (265 m) around the outside of the tower.

Fremont Street Experience

Bordered by Charles & Stewart Sts. ((702) 678-5777. ○ daily.
Las Vegas's first gaming license was issued on Fremont Street in the 1930s. Over the years, this downtown area became known as "Glitter Gulch," due to its profusion of neon signs and lights. Now five blocks of Fremont, stretching from Main Street to Las Vegas Boulevard, have been transformed into the Fremont Street Experience – a covered pedestrian promenade. Casinos line the street. A spectacular light and sound show is held each night, using more than two million computer-controlled lights.

ENVIRONS: Lake Mead, which lies 25 miles (40 km) east of Las Vegas, was created by the construction of Hoover Dam, completed in 1931. The lake extends 110 miles (175 km) and has more than 500 miles (800 km) of shoreline. Scuba-diving, boating, water-skiing, and fishing facilities are all available. There are daily tours of the 726-ft (220-m) high dam and a visitors' center with exhibits on the region's natural history. The Valley of Fire State Park, 55 miles (88 km) northeast of Las Vegas, has stunning orange sandstone formations. Petroglyphs and other remains of an ancient Native American civilization can still be seen. Red Rock Canyon (not the same as the park on *page 274*), 15 miles (24 km) west of Las Vegas, has 3,000-ft (900-m) high escarpments, and ridges, and trails for all levels of hikers.

Stratosphere Tower

VISITORS' CHECKLIST

Road map E4. 🚶 1,200,000. ✈ McCarran International Airport, 4 miles (6.5 km) S of Las Vegas. 🚌 200 S Main St. 🚆 1 Main St. 🛈 3150 Paradise Rd (702 892-0711). **Treasure Island Hotel and Casino** 3300 Las Vegas Blvd. ((702) 894-7111. **Mirage Hotel and Casino** 3400 Las Vegas Blvd. ((702) 791-7111. **Luxor Las Vegas Hotel and Casino** 3900 Las Vegas Blvd. ((702) 262-4000. **MGM Grand Hotel, Casino and Theme Park** 3799 Las Vegas Blvd. ((702) 891-7777.

Death Valley National Park 🟒

THROUGHOUT THE SUMMER MONTHS, Death Valley National Park has the highest mean temperature of anywhere on the planet. This is a land of wrenching extremes, a sunken trough in the earth's crust that reaches the lowest point in the Western Hemisphere. The valley is guarded on both sides by ranges of rugged mountains. The range on the western side soars 11,000 ft (3,350 m) to form razor-sharp peaks. Even though it is always inhospitable, Death Valley is also a place of subtle colors and polished canyons, of burning salt flats and delicate rock formations. It is now one of the most unique and popular tourist destinations in the state of California.

Central Death Valley

Furnace Creek, with its various provisions and accommodation centers, is located in the heart of Death Valley. Many of the most impressive sights in the park are within easy reach of this visitors' complex.

🐟 Salt Creek

Salt Creek supports the hardy pupfish. Endemic to Death Valley, the pupfish can live in water almost four times as salty as the sea and withstand temperatures of up to 111° F (44° C). The fish attract other wildlife, including great blue herons. Wooden walkways allow visitors to explore this unique site without disturbing the fragile habitat.

🏛 Borax Museum

Furnace Creek Ranch. ☎ (760) 786-2345. ◯ *daily.*

Borax was discovered in Death Valley in 1873, but mining did not begin until the 1880s when crystallized borate compounds

Ruins of the Harmony Borax Works processing plant

were taken to the Harmony Borax Works to be purified. They were then loaded onto wagons and hauled by teams of 20 mules the 165 miles (265 km) to Mojave Station. Each team of mules pulled two wagons carrying up to 10 tons of borax each. The wagons carried their heavy mineral loads from 1883 to 1888.

Used for producing glass that is heat-resistant, borax is more commonly used today as an ingredient in washing powder.

The Borax Museum has displays of mining tools and transport machinery used at the 19th-century refinery. On Hwy 190, 1 mile (1.5 km) north of the Death Valley Visitor Center, the eerie ruins of the Harmony Borax Works can still be seen

🏛 Death Valley Museum and Visitor Center

Rte 190, Furnace Creek. ☎ (760) 786-2331. ◯ *daily.* ● *Jan 1, Dec 25, Thanksgiving.* 🎫

Interesting exhibits and a slide show every 30 minutes explain the natural and human history of Death Valley. Evening park-ranger programs and guided walks are available in winter.

Furnace Creek

At Furnace Creek, millennia of winter floods have carved a natural gateway into Death Valley through the hills to the east. The springs here once drew Shoshone Indians each winter. Today, the same abundant springs make Furnace Creek a desert oasis and the de facto center of Death Valley. Shaded by date-bearing palms are a variety of restaurants and motels. The world's lowest golf course can also be found here, lying at 214 ft (65 m) below sea level. The Furnace Creek Inn *(see p522)*, a four-star hotel built in the 1920s, sits above the valley on a small mesa.

Historic Furnace Creek Inn, set in lush surroundings

Salt formations at the Devil's Golf Course

Southern Death Valley
Some of the valley's most breathtaking natural features are to be found in this area south of Furnace Creek.

Golden Canyon
Just over 3 miles (5 km) south of Furnace Creek on Hwy 178, a one-mile (1500-m) hike leads into Golden Canyon. The mustard-colored walls, after which the canyon was named, are best seen in the afternoon sun. Native Americans used the red clay at the canyon mouth for face paint. These layers of rock were originally horizontal, but geological activity has now tilted them to an angle of 45°.

A paved road once led to the Golden Canyon, but it was washed out by a sudden storm in 1976. The battered state of the few remaining stretches of the road demonstrate the sheer power of fast-flowing water.

Devil's Golf Course
This expanse of salt pinnacles is located 12 miles (19 km) south of Furnace Creek, off Hwy 178. Until approximately 2,000 years ago, successive lakes covered this area. When the last lake evaporated, it left behind alternating layers of salt and gravel deposits, at least 1,000 ft (305 m) deep and covering 200 sq miles (520 sq km). As surface moisture continued to evaporate, ridges and spires of crystallized salt were formed. The ground is now 95 percent pure salt. Visitors can hear the salt expand and contract in the continual changes of temperature. New crystals (recognized by their whiter hue) are constantly forming.

Badwater
Temperature increases as elevation decreases, so the air at Badwater can reach 120° F (49° C). With the ground temperature 50 percent higher than the air temperature, it really is possible to fry an egg on the ground here. Rain is very rare, although flash flooding, caused by rainstorms, is common. In spite of its inhospitable environment, Badwater is home to several species of insect and to the endangered Death Valley snail.

Northern Death Valley
This area includes Ubehebe Crater *(see p282)*, where only a few tourists venture, despite the beauty of the landscape. Scotty's Castle, which has more visitors per year than any other sight in the park, is also here.

Scotty's Castle
Hwy 267. *(760) 786-2392.*
Castle daily. **Grounds** daily.
Albert Johnson began work on his "Death Valley Ranch" in 1922 after rejecting an original design by Frank Lloyd Wright. Materials were hauled from a railroad line 20 miles (32 km) away. When work ended in 1931 the castle covered more than 30,000 sq ft (2,800 sq m). Johnson died in 1948. "Death Valley Scotty" *(see p282)*, who lent his name to Johnson's ranch, was allowed to remain there until his death in 1954.

Western Death Valley
Sand dunes cover 15 sq miles (39 sq km) on this side of the park, not far from the second-largest outpost in Death Valley, Stovepipe Wells *(see p282)*.

Sand Dunes
A walk along the 14 sq miles (36 sq km) of undulating sand dunes, north of Stovepipe Wells, is one of the greatest experiences of Death Valley. Shifting winds blow the sand into the classic crescent dune configuration. Mesquite trees dot the lower dunes. A variety of wildlife feeds on the seeds of these trees, such as kangaroo rats and lizards. Included among the region's other, mainly nocturnal, creatures are the rattlesnake, the chuckwalla lizard, and the coyote.

Impressive sand dunes north of Stovepipe Wells

A Tour of Death Valley

THE NATIVE AMERICANS called the valley Tomesha, "the land where the ground is on fire" – an apt name for the site of the highest recorded temperature in the United States: 134° F (57° C) in the shade, in July 1913. Death Valley stretches for some 140 miles (225 km) north to south and was once an insurmountable barrier to miners and emigrants. The valley and surrounding area were declared a National Park *(see pp280–81)* in 1994. Death Valley is now accessible to visitors, who can discover this stark and unique landscape by car and by taking short walks from the main roads to spectacular viewpoints. However, this remains the California desert at its harshest and most awe-inspiring.

Scotty's Castle ⑧

This incongruous Moorish-style castle was commissioned by Albert Johnson at a cost of $2.4 million. However, the public believed it belonged to Walter Scott, an eccentric prospector. The house remained unfinished after Johnson lost his money in the Wall Street Crash of 1929. In 1970 the building was bought by the National Park Service, who now hold hourly guided tours of the interior *(see p281)*.

Ubehebe Crater ⑦

This is one of a dozen volcanic craters in the Mojave area. The Ubehebe Crater is 3,000 years old. It is more than 900 yds (800 m) wide and 500 ft (150 m) deep.

Death Valley Wash

North Hwy

Titus Canyon Rd

Sand Dune

PANAMINT SPRINGS

190

Stovepipe Wells ⑥

Stovepipe Village, founded in 1926, was the valley's first tourist resort. According to legend, a lumberjack traveling west struck water here and stayed. An old stovepipe, similar to the ones that were then used to form the walls of wells, marks the site.

DEATH VALLEY SCOTTY

Walter Scott, would-be miner, beloved charlatan, and sometime performer in Buffalo Bill's Wild West Show, liked to tell visitors to his home that his wealth lay in a secret gold mine. That "mine" was, in fact, his friend Albert Johnson, a Chicago insurance executive, who paid for the castle where Scott lived and received visitors. Built during the 1920s by European craftsmen and local Native American labor, the castle represents a mixture of architectural styles and has a Moorish feel. Scott never owned the land or the building, and Johnson paid all his bills. "He repays me in laughs," said Johnson. Although Scott died in 1954, the edifice is still known as Scotty's Castle.

Grandiose Scotty's Castle

KEY

▬▬	Tour route
═══	Other roads
ℹ	Tourist information
🚶	Ranger station
⛽	Gas station

Zabriskie Point [2]
Made famous by Antonioni's 1960s film of the same name, Zabriskie Point offers views of the multicolored mud hills of Golden Canyon *(see p281)*. The spot was named after a former general manager of the borax operations in Death Valley *(see p280)*.

Furnace Creek [1]
The springs here are one of the few freshwater sources in the desert. They are thought to have saved the lives of hundreds of gold prospectors crossing the desert on their way to the Sierra foothills. The full-service visitors' complex here *(see p280)* is the valley's main population center.

Dante's View [3]
At 5,475 ft (1,650 m), the view takes in the entire valley floor and is best seen in the morning. The name of the viewpoint was inspired by Dante's *Inferno*. In the distance is Telescope Peak in the Panamint Range.

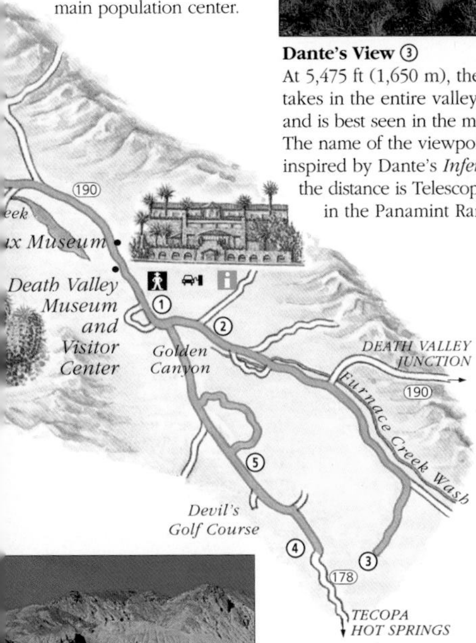
190
eek
ıx Museum
Death Valley Museum and Visitor Center
Golden Canyon
DEATH VALLEY JUNCTION
190
Furnace Creek Wash
Devil's Golf Course
178
TECOPA HOT SPRINGS

Tips for Drivers

Tour length: *236 miles (380 km).*
When to go: *The best time to visit is October to April, when temperatures average 65° F (18° C). May to September, when the ground temperature can be extremely hot, should be avoided. Try for an early start, especially if you are planning to take any hikes. Always wear a hat and use plenty of sunblock.*
Precautions: *Check the weather forecast before you leave and always carry water, a map, a first aid and snake-bite kit, a cell phone, a jack, and a spare tire. Remain near your vehicle if you break down. If you plan to travel in remote areas, inform someone of where you are going and when you plan to return. The area is not suitable for rock climbing. Do not feed wild animals or reach into burrows or holes.*
Stopping-off points: *Furnace Creek Ranch, Furnace Creek Inn, Stovepipe Wells Village (see p522), and Panamint Springs are the only lodging and eating places in the park. Shoshone, Amargosa, and Tecopa, outside the park, also have motels.*
Emergency: *Phone park rangers on 911 or (760) 786-2331.*
[W] www.nps.gov/deva

Badwater

Badwater [4]
Badwater *(see p281)* is the lowest point in the western hemisphere. It lies 282 ft (85 m) below sea level and is one of the world's hottest places. The water is not poisonous, but it is unpalatable, filled with sodium chloride and sulfates.

Artist's Palette [5]
These multicolored hills of cemented gravels were created by mineral deposits and volcanic ash. The colors are at their most intense in the late afternoon sun.

0 kilometers 10

0 miles 10

SAN FRANCISCO AND THE BAY AREA

San Francisco and the Bay Area at a Glance

SAN FRANCISCO IS A COMPACT CITY and much of the central area can be explored on foot. The many hills give rise to some strenuous climbing, but are useful landmarks for orientation and offer superb views. A rich ethnic mix adds a distinctive character to the city's many neighborhoods. The smaller cities of Oakland and Berkeley on the East Bay are reached via the Bay Bridge, while to the north, Golden Gate Bridge links the peninsula to the Marin Headlands and the Point Reyes National Seashore. To the south are the colonial city of San Jose and rugged stretches of coastline inhabited by a variety of flora and fauna.

LOCATOR MAP

■ San Francisco & the Bay Area

Golden Gate Bridge
Over 60 years old, the bridge is as much a part of the landscape as the craggy Marin Headlands and the idyllic bay (see pp370–71).

**GOLDEN GATE PARK
AND THE PRESIDIO**
(see pp354–71)

Palace of Fine Arts
Built for the Panama-Pacific Exposition of 1915, this Neo-Classical monument was fully restored in 1962 (see p339).

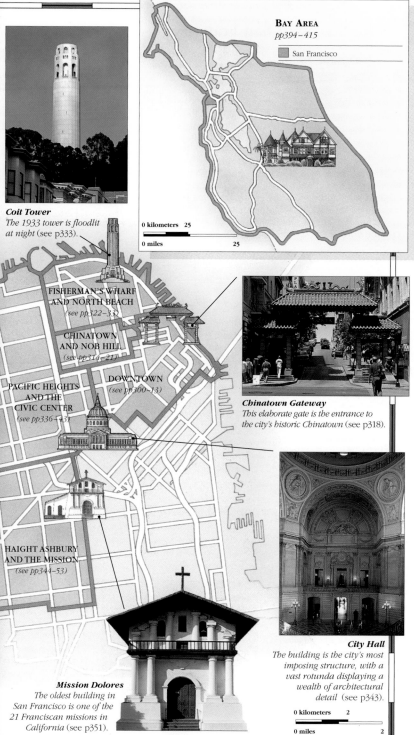

Coit Tower
The 1933 tower is floodlit at night (see p333).

BAY AREA
pp394–415

San Francisco

0 kilometers 25

0 miles 25

FISHERMAN'S WHARF
AND NORTH BEACH
(see pp322–33)

CHINATOWN
AND NOB HILL
(see pp314–21)

DOWNTOWN
(see pp300–13)

PACIFIC HEIGHTS
AND THE
CIVIC CENTER
(see pp336–43)

HAIGHT ASHBURY
AND THE MISSION
(see pp344–53)

Chinatown Gateway
This elaborate gate is the entrance to the city's historic Chinatown (see p318).

City Hall
The building is the city's most imposing structure, with a vast rotunda displaying a wealth of architectural detail (see p343).

Mission Dolores
The oldest building in San Francisco is one of the 21 Franciscan missions in California (see p351).

0 kilometers 2

0 miles 2

The Shape of San Francisco

San Francisco
road sign

SAN FRANCISCO, with its estimated 43 hills, sits at the tip of a peninsula, surrounded by the Pacific Ocean to the west and San Francisco Bay to the east. To the north, linked by the Golden Gate Bridge, are the rugged Marin Headlands and the protected wildlife area of the Point Reyes Peninsula. The Diablo Coast Range, with the 3,850-ft (1,170-m) Mount Diablo at its heart, forms a mountainous backdrop to the heavily populated cities of Richmond, Oakland, and Berkeley in the East Bay, and divides the region from the flat plains of the Central Valley. To the south, the coastal mountains enclose the industrial Silicon Valley and run along the coastline toward Big Sur.

Vallejo
This town, in the north of the bay, is home to Marine World Africa wildlife park and oceanarium, which includes dolphin displays (see p399).

Red and White ferries

Sausalito
This former fishing community, across the Golden Gate Bridge, is lined with Victorian houses looking out toward the bay (see p398).

RICHMOND

RICHMOND BRIDGE

TIBURON

29

37

101

SONOMA MOUNTAINS

MOUNT TAMALPAIS

1

POINT REYES NATIONAL SEASHORE

PACIFIC OCEAN

Point Reyes Peninsula
The rugged coastline of the peninsula, situated on the San Andreas Fault and only partly attached to the mainland, is abundant with wildlife and is a very productive dairy farming community (see p398).

The Marin Headlands
are part of the Golden Gate National Recreation Area. These green hills and quiet beaches offer perfect relaxation away from the city, with hiking, fishing, and bird-watching opportunities *(see pp400–401).*

Downtown
One of the major financial districts in the United States is located in San Francisco's Downtown area. Its skyline is dominated by the Transamerica Pyramid (see pp300–313).

Livermore
This rural community is home to the world's largest wind farm, making use of the area's strong winds to produce natural energy (see p410).

Berkeley includes the University of California at Berkeley campus, once known for its radicalism *(see pp402–405).*

The Diablo Coast Range separates the East Bay from the Central Valley. Mount Diablo is at the heart of the range *(see p410).*

DIABLO COAST RANGE

580

680

880

SAN MATEO BRIDGE

84

BRIDGE

280

Golden Gate Bridge

1

GOLDEN GATE NATIONAL RECREATION AREA

SAN BRUNO MOUNTAINS

San Jose was originally a Spanish colonial city and preserves its history. It is still home to a large Mexican–American population *(see pp412–13).*

...land
...busy city has a multicultural ...lation and many historic landmarks. ...inked to San Francisco by the Bay ...ge (see pp406–409).

Palo Alto
This town was built up specifically to serve the Stanford University campus, which was created by railroad baron Leland Stanford in 1891 (see p411).

Victorian Houses in San Francisco

Italianate window

DESPITE EARTHQUAKES, fires, and the inroads of modern life, thousands of ornate, late-19th-century houses still line the streets of San Francisco. In fact, in many neighborhoods they are by far the most common type of houses. Victorian houses are broadly similar, in that they all have wooden frames, elaborately decorated with mass-produced ornamentation. Most were built on narrow plots to a similar floor plan, but they differ in the features of the façade. Four main styles prevail in the city, although in practice many houses, especially those constructed in the 1880s and 1890s, combine aspects of two or more styles.

Detail of Queen Anne-style gateway at Chateau Tivoli

GOTHIC REVIVAL (1850–80)

Gothic Revival houses are the easiest to identify, as they always have pointed arches over the windows and sometimes, over the doors. Other features are pitched gabled roofs, decorated vergeboards (again, with pointed arch motifs), and porches that run the width of the building. The smaller, simpler houses of this type are often painted white, rather than the vibrant colors of later styles.

No. 1111 Oak Street is one of the city's oldest Gothic Revival buildings. Its front garden is unusually large.

The pitched roof over the main façade often runs lengthwise, allowing the use of dormer windows.

A gabled roof with ornate verge-boards is the clearest mark of Gothic Revival.

Gothic porch with cross bracing at No. 1978 Filbert Street

Full-width porches are reached by a central stair.

Balustrades on the porch betray the Deep South origins of the style.

ITALIANATE (1850–85)

Italianate houses were more popular in San Francisco than elsewhere in the US, perhaps because their compact form was suited to the city's high building density. The most distinctive feature of the style is the tall cornice, usually with a decorative bracket, which adds a palatial air even to modest homes. Elaborate decoration around windows and doors is also typical of the style.

No. 1913 Sacramento Street displays a typical formal Italianate façade, modeled on a Renaissance palazzo. The wood boarding is made to look like stone.

Tall cornices, often with decorative brackets, conceal a pitched roof.

Imposing entrance with Italianate porch

Symmetrical windows are capped by decorative arches.

Neo-Classical doorways, sometimes with ornate pedimented porches, are a typical Italianate touch.

STICK (1860–90)

This architectural style, with its ungainly name, is perhaps the most prevalent among Victorian houses in the city. Sometimes also called "Stick–Eastlake" after London furniture designer Charles Eastlake, this style was intended to be more architecturally "honest." Vertical lines are emphasized, both in the wood-frame structure and in ornamentation. Bay windows, false-gabled cornices, and square corners are key identifying features.

No. 1715–17 Capp Street is a fine example of the Stick–Eastlake style, with a plain façade enlivened by decorative flourishes.

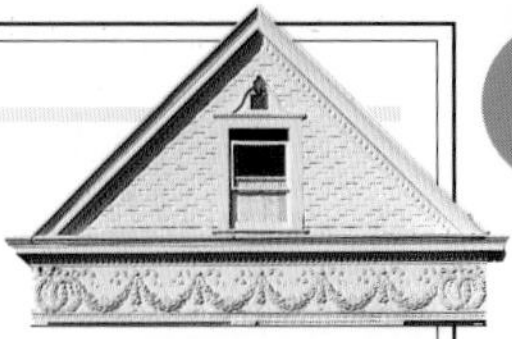

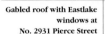

Gabled roof with Eastlake windows at No. 2931 Pierce Street

Wide bands of trim often form a decorative truss, emphasizing the underlying structure of Stick houses.

Decorative gables filled with "sunburst" motifs are used on porches and window frames.

Adjoining front doors can be protected by a single projecting porch.

QUEEN ANNE (1875–1905)

The name "Queen Anne" does not refer to a historical period; it was coined by the English architect Richard Shaw. Queen Anne houses combine elements from many decorative traditions but are marked by their towers, turrets, and large decorative panels on wall surfaces. Many of the houses display intricate spindle-work on balustrades, porches, and roof trusses *(see pp26–7)*.

Palladian windows were used in gables to give the appearance of an extra floor.

Queen Anne gable filled with ornamental panels at No. 818 Steiner Street

Queen Anne turret topped by a finial at No. 1015 Steiner Street

Round, square, and polygonal turrets and towers are typical of Queen Anne-style houses.

Gable pediments hold ornamental windows and decorative panels.

The curved window frame is not itself characteristic of Queen Anne style, but many houses include features borrowed from other styles.

The asymmetrical façade of No. 850 Steiner Street, together with its eclectic ornament, is typical of a Queen Anne house. Such features are often painted in various bright colors.

WHERE TO FIND VICTORIAN HOUSES

1715–1717 Capp St.
   Map 10 F4.
Chateau Tivoli, 1057 Steiner St.
   Map 4 D4.
1978 Filbert St. **Map 4 D2.**
1111 Oak St. **Map 9 C1.**
2931 Pierce St. **Map 4 D3.**
1913 Sacramento St.
   Map 4 E3.
818 Steiner St. **Map 4 D5.**
850 Steiner St. **Map 4 D5.**
1015 Steiner St. **Map 4 D5.**
2527–2531 Washington St.
   Map 4 D3.
Alamo Square *p343.*
Clarke's Folly *p353.*
Haas-Lilienthal House *p338.*
Liberty Street. **Map 10 E3.**
Masonic Avenue. **Map 3 C4.**
Octagon House *p341.*
Spreckels Mansion *p338.*

San Francisco's Cable Cars

THE CABLE CAR system was launched in 1873, and its inventor Andrew Hallidie rode in the first car. He was inspired to tackle the problem of transporting people up the city's steep slopes after witnessing a bad accident, when a horse-drawn tram slipped down a hill, dragging the horses with it. His system was a success, and by 1889 cars were running on eight lines. Before the 1906 earthquake *(see pp48–9)*, more than 600 cars were in use. With the advent of the internal combustion engine, cable cars became obsolete, and in 1947 attempts were made to replace them with buses. After a public outcry the present three lines, using 17 miles (25 km) of track, were retained.

Cable car traffic lights

The Cable Car Barn *garages the cars at night, and is a repair shop, museum, and powerhouse for the entire cable car system* (see p321).

The gripman *has to be strong, with good reflexes. Only a third of candidates pass the training course.*

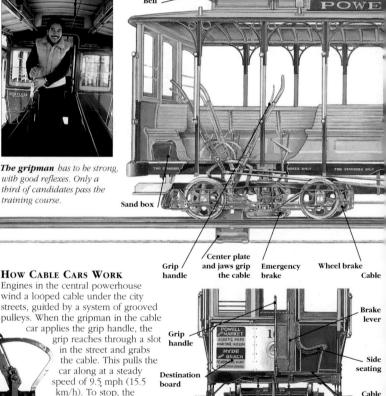

Bell

POWE

Sand box

Grip handle

Center plate and jaws grip the cable

Emergency brake

Wheel brake

Cable

HOW CABLE CARS WORK

Engines in the central powerhouse wind a looped cable under the city streets, guided by a system of grooved pulleys. When the gripman in the cable car applies the grip handle, the grip reaches through a slot in the street and grabs the cable. This pulls the car along at a steady speed of 9.5 mph (15.5 km/h). To stop, the gripman releases the grip and applies the brake. Great skill is needed at corners where the cable passes over a pulley. The gripman must release the grip to allow the car to coast over the pulley.

Cable car grip mechanism

Grip handle

Destination board

Wooden beams

Grip crotch

POWELL AND MARKET
AQUATIC PARK MARITIME MUSEUM
HYDE AND BEACH

Brake lever

Side seating

Cable car floor

Paving stones

Yoke

Hatch House *is the name given to a four-story house that needed to be moved in its entirety in 1913. Herbert Hatch used a system of jacks and hoists to maneuver the house across the cable car line without causing any cessation of the service.*

A cable car celebration *was held in 1984 after a two-year-long system refurbishment. Each car was refitted, and all lines were replaced with reinforced tracks. The system should now work safely for the next 100 years.*

A cable car bell-ringing contest *is held at Union Square every July, when conductors ring out their most spirited rhythms. On the street, the bell signals a warning to other traffic.*

Brake block   **Brake shoe**

The original *San Francisco cable car, tested by Hallidie on Clay Street on August 2, 1873, is on display in the Cable Car Barn (see p321). The cable car system has remained essentially unchanged since its invention.*

Rebuilding the cable cars *has to be done with attention to historical detail, since they are designated historic monuments.*

ANDREW SMITH HALLIDIE

Andrew Smith was born in London in 1836 and later adopted his uncle's surname. He trained as a mechanic, moved to San Francisco in 1852, and formed a company that made wire rope. In 1873 he tested the first cable car, which soon became profitable by opening the hills of the city to development.

San Francisco's Best: Museums and Galleries

MUSEUMS AND GALLERIES in the city range from the encyclopedic MH de Young (closed until 2006) and the California Palace of the Legion of Honor, to the contemporary art of the Museum of Modern Art and its neighbor, the Yerba Buena Center for the Arts. There are several excellent science museums, including the Exploratorium and the California Academy of Sciences. Other museums celebrate the city's heritage, including its ancestral Native American culture, and the people and events that made the city what it is today.

The Exploratorium *is one of the best science museums in the US. Here visitors experiment with* Sun Painting, *a feast of light and color. (See p339.)*

California Palace of the Legion of Honor *houses a collection of European art from the Middle Ages to the 19th century, including* Sailboat on the Seine *(c.1874) by Claude Monet. (See pp364–5.)*

Golden Gate Park and the Presidio

Pacific and th Cer

MH de Young Museum *is undergoing a rebuilding and renovation and will be closed until 2006. Many of the well-known exhibits are now at the Legion of Honor while the de Young is under construction.*

0 kilometers 2

0 miles 1

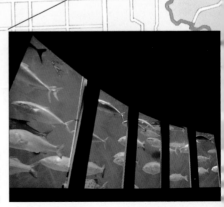

California Academy of Sciences *has something of interest, from alligators to astronomy, for all who visit. The Fish Roundabout is a circular aquarium. (See pp360–61.)*

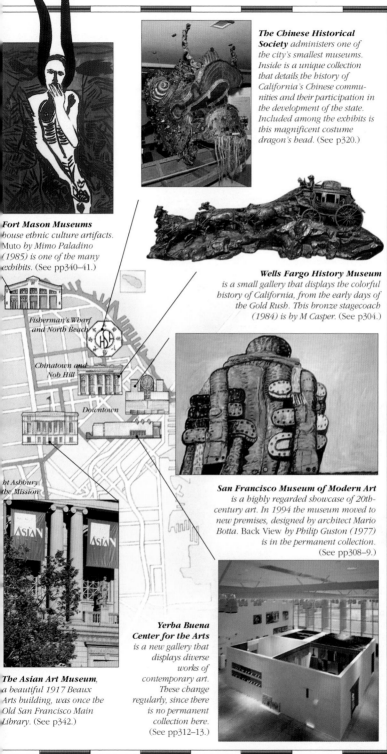

The Chinese Historical Society *administers one of the city's smallest museums. Inside is a unique collection that details the history of California's Chinese communities and their participation in the development of the state. Included among the exhibits is this magnificent costume dragon's head. (See p320.)*

Fort Mason Museums *house ethnic culture artifacts. Muto by Mimo Paladino (1985) is one of the many exhibits. (See pp340–41.)*

Fisherman's Wharf and North Beach

Chinatown and Nob Hill

Downtown

ht Ashbury the Mission

Wells Fargo History Museum *is a small gallery that displays the colorful history of California, from the early days of the Gold Rush. This bronze stagecoach (1984) is by M Casper. (See p304.)*

San Francisco Museum of Modern Art *is a highly regarded showcase of 20th-century art. In 1994 the museum moved to new premises, designed by architect Mario Botta. Back View by Philip Guston (1977) is in the permanent collection. (See pp308–9.)*

The Asian Art Museum, *a beautiful 1917 Beaux Arts building, was once the Old San Francisco Main Library. (See p342.)*

Yerba Buena Center for the Arts *is a new gallery that displays diverse works of contemporary art. These change regularly, since there is no permanent collection here. (See pp312–13.)*

San Francisco's Murals

SAN FRANCISCO IS PROUD of its reputation as a culturally rich and cosmopolitan city, and these qualities are evident in the bright murals that decorate walls and other public places in several areas of the city. Many were painted in the 1930s and many more in the 1970s, with some appearing spontaneously, while others were specially commissioned. One of the best is the *Carnaval Mural* on 24th Street in the Mission District *(see p352)*; other examples are shown here.

503 Law Office at Dolores and 18th streets

SCENES FROM HISTORY

Some of the best examples of San Francisco's historical mural art can be found inside Coit Tower *(see p333)*, where a series of panels, funded during the Great Depression of the 1930s by President Roosevelt's New Deal program, is typical of the period. Many local artists participated in creating the work, and themes include the struggles of the working class and the rich resources of California. The city also boasts three murals by Diego Rivera, the Mexican artist who revived fresco painting during the 1930s and 1940s.

Detail from Coit Tower mural illustrating the rich resources of California

The making of a mural depicted by Diego Rivera at San Francisco Art Institute

Architect Frank Lloyd Wright

Emmy Lou Packard, Rivera's assistant on the mural

Otto Diechman, architect

Mussolini, as portrayed by Jack Oakie in *The Great Dictator*

Coit Tower mural showing life during the Great Depression

Adolf Hitler

Benito Mussolini

The 1940 Diego Rivera mural at City College has a theme of Pan-American unity, and features many important historical figures. The section illustrated here lays emphasis on creative endeavor in the United States and on the role played by artists in the fight against Fascism.

Edward G Robinson

Joseph Stalin

Charlie Chaplin in *The Great Dictator*, a film made in 1940 that poked fun at Fascism. Chaplin had two parts, playing both a Jewish barber and Hitler.

MODERN LIFE

Life in the modern metropolis is one of the major themes of mural art in San Francisco, as much now as it was in the 1930s. In the Mission District particularly, every aspect of daily life is illustrated on the walls of banks, schools, and restaurants, with lively scenes of the family, community, political activity, and people at work and play. The Mission District contains about 200 murals, many painted in the 1970s, when the city government paid rebellious young people to create works of art in public places. The San Francisco Arts Commission continues to foster this art form.

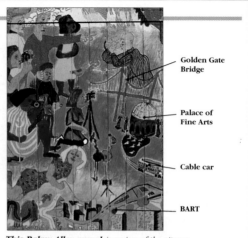

Golden Gate Bridge

Palace of Fine Arts

Cable car

BART

This Balmy Alley mural is a view of the city as tourists see it. The alley, in the Mission District, is decorated with numerous vivid murals, first painted by local children, artists, and community workers in the 1970s. The works are now a major attraction.

The Learning Wall, Franklin St, depicts education and art

Positively Fourth Street, a weathered mural at Fort Mason

THE MULTICULTURAL CITY

San Francisco's heritage of diversity and tolerance comes alive in the murals that enliven its ethnic neighborhoods. In Chinatown, Chinese-American artists evoke memories of the "old country." The Mission District is filled with art, some of it politically inspired, which celebrates the struggles and achievements of its Mexican and Latin American population.

Mexican-American dancer

Native American drummer

Caucasian bass player

African-American maracas player

Multicultural San Francisco is celebrated at Park Branch Library in Haight Ashbury.

Mural in Washington Street encapsulating life in China

WHERE TO FIND THE MURALS

Balmy Alley, 24th & 25th Sts.
City College of San Francisco
    50 Phelan Ave.
Coit Tower *p333.*
Dolores and 18th St. **Map 10 E3.**
Fort Mason *pp340–41.*
Franklin Street. **Map 4 E1.**
Park Branch Library
    1833 Page St. **Map 9 B1.**
San Francisco Art
    Institute *pp330–31.*
Washington Street. **Map 4 E3.**

The 49-Mile Scenic Drive

Official sign

Linking the city's most intriguing neighborhoods, fascinating sights and spectacular views, the 49-Mile Scenic Drive (79 km) provides a splendid overview of San Francisco. Keeping to the well-marked route is easy – just follow the blue-and-white seagull signs. Some of these are hidden by overhanging vegetation, so you need to be alert. Set aside a whole day for this trip; there are plenty of places to stop to take photographs or admire the views.

The Palace of Fine Arts and the Exploratorium ②
The grand Neo-Classical building and its modern science museum stand near the entrance to the Presidio.

Stow Lake ⑤
There is a waterfall and a Chinese pavilion on the island in this picturesque lake. Boats can be rented.

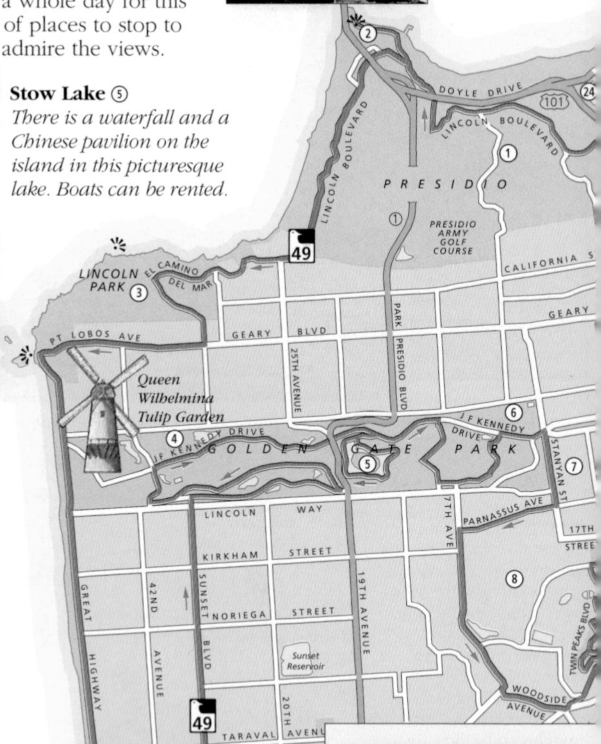

Sutro Tower ⑧
This distinctive orange and white tower is visible from all over the city.

0 kilometers 2

0 miles 1

Key

— 49-Mile Scenic Drive

✲ Viewpoint

Five-tiered pagoda in Japantown

Coit Tower ⑳
Overlooking North Beach, Telegraph Hill is topped by this tower, which has fine murals and an observation deck.

Marina Green ㉓
This is an excellent vantage point from which to view or photograph Golden Gate Bridge.

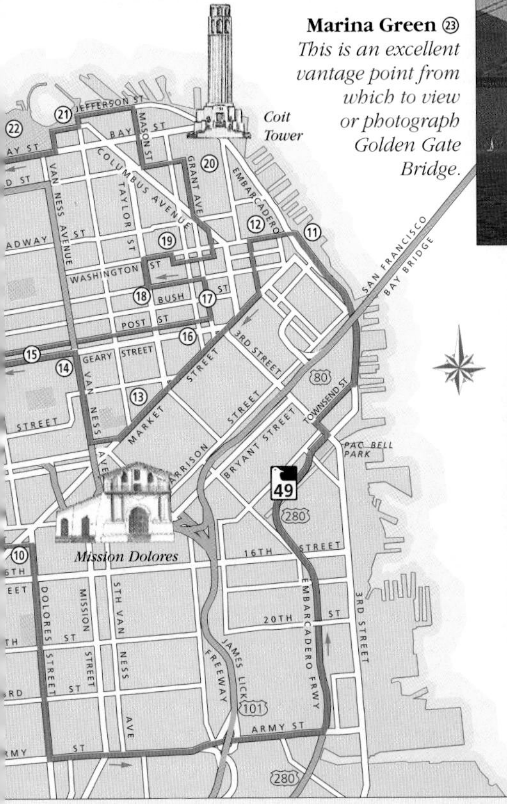

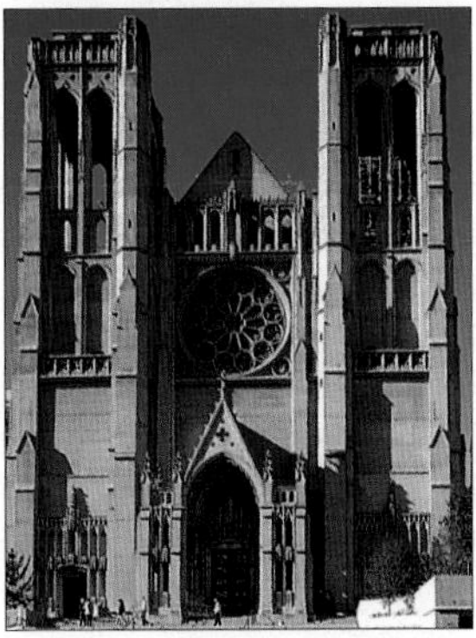

Grace Cathedral ⑱
This impressive cathedral, based on Notre Dame in Paris, dominates the summit of the city's steepest hill, Nob Hill.

Tips for Motorists

***Starting point**: Anywhere. The circuit is designed to be followed in a counterclockwise direction starting and ending at any point.*
***When to go**: Avoid driving during rush hours: 7–9am, 4–7pm. Most of the views are as spectacular by night as by day.*
***Parking**: Use the parking lots that are situated around the Financial District, the Civic Center, Japantown, Nob Hill, Chinatown, North Beach, and Fisherman's Wharf. Elsewhere, street parking is usually easily available.*

Finding the Sights

① Presidio *pp366–7*
② Fort Point *p368*
③ California Palace of the Legion of Honor *pp364–5*
④ Queen Wilhelmina Tulip Garden *p359*
⑤ Stow Lake *p358*
⑥ Conservatory of Flowers *p358*
⑦ Haight Street *p348*
⑧ Sutro Tower *p353*
⑨ Twin Peaks *p353*
⑩ Mission Dolores *p351*
⑪ Ferry Building *p306*
⑫ Embarcadero Center *p304*
⑬ Civic Center *pp342–3*
⑭ St. Mary's Cathedral *p342*
⑮ Japan Center *p342*
⑯ Union Square *p310*
⑰ Chinatown Gateway *p318*
⑱ Grace Cathedral *p321*
⑲ Cable Car Barn *p321*
⑳ Coit Tower *p333*
㉑ San Francisco National Maritime Museum *p327*
㉒ Fort Mason *pp340–41*
㉓ Marina Green *p340*
㉔ Palace of Fine Arts and the Exploratorium *p341*

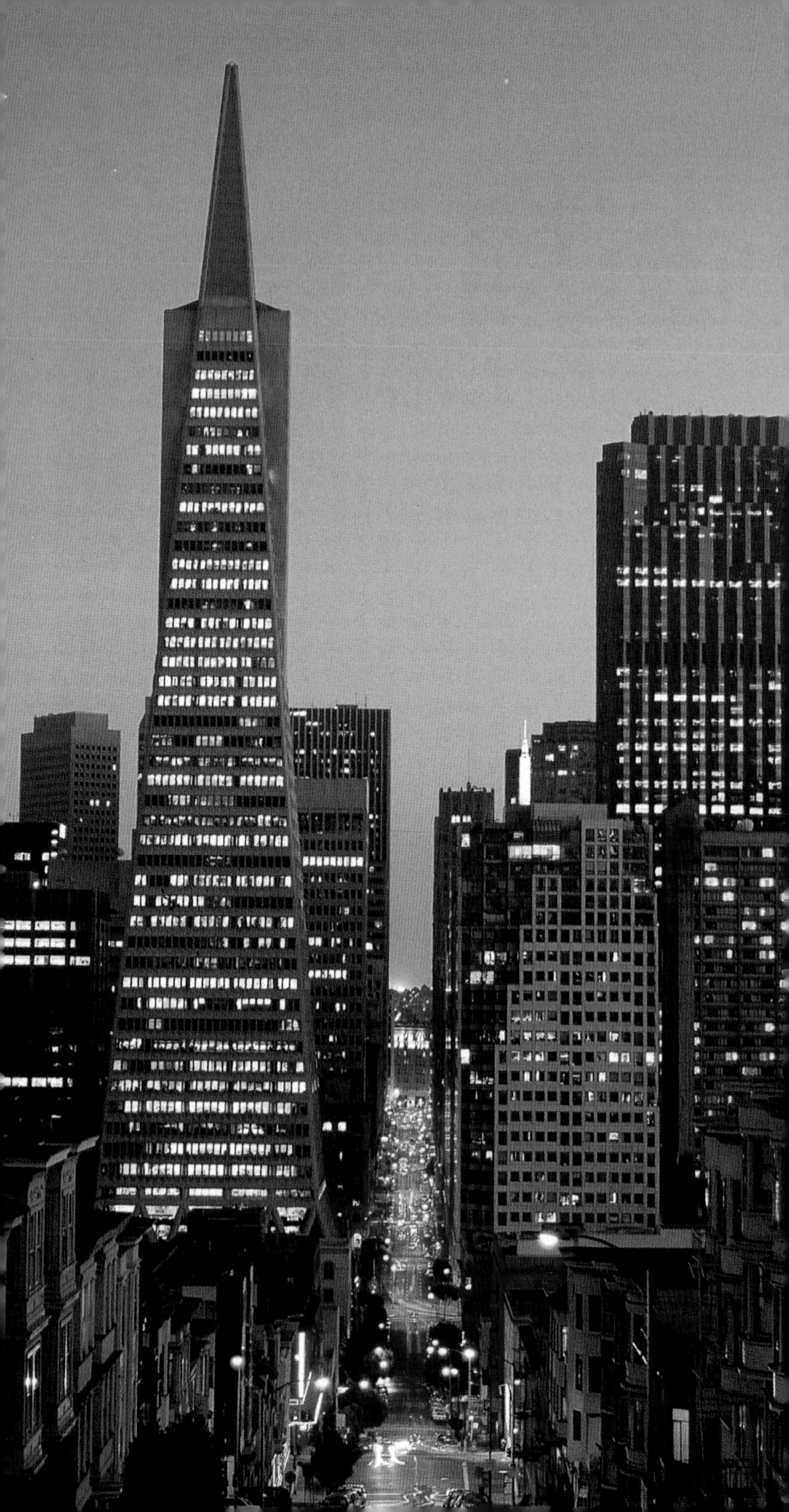

DOWNTOWN SAN FRANCISCO

MONTGOMERY STREET, now right in the heart of the Financial District, was once a street of small shops, where miners came to weigh their gold dust. Wells Fargo built the city's first brick building on the street during the Gold Rush *(see pp44–5)*. Today, old-fashioned

Motif on Union Bank

banks stand in the shadow of modern skyscrapers. Union Square is the city's main shopping district and has a wealth of fine department stores. SoMa (South of Market) has become the city's "artists' quarter," with its old warehouses converted into studios, bars and avant-garde theaters.

SIGHTS AT A GLANCE

Historic Streets and Buildings
Bank of California **6**
California Historical Society **12**
Ferry Building **10**
Jackson Square Historical District **2**
Merchant's Exchange **7**
Old United States Mint **24**
Pacific Coast Stock Exchange **8**
Powell Street Cable Car Turntable **22**

Shops
Crocker Galleria **17**
Gump's **18**
San Francisco Center **23**
Union Square Shops **21**

Modern Architecture
Bank of America **4**
Embarcadero Center **1**
Rincon Center **11**
Transamerica Pyramid **5**
Yerba Buena Gardens pp312–13 **14**

Theaters
Theater District **20**

Hotels
Sheraton Palace Hotel **16**

Museums and Galleries
Museum of Cartoon Art **15**
Museum of Modern Art pp308–9 **13**
Wells Fargo History Museum **3**

Parks and Squares
Justin Herman Plaza **9**
Union Square **19**

GETTING THERE

All streetcar, cable car, and BART lines, and most ferries and bus lines, converge at some point on Market Street – the heart of this section. From Market Street, bus lines reach all parts of the district.

0 meters   400
0 yards   400

KEY

	Street-by-Street map *See pp302–3*
	Cable car terminus
	BART station
P	Parking
	Ferry terminus

◁ **A view of downtown San Francisco at night**

Street-by-Street: Financial District

SAN FRANCISCO'S economic engine is fueled predominantly by the Financial District, one of the chief commercial centers in the US. It reaches from the imposing modern towers and plazas of the Embarcadero Center to staid Montgomery Street, called the "Wall Street of the West." All the principal banks, brokers, and law offices are situated within this area. The Jackson Square Historical District, north of Washington Street, was once the heart of the business community.

★ **Embarcadero Center**
The center houses commercial outlets and offices. A shopping arcade occupies the first three tiers of the towers ❶

La Chiffonière (1978)
by Jean de Buffet,
Justin Herman Plaza

Hotaling Place is a narrow alley known for its many excellent antique shops.

Jackson Square Historical District
This district, more than any other, recalls the Gold Rush era ❷

The Golden Era Building was built during the Gold Rush and housed the paper *Golden Era*, for which Mark Twain wrote.

Bus stop
(No. 41)

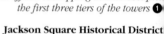

WASHINGTON STREET
BATTERY STREET
SANSOME STREET
MONTGOMERY STREET

★ **Transamerica Pyramid**
This 853-ft (260-m) skyscraper is now the tallest on the city's skyline ❺

Bank of California
This enormous bank is guarded by fierce stone lions carved by sculptor Arthur Putnam ❻

Merchant's Exchange
Paintings of shipping scenes line the walls ❼

Wells Fargo History Museum
An old stagecoach, evoking the Wild West days, is one of the exhibits in this transportation and banking museum ❸

Bank of America
There are fine views from the 52nd floor of this important banking institution ❹

0 meters   100
0 yards   100

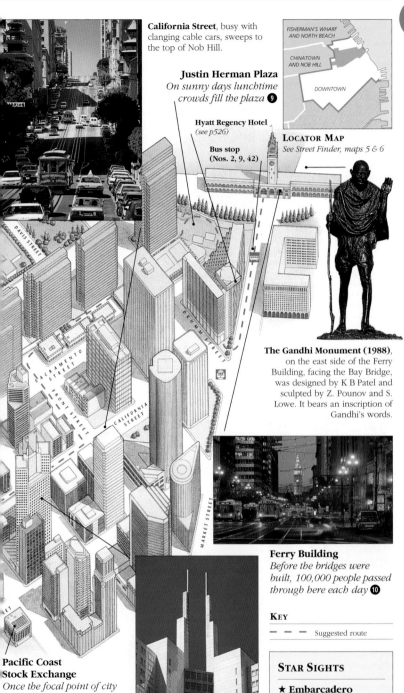

California Street, busy with clanging cable cars, sweeps to the top of Nob Hill.

Justin Herman Plaza
On sunny days lunchtime crowds fill the plaza ❾

Hyatt Regency Hotel
(see p526)

Bus stop
(Nos. 2, 9, 42)

FISHERMAN'S WHARF AND NORTH BEACH

CHINATOWN AND NOB HILL

DOWNTOWN

LOCATOR MAP
See Street Finder, maps 5 & 6

The Gandhi Monument (1988), on the east side of the Ferry Building, facing the Bay Bridge, was designed by K B Patel and sculpted by Z. Pounov and S. Lowe. It bears an inscription of Gandhi's words.

DAVIS STREET

SACRAMENTO STREET

FRONT STREET

CALIFORNIA STREET

DRUMM STREET

MARKET STREET

Ferry Building
Before the bridges were built, 100,000 people passed through here each day ❿

KEY

– – – Suggested route

Pacific Coast Stock Exchange
Once the focal point of city trade, it is now closed due to electronic trading. ❽

First Interstate Center towers are linked by glass "sky-bridges."

STAR SIGHTS

★ **Embarcadero Center**

★ **Transamerica Pyramid**

Embarcadero Center ❶

Map 6 D3. 🚌 *1, 32, 42.*
🚋 *J, K, L, M, N.* 🚞 *California St.*
See **Shopping** *p376–79* and **Where to Stay** *p504–37.*

COMPLETED IN 1981 after a decade of construction, San Francisco's largest re-development project stretches from Justin Herman Plaza to Battery Street. Office workers and shoppers use its open spaces to relax in the sun and eat their lunch. Four high-rise towers reach 35 to 45 stories above the landscaped plazas and elevated walkways.

The Embarcadero Center's most spectacular interior is the foyer of the Hyatt Regency Hotel *(see p525)*. Its 17-story atrium contains an immense sculptured globe by Charles Perry entitled *Eclipse*. Glass elevators glide up and down one wall, carrying visitors to and from the Equinox, a re-volving rooftop restaurant that completes a full circle every 40 minutes.

Lobby of the Hyatt Regency Hotel at the Embarcadero Center

Hotaling Place in Jackson Square

Jackson Square Historical District ❷

Map 5 C3. 🚌 *12, 15, 42, 83.*

RENOVATED IN the early 1950s, this neighborhood con-tains many historic brick, cast-iron, and granite façades dating from Gold Rush days. From 1850 to 1910 it was known as the Barbary Coast, notorious for its squalor and the crude-ness of its inhabitants. The old Hippodrome theater at No. 555 Pacific Street contains bawdy relief sculptures in the recessed front, which recall the risqué shows that were performed there. Today the buildings are used as show-rooms, law offices, and fine antique shops; the best ones can be seen in Jackson Street, Gold Street, Hotaling Place, and Montgomery Street.

Wells Fargo History Museum ❸

420 Montgomery St. **Map** 5 C4.
🕿 *(415) 396-2619.* 🚌 *1, 12, 15, 42.* 🚞 *California St.* 🕘 *9am–5pm Mon–Fri.* ⬤ *public hols.* ♿

FOUNDED IN 1852, Wells Fargo & Co. became the greatest banking and trans-portation company in the West and was influential in the development of the American frontier.

The company moved people and goods from the East to the West Coast, and between the mining camps and towns of California. It also transported gold from the West Coast to the East, and delivered mail, placing mailboxes in convenient locations to enable the messengers to sort letters en route. The Pony Express was another mail venture in which Wells Fargo & Co. played a major role.

The splendid stagecoaches on display are famous, particu-larly for the legendary stories of their heroic drivers and the bandits who robbed them. The best-known bandit was Black Bart, who left poems at the scene of his crimes. He stalk-ed the many lonely roads from Calaveras County up to the Oregon border from 1875 to 1883. In one holdup he mistakenly left behind his handkerchief. Its distinctive laundry mark revealed him as mining engineer Charles Boles *(see p463).*

Museum visitors can experience how it felt to sit for days in a jostling stage-coach, and listen to the recorded diary of an immigrant called Francis Brocklehurst. Exhibits include Pony Express mail, photo-graphs, bills of exchange, early checks, gold nug-gets, and the imperial currency of Emperor Norton *(see p47).*

Black Bart, the poet bandit

Bank of America ❹

55 California St. **Map** 5 C4.
(415) 433-7500 (Carnelian Room).
1, 15. California St.

THE RED granite-clad building
housing the headquarters
of the Bank of America opened in 1972. Its 52 floors make
it the tallest skyscraper in San
Francisco, and incredible
views from the Carnelian
Room on the 52nd floor show
the fascinating workings of
city life. The Bank of America

was originally the Bank of
Italy, which was founded by
AP Giannini in San Jose *(see
pp412–13)*. It built up a huge
clientele early in the 20th
century by catering to immigrants and investing in the
booming farmlands and small
towns. In the great fire of
1906 *(see pp48–9)*, Giannini
personally rescued his bank's
deposits, carrying them to
safety by hiding them in fruit
crates, so there were sufficient
funds for the bank to invest
in the rebuilding of the city.

***Transcendence* by Masayuki Nagari
(1972) at the Bank of America**

Transamerica Pyramid ❺

600 Montgomery St. **Map** 5 C3.
1, 15, 42. 8:30am–4:30pm
Mon–Fri. public hols.
www.tapyramid.com

CAPPED WITH a pointed
spire on top of its
48 stories, the pyramid
reaches 853 ft (260 m)
above sea level. It is the
tallest and most widely
recognized building in
the city, and although
San Franciscans disliked
it when it opened in
1972, they have since
accepted it as part of
their city's skyline.
  Designed by William
Pereira & Associates, the
pyramid houses 1,500
office workers on a site
that is historically one of
the richest in the city.
The Montgomery Block,
which contained many
important offices and
was the largest building
west of the Mississippi,
was built here in 1853.
In the basement was
the Exchange Saloon,
which was frequented
by Mark Twain/
Samuel Clemens. The
Financial District was
extended south in the
1860s, and artists and
writers took up
residence in the
Montgomery Block.
The Pony Express
terminus, marked
by a plaque, was
at Merchant
Street, opposite
the pyramid.

The spire is hollow, rising 212 ft (64 m) above the
top floor. Lit from inside, it casts a warm, yellow
glow at night. Its purpose is purely decorative.

The vertical wings *of the
building rise from the middle of
the ground floor and extend
beyond the frame, which tapers
inward. The eastern wing houses
18 elevator shafts, and the
western wing houses a smoke
tower and emergency stairs.*

**The observation
deck** *is situated on the
ground floor. Here, a
bank of monitors
provides visitors with
stupendous views
beamed down from
four cameras that
revolve at the
apex of the spire.*

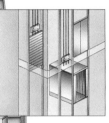

Earthquake protection
*is ensured by white precast
quartz aggregate, interlaced
with reinforcing rods at
four places on each floor,
that cover the exterior of
the pyramid. Clearance
between the panels allows
for lateral movement in
case of an earthquake.*

The shape *of the
building tapers so that it casts
a smaller shadow than a
conventional design.*

The 3,678 windows
take cleaners an entire
month to wash.

The foundations rest on a steel and
concrete block, sunk 52 ft (15.5 m)
into the ground and designed to
move with earth tremors.

Bank of California ❻

400 California St. **Map** 5 C4. 📞 *(415) 765-0400.* 🚌 *1, 42.* 🚃 *California St.* **Museum of American Money** ☐ *10am–4pm Mon–Thu, 10am–5pm Fri.* ⬤ *public hols.* ♿

Wᴵᴸᴸᴵᴀᴹ ʀᴀʟsᴛᴏɴ and Darius Mills founded this bank in 1864. Ralston, known as "the man who built San Francisco," invested profitably in the Comstock mines *(see p45)*. He used the bank and his personal fortune to finance many civic projects in San Francisco, including the city's water company, a theater, and the Palace Hotel *(see p526)*. When economic depression struck in the 1870s, Ralston's empire collapsed.

The present colonnaded building was completed in 1908. In the basement, the Museum of American Money displays gold, coins, old banknotes, and diagrams of the Comstock mines.

Classical façade of the Bank of California

Merchant's Exchange ❼

465 California St. **Map** 5 C4. 📞 *(415) 421-7730.* 🚌 *3, 4, 15.* ☐ *by appointment only* ⬤ *public hols.* ♿

Tʜᴇ ᴇxᴄʜᴀɴɢᴇ, designed by Willis Polk in 1903 survived the great fire of 1906 with little damage *(see pp48–9)*. Inside, fine seascapes by the Irish painter William Coulter line the walls, depicting epic maritime scenes from the age of steam and sail. This was the focal point of San Francisco's commodities exchange in the early 20th century, when look-outs in the tower relayed

news of ships arriving from abroad. Now dwarfed by skyscrapers, the Exchange once dominated the skyline.

Pacific Coast Stock Exchange ❽

301 Pine St. **Map** 5 C4. 📞 *(415) 393-4000.* 🚌 *3, 4, 15, 42.* ⬤ *to the public, except by prearranged tour.*

Tʜɪs ᴡᴀs ᴏɴᴄᴇ America's largest stock exchange outside New York. Founded in 1882 it occupied these buildings, which were re-modeled in 1930 by Miller and Pflueger from the existing US Treasury. The monumental granite statues that flank the Pine Street entrance were sculpted by Ralph Stackpole, also in 1930. The building is now closed, its once-frantic trading floor silent due to the emergence of electronic and Internet trading.

Justin Herman Plaza ❾

Map 6 D3. 🚌 *many buses.* 🚃 *F, J, K, L, M, N.* 🚃 *California St.*

Pᴏᴘᴜʟᴀʀ ᴡɪᴛʜ lunchtime crowds from the nearby Embarcadero Center *(see p304)*, this plaza is best known for its avant-garde Vaillancourt Fountain, built in 1971 by the Canadian artist Armand Vaillancourt. The fountain is modeled from huge concrete blocks, and some people find it ugly, especially when it is allowed to run dry during times of drought. However, you are allowed to climb on and through it, and with its splashing pools and columns of falling water, it is an intriguing public work of art when functioning as intended.

The area is often rented out to musicians during the lunch hour – the popular rock band U2 performed a

The Vaillancourt Fountain in Justin Herman Plaza

lunchtime concert here in 1987, after which they spray-painted the fountain.

Ferry Building ❿

Embarcadero at Market St. **Map** 6 E3. 🚌 *many buses.* 🚃 *J, K, L, M, N.* 🚃 *California St.*

Cᴏɴsᴛʀᴜᴄᴛᴇᴅ ʙᴇᴛᴡᴇᴇɴ 1896 and 1903, the Ferry Building survived the great fire of 1906 through the intercession of fireboats pumping water from the bay. The clock tower is 235 ft (71 m) high and was inspired by the Moorish bell tower of Seville Cathedral in Spain. In the early 1930s more than 50 million passengers a year passed through the building. Many of these were travelers to and from the transcontinental railroad terminal in Oakland, while others were commuters using the 170 daily ferries between the city and their homes across the bay. With the opening of the Bay Bridge in 1936 *(see pp406–7)*, the Ferry Building ceased to be the city's main point of entry and began to deteriorate. A few ferries still cross the bay, to Tiburon and Sausalito in Marin County *(see pp398–9)* and Oakland in the East Bay *(see pp406–7)*.

The clock tower on the Ferry Building

Rincon Annex mural depicting the Spanish discovery of San Francisco

Rincon Center ⓫

Map 6 E4. 🚌 14. See **Shopping** pp376–9.

THIS SHOPPING CENTER, with its soaring atrium and its 90-ft (27-m) fountain, was added on to the old Rincon Annex Post Office Building in 1989. The Rincon Annex dates from 1940 and is well known for its murals by the Russian-born artist Anton Refregier, showing aspects of the history of San Francisco. Some of the works depict harsh images of important events and people of the city, which caused much controversy when first shown.

California Historical Society ⓬

678 Mission St. **Map** 6 D5. 📞 (415) 357-1848. 🚊 J, K, L, M, N. 🕐 11am–5pm Tue–Sun. 🖥 www.calhist.org

THE CALIFORNIA Historical Society is dedicated to preserving and interpreting Californiana. The Society offers a reference and research library, museum galleries, and a well-stocked bookstore. There is also an impressive photographic collection, more than 900 oil paintings and watercolors by American artists, a decorative arts exhibit, and a unique costume collection.

Museum of Modern Art ⓭

See pp308–9.

Yerba Buena Gardens ⓮

See pp312–13.

Cartoon art on a US stamp

Museum of Cartoon Art ⓯

655 Mission St. 📞 (415) 227-8666. 🕐 11am–5pm Wed–Fri, 10am–5pm Sat, 1–5pm Sun. 🖼 📷

FOUNDED IN 1984, this is the only museum of original cartoon art on the West Coast. The 10,000 pieces in the collection date from the 18th century to the present day and include the original artwork for such well-known cartoon characters as Popeye, Charlie Brown, L'il Abner, Little Orphan Annie, and Walt Disney's numerous creations. Exhibitions change every four months. The museum also includes a children's area and a CD-ROM gallery.

Sheraton Palace Hotel ⓰

2 New Montgomery St. **Map** 5 C4. 📞 (415) 512-1111. 🚌 7, 8, 9, 21, 31, 66, 71. 🚊 J, K, L, M, N. See **Where to Stay** p526.

THE ORIGINAL Palace Hotel was opened by William Ralston, one of San Francisco's best-known financiers, in 1875. It was the most luxurious of San Francisco's early hotels, with 7 floors, 700 windows, an inner courtyard, and exotic international décor. It was regularly frequented by the rich and famous. Among its patrons were the actress Sarah Bernhardt and writers Oscar Wilde and Rudyard Kipling. The celebrated tenor Enrico Caruso was a guest at the hotel at the time of the earthquake of 1906 when the hotel, like much of the city, caught fire. It was rebuilt shortly after under the direction of the architect George Kelham, and reopened in 1909. The Garden Court dining room can seat nearly 1,000 people and is lit by 20 crystal chandeliers. In 1988 the building was completely refurbished at a cost of $100 million.

The Garden Court at the Sheraton Palace Hotel

San Francisco Museum of Modern Art ⑮

THIS DRAMATIC museum forms the nucleus of San Francisco's reputation as a leading center of modern art. Created in 1935 with the aim of displaying works from 20th-century artists, it moved into its new quarters in 1995. The focus of Swiss architect Mario Botta's modernist building is the 125-ft (38-m) cylindrical skylight, which channels light down to the first-floor atrium court. More than 17,000 works of art are housed in its 50,000 sq ft (4,600 sq m) of gallery space on four floors. The museum offers a dynamic schedule of changing exhibits from around the world.

Zip Light (1990) by Sigmar Willnauer

Personal Values
Belgian Surrealist René Magritte created this late masterpiece in 1952. It features his use of everyday objects in strange and often unsettling surroundings, all painted in a realistic style.

MUSEUM GUIDE
The museum shop, auditorium, café and special events space are on the first floor. On the second floor are works from the permanent collection of paintings, sculptures, California art, architecture and design. Photography and other works on paper are displayed on the third floor, with media arts on the fourth floor. Contemporary works are displayed in fourth and fifth floor special exhibition halls, along with temporary exhibits and recent gifts and purchases. The museum's entire collection rotates regularly.

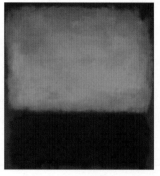

★ **No. 14, 1960**
This oil on canvas was painted by Mark Rothko, a leading Abstract Impressionist. The background color is subtly related to those of the two rectangles.

PM Magazine
Television screens show Dara Birnbaum's innovative 1982 video work.

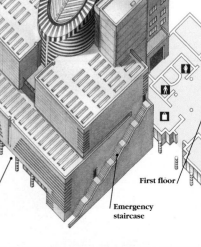

125-ft (38-m) tall cylindrical skylight

Second floor

Auditorium

First floor

Main entrance

Emergency staircase

KEY TO FLOOR PLAN

- ☐ Painting and sculpture
- ☐ Architecture and design
- ☐ Photography and works on paper
- ☐ Media arts
- ☐ Special exhibitions and events
- ☐ Non-exhibition space

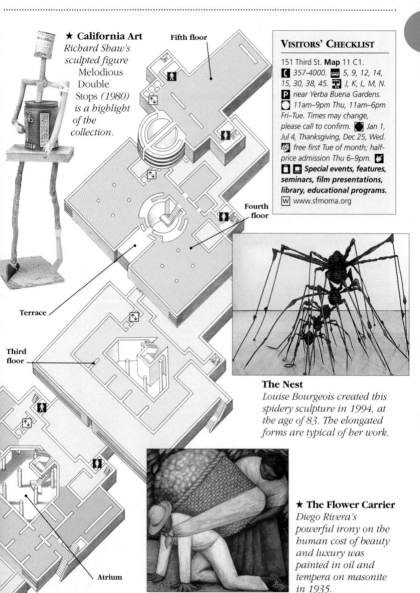

★ **California Art**
Richard Shaw's sculpted figure Melodious Double Stops *(1980) is a highlight of the collection.*

Fifth floor

Fourth floor

Terrace

Third floor

Atrium

VISITORS' CHECKLIST

151 Third St. **Map** 11 C1.
357-4000. 5, 9, 12, 14, 15, 30, 38, 45. J, K, L, M, N.
near Yerba Buena Gardens.
11am–9pm Thu, 11am–6pm Fri–Tue. Times may change, please call to confirm. Jan 1, Jul 4, Thanksgiving, Dec 25, Wed.
free first Tue of month; half-price admission Thu 6–9pm.
Special events, features, seminars, film presentations, library, educational programs.
www.sfmoma.org

The Nest
Louise Bourgeois created this spidery sculpture in 1994, at the age of 83. The elongated forms are typical of her work.

★ **The Flower Carrier**
Diego Rivera's powerful irony on the human cost of beauty and luxury was painted in oil and tempera on masonite in 1935.

Country Dog Gentlemen
Bay Area artist Roy De Forest painted this fantasy of a universe guarded by animals in 1972.

STAR EXHIBITS

★ The Flower Carrier

★ No14, 1960 (Rothko)

★ California Art

Central plaza of the Crocker Galleria

Crocker Galleria 🄗

Between Post, Kearny, Sutter, and Montgomery Sts. **Map** 5 C4. 🚌 2, 3, 4. 🚋 J, K, L, M, N. See **Shopping** pp376–9.

THE CROCKER GALLERIA was built in 1982. Inspired by Milan's Galleria Vittorio Emmanuelle, the building features a central plaza under an arched atrium. More than 50 shops and restaurants are housed here on three floors, with displays promoting the best of European and American designers.

Gump's 🄘

135 Post St. **Map** 5 C4. 🄲 (415) 982-1616. 🚌 2, 3, 4, 30, 38, 45. 🚋 J, K, L,M, N. 🚋 Powell–Mason, Powell–Hyde. ◯ 10am–6pm Mon–Sat. ♿ See **Shopping** pp376–9.

FOUNDED IN 1861 by German immigrants who were once mirror and frame merchants, this indigenous San Francisco department store has now become a local institution. Many of the city's couples register their wedding present list with the store.

Gump's houses the largest collection of fine china and crystal in the United States; it includes such prestigious designers as Baccarat, Steuben, and Lalique.

The store is also celebrated for its oriental treasures, furniture, and the rare works of art in the art department. The Asian art is particularly fine, especially the jade collection, which enjoys an international reputation. In 1949 Gump's imported a great bronze Buddha and presented it to the Japanese Tea Garden *(see pp356–7)*.

Gump's has a refined atmosphere and is often frequented by the rich and famous. It is renowned for its colorful and extravagant window displays, which change regularly and feature different themes.

Union Square 🄙

Map 5 C5. 🚌 2, 3, 4, 30, 38, 45. 🚋 J, K, L, M, N. 🚋 Powell–Mason, Powell–Hyde.

UNION SQUARE was named after the big, pro-Union rallies held here during the Civil War of 1861–65. The rallies galvanized popular support in San Francisco for the Northern cause, and this was instrumental in bringing California into the war on the side of the Union. The original churches, gentlemen's clubs, and a synagogue were eventually overtaken by shops and offices. This green square, lined with palm trees, is now at the heart of the city's shopping district and marks the edge of the Theater District. It is bordered on the west side by the luxurious Westin St. Francis Hotel *(see p526)*. In the center there is a bronze statue of the Goddess of Victory. Sculpted by Robert Aitken in 1903, she stands at the top of a 90-ft (27-m) Corinthian column. The monument was erected to commemorate Admiral Dewey's naval victory at Manila Bay during the Spanish–American War of 1898. Union Square also had the world's first multilevel underground parking lot, constructed in 1942.

Theater District 🄴

Map 5 B5. 🚌 2, 3, 4, 38. 🚋 Powell–Mason, Powell–Hyde. See **Entertainment** pp372–5.

SEVERAL THEATERS are located near Union Square, all within a six-block area. The two largest are on Geary Boulevard: the Curran Theater, designed in 1922 by Alfred Henry D Jacobs, which imports Broadway shows, and the Geary Theater, with its Edwardian façade, now home to the American Conservatory Theater (ACT). The Theater on the Square mounts avantgarde, off-Broadway shows. The city has a fine reputation for the variety of performances it offers and has always attracted great actors. Isadora Duncan, the innovative 1920s dancer, was born nearby at No. 501 Taylor Street, which is now marked by a plaque.

Union Square Shops 🄵

Map 5 C5. 🚌 2, 3, 4, 30, 38, 45. 🚋 J, K, L, M, N. 🚋 Powell–Mason, Powell–Hyde. See **Shopping** pp376–9.

MANY OF San Francisco's largest department stores can be found here, including Macy's, Saks Fifth Avenue, and

Department stores overlooking Union Square

Rotating a cable car on the Powell Street Turntable

San Francisco Center ㉓

Market St and Powell St. **Map** 5 C5.
📞 *(415) 512-6776.* 🚌 *5, 7, 8, 9, 14, 21, 71.* 🚋 *J, K, L, M, N.* 🚋 *Powell–Mason, Powell–Hyde.*
🕐 *9:30am–8pm Mon–Sat, 11am–6pm Sun. See* **Shopping** *pp376–9.*

S HOPPERS ARE CARRIED upward on semispiral escalators through this vertical mall, with its nine floors of shops. It is topped by a retractable dome that is opened on fine days. The basement levels provide access to Powell Street Station. Nordstrom, a fashion store, occupies the top four levels. Entrances to Emporium, a department store famous for its Classical rotunda, are on the lower floors.

Old United States Mint ㉔

Fifth St and Mission St. **Map** 5 C5.
🚌 *14, 14L, 26, 27.* 🚋 *J, K, L, M, N.*
⬤ *to the public.*

S AN FRANCISCO'S Old Mint produced its last coins in 1937. It was built of granite in the Classical style by AB Mullet between 1869 and 1874, hence its nickname, the "Granite Lady." Its windows were fortified by iron shutters, and its basement vaults impregnable. The building was one of the few to survive the 1906 earthquake *(see pp48–9).* From 1973 to 1994 the building housed a museum, but today it is considered to be seismically unsafe. Closed for an indefinite period, its future is now uncertain.

Gump's. The Nieman Marcus store, at the request of San Franciscans, has preserved the 1900 rotunda and skylight from the City of Paris. The latter was the city's most elegant store at the end of the 19th century but was demolished in 1982. As well as the larger stores, the area houses many antiquarian bookshops and smaller boutiques. The Circle Gallery Building, at 140 Maiden Lane, is a contemporary art gallery. Designed by Frank Lloyd Wright in 1947, it was the precursor to his Guggenheim Museum in New York *(see p29).*

Powell Street Cable Car Turntable ㉒

Hallidie Plaza, Powell St at Market St. **Map** 5 C5. 🚌 *many buses.* 🚋 *J, K, M, N.* 🚋 *Powell–Mason, Powell–Hyde.*

T HE POWELL–HYDE and the Powell–Mason cable car lines are the most spectacular routes in San Francisco. They start and end their journeys to Nob Hill, Chinatown, and Fisherman's Wharf at the corner of Powell Street and Market Street. Unlike the double-ended cable cars that are found on the California Street line, the Powell Street cable cars were built to move in one direction only – hence the need for a turntable at the end of each line.

After the last passengers have disembarked, the car is pushed onto the turntable and rotated manually by the conductor and gripman. The next passengers for the return journey wait for the half-circle to be completed amid an ever-moving procession of street musicians, local shoppers, and office workers.

The impregnable "Granite Lady" Old Mint

Yerba Buena Center ⑭

THE CONSTRUCTION of the Moscone Center, San Francisco's largest venue for conventions, heralded the beginning of ambitious plans for Yerba Buena Gardens, now the Yerba Buena Center for the Arts. New housing, hotels, museums, and shops have followed, rejuvenating a once depressed area. The development is far from complete, but it is already contributing to the city's cultural and economic life.

★ Center for the Arts Galleries
Galleries for the visual arts and a sculpture court feature displays of contemporary art.

Esplanade Gardens
Visitors can wander along the paths or relax on benches.

The Martin Luther King Jr Memorial has words of peace in several languages.

Zeum
Zeum is located at the Yerba Buena Rooftop. It has an ongoing program of events and provides opportunities for youngsters and artists to collaborate in the design and creation of anything from airplanes, robots, and futuristic buildings to mosaics and sculptures.

STAR SIGHTS

★ **Yerba Buena Center for the Arts**

★ **SF Museum of Modern Art**

MOSCONE CENTER

Engineer TY Lin found an ingenious way to support the rooftop garden above this huge underground hall without a single interior column. The bases of the eight steel arches are linked, like an archer's bow strings, by cables under the floor. By tightening the cables, the arches exert enormous upward thrust.

Center for the Arts Theater
Works reflecting the cultural diversity of San Francisco are presented in the 755-seat indoor theater. There is also an outdoor stage with lawn seating for 3,000.

North entrance to Moscone Center

East Garden

★ **San Francisco Museum of Modern Art**
Orange Sweater (1955) by Elmer Bischoff is among the many modern works of art in this privately funded museum.

South entrance to Moscone Center

Moscone Ballroom is part of San Francisco's extensive convention facilities. It is available for large conferences and symposia.

The children's center is equipped with facilities that will help to encourage imaginative play.

Ice-skating rink

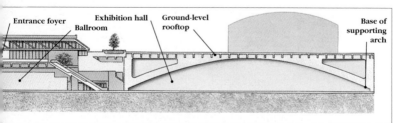

Entrance foyer
Ballroom
Exhibition hall
Ground-level rooftop
Base of supporting arch

擎天酒樓

KING T
RESTAURA

家

CHINATOWN AND NOB HILL

THE CHINESE settled in the plaza on Stockton Street during the 1850s; the steep hills had made the area unpopular among wealthier San Franciscans. Today the district recalls the atmosphere of a typical southern Chinese town, although the architecture, customs, and public events are distinctly American hybrids on a Cantonese theme. This densely populated neighborhood has been called the "Gilded Ghetto," because its colorful façades and teeming markets screen a much harsher

Chinese symbol outside the Bank of America

world of sweatshops, cramped living quarters, and poor inhabitants.

Nob Hill is San Francisco's most celebrated hilltop, famous for its cable cars, plush hotels, and views. In the late 19th century, the "Big Four," who built the first transcontinental railroad, were among its richest tenants in their large mansions on the hill. In 1906, the earthquake and fire *(see pp48–9)* leveled all but one of these houses, but today's luxury hotels still recall the opulence of the Victorian era *(see p523)*.

SIGHTS AT A GLANCE

Historic Streets and Buildings
Chinatown Alleys ❺
Chinatown Gateway ❶
Grant Avenue ❻
Nob Hill ❿

Galleries and Museums
Cable Car Barn ⓫
Chinese Historical Society ❾
Pacific Heritage Museum ❽

Churches and Temples
Grace Cathedral ⓬
Kong Chow Temple ❸
Old St. Mary's Church ❷
Tin How Temple ❹

Parks and Squares
Portsmouth Plaza ❼

KEY

Street-by-Street map
See pp316–17

Cable car turntable

P Parking

0 meters   500
0 yards   500

GETTING THERE

Visit on foot if possible. Car drivers can sometimes park in one of the Nob Hill hotel garages, under Portsmouth Plaza, or at St. Mary's Square in Chinatown. All cable car lines go to Nob Hill and Chinatown.

◁ **Colorful oriental architecture along Chinatown's streets**

Street-by-Street: Chinatown

A street lamp in Chinatown

GRANT AVENUE is the Chinatown for tourists, with dragon lampposts, up-turned roofs, and neighborhood hardware stores selling everything from kites to cooking utensils. Locals shop on Stockton Street, where boxes of the freshest vegetables, fish, and other produce spill over onto crowded sidewalks. In the alleys in between, look for temples, laundries, and family-run restaurants.

★ Chinatown Alleys
Authentic sights and sounds of the Orient echo in these busy alleys 5

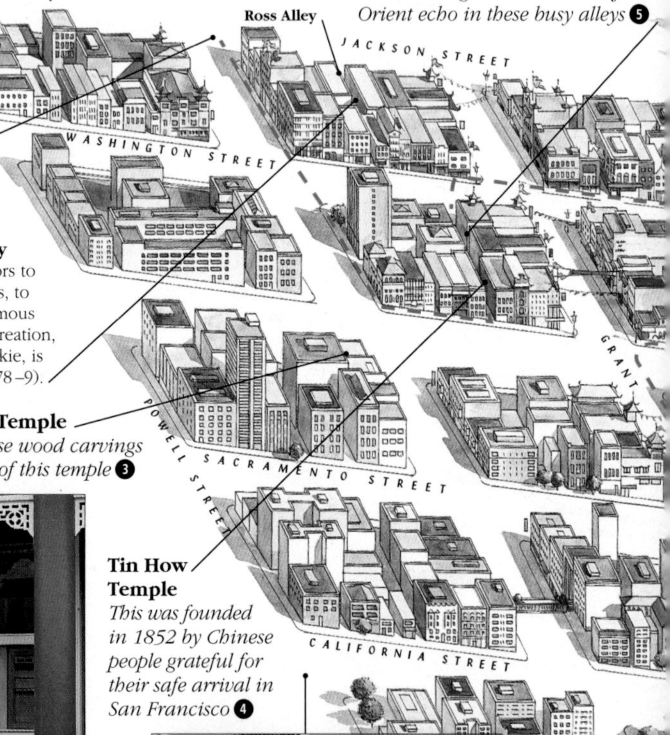
JACKSON STREET
WASHINGTON STREET
SACRAMENTO STREET
POWELL STREET
CALIFORNIA STREET
GRANT
STOCKTON
BUSH ST
0 meters 100
0 yards 100

Ross Alley

To bus no. 83

The Fortune Cookie Factory welcomes visitors to its tiny premises, to see how the famous San Francisco creation, the fortune cookie, is made (see pp378–9).

Kong Chow Temple
Fine Cantonese wood carvings are a feature of this temple 3

Tin How Temple
This was founded in 1852 by Chinese people grateful for their safe arrival in San Francisco 4

廣東銀行中國城分行

The Bank of Canton was home to Chinatown's telephone exchange until 1946. The operators spoke five Chinese dialects.

Cable Cars run down two sides of Chinatown and are an essential part of the area's bustling atmosphere. Any of the three lines will take you there.

STAR SIGHTS

- **★ Chinatown Alleys**
- **★ Chinatown Gateway**
- **★ Grant Avenue**

Portsmouth Plaza
Laid out in 1839, this was the social center for the village of Yerba Buena. Today it is a gathering place for players of cards and mahjong **7**

★ **Grant Avenue**
In the 1830s and early 1840s this was the main thoroughfare of Yerba Buena. It is now the busy commercial center of Chinatown **6**

LOCATOR MAP
See Street Finder, map 5

KEY

– – – Suggested route

The Chinese Cultural Center
contains an art gallery and a small crafts shop. It sponsors a lively program of lectures and seminars.

Chinese Historical Society
The society's collection of historical artifacts, documents, and photographs is exhibited here **9**

Pacific Heritage Museum
Housed in an elegant building below the Bank of Canton, this small museum has fine exhibitions of Asian art, which are regularly changed **8**

Old St. Mary's Church
The clock tower of this church, built while the city was still in its infancy, bears an arresting inscription **2**

SON.OBSERVE THE TIME AND FLY FROM EVIL. E(C.IV.23.

St. Mary's Square is a quiet haven in which to rest.

To bus nos. 31, 38

★ **Chinatown Gateway**
Also known as the "Dragons' Gate," this marks Chinatown's south entrance **1**

Chinatown Gateway ❶

Grant Ave at Bush St. **Map** 5 C4.
🚌 *2, 3, 4, 15, 30, 45.*

THIS ORNATE PORTAL, opened in 1970, was designed by Clayton Lee as an arch over the entrance to Chinatown's main tourist street, Grant Avenue. It was inspired by the ceremonial entrances of traditional Chinese villages. The three-arched gateway is capped with green roof tiles and a host of propitiatory animals, all of glazed ceramic. The gate was erected by an American institution, the Chinatown Cultural Development Committee. The materials were donated by Taiwan (Republic of China).

It is guarded by two stone lions that are suckling their cubs through their claws, in accordance with ancient lore. Once through the gate, visitors can buy antiques, embroidered silks, and gems, though prices are aimed at tourists.

Stone lions decorating the Chinatown gateway

Old St. Mary's Church ❷

660 California St. **Map** 5 C4.
📞 *(415) 288–3800.* 🚌 *1, 15, 30, 45.* 🚋 *California St.* **Mass** 5pm Sat, 8.30am Sun. 📷

SAN FRANCISCO's first Catholic cathedral, Old St. Mary's, was consecrated on Christmas Day 1854 as the seat of the Roman Catholic bishop of the Pacific Coast. Until 1891 it served a largely Irish congregation, when the new St. Mary's Cathedral was built on Van Ness Avenue. Because of the unavailability of the right building materials in California, the bricks and iron for the church were imported from the East Coast, while the granite foundation stones came from China. The clock tower of the church bears a large inscription, "Son, observe the time and fly from evil," said to have been directed at the brothels that stood across the street at the time it was built. It was one of the few buildings to remain unharmed by the 1906 earthquake and retains its original foundations and walls. The interior, with stained-glass windows and a balcony, was completed in 1909.

Entrance to Old St. Mary's Church below the clock tower and its inscription

Kong Chow Temple ❸

4th floor, 855 Stockton St. **Map** 5 B4.
📞 *(415) 788-1339.* 🚌 *30, 45.* ⭕ *10am–4pm daily.* **Donation.** ♿

FROM THE TOP FLOOR above the district's post office, the Kong Chow Temple looks out over Chinatown and the Financial District. Although the building itself dates from only 1977, the temple altar and statuary are thought to form the oldest Chinese religious shrine in the United States. One altar was hand-carved in Guangzhou (Canton) and shipped to San Francisco in the 19th century. The main shrine is presided over by a carved wooden statue of Kuan Di, also dating from the 19th century. He is the deity most often found in shrines in Cantonese cities.

Kuan Di is also frequently seen in the city's Chinatown

Carved statue of Kuan Di inside the Kong Chow Temple

district: his highly distinctive face looks down from Taoist shrines in many of the area's restaurants. He is typically depicted holding a large sword in one hand and a book in the other. These are symbols of his unswerving dedication to both the martial and the literary arts.

Tin How Temple ❹

Top floor, 125 Waverly Pl. **Map** 5 C3. 🚌 1, 15, 30, 45. ⬛ 10am–5pm daily. **Donation**.

THIS UNUSUAL temple is dedicated to Tin How (Tien Hau), the Queen of Heaven and protector of seafarers and visitors, and is the oldest operating Chinese temple in the United States. The sanctuary was originally founded in 1852 by a group of Chinese sailors, in gratitude for their safe voyage across the Pacific Ocean from their homeland to San Francisco. The temple is now situated at the top of three steep, wooden flights of stairs, which are considered to place it closer to heaven. The narrow space is filled with the smoke from both incense and burned paper offerings, and is brightly decorated with hundreds of gold and red lanterns. It is lit by red electric light bulbs and burning wicks floating in oil. Gifts of fruit lie on the carved altar in front of the wooden statue of the temple's namesake deity.

A view along Chinatown's main street, Grant Avenue

The impressive façade of the Tin How Temple on Waverly Place

Chinatown Alleys ❺

Map 5 B3. 🚌 1, 30, 45.

CONTAINED WITHIN a busy neighborhood, the Chinatown Alleys are situated between Grant Avenue and Stockton Street. These four narrow lanes intersect at Washington Street within half a block of each other. Of these, the largest is Waverly Place, known as the "Street of Painted Balconies" for reasons that are apparent to every passerby. Its other nickname, "15 Cents Street," derives from the cost of a haircut by the Chinese barbers trading here at the turn of the century. Nearby, Sun Yat-sen spent many years in exile at No. 36 Spofford Alley.

The alleys contain many old buildings, as well as traditional shops and restaurants. There are also atmospheric, old-fashioned herbalist shops, displaying elk antlers, sea horses, snake wine, and other exotic wares in their windows. Numerous small restaurants, above and below street level, serve cheap and delicious home-cooked food.

Grant Avenue ❻

Map 5 C4. 🚌 1, 30, 45. 🚋 California St.

GRANT AVENUE is historically important for being the first street of Yerba Buena, the village that preceded San Francisco. A plaque at No. 823 marks the site of the first dwelling, a canvas tent that was erected on June 25, 1835. By 1836 the tent was replaced with a wooden structure and by 1837 with an adobe house. The street was then named Calle de la Fundacíon, the "Street of the Foundation."

An estimated 25,000 Chinese arrived in San Francisco during the Gold Rush era (see pp44–5). They settled in this area on the undesirable lower east slopes of Nob Hill, which were too steep for horse-drawn carriages. In 1885 the street was renamed Grant Avenue, in memory of Ulysses S Grant, the US president who died that year.

Most of the buildings on Grant Avenue were built after the 1906 earthquake in an Oriental Renaissance style. They now form the main tourist street in Chinatown.

Portsmouth Plaza, at the hub of Chinatown life

Portsmouth Plaza **❼**

Map 5 C3. 🚌 *1, 15.*

SAN FRANCISCO'S original town square was laid out in 1839. It was once the social center for the village of Yerba Buena. On July 9, 1846, just after US rebels in Sonoma had declared California's independence from Mexico *(see pp448–9)*, marines raised the American flag above the plaza, officially seizing the port as part of the United States. Two years later, Sam Brannan announced the discovery of gold in the Sierra Nevada Mountains *(see pp44–5)* here. In the 1850s the area was the hub of this new dynamic city, but in the 1860s the business district shifted to flatlands reclaimed from the bay and the plaza declined in civic importance.

Today Portsmouth Plaza is the social center of Chinatown. In the morning people practice *t'ai chi*, and from noon to evening gather to play cards.

Pacific Heritage Museum **❽**

608 Commercial St. **Map** 5 C3. 📞 *(415) 399-1124.* 🚌 *1, 15.* 🕐 *10am–4pm Mon–Sat, except public hols.* ♿

THE MUSEUM BUILDING is as elegant as the changing collections of Asian arts displayed inside. It is a synthesis of two buildings. The US Sub-Treasury was erected here in 1875–77 by William Appleton Potter, on the site of the city's first mint. Old coin vaults can still be seen in the basement.

In 1984 the 17-story Bank of Canton headquarters were built above the Treasury, incorporating the old façade and basement. The result is a building of great refinement.

Chinese Historical Society **❾**

965 Clay St. **Map** 5 C3. 📞 *(415) 391-1188.* 🚌 *1, 15.* 🕐 *9am–5pm Mon–Fri.* 🅿
🌐 www.chsa.org

AMONG THE EXOTIC exhibits in this museum are a ceremonial dragon costume and a "tiger fork." This triton was wielded in one of the battles during the reign of terror known as the Tong Wars. The tongs were rival Chinese clans who fought over the control of gambling and prostitution in the city in the late 19th century. Other objects, documents and photographs illuminate the daily life of Chinese immigrants in San Francisco. There is a yearbook of the neighborhood written in Chinese, as well as the original Chinatown telephone directory, written by hand.

The contribution of the Chinese to California's development was extensive despite the antagonism and poor treatment they were met with, as the many museum displays make clear. Chinese workers made the perilous voyage to

Dragon's head in the Historical Society

California in the thousands to find gold and escape the economic difficulties of their homeland. Rich merchants used them as cheap labor in the gold mines, and later they were used to build the western half of the transcontinental railroad *(see pp46–7)*. They also constructed dikes in the Sacramento River delta, were great pioneers in the fishing industry, and planted the first vines in many of California's early vineyards.

Nob Hill **❿**

Map 5 B4.

NOB HILL is the highest summit of the city center rising 338 ft (103 m) above the bay. Its steep slopes kept prominent citizens away until the opening of the California Street cable car line in 1878. The rich then flocked to build homes here, including the "Big Four" railroad barons *(see pp456–7)*. Its name is thought to come from the Hindi word *nabob*, meaning governor. Sadly, all the mansions were burned down in the fire of 1906 *(see pp48–9)*, except the home of James C Flood, now the Pacific Union Club. Nob Hill still attracts the affluent to its splendid hotels which benefit from spectacular views of the city.

A panoramic view of the city from a penthouse bar on Nob Hill

Cable Car Barn ⓫

01 Mason St. **Map** 5 B3. 🚋 *(415)*
4-1887. 🚌 *1.* 🚋 *Powell–Mason,*
well–Hyde. ⭕ *10am–6pm daily*
0am–5pm in winter). ● *Jan 1,*
anksgiving, Dec 25. ♿ *mezzanine*
ly. **Video show.** 📷
🔗 www.cablecarmuseum.com

THIS IS BOTH a museum and
the powerhouse of the
ble car system *(see pp292–*
). Anchored to the floor are
the wheels that wind the cables
through the system of channels and pulleys beneath the
city's streets. You can observe
them from the mezzanine, then
walk downstairs to see under
the street. The museum also
houses an early cable car and
specimens of the mechanisms
that control the movements of
individual cars. The cable car
system is the last of its kind
in the world. The brick building was constructed in 1909.

**The entrance to the Cable Car
Barn Museum**

Grace Cathedral ⓬

00 California St. **Map** 5 B4. 🚋
5) 749-6300. 🚌 *1.* 🚋 *California*
🎵 *Choral evensong 5:15pm Thu,*
30pm Sun; Choral Eucharist 7:30am,
30am, 11am Sun. ♿ 📷 *12:30–*
m Sun, 1–3pm Mon–Fri, 11:30am–
30pm Sat. 📷

GRACE CATHEDRAL is the main
Episcopal church in San
ancisco. It was designed by
ewis P Hobart. Preparatory
ork began in February 1927,
d building started in
eptember 1928, but the
thedral was not completed
til 1964. Despite its modern
construction, the building
is inspired by Notre
Dame in Paris, using
traditional materials.
The interior is
replete with marble,
and the leaded
windows were
designed by
Charles Connick,
using the blue
glass of Chartres as
his inspiration. The
rose window is
made using 1-
inch (2.5-cm)
thick faceted
glass, which is
illuminated

**Cast figure from
the main
entrance**

from inside the building
at night. Other windows
were executed by Henry
Willet and Gabriel Loire.
These include depic-
tions of modern
heroes such as Albert
Einstein and astronaut
John Glenn. Objects in
the cathedral include a
13th-century Catalonian
crucifix and a 16th-
century Brussels
tapestry. The entrance
doors are cast from
molds of Ghiberti's
"Doors of Paradise,"
made for the Bap-
tistry in Florence.

he New Testament Window,
ade in 1931 by Charles
onnick, is placed
the south
de of the
urch.

The Rose Window
was made in Chartres by
Gabriel Loire in 1964.

The Carillon Tower
houses 44 bells made
in England in 1938.

**he Chapel of
race,** funded by
e Crocker family,
s a 15th-century
ench altarpiece.

**The Doors of
Paradise** are decorated
with scenes from the bible
and portraits of Ghiberti
and contemporaries.

Entrances

FISHERMAN'S WHARF AND NORTH BEACH

FISHERMEN FROM Genoa and Sicily first arrived in the Fisherman's Wharf area in the late 19th century and founded the San Francisco fishing industry. The district has slowly given way to tourism since the 1950s, but brightly painted boats still set out from the harbor on fishing trips early each morning. To the south of

Fisherman's Wharf entrance sign

Fisherman's Wharf lies North Beach, sometimes known as "Little Italy." This lively part of the city has an abundance of delis, bakeries, and cafés, from which you can watch the crowds. It is home to many Italian and Chinese families, with a sprinkling of writers and bohemians; Jack Kerouac *(see pp22–3)*, among others, found inspiration here.

SIGHTS AT A GLANCE

Museums and Galleries
North Beach Museum **13**
Ripley's Believe It Or Not! Museum **5**
San Francisco Art Institute **10**
San Francisco National Maritime Museum **8**
USS *Pampanito* **3**
Wax Museum **4**

Historic Streets and Buildings
Alcatraz Island pp328–9 **1**
Lombard Street **9**
Pier 39 **2**
Vallejo Street Stairway **11**

Shopping Centers
The Cannery **6**
Ghirardelli Square **7**

Restaurants and Bars
Club Fugazi **12**

Parks and Gardens
Levi's Plaza **17**
Telegraph Hill **16**
Washington Square **14**

Churches
Saints Peter and Paul Church **15**

KEY

▢	Street-by-Street map See pp324–5
🚋	Cable car turntable
⛴	Ferry terminal
P	Parking
🚃	Historical trolley line

0 meters   500
0 yards   500

GETTING THERE
The Powell–Hyde cable car line goes to Ghirardelli Square and Russian Hill. The Powell–Mason line passes through North Beach, to Fisherman's Wharf and Pier 39. Many buses run through the district.

◁ **View of Fisherman's Wharf and Alcatraz Island from the Powell–Hyde cable car**

Street-by-Street: Fisherman's Wharf

ITALIAN SEAFOOD restaurants have now replaced fishing as the primary focus of the Fisherman's Wharf local economy. Both the expensive restaurants and the cheap outdoor crab pots serve San Francisco's celebrated Dungeness crab, in season from November to June. As well as sampling the seafood, visitors also enjoy taking in the many shops, museums, and other attractions for which Fisherman's Wharf is noted.

★ **USS _Pampanito_**
A tour gives an idea of the hardships endured by sailors in this World War II submarine ❸

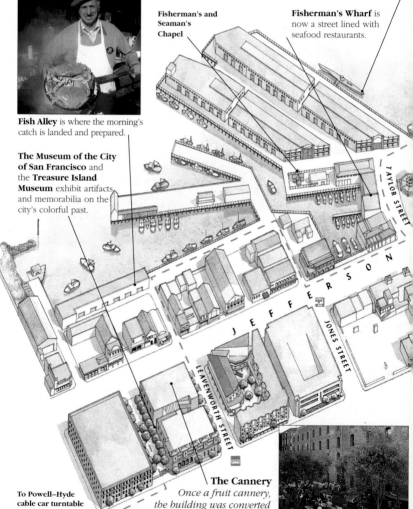

Fisherman's and Seaman's Chapel

Fisherman's Wharf is now a street lined with seafood restaurants.

Fish Alley is where the morning's catch is landed and prepared.

The Museum of the City of San Francisco and the **Treasure Island Museum** exhibit artifacts and memorabilia on the city's colorful past.

To Powell–Hyde cable car turntable (1 block)

The Cannery
Once a fruit cannery, the building was converted to a mall, with restaurants, fine shops, and museums ❻

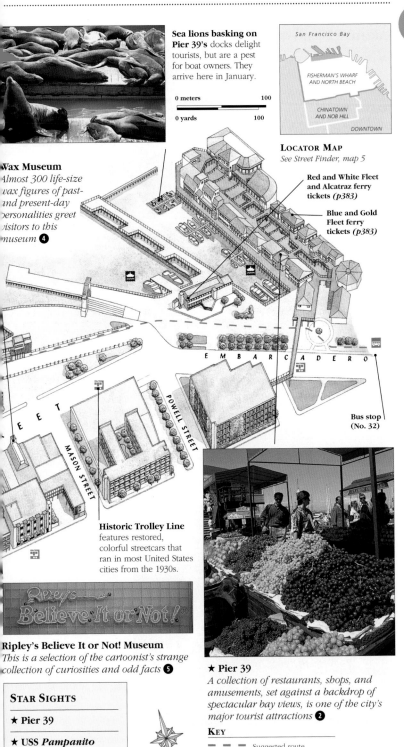

Sea lions basking on Pier 39's docks delight tourists, but are a pest for boat owners. They arrive here in January.

| 0 meters | | 100 |
| 0 yards | | 100 |

San Francisco Bay

FISHERMAN'S WHARF AND NORTH BEACH

CHINATOWN AND NOB HILL

DOWNTOWN

LOCATOR MAP
See Street Finder, map 5

Wax Museum
Almost 300 life-size wax figures of past-and present-day personalities greet visitors to this museum ❹

Red and White Fleet and Alcatraz ferry tickets *(p383)*

Blue and Gold Fleet ferry tickets *(p383)*

EMBARCADERO

POWELL STREET

MASON STREET

E E T

Bus stop (No. 32)

Historic Trolley Line features restored, colorful streetcars that ran in most United States cities from the 1930s.

Ripley's Believe It or Not! Museum
This is a selection of the cartoonist's strange collection of curiosities and odd facts ❺

★ Pier 39
A collection of restaurants, shops, and amusements, set against a backdrop of spectacular bay views, is one of the city's major tourist attractions ❷

KEY

— — — Suggested route

STAR SIGHTS

★ **Pier 39**

★ **USS Pampanito**

Alcatraz Island **❶**

See pp328–9.

Pier 39 **❷**

Map 5 B1. 🚌 *32, 25.*
See **Shopping** pp376–9.

R EFURBISHED IN 1978 to
resemble a quaint wooden
fishing village, this 1905 cargo
pier now houses many tourist
shops and specialty stores
spread over two levels.

The pier's street performers
and amusements are popular
and appealing, particularly to
families with children. You
can ride on the two-level
carousel, or brave the Turbo
Ride, a roller-coaster simulator
where a film gives the illusion
of speed and danger.

A sensational multimedia
show called the San Francisco
Experience takes visitors
through a whirlwind historical
tour of the city, complete with
Chinese New Year celebrations
and an earthquake.

USS *Pampanito*'s torpedo room

USS *Pampanito* **❸**

Pier 45. **Map** 4 F1. 📞 *(415) 775-1943.*
🚌 *32.* 🕐 *May–Oct: 9am– 9pm;
Sun–Thu: 9am–8pm Fri–Sat.* 🎿 🔊
🌐 *www.maritime.org*

T HIS WORLD WAR II submarine
fought in, and survived,
several bloody battles in the
Pacific, sinking six enemy
ships and severely damaging
others. Tragically for the
Allies, two of its fatal targets
were carrying British and
Australian prisoners of war.
The *Pampanito* managed to
rescue 73 men, however, and
carry them to safety in the
United States. A tour of the
ship takes visitors from stern
to bow and includes visits to
the torpedo room, the claus-
trophobic galley, and officers
quarters. In the days when th
USS *Pampanito* was in service
it had a crew of ten officers
who were in command of 70
enlisted seamen.

Wax Museum **❹**

145 Jefferson St. **Map** 5 B1. 📞 *(80
439-4305.* 🚌 *32.* 🕐 *10am–9pm
Mon–Fri; 9am–9pm Sat & Sun.* 🎿 🔊
🚹 *limited.*
🌐 *www.waxmuseum.com*

O NE OF THE WORLD's largest
and most absorbing col-
lections of life-size wax
figures is displayed here. All
aspects of life and history are
displayed here, from the
gruesome Chamber of
Horrors to the inspiring Hall
of Religions and the Library o
US Presidents. In the Palace
of Living Art, world-famous
portraits are rendered in wax
The entire Lower Lobby is
dedicated to a *Titanic* exhibi

A gallery of wax figures
includes such diverse
personages as members of th
British Royal Family, Elvis
Presley, Beethoven, Neil
Armstrong, Marilyn Monroe,
and Martin Luther King Jr.
The building is also home to
the Rainforest Cafe with its
waterfall and theme shops.

Ripley's Believe It Or Not! Museum **❺**

175 Jefferson St. **Map** 4 F1. 📞 *(415
771-6188.* 🚌 *32.* 🕐 *10am–10pm
Sun–Thu, 10am–midnight Fri–Sat.*
🎿 🚹
🌐 *www.ripleys.com*

C ALIFORNIAN NATIVE Robert L
Ripley, was an illustrator
who collected peculiar facts
and artifacts and earned his
fame from syndicating his
celebrated US newspaper
cartoon strip, called "Ripley's
Believe It Or Not!" Among
the 350 oddities on display
are a cable car built of
275,000 matchsticks, a two-
headed calf, tombstones
with wry epithets, and a life-
size replica of a man with
two pupils in each eyeball.

The two-level Venetian Carousel on Pier 39

The Cannery ⑥

2801 Leavenworth St. **Map** 4 F1.
🚎 19, 30, 32. 🚋 Powell–Hyde.
🕐 10am–4pm daily. ⚐ See
Shopping pp376–9.

THE INTERIOR of this 1909 fruit-canning plant was redeveloped in the 1960s. It now incorporates footbridges, rambling passages, and sunny courtyards, with restaurants and shops selling clothing, collector dolls, and Native American arts and crafts.

The Cannery also houses the Treasure Island Museum. Chief among its displays are memorabilia from the 1939 World's Fair, which celebrated the unity of Pacific cultures. Other permanent displays include the China Clippers – the silver Pan American Airways seaplanes which flew between Treasure Island and the Far East during World War II – and a Fresnel lens once used at the Farallon Island lighthouse.

Ghirardelli Square

Ghirardelli Square ⑦

900 North Point St. **Map** 4 F1.
🚎 19, 30, 32, 47, 49.
🚋 Powell–Hyde. See **Shopping** pp376–9.

THIS FORMER chocolate factory and woolen mill is the most attractive of the city's many refurbished sites, with elegant shops and restaurants. The clock tower and roof sign from the original building still remain. The Ghirardelli Chocolate Manufactory on the plaza houses old chocolate-making machinery and sells the confection, but the chocolate bars are now made in San Leandro, across the bay.

Fountain Plaza is a colorful focal point for shoppers, at any time of day and evening.

San Francisco National Maritime Museum ⑧

900 Beach St. **Map** 4 F1. ⚏ (415) 556-8177. **Hyde Street Pier** ⚏ 556-3002. 🚎 19, 30, 32. 🚋 Powell–Hyde. 🕐 mid-May–mid-Sep: 10am–6pm daily; mid-Sep–mid-May: 9:30am–5pm daily. 💶 pier. ⚐ pier and museum. 🎟 **Lectures, maritime demonstrations, activities.** ☎ ⚑ www.maritime.org

RESEMBLING a beached ocean liner, this 1939 building first housed the Maritime Museum in 1951. On display is a collection of ship models, vintage nautical instruments, paintings, and

Hyde Street Pier

photographs illustrating local nautical history. Moored at the nearby Hyde Street Pier is one of the world's largest collections of old ships.

Among the most spectacular is the *C.A. Thayer*, a three-masted schooner built in 1895. It carried lumber along the northern California coast and later was used as a fishing boat in Alaska. Also at the pier is the 2,320-ton side-wheel ferryboat, *Eureka*, built in 1890 to ferry trains between Hyde Street Pier and the counties north of San Francisco Bay. It carried 2,300 passengers and 120 cars and was the largest passenger ferry of its day.

Mainmast

BALCLUTHA
This ship is the star of Hyde Street Pier. Launched in 1886, she sailed twice a year between Britain and California, trading wheat for coal.

Mizzenmast

Foremast

Quarterdeck

Bowsprit

Alcatraz Island ❶

ALCATRAZ MEANS "pelican" in Spanish and refers to the first inhabitants of this rocky, steep-sided island. Lying 3 miles (5 km) east of the Golden Gate, its location is both strategic and exposed to ocean winds. In 1859, the US army established a fort here that guarded San Francisco Bay until 1907, when it became a military prison. From 1934 to 1963, it served as a maximum-security Federal Penitentiary. In 1969 the island was seized by members of the Native American Movement *(see p52)* claiming it as their land. They were expelled in 1971, and Alcatraz is now part of the Golden Gate National Recreation Area.

Badge on entrance to cellhouse

★ Cell Block
The cell house contains four cell blocks. No cell has an outside wall or ceiling. The dungeonlike foundation of the prison block shares the original foundation of the old military fortress.

Alcatraz Island from the Ferry
"The Rock" has no natural soil. Soil was shipped from Angel Island to make garden plots.

The officers' apartments stood here.

Military parade ground

Barracks buildings

| 0 meters | 75 |
| 0 yards | 75 |

KEY

– – – Suggested route

STAR SIGHTS

★ **Cell Block**

★ **Exercise Yard**

The Warden's House was fire damaged during the 1969–71 siege.

Alcatraz Pier
Most prisoners took their first steps ashore here; no other wharf served the steep-sided island. Now visitors alight at this pier.

★ **Exercise Yard**
Meals and a walk around the exercise yard were the highlights of a prisoner's day. The walled yard featured in films made at the prison.

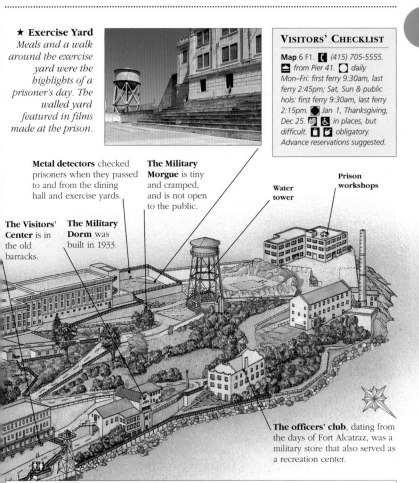

Metal detectors checked prisoners when they passed to and from the dining hall and exercise yards.

The Military Morgue is tiny and cramped, and is not open to the public.

Water tower

Prison workshops

The Visitors' Center is in the old barracks.

The Military Dorm was built in 1933.

The officers' club, dating from the days of Fort Alcatraz, was a military store that also served as a recreation center.

FAMOUS INMATES

Al Capone

The Prohibition gangster, "Scarface" Capone was actually convicted in 1934 for income tax evasion! He spent much of his five-year sentence on Alcatraz in an isolation cell, and left the prison mentally unstable.

Robert Stroud

The original *"Birdman of Alcatraz"* spent the majority of his 17 years on The Rock in solitary confinement.

Carnes, Thompson, and Shockley
In May 1946, prisoners led by Clarence Carnes, Marion Thompson, and Sam Shockley overpowered guards and captured their guns. The prisoners failed to break out of the cell house, but three inmates and two officers were killed in what became known as the "Battle of Alcatraz." Carnes received an additional life sentence, and Shockley and Thompson were executed at San Quentin prison for their part in the insurrection.

Anglin Brothers

John and Clarence Anglin, together with Frank Morris, chipped through the walls of their cells, and hid the holes with cardboard grates. Leaving dummy heads in their beds, they made a raft to enable their escape and were never caught. Their story was dramatized in the film *Escape from Alcatraz* (1979).

Cars negotiating the steep and crooked section of Lombard Street

Lombard Street ❾

Map 5 A2. 🚌 *45.* 🚋 *Powell–Hyde.*

BANKED AT a natural incline of 27°, this hill proved too steep for vehicles to climb. In the 1920s the section of Lombard Street close to the summit of Russian Hill was revamped, and the severity of its gradient was lessened by the addition of eight curves.

Today it is known as "the crookedest street in the world." Cars can travel downhill at a speed of only 5 miles per hour (8 km/h), while pedestrians use steps. There are spectacular views of San Francisco from the summit.

San Francisco Art Institute ❿

800 Chestnut St. **Map** 4 F2. ☎ *(415) 771-7021.* 🚌 *30.* **Diego Rivera Gallery** 🕐 *8am–9pm daily.* ⛔ *public hols.* ♿ *partial.* 🛍 ☕

SAN FRANCISCO'S Art Institute dates from 1871 and once occupied the immense

A 30-Minute Walk through North Beach

SETTLERS ORIGINALLY FROM CHILE, and more recently Italy, have brought their enthusiasm for nightlife to North Beach, earning this quarter its vibrant reputation. Its café-oriented atmosphere has long appealed to bohemians, particularly the 1950s Beat Generation *(see pp22–3)*.

Columbus Café ⑪

The Beat Neighborhood
Start the walk from the southwest corner of Broadway and Columbus Avenue at City Lights Bookstore ①. Owned by Beat poet Lawrence Ferlinghetti, City Lights was the first bookshop in the US to sell paperbacks exclusively. The author Jack Kerouac, a friend of Ferlinghetti, coined the word "Beat," later referred to as "Beatnik."

One of the most popular Beat bars was Vesuvio ②, south of City Lights, across Jack Kerouac Alley. Welsh poet Dylan Thomas was a patron here, and it is still a favorite with poets and artists. From here travel south to Pacific Avenue, cross to the opposite side of Columbus Avenue and walk back toward Broadway, stopping at Tosca ③. The walls of this bar and café display murals of Tuscany, and a jukebox plays selections from Italian opera. A few steps north bring you to Adler Alley. Specs ④, a lively bar filled with memorabilia of the Beat era, is at No. 12. Walking back to Columbus Avenue, turn right into Broadway and at the corner of Kearny Street cross over to Enrico's Sidewalk Café ⑤.

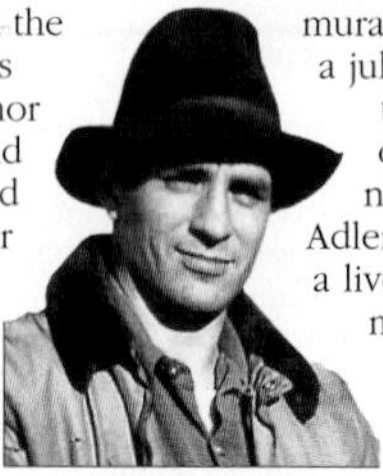
Jack Kerouac

The Strip
Enrico's celebrated outdoor café is the best place from which to watch the action on this stretch of Broadway, called The Strip ⑥, noted for its "adult entertainment." At the junction of Broadway and Grant Avenue is the former Condor Club ⑦, where the world's first topless stage show was performed in June 1964.

wooden mansion built for the family of railroad baron Mark Hopkins on Nob Hill (see p320), which burned down in the fire of 1906 (see pp48–9). Its students today are housed in a Spanish Colonial-style building that was constructed in 1926, complete with cloisters, a courtyard fountain, and bell tower. A modern extension was added at the rear of the building in 1969. The Diego Rivera Gallery, named after the famous Mexican muralist (see pp296–7), can be found to the left of the main entrance.

The Institute holds temporary exhibitions of works by its young artists.

Diego Rivera's *Making of a Mural* (1931), San Francisco Art Institute

Vallejo Street Stairway ⓫

Mason St and Jones St. **Map** 5 B3. 🚌 30, 45. 🚋 Powell–Mason.

THE STEEP CLIMB from Little Italy to the summit of Russian Hill reveals some of the best views of Telegraph Hill, North Beach, and the bay. The street gives way to steps at Mason Street, which climb up through Ina Coolbrith Park.

Above Taylor Street, there are lanes, with several Victorian houses (see pp290–91). At the crest of the hill is one of the rare parts of the city not destroyed in the earthquake of 1906 (see pp48–9).

Club Fugazi ⓬

678 Green St. **Map** 5 B3. 🄲 (415) 421-4222. 🚌 15, 30, 45. 🕐 Wed–Sun. See **Entertainment** pp372–5.

BUILT IN 1912 as a North Beach community hall, the Club Fugazi is the venue for the musical cabaret *Beach*

Blanket Babylon. This is a lively show that has been running for more than two decades and has become an institution among San Franciscans. It is popular with locals and tourists alike and is famous for its topical and outrageous songs, and for the bizarre hats often worn by the performers.

North Beach Museum ⓭

1435 Stockton St. **Map** 5 B3. 🄲 (415) 626-7070. 🚌 15, 30, 45. 🕐 9am–4pm Mon–Thu, 9am–6pm Fri, 9am–1pm Sat. ⬤ public hols.

THIS SMALL MUSEUM, on the second floor of the Eureka Bank, documents the history of North Beach and Chinatown through exhibitions of old photographs. These celebrate the heritage of the Chilean, Irish, Italian, and Chinese immigrants who have arrived in the area since the 19th century. Other photographs illustrate the bohemian community of North Beach.

Upper Grant Avenue
Turn right into Grant Avenue where you will find The Saloon ⑧ with its original 1861 bar. On the corner of Vallejo Street is Caffè Trieste ⑨, the oldest coffee house in San Francisco, and a

genuine Beat rendezvous since 1956. Very much a part of Italian-American culture, it offers live opera on Saturday afternoons. Follow Grant Avenue north past the Lost and Found Saloon ⑩, now a blues club but formerly the Coffee Gallery, another of the Beat haunts. Turn left at Green Street and look for Columbus Café ⑪, whose exterior

Vesuvio, a popular Beat bar ②

walls are decorated with attractive murals. Turning left again at Columbus Avenue, follow this main street of North Beach south past many more Italian coffee houses, to return to your starting point.

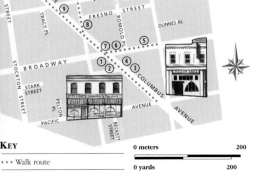

TIPS FOR WALKERS

Starting point: Corner of Broadway and Columbus Avenue.
Length: 1 mile (1.6 km).
Getting there: Muni bus No. 15 runs along Columbus Avenue.
Stopping-off points: All the bars and cafés mentioned are worth visiting for a drink and the atmosphere. Children are not usually allowed in bars.

KEY

••• Walk route

0 meters 200
0 yards 200

The façade of Saints Peter and Paul Church, Washington Square

notable for its many columns and ornate altar. There are also statues and mosaics illuminated by stained-glass windows. The concrete and steel structure of the church, with its twin spires rising over the surrounding rooftops, was completed in 1924.

Cecil B De Mille filmed the workers working on the foundations of Saints Peter and Paul, and used the scene to show the building of the Temple of Jerusalem in his film *The Ten Commandments*, made in 1923.

The church is sometimes referred to as the Fishermen's Church (many Italians once earned their living by fishing), and there is an annual mass and procession from Columbus Avenue to Fisherman's Wharf to celebrate the Blessing of the Fleet in October. Masses in the church can still be heard in Italian and Cantonese as well as English.

Telegraph Hill ⓰

Map 5 C2. **Coit Tower** Telegraph Hill Blvd. 📞 *(415) 362-0808.* 🚌 *39.* 🕙 *10am–6pm (7:30pm summer) daily.* 📷 ♿ *murals only.* 🚻

ORIGINALLY CALLED Alta Loma by the Mexicans, then Goat Hill after the animals that grazed on its slopes, Telegraph Hill was renamed in 1850 after the semaphore installed on its crest. This alerted the city's merchants to the arrival of ships through the Golden Gate. On the eastern side,

Washington Square ⓮

Map 5 B2. 🚌 *15, 30, 39, 45.*

THE SQUARE CONSISTS of a simple expanse of lawn, surrounded by benches and trees, set against the twin towers of Saints Peter and Paul Church. It has an almost Mediterranean atmosphere, appropriate for the "town square" of Little Italy. Near the center of the square stands a statue of Benjamin Franklin. A time capsule was buried under the statue in 1979 and is scheduled to be reopened in 2079. It is said to contain some Levi's jeans, a bottle of wine, and a poem written by Lawrence Ferlinghetti, one of San Francisco's famous beat poets *(see pp22–3).*

Saints Peter and Paul Church ⓯

666 Filbert St. **Map** 5 B2. 📞 *(415) 421-0809.* 🚌 *15, 30, 39, 45.* ✝ *Italian mass and choir 11:30am Sun; phone for other masses.* ♿

STILL KNOWN by many as the Italian Cathedral, this large church is situated at the heart of North Beach, and many Italians find it a welcome haven when they first arrive in San Francisco. It was here that the local baseball hero, Joe Di Maggio, was photographed after his marriage to the actress Marilyn Monroe in 1957, although the actual wedding ceremony was held elsewhere. The building, designed by Charles Fantoni, has an Italianesque façade, with a complex interior

Coit Tower mural showing Fisherman's Wharf in the 1930s

Steps at the bottom of Filbert Street leading up to Telegraph Hill

which, until 1914, was regularly dynamited to provide rocks for landfill and paving, the hill falls away abruptly to form steep paths, bordered by leafy gardens.

The western side slopes more gradually into the area known as "Little Italy," around Washington Square, although in recent years the city's Italian population has begun to settle in the Marina District. In the past the hill has been a neighborhood of immigrants living in wooden cabins, and of struggling artists, who appreciated the panoramic views. These days, however, the quaint pastel clapboard homes are much sought after, and this is one of the city's prime residential areas.

Coit Tower was built in 1933 at the top of 284-ft (86-m) high Telegraph Hill, with funds left to the city by Lillie Hitchcock Coit, an eccentric San Franciscan pioneer and philanthropist. The 210-ft (64-m) reinforced concrete tower was designed as a fluted column by the architect Arthur Brown. When floodlit at night, its glow can be seen from most of the eastern half of the city. The encircling view around the North Bay Area from the observation platform (reached by an elevator) is quite spectacular.

In the lobby of the tower are absorbing murals (see pp296–7). These were sponsored in 1934 by a government-funded program designed to keep artists in employment during the Great Depression. Twenty-five

artists worked together on the vivid portrait of life in modern California. Scenes range from the busy streets of the city's Financial District (with a robbery in progress) to factories, dockyards, and the Central Valley wheat fields. There are a number of fascinating details – a car crash, a family of immigrants encamped by a river, newspaper headlines, magazine covers, and book titles. There is a sense of frustration, satire, and whimsy in the pictures. Various political themes also feature. Many of the faces in the paintings are those of the artists and their friends, along with local figures such as Colonel William Brady, the caretaker of Coit Tower. The work's political subject matter caused some public controversy and delayed its official unveiling.

On the eastern side of Telegraph Hill the streets become steep steps. Descending from Telegraph Hill Boulevard, Filbert Street is a rambling stairway, constructed of wood, brick, and concrete, where rhododendron, fuschia, bougainvillea, fennel, and blackberries thrive.

Levi's Plaza ⑰

Map 5 C2. 🚌 42.

THIS SQUARE is where the headquarters of Levi Strauss & Co., the manufacturers of blue jeans, can be found. The square was landscaped by Lawrence Halprin in 1982, with the intention of recalling the company's long history in the state. The plaza is studded with granite rocks and cut by flowing water, thus symbolizing the Sierra Nevada canyon scenery in which the miners who first wore the jeans worked. Telegraph Hill in the background adds a more natural mountainous element.

LEVI STRAUSS AND HIS JEANS

First manufactured in San Francisco in the days of the Gold Rush (see pp44–5), denim jeans have had a great impact on popular culture, and they are just as fashionable today as they were when they first appeared. One of the leading producers of jeans is Levi Strauss & Co., founded in the city in the 1860s.

Levi Strauss

The company's story started in 1853, when Levi Strauss left New York to establish a dry goods business with his brother-in-law in San Francisco. In the 1860s, though still primarily a seller of dry goods, he pioneered the use of a durable, brown,

canvaslike material to make work trousers, sold directly to miners. In the 1870s his company began to use metal rivets to strengthen the stress points in the garments, and demand increased. The company then expanded, and early in the 20th century it moved to 250 Valencia Street in the Mission District. Levi's jeans are now an institution, and are produced, sold, and worn all over the world. The company that was first founded by Levi Strauss is still owned and managed by his descendants.

Two miners sporting their Levis at the Last Chance Mine in 1882

Pacific Heights and the Civic Center

Pacific Heights is an exclusive neighborhood, rising 300 ft (90 m) above the city. After cable cars linked it with the city center in the 1880s, it quickly became a desirable place to live, and many fine Victorian houses now line its streets. To the north of Broadway, the streets drop steeply down to the Marina District, with its smart shops, fashionable cafés, and two prestigious yacht clubs. To the south of Pacific Heights is the Civic Center, which was built after the earthquake of 1906. It includes some of the best Beaux-Arts architecture in the city, and in 1987 the area was declared a historic site. The Civic Center is perhaps the most elegant city complex in the US.

Fort Mason logo

Sights at a Glance

Historic Streets and Buildings

Alamo Square 18
Asian Art Museum 14
Bill Graham Civic Auditorium 15
City Hall 16
Cow Hollow 9
Fort Mason 7
Haas-Lilienthal House 1
Octagon House 10
Palace of Fine Arts and the Exploratorium 5
Spreckels Mansion 2
University of San Francisco 19

Shopping Areas

Chestnut Street 8
Fillmore Street 11
Hayes Valley 17

Modern Architecture

Japan Center 12

Churches

St. Mary's Cathedral 13

Parks and Gardens

Alta Plaza 4
Lafayette Park 3
Marina Green 6

Getting There

Muni buses 1 and 12, and the California Street cable car serve the Pacific Heights area. The Civic Center BART/Muni station on Market Street is two blocks east of City Hall. Buses 5, 8, and 19 all travel into the Civic Center.

Key

Street-by-Street map *See pp336–7*
Cable car terminus
BART station
Parking
Streetcar terminus

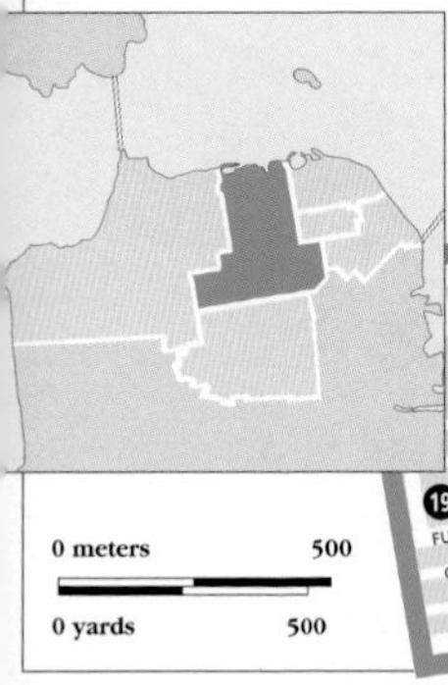

◁ View from Alamo Square across the Civic Center toward the Financial District

Street-by-Street: Pacific Heights

T HE STEEP blocks between Alta Plaza and Lafayette Park are set in the heart of the exclusive Pacific Heights district. The streets here are quiet and tidy, lined with stylish apartment blocks and palatial Victorian houses. Some of these date from the late 19th century, while others were built after the great earthquake and fire of 1906 *(see pp48–9)*. To the north of this area, the streets drop steeply down toward the residential Marina District and offer outstanding views of San Francisco Bay. Wander through the two large landscaped parks and past the luxurious gardens of the private mansions in between, then visit one of the many fashionable bars, cafés, and restaurants along Fillmore Street *(see pp565–6)*.

The Webster Street Row houses have been declared a historic landmark. They were built for a middle-class clientele in 1878 and have since been restored to their original splendor.

Washington Street lies to the east of Alta Plaza. Here the Victorian houses, built in various architectural styles, fill an entire block.

★ Alta Plaza
Set aside as a public park in the 1850s, this hilltop green space has a playground, tennis courts, and spectacular views of San Francisco ❹

To bus no. 12

WEBSTER STREET

FILLMORE STREET

STEINER STREET

0 meters   100

0 yards   100

KEY

– – – Suggested route

STAR SIGHTS

★ Alta Plaza

★ Spreckels Mansion

Haas-Lilienthal House
Furnished in Victorian style, this mansion is the headquarters of the Architectural Heritage Foundation ❶

LOCATOR MAP
See Street Finder maps 3, 4

To bus nos. 47, 76

No. 2151 Sacramento Street is an ornate French-style mansion. A plaque commemorates a visit by the author Sir Arthur Conan Doyle in 1923.

JACKSON STREET

LAGUNA STREET

WASHINGTON STREET

CLAY STREET

GOUGH STREET

SACRAMENTO STREET

Mansions Hotel
(see p527)

Lafayette Park
This quiet park offers good views of the Victorian houses that surround it ❸

★ Spreckels Mansion
This impressive limestone building, constructed on the lines of a French Baroque palace, has been home to best-selling novelist Danielle Steele since 1990 ❷

No. 2004 Gough Street, one of the more elaborate Victorian houses in Pacific Heights, was built in 1889.

The Haas-Lilienthal House, a Queen Anne mansion from 1886

Haas-Lilienthal House ❶

2007 Franklin St. **Map** 4 E3.
📞 *(415) 441-3004.* 🚌 *1, 19, 27, 47, 49, 83.* ⏰ *noon–3pm Wed, 11am–4pm Sun.* ♿ 📷 🚪

T HIS ATTRACTIVE Queen Anne-style mansion *(see pp290–91)* was built in 1886 for the rich merchant William Haas. Alice Lilienthal, his daughter, lived here until 1972, when it was given to the Foundation for San Francisco's Architectural Heritage. It is the only intact private home of the period in San Francisco, now open as a museum, and it is complete with authentic furniture. A fine example of an upper-middle-class Victorian home, Haas-Lilienthal House has elaborate wooden gables, a circular corner tower, and luxurious ornamentation.

A display of photographs in the basement describes the history of the building and reveals that this grandiose house was modest in comparison with some of the mansions destroyed in the great fire of 1906 *(see pp48–9)*.

Spreckels Mansion ❷

2080 Washington St. **Map** 4 E3.
🚌 *1, 47, 49.* 🚫 *to the public.*

D OMINATING the north side of Lafayette Park, this imposing Beaux-Arts mansion is sometimes known as the "Parthenon of the West." It was built in 1912 for the flamboyant Alma de Bretteville Spreckels and her husband, Adolph, heir to the sugar fortune of Claus Spreckels *(see p348)*. The house contains 26 bathrooms, and a large swimming pool in which Alma Spreckels swam daily until the age of 80. Her love of French architecture inspired the design. The architect of Spreckels mansion was George Applegarth, who in 1916 also designed the California Palace of the Legion of Honor in Lincoln Park *(see pp364–5)*. The Palace was donated to the city by the Spreckelses in 1924.

Today Spreckels Mansion is privately owned. It occupies a block of Octavia Street, which is paved and landscaped in a similar style to curvy Lombard Street *(see p330)*.

Façade of the impressive Spreckels Mansion

Lafayette Park ❸

Map 4 E3. 🚌 *1, 12.*

O NE OF San Francisco's prettiest hilltop gardens, Lafayette Park is a leafy green haven of pine and eucalyptus trees, although its present tranquillity belies its turbulent history. Along with Alta Plaza and Alamo Square *(see p343)* the land was set aside in 1855 as a city-owned open space. Then squatters and others, including a former City Attorney, laid claim to the land and began to build their houses on it. The largest of these houses remained standing at the center of the hilltop park until 1936, the squatter who had built it refusing to move. It was finally demolished after the city authorities agreed to swap it for other land on nearby Gough Street. Steep stairways now lead to the summit of the park and its delightful views.

In the streets surrounding Lafayette Park there are a number of other palatial Victorian buildings. Particularly ornate examples are situated along Broadway, Jackson Street, and Pacific Avenue going east-west, and Gough, Octavia, and Laguna streets going north-south.

Alta Plaza ❹

Map 4 D3. 🚌 *1, 3, 12, 22, 24.*

S ITUATED IN the center of Pacific Heights, Alta Plaza is a landscaped urban park, where the San Franciscan elite come to relax. The stone steps rising up from Clay Street on the south side of the park offer good views of Haight Ashbury *(see pp344–53)*, the Fillmore district, and Twin Peaks *(see p353)*. The steps may be familiar to film buffs – Barbra Streisand drove down them in *What's Up Doc?* There are also tennis courts and a playground.

From the north side of the park some splendid Victorian mansions are visible, including Gibbs House, at No. 2622 Jackson Street, built by Willis Polk in 1894. Smith House, at No. 2600 Jackson Street, was

Relaxing in the peaceful Alta Plaza park

one of the first houses in San Francisco to be supplied with electricity in the 1890s.

Palace of Fine Arts and the Exploratorium ❺

3601 Lyon St. **Map** 3 C2. **🅒** (415) 561 0360. 🚌 22, 28, 29, 30, 43, 45, 47, 49. ⭕ Oct–Apr: 10am–5pm Tue–Sun, 10am–9pm Wed; May–Aug: 10am–6pm Thu–Tue, 10am–9pm Wed. 🎟️ 🚻 **Tactile Dome** 🅒 (415) 561-0362 (reservations). 🆆 www.exploratorium.com

Sole survivor of the many grandiose monuments built as part of the 1915 Panama-Pacific Exposition, the Palace of Fine Arts is a Neo-Classical folly. It was designed by the architect Bernard R Maybeck, who was inspired by the drawings of the Italian architect Piranesi and by the painting *L'Isle des Morts* by Swiss artist, Arnold Böcklin. Originally built of wood and plaster, the Palace eventually began to crumble, until one concerned citizen raised funds for its reconstruction in 1959. It was restored to its original splendor between 1962 and 1975 using reinforced concrete.

The central feature is the rotunda, perched on the edge of a landscaped, swan-filled lagoon. Its dome is decorated with allegorical paintings, all depicting the defense of art against materialism. On top of the many Corinthian columns, nymphs with bent heads are symbolic of the "melancholy of life without art."

The Palace's auditorium can hold up to 1,000 spectators, and its most important annual event is the May Film Festival, which highlights the work of new directors, particularly those from the Third World.

An elongated industrial shed inside the Palace houses the Exploratorium Museum, one of the most entertaining science museums in the United States. Established in 1969 by the physicist Frank Oppenheimer (whose brother Robert helped to develop the atom bomb), it is filled with more than 650 interactive exhibits, exploring the world of science and the senses. The exhibits, on two floors, are divided into 13 subject areas, each one color-coded by an overhead sign. These include a room for Electricity, where balls of lightning are produced in a tube; Vision, Color, and Light, where optical illusions are explained; and Motion, featuring the thrilling Momentum Machine. The Tactile Dome offers a sensory journey taken in total darkness.

The gardens form a relaxing and attractive backdrop to this imitation Roman ruin, which is a firm favorite with San Francisco residents.

The world of science explained in the Exploratorium Museum

Classical rotunda of the Palace of Fine Arts

PANAMA-PACIFIC EXPOSITION

In 1915 San Francisco celebrated its successful recovery from the 1906 earthquake and fire with a monumental fair. Officially, it was intended to celebrate the opening of the Panama Canal, and was designed to be the most splendid world's fair ever held. Its grand structures were indeed described by one highly enthusiastic visitor as "a miniature Constantinople."

The halls and pavilions of the fair were constructed on land reclaimed from San Francisco Bay, on the site of today's Marina District. They were donated by all the states and by 25 foreign countries, and lined a concourse 1 mile (1.6 km) long. Many of the buildings were based on such architectural gems as a Turkish mosque and a Buddhist temple from Kyoto. The brilliant Tower of Jewels, at the center of the concourse, was encrusted with glass beads and lit by spotlights. To the west stood the beautiful Palace of Fine Arts, which visitors reached by gondola across a landscaped lagoon.

Marina Green ❻

Map 4 D1. 🚌 *22, 28, 30.*

A LONG THIN STRIP of lawn running the length of the Marina District, Marina Green is popular with kite-flyers and picnickers, especially on the Fourth of July, when the city's largest fireworks display can be seen from here. Paths along the waterfront are the city's prime spots for cyclists, joggers, and skaters. Golden Gate Promenade leads from the west end of the green to Fort Point, or you can turn east to the Wave Organ at the end of the harbor jetty.

Chestnut Street ❽

Map 4 D1. 🚌 *22, 28, 30, 43.*

T HE MAIN SHOPPING and night-life center of the Marina District, Chestnut Street has a varied mix of movie theaters, markets, and restaurants, catering more to the local residents than to visitors. The

strip stretches just a few blocks from Fillmore Street west to Divisadero Street, after which the neighborhood becomes residential in character.

Cow Hollow ❾

Map 4 D2. 🚌 *22, 41, 45.*

C OW HOLLOW is a shopping district along Union Street. It is so called because it was used as grazing land for the city's dairy cows up until the 1860s. It was then taken over for development and turned into a residential neighborhood. In the 1950s the area became fashionable, and chic boutiques, antique shops, and art galleries took over the old neighborhood stores. Many of these are in restored 19th-century buildings, lending an old-fashioned air to the district, in stark contrast to the sophistication of the merchandise on display.

Union Street itself has more than 300 boutiques, and open-air arts, crafts, and food fairs are held regularly in the area.

View from Fillmore Street, overlooking Cow Hollow

Fort Mason ❼

Map 4 E1. 🛈 *(415) 979-3010.* **Events** *441-3400.* 🚌 *22, 28, 30, 42, 43.* ♿ *partial.* 🅦 *www.fortmason.org*

F ORT MASON reflects the military history of San Francisco. The original buildings were private houses, built in the late 1850s, which were confiscated by the US Government when the site was taken over by the US army during the American Civil War (1861–65).

The Fort was an army command post until the 1890s. It later housed refugees whose homes had been destroyed in the 1906 earthquake *(see pp48–9).* During World War II, it was the embarkation point for around 1.6 million soldiers.

The Fort was converted to peaceful use in 1972 although some of the white-painted mid-19th-century buildings still house military personnel. Other buildings, however, are open to the public. These include the original barracks, and the old hospital, which

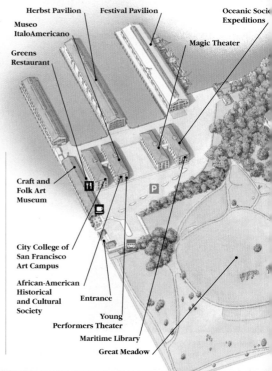

Herbst Pavilion

Festival Pavilion

Oceanic Socie Expeditions

Museo ItaloAmericano

Magic Theater

Greens Restaurant

Craft and Folk Art Museum

City College of San Francisco Art Campus

African-American Historical and Cultural Society

Entrance

Young Performers Theater

Maritime Library

Great Meadow

Octagon House ⑩

2645 Gough St. **Map** 4 E2. 📞 *(415) 441-7512.* 🚌 *41, 42, 45, 47, 49.* ◯ *noon–3pm on second Sun and second and fourth Thu of the month, except Jan.* **Donation.** 📷 ♿ *limited.*

Built in 1861, the Octagon House, with its eight-sided cupola, is a well-preserved example of a house style that was once popular throughout the United States. The ground floor has now been opened up into one large room, and this and the first floor house a small but engaging collection of decorative arts as well as historic documents of the Colonial and Federal periods of the United States. Among the exhibits are furniture, paintings, porcelain, silver, pewter, samplers, playing cards from the American Revolution era, and signatures of 54 of the 56 signatories to the Declaration of Independence. The house now serves as the headquarters of the National Society of Colonial Dames of America.

Octagon House's cupola ensures sunlight in each room

Fillmore Street ⑪

Map 4 D4. 🚌 *1, 2, 3, 4, 22, 24.*

Fillmore street managed to survive the 1906 earthquake and fire virtually intact, so for several years afterward it was forced to serve as the civic heart of the ruined city. Government departments, as well as several independent businesses, were housed in local shops, homes, and even churches. Today the main commercial district linking Pacific Heights and the Civic Center is located here, from Jackson Street to the outskirts of the Japan Center (*see p342*) around Bush Street. This area is filled with fine bookstores, fashionable restaurants, and exclusive boutiques.

---

serves both as a Visitors' Center and as the headquarters of the Golden Gate National Recreation Area (GGNRA). Besides being rich in history and culture, Fort Mason also offers some of the city's finest views, looking across the bay toward Golden Gate Bridge (*see pp370–71*) and Alcatraz Island (*see pp328–29*).

Starting from the west gate of the Fort, Golden Gate Promenade winds eastward to Aquatic Park and then to Fisherman's Wharf (*see pp324–5*).

Fort Mason Center
Part of the Fort is now occupied by one of San Francisco's major art complexes. The Fort Mason Center houses about 50 cultural organizations, which include art galleries, museums, and theaters, such as the Cowell Dance Theater and the Bayfront Improv. Italian and Italian-

American artists display their works at the Museo Italo-Americano. The Magic Theater is an experimental theater, and the Young Performers Theater is a playhouse for children. The Maritime Library holds a wonderful collection of books, oral histories, and ships' plans. The Maritime Museum itself is located near Fishermans Wharf (*see p327*).

The Fort Mason Center produces a monthly calendar of current events. Call the Events Line or visit their website for more information.

International Youth Hostel

Fort Mason Officers' Club

Chapel

Visitors' Center

Golden Gate National Recreation Area headquarters

Meta III (1985) by Italo Scanga at Museo ItaloAmericano Chapel

The SS *Balclutha*, at Hyde Street Pier, part of the Maritime Museum

The pagoda in the Japan Center's Peace Plaza

Japan Center ⑫

Post St & Buchanan St. **Map** 4 E4.
📞 (415) 922-6776. 🚌 2, 3, 4, 22, 38. ⏰ 10am–5:30pm daily.

THE JAPAN CENTER was built as part of an ambitious 1960s scheme to revitalize the Fillmore District. Many blocks of aging Victorian houses were demolished and replaced by the Geary Expressway and the large shopping complex of the Japan Center. The neighborhood has been the heart of the Japanese community for some 75 years.

At the heart of the complex, and centered upon a five-tiered, 75-ft (22-m) concrete pagoda, is the newly remodeled Peace Plaza. Taiko drummers and others perform here at the annual Cherry Blossom festival each April. Each side of the pagoda are malls lined with Japanese shops, sushi bars, bathhouses, and *Shiatsu* massage centers, all modeled on Tokyo's Ginza district. One of the city's best movie theaters, the eight-screen AMC Kabuki *(see pp374–75)*, is also found here. More Japanese shops line the open-air mall across Post Street, flanked by twin steel sculptures by Ruth Asawa.

St. Mary's Cathedral ⑬

1111 Gough St. **Map** 4 E4. 📞 (415) 567-2020. 🚌 2, 3, 4, 38. ⏰ 8:30am–4:30pm Mon–Fri, 9am–3pm Sat–Sun. ✝ 6:45am, 8am, 10pm Mon–Sat, 7:30am, 9am, 11am, 1pm Sun. 📷 during services. ♿

SITUATED AT THE summit of Cathedral Hill, St. Mary's is one of San Francisco's most prominent architectural landmarks. Designed by Pietro Belluschi and Pier Luigi Nervi, it was completed in 1971.

The four-part arching paraboloid roof stands out like a white-sailed ship on the horizon. The 200-ft (60-m) high concrete structure, which seems to hover effortlessly above the nave, supports the cross-shaped stained-glass ceiling representing the four elements. A canopy of aluminium rods sparkles above the stone altar, from which the priest faces the congregation.

Asian Art Museum ⑭

Larkin at Grove St. **Map** 4 F5. 📞 (415) 379-8800. 🚌 5, 8, 19, 21, 26, 47, 49. 🚇 J, K, L, M, N. ⏰ 9am –5pm Wed–Sun. 📷 ♿ 🎫 🍴 🖥

THE NEW Asian Art Museum is located on Civic Center Plaza in a building that was the crown jewel of the Beaux Arts movement. The former Main Library, built in 1917, has undergone seismic strengthening and adaptive reuse of the original space to create the largest museum outside Asia devoted exclusively to Asian art. The new museum's exhibits include 12,000 art objects spanning 6,000 years of history and representing more

than 40 Asian nations. In addition to increased gallery space, there are performance venues and a hands-on discovery center. The terrace cafe overlooks the Civic Center and Fulton Street mall.

Bill Graham Civic Auditorium ⑮

99 Grove St. **Map** 4 F5. 📞 (415) 974-4060. 🚌 5, 8, 19, 21, 26, 47, 49. 🚇 J, K, L, M, N.

DESIGNED IN Beaux-Arts style by architect John Galen Howard, the city's Civic Auditorium was opened in 1915 and has since become one of San Francisco's major performance venues. It was inaugurated by the French pianist and composer Camille Saint-Saëns. The building was completed along with City Hall, during the architectural renaissance that followed the great earthquake of 1906 *(see pp48–9)*. It was built, together with the adjoining Brooks Exhibit Hall, beneath the Civic Center Plaza.

The civic auditorium now serves as the city's main conference center, and seats 7,000 people. In 1964 its name was changed in honor of Bill Graham *(see p349)*, the local rock music impresario.

Grand staircase in the Asian Art Museum

The imposing façade of City Hall in San Francisco's Civic Center

City Hall ⑯

400 Van Ness Ave. **Map** 4 F5.
📞 (415) 554-4000. 🚌 5, 8, 19, 21,
26, 47, 49. 🚇 J, K, L, M, N.
🕐 8am–5pm Mon–Fri. ♿
🎥 phone (415) 557-4266.

CITY HALL, completed in
1915, just in time for the
Panama-Pacific Exposition
(see p339), was designed by
the architect Arthur Brown at
the height of his career. Its
grand Baroque dome was
modeled after St. Peter's in
Rome and is higher than that
of the US Capitol in
Washington, DC.

The newly renovated building stands at the heart of the
Civic Center complex, and is a
magnificent example of the
Beaux-Arts style. Allegorical
figures evoking the city's
Gold Rush past fill the pediment above the Polk Street
entrance, which leads into the
rotunda, one of the city's
finest interior spaces.

Hayes Valley ⑰

Map 4 E5. 🚌 21, 22.

SITUATED WEST of City Hall,
these few blocks of Hayes
Street have become one of
San Francisco's trendier shopping districts. After US 101
highway was damaged in the
1989 Loma Prieta earthquake
(see p489) the road was
demolished. The former

highway had previously divided Hayes Valley from the
wealthy power-brokers and
theatergoers who frequented
the rest of the Civic Center. A
small number of adventurous
cafés and restaurants, such as
Ivy's and Mad Magda's Russian
Tea Room, had already established themselves alongside
Hayes Street's second-hand
furniture and reject shops.
Today a new influx of art galleries, interior design shops,
trendy cafés, and exclusive
boutiques has made the area
noticeably more stylish.

**View from Alamo Square toward
the Downtown skyscrapers**

Alamo Square ⑱

Map 4 D5. 🚌 21, 22.

THE MOST photographed row
of Victorian houses in the
city lines the eastern side of
this sloping green square. It is

set 225 ft (68 m) above the
Civic Center, offering great
views of City Hall and the
Downtown skyscrapers. The
square was laid out at the
same time as the beautiful
squares in Pacific Heights, but
it developed later, with speculators building nearly
identical houses.

The "Six Sisters" Queen
Anne-style houses built in
1895 at 710–20 Steiner Street
on the east side of the square
appear on numerous post-
cards of San Francisco. The
city has now declared the
area to be a historic district. '

University of San
Francisco ⑲

2130 Fulton St. **Map** 3 B5. 📞 (415)
422-5555. 🚌 5, 31, 33, 38, 43.
🕐 8am–5pm Mon–Fri.

ORIGINALLY FOUNDED in 1855
as St. Ignatius College,
the University of San Francisco
(USF) remains a Jesuit-run
institution, though classes are
now coeducational and non-
denominational. The land-
mark of the campus is the St.
Ignatius Church, completed in
1914. Its buff-colored twin
towers are visible from the
western half of San Francisco,
especially when lit up at night.
The campus and the surrounding residential area occupy
land that was once San Francisco's main cemetery district,
on and around Lone Mountain.

Haight Ashbury and the Mission

To the north of Twin Peaks – two windswept hills rising 900 ft (274 m) above the city – lies Haight Ashbury. With its rows of Victorian houses *(see pp290–91)*, it is mostly inhabited by the wealthy middle classes, although this is where thousands of hippies lived in the late 1960s *(see p349)*. The Castro District, to the east, is the center of the city's gay community. Well known for its hedonism in the 1970s, the area has become far quieter in recent years, although its cafés and shops are still lively. The Mission District, even farther east, was first founded by Spanish monks *(see pp42–3)* and is home to many Latin Americans.

Figure from Mission Dolores

Sights at a Glance

Historic Streets and Buildings
Castro Street 8
Clarke's Folly 15
Dolores Street 10
Haight Ashbury 2
Lower Haight Neighborhood 5
Noe Valley 14
(Richard) Spreckels Mansion 3

Churches
Mission Dolores 9

Landmarks
Sutro Tower 18

Parks and Gardens
Buena Vista Park 4
Corona Heights Park 6
Dolores Park 11
Golden Gate Park Panhandle 1
Twin Peaks 16
Vulcan Street Steps 17

Museums and Galleries
Carnaval Mural 13
Mission Cultural Center for the Latino Arts 12

Theaters
Castro Theater 7

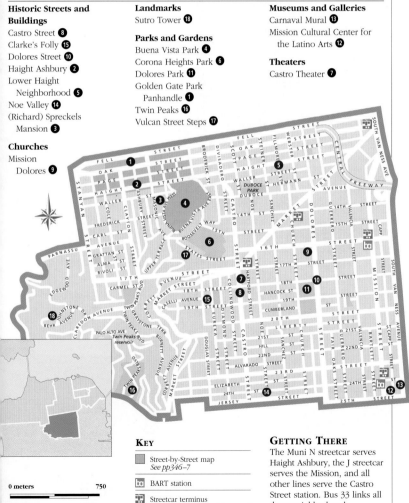

Key

Street-by-Street map
See pp346–7

BART station

Streetcar terminus

0 meters 750
0 yards 750

Getting There

The Muni N streetcar serves Haight Ashbury, the J streetcar serves the Mission, and all other lines serve the Castro Street station. Bus 33 links all three neighborhoods.

◁ **Street scene in Haight Ashbury**

Street-by-Street: Haight Ashbury

STRETCHING FROM Buena Vista Park to
the flat expanses of Golden Gate Park,
Haight Ashbury was a place to escape to
from the city center in the 1880s. It then
developed into a residential area, but
between 1930 and 1960 it changed
dramatically from a middle-class suburb
to the center of the "Flower Power" world,
with a free clinic to treat hippies without
medical insurance. It has now settled
into being one of the liveliest and most
unconventional places in San Francisco,
with an eclectic mix of people, excellent
book and music shops, and good cafés.

Haight Ashbury
In the 1960s, hippies met at this crossroads
which gives the area its name 🐾

Golden Gate Panhandle
This thin green strip runs west
into the heart of Golden
Gate Park ❶

Cha Cha Cha is one of the
liveliest places to eat in
San Francisco, serving
Latin American food in a
series of small dishes
(see p564).

HAIGHT STREET

To bus nos. 7, 33

STAR SIGHTS

★ **Buena Vista Park**

★ **(Richard) Spreckels**
Mansion

The Red Victorian
Hotel is a relic of the
1960s hippie era. It
now caters to a New
Age clientele, with
health food and rooms
with transcendental
themes *(see p527)*.

No. 1220 Masonic Avenue is one of many ornate Victorian mansions built on the steep hill that runs down from Golden Gate Park Panhandle to Haight Street.

LOCATOR MAP

PACIFIC HEIGHTS AND THE CIVIC CENTER

HAIGHT ASHBURY AND THE MISSION

LOCATOR MAP
See Street Finder, map 10

KEY

– – – – Suggested route

★ **(Richard) Spreckels Mansion**
This grand home at No.737 Buena Vista Avenue was built in 1897 ❸

OAK STREET

CENTRAL STREET

LYON STREET

BUENA VISTA WEST

★ **Buena Vista Park**
Through its mass of twisting, matted trees, this dramatic park offers magnificent views over the city ❹

0 meters   100

0 yards   100

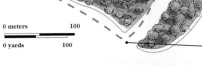

To bus no. 37

Golden Gate Park Panhandle ❶

Map 9 C1. 🚌 *6, 7, 21, 43, 66, 71.*

THIS ONE-BLOCK-WIDE and eight-block-long stretch of parkland forms the narrow "Panhandle" to the giant rectangular pan that is Golden Gate Park *(see pp356–9)*. It was the first part of the park to be reclaimed from the sand dunes that rolled across west San Francisco, and its eucalyptus trees are among the oldest and largest in the city.

The Panhandle's winding carriage roads and bridle paths were first laid out in the 1870s, and the upper classes came here to walk and ride. They built large mansions on the outskirts of the park, many of which can still be seen today. In 1906 the Panhandle was used as a refuge for families made homeless by the earthquake *(see pp48–9)*. Today the old roads and paths are frequented regularly by large crowds of joggers and cyclists.

The Panhandle is still remembered for its "Flower Power" heyday of the 1960s. The era's young hippies flocked to the park to listen to impromptu free concerts held here by the new psychedelic bands from Haight Ashbury. The area is still a popular spot for the city's street musicians and hippie guitarists.

Haight Ashbury ❷

Map 9 C1. 🚌 *6, 7, 33, 37, 43, 66, 71.* 🚋 *N.*

TAKING ITS NAME from the junction of two major streets, Haight and Ashbury, this district contains alternative bookshops, large Victorian houses, and numerous cafés. Following the reclamation of Golden Gate Park *(see pp356–9)* and then the opening of a large amusement park called The Chutes, the area was rapidly built up in the 1890s as a middle-class suburb – hence the dozens of elaborate Queen Anne-style houses *(see pp290–91)* lining its streets. The Haight district survived the 1906 earthquake and fire *(see pp48–9)*, and then experienced a brief boom, which was followed by a long period of decline.

After the tram tunnel underneath Buena Vista Park was completed in 1928, the middle classes began their exodus to the suburbs in the Sunset. The area reached its lowest ebb in the years after World War II. The big Victorian houses were divided into apartments and low rents attracted a disparate population. By the 1960s the Haight had become host to a bohemian community that was a hotbed of anarchy. A component of this "hippie scene" was the music of rock bands such as the Grateful Dead, but the area stayed fairly quiet until 1967. Then the "Summer of Love," fueled by the media, brought some 75,000 young people in search of free love, music, and drugs, and the area became the focus of a worldwide youth culture.

Haight retains its radical atmosphere, but now there are problems with crime, drugs, and homelessness. However, from the cafés to the second-hand clothing shops, there is still an "only in San Francisco" experience to be found here.

Junction of Haight and Ashbury streets

Late-Victorian mansion built for Richard Spreckels

(Richard) Spreckels Mansion ❸

737 Buena Vista West. **Map** 9 C2. 🚌 *6, 7, 37, 43, 66, 71.* ⬤ *to the public.*

THIS HOUSE SHOULD not be confused with the grander Spreckels Mansion situated on Washington Street *(see p338)*. It was, however, also built by the millionaire "Sugar King" Claus Spreckels, for his nephew Richard. The elaborate Queen Anne-style house *(see pp290–91)*, built in 1897 is a typical late-Victorian Haight Ashbury home. It was once a guesthouse, whose guests included the acerbic journalist and ghost-story writer Ambrose Bierce, and the adventure writer Jack London, who wrote *White Fang* here in 1906 *(see p22)*. The house is now in private hands.

Buena Vista Park ❹

Map 9 C1. 🚌 *6, 7, 37, 43, 66, 71.*

BUENA VISTA PARK rises steeply 570 ft (174 m) above the geographical center of San Francisco with views over the Bay Area. First landscaped in 1894, it is a pocket of land left to nature. Numerous overgrown and eroded paths wind up from Haight Street to the crest, but there is a paved route from Buena Vista Avenue. It is best to avoid the park at night.

Lower Haight Neighborhood ❺

Map 10 D1. 🚌 6, 7, 22, 66, 71.
🚋 K, L, M.

HALFWAY BETWEEN City Hall and Haight Ashbury, and marking the southern border of the predominantly African-American Fillmore District, the Lower Haight is an area in transition. Unusual art galleries and boutiques, including the Used Rubber USA shop, which sells clothes and accessories made entirely of recycled rubber, began to open here in the mid-1980s. These were in addition to the inexpensive cafés, bars, and restaurants serving a bohemian clientele already in business in the area. This combination has created one of the most lively districts in San Francisco.

As in nearby Alamo Square *(see p343)*, the Lower Haight has dozens of houses known as "Victorians" *(see pp290–91)* built from the 1850s to the early 1900s, including picturesque cottages such as the Nightingale House at No. 201 Buchanan Street, built in the 1880s. The 1950s public housing blocks have discouraged wholesale gentrification. The area is safe during the day but, like Alamo Square, it can seem threatening after dark.

Sign from Cha Cha Cha restaurant on Haight Street *(see p564)*

Corona Heights Park ❻

Map 9 D2. 📞 *(415) 554-9600.* 🚌 24, 37. **Randall Museum Animal Room** ⬜ *10am–1pm, 2–5pm Tue–Sat.* ♿ *limited.*

CORONA HEIGHTS PARK is a dusty and undeveloped rocky peak. Clinging to its side is an unusual museum for children. The Randall

View from Corona Heights across the Mission

Museum at No. 199 Museum Way has an extensive menagerie of raccoons, owls, snakes, and other animals, many of which the children can handle and stroke. The emphasis of the museum is on participation, with many hands-on exhibits and workshops. Children also enjoy climbing

on the craggy outcrops in the park. Corona Heights was gouged out by brick-making operations in the 19th century. It was never planted with trees, so its red rock peak has an unimpeded panorama over the city. There is a good view of the winding streets of Twin Peaks *(see p353)*.

THE SOUNDS OF 1960S SAN FRANCISCO

During the late 1960s, and most notably during the 1967 "Summer of Love," young people from all over the country flocked to the Haight Ashbury district. They came not just to "turn on, tune in, and drop out," but also to listen to bands such as Janis Joplin's Big Brother and the Holding Company, Jefferson Airplane, and the Grateful Dead, all of whom emerged out of a thriving music scene. They established themselves at the city's new music venues.

Premier music venues
The Avalon Ballroom, now the Regency II theater on Van Ness Avenue, was the first and most significant venue. Run by Chet Helms and the Family Dog collective, the Avalon pioneered the use of colorful psychedelic posters by designers such as Stanley Mouse and Alton Kelly *(see pp424–5)*.
Fillmore Auditorium, facing the Japan Center *(see p342)* and a former church hall, was taken over by impresario

Bill Graham in 1965, after whom the Civic Auditorium *(see p342)* is named. He put unlikely pairs such as Miles Davis and the Grateful Dead on the same bill, and brought in big-name performers from Jimi Hendrix to The Who. The Fillmore Auditorium was damaged in the 1989 earthquake but has recently reopened.

By the time Bill Graham died in 1992 he had become the most successful rock music promoter in the US.

Janis Joplin (1943–70), hard-edged blues singer

Castro Theater ●

429 Castro St. **Map** 10 D2. *621-6120.* 8, 24, 33, 35, 37. F, K, L, M. See **Entertainment** pp374–5.

COMPLETED IN 1922, this brightly lit neon marquee is a Castro Street landmark. It is the most sumptuous and best preserved of San Francisco's neighborhood film palaces, and one of the first commissions of the architect Timothy Pflueger. With its Arabian Nights interior, complete with a glorious Wurlitzer organ that rises from the floor between the screenings, it is well worth the price of admission. The ceiling of the auditorium is cast in plaster and resembles the interior of a large tent, with imitation swathes of fabric, rope, and tassels. The theater seats 1,500 and shows mainly revival classics. It also hosts the Gay and Lesbian Film Festival, held each June.

Historic and ornate Castro Theater

Castro Street ●

Map 10 D2. 8, 24, 33, 35, 37. F, K, L, M.

THE HILLY neighborhood around Castro Street between Twin Peaks and the Mission District is the heart of San Francisco's high-profile gay and lesbian community. Focused on the intersection of Castro Street and 18th Street, the self-proclaimed "Gayest Four Corners of the

World" emerged as a homosexual nexus during the 1970s. Gays of the Flower Power generation moved into this predominantly working-class district and began restoring Victorian houses and setting up businesses such as the bookshop, A Different Light, at No. 489 Castro Street. They also opened gay bars such as the Twin Peaks on the corner of Castro Street and 17th Street. Unlike earlier bars, where lesbians and gays hid in dark corners out of public view, the Twin Peaks installed large windows. Though the many shops and restaurants attract all kinds of people, the area's openly homosexual identity has made it a place of pilgrimage for gays and lesbians. It symbolizes for this minority group a freedom not often found in cities elsewhere.

The city's first openly gay politician, Harvey Milk, was known as the Mayor of Castro Street before his assassination on November 28, 1978. He and Mayor George Moscone were killed by an ex-policeman, whose lenient sentence caused rioting in the city. Milk is remembered with a plaque outside the Muni stop on Market Street and a candlelit procession from Castro Street to City Hall every year.

Over a quarter of a million people come to the area for the Castro Street Fair, which is held each October. Arts, crafts, beer, food, and music are all provided, and proceeds go towards helping the local community.

AIDS Memorial Quilt on display in Washington, DC in 1992

THE NAMES PROJECT

The NAMES Project's AIDS Memorial Quilt was conceived by San Francisco gay rights activist Cleve Jones, who organized the first candlelit procession on Castro Street for Harvey Milk in 1985. Jones and his fellow marchers wrote the names of all their friends who had died of AIDS on placards, which they then taped to the San Francisco Federal Building. The resulting "patchwork quilt" of names inspired Jones to create the first panel for the AIDS Memorial Quilt in 1987. Public response to the quilt was immediate – both in the US and across the world. It is now made up of over 60,000 panels, some sewn by individuals and others by "quilting bees" – friends and relatives who have come together to commemorate a person lost to AIDS. All panels are the same size – 3 by 6 ft (90 by 180 cm) – but each is different: the design, colors, and material reflect the life and personality of the person commemorated. In 2002 the Memorial Quilt moved from its base in San Francisco to permanent headquarters in Atlanta, Georgia.

Mission Dolores ❾

16th St and Dolores St. **Map** 10 F3.
📳 621-8203. 🚌 22. 🚇 J. ⬤
9am–4pm (May 1–Oct
31: 4:30 pm) daily.
⬤ Thanksgiving, Dec
25. 🎞 📷 ♿ 🚻

PRESERVED INTACT
since it was built
in 1791, Mission
Dolores is the oldest
building in the city and
an embodiment of San
Francisco's religious
Spanish colonial roots
(see pp42–3). The mission
was founded by Father
Junípero Serra and is
formally known as the
Mission of San Francisco
de Asis. The name Dolores

Figure of saint in the mission

reflects its proximity to
Laguna de los Dolores (Lake
of Our Lady of Sorrows), an
ancient insect-plagued swamp.
The building is modest
by mission standards,
but its 4-ft (1.2-m) thick
walls have survived the
years without any
serious decay. Paint-
ings by Native
Americans adorn
the ceiling, which
has been restored.
There is a fine
Baroque altar and
reredos, and a
display of histor-
ical documents in
the small museum.
Most services are
now held in the
basilica, built next

to the mission in 1918. The
cemetery contains graves of
San Franciscan pioneers.
A statue marking the mass
grave of 5,000 Native Americans, most of whom died in
the measles epidemics of 1804
and 1826, was later stolen. All
that now remains is a pedestal,
reading "In Prayerful Memory
of our Faithful Indians."

***The painted and gilded
altarpiece** was imported from
Mexico in 1780.*

The statue of Father Junípero Serra
is a copy of the work of local
sculptor Arthur Putnam.

The ceramic mural was created by
Guillermo Granizo, a native San
Francisco artist.

**Museum and
display**

The ceiling paintings
are based on original
Ohlone designs using
vegetable dyes.

**Entrance for
the disabled**

**The mission
cemetery** originally
extended across
many streets. The
earliest wooden
grave markers have
disintegrated, but
the Lourdes Grotto
commemorates the
forgotten dead.

**Statue of Our Lady
of Mount Carmel**

**Entrance
and gift
shop**

**The mission
façade** has four
columns which
support niches for
three bells,
inscribed with their
names and dates.

Spanish–American War memorial on Dolores Street

Dolores Street ⑩

Map 10 E2. 🚌 8, 22, 33, 48. 🚇 J.

LINED BY lovingly maintained late-Victorian houses *(see pp290–91)* and an island of palm trees, this street is one of the city's most attractive public spaces. The broad street runs parallel to Mission Street, forming the western border of the Mission District. It starts at Market Street, where a statue honoring soldiers of the Spanish–American War is overwhelmed by the US Mint.

Mission High School, with the white walls and red tile roof typical of Mission-style architecture *(see p26)*, and Mission Dolores *(see p351)* are both situated on Dolores Street. The street ends in the Noe Valley district.

Dolores Park ⑪

Map 10 E3. 🚌 22, 33. 🚇 J.

ORIGINALLY THE SITE of San Francisco's main Jewish cemetery, Dolores Park was transformed in 1905 into one of the Mission District's few large open spaces. Ringed by Dolores, Church, 18th, and 20th streets, it is situated high on a hill with an excellent view of the city center.

Dolores Park is very popular during the day with tennis players, sunbathers, and dog walkers, but after dark it is a haven for drug dealers. Above the park to the south and west, the streets rise so steeply that

many turn into pedestrian-only stairways. Some of the city's finest Victorian houses can also be seen here.

Mission Cultural Center for the Latino Arts ⑫

2868 Mission St. **Map** 10 F4. 📞 (415) 821-1155. 🚌 14, 26, 48, 49. 🚇 J. ⭕ 10am–4pm Tue–Sat. ♿

THIS DYNAMIC arts center is partly funded by the city, and caters to the local, predominantly Latino population. It offers classes and workshops, and stages theatrical events and exhibitions. Among these is the festival held in November to celebrate the Day of the Dead *(see p34)*.

Detail from the *Carnaval Mural*

Carnaval Mural ⑬

24th St and South Van Ness Ave. **Map** 10 F4. 🚌 12, 14, 48, 49, 67. 🚇 J.

ONE OF THE MANY brightly painted murals on the walls of the Mission District, the *Carnaval Mural* celebrates the diverse people who come together for the Carnaval festival *(see p32)*. This annual spring event is the highlight of the year.

Guided tours of the other murals, some with political themes, are given by civic organizations. There is also an outdoor gallery with murals in Balmy Alley *(see pp296–7)*.

Noe Valley ⑭

🚌 24, 35, 48. 🚇 J.

NOE VALLEY is often referred to as "Noewhere Valley" by its residents, who remain determined to keep it off the tourist map. It is a pleasant, comfortable neighborhood, largely inhabited by young professionals. Its spotless streets and safe atmosphere seem at odds with the surrounding, densely populated Mission District.

The area was named after its original land-grant owner, José Noe, the last *alcalde* (mayor) of Yerba Buena, the Mexican village that eventually grew into San Francisco. The valley was first built up during the 1880s after a cable car line over the steep Castro Street hill was completed. The low rents attracted mostly working-class Irish families. Then, like so many other areas of San Francisco, this once blue-collar district underwent gentrification in the 1970s, raising the value of the properties and resulting in today's engaging mix of boutiques, bars, and restaurants. The Noe Valley Ministry, found at No. 1021 Sanchez Street, is a late 1880s Presbyterian church in the "Stick Style" *(see pp290–91)*, the most prevalent architectural style in the city, with its emphasis on vertical lines. The ministry was converted into a community center in the 1970s.

Victorian façade of the Noe Valley Ministry on Sanchez Street

Nobby Clarke's Folly

Clarke's Folly ⑮

250 Douglas St. **Map** 10 D3. 🚌 8, 33, 35, 37, 48. ● to the public.

THIS RESPLENDENT white manor house was at one time set in its own extensive grounds. It was built in 1892 by Alfred Clarke, known locally as Nobby. Clarke had worked for the San Francisco Police Department at the time of the Committee of Vigilance in 1851, when a group of local citizens attempted to control the city's growing lawlessness *(see pp44–5)*. The house is said to have cost $100,000 to build, a huge sum in the 1890s.

Although it is now surrounded by other buildings, the house is a fine example of Victorian domestic architecture. The turrets and the gabled roof are typical of the Queen Anne style, while the shingled walls and front porch adopt the elements of Eastlake architecture *(see pp290–91)*.

Today the house is divided into private apartments.

Twin Peaks ⑯

Map 9 C4. 🚌 33, 36, 37.

THESE TWO HILLS were first known in Spanish as *El Pecho de la Chola*, the "Bosom of the Indian Girl." They lie at the heart of San Francisco, and reach a height of 900 ft

(274 m) above sea level. At the top there is an area of parkland with steep, grassy slopes, from which incomparable views of the whole of San Francisco can be enjoyed.

Twin Peaks Boulevard circles both hills near their summits; there is a parking lot and viewing point that overlooks the city. Those who are prepared to climb up the steep path to the very top on foot can leave the crowds behind and get a breathtaking 360-degree view.

Twin Peaks are the only hills in the city left in their original state. The residential districts on the lower slopes have curving streets that wind around the contours of the hills, rather than the grid system that is more common in the rest of San Francisco.

Vulcan Street Steps ⑰

Vulcan St. **Map** 9 C2. 🚌 37.

APART FROM a tiny figure of Spock standing on a mailbox, there is no connection between the cult television program *Star Trek* and this block of houses climbing between Ord and Levant Streets. However, the Vulcan Steps do feel light years away from the busy Castro District below. The small, picturesque gardens of the houses spill out and soften the edges of the steps, and a canopy of pines muffles the city sounds. There are great views of the Mission District and the southern waterfront.

Sutro Tower ⑱

Map 9 B3. 🚌 36, 37. ● to the public.

MARKING THE SKYLINE like an invading robot, Sutro Tower is 970 ft (295 m) high. It was named after the local philanthropist and landowner Adolph Sutro, and it carries antennae for the signals of most of San Francisco's TV and radio stations. Built in 1973, it is still much used, despite the rise of cable networks. The tower is visible from all over the Bay Area, and sometimes seems to float above the summer fogs that roll in from the sea. On the north side of the tower there are dense eucalyptus groves, first planted in the 1880s by Adolph Sutro.

View of the city and of Twin Peaks Boulevard from the top of Twin Peaks

GOLDEN GATE PARK AND THE PRESIDIO

THE SPECTACULAR Golden Gate Park is one of the world's largest urban parks, created in the 1890s out of sandy wasteland. It houses three museums and a range of sports facilities. Land's End, the city's wildest region and scene of many shipwrecks, is accessible from the park.

Cannon from the Presidio

To the north of Golden Gate Park, the Presidio, overlooking San Francisco Bay, was established as an outpost of Spain's New World empire in 1776, and for many years was a military base. In 1993 it became a National Park, and visitors can now stroll through its acres of woodland full of wildlife.

SIGHTS AT A GLANCE

Historic Streets and Buildings
Clement Street **12**
Golden Gate Bridge pp370–71 **17**
Presidio Community Club **14**

Parks and Gardens
Buffalo Paddock **8**
Conservatory of Flowers **5**
Japanese Tea Garden **3**
Queen Wilhelmina Tulip Garden **9**
Shakespeare Garden **2**
Stow Lake **7**
Strybing Arboretum **6**

Museums and Galleries
California Academy of Sciences pp360–61 **1**
California Palace of the Legion of Honor pp364–5 **10**
Fort Point **16**
MH de Young Memorial Museum **4**
Presidio Visitor Center **15**

Churches and Temples
Holy Virgin Cathedral **11**
Temple Emanu-El **13**

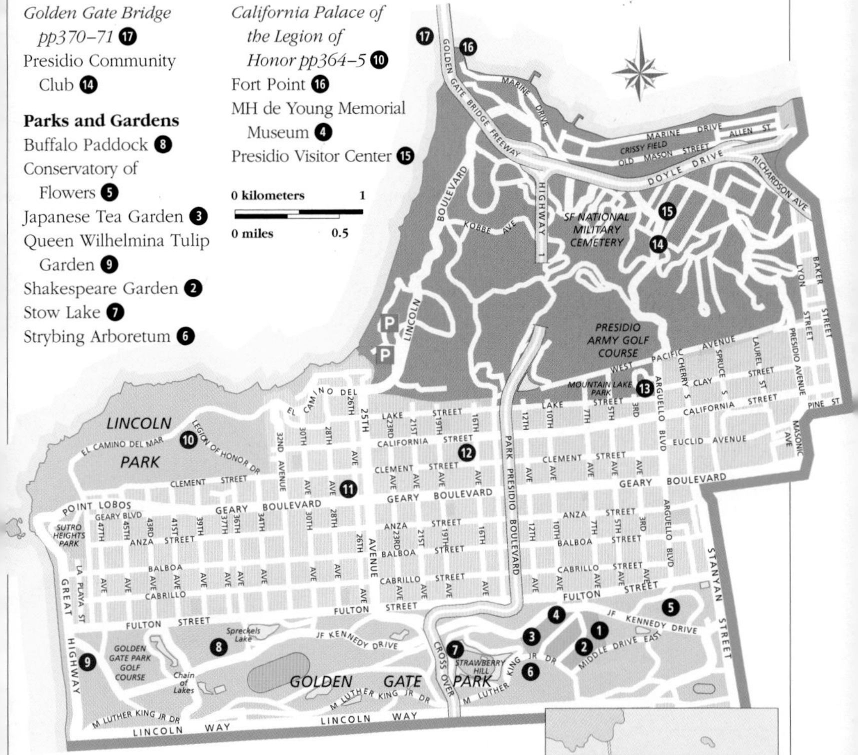

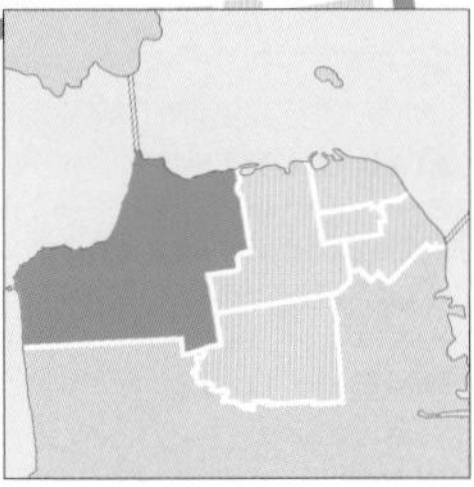

0 kilometers   1

0 miles   0.5

GETTING THERE
For Golden Gate Park, take buses 5, 7, 21, 71, or 73, or the N streetcar. The Presidio is best seen by car, but Muni bus 29 stops at the main sights, bus 43 serves the eastern end, and bus 28 the northern boundary.

KEY
Street-by-Street map
See pp356–7

The Presidio
see pp366–7

P Parking

◁ **Golden Gate Bridge from Fort Point**

Street-by-Street: Golden Gate Park

GOLDEN GATE PARK is 3 miles (5 km) long and almost 1 mile (1.6 km) across. It stretches from the Pacific Ocean to the center of San Francisco, forming an oasis of greenery and calm in which to escape from the bustle of city life. Within the park an amazing number of activities are catered to, both sporting and cultural. The landscaped area around the Music Concourse, with its fountains, plane trees, and benches, is the most popular and developed section. Here you can enjoy free Sunday concerts at the Spreckels Temple of Music. A total of three museums stand on either side of the Concourse, and the Japanese and Shakespeare gardens are within walking distance.

Lamp in the Japanese Tea Garden

★ **MH de Young Museum**
The de Young Museum is closed for renovation until 2006. Many exhibits are on display at the California Palace of the Legion of Honor (see p364) ❹

The Great Buddha reaches almost 11 ft (3 m) in height.

Japanese Tea Garden
This exquisite garden, with its well-tended plants and pretty lake, is one of the most attractive parts of the park ❸

HAGIWARA

MARTIN LUTHER KING DR

KEY

– – – Suggested route

0 meters   80
0 yards   80

STAR SIGHTS

★ **California Academy of Sciences**

★ **MH de Young Museum**

Shakespeare Garden
This tiny garden holds more than 150 species of plants, all mentioned in Shakespeare's poetry or plays ❷

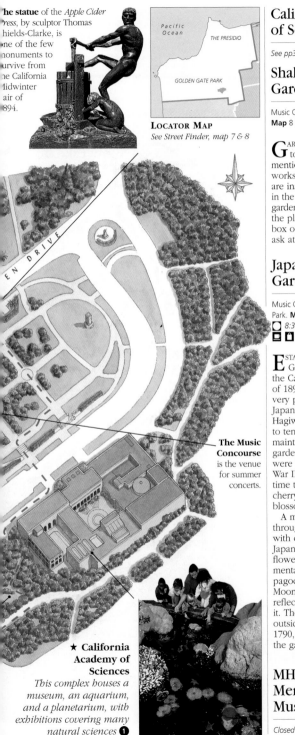

The statue of the *Apple Cider Press*, by sculptor Thomas Shields-Clarke, is one of the few monuments to survive from the California Midwinter Fair of 1894.

Pacific Ocean

THE PRESIDIO

GOLDEN GATE PARK

LOCATOR MAP
See Street Finder, map 7 & 8

The Music Concourse is the venue for summer concerts.

★ **California Academy of Sciences**
This complex houses a museum, an aquarium, and a planetarium, with exhibitions covering many natural sciences ❶

California Academy of Sciences ❶

See pp360–61.

Shakespeare Garden ❷

Music Concourse, Golden Gate Park. **Map** 8 F2. 🚌 44.

GARDENERS HERE have tried to cultivate all the plants mentioned in Shakespeare's works. Relevant quotations are inscribed on plaques set in the wall at the back of the garden. A 19th-century bust of the playwright is kept in a box opened only occasionally; ask at the Lodge.

Japanese Tea Garden ❸

Music Concourse, Golden Gate Park. **Map** 8 F2. 🚌 44.
🕐 8:30am–6pm daily. 📷
📷 📷

ESTABLISHED BY the art-dealer George Turner Marsh for the California Midwinter Fair of 1894, this garden was a very popular attraction. A Japanese gardener, Makota Hagiwara, was later contracted to tend it. He and his family maintained and expanded the garden until 1942, when they were interned during World War II. The most spectacular time to visit is when all the cherry trees break into blossom in April.

A maze of paths winds through the gardens, lined with carefully manicured Japanese trees, shrubs, and flowers. There are also orna-mental ponds and a wooden pagoda. The steeply arched Moon Bridge forms a circular reflection in the pond below it. The largest bronze Buddha outside Asia, cast in Japan in 1790, is seated at the top of the garden stairs.

MH de Young Memorial Museum ❹

Closed for refurbishment until 2006.

Conservatory of Flowers ❺

John F Kennedy Drive, Golden Gate Park. **Map** 9 A1. 📞 *(415) 750-5105.* 🚌 *33, 44.* ⬤ *to the public.* 📷 🅰️ ♿ *limited.* 🔲

THIS ORNATE greenhouse, inspired by the one in London's Kew Gardens, is the oldest building in Golden Gate Park. A property developer, James Lick, imported the frame from Ireland, but he died before its erection in 1879. A jungle of ferns, palms, and orchids thrived here for more than a century, but a hurricane hit the city in December 1995 and largely destroyed the conservatory. San Franciscans are currently campaigning for its much-needed repair.

Strybing Arboretum ❻

9th Ave at Lincoln Way, Golden Gate Park. **Map** 8 F2. 📞 *661 1316.* 🚌 *44, 71.* ⬤ ⏰ *8am–4:30pm Mon–Fri, 10am–5pm weekends and public hols.* 📷 ♿ ✓ 🔲

ON DISPLAY in the Strybing Arboretum are 7,500 species of plants, trees, and shrubs from many different countries. There are Mexican, African, South American, and Australian gardens, and one

Garden of Fragrance in the Strybing Arboretum

that is devoted entirely to native California plants.

Well worth a visit is the enchanting Moon-Viewing Garden. It exhibits Far Eastern plants in a setting that, unlike that of the Japanese Tea Garden *(see p357)*, is naturalistic rather than formal. Both medicinal and culinary plants are grown in the Garden of Fragrance, which is specifically designed for blind plant-lovers. Here the emphasis is on the senses of taste, touch, and smell, and all the plants are identified in Braille.

Another area, with a stream winding through it, is planted with indigenous California redwood trees. This re-creates the flora and the atmosphere of a northern Californian coastal forest. There is also a New World Cloud Forest,

with flora from the mountains of Central America. Surprisingly, all these gardens thrive in the Californian fogs.

The Arboretum has a small shop selling seeds and books, and it also houses the Helen Crocker Horticultural Library, which is open to the public. A colorful flower show is held in the summer.

Stow Lake ❼

Stow Lake Drive, Golden Gate Park. **Map** 8 E2. 🚌 *28, 29.* 🔲 ⬇️

IN 1895, the President of the Park Commission, WW Stow, ordered the construction of this artificial lake, the largest in the park. It was created encircling Strawberry Hill (named after the wild fruit that once grew here), so that the summit of the hill now forms an island in the lake. It is linked to the mainland by two stone-clad bridges. Stow Lake's circular stream makes an ideal course for rowing laps from the boathouse, although the tranquil atmosphere makes leisurely drifting seem more appropriate. A Chinese pavilion on the island's shore was a gift to San Francisco from its sister city in Taiwan, Taipei. The red and green pavilion arrived in San Francisco by ship in 6,000 pieces and then was reassembled on the island.

Chinese moon-watching pavilion on Stow Lake

The millionaire railway baron Collis Porter Huntington *(see pp46–7)* donated the money in 1894 to create the reservoir and the waterfall that cascades into Stow Lake. These are known as Huntington Falls. Damaged in the 1906 earthquake *(see pp48–9)*, it was restored in the 1980s and is now one of the park's most attractive features.

Buffalo Paddock ❽

John F Kennedy Drive, Golden Gate Park. **Map** 7 C2. 🚌 *5, 29.*

T HE SHAGGY BUFFALO grazing in this specially designed paddock are the largest of all North American land animals. Immediately recognizable by their short horns and humped backs, buffaloes are the symbol of the American plains, and are more properly known as the American bison.

This paddock was opened in 1892, with the aim of protecting the species, then on the verge of extinction. The first herd, however, brought in from Wyoming, all died of a tuberculosis epidemic and had to be replaced. In 1902 William Cody, the American scout and showman "Buffalo Bill," traded one of his bulls for one from the Golden Gate Park herd. Both parties thought that they had rid themselves of an aggressive beast, but Cody's newly purchased bull jumped a high fence once it was back at his encampment and escaped. According to one newspaper, the *San Francisco Call*, it took 80 men to recapture it.

Buffalo in the Buffalo Paddock

Queen Wilhelmina Tulip Garden and the Dutch Windmill

Queen Wilhelmina Tulip Garden ❾

Map 7 A2. 🚌 *5, 18.* **Windmill** ♿

T HIS GARDEN was named after the Dutch Queen Wilhelmina, and hundreds of tulip bulbs are donated each year by the Dutch Bulb Growers' Association. In the spring months, the area is carpeted with the flowers in full bloom. The Dutch Windmill, near the northwest corner of Golden Gate Park, was built in 1903. Its purpose, along with its companion, the Murphy Windmill, erected in the park's southwest corner in 1905, was to pump water from a source underground, in order to irrigate the park. The increasing volume of water required – about 5 million gallons, or 230 million liters per day – soon made the windmills obsolete, and they are no longer in use.

JOHN MCLAREN

Although Golden Gate Park was designed by William Hammond Hall, the park's current status owes the most to his successor, John McLaren.

McLaren was born in Scotland in 1846 and studied botany before emigrating to California in the 1870s. He succeeded Hall as administrator in 1887 and devoted the rest of his life to the park.

An expert landscape gardener and botanist, McLaren succeeded in importing exotic plants from all over the world and making them thrive, despite the poor soil and foggy climate. He planted thousands of trees and chose the right shrubs to make sure the park was in full bloom all year long.

John McLaren Lodge, a sandstone villa situated on the park's east side, was built in 1896 as a home for McLaren and his family. As McLaren lay dying in 1943, he requested that the cypress tree outside the lodge be lit with Christmas lights, and his request was granted, despite a wartime blackout being in force. The tree is still referred to as "Uncle John's Christmas Tree" and is lit every December in his honor. He is buried in a tomb in the San Francisco City Hall. Golden Gate Park still remains true to his vision – a place in which to escape from city life.

California Academy of Sciences ●

THIS EXPANSIVE MUSEUM was erected in several installments between 1916 and 1968, yet maintains a unified design around a central courtyard. The original building, located downtown, was severely damaged in the 1906 earthquake. The exhibits in two of the rooms were salvaged, however, becoming the foundation of an exciting new collection. The trademark fountain of the Academy, *Mating Whales*, sculpted by Robert Howard for the 1939 World's Fair on Treasure Island *(see pp50–51)*, spouts at the heart of the courtyard.

A penguin in the Steinhart Aquarium

Façade of the California Academy of Sciences

MUSEUM GUIDE
The widely varied collections, arranged by subject, are housed in different halls on the first floor around the central courtyard. Several areas are allocated for the display of special exhibitions. The Academy Store, selling books and gifts, has a shop in Cowell Hall and another outside the Auditorium. The Academy library, which contains 70,000 volumes, is on the second floor.

Reptiles and Amphibians

Fish

Wattis Hall

Far Side of Science Gallery

Elkus Collection

Morrison Planetarium
One of the world's most precise star projectors transforms the ceiling here into a night sky.

Auditorium

KEY TO FLOOR PLAN

- African Hall
- Earth and Space
- Wallis Hall
- Life Through Time
- Steinhart Aquarium
- Gem and Mineral Hall
- Wild California
- Special exhibitions
- Nonexhibition space

★ Earthquake!
Experience the power and movement of great earth tremors, while learning of their destructive power.

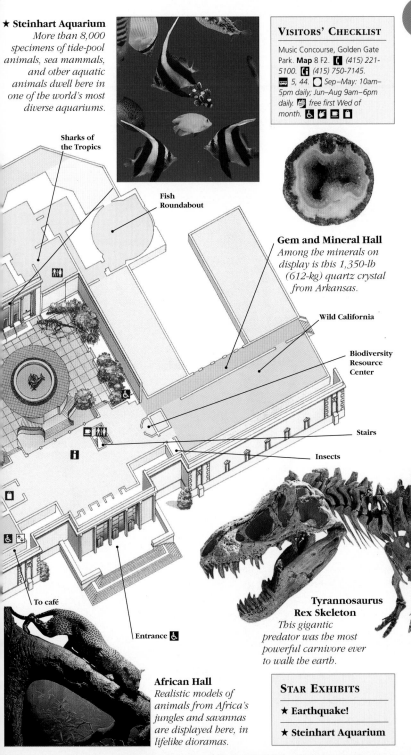

★ Steinhart Aquarium
More than 8,000 specimens of tide-pool animals, sea mammals, and other aquatic animals dwell here in one of the world's most diverse aquariums.

VISITORS' CHECKLIST

Music Concourse, Golden Gate Park. **Map** 8 F2. ☎ *(415) 221-5100.* 🔗 *(415) 750-7145.* 🚌 *5, 44.* 🕐 *Sep–May: 10am–5pm daily; Jun–Aug 9am–6pm daily.* 🎟 *free first Wed of month.* ♿ ✔ 📷 🎦 🏪

Sharks of the Tropics

Fish Roundabout

Gem and Mineral Hall
Among the minerals on display is this 1,350-lb (612-kg) quartz crystal from Arkansas.

Wild California

Biodiversity Resource Center

Stairs

Insects

Tyrannosaurus Rex Skeleton
This gigantic predator was the most powerful carnivore ever to walk the earth.

To café

Entrance ♿

African Hall
Realistic models of animals from Africa's jungles and savannas are displayed here, in lifelike dioramas.

STAR EXHIBITS

★ **Earthquake!**

★ **Steinhart Aquarium**

Golden Gate Bridge from Lincoln Park golf course ▷

California Palace of the Legion of Honor ❿

INSPIRED BY the Palais de la Légion d'Honneur in Paris, Alma de Bretteville Spreckels built this museum in the 1920s to promote French art in California. Designed by the architect George Applegarth, it contains works of European art from the last eight centuries, with paintings by Monet, Rubens, and Rembrandt, and more than 70 statues by Rodin. The Achenbach Foundation, a famous collection of graphic works, occupies part of the gallery.

Old Woman
French artist Georges de la Tour painted this female portrait in about 1618.

Florence Gould Theater

The Porcelain Gallery
contains figurines, china, and other pieces dating from the 18th century.

Stairs down from first floor

Virgin and Child
This oil-on-panel by the Flemish artist Dieric Bouts dates from the 15th century. It forms part of a series of four panels titled Life of the Virgin.

STAR FEATURES

★ **The Thinker**

★ **Waterlilies**

The Tribute Money *(1612)*
*The use of primary colors in this
oil-on-canvas is typical of the
Flemish artist Peter
Paul Rubens.*

The Impresario
*In this portrait from around
1877, artist Edgar Degas
emphasizes the subject's size
by making him appear too
large for the frame.*

Entrance

★ Waterlilies
*Claude Monet's work from
between 1914 and 1917 is
one of a series depicting the
lily pond in his gardens in
Giverny, near Paris.*

GALLERY GUIDE
*The museum's permanent
collection of European art is
displayed throughout 19
galleries on the first floor.
Works are arranged
chronologically, from the
medieval period, left of the
main entrance, through the
Renaissance, and on to the
20th century. Temporary
exhibitions, graphic art, and
the porcelain collection are
on the lower level.*

KEY TO FLOOR PLAN

- [ ] Permanent displays
- [ ] Achenbach Foundation Library
- [ ] Porcelain gallery
- [ ] Theater storage
- [ ] Temporary displays
- [ ] Nonexhibition space

★ The Thinker
*The original bronze casting of
Rodin's* Le Penseur *(1904) is at
the center of the colonnaded
Court of Honor. It is one of
five castings of the statue in
collections around the world.*

The Presidio

**Presidio
Park sign**

THE WINDING ROADS and lush green landscaping of the Presidio belie its long military history. This prominent site has played a key role in San Francisco's growth, and it has been occupied longer than any other part of the city. Remnants of its military past, including the well-preserved barracks, artillery emplacements, and a museum, can be seen everywhere, and there are many hiking trails, bike paths, and beaches. The coastal path is one of the most popular walks and picnic areas in the city. The striking Golden Gate Bridge crosses the bay from the northwest corner of the Presidio to Marin County.

Fort Point
This impressive brick fortress, now a national historic site, guarded the Golden Gate during the Civil War of 1861–5 16

★ **Golden Gate Bridge**
Opened in 1937, the bridge has a single span of 4,200 ft (1,280 m) 17

Mountain Lake is a large spring-fed lake and a popular picnic spot. The original Presidio was established nearby in 1776 to defend the bay area and Mission Dolores (*see p351*).

Crissy Field was reclaimed from marshland for the 1915 Panama-Pacific Exposition *(see p341)*. It was used as an airfield from 1919 to 1936 and has been recently restored.

LOCATOR MAP
See Street Finder, map 2 & 3

The Military Cemetery holds the remains of almost 15,000 American soldiers killed during several wars.

The Tidal Marsh is part of the restoration of the Presidio area.

Arguello Gate
This decorative gate with its military symbols marks the entrance to the former army base, now open to the public.

★ Presidio Visitor Center
The visitor center on Montgomery Street is in the Main Post area of the Presidio .

STAR SIGHTS

★ **Golden Gate Bridge**

★ **Presidio Visitor Cntr**

| 0 meters | 500 |
| 0 yards | 500 |

Holy Virgin Cathedral ⓫

6210 Geary Blvd. **Map** 8 D1. 221-3255. 2, 29, 38. 8am, 6pm daily, extra services 8am, 9:45am Sun.

Shining gold onion-shaped domes crown the Russian Orthodox Holy Virgin Cathedral of the Russian Church in Exile, a startling landmark in the suburban Richmond District. Built in the early 1960s, it is generally open to the public only during services. In contrast to those of many other Christian denominations, the services in this cathedral are conducted with the congregation standing, so there are no pews or seats.

The cathedral and the many Russian-owned businesses surrounding it, such as the lively Russian Renaissance restaurant, are situated at the heart of San Francisco's extensive Russian community *(see p31)*. This has flourished since the 1820s, but it reached its highest population influx when a large number of new immigrants arrived after the Russian Revolution of 1917. It has since boomed twice more: in the late 1950s and late 1980s.

Clement Street ⓬

Map 1 C5. 2, 28, 29, 44.

This is a bustling main thoroughfare of the otherwise sleepy Richmond District. Bookshops and small boutiques flourish here, and the inhabitants of the neighborhood meet together in a lively mix of bars, fast-food cafés, and ethnic restaurants. Most of these are patronized more by locals than by tourists.

Clement Street is surrounded by an area known as New Chinatown, home to more than one-third of the Chinese population of San Francisco. As a result, some of the city's best Chinese restaurants can be found here, and the emphasis in general is on Far Eastern cuisine *(see p564)*.

The area is also known for the diversity of its restaurants, and Danish, Peruvian, and French establishments, among others, flourish here. The street stretches from Arguello Boulevard to the north/south cross-streets that are more commonly known as "The Avenues." It ends near the California Palace of the Legion of Honor *(see pp364–5)*.

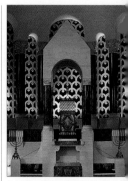

Interior of Temple Emanu-El, showing the Holy Ark

Temple Emanu-El ⓭

Lake St and Arguello Blvd. **Map** 3 A4 751-2535. 8:30am–5:30pm Mon–Thu, 8:30am–5pm Fri (8:30am–7:30pm first Fri of month). 5:30pm Fri, 10:30am Sat. during services.

After World War I hundreds of Jews from Russia and Eastern Europe moved into the Richmond District and built major religious centers. Among these is the Temple Emanu-El, its dome inspired by that of the 6th-century Hagia Sophia in Istanbul.

The temple stands out as a majestic piece of architecture. It was built in 1925 for the longest established congregation of Jews in the city, founded in 1850. The architect was Arthur Brown, who also designed City Hall *(see p342)*. The temple is an architectural hybrid: Mission style *(see pp26–7)*, Byzantine ornamentation, and Romanesque arcades. Its interior, which accommodates nearly 2,000 worshipers, is especially fine when sunlight shines through the stained-glass windows.

Presidio Officers' Club ⓮

50 Moraga Ave. **Map** 3 A2. (415) 561-2582. 29. to the public.

Looking out across the original parade grounds of the Presidio and the 19th-century wooden barracks, the Officers' Club was built in the Spanish Mission style *(see*

The Russian Orthodox Holy Virgin Cathedral

26–7). Although it dates
 om the 1930s, it was care-
ly built around the adobe
 un-dried brick) remains of
 e original 18th-century
 anish fort. Exhibits are
 metimes held here, which
 e open to the public. Phone
 ead to check the schedule.

residio Visitor
 enter **⑮**

 2 Montgomery St at Lincoln Blvd
 p 3 A2. **[** (415) 561-4323.
 9am–5pm daily. **⊙ &**

 THE PRESIDIO MUSEUM, once
  housed in a white wooden
 ilding dating from the 1860s,
 at served as the Presidio
 spital, is now part of the
 w Mott Visitor Center.
 cated in a brick barracks
 Infantry Row, the Center
 uses exhibits and artifacts
 sociated with the long
 story of the Presidio. The
 splays focus on eyewitness
 counts of the evolution of
 e city of San Francisco,
 m the small frontier
 tpost in the 1770s to the
 ajor metropolis it is today.
 her exhibits of uniforms,
 eapons, and newspaper
 counts of the 1906 earth-
 ake and fire are on display
 other Presidio buildings.
 Two small cabins stand
 hind the Old Post Hospital
 e p367) and are represen-
 ive of the hundreds of
 nporary shelters set up here
 llowing the great earthquake
 1906 (see pp48–9).

 nnon near the Old Post Hospital
 the grounds of the Presidio

Golden Gate Bridge, seen from Fort Point

Fort Point **⑯**

Marine Drive. **Map** 2 E1.
[556-1693. **⊙** 10am–5pm daily.
⊙ & partial.

COMPLETED BY the US army
in 1861, this fort was built
partly to protect San Francisco
Bay from any impending
military attack, and partly to
defend ships carrying gold
from the Californian mines
(see pp44–5). It is the most
prominent of the many forti-
fications constructed along the
Pacific coastline and is a
classic example of a pre-Civil
War brick and granite fortress.
The building soon became
obsolete, its 10-ft (3-m) thick
brick walls not being strong
enough to stand up to powerful modern weaponry. It was
closed in 1900, never having
come under attack.

The fort's brickwork vault-
ing is extremely unusual for
San Francisco, where the
ready availability of good
timber was an incentive to
build wood-frame constructions. This may have saved
the fort from collapse in the
1906 earthquake (see pp48–9).
It was nearly demolished in
the 1930s to make way for
the Golden Gate Bridge, but
it survived and is now a good
place from which to view the
bridge. Restored in the 1970s,
the fort now houses a museum
displaying military uniforms
and arms. Park Rangers
dressed in Civil War costume
conduct guided tours.

A HISTORY OF THE PRESIDIO

In 1776 José Joaquin
Moraga, one of the
first Spanish settlers,
founded a presidio.
His aim in erecting
this camp of adobe
buildings on the
edge of San Fran-
cisco Bay was to
defend the Mission

The Presidio in the 19th century

Dolores (see p351). Following Mexican independence from
Spain, the site remained the northernmost fort of the short-
lived republic until the United States took it over in 1847.
The Presidio was used for military purposes until 1990.

From the 1850s to the 1930s, the adobe buildings were
replaced, first with wooden barracks, and later with concrete Mission- and Georgian-style cottages for the officers
and their families. These buildings remain.

The site covers 1,400 acres (567 ha), and its landscaped
forests of eucalyptus and cypress trees are not found on
any other army base in the world. The Presidio has now
been declared an historic site and is a protected member of
the Golden Gate National Recreation Area (GGNRA).

Golden Gate Bridge ⑰

NAMED AFTER THAT PART of San Francisco Bay called "Golden Gate" by John Frémont in 1844, the bridge opened in 1937, connecting the city with Marin County. It took just over four years to build at a cost of $35 million. Breathtaking views are offered from this spectacular, world-famous landmark, which has six lanes for vehicles plus a free pedestrian walkway. It is the world's third largest single-span bridge and, when it was built, it was the world's longest and tallest suspension structure.

Bridge builder wearing protective mask

The twin steel towers rise to a height of 746 ft (227 m) above the water. The towers are hollow.

Catching the Hot Rivets
Working in gangs of four, one man heated the rivets and threw them to another, who caught them in a bucket. The other two fastened sections of steel with the hot rivets.

The Foundations
The foundations of the twin towers are a remarkable feat of engineering. The south pier, 1,125 ft (343 m) offshore, was sunk 100 ft (30 m) into the sea bed.

Pier base 65-ft (20-m) thick
Fender 155-ft (47-m) high
Reinforcing iron frame

The roadway 220 ft (67 ▶ above water 318 (97-m) dee

The Concrete Fender
During construction, the south pier base was protected from the force of the tides by a fender of concrete. Water was pumped out to create a vast watertight locker.

THE GOLDEN GATE BRIDGE
AT SAN FRANCISCO

The Roadway
The original steel-supported concrete roadway was constructed from the towers in both directions, so that weight on the suspension cables was evenly distributed.

Joseph Strauss
Chicago engineer Joseph Strauss is officially credited as the bridge's designer, and he led the opening ceremony in April 1937. He was assisted by Leon Moisseiff and Charles Ellis. Irving F Morrow acted as consulting architect.

The length of the bridge is 1.7 miles (2.7 km), the span is 4,200 ft (1,280 m), and the roadway is 220 ft (67 m) above the water.

View from Vista Point
The best view of both the bridge and the San Francisco skyline is from the Marin County side.

THE BRIDGE IN FIGURES

• Every year more than 40 million vehicles cross the bridge; every day about 118,000 vehicles use it.
• The original coat of paint lasted for 27 years, needing only touch-ups. But since 1965, a crew has been stripping off the old paint and applying a more durable coating.
• The two great 7,650-ft (2,332-m) cables are more than 3 ft (1 m) thick, and contain 80,000 miles (128,744 km) of steel wire, enough to circle the earth at the equator three times.
• The volume of concrete poured into the piers and anchorages during the bridge's construction would be enough to lay a 5-ft (1.5 m) wide sidewalk from New York to San Francisco, a distance of more than 2,500 miles (4,000 km).
• The bridge can withstand 100 mph (160 km/h) winds.
• Each pier has to withstand a tidal flow of more than 60 mph (97 km/h), while supporting a 44,000-ton steel tower.

Painting the bridge

ENTERTAINMENT IN SAN FRANCISCO

S AN FRANCISCO has prided itself on being the cultural capital of the West Coast since the city first began to prosper in the 1850s, and the entertainment offered is generally of high quality. The performing arts complex of the Civic Center, opposite the City Hall, is the principal venue for classical music, opera, and ballet. The latest addition to the city's cultural life is the highly rated Center for the Arts Theater at Yerba Buena Gardens. Many international touring shows can be seen

Beach Blanket Babylon
(see p331)

here. There are numerous repertory movie theaters offering filmgoers a wide range of programs but theater, except for some of the "alternative" venues is not the city's strongest suit. Popular music, in particular jazz and blues, is where San Francisco really excels, and you can hear good bands for the price of a drink or at the street fairs and music festivals that are held during the summer months. Facilities are also available for a wide variety of sports, from cycling to golf, tennis, and sailing.

INFORMATION SOURCES

C OMPLETE LISTINGS of what's on and where are given in the *San Francisco Chronicle* and *Examiner* newspapers. The *Chronicle's* Sunday edition is very useful. Other good sources are the free weekly newspapers, such as the *San Francisco Weekly* (available in most cafés and bars) or the *San Francisco Bay Guardian*. These give both listings and reviews, especially of live music, films, and nightclubs.

Visitors planning farther in advance will find the *San Francisco Book* very helpful. This is published twice yearly by the **San Francisco Convention and Visitors' Bureau** and is available free at the **Visitors' Information Center** at Hallidie Plaza or for $2 if mailed out. You can also phone the visitors' bureau's Events Line for recorded information. Numerous free magazines for visitors are available, as well as calendars of events. Among these are *Key This Week San Francisco* and *Where San Francisco*.

BUYING TICKETS

T HE MAIN SOURCE for tickets to concerts, theater, and sporting events is **Ticketmaster**, which has a virtual monopoly on ticket sales, running an extensive charge-by-phone operation with outlets in the Tower and Wherehouse record shops *(see pp584–5)* all over Northern California. There is

Storefront of San Francisco ticket agency

a "convenience charge" of about $4 per ticket. An alternative to Ticketmaster is to buy directly from the box offices, though many of these are only open just before the start of evening performances.

To see productions by the reputable San Francisco Symphony, Ballet, and Opera companies, advance planning is essential. All have subscription programs, which are useful if you are planning to stay in the city for a lengthy period of time.

There are only a few ticket agencies in San Francisco, and they mostly specialize in selling limited seats at marked-up prices. They are all listed in the Yellow Pages of the telephone directory, found in most public pay phones. Ticket scalpers are invariably found outside sold-out events, offering seats at extortionate prices. If you are willing to bargain (and risk missing the start of the game or the opening act) it is often possible to get a good deal this way.

Front entrance of the War Memorial Opera House

Outdoor chess, popular in
Portsmouth Plaza, Chinatown

DISCOUNT TICKETS

DISCOUNT TICKETS for some
selected events are available from **TIX Bay Area**,
offering half-price seats from a
booth on the east side of
Union Square (see p310).
Tickets are sold starting at
11am, on the day of the performance only. Occasionally,
there are also some half-price
tickets available on Saturdays
for those events that are
taking place on the following
Sunday and Monday.

TIX Bay Area is also a full-
service Ticketmaster outlet
selling full-price tickets; it
accepts all major credit cards
for advance sales. It is open
on Tuesdays, Wednesdays,
and Thursdays from 11am to
6pm, and on Fridays and
Saturdays from 11am to 7pm.

FREE EVENTS

IN ADDITION to San Francisco's
many ticket-only events, a
number of free concerts and
performances are regularly
staged all over the city. Many
of these take place during the
day and outdoors in the summer; they can offer a welcome change of pace from
the usual standard fare.

The San Francisco Symphony
Orchestra (see pp374–5) gives
a series of late-summer Sunday
concerts at Stern Grove, south
of the Sunset District. The
same venue is also occasionally used for ballets.

Cobb's Comedy Club (see
pp374–5) hosts the popular
San Francisco International
Comedy Competition in
August and September.

Performers from the San
Francisco Opera (see pp374–
5) can be heard singing some
favorite arias in the Financial
District as part of the "Brown
Bag Operas" series and in
Golden Gate Park in "Opera
in the Park" events. In the
summer the park is also host
to the Shakespeare Festival,
Comedy Celebration Day, and
the San Francisco Mime
Troupe. A series of concerts
called "Music in the Park" is
held on summer Fridays at
noon, in the redwood grove
behind the Transamerica
Pyramid (see p305). At Grace
Cathedral (see p321) the fine
cathedral choir sings choral
music at Evensong, at 5:15pm
on Thursdays.

FACILITIES FOR THE DISABLED

CALIFORNIA is a national
leader in providing facilities for the handicapped. Most
theaters and concert halls in
San Francisco are therefore
fully accessible and have open
areas set aside for wheelchair-
users. Some smaller venues
may require the use of special
entrances, or elevators to
reach the upper tiers. Many
movies offer amplifying head-
phones. Contact the theaters
to be sure of their facilities.

The Presidio Cinema

Pac Bell Park, home of the San Francisco Giants (see pp374–5)

Entertainment Venues

With a variety of entertainment options, San Francisco is one of the most enjoyable cities in the world. Whatever your cultural preferences, what you see here is sure to be good. Besides housing the West Coast's best opera and ballet companies, it has a highly regarded symphony orchestra. The city also offers a wide range of jazz and rock music, diverse theater companies, and specialty movie houses. For the sports fan there are also plenty of opportunities to both watch and take part.

FILM AND THEATER

San Francisco has an avid film-going community. One of the city's best movie houses is the **AMC Kabuki**, an eight-screen complex in the Japan Center (*see p342*), which also hosts the **San Francisco International Film Festival** each May. A main venue for first-run foreign films is the **Opera Plaza**. The **Castro** (*see p350*) shows Hollywood classics and other revivals, with a program that changes daily.

For theater goers, major shows are staged at the main Theater District venues (*see p310*). Of the smaller theaters the best is the **Mason Street Theater**. The most respected company is the **American Conservatory Theater (ACT)**, which performs from October to May.

The Geary Theater (*see p310*)

OPERA, CLASSICAL MUSIC, AND DANCE

The main season of the **San Francisco Opera Association** runs from September to December; tickets can cost

Louise M Davies Symphony Hall

more than $100, but there is a summer season, with less expensive tickets.

The main venue for opera, classical music and dance is the Civic Center arts complex on Van Ness Avenue. The **Louise M Davies Symphony Hall** is home to the city's symphony orchestra, which performs up to five concerts a week during its winter season.

The **San Francisco Ballet** season of classical and new works runs from February to April. The Center for the Arts (*see pp312–13*) is home to the **LINES Contemporary Ballet**.

ROCK, JAZZ, AND BLUES

Two of the best rock clubs, **Slim's** and the smaller **Paradise Lounge**, are opposite one another in the SoMa district. Another popular place is the reopened **Fillmore Auditorium**, the legendary birthplace of psychedelic rock during the 1960s (*see p349*).

There are a number of places to hear live jazz, such as **Jazz at Pearl's**. The entertainment is usually free, if you buy dinner or drinks.

Live blues is played in bars such as **The Saloon** and the **Boom Boom**

Banner for the Jazz Festival (*see p34*)

Room. The annual San Francisco Blues Festival (*see p34*) attracts blues bands from all over the country.

CLUBS

San Francisco's largest disco is **Polly Esther's**, with its multiple dance floors, flashy décor, and mainstream clientele. The **Covered Wagon** is also a great place to dance the night away. Some of the most popular clubs are primarily, though rarely exclusively, gay. These include **Endup** and **Rawhide II**, which has square dancing every night.

Piano bars all have nightly live music that you can enjoy for the price of a drink. One of the best is the beautiful Art Deco-style **Top of the Mark** at the top of the Mark Hopkins InterContinental Hotel (*see p523*). **Julie's Supper Club** serves up good live jazz and R&B along with tasty Cajun food. Some of the best stand-up comedy shows take place at **Tommy T's Comedy House** and **Cobb's Comedy Club**.

SPORTS AND OUTDOOR ACTIVITIES

The home ground of the **San Francisco 49ers** is 3 Com Park; the **Oakland Raiders** play at **Network Associates Coliseum** in Oakland. Other football teams are supported by local colleges, the **University of California** at Berkeley (*see p402*) and **Stanford University** (*see p411*). Two professional baseball teams play in the Bay Area, the National League **San Francisco Giants** and the American League **Oakland Athletics**. The Giants play at the new **Pacific Bell Park**, and the Athletics home field is the Network Associates Coliseum.

Golfers have a range of courses to choose from, including the municipal links in **Lincoln Park**. Most of the public swimming pools are situated on the suburban fringes; for details contact the **City of San Francisco Recreation and Parks Department**. To swim in the chilly ocean, head out to China Beach.

There are tennis courts in almost all the public parks in San Francisco, with the largest ones in Golden Gate Park *(see pp356–9)*. **Claremont Resort Spa and Tennis Club** *(see p402)* in Berkeley offers fine courts with unlimited playing time even to non-guests.

Golden Gate Bridge from Lincoln Park golf course

DIRECTORY

FILM AND THEATER

AMC Kabuki
Map 4 E4.
(415) 931-9800.

American Conservatory Theater (ACT)
Map 5 B5.
(415) 749-2228.

Castro
Map 10 D2.
(415) 621-6120.

San Francisco Film Society International Film Festival
(415) 561-5000.
FAX *(415) 551-5099.*
W www.sffs.org

Mason Street Theater
Map 5 B5.
(415) 982-5463.

Opera Plaza
Map 4 F5.
(415) 352-0810.

OPERA, CLASSICAL MUSIC, AND DANCE

LINES Contemporary Ballet
Yerba Buena Center for the Arts,
700 Howard St.
Map 5 C5.
(415) 978-2787.

Louise M Davies Symphony Hall Box Office
201 Van Ness Ave.
Map 4 F5.
(415) 864-6000.

San Francisco Ballet
455 Franklin St.
Map 4 F4.
(415) 861-5600.

San Francisco Opera Association
301 Van Ness Ave.
Map 4 F5.
(415) 861-4008.

San Francisco Symphony Association
201 Van Ness Ave.
Map 4 F5.
(415) 864-6000.

ROCK, JAZZ, AND BLUES

Boom Boom Room
1601 Fillmore St.
Map 10 F2.
(415) 621-1912.

Fillmore Auditorium
1085 Geary at Fillmore St.
Map 4 D4.
(415) 346-6000.

Jazz at Pearl's
256 Columbus Ave.
Map 5 C3.
(415) 291-8255.

Paradise Lounge
308 11th St.
Map 10 F1.
(415) 861-6906.

The Saloon
1232 Grant Ave.
Map 5 C3.
(415) 989-7666.

San Francisco Blues Festival
Fort Mason.
Map 4 E1.
(415) 826-6837.

Slim's
333 11th St.
Map 10 F1.
(415) 255-0333.

CLUBS

Cobb's Comedy Club
The Cannery at
Beach St. **Map** 5 A1.
(415) 928-4320.

Covered Wagon
917 Folsom St.
Map 11 B1.
(415) 974-1585.

Endup
401 6th St.
(415) 357-0827.

Julie's Supper Club
1123 Folsom St.
(415) 861-0707.

Polly Esther's
181 Eddy St.
Map 5 B5.
(415) 885-1977.

Rawhide
280 7th St.
(415) 621-1197.

Tommy T's Comedy House
1655 Willow Pass Rd.
(925) 686-6809.

Top of the Mark
Mark Hopkins
Inter-Continental Hotel.
1 Nob Hill.
Map 5 B4.
(415) 616-6916.

SPORTS AND OUTDOOR ACTIVITIES

Recreation and Parks Department
Tennis Information.
(415) 753-7100.

Swimming Information.
(415) 831-2747.

Lincoln Park
(Municipal 18 hole)
Map 1 C5.
(415) 221-9911.

Oakland Athletics, Oakland Raiders
Network Associates.
Coliseum, Oakland
(800) 949-2626.

San Francisco 49ers
3Com Park.
(415) 656-4900.

San Francisco Giants
Pacific Bell Park
(800) 5-GIANTS.

Stanford University Athletics
Stanford University.
(1 800) 232-8225.

UC Berkeley Intercollegiate Athletics
UC Berkeley.
(1 800) 462-3277.

SHOPPING IN SAN FRANCISCO

SHOPPING in San Francisco is much more than simply making a purchase, it's a whole experience that allows a glimpse into the city's culture. It is the diversity of San Francisco that makes buying anything here an adventure. An enormous range of goods is available, from the practical to the more eccentric, but you can take your time in choosing, since browsers

Clock over entrance to Tiffany's

are generally made to feel welcome, particularly in the many small specialty shops and boutiques of the city. If you want convenience, the numerous shopping centers and department stores are excellent. For those in search of local color, every neighborhood shopping district has a charm and personality of its own, with each reflecting a different aspect of the city.

MALLS AND SHOPPING CENTERS

IN CONTRAST to a great many suburban shopping malls, those of San Francisco have character, and one or two of them are of considerable architectural interest. The Embarcadero Center (see p304) has more than 125 shops, in an area covering eight blocks. Ghirardelli Square (see p327) was a well-known chocolate factory from 1893 until early in the 1960s. It is now a mall that is very popular with visitors, and it houses more than 70 shops and several restaurants, overlooking San Francisco Bay.

The San Francisco Center (see p311) has nine levels and more than 100 shops. Pier 39 (see p326) is a marketplace on the waterfront, with restaurants, a double-decker Venetian merry-go-round, a marina, and many specialty boutiques. In the Cannery (see p327), located at Fisherman's Wharf, you will find a variety of charming small shops. The beautiful

Emporio Armani

Crocker Galleria (see p310) is one of the city's most spectacular malls, with three floors set under a high glass dome built around a central plaza.

The Japan Center (see p342), complete with pagoda, offers exotic foods, goods, and art from the East, as well as a Japanese-style hotel and traditional baths. The Rincon Center (see p307), with a 90-ft (27-m) water column at its center, is an Art Deco haven for shopping and eating.

DEPARTMENT STORES

MOST OF San Francisco's major department stores are in or near Union Square. They are huge retail stores that offer their customers an outstanding selection of goods and services.

Macy's department store spans two city blocks. It stocks an enormous range of goods, all beautifully presented and sold by enthusiastic sales people. It offers a wide range of extra facilities, including a currency exchange and an interpreting service. The men's department is particularly extensive.

Neiman Marcus is another stylish emporium. Its modern building caused a furor when it was opened in 1982, replacing a popular store built in the 1890s. The huge stained-glass dome in its Rotunda Restaurant was part of the original building and is well worth coming to see.

Nordstrom, known for its fashion and shoes, is often called the "store-in-the-sky"; it is located in the top five floors of the innovative San Francisco Shopping Center.

Flags flying in front of the pagoda at the Japan Center

SHOPPING AROUND UNION SQUARE

SERIOUS SHOPPERS should concentrate on the blocks bordered by Geary, Powell, and Post Streets, and on the surrounding blocks between Market and Sutter Streets. Here luxurious shops and inexpensive boutiques sell anything from designer bed linens to pedigree dogs to souvenirs. Exclusive hotels, chic restaurants, and colorful flower stalls all add to the fashionable atmosphere.

SHOPS FOR A GOOD CAUSE

SAN FRANCISCANS take great pleasure in shopping for a good cause. The **Planet-weavers Treasure Store** is the official UNICEF shop, where crafts and clothes made in developing countries are sold, as well as educational toys from around the world.

Flower stall on Union Square

UNICEF receives 25 percent of net profits. The **Golden Gate National Park Store** offers gifts and memorabilia; proceeds go to all national parks, including Golden Gate National Park. All the profits that are made at **Under One Roof** benefit the various groups set up to help combat AIDS. Those who want to protect the environment head for the **Greenpeace Store**, which sells jewelry, prints, and a variety of other gifts.

SOUVENIRS

MANY SOUVENIRS, such as T-shirts, keyrings, mugs, and Christmas ornaments, are decorated with motifs symbolizing San Francisco at **Only in San Francisco** and the **Bay Company**. Souvenir and novelty hats of every color, size, and shape are available at **Krazy Kaps**, while the store entrances on Grant Avenue *(see p319)* and Fisherman's Wharf *(see pp324–5)* are lined with baskets filled with inexpensive gifts.

BEST BUYS

GOURMET SHOPPERS should look for seafood, one of the city's specialties. Wine from the Napa Valley *(see pp446–7)* is another good buy. You will find blue jeans at competitive prices, also vintage clothing, ethnic art, books, and records.

SHOPPING TOURS

SHOPPERS who want to be guided to the best shops for their own particular needs can go on a special tour, organized by companies such as **A Simple Elegance Shopping Tour** or **Shopper Stopper Shopping Tours**. A guide takes you from shop to shop to find unusual items.

MUSEUMS

MUSEUM SHOPPING offers exquisite gifts to suit all budgets. Among the city's best are the **Academy Store** in the California Academy of Sciences *(see pp360–61)*, the **Museum Store** at the Palace of the Legion of Honor, *(see pp364–5)*, and the **San Francisco MOMA Museum Store** *(see pp308–9)*.

Grant Avenue, Chinatown

San Francisco Specials

ENTREPRENEURIAL SPIRIT in San Francisco is strong and innovative, and the city's sophisticated image is very much deserved. Whether it is a small souvenir, a designer outfit, an antique, or a mouthwatering snack that is required, visitors will never be disappointed amid the shops and markets of San Francisco. The city is also home to many dedicated "foodies," gastronomes whose liking for fine wine and gourmet meals have resulted in unusual and delicious grocery stores. All this creates an environment that makes shopping in San Francisco an exciting experience.

SPECIALTY SHOPS

IF YOU WANT to laugh, go to **Smile–A Gallery with Tongue in Chic**, where humorous art to wear or display is sold, including many objects made by Bay Area artists. **Malm Luggage** has sold luggage, briefcases, and leather goods since the Gold Rush days. You can describe the city's attractions on a designer card from **Flax Art and Design**, a sixty-year-old business offering a huge selection of hand-made papers, artists' tools, and customised stationery. The city's main toy shop, **FAO Schwartz**, is a three-floor fantasy world for children.

Doorman at FAO Schwartz

CLOTHES

SAN FRANCISCO designer shops include **Diana Slavin** for classics, **Joanie Char**'s for sportswear, and **Wilkes Bashford** for up-and-coming designs. **Levi Strauss & Co** has been in business since 1853, offering a broad range of clothes, all of which can be worn with their famous jeans (*see p333*). For discount designer clothes, head to the trendy SoMa district.

Brooks Brothers is well known for its conservative men's suits and button-down shirts. Fashionable outdoor clothing is available from **Eddie Bauer**.

Small Frys is the locals' favorite for cotton children's clothes, and **Nike Town** is a megastore for training shoes, with televised sporting events to entertain shoppers.

BOOKS, MUSIC, ART, AND ANTIQUES

THE LARGEST independent bookshop in the city is **A Clean Well-Lighted Place for Books**, carrying the latest titles, plus classics and works by local authors. Beats once met to talk about the country's emerging 1960s social revolution at the **City Lights Bookstore** (*see pp330–31*), which stays open late and is a famous San Francisco institution.

A wide selection of music is offered at various branches of **Tower Records** and the **Virgin Megastore**. More obscure music can usually be found at **Recycled Records**.

Art lovers will find something to their liking in the city's hundreds of galleries. The **John Berggruen Gallery** has the city's largest collection of works by both emerging and more established artists. **Eleonore Austerer Gallery** sells limited edition prints by such modern masters as Picasso, Matisse, and Miró. For a local perspective, pay a visit to **SF Artisan's Gallery** for the Art Nouveau period and the early California artists.

Jackson Square is San Francisco's main area for antiques (*see p304*).

Last touches in the Cookie Factory

FOOD AND WINE

FROM ABALONE to zucchini, and from fresh California produce to imported specialty foods, the gourmet grocery **Whole Foods** carries a wide variety of items. **Williams-Sonoma** has jams, mustards, and much more for gifts or as a special treat. The Italian **Molinari Delicatessen** is famous for its fresh ravioli and tortellini, ready to throw into a saucepan. It is well worth going to Chinatown (*see pp316–17*) for Far Eastern

City Lights Bookstore (*see p330*) on Columbus Avenue

food products. The district's produce stores have the feel of an exotic farmers' market and are open every day. For an authentic atmosphere of Chinatown go to the **Golden Gate Fortune Cookie Company** *(see p316)* where customers can sample the famous San Francisco Chinatown invention. At **Casa Lucas Market** you will find a variety of Spanish and Latin American food specialties. A baguette of fresh sourdough bread from **Boudin Bakery** is a long-standing addiction with locals and a tradition with visitors. Chocoholics are catered to at San Francisco's own **Ghirardelli's**.

San Franciscans are coffee connoisseurs, and there are many specialty houses. **Caffè Trieste** is the city's oldest coffee house and sells a range of custom-roasted and blended coffees and a variety of brewing equipment.

The **Napa Valley Winery Exchange** features selections from the many Californian wineries, including the smaller local producers.

Locally grown fruit and vegetables arrive by the truckload at the regular farmers' markets in the center of the city. Stalls are erected for the day, and the farmers sell their goods directly to the public. The **Heart of the City** is open on Wednesdays and Sundays from 7am to 5pm, and **Ferry Plaza Farmers' Market** is held on Saturdays from 9am to 2pm.

Ghirardelli Square, home to San Francisco's famous chocolate

DIRECTORY

SPECIALTY SHOPS

FAO Schwartz
48 Stockton St.
Map 5 C5.
℡ *(415) 394-8700.*

Flax Art and Design
1699 Market St.
Map 10 F1.
℡ *(415) 522-2355.*

Malm Luggage
222 Grant Ave.
Map 5 C4.
℡ *(415) 392-0417.*

Smile–A Gallery with Tongue in Chic
500 Sutter St.
Map 5 B4.
℡ *(415) 362-3436.*

CLOTHES

Brooks Brothers
201 Post St.
Map 5 C4.
℡ *(415) 397-4500.*

Diana Slavin
3 Claude Lane.
Map 5 C4.
℡ *(415) 677-9939.*

Eddie Bauer
250 Post St. **Map** 5 C4.
℡ *(415) 986-7600.*

Joanie Char
285A Sutter St.
Map 5 C4.
℡ *(415) 399-9867.*

Levi Strauss & Co
250 Valencia St.
Map 10 F1.
℡ *(415) 565-9159.*

Nike Town
278 Post St. **Map** 5 C4.
℡ *(415) 392-6453.*

Small Frys
4066 24th St.
Map 10 D4.
℡ *(415) 648-3954.*

Wilkes Bashford
375 Sutter St. **Map** 5 C4.
℡ *(415) 986-4380.*

BOOKS, MUSIC, ART, AND ANTIQUES

SF Artisan's Gallery
2 Embarcadero. **Map** 6 D3.
℡ *(415) 388-2044.*

City Lights Bookstore
261 Columbus Ave.
Map 5 C3.
℡ *(415) 362-8193.*

A Clean Well-Lighted Place for Books
601 Van Ness Avenue.
Map 4 F5.
℡ *(415) 441-6670.*

Eleonore Austerer Gallery
540 Sutter St.
Map 5 B4.
℡ *(415) 986-2244.*

John Berggruen Gallery
228 Grant Ave.
Map 5 C4.
℡ *(415) 781-4629.*

Recycled Records
1377 Haight St.
Map 9 C1.
℡ *(415) 626-4075.*

Tower Records
Columbus Ave & Bay St.
Map 5 A2.
℡ *(415) 885-0500.*
One of several branches.

Virgin Megastore
Stockton St. & Market St.
Map 5 C5.
℡ *(415) 397-4525.*
One of several branches.

FOOD AND WINE

Boudin Bakery
4 Embarcadero Center.
Map 6 D3.
℡ *(415) 362-3330.*

Caffè Trieste
601 Vallejo St. **Map** 5 C3.
℡ *(415) 982-2605.*

Casa Lucas Market
2934 24th St. **Map** 9 C3.
℡ *(415) 826-4334.*

Ferry Plaza Farmers' Market
Market St at the Embarcadero. **Map** 6 D3.

Ghirardelli's
Ghirardelli Square.
Map 4 F1.
℡ *(415) 474-3938.*

44 Stockton St.
Map 5 C1.
℡ *(415) 397-3615.*

Golden Gate Fortune Cookie Company
56 Ross Alley.
Map 5 C3.
℡ *(415) 781-3956.*

Heart of the City Farmers' Market
United Nations Plaza.
Map 10 A1.
℡ *(415) 558-9455.*

Molinari Delicatessen
373 Columbus Ave.
Map 5 C3.
℡ *(415) 421-2337.*

Napa Valley Winery Exchange
415 Taylor St. **Map** 5 B5.
℡ *(415) 771-2887.*

Whole Foods
1765 California St.
Map 4 F4.
℡ *(415) 674-0500.*

Williams-Sonoma
150 Post St. **Map** 5 C4
℡ *(415) 362-6904.*

GETTING AROUND
SAN FRANCISCO

S AN FRANCISCO occupies a compact area, making it a sightseer's dream. Many of the sights featured on visitors' itineraries are only a short walk from each other. The public transportation system is also easy to use and efficient. Few visitors can resist a cable car ride. Bus routes crisscross town and pass many attractions. Muni Metro streetcars and BART lines serve the suburbs and the outlying neighborhoods. Taxis are affordable and recommended (but often hard to find) for trips after dark or during the day through certain areas. Passenger ferries and boat trips run regularly east and north across the bay. If driving in San Francisco see page 603 for details on the city's parking laws.

Do not cross the street   **You may cross the street**

WALKING IN SAN FRANCISCO

T HE BEST WAY to explore San Francisco is on foot. The main tourist areas are within 15 to 20 minutes of each other walking at average speed. The hills can be a struggle, but the views over the city and the bay make them well worth the strenuous climb.

Most road intersections are marked with a green and white sign bearing the name of the cross street, or names are imprinted in the concrete pavement at street corners.

Vehicles are driven on the right-hand side of the road and are allowed to turn right on a red light if the road is clear, so be careful when crossing at traffic lights. Never rely solely on a pedestrian "Walk" signal.

Jaywalking is common but illegal. Using a crossing when the "Don't Walk" signal is showing can result in a minimum $50 fine.

TAKING A TAXI

T AXIS IN SAN FRANCISCO are licensed and operate 24 hours a day. To catch a cab, wait at a taxi stand, call for a pick-up, or hail a cab when its rooftop sign is illuminated.

There is a flat fee (about $2.00) for the first mile (1.6 km). This increases by about $2 for each additional mile or 35 cents a minute while waiting at an address or in heavy traffic. Pay with bills of $20 or smaller and add a 15 percent tip onto the fare.

BICYCLING

C YCLING IS VERY popular in San Francisco, and it is possible to find routes that avoid hills, especially along the waterfront. Bicycles can be rented for around $25 a day or $125 a week. There are cycle lanes in parts of the city, and some buses are equipped to carry bikes strapped to the outside. Details of scenic routes in the area are available from **Start to Finish** and **Wheel Escapes**.

OTHER WAYS TO GET AROUND

P EDICABS and horse-drawn carriages can be found on The Embarcadero, especially near Fisherman's Wharf (*see* *pp324–5*). A fleet of motorized cable cars dash around the city giving guided tours of all the sights, and passengers can get on or off where they choose. Sightseeing coach tours are offered as either half- or full-day excursions.

Pedicabs are popular

Pedestrian crossing

Traveling by Bus and Muni Metro Streetcar

SAN FRANCISCO MUNICIPAL RAILWAY, or Muni as it is more commonly called, is the organization that runs the city's public transportation system. You can use one interchangeable pass – Muni Passport – to travel on Muni buses, Muni Metro streetcars (electric trams), and the three cable car lines. Buses and streetcars serve most tourist attractions and all neighborhoods.

FARES AND TICKETS

BUSES AND STREETCARS both cost $1 per ride; for this fare, you can request a free transfer allowing you to change vehicles twice within two hours. There is a supplement for express or limited-stop buses. Reduced fares are available for both senior citizens and children aged 5 to 17. Children under 5 travel free.

If you are planning to make a number of trips by Muni, a Muni Passport, valid for 1, 3, or 7 days, allows unlimited travel on the city's buses, streetcars, and cable cars. Muni passports are available from the information kiosk at City Hall (see p343), the **Visitors' Information Center**, and the Muni kiosk situated at the Powell–Hyde cable car turntable (see p311).

USING BUSES AND STREETCARS

BUSES STOP only at their designated bus stops, placed every two or three blocks. The route number and the destination are printed on the front and side of each bus. Route numbers that are followed by a letter (L, EX, A, B, etc.) are express services.

On boarding, put the exact change or tokens in the fare box or show your Muni Passport to the driver. To indicate that you want to

A Muni Metro streetcar

Muni Passports

get off at the next stop, pull the cord that runs along the windows or inform the driver. The "Stop Requested" sign above the front window will light up. Bus stops are indicated by signs displaying the Muni logo. Route numbers of buses that stop there are listed below the sign, and route maps and timetables are located on the inside walls of bus shelters. Along Market Street routes alternate between stops at the curb or at islands in the street.

Muni Metro streetcars and BART trains (see p382) both use the same underground terminals along Market Street. Orange, yellow, and white illuminated signs mark their entrances. Once you are inside the terminal, look for the separate "Muni" entrance.

To travel to the west of the city, choose "Outbound"; to travel east, choose "Downtown." Electronic signs indicate which streetcar is about

to arrive. Doors open automatically on boarding; push the bar by the door when exiting. Stops above ground level have an orange-and-brown flag or a yellow band around a pole, marked "Muni" or "Car Stop."

SIGHTSEEING BY BUS

POPULAR BUS ROUTES for visitors include numbers 8, 15, 30, 32, 39, and 45. Route 38 runs to the hills above Ocean Beach, and Golden Gate Park (see pp356–9) is on route No. 21. For Chinatown and Nob Hill (see pp314–21) take Route 45; for Haight Ashbury and the Mission District (see pp344–53) take Route 8. The Bay Area (see pp394–415) can be reached within 30 to 45 minutes, depending on traffic.

A Muni "Tours of Discovery" sightseeing brochure is available from the Muni office itself or the city's **Visitors' Information Center**.

Muni bus shelter with pay phones

DIRECTORY

MUNI INFORMATION

☎ (415) 673-6864.
Ⓦ www.sfmuni.com

MUNI PASSPORTS

Visitors' Information Center
Hallidie Plaza. **Map** 5 C5.
☎ (415) 391-2000.
Ⓦ www.transitinfo.org

A Muni bus

Traveling by Cable Car, BART, and Ferry

SAN FRANCISCO's cable cars are world famous (see pp292–3) and every visitor will want to ride one at least once. San Francisco peninsula and the East Bay are linked by BART (Bay Area Rapid Transit), a 71-mile (114-km) light rail system with a high speed, efficient fleet of trains, all wheelchair accessible. Boats and passenger ferries are also a favorite way to see the city's shoreline and get around.

Riding down Hyde Street to the bay

USING THE CABLE CARS

THE CITY'S CABLE CAR service operates from 6:30am to 12:30am daily. There is a flat fare of about $2 for each journey. Cable cars run along three routes. The name of the line is displayed on the front, back, and sides of every cable car. The Powell–Hyde line is the most popular, starting at the Powell and Market turntable (see p311) and ending on Hyde Street, near Aquatic Park. The Powell–Mason line also begins at Powell and Market streets and ends at Bay Street. Sit facing east on the Powell

lines and you will see the best sights as you travel. The California line runs from the base of Market Street, then through part of the Financial District and Chinatown, ending at Van Ness Avenue. Cable cars run at 15-minute intervals.

To catch a cable car, you should be prepared to jump on board quickly. Stops are marked by maroon signs that display the outline of a cable car in white, or by a yellow line painted on the road at right angles to the track.

If you have not already purchased a Muni Passport (see p381), either pay the conductor on board the car or buy a souvenir ticket. These are available at ticket machines or a booth at the terminus, shops along the route, Muni kiosks, or at the city Visitor Information Center (see p381). Tickets are collected by the conductor when you board. Fares are for a single trip only.

Commuters like to use cable cars too, so try to avoid traveling during rush hours. Whenever you travel you are more likely to get a seat if you board the car at the end of the line you have chosen.

Cable car ticket machine

Nob Hill, main cable car junction

SIGHTSEEING BY CABLE CAR

THE CITY'S HILLS present no problem to the cable cars. They tackle precipitous slopes effortlessly, passing sights and areas popular with tourists. The most thrilling descent is the final stretch of the Powell–Hyde line as it dips down from Nob Hill to the bay.

TRAVELING SAFELY IN A CABLE CAR

IF THERE IS NOT a crowd, you can choose whether to sit or stand inside, sit outside on a bench, or stand on a side running board. Wherever you find a place, hold on tight.

Try not to get in the way of the gripman; he needs a lot of room to operate the grip lever. This off-limits area is marked by yellow lines on the floor. Use caution while on board. Passing other cable cars is exciting, but be careful not to lean out too far because they get very close to one another. Be careful when boarding or getting off. Often cable cars stop at an intersection, and you have to get on or off between the car and other vehicles. All passengers must get off at the end of the line.

USEFUL NUMBERS

Cable Car Barn
1201 Mason St. **Map** 5 B3.
((415) 474-1887.

Muni Information
((415) 673-6864. Cable car information, fares, Muni Passports.

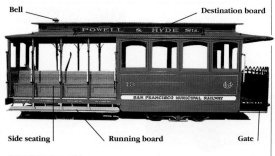

Bell ——— Destination board

POWELL & HYDE Sts.

13

SAN FRANCISCO MUNICIPAL RAILWAY

Side seating | Running board | Gate

A San Francisco cable car

MAKING A JOURNEY BY BART

The BART logo

BART trains operate daily from early morning until midnight. During rush hours, 7am to 9am and 4pm to 7pm, they run at full capacity. The trains are clean and well kept, and the service is efficient.

BART trains stop at five city center stations, all beneath Market Street – Van Ness, Civic Center, Powell, Montgomery, and Embarcadero – but glide above ground in the majority of outlying areas.

All trains from Daly City stop at city center stations before heading for the East Bay through a dark, 4-mile (6-km) underwater tunnel.

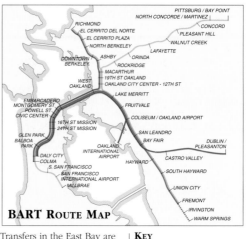

BART ROUTE MAP

Transfers in the East Bay are best done at two stations: MacArthur and Oakland City.

To explore the BART system without buying a new ticket for each trip, you can buy an excursion fare. All BART stations have personnel on hand to assist passengers.

KEY

— Colma–Richmond Line

— Millbrae–Bay Point Line

— Daly City–Fremont Line

— Richmond–Fremont Line

— Daly City–Pleasanton Line

FERRY SERVICES AND BAY TRIPS

RESIDENTS OF THE Bay Area adore their ferries, and they are used as much by local commuters to and from the city as they are by tourists. Although these ferries do not have audio tours to point out and describe the sights, they are less expensive than sightseeing cruises. The Ferry Building (*see p306*) is the terminal for **Golden Gate Ferries**.

Bay sightseeing cruises from Fisherman's Wharf are operated by **Blue & Gold Fleet** and **Red & White Fleet**. Trips offered include Angel Island, Alcatraz (*see pp328–9*), and towns that lie on the north shore of the bay (*see pp398–9*). There are also combined boat and bus tours to Six Flags Marine World and Muir Woods (*see p398*).

You can dine and dance aboard one of several cruisers that ply the bay's waters.

Sign for bay cruise tickets

Hornblower Dining Yachts offer lunch on Friday, brunch on weekends, and dinner daily on their cruises. Meals are also served at bayside tables that offer diners spectacular views of the waterfront. The **Oceanic Society** offers trips with an onboard naturalist around the Farallon Islands, 25 miles (40 km) off San Francisco (*see pp396–7*). Whale-watching expeditions off the city's west

coast (*see p580*) are also available. Check with individual operators for seasonal details.

Red & White Fleet ferry

DIRECTORY

FERRIES

Golden Gate Ferries
((415) 923-2000.

Red & White Fleet
Pier 41 & 43½.
Map 5 B1.
((415) 447-0597,
or (1 888) 732-3483.
45-minute tour.

BAY TRIPS

Blue & Gold Fleet
Pier 39. **Map** 5 B1.
((415) 773-1188.
75-minute tour.

Hornblower Dining Yachts
Pier 33. **Map** 5 C1.
((415) 394-8900, ext. 7.

Oceanic Society Expeditions
((415) 441-1104.

SAN FRANCISCO STREET FINDER

MAP REFERENCES given with sights, entertainment venues, shops and Practical Information addresses described in the San Francisco section refer to the maps on the following pages. Map references for hotels and restaurants in the city (see pp523–9 and pp560–68) also apply to these pages. The key map below shows the are covered by the Streetfinder, including the sightseeing areas and othe districts important for restaurant hotels, and entertainment venues. large scale map of the city cente appears on pages 5 and 6. The symbols used on the Street Finder map are listed in the key below.

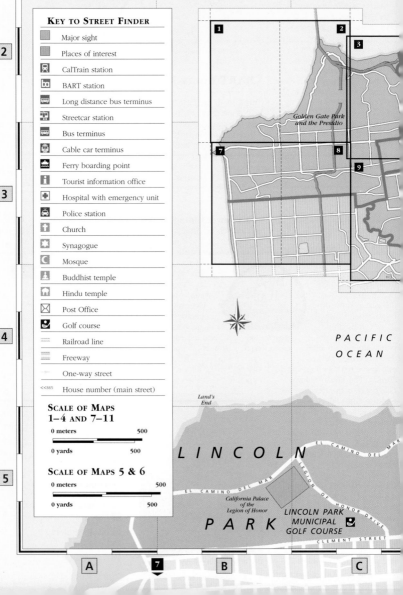

KEY TO STREET FINDER	
	Major sight
	Places of interest
🚃	CalTrain station
🚇	BART station
🚌	Long distance bus terminus
🚋	Streetcar station
🚍	Bus terminus
🚠	Cable car terminus
⚓	Ferry boarding point
🅸	Tourist information office
✚	Hospital with emergency unit
🚓	Police station
✝	Church
✡	Synagogue
☪	Mosque
卍	Buddhist temple
🛕	Hindu temple
⊠	Post Office
⛳	Golf course
═══	Railroad line
▬▬	Freeway
→	One-way street
<<665	House number (main street)

SCALE OF MAPS 1–4 AND 7–11

0 meters   500

0 yards   500

SCALE OF MAPS 5 & 6

0 meters   500

0 yards   500

Golden Gate Park and the Presidio

PACIFIC OCEAN

Land's End

LINCOLN PARK

EL CAMINO DEL MAR

California Palace of the Legion of Honor

LINCOLN PARK MUNICIPAL GOLF COURSE

CLEMENT STREET

1

Alcatraz
Island

2

San Francisco
Bay

Pier 19

Pier 17

Pier 15

Pier 9

Pier 7

Pier 5

Pier 3

Pier 1

DAVIS STREET

THE EMBARCADERO

DRUM STREET

EMBARCADERO
PLAZA PARK

JUSTIN
HERMAN
PLAZA

World Trade Center

Pier 2

Ferry Building

3

cadero Center

FRONT ST

DAVIS ST

STEUART STREET

Hyatt Regency
Hotel

Embarcadero
Station

Rincon
Center

SPEAR STREET

MAIN STREET

STEUART STREET

Pier 24

MISSION STREET

BEALE STREET

HOWARD STREET

1ST STREET

FREMONT STREET

Folsom
Station

4

Amtrak
Terminal
Ticket

Greyhound
Bus Depot

Transbay
Terminal

FOLSOM STREET

ELMART ST

Pier 26

Pier 28

TEHAMA STREET

CLEMENTINA ST

GROTE

GUY PL

LANSING ST

ESSEX ST

FOLSOM STREET

Pier 30

Pier 32

THE EMBARCADERO

5

m of
a Art

HAWTHORNE STREET

DON PL

HAMPTON PL

VERONICA PL

HARRISON STREET

STILLMAN ST

BRYAN

RINCON ST

DE BOOM ST

BRANNAN STREET

1ST STREET

Brannan
Station

Pier 34

Pier 36

Pier 38

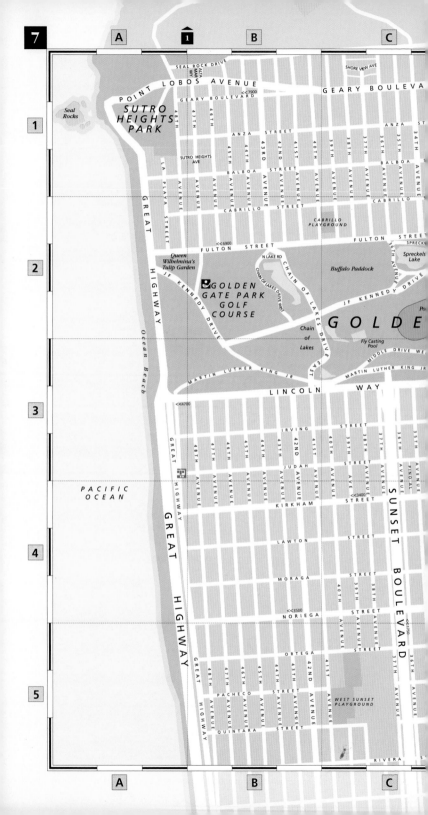

7

A   B   C

SEAL ROCK DRIVE
ALTA
MAR
WY

POINT LOBOS AVENUE

SHORE VIEW AVE

GEARY BOULEVA

Seal
Rocks

SUTRO
HEIGHTS
PARK

GEARY BOULEVARD

<<7900

48TH

47TH

46TH

45TH

44TH

43RD

42ND

41ST

40TH

39TH

38TH

37TH

36TH

35TH

34TH

AVENUE

ANZA

ST

1

SUTRO HEIGHTS
AVE

ANZA

STREET

LA
PLAYA
STREET

BALBOA

AVENUE

AVENUE

STREET

BALBOA

S

CABRILLO

STREET

CABRILLO

CABRILLO
PLAYGROUND

FULTON

STREET

FULTON

STREET

SPRECKE

<<6900

2

G R E A T

H I G H W A Y

Queen
Wilhelmina's
Tulip Garden

JF KENNEDY DRIVE

N LAKE RD

CHAIN OF LAKES DRIVE WEST

Buffalo Paddock

42ND AVENUE

Spreckels
Lake

GOLDEN
GATE PARK
GOLF
COURSE

Chain
of
Lakes

CHAIN OF LAKES DRIVE EAST

JF KENNEDY DRIVE

G O L D E

Po

Ocean Beach

Fly Casting
Pool

MIDDLE DRIVE WE

MARTIN LUTHER KING JR

MARTIN LUTHER KING JR

LINCOLN

WAY

<<4700

3

PACIFIC
OCEAN

G R E A T

H I G H W A Y

48TH

47TH

46TH

45TH

44TH

43RD

42ND

41ST

40TH

39TH

38TH

37TH

36TH

35TH

AVENUE

IRVING

STREET

AVENUE

AVE

AVENUE

AVENUE

JUDAH

STREET

PINO AL

<<3400

KIRKHAM

STREET

LAWTON

STREET

4

MORAGA

STREET

40TH

39TH

38TH

AVENUE

<<3500

NORIEGA

STREET

37TH

36TH

SUNSET   BOULEVARD

<<1750

ORTEGA

STREET

48TH

47TH

46TH

45TH

44TH

43RD

42ND

41ST

AVENUE

STREET

37TH

36TH

AVENUE

5

PACHECO

STREET

AVENUE

WEST SUNSET
PLAYGROUND

G R E A T   H I G H W A Y

QUINTARA

STREET

RIVERA

A   B   C

THE BAY AREA

MANY OF THE SETTLEMENTS encircling San Francisco Bay were once summer retreats for the city's residents, but today they are sprawling suburbs or cities in their own right. Two of the most popular destinations in the East Bay are Oakland's museum and harbor and Berkeley's gardens and famous university. Farther south, San Jose has emerged as the region's newest commercial and cultural center, combining the technology of Silicon Valley with fine museums and preserved architecture of its Spanish Colonial past. Smaller towns such as Tiburon, Pescadero, and Sausalito, however, have managed to retain their village atmosphere, despite their closeness to the city. The area also has the advantage of its coastal landscapes: the cliffs of Point Reyes and the Marin Headlands, with their abundance of wildlife, offer perfect afternoon retreats away from the metropolis.

**Detail from
Sather Gate, Berkeley**

SIGHTS AT A GLANCE

Historic Towns
Benicia **8**
Berkeley **9**
Livermore **13**
Oakland **10**
Pescadero **16**
San Jose **17**
Sausalito **5**
Tiburon **6**

Theme Parks
Six Flags
  Marine World **7**

Historic Buildings
Filoli **15**
Stanford University **14**
Tao House **11**

Parks and Beaches
John Muir National Historic
  Site **2**
Marin Headlands **4**
Mount Diablo State Park **12**
Muir Woods and Beach **3**
Point Reyes National
  Seashore **1**

| 0 kilometers | 25 |
| 0 miles | 25 |

KEY

- Central San Francisco
- Urban areas
- Airport
- Amtrak station
- Major road
- Minor road

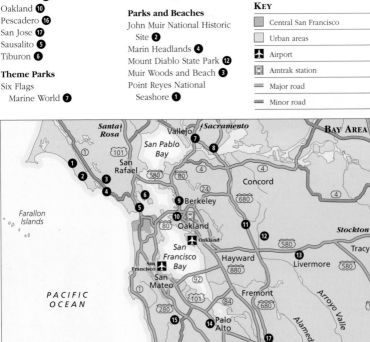

◁ **Houseboats in the picturesque town of Sausalito**

The Bay Area Coastline

THE COASTLINE AROUND San Francisco varies a great deal, its rugged cliffs alternating with sandy beaches. Since the ocean water hovers around 60° F (15° C) all year, nobody swims or surfs without a wet suit, but for sunbathing or aimless beachcombing strolls, the Bay Area beaches are hard to beat. Much of the coast is protected by a series of state and federal parks, such as the Point Reyes National Seashore *(see p398)*, the Marin Headlands section of the Golden Gate National Recreation Area *(pp400–401)*, and the many state beaches that line the southern coast.

Tomales Road

① *Point Reyes Station*

Pacifica *was once the agricultural outpost of Mission Dolores* (see p351). *The two-story Sanchez Adobe in the town now houses a museum of 19th-century farming equipment.*

★ Point Reyes National Seashore ①
This protected stretch of land is noted for its diverse ecosystems and its 360 species of birds *(see p398)*.

Bolinas ②
Following the Gold Rush *(see pp44–5)*, Bolinas became a summer haven for San Franciscans, and some Victorian buildings still survive. The town is also a winter home to monarch butterflies.

Marin Headlands ④
The Marin Headlands benefit from stunning views of San Francisco as well as a wilderness rife with diverse birdlife *(see pp400–401)*.

Treasure Island ⑥
At the center of the Bay Bridge *(see pp406–407)*, the island was the site of the 1939 World's Fair. Connected to Yerba Buena Island, Treasure Island is now an upscale community.

Fort Funston ⑦
The bluff overlooking this beach, which is also used as an observation site, is a favorite launch site for professional and amateur hang gliders.

Colma ⑧
This unusual town consists almost entirely of cemeteries, containing the graves of former San Franciscans and Bay Area residents. Cemeteries are prohibited within the city of San Francisco.

Pillar Point Harbor ⑨
This is the only naturally protected harbor located between San Francisco and Santa Cruz. In the late 19th century it was used as a whaling station.

⑫

★ Farallon Islands ⑫
Twenty-seven miles (44 km) west of Point Bonita, the islands are the most important nesting site for sea birds and stopover point for migratory birds in California. They are also a breeding ground for elephant seals. There is no public access.

Muir Woods National Monument *is the last remaining redwood forest in the Bay Area. The others were cut down for lumber during the 19th century (see p398).*

Mount Tamalpais, reaching a height of 2,604 ft (794 m), is the habitat of various flora and fauna, including the rarely sighted mountain lion. The Mountain Theater is set in a natural bowl overlooking the bay.

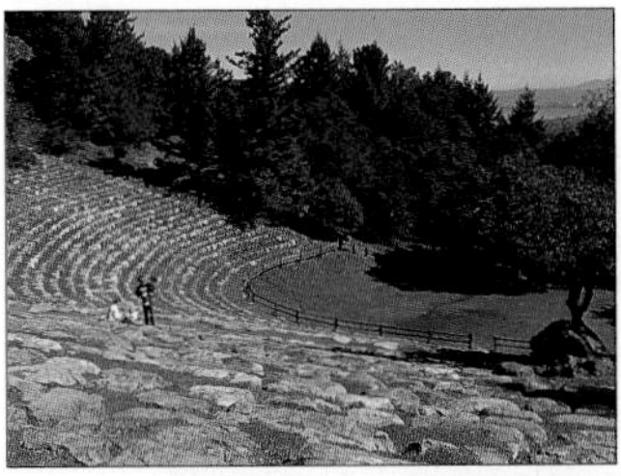

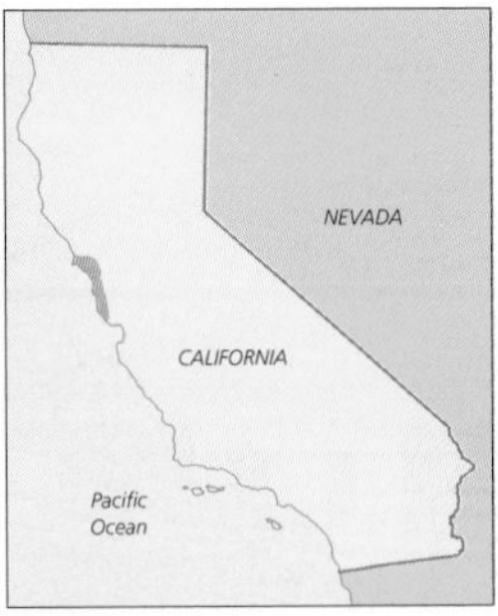

Locator Map

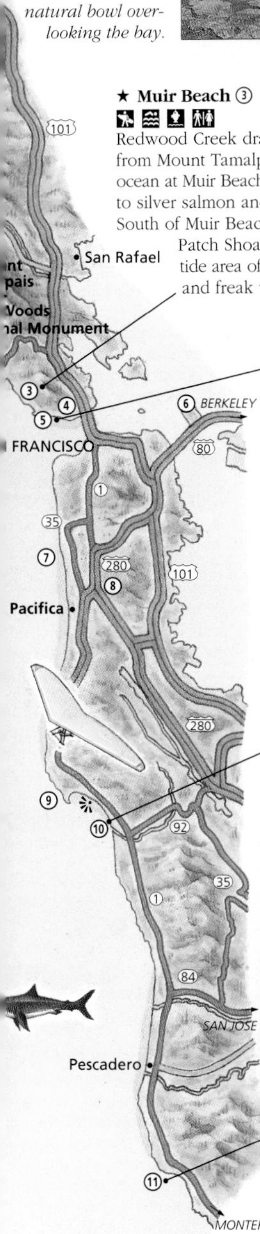

★ Muir Beach [3]

🏄 🌊 ⛑ 🚻

Redwood Creek drains down from Mount Tamalpais to the ocean at Muir Beach. It is home to silver salmon and crayfish. South of Muir Beach, Potato Patch Shoal is a low-tide area of turbulence and freak waves.

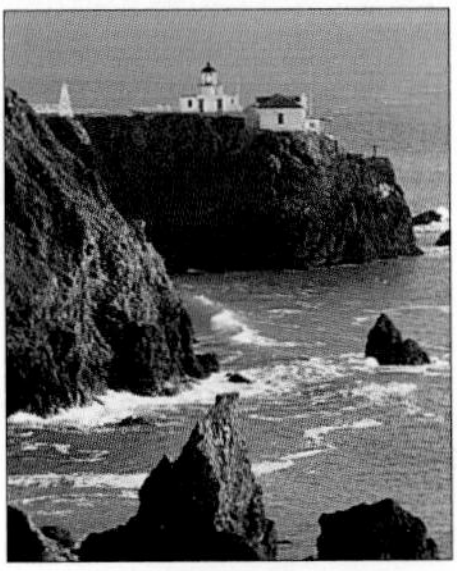

★ Point Bonita [5]

Point Bonita's lighthouse on this rugged clifftop was the last manually operated lighthouse in the state, only changing to automation in 1980. The lighthouse is reached via a tunnel carved through solid rock or over a surf-lashed bridge.

★ Half Moon Bay [10]

🏄 🌊 ⛑ ♿ 🚻 ✋

The oldest town in San Mateo County, the area's soil is ideal for growing artichokes, broccoli, and pumpkins. The town holds a pumpkin festival each October in celebration of its prime crop.

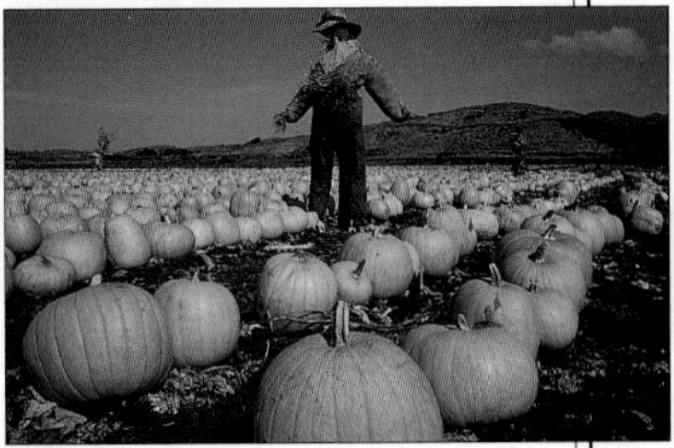

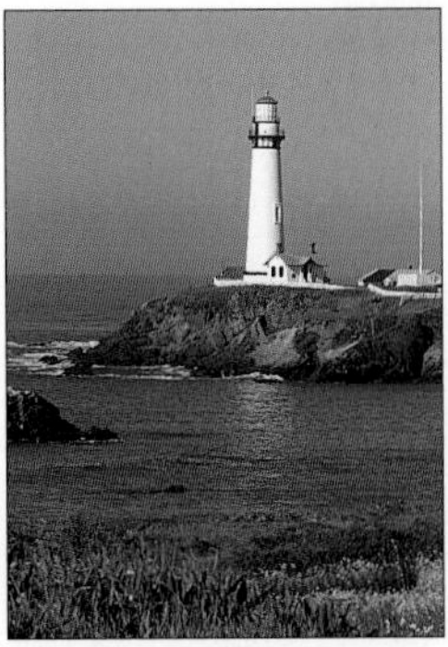

★ Pigeon Point [11]

🏄 🌊 ⛑

Following numerous shipwrecks in the area, including the *Carrier Pigeon,* which gave the area its name, a 115-ft (35-m) lighthouse was erected in 1872. Sea lions can often be spotted offshore.

0 kilometers 10

0 miles 10

Key

Freeway

Major road

Minor road

River

Viewpoint

Dairy farm at picturesque Point Reyes

Point Reyes National Seashore ❶

Road map A3. 🚌 *from San Rafael Center (weekends only).* **Bear Valley Visitors' Center** *Bear Valley Rd, main entrance to National Seashore, Point Reyes.* ☎ *(415) 464-5100.* ◯ *9am–5pm daily.*

THIS TRIANGULAR-SHAPED area of land, only half attached to the San Franciscan coastline, has been gradually drifting northward along the California coast for more than six million years.

POINT REYES
NATIONAL SEASHORE
United States Department of the Interior
National Park Service
Signpost to Point Reyes

Situated due west of the San Andreas Fault, the peninsula moved a full 20 ft (6 m) north of the mainland during the 1906 earthquake *(see pp48–9).* A displaced fence on the Earthquake Trail near Bear Valley Visitor Center is evidence of this overnight movement. The visitors' center itself contains interesting displays on local geology and geography and supplies and trail maps for hikers.

A notable feature of this stretch of coastline is its abundance of wildlife, including a herd of tule elk. The area has cattle and dairy ranches, and three small towns: Point Reyes Station, Olema, and Inverness.

Drake's Bay is named after the English explorer Sir Francis Drake, who is thought to have anchored here in 1579. He named the land Nova Albion and briefly claimed it for England *(see pp42–3).*

John Muir National Historic Site ❷

4202 Alhambra Ave, Martinez. ☎ *(925) 228-8860.* ◯ *10am–4:30pm Wed–Sun.* ⬤ *Jan 1, Thanksgiving, Dec 25.* 🎟 ♿ *1st floor & grounds only.*

SET AMID the suburban neighborhood of Martinez, the John Muir National Historic Site preserves the home where the naturalist and writer lived from 1890 until his death in 1914. The 17-room Italianate house is typical of a late Victorian upper-middle-class dwelling, conveying little of Muir's simple tastes and back-to-nature inclinations. Only the library, which Muir called his "scribble den," gives a real sense of the man. The house was once surrounded by 2,600 acres (1,052 ha) of fruit trees, only one of which survives. In season, rangers pick fruit for visitors to sample.

John Muir (1838–1914)

Muir Woods and Beach ❸

🚌 *Mill Valley.* **Visitors' Center** *Hwy 1, Mill Valley.* ☎ *(415) 388-2595.* ◯ *8am–5pm daily.*

NESTLING AT the foot of Mount Tamalpais *(see pp396–7)* is Muir Woods National Monument, one of the few remaining stands of old-growth coastal redwoods. Before the 19th-century lumber industry flourished, these tall trees (the oldest is at least 1,000 years old) once completely covered the coastal area of California. The woods were named in honor of John Muir, the 19th-century naturalist responsible for turning Yosemite into a national park *(see pp472–5).*

Redwood Creek bubbles out of Muir Woods and makes its way down to the ocean at Muir Beach, a wide expanse of sand popular with beachcombers and picnickers *(see pp396–7).* Along the road to the beach is the incongruous Pelican Inn, a 16th-century-style English inn – proud of its traditional English menu, with items such as roast beef, and offering visitors a warm welcome *(see p529).*

Muir Beach is likely to be crowded at weekends, especially during the summer, but visitors who are prepared to walk for 15 minutes or more along the sand are rewarded with peace and quiet.

Marin Headlands ❹

See pp400–401.

Sausalito ❺

Road map inset B. 🚶 *7,300.* 🚌 🚢 🚆 ℹ️ *777 Bridgeway Ave, 4th flr (415 332-0505).*

IN THIS SMALL TOWN that was once a fishing community, Victorian bungalows cling to steep hills rising from San Francisco Bay. Parallel to the waterfront, Bridgeway Avenue serves as a promenade for the weekend crowds that come to patronize the restaurants and shops and enjoy the views.

Harbor scene in Sausalito

"arks." These unique buildings are in fact houseboats from the early 20th century that have been pulled ashore and innovatively refurbished. They now stand in what is called "Ark Row."

Less hectic than nearby Sausalito, Tiburon is a good town for walking. Parks are situated along the waterfront from which you can contemplate the bay. At night, the harbor shines with fairy lights.

Village Fair is an eclectic assembly of trendy shops located in an old warehouse. The **Bay Model** simulates the movement of the bay's tides and currents.

🏛 Village Fair
777 Bridgeway Ave. **[** (415) 332-1902. ☐ daily. ● public hols.

🏛 Bay Model
2100 Bridgeway Ave. **[** (415) 332-3870. ☐ Sep–May: Tue–Fri; Jun–Aug: Tue–Sun. ● public hols.

Tiburon ❻

Road map inset B. 🏃 8,200. ☐ ☒
☒ **ℹ** 96B Main St (415 435-5633).

THE MAIN STREET of this elegant waterfront town is lined with fashionable shops and restaurants housed in

Six Flags Marine World ❼

Road map inset B. **[** (707) 643-6722. ☒ ☒ ☒ ☒ ☒ from San Francisco. ☐ Jun–Aug: 10am–8pm Sun–Fri, 10am–7pm Sat; Mar–May: 10am–7pm Wed–Sun. ● Thanksgiving, Dec 25. 🎫 ♿ ✔

THE MOST UNIQUE wildlife park and oceanarium in Northern California, Six Flags Marine World attracts 1.6 million visitors each year. Its lush 160-acre (65-ha) site is located along I-80 at Hwy 37 on the outskirts of Vallejo.

There is equal emphasis on education and entertainment

Sign for Marine World

in the park, but the primary attractions are the shows featuring marine mammals. Arenas housing large pools showcase killer whales, sea lions, and dolphins. In the Shark Experience, visitors walk by way of a transparent tunnel through a tank filled with large sharks and tropical fish swimming overhead.

Land animal attractions include shows featuring Bengal tigers and baboons, an aviary of exotic birds, and a collection of brilliantly colored tropical butterflies.

Benicia ❽

Road map inset B. 🏃 24,400. ☒
☒ ☒ **ℹ** Benicia Chamber of Commerce, 601 1st St (707 745-2120).

SET ON the north side of the Carquinez Straits, the narrow waterway through which the Sacramento and the San Joaquin rivers flow from the Sierra Nevada to San Francisco Bay, Benicia is one of California's most historic small towns.

From February 1853 until February 1854, Benicia served as an early state capital. The Greek Revival building that once housed the government has been preserved as a state historic park, complete with many original fixtures and furnishings. Next door to the former capitol, the Fisher-Hanlon House, a former Gold Rush hotel, has also been restored to its original condition as part of **Benicia State Historic Park**.

At the other end of Main Street from the capitol complex is the Benicia waterfront where ferries shuttled to Port Costa during the 1850s. The former Benicia Arsenal, which stored army weapons from the 1850s to the 1950s, has now been converted into studio space for local artists and craftspeople.

🏛 Benicia State Historic Park
1st & G Sts. **[** (707) 745-3385.
☐ 10am–5pm daily. ● Jan 1, Thanksgiving, Dec 25. 🎫

Attractive main street of Tiburon

A 90-Minute Walk through the Marin Headlands

At its northern end, the Golden Gate Bridge is anchored in the rolling green hills of the Marin Headlands. This is an unspoiled wild area of windswept ridges, sheltered valleys, and deserted beaches, once used as a military defense post and now part of the vast Golden Gate National Recreation Area. From several vantage points there are spectacular views of San Francisco and vast panoramas of the sea, and, on autumn days you can see migrating eagles and ospreys gliding past Hawk Hill.

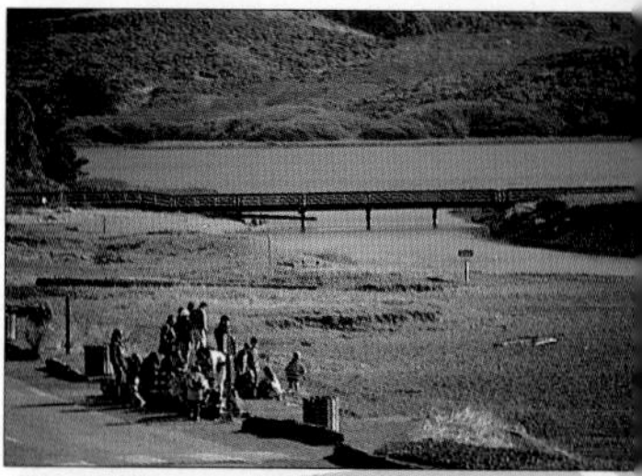

Schoolchildren on a trip to the Marin Headlands

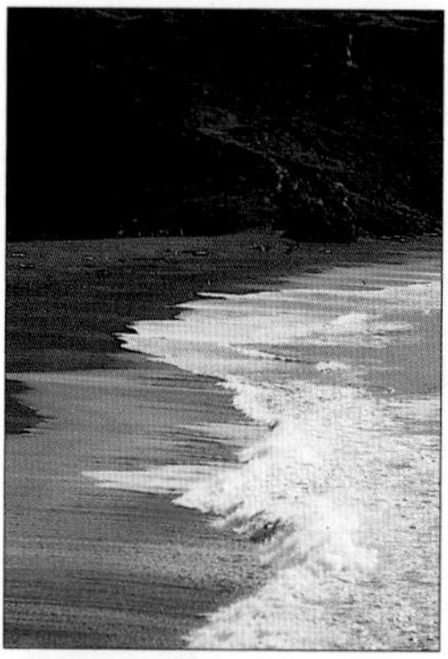

Rodeo Beach ③

Visitors' Center to Rodeo Beach

Before starting this walk, pause a while at the steepled Visitors' Center ①, which was once the interdenominational chapel for Fort Cronkhite. It has since been refurbished and is now a museum and information center, with a natural history bookshop that specializes in books on birds. Here you can discover the history of the Marin Headlands and see a Coast Miwok Indian shelter. The walk, which will take you around Rodeo Lagoon ②, begins at the gate on the west, ocean side, of the parking lot. Take the path to the left that leads to the sea. This part of the trail is thick with trees and shrubs, including poison oak, of which visitors should be aware. The songs of birds fill the air and around the edges of the lagoon you will see brown pelicans, snowy egrets, and mallards.

A 15-minute walk will bring you to the sandy, wind-blown Rodeo Beach ③, and from here you can see Bird Island ④ lying offshore

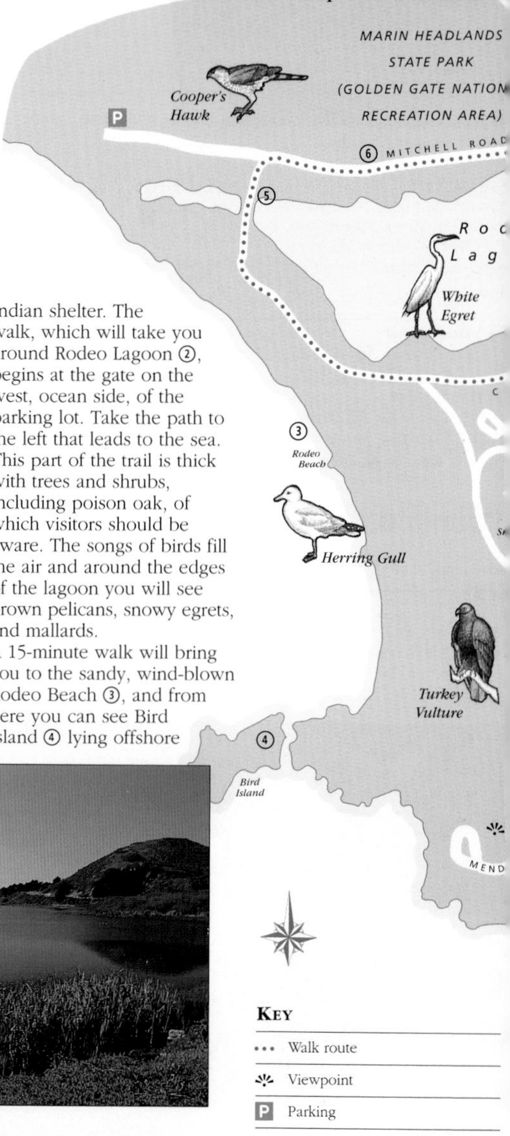
MARIN HEADLANDS
STATE PARK
(GOLDEN GATE NATION
RECREATION AREA)
Cooper's Hawk
⑥ MITCHELL ROAD
⑤
White Egret
③
Rodeo Beach
Herring Gull
Turkey Vulture
④
Bird Island
KEY
Walk route
Viewpoint
Parking

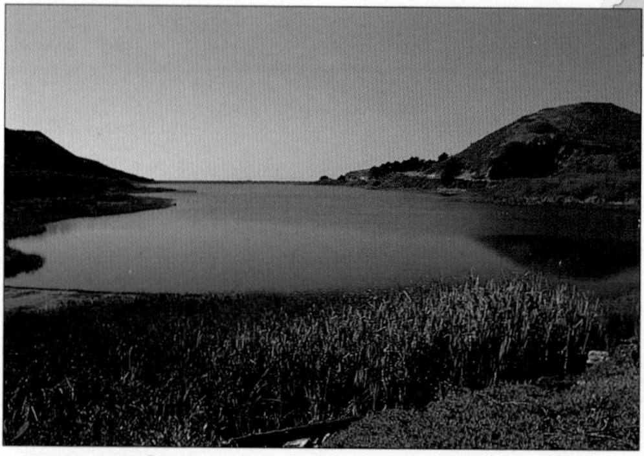

Rodeo Lagoon ②

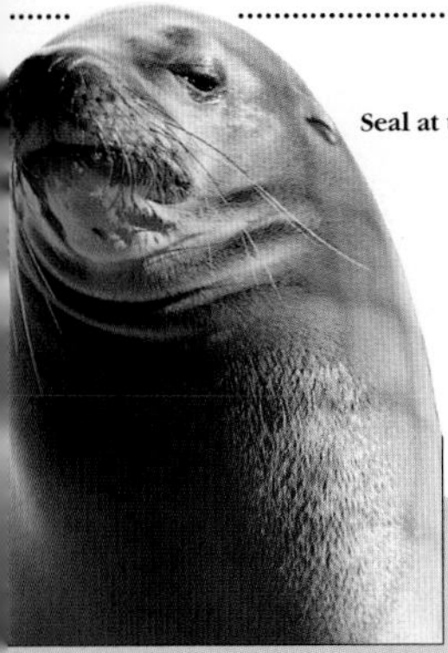

Seal at the Marine Mammal Center ⑦

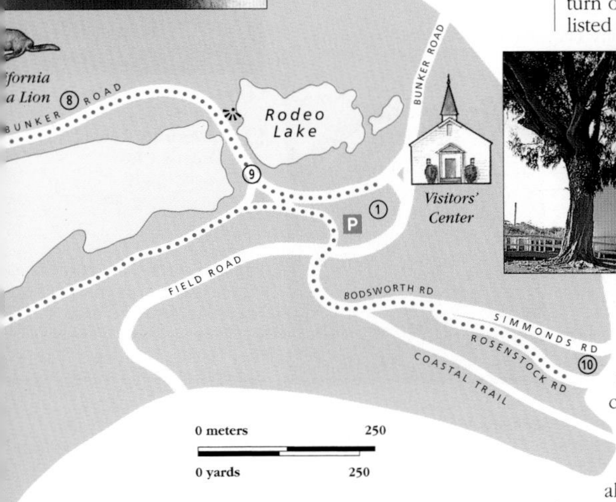

to the south. Fishing boats may be seen bobbing out at sea, but the beach is mostly empty of people, although sometimes you might see groups of children working on coastal ecology programs. These are run by the Headlands Institute, which is based in the nearby clutch of former army barracks.

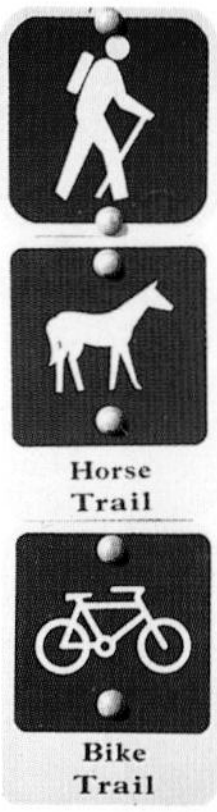

Sign marking a trail

Barracks to the California Marine Mammal Center

From the beach, turn inland again as you approach the tip of the lagoon, crossing a wooden footbridge ⑤. Here there are lavatories, and barracks ⑥ housing various offices, among them the Headlands District Office, the Raptor Observatory, and an energy and resources center. Walking past the barracks, continue along the path, then turn left at the road that climbs a steep hill to the California Marine Mammal Center ⑦. This was used as a missile defense site during the Cold War, but is now run by volunteers who rescue and care for sick or injured marine mammals. Sea lions and seals, including the rare elephant seals are examined and treated here, in specially designed pens. They are then returned to the sea when they have recovered. You can watch the vets at work and get a close view of the mammals, many of which are orphaned pups. There are also some displays of the marine ecosystem.

Lagoon to the Golden Gate Hostel

Make your way back down the hill and return to the paved road that runs past Rodeo Lagoon ⑧. There is a separate pathway beside the road for hikers, but you have to climb over a guard rail to get to it. Just before the road crosses a bridge, there is a large bench where you can view the water birds. There are plenty of birds to be seen in this brackish lagoon with its tall grasses.

Cross the bridge, not on the roadway but on the separate footpath at the side. Before the guard rail ends, a path ⑨ plunges down to the right into the dense shrubbery. From here, continue up the hill again, via a series of steps that will return you to the path at the end of the Visitors' Center parking lot. Walk across the lot and up the hill to a three-story wooden building, constructed at the turn of the century. This is listed on the National Historic

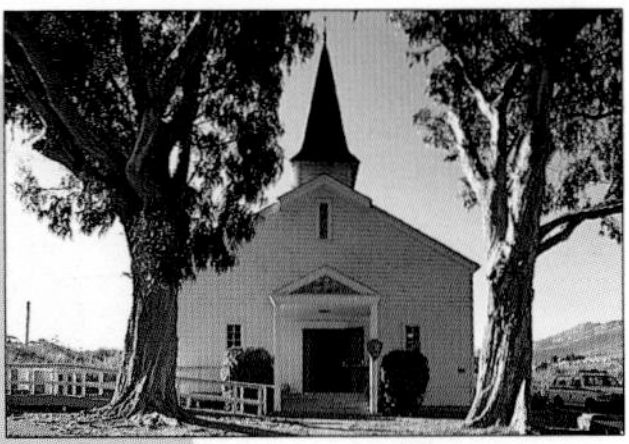

Visitors' Center ①

Registry and has been officers' headquarters, a hospital, and a missile command center. It is now the Golden Gate Hostel ⑩ for travelers. The Marin Headlands also offer a wide range of longer, more challenging walks. Wolf Ridge and Bobcat Trail are two popular routes you may want to try.

Tips for Walkers

***Starting point**: The Visitors' Center at Fort Cronkhite.*
***Length**: 2 miles (3 km).*
***Getting there**: San Francisco Muni bus 76 leaves from the intersection of Fourth Street and Townsend Street on Sundays and some holidays, ☎ (415) 673-6864. By car, drive across the Golden Gate Bridge, taking the Alexander Avenue exit. Turn under the freeway, following signs for the Headlands, Fort Cronkhite and Fort Barry.*
***Stopping-off points**: Water is available, but there are no refreshment facilities or restaurants in the Marin Headlands. You will need to bring your own picnic lunch, which can be enjoyed at any number of tables dotted along the trails and along the beaches.*

Berkeley 🟢

BERKELEY BEGAN to boom following the earthquake of 1906 *(see pp48–9)*, when many San Franciscans fled their ruined city and settled on the east side of the bay. Berkeley did not really find its own voice, however, until the birth of the Free Speech Movement and the student uprisings against the Vietnam War during the 1960s, earning itself the nickname "Beserkeley." Many stores and market stalls still hark back to the hippie era with their psychedelic merchandise, but in recent years Berkeley has begun to raise its profile. Stylish restaurants and cafés have emerged, as well as a reputation for fine food – it was here that the popular California cuisine was born. Today the city blends idealism and style in unique harmony.

Claremont Resort Hotel

🏛 University of California at Berkeley
🅲 *(510) 642-6000.* **Hearst Museum of Anthropology** 🅲 *(510) 643-7648.* ⭕ *10am–4:30pm Wed–Sun (until 9pm Thu).* ● *public hols.*
Berkeley Art Museum and Pacific Film Archive 🅲 *(510) 642-0808.* ⭕ *11am–5pm Wed–Sun (until 9pm Thu).* ● *public hols.* 🎞 ♿
The reputation of UC Berkeley for counter-cultural movements sometimes eclipses its academic reputation, yet it is one of the largest and most prestigious universities in the world. Founded in 1868, Berkeley numbers at least ten Nobel laureates among its professors. The campus *(see pp404–405)* was laid out by the architect Frederick Law Olmsted. There are more than 30,000 students and a wide range of museums, cultural amenities, and buildings of note to visit. These include the University Art Museum *(see p405)*, Sather Tower, (the Campanile), and the Hearst Museum of Anthropology.

Model of DNA at the Lawrence Hall of Science

🏛 Lawrence Hall of Science
Centennial Drive, UC Berkeley.
🅲 *(510) 642-5132.* ⭕ *10am–5pm daily.* ♿ 🎞
Science is fun here. Hands-on exhibits tempt visitors to manipulate a hologram, track earthquakes, or plot stars in the planetarium. There are also changing exhibitions.
At night, the view of the lights around the northern Bay Area from the Hall's plaza is an extraordinary sight.

🧖 Claremont Resort Spa and Tennis Club
41 Tunnel Rd, Oakland.
🅲 *(510) 843-3000.* ♿
The Berkeley hills form a backdrop to this half-timbered, fairytale castle. The enormous Claremont Resort construction began in 1906 and ended in 1915. In the early years the hotel failed to prosper, partly due to a law that forbade the sale of alcohol within a 1-mile (1.6-km) radius of the UC Berkeley campus. In 1937 an enterprising student actually measured the distance and discovered that the radius line passed through the *center* of the building. The Terrace Bar was opened beyond the line, in the same corner of the hotel that it occupies today.
The Bay Area's plushest hotel is a good place to have a drink and enjoy the views.

🌿 University of California Botanical Garden
Centennial Drive, Berkeley. 🅵 *(510) 643-2755.* ⭕ *9am–5pm daily.* ● *1st Tue of month, Dec 25.* ♿ *limited.*
More than 12,000 species from all over the world thrive in the Mediterranean-style climate of Berkeley's Strawberry Canyon. Although primarily used for research, the collections are arranged in thematic gardens linked by paths. Particularly noteworthy are the Asian, African, South American, European, and California sections. The Chinese medicinal herb garden, the orchid houses, cactus garden, and the carnivorous plants are also well worth a visit.

Wellman Hall on the University of California campus

🌳 Tilden Park

☎ *(510) 843-2137.* **Steam trains** *run 11am–6pm Sat & Sun, and daily during summer.* 🎟 **Carousel** 🕐 *10am–5pm Sat & Sun, 11am–5pm daily during summer.* 🎟 **Botanical Garden** *open 8:30am–5pm daily.* ♿ *limited.*

Though preserved for the most part in a natural wild condition, Tilden Park offers a variety of attractions. It is noted for the enchantingly landscaped Botanical Garden, specializing in California plants. Visitors can stroll from alpine meadows to desert cactus gardens by way of a redwood glen, and there are guided nature walks. If you have children, don't miss the carousel, the miniature farmyard, and the model steam train.

🏛 Judah L Magnes Museum

2911 Russell St, Berkeley. ☎ *(510) 549-6950.* 🕐 *10am–4pm Sun–Thu.* ● *Jewish and federal hols.* ♿ *arrange in advance.*

Located in a rambling old mansion, this is California's largest collection of art and historical artifacts pertaining to Jewish culture from ancient times to the present day. Among the exhibits are art treasures from Europe, Turkey, and India, and graphic works and paintings by Marc Chagall, Max Liebermann, and others. There are also mementos of the experience of Jews during the Holocaust, such as a burned Torah scroll rescued from a German synagogue.

Lectures, videos, and temporary exhibitions often enliven the museum's halls.

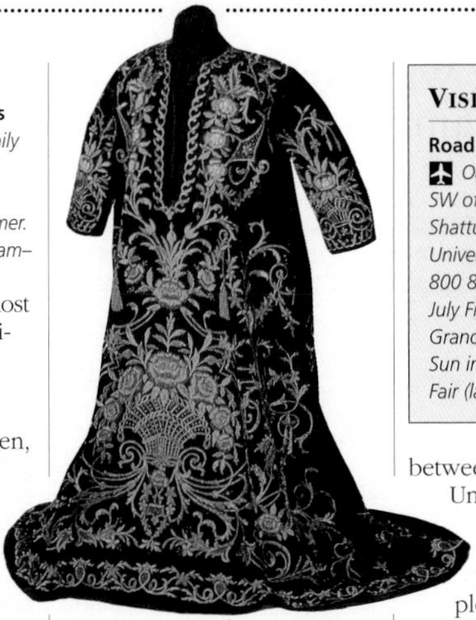

19th-century Jewish ceremonial dress, Judah L Magnes Museum

🏪 Telegraph Avenue

Berkeley's most fascinating street is Telegraph Avenue, especially the blocks between Dwight Way and the University. It has one of the highest concentrations of bookstores in the country, and a plethora of coffee houses and cheap eateries. The district was the center of student protest during the 1960s. It still swarms with students from dawn to dark, along with street vendors, musicians, protesters, and eccentrics.

> **Visitors' Checklist**
>
> **Road map** inset B. 👥 *104,900.* ✈ *Oakland, 12 miles (19 km) SW of Berkeley.* 🚌 🚆 *2160 Shattuck Ave.* ℹ *1834 University Ave (510 549-7040, 800 847-4823).* 🎉 *Fourth of July Fireworks; Farmers' Market Grand Opening & Parade (2nd Sun in Jul); Telegraph Ave Book Fair (late Jul).*

🏪 Fourth Street

This gentrified enclave north of University Avenue is characteristic of Berkeley's fine craftsmanship and taste. Here you can buy everything from stained-glass windows and furniture, to organically grown lettuce and designer garden tools. There is also a handful of good restaurants *(see p566)*.

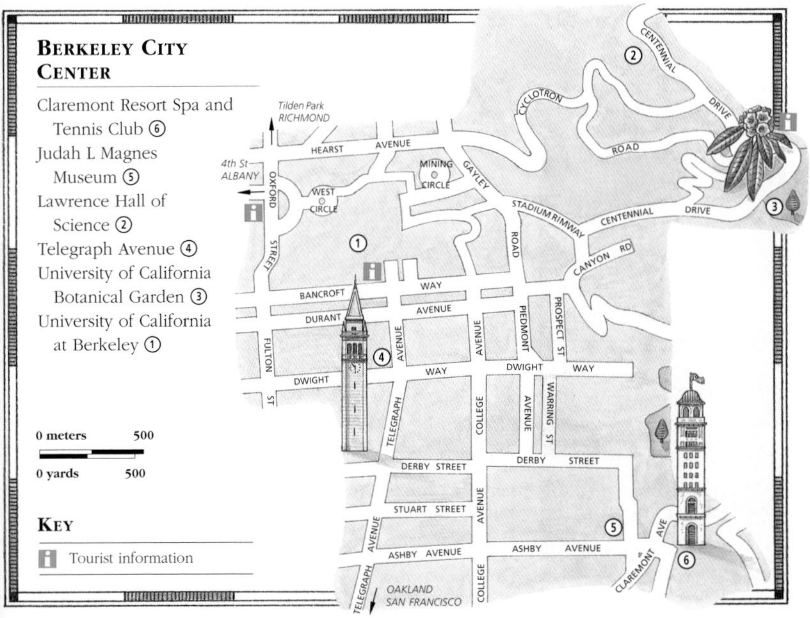
Berkeley City Center
Claremont Resort Spa and Tennis Club ⑥
Judah L Magnes Museum ⑤
Lawrence Hall of Science ②
Telegraph Avenue ④
University of California Botanical Garden ③
University of California at Berkeley ①
0 meters 500
0 yards 500
Key
Tourist information
Tilden Park RICHMOND
4th St ALBANY
OAKLAND SAN FRANCISCO
HEARST AVENUE
MINING CIRCLE
WEST CIRCLE
GAYLEY
CYCLOTRON
CENTENNIAL DRIVE
ROAD
STADIUM RIMWAY
CENTENNIAL DRIVE
CANYON RD
OXFORD STREET
ROAD
BANCROFT WAY
DURANT AVENUE
PIEDMONT
PROSPECT ST
FULTON ST
DWIGHT WAY
DWIGHT WAY
TELEGRAPH AVENUE
COLLEGE AVENUE
WARRING ST
DERBY STREET
DERBY STREET
STUART STREET
ASHBY AVENUE
ASHBY AVENUE
CLAREMONT AVE

A 90-Minute Walk around the University of California Campus in Berkeley

THIS WALK CONCENTRATES on a distinct area of Berkeley, the famous main campus of the University of California. It allows a stimulating glimpse into the intellectual, cultural, and social life of this vibrant university town *(see pp402–403)*.

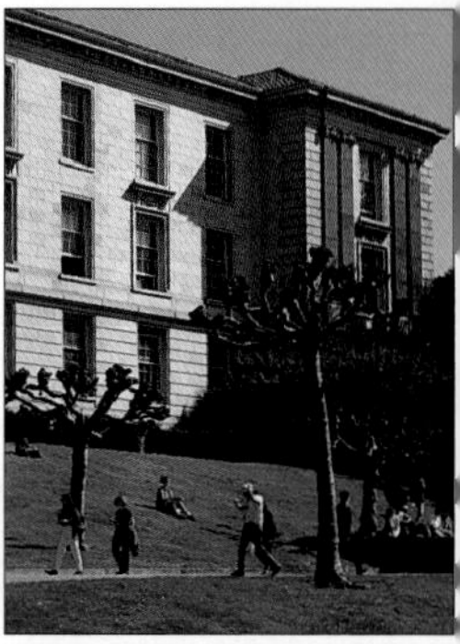

Students outside Wheeler Hall on Cross Campus Road ④

West Entrance to Sather Tower

From University Avenue ①, cross Oxford Street and walk along University Drive past the Valley Life Sciences Building ②. Wellman Hall can be seen on the north fork of Strawberry Creek as you follow the road to the right, keeping California Hall ③ on your right. Take a left turn on Cross Campus Road ④. Wheeler Hall lies to the right, and ahead is the main campus landmark, the 307-ft (94-m) tall Sather Tower ⑤. Built by John Galen Howard in 1914, it was based on the campanile in the Piazza San Marco in Venice.

Before visiting the bell tower, go to the Doe Library ⑥ then the AF Morrison Memorial Library ⑦ in the north wing. The adjacent Bancroft Library houses the plate supposedly left by Sir Francis Drake in 1579, when he claimed California for England *(see pp42–3)*.

Return to Sather Tower, open 10am–3:30pm Monday to Saturday. There are fine views of the bay from the top of the tower. Across the way lies South Hall ⑧, the oldest building on campus.

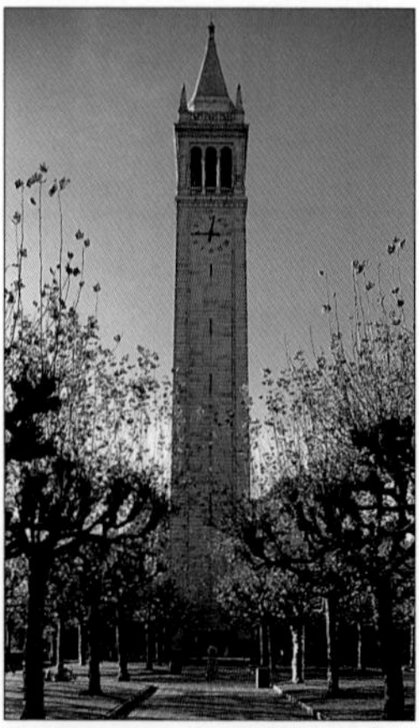

Esplanade near Sather Tower ⑤

Hearst Mining Building to the Greek Theater

Continuing north, walk past LeConte Hall then cross over University Drive to the Mining Circle. Here is the Hearst Mining Building ⑨, built by Howard in 1907. Inside are ore samples and pictures of old mining operations. Return to University Drive, turn left out of East Gate to the Hearst Greek Theater ⑩.

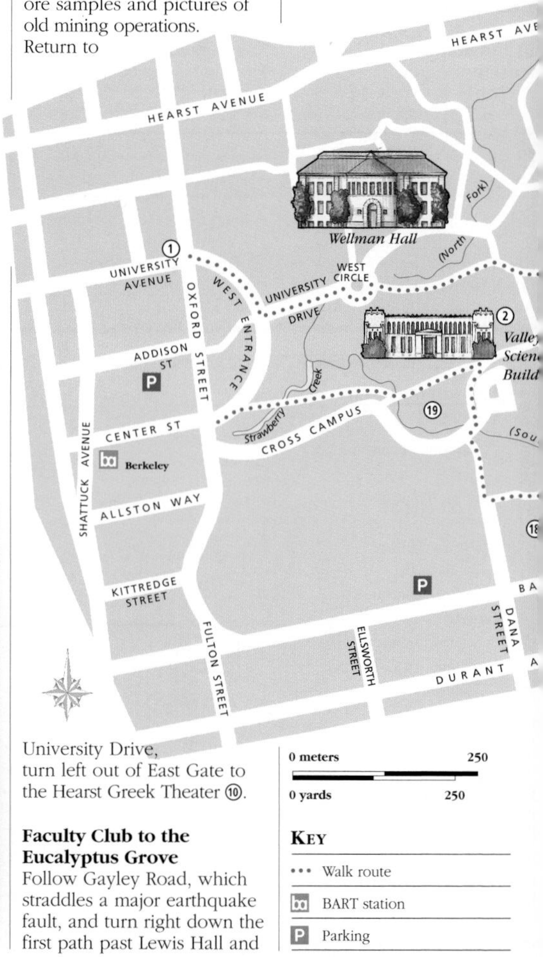
HEARST AVENUE
HEARST AVE
Wellman Hall
(North Fork)
WEST CIRCLE
UNIVERSITY AVENUE
OXFORD STREET
WEST ENTRANCE
UNIVERSITY DRIVE
Valley Scien Build
ADDISON ST
Strawberry Creek
CROSS CAMPUS
CENTER ST
SHATTUCK AVENUE
Berkeley
ALLSTON WAY
KITTREDGE STREET
FULTON STREET
ELLSWORTH STREET
DANA STREET
DURANT
0 meters 250
0 yards 250
KEY
Walk route
BART station
Parking

Faculty Club to the Eucalyptus Grove

Follow Gayley Road, which straddles a major earthquake fault, and turn right down the first path past Lewis Hall and

Hildebrand Hall, then left over a footbridge. The path winds between a log house and the Faculty Club ⑪. This rambling, rustic building was partly designed by Bernard Maybeck and dates from 1903. Faculty Glade ⑫ in front of the club is a favorite picnic and resting place with students and visitors alike.

The path now swings to the right, then sharp left. Take a look at Hertz Hall ⑬, then go down the diagonal walk that passes Wurster Hall to Kroeber Hall. Here you can visit the Hearst Museum of Anthropology (see p402).

Included in the museum are artifacts made by Ishi, the last surviving Yahi Indian who was brought by scientists to live on the campus from 1911 until his death in 1916. Cross Bancroft Way to the Caffè Strada ⑭ and then proceed to the University Art Museum ⑮, which includes Picassos and Cézannes among its exhibits (see p402). Continue along Bancroft Way to Telegraph Avenue ⑯, famous for the student riots of the 1960s and '70s (see p403).

The entrance to the university opposite Telegraph Avenue opens on to Sproul Plaza ⑰, which is often

Within (1969) by A Lieberman at UCB Art Museum ⑮

enlivened by street musicians. Step into the lower courtyard with its modern Zellerbach Hall ⑱, then, noting the state-of-the-art Harmon Gym, pass Alumni House and turn right. Cross over the south fork of Strawberry Creek at Bay Tree Bridge and bear left for the nature area, with some of the world's tallest eucalyptus trees ⑲. The path ends at Oxford Street, near the start of the walk.

TIPS FOR WALKERS

Starting point: The West Gate at University Avenue and Oxford Street.
Length: 2.5 miles (4 km).
Getting there: San Francisco–Oakland Bay Bridge, Hwy 80 north, University Avenue exit. By BART, Berkeley stop.
Stopping-off points: The upscale Caffè Strada, on Bancroft Way, is always crowded with students sipping cappuccinos or eating bagels and cakes. A few steps down the street, in the University Art Museum, is the Café Grace, which looks out on to the sculpture garden. You may want to browse in the bookstores on Telegraph Avenue that also have coffee shops, or try one of the food carts that crowd the entrance to Sproul Plaza. Here you could sample a "smoothie" (blended fruit and ice) or a wide selection of Mexican food. In the lower Sproul Plaza of the University, amid a phalanx of bongo drummers, there are several other inexpensive cafés.

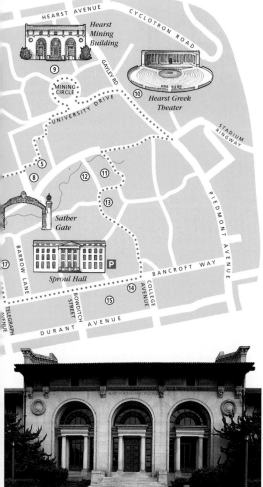

The Hearst Mining Building around the Mining Circle ⑨

Oakland ⑩

A**T ONE TIME** a small, working-class suburb of San Francisco, Oakland grew into a city in its own right when it became the West Coast terminus of the transcontinental railroad. With access to the town, businesses inevitably boomed, and it soon became one of the largest container ports in the United States. Many of the African-Americans who worked on the railroad then settled in Oakland, later followed by a Hispanic population, giving the city a multicultural atmosphere that continues to this day. Oakland's literary associations, including Jack London and Gertrude Stein, have also enhanced the area as a cultural center.

VISITORS' CHECKLIST

Road map inset B. 🚉 *387,000.*
✈ *Oakland, 5 miles (8 km) SW of Oakland.* 🚉 *1245 Broadway St.* ℹ *475 14th St (510 874-4800).* 📷 *Festival at the Lake (early Jun).*

Façade and gardens of the Mormon Temple

🛕 Mormon Temple

4770 Lincoln Ave. ☎ *(510) 531-1475.* **Visitors' Center** 🕐 *9am–9pm daily.* **Temple** 🕐 *6:30am– 8pm Tue–Thu, 6:30am–9pm Fri, 5:30am–1pm Sat.* ♿
Designed in 1963 and built on a hilltop, this is Northern California's only Mormon temple. Its full name is the Oakland Temple of the Church of Jesus Christ of Latter Day Saints. Floodlit at night, it can be seen from Oakland and San Francisco. The central ziggurat is surrounded by four shorter terraced towers, all clad with white granite and capped by glistening golden pyramids.
   From the temple there are magnificent views over the entire Bay Area.

📷 Lake Merritt

Formed when a saltwater tidal estuary was dredged, embanked, and partly dammed, Lake Merritt and its surrounding park form an oasis of rich blue and green in the urban heart of Oakland. Designated in 1870 as the first state game refuge in the US, the lake still attracts migrating flocks of birds. Boats can be rented from two boathouses on the west and north shores, and joggers and cyclists can circle the lake on a 3-mile (5-km) path. The north shore at Lakeside Park has flower gardens, an aviary, and a Children's Fairyland with pony rides, puppet shows, and nursery rhyme scenes.

🏛 Jack London Square

Author Jack London, who became famous for his adventure novels *The Call of the Wild* and *White Fang (see pp22–3)*, grew up in Oakland in the 1880s and was a frequent visitor to the Oakland waterfront. Today the area

🏛 Bay Bridge

Map 6 E4

The compound, high-level San Francisco–Oakland Bay Bridge was designed by Charles H Purcell. It has two distinct structures, joining at Yerba Buena Island in the middle of the Bay, and reaches 4.5 miles (7.2 km) from shore to shore. Its completion in 1936 heralded the end of the age of ferry boats on San Francisco Bay by linking the peninsular city at Rincon Hill to the Oakland "mainland." Train tracks were removed in the 1950s, leaving the bridge for use by more than 250,000 vehicles a day. It is five traffic lanes wide and has two levels. The westbound traffic uses the top deck, eastbound the lower. The eastern cantilever is raised on more than 20 piers, climbing up from the toll plaza causeway in Oakland to 191 ft (58 m) above Yerba Buena Island.
   In 1989 the bridge was closed for a month after the Loma Prieta earthquake *(see p489)* when a 50-ft (15-m) segment disconnected where the cantilever span meets the approach ramp from Oakland. Two suspension

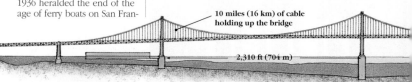
10 miles (16 km) of cable holding up the bridge

2,310 ft (704 m)

The West Bay Crossing section of Bay Bridge

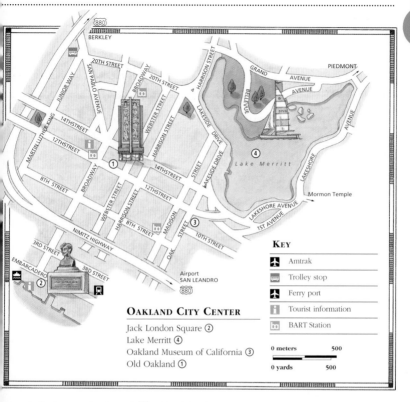

OAKLAND CITY CENTER

Jack London Square ②
Lake Merritt ④
Oakland Museum of California ③
Old Oakland ①

KEY

✈	Amtrak
🚋	Trolley stop
⚓	Ferry port
ℹ️	Tourist information
🚇	BART Station

0 meters	500
0 yards	500

named after him is a bright promenade of shops, restaurants with outdoor tables, and pleasure boats. London's footsteps can be traced to the First and Last Chance Saloon, now sunken with age into the street, and the Yukon cabin occupied by London in 1898.

🏛 Old Oakland

Farmers' Market 📞 *(510) 745-7100.* 🕐 *8am–2pm Fri.*
Housewives' Market 📞 *(510) 444-4396.* 🕐 *9am–6pm Mon–Sat.*
Also known as Victorian Row, these two blocks were erected between the 1860s and 1880s and renovated in the 1980s. Crowds of shoppers visit the

Outdoor Market on Fridays, and the Housewives' Market at Clay and 9th streets offers an array of ethnic foods.

At night, try Rattos, at No. 827 Washington Street, an Italian delicatessen famed for its weekend "Pasta Operas," when the management serenades the clientele.

spans join at the central anchorage, which is sunk deeper in the water than that of any other bridge. Now there are plans to completely rebuild the East Bay crossing. Treasure Island, the larger part of Yerba Buena Island, hosted the 1939–40 World's Fair to celebrate the bridge's completion. This small island is now home to small parks and an upscale community.

East Bay Crossing

Central anchorage

5-lane double-level roadway

Pylons supporting both road decks

400 ft (122 m)

2,310 ft (704 m)

Oakland Museum of California

California gold miner's banjo

CALIFORNIA's only museum exclusively dedicated to documenting the state's art, history, and ecology first opened in 1969. The building, handsomely terraced and landscaped with courtyards and gardens, was designed by architect Kevin Roche and encompasses three disciplines: the art, social, and natural history of California. The natural history dioramas in the Hall of California Ecology are among the most impressive in the entire country. The Cowell Hall of California History has one of the largest collections of California artifacts in the state, and the Gallery of California Art is famous for its early oil paintings of Yosemite and San Francisco.

Welcome to California
This display celebrates past and present-day life in California.

Roof and gardens

The Great Hall is used for special exhibitions and functions.

Art Gallery
Modern art includes the painting Spring Nude *(1962) by Nathan Oliveira.*

Level 3

Level 2

10th Street entrance

★ **Dream on Wheels**
A drive-in restaurant sign and jukebox in the 1951 diorama capture the atmosphere of postwar California.

KEY TO THE OAKLAND MUSEUM LEVELS

☐ Art Gallery   ☐ History   ☐ Natural Sciences

California Mud Wagon
*Developed for rural life during the mid-
19th century, this multipurpose vehicle
could be converted easily from a field
wagon to a stylish carriage.*

Food Chain Diorama
*This diorama features a
mountain lion and its
prey, to show how
wildlife competes
to survive.*

MUSEUM GUIDE
*Level 1 contains the shop and the Hall
of Ecology, where the exhibits show
the changes in the state's ecology
from west to east. Artifacts in
the Cowell Hall on level 2 are
arranged chronologically.
Level 2 has the cafeteria,
level 3 the Art Gallery.*

Level 1

**The Great
Court** has outdoor
exhibitions and is also a
popular spot for a picnic.

★ Delta Waters Diorama
*This diorama of a Sacramento delta
marsh, showing fish, bird, and
insect life, typifies the high caliber of
the Aquatic California Gallery.*

STAR EXHIBITS

★ **Delta Waters
Diorama**

★ **Dream on
Wheels**

Eugene O'Neill's beautiful Tao House, in Danville

Tao House **⓫**

Road map inset B. **☎** *(925) 838-0249.* **☐** *10am–noon, 12:30pm–2:30pm Wed–Sun, by reservation only.* **♿ ✔** *obligatory.*

WHEN THE AMERICAN playwright Eugene O'Neill (1888–1953) won the Nobel Prize for Literature in 1936, he used the stipend to build a home for himself and his wife in the then-rural San Ramon Valley at the foot of Mount Diablo. Tao House, a hybrid of Spanish Colonial and oriental styles, was completed in 1937. Over the next six years O'Neill worked in this house on what is now considered his best work, the semi-autobiographical series of tragic plays, including *The Iceman Cometh, A Moon for the Misbegotten,* and *Long Day's Journey Into Night.* In 1944, however, O'Neill was struck down with Parkinson's disease. The remote location of the house and the lack of available nursing staff due to the war forced the disabled O'Neill to abandon his beloved home. He died in a Boston hotel in 1953.

Mask used in O'Neill's stage plays

Although the surrounding valleys have now been developed into suburbs of San Francisco, Tao House and its beautiful landscaped grounds have been turned into a National Historic Site, operated by the National Park Service. Both have been preserved in the condition in which the playwright left them.

Mount Diablo State Park **⓬**

Road map inset B. **🚌 🚆** *Walnut Creek.* **ℹ** *Walnut Creek (925) 837-2525).* **☎** *(925) 837-6119.* **☐** *11am–5pm Wed–Sun.*

RISING VOLUMINOUSLY over the inland suburbs, the 3,849-ft (1,173-m) high Mount Diablo dominates the East Bay region. Its summit offers one of the most impressive panoramas in North America. On a fine and clear day it is possible to see for more than 200 miles (320 km) in each direction, stretching from Mount Lassen *(see p437)* and the Cascade Mountains in the north to Mount Hamilton in the south, and from the Sierra Nevada mountains in the east to the Farallon Islands *(see pp396–7)* in the Pacific Ocean to the west.

Almost 20,000 acres (8,000 ha) of land surrounding the summit have now been set aside as a state park, and there is a wide range of hiking trails. A twisting road takes car drivers within 50 ft (15 m) of the summit, which is a popular picnic spot. The park's Visitors Center at the summit offers information on the mountain's fauna and flora, including the wildflowers that cover the mountainside in spring and the abundant oak trees.

Livermore **⓭**

Road map inset B. **🚶** *67,000.* **🚌 🚆 ℹ** *2157 First St (925) 447-1606).*

FOUNDED IN the 1870s as a cattle-ranching and grape-producing community, Livermore in recent years has grown into an outlying suburb of San Francisco.

Still rural in feel and retaining a few ranches and vineyards, the town is now best known as the home of the Lawrence Livermore National Laboratory. This state-of-the-art technology research center is operated by the University of California on behalf of the United States Department of Energy. During the Cold War era the laboratory had primary responsibility for the design of the nation's nuclear weapons arsenal, but today it has diversified into civilian applications.

To the east of Livermore, along I-580 as it climbs over hilly Altamont Pass, are hundreds of shining high-tech windmills. This is the world's largest wind farm, producing natural, nonpolluting energy from the area's constant winds. The windmills are all privately owned and operated, with no

Windmills producing natural energy at Livermore's wind farm

overnment funding. They onsist of two main types: the additional propeller type, and the more unusual vertical axis windmills, which resemble giant egg-whisks.

tanford University ⑭

Juniper Serra St. **Road map** inset B.
(650) 723-2053. **Visitors' Center**
9am–5pm daily. university
tours; call ahead.
www.stanford.edu

AMONG THE MOST pleasant of the Bay Area suburbs, the town of Palo Alto grew up specifically to serve Stanford University, one of the most reputed centers of higher education in the country.
Founded by the railroad tycoon Leland Stanford *(see pp46–7)* in honor of his son who died in 1885 at the age of 16, Stanford University opened in 1891. The campus occupies the former Stanford family farm, covering 8,200 acres (3,320 ha) at the foot of the coastal mountains – larger than the entire downtown district of San Francisco. It was designed in a mixture of Romanesque and Mission styles *(see pp26–7)* by the architect Frederick Law Olmsted, and its sandstone buildings and numerous arcades are topped by

red-tiled roofs. At the heart of the university campus is the Main Quadrangle, where the Memorial Church is decorated with a gold-leaf and tile mosaic. Also on the campus is the Stanford Museum of Art. This small but intriguing museum holds one of the largest collections of sculptures by Auguste Rodin, including the impressive *Gates of Hell*.

Filoli ⑮

Canada Rd. **Road map** inset B.
(650) 364-2880, ext 507.
9am–4pm Mon–Fri. public
hols.

ONE OF THE MOST impressive mansions in Northern California open to the public, the Filoli estate was the home of gold mining millionaire William Bourn, owner of the Empire Gold Mine *(see p454)*. It was designed in Palladian style by Willis Polk in 1916. The redbrick exterior resembles a Georgian terrace and encloses more than 18,000 sq ft (1,672 sq m) of living space on two fully furnished floors.
The house is surrounded by 16 acres (6.5 ha) of formal gardens, landscaped to provide blooms of varying colors through the year – 25,000 tulips and daffodils in spring, roses in summer, and the brilliant russet maple leaves

in the autumn. The estate's name, Filoli, is an acronym for the motto "Fight for a just cause, Love your fellow man, Live a good life," which commemorates William Bourn's love for the Irish.

Picturesque church in the tiny village of Pescadero

Pescadero ⑯

Road map inset B. 360. 520 Kelley Ave, Half Moon Bay (650 726-5202).

ONLY HALF AN HOUR'S drive from San Francisco to the north and the Silicon Valley *(see p412)* to the south, the tiny town of Pescadero seems light years away from the surrounding modern world.
Pescadero is a sleepy little farming community that produces an abundance of vegetables such as asparagus, pumpkins, and Brussels sprouts. It contains little more than a whitewashed church (the oldest in the county), a general store, a post office, and the popular Duarte's Tavern *(see p567)* along its two main streets. Its many whitewashed buildings follow a tradition that goes back to the 19th century, when a cargo of white paint was rescued from a nearby shipwreck.
Eight miles (13 km) south of town, the Pigeon Point Lighthouse is well worth a visit. The lighthouse also operates as a hostel *(see pp396–7)*.

Façade of the Memorial Church at Stanford University

San Jose ⓱

THE ONLY OTHER ORIGINAL Spanish Colonial town in California after Los Angeles (see pp54–183), San Jose was founded in 1777 by Felipe de Neve and has grown to become the state's third largest city, its population exceeding that of San Francisco. Now the commercial and cultural center of the South Bay and civic heart of the Silicon Valley region, San Jose is a bustling and modern city that has only recently taken action to preserve its history. High-rise offices and high-tech factories now stand on what was only farmland in the 1950s, yet the city's fine museums and historic sites offer genuine attractions to the visitor, despite the suburban sprawl.

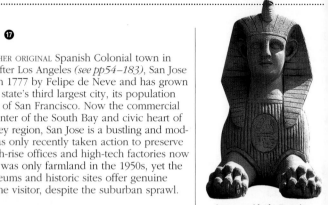

Statue outside the Egyptian Museum and Planetarium

Exploring San Jose

San Jose's colonial pueblo was situated on what is now Plaza Park, off Market Street. During 1849–50, California's first State Capitol was located in a hotel on the east side of the plaza, roughly on the site of the present Fairmont Hotel (see p529).

Other historic sites along Market Street include the San Jose Museum of Art and the birthplace of Amadeo P Giannini (see p305).

The well-known Winchester Mystery House (see pp414–15), is located on the town's outskirts.

🏛 Peralta Adobe

175 W St John St. [(408) 993-8182. ⬤ Tue–Sun. ⬤ public hols. 🌐 & first floor only.
One block to the left of Market Street is San Jose's oldest surviving

building, the Peralta Adobe. Built in 1797 it is the sole remnant of the Spanish pueblo. Upscale bars and cafés now surround the area.

⛪ Mission Santa Clara de Asis

500 El Camino Real. [(408) 554-4023. ⬤ daily.
On the campus of the Jesuit University of Santa Clara, 5 miles (8 km) northwest of downtown San Jose, this mission church is a modern replica of the adobe original, first built in 1777 and reconstructed many times thereafter. Relics on display include bells given to the missionaries by the Spanish monarchy. The gardens adjacent to the church are carefully maintained in their original splendor.

Mission Santa Clara detail

🏛 Rosicrucian Egyptian Museum and Planetarium

Naglee & Park Aves. [(408) 947 3600. ⬤ Tue–Sun. ⬤ Jan 1, Easter Sunday, Thanksgiving, Dec 25. 🌐
This large museum displays the most extensive collection of ancient Egyptian artifacts west of the Mississippi. Housed in a complex of Egyptian- and Moorish-style buildings, each gallery represents a different aspect of Egyptian culture, from mummies, burial tombs, and canopic jars to domestic implements and a variety of children's toys, some of which date back to 1500 BC. There are also replicas of the sarcophagus in which Tutankhamen was discovered in 1922, and of the Rosetta Stone.

The museum is operated by a nonsectarian organization known as the Rosicrucian Order, which is dedicated to spiritual development by combining modern science with the ancient wisdoms.

🏛 Tech Museum of Innovation

201 S Market St. [(408) 279-7150. ⬤ Sep–May: Tue–Sun; Jun– Aug: Mon– Sun. ⬤ Jan 1, Easter, Thanksgiving, Dec 25. 🌐
Located in the heart of San Jose, this fascinating science museum has its eyes set on the future. The Tech Museum is crowded with hands-on exhibits, which encourage visitors of all ages to discover how various technological inventions work. Its main focus is on understanding the workings of computer hardware and software. The Imax Dome Theater is also worth a visit.

SILICON VALLEY

The world-famous center of the computer industry, Silicon Valley covers approximately 100 sq miles (260 sq km) from Palo Alto to San Jose. However, the term refers to myriad businesses rather than to a defined geographical location.

The name, based on the material used in the manufacture of semiconductors, was first used in the early 1970s to describe the area's expanding hardware and software industries. The seeds, however, were sown a decade earlier, at Stanford University and the Xerox Palo Alto Research Center, as well as in the garages of computer pioneers William Hewlett, David Packard, and later Steve Jobs and Stephen Wozniak, who invented the Apple personal computer.

Many world-class high-tech firms are based here, including Intel, Silicon Graphics, and Cisco Systems.

Silicon chip circuitry

San Jose Museum of Art

10 S Market St. ((408) 271-6840.
◻ Tue–Sun. ● Jan 1, Thanksgiving,
Dec 25. 📷 W www.sjmusart.org
This small but daring art museum is known for some of the Bay Area's most interesting and popular art exhibits. The permanent collection focuses on well-known contemporary California artists.

Children's Discovery Museum of San Jose

180 Woz Way. ((408) 298-5437.
◻ Tue–Sun. ● Jan 1, Dec 25. 📷
W www.cdm.org
This large purple building, designed by Mexican architect Ricardo Legoretta, offers interactive exhibits and programs for children and their families. Arts and technology are featured in this warm, inviting space.

De Saisset Museum

500 El Camino Real. ((408) 554-4528. ◻ Tue–Sun. ● Jan 1, Thanksgiving, Dec 25. **Donation**.
Next to the Santa Clara Mission, this museum exhibits artifacts from the 18th-century mission and other eras of California history, along with a vast collection of paintings, prints, and photographs.

Trolley car at the San Jose Historical Museum

San Jose Historical Museum

1650 Senter Rd. ((408) 287-2290.
◻ Noon–5pm Tue–Sun.
● Thanksgiving, Dec 25. 📷
One mile (1.5 km) southeast of downtown San Jose, in Kelley Park, more than two dozen historic structures of San Jose have been reassembled into an outdoor museum. Highlights include a trolley car, a gas station from the 1920s, and 19th-century business premises including a doctor's office, a hotel, and the original Bank of Italy.

By 2001 the museum aims to have 75 structures, completing this life-size model of San Jose as it used to be.

VISITORS' CHECKLIST

Road map inset B. 🚶 846,000.
✈ San Jose International Airport, 2 miles (3 km) NW of San Jose. 🚊 65 Cahill St.
🚌 70 Almeden St. 🛈 180 S Market St (408 291-5250).
🎭 Festival of the Arts (Sep).

Paramount's Great America Amusement Park

2401 Agnew Rd. ((408) 988-1776.
◻ mid-Mar–Jun: Sat & Sun; Jul–mid-Oct: daily. 📷
The best amusement park in Northern California packs a wide variety of attractions into its 100-acre (40-ha) site.

The park is divided into several different areas, each one designed to evoke various regions of the United States. These include Orleans Place, Yankee Harbor, and the Yukon Territory. Along with high-speed roller coasters, such as the Demon and the Tidal Wave, many rides incorporate themes from films and television shows produced by Paramount Studios, including *Top Gun* and *Star Trek*. Open-air pop concerts are often held on summer evenings in the large amphitheater.

SAN JOSE CITY CENTER

De Saisset Museum ①
Mission Santa Clara de Asis ②
Rosicrucian Egyptian Museum and Planetarium ③
San Jose Museum of Art ④
Tech Museum of Innovation ⑤
Winchester Mystery House
pp414–15 ⑥
Children's Discovery Museum ⑦

KEY

🚊 Amtrak station
🚌 Bus stop
🛈 Tourist information

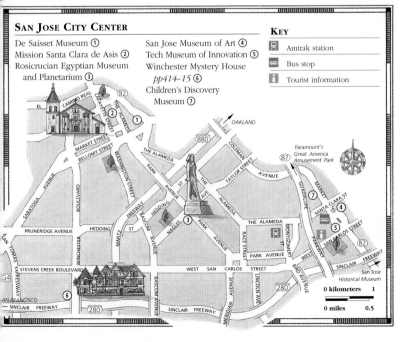

San Jose: Winchester Mystery House

WINCHESTER MYSTERY HOUSE is a mansion with a remarkable history. Sarah Winchester, heiress of the Winchester Rifle fortune, moved from Connecticut to San Jose in 1884 and bought a small farmhouse. Convinced by a medium that its expansion would exorcise the spirits of those killed by the rifle, she kept builders laboring on the house 24 hours a day, 7 days a week, for 38 years, until her death in 1922. The result is a bizarre complex of 160 rooms, including stairs that lead nowhere and windows set into floors. The total cost of the construction amounted to $5.5 million. The house has been refurbished with replica 19th-century furniture.

Stone cherub fountain

★ Main Bedroom
Sarah Winchester eventually died in her plush bedroom. The flooring is English mitered herringbone. At night she would play the harmonium situated opposite the elaborately carved bed.

The Greenhouse
incorporates 13 glass cupolas.

Tiffany Stained-Glass Window
The full beauty of the multi-colored Tiffany glass in this window is lost by its placement on an inside wall.

FACTS AND FIGURES

- The house contains 2,000 doors, 10,000 windows, 47 fireplaces and 17 chimneys.
- The number 13 is used superstitiously throughout – 13 bathrooms, 13 windows in a room, and 13 lights in the chandeliers.
- When the top of the house collapsed during the 1906 earthquake, building continued outward rather than upward.
- Mrs. Winchester's height of 4 ft 10 in (147 cm) explains hallways 2 ft (0.6 m) wide and doors only 5 ft (152 cm) high.
- Mrs. Winchester selected a new bedroom out of the 40 in the house each night, to confuse the spirits.

★ Grand Ballroom
This elaborate organ is one of the main features of the Grand Ballroom. Other features include artglass windows, a paneled ceiling, and hand-carved woodwork.

Switchback Stairs
Each of these 44 steps is only 1.5 inches (3.8 cm) high, and the entire staircase rises only 9 ft (2.7 m) from start to finish. It is thought they were built in this way to ease Sarah Winchester's arthritis.

Tour entrance

★ Winchester Firearms Museum
Included in this small display are the Winchester Repeating Rifle and the Model 1873, which came to be known as "The Gun that Won the West." Commemorative rifles include the Theodore Roosevelt and the John Wayne.

The Winchester Products Museum contains items, other than rifles, produced by the company, including roller skates, electric irons, and lawn mowers.

STAR FEATURES

★ **Grand Ballroom**

★ **Main Bedroom**

★ **Winchester Firearms Museum**

Stairwell to the Ceiling
This stairway leading nowhere is just one of the many unexplained oddities within the house.

NORTHERN
CALIFORNIA

Northern California at a Glance

Northern California stretches for more than 500 miles (800 km), from the sparsely populated border with Oregon to the high-tech urban civilization that marks the beginning of Southern California. Vast areas of wilderness cover the region, including volcanic landscapes and dense forests, imposing mountain ranges and rugged coastlines, proudly preserved by a series of national parks. Northern California also has a rich history, from the first European settlers in Monterey to the celebrated Gold Rush of 1849. Its natural beauty is enhanced by equally picturesque and significant towns, including the state's capital, Sacramento.

THE NORTH
(see pp426–37)

Redwood National Park *(see p434) is a protected landscape of dense, awe-inspiring redwood forests, including the world's tallest tree, which reaches a height of 368 ft (112 m). The area is perennially popular with anglers, hikers, birdwatchers, and campers.*

WINE COUNTRY
(see pp438–49)

Sonoma *(see pp448–9) was the site of the Bear Flag Revolt in 1846, when Americans rebelled against Mexican rule and tried to turn California into a republic. The vineyards of Sonoma County and the Napa Valley (see pp446–7), benefiting from good soil and an ideal climate, produce world-class wines.*

Carmel Mission *(see pp496–7) was founded in 1770 by Junípero Serra and became the most important of all the 21 Franciscan missions, serving as the administrative center for Northern California. Today, restored to its original splendor, it is considered to be the state's most beautiful church.*

0 kilometers 50

0 miles

Lassen Volcanic National Park (see p437) *was formed in 1914, when more than 300 eruptions resulted in a new landscape of mudflows and sulfurous streams heated by molten lava. Mount Lassen, part of the Cascade Mountain Range, is considered to be still active.*

Sacramento (see pp456–9) *has been the state capital since 1854, and the Capitol is one of California's finest buildings. Old Sacramento preserves its historic structures from the 1860s and 1870s, when the town was the western terminus of the transcontinental railroad.*

Yosemite National Park (see pp472–5) *is an unforgettable wilderness of forests, alpine meadows, breathtaking waterfalls, and imposing granite rocks. In 1864 it became the first protected park in the US.*

GOLD COUNTRY
AND THE
CENTRAL VALLEY
(see pp450–65)

THE HIGH SIERRAS
(see pp466–81)

NORTH CENTRAL
CALIFORNIA
(see pp482–501)

Columbia State Historic Park (see pp464–5) *was once the second largest town in California and is now the best preserved of the old gold mining centers.*

Wildlife and Wilderness

Eons ago, most of Northern California was under water, until geological forces pushed up the floor of the Central Valley, causing the Pacific Ocean to recede. Diverse terrains and ecosystems then emerged and Northern California is now a land of peaks, canyons, and headlands. Unique flora grows here, such as giant sequoias in the High Sierras *(see pp480–81)* and Monterey cypress trees *(see p495)*. Black bears roam redwood groves and hawks hover above Yosemite Valley *(see pp472–3)*. Legend has it that Bigfoot, America's version of the Yeti, makes his home in these parts. In order to protect this landscape, the environment-friendly Sierra Club began here in 1892 and is still active today.

Prairie Creek State Park has a herd of protected Roosevelt elk, which roam the dunes of Gold Bluff Beach.

Six Rivers National Forest

Trinity National Forest

Kla Natio

Clair Engle Lake Shas Na Fo

• Eureka

THE NORTH

Redwood National Park
(see pp432–3) *contains the world's tallest redwood tree, reaching 368 ft (112 m). These evergreens soak up the winter's heavy rainfall and are kept moist in summer by fogs, which move in from the ocean. Woodpeckers, spotted owls, mule deer, squirrels, and banana slugs frequent the groves.*

Sinkyone Wilderness

Eel River

Mendocino National Forest

The Sacramento National Wildlife Refuges protect the many birds that stop off on the Pacific Flyway.

Mendocino

Sutte Wildl Clear Lake

WINE COUNTRY

Lake Sonoma

Point Reyes Peninsula
(see pp396–7) *is a small "island," almost separated from the mainland by the San Andreas Fault. Its forested ridges, littoral rocks, and rock pools are a prime habitat for crustaceans such as the Pacific rock crab.*

Sonoma •

San Francisco •

BA

San Jo

The Farallon Islands
(see pp396–7) *are an important breeding ground for sea birds, including the puffin, and elephant seals. Visitors are not permitted on the islands.*

Año Nuevo State Reserve *(see p488)* is occupied every winter by hundreds of breeding elephant seals.

Poi

The Monterey Peninsula
(see pp494–5) is the winter home of the beautiful migratory monarch butterfly.

Key

☐	National Park
☐	State Park
☐	National Forest
☐	Wildlife refuge
- - -	River

0 kilometers 25

0 miles   25

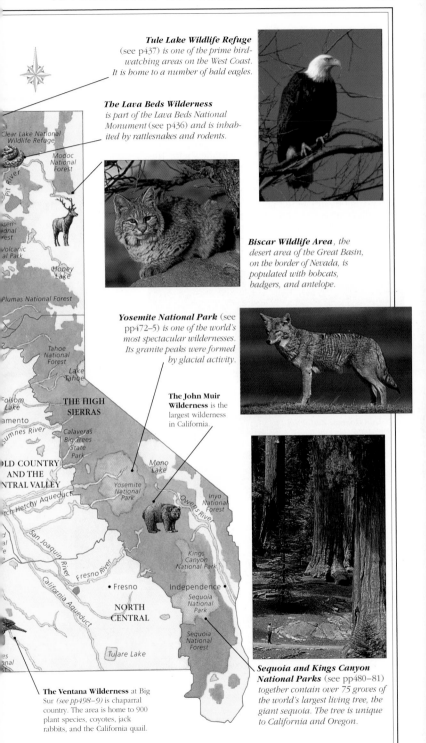

Tule Lake Wildlife Refuge
(see p437) *is one of the prime bird-watching areas on the West Coast. It is home to a number of bald eagles.*

The Lava Beds Wilderness
is part of the Lava Beds National Monument (see p436) and is inhabited by rattlesnakes and rodents.

Clear Lake National
Wildlife Refuge

Modoc
National
Forest

Pit River

ssen
onal
rest

olcanic
al Park

Honey
Lake

Plumas National Forest

Biscar Wildlife Area, *the desert area of the Great Basin, on the border of Nevada, is populated with bobcats, badgers, and antelope.*

Tahoe
National
Forest

Lake
Tahoe

Folsom
Lake

THE HIGH
SIERRAS

amento

Calaveras
Big Trees
State
Park

umnes River

OLD COUNTRY
AND THE
NTRAL VALLEY

Mono
Lake

Yosemite
National
Park

tch Hetchy Aqueduct

San Joaquin River

Fresno River

California Aqueduct

• Fresno

NORTH
CENTRAL

Tulare Lake

Inyo
National
Forest

Owens River

Kings
Canyon
National Park

Independence •

Sequoia
National
Park

Sequoia
National
Forest

Yosemite National Park (see pp472–5) *is one of the world's most spectacular wildernesses. Its granite peaks were formed by glacial activity.*

The John Muir Wilderness is the largest wilderness in California.

Sequoia and Kings Canyon National Parks (see pp480–81) *together contain over 75 groves of the world's largest living tree, the giant sequoia. The tree is unique to California and Oregon.*

The Ventana Wilderness at Big Sur *(see pp498–9)* is chaparral country. The area is home to 900 plant species, coyotes, jack rabbits, and the California quail.

The Wine of Northern California

CALIFORNIA IS THE MOST important wine-growing area in the United States, producing 90 percent of the nation's wine. More than 327,000 acres (132,000 ha) of the state's land is used for viticulture. Half of the grapes grown here are harvested from the fertile soil of the interior region, particularly the stretch of land bordered by the Sacramento Valley to the north and the San Joaquin Valley to the south. The north coast region accounts for less than a quarter of California's total wine-growing acreage, but many of the country's best Chardonnay, Sauvignon Blanc, Cabernet Sauvignon, and Merlot grapes are grown here. The north coast is also home to most of the state's 800 wineries. Chardonnay and Pinot Noir grapes are the mainstays of the central coast region, which extends from the San Francisco Bay Area to Santa Barbara.

LOCATOR MAP

▢ *Northern California wine region*

Grape harvest at V. Sattui Winery near St. Helena in Napa Valley

Late Harvest Zinfandel from the Hop Kiln Winery is a red dessert wine made from grapes left on the vine longer than usual to increase their sweetness. The winery is housed in an historic hop kiln barn.

• Fort Bragg

Ukiah •

Healdsburg •

• San

SAN FRANCISCO

THE STORY OF ZINFANDEL

The story of Zinfandel is one of the great success stories of California wine. This versatile grape is thought to have been brought to America from Croatia's Dalmatian coast. Zinfandel arrived in California in the 1850s, but only gained widespread popularity relatively recently. The Zinfandel reds, particularly those from the Dry Creek and Russian River valleys, are now in great demand. Some have oaky flavors while others have strong fruity flavors. The rosé White Zinfandel was created by winemakers to use up their surplus red grapes.

Saintsbury's Vin Gris is a Burgundy-style rosé wine, which is made from the juice of Pinot Noir grapes.

KEY

▢ Lake County	▢ Carneros Valley
▢ Anderson Valley	▢ Santa Cruz Mountains
▢ Alexander Valley	▢ Livermore Valley
▢ Dry Creek Valley	▢ Lodi Valley
▢ Russian River Valley	▢ El Dorado Valley
▢ Napa Valley	▢ Redwood–Ukiah Valley
▢ Sonoma Valley	▢ San Joaquin Valley

KEY FACTS ABOUT CALIFORNIA WINES

Location and Climate

California's latitude, proximity to the ocean, and sheltered valleys create a mild climate. Winters tend to be short and mild, while the growing season is long and hot but cooled by summer fogs. Combined with fertile soil, these factors mean that large areas have ideal grape-growing conditions.

Grape Varieties

California's most widely planted grape variety is **Chardonnay**, used to make a dry wine with a balance of fruit, acidity, and texture. Other popular whites include **Sauvignon Blanc** (also known as **Fumé Blanc**), **Chenin Blanc, Pinot Blanc, Gewürztraminer**, and **Johannisberg Riesling**. California's red wines are typically dry with some tannic astringency and include the rich, full-bodied **Cabernet Sauvignon**, **Merlot**, **Petite Sirah**, **Pinot Noir**, and **Zinfandel**.

Good Producers

Chardonnay: Acacia, Byron, Château Montelena, Ferrari-Carano, Kendall-Jackson, Kistler, Kunde Estate, Sonoma-Cutrer *Cabernet Sauvignon:* Beaulieu, Beringer, Grgich Hills, Heitz, The Hess Collection, Jordan, Joseph Phelps, Silver Oak, Robert Mondavi, Stag's Leap, Wente, Whitehall Lane. *Merlot:* Clos du Bois, Duckhorn, Frog's Leap, Silverado, Sterling. *Pinot Noir:* Dehlinger, Etude, Gary Farrell, Saintsbury, Sanford. *Sauvignon Blanc:* Duckhorn, Glen Ellen, Kenwood, Matanzas Creek, J Rochioli. *Zinfandel:* Dry Creek, Lake Sonoma, De Loach, Hop Kiln, Ridge, Rosenblum, Sebastiani.

Good Vintages

(Reds) 1994, 1993, 1992, 1991, 1990, 1987, 1986, 1985, 1984. *(Whites)* 1994, 1997, 1992, 1991, 1990, 1988, 1987, 1986, 1985.

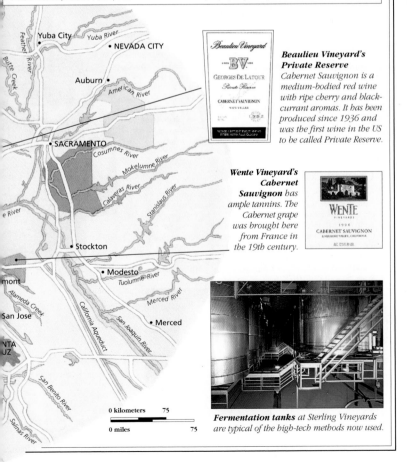

Beaulieu Vineyard's Private Reserve

Cabernet Sauvignon is a medium-bodied red wine with ripe cherry and black-currant aromas. It has been produced since 1936 and was the first wine in the US to be called Private Reserve.

Wente Vineyard's Cabernet Sauvignon *has ample tannins. The Cabernet grape was brought here from France in the 19th century.*

Fermentation tanks *at Sterling Vineyards are typical of the high-tech methods now used.*

0 kilometers   75

0 miles   75

The Bohemian North

PERHAPS BECAUSE the region attracted a wide range of people and enjoyed enormous wealth during the Gold Rush *(see pp44–5)*, Northern California has always tended to be nonconformist and somewhat hedonistic. This has caused some anguish over the years, as charlatans and crackpots have taken advantage of the region's broad-mindedness, but it has certainly made the area a colorful place. During the late 19th century San Francisco's Barbary Coast was home to casinos, opium dens, and brothels *(see p304)*. Utopian communities, organized around humanitarian, religious, or dietary principles, have been another facet of Northern California life. In the 1960s, the area's air of liberality made it a haven for members of the "Make Love, Not War" generation *(see p349)*. It has since attracted everybody from nudists and hot-tub lovers, to religious gurus and the latter-day hippies who helped turn marijuana into a chief crop of Humboldt County.

Spiritual guidance became popular during the 1850s, and 1860s. San Francisco attracted many spiritualist "mediums," who held regular seances. There are still a few spiritualist churches operating in the Bay Area.

Sally Stanford, born in 1903, was a virtual pariah in Sausalito when she took over the Valhalla (now the Chart House), the town's oldest restaurant, in 1950. Local citizens didn't approve of her previous occupation as a San Francisco madam. But Sally's personality eventually won the town over, and she served one term as the town's mayor (1976–8). She died in 1982.

UTOPIAN COMMUNITIES

From the 1850s to the 1950s, more Utopian communities were founded in Northern California than in any other place in the nation. William Riker's Holy City was established in 1918 in the Santa Cruz Mountains. Riker, a racist and forecaster of apocalypses, called his totalitarian community the "headquarters for the world's perfect government." It eventually died out because the community was celibate.

Fountain Grove was a Utopian outpost north of Santa Rosa, founded in 1875 by New York mystic Thomas Lake Harris. Harris's theory was that God was bisexual and Christ was the Divine Man-Woman. Under attack for alleged sexual and financial abuses, Harris was forced to close his commune in 1892.

William Riker

Young and old lived and traveled together in communties.

Bright colors and childlike designs were influenced by the lights and patterns experienced during drug-induced hallucinatory "trips."

Psychedelic Pop Art *posters of the 1960s were distinctive for their inflated, crammed typeface, developed by artist Wes Wilson.*

JIM JONES AND THE PEOPLE'S TEMPLE

The Reverend Jim Jones (1931–78) was a popular cult leader in the Bay Area during the 1970s, preaching an amalgam of racial and religious egalitarianism, political empowerment, doomsday visions, and sexual freedom. He was alternately a fundamentalist, supposedly "healing" people through touch, and a modern minister, with his services accompanied by music and dance. But he was also a self-proclaimed messiah. After building up a congregation of some 20,000 at his People's Temple in San Francisco, in 1978 he moved almost 1,000 of them to an isolated agricultural mission in Guyana, South America. After rumors of physical abuse and weapons caches at the colony brought international scrutiny, Jones ordered a mass suicide. Investigators later found hundreds of his followers' corpses in the jungle; they had all drunk a cyanide-laced fruit drink and the despotic reverend had been shot in the head.

Jim Jones

Hippies from the 1960s

PSYCHEDELIA

The term "psychedelic" originally referred to ideas or approaches that were somehow outrageous, non-conformist, or "mind-expanding." But after San Francisco witnessed the opening of the Psychedelic Shop on Haight Street in 1966 *(see p348)*, the word became associated with the hallucinatory drugs popular among the region's hippie generation.

Psychedelia then turned into a symbol of an entire lifestyle: young hippie communities rejecting conformity and traveling from one gathering to another on brightly painted buses, taking drugs, and preaching peace.

The Esalen Institute (see p499) *became famous in the 1960s as the center of the "human potential movement," a philosophy emphasizing individual responsibility for both the good and bad events in life. Today it is an expensive retreat where former flower children and stressed corporate executives all discuss spiritual insights while reclining in hot springs overlooking the Pacific Ocean.*

THE NORTH

R ANGING FROM DESERTED BEACHES *strewn with giant driftwood logs to dense forests at the foot of alpine peaks, the far north of California is the state at its most wild and rugged. The landscape is as diverse as any continent – lush redwood groves, the volcanic Cascade Mountains, the arid plains at the edge of the Great Basin – yet all this is confined within one-quarter of the state.*

Native Americans settled in extreme Northern California around 10,000 BC. They coexisted peacefully with each other and with the earth, leaving behind few signs of their existence apart from discarded sea shells and pictographs on cave walls. When the Europeans arrived in the area in the 19th century, things changed swiftly.

The first to come were fur trappers, in search of beavers, sea otters, and other pelts. Soon afterward gold seekers descended upon the region's rivers, hoping for similar riches to those found in the Sierra Nevada *(see pp44–5)*. Some gold was found, but the real wealth was made at the end of the century when lumber companies began to harvest the forests of coastal redwoods. These giant redwood trees *(Sequoia sempervirens)* are the region's defining feature. The finest forests have been protected by state and national parks and exude a palpable sense of history.

Inland, an even more ancient sight confronts visitors to the strange volcanic areas of Mount Lassen and the Lava Beds National Monument. Millions of years worth of geological activity has formed a stunning landscape that is devoid of civilization.

Far Northern California is sparsely populated, with a few medium-sized towns, such as Redding and Eureka. The prime attractions are natural, and life here, for visitors and residents, revolves around the great outdoors.

Lost Creek in Redwood National Park

◁ **Imposing snow-capped peak of Mount Shasta**

Exploring the North

RUGGED, WILD, AND SPARSELY POPULATED, California's northern extremes have more in common with neighboring Oregon and Washington than they do with the rest of the state. Dense forests of pine, fir, and redwood trees cover more than half the landscape, and two parallel mountain ranges, the Coast Range and, farther inland, the Sierra Nevada Mountains, divide the north into three very different sections. Along the coast, Cape Mendocino makes a good base for exploring the often deserted beaches and coastal redwood groves. Inland, the Sacramento Valley provides access to the beautiful snow-capped Mount Shasta, the volcanic spectacles of Lassen Volcanic National Park, and the Lava Beds National Monument.

SIGHTS AT A GLANCE

Arcata ❷
Avenue of the Giants ❼
Eureka ❸
Ferndale ❺
Lassen Volcanic
    National Park ⓯
Lava Beds National
    Monument ⓮
Mount Shasta ⓬
Samoa Cookhouse ❹
Scotia ❻
Shasta Dam ❿
Shasta State Historic Park ⓫
The Lost Coast ❽
Tule Lake National
    Wildlife Refuge ⓭
Weaverville ❾

Tour
Redwood National
    Park *pp432–3* ❶

Patrick's Point State Park in Humboldt County

GETTING AROUND

A car is essential for visiting northern California. Two north–south routes run parallel up and down the region, but the only comfortable route through the mountains east–west is Hwy 299. Bisecting the north, I-5 runs through the Sacramento Valley, while to the west US Hwy 101 runs through the lush valleys of the Russian and Eel Rivers. Public transportation is limited to Greyhound buses along the two main highways and a midnight train through the Sacramento Valley to Seattle.

KEY

Freeway

Major road

Minor road

Scenic route

River

☆ Viewpoint

SEE ALSO

- *Where to Stay* pp530–31

- *Where to Eat* pp568–9

Impressive peak of Mount Shasta

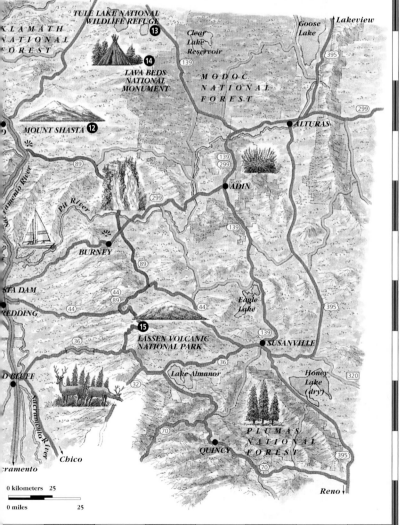

fford   **Klamath Falls**

KLAMATH NATIONAL FOREST

TULE LAKE NATIONAL WILDLIFE REFUGE **13**

Clear Lake Reservoir

Goose Lake

Lakeview

(139)

(395)

14 LAVA BEDS NATIONAL MONUMENT

MODOC NATIONAL FOREST

(299)

MOUNT SHASTA **12**

(89)

(139) (299)

●**ALTURAS**

●**ADIN**

(299)

(139)

Sacramento River

Pit River

☆

BURNEY

(89)

STA DAM

REDDING●

(44)

(89)

(44)

(44)

Eagle Lake

(395)

15

LASSEN VOLCANIC NATIONAL PARK

●**SUSANVILLE**

(139)

(36)

Lake Almanor

Honey Lake (dry)

(320)

D BLUFF●

(32)

(70)

PLUMAS NATIONAL FOREST

(395)

Sacramento River

ramento

Chico

●**QUINCY**

(70)

Reno ↓

0 kilometers   25

0 miles   25

Redwood National Park ❶

See pp432–3.

Arcata ❷

Road map A2. 🏛 *16,400.* 🚌
✈ *Arcata/Eureka Airport, 8 miles (13 km) N of Arcata.* ℹ *62 G St (707 822-3619).*

ARCATA IS A small town and its life revolves around Humboldt State University, in the hills above. Arcata's main square, with palm trees and a statue of President McKinley (1843–1901), is filled with bookstores and cafés. The town is a pleasant base for exploring the redwood region.

The forests east of Arcata are thought to be the stomping grounds of Bigfoot, the US equivalent to Asia's Yeti. No one has yet proved its existence, but footprints larger than those of the biggest bear have been found.

Eureka ❸

Road map A2. 🏛 *27,600.* 🚌
✈ *Arcata/Eureka Airport, 15 miles (24 km) N of Eureka.* ℹ *2112 Broadway (707 442-3738).*

EUREKA WAS founded by gold miners in 1850, who were so excited by their find that they proudly named it after

Ornate Carson Mansion in Eureka

REDWOODS AND THE LUMBER INDUSTRY

The tallest tree on earth, the coniferous coastal redwood *(Sequoia sempervirens)* is unique to northern California and southern Oregon, although it is also related to the giant sequoia *(Sequoiadendron gigantea)* of the High Sierras and the *Metasequoia glyptostrobiodes* species, native to China. Redwoods can live for 2,000 years and reach 350 ft (107 m), despite roots that grow up to 200 ft (61 m) horizontally but only 4–6 ft (1–2 m) deep.

The redwood's fast growth and resistance to disease makes it ideal for commercial use. By the 1920s, logging had destroyed 90 percent of the groves. The Save the Redwoods League was formed, buying land now protected in state parks. However, some groves are still owned by lumber companies, and their future is a major issue on both local and national levels.

Stacked redwood lumber

the state's ancient Greek motto meaning "I have found it." It has since expanded into the northern coast's largest industrial center, with extensive logging and fishing operations surrounding the state protected natural harbor.

West of US 101, between E and M streets along the waterfront, is Eureka's interesting Old Town. Its restored 19th-century buildings, many of them with cast-iron façades, have now been converted into fashionable cafés, bars, and restaurants.

Situated at M and Second streets is the extravagant Victorian architecture of Carson Mansion *(see pp26–7).* It was built in 1885 for millionaire lumber baron William Carson. Its whimsical Gothic design is enhanced by its redwood construction typical of the area, painted to resemble the more expensive medium of stone. Carson Mansion is now a gentlemen's club and is unfortunately closed to the general public.

Samoa Cookhouse ❹

79 Cookhouse Ln & Samoa Rd, Eureka. **Road map** A2. 📞 *(707) 442-1659.* ◯ *daily.* ● *Dec 25.* ♿

THE SAMOA COOKHOUSE was built in 1900 as a dining room for workers at the adjacent Louisiana Pacific pulp mill, one of many lumber mills standing on the narrow Samoa Peninsula. It was opened to the public in the 1960s, when automation in the mills had reduced the size of the workforce and the need for on-site dining facilities. The restaurant has retained its rustic décor and its giant-sized portions of ham and eggs, fried chicken, and other traditional American dishes. Old photographs and antique logging equipment add to the unique ambience.

Ferndale ❺

Road map A2. 🏛 *1,400.*
✈ *Arcata/Eureka Airport, 40 miles (64 km) N of Ferndale.* ℹ *PO Box 325, Ferndale (707 786-4477).*

LOCATED ON a flood plain near the mouth of the Eel River, Ferndale is a pastoral respite from the wilderness of

California's northern coast. The town was founded in 1852 by Danish, Swiss-Italian, and Portuguese immigrants who together established a lucrative dairy industry here. Many of Ferndale's Victorian houses have now been converted into inns and restaurants. In 1992, Ferndale was hit by one of the most powerful earthquakes in California's recent history, measuring 7.1 on the Richter scale, but damage was limited. Exhibits of the town's history can be seen in the **Ferndale Museum**.

The town is perhaps best known as the host of the annual Kinetic Sculpture Race, during which contestants ride their self-made vehicles from Arcata to Centerville County Beach, outside Ferndale.

🏛 **Ferndale Museum**
Shaw & 3rd St. [] (707) 786-4466.
⬜ Feb–Sep: Wed–Sun.

Gingerbread Mansion, one of Ferndale's Victorian houses

Scotia ❻

Road map A2. 🚶 2,500. 🚌
✈ Arcata/Eureka Airport, 40 miles (64 km) N of Scotia. 🛈 715 Wildwood Ave (707 764-3436).

THE TOWN OF SCOTIA was built in 1887 to house the workers from the **Pacific Lumber Company**'s massive redwood mill, which dominates the south end of town. Palco, as the company is better known, was established in 1869 and owns and manages nearly 200,000 acres (80,000 ha) of prime redwood forest along the banks of the Eel River and its tributaries. Incorporating two sawmills, a school, medical clinics, and housing for nearly 300 lumber

Palco's redwood visitors' center in Scotia

employees and their families, Scotia is the only complete lumber community still in existence in California.

Exhibits on the history of Scotia, and on the redwood lumber industry as a whole, are displayed in a small museum in the center of town, which also dispenses passes for self-guided tours of the lumber mill. Here visitors can see each stage of the milling process: huge logs are debarked by powerful jets of water, sliced by laser-guided saws into lumber, then dried and stacked ready for shipping.

🏭 **Pacific Lumber Company**
125 Main St. [] (707) 764-2222.
⬜ Mon–Fri. ♿

Avenue of the Giants ❼

🚌 Garberville. 🛈 Weott (Mar–Oct: daily; Nov–Feb: Thu–Sun) (707 946-2263).

THE WORLD'S tallest redwood trees and the most extensive primeval redwood groves stand along the banks of the Eel River within the impres-

sive 50,000-acre (20,200-ha) Humboldt Redwoods State Park *(see p432)*. The best overall sense of these redwoods can be seen by driving along the 33-mile (53-km) Avenue of the Giants, a winding two-lane highway running parallel to US 101 through the park. For the best experience, however, leave your car in one of the many parking areas provided and walk around the groves, taking in the full immensity and magnificence of the trees.

The tallest individual specimen, the 364-ft (110-m) Dyersville Giant, was blown over during a storm in the winter of 1991, but its size is perhaps even more astounding now, lying on its side in Founder's Grove at the north end of the park. Currently the tallest and largest trees stand within the Rockefeller Forest above the west bank of the river.

The visitors' center, halfway along the Avenue of the Giants on US 101, exhibits displays on the natural history of these mighty forests. It also supplies maps and detailed information on the many hiking and camping facilities available within the park.

Avenue of the Giants, in Humboldt Redwoods State Park

A Tour of Redwood National Park ❶

REDWOOD NATIONAL PARK protects some of the largest original redwood forests in the world, stretching along the coastline of Northern California. Established by President Johnson in 1968 to promote tourism to the area, the 58,000-acre (23,500-ha) park includes smaller areas that had already been established as state parks. A tour of the area takes one full day, although two days allows time to walk away from the roads and experience the tranquillity of these majestic groves.

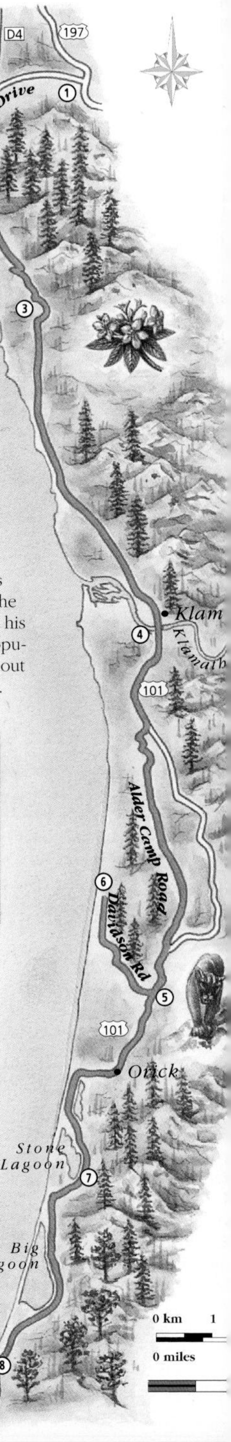

Fort Dick
D3
D4
197
Parkway Drive
101
Klam
Alder Camp Road
Davison Rd
Orick
Stone Lagoon
Big Lagoon
0 km 1
0 miles

Coastal redwood trees

Del Norte Coast Redwood State Park ③
This park became the first protected area in 1926. Part of the old Redwood Highway has been maintained as a hiking trail. In spring, wildflowers cover the hillsides.

Trees of Mystery ④
A major tourist attraction of the area is marked by giant fiberglass statues of the mythical lumberjack Paul Bunyan and his ox, Babe. The two characters were popularized in early 20th-century stories about their journey from Maine to California.

Tall Trees Grove ⑤
The world's tallest tree, a 368-ft (112-m) giant, stands in the aptly named Tall Trees Grove, at the southern end of the park. The park provides a habitat for one of the world's last remaining herds of Roosevelt elk.

Gold Bluffs Beach ⑥
This 11-mile (18-km) beach is rated by many as the most beautiful in Northern California.

Humboldt Lagoons State Park ⑦
Big Lagoon, a freshwater lake stretching for 3 miles (5 km), and two other estuaries form Humboldt Lagoons State Park.

Patrick's Point State Park ⑧
In winter, the headlands are a good place to watch for migrating gray whales. Rock pools abound with smaller marine life.

Jedediah Smith Redwoods State Park ①

Found among the 9,200 acres (3,720 ha) of this park are the most awe-inspiring coastal redwoods. The park was named after the fur-trapper Jedediah Smith, the first white man to walk across the US. He explored this region in 1828 *(see p42)*.

Crescent City ②

This northern town is the site of the headquarters and main information center for Redwood National Park.

Key

| Tour route |
| Other roads |

TIPS FOR DRIVERS

Tour length: Arcata to Crescent City is 78 miles (125 km). US 101 is the quickest route.

Duration of trip: One could drive the entire route in under two hours one-way, but to experience a more satisfying and relaxing visit to the Redwood National Park area, allow at least a full day.

When to go: September and October are ideal months to travel. Spring and summer can be foggy, but the best flowering plants are on view during these months. Winter is often rainy but best for whale-watching. Summer is the prime tourist season, although crowds are rarely a problem in this remote area of the state.

Where to stay and eat: Tourist services are comparatively few and far between in this region. However, there is a limited range of restaurants and motels available in Orick and Klamath, while a much wider range of facilities is available in Crescent City (see pp530 & 568) and Arcata, south of the park (see p430).

Visitor information: Redwood Empire Association, 2801 Leavenworth Street, San Francisco, CA 94133. (415) 394-5991. W www.redwood.nationalpark.com

The Lost Coast, near Crescent City

The Lost Coast ❽

Road map A2. 🚌 *Garberville.* ℹ️ *Shelter Cove (707 923-2613).*

COVERING a small section of coastline so craggy and wild that no road could reasonably be built along it, the so-called Lost Coast is the largest remaining stretch of undeveloped shoreline in California. Protected by the United States government within the Sinkyone Wilderness State Park and the King Range National Conservation Area, the Lost Coast region stretches for more than 40 miles (64 km).

The salmon-fishing port of Shelter Cove, tucked away within a tiny bay, is at the center of the Lost Coast. Its remote location has kept the village small, but it remains a good base for hikers and wildlife enthusiasts. Sixteen miles (25 km) of hiking trails, inhabited only by fauna such as black bears, deer, mink, and bald eagles, run along the clifftops, interspersed with free camp sites. Shelter Cove is accessible only via a winding but well-maintained road.

A good feel for the Lost Coast can be had by taking Hwy 211 west of US 101 and then following the scenic road between Humboldt Redwoods State Park and Ferndale *(see p430)*. This beautiful 50-mile (80-km) road runs to the edge of the Pacific Ocean around Cape Mendocino, the westernmost point on the coast of California.

Weaverville ❾

Road map A2. 🏘️ *3,500.* ✈️ *Redding Municipal Airport, 40 miles (64 km) E of Weaverville.* ℹ️ *317 Main St (530 623-6101).*

THE SMALL rural town of Weaverville, set back in the mountains between the coast and the Central Valley, has changed little in the 150 years since it was founded by gold prospectors.

At the heart of the small commercial district, which boasts the state's oldest drugstore, is the **Jake Jackson Museum**. This small museum has displays tracing both the history of Weaverville and its surrounding gold-mining and lumber region. Adjacent to the museum, the Joss House State Historic Site is the oldest and best-preserved Chinese Temple in the country. Built in 1874, it serves as a reminder of the many Chinese immigrants who arrived in the US to mine gold and stayed in the state as cheap labor building the California railroads *(see pp46–7)*.

North of Weaverville, the Trinity Alps, part of the Salmon Mountain Range, rise up at the center of a beautiful mountain wilderness. They are popular with hikers and backpackers in the summer and with cross-country skiers during the winter months.

🏛 **Jake Jackson Museum**
508 Main St. 📞 *(530) 623-5284.* ⏰ *Apr–Nov: daily; Dec–Mar: Tue & Sat only.* **Donation**.

Shasta Dam, controlling the North's water supplies

Shasta Dam ⓾

🚉 *Redding.* **Visitors' Center** 📞 *(530) 225-4100, (800) 874-7562.*

IN ORDER TO provide a steady supply of water for agriculture, a cheap source of electricity for manufacturers, prevent flooding in the valley, and offer jobs for workers who had been left unemployed by the downturn in local mining industries, the US government funded the Central Valley Project. This was a network of dams, canals, and reservoirs, set up during the Depression of the 1930s and centered upon the 602-ft (183-m) high, 3,460-ft (1,055-m) long Shasta Dam. With a spillway three times as high as Niagara Falls, the dam is one of the most impressive civil engineering achievements in the country to this day.

Shasta State Historic Park ⓫

Road map A2. 🚉 *Redding.* **Visitors' Center** 📞 *(530) 225-2065.* 🕐 *Wed–Sun.*

DURING THE 1850s, Shasta was one of the largest gold mining camps in the state and the base of operations for prospectors working along the Sacramento, Trinity, McCloud, and Pit Rivers. As the Gold Rush faded, however, the town faded too, especially after the railroad was rerouted through the town of Redding, 5 miles (8 km) to the east.

Shasta is now a ghost town, but in the early 1920s the state of California, realizing its historical importance, took over the site and began to restore it. Numerous old brick buildings are preserved in a state of arrested decay, and the old **Shasta Courthouse** has been restored to its original condition. A small visitors' center has exhibits tracing the history of the town.

One mile (1.5 km) west of Shasta town, the land around Lake Whiskeytown forms the smallest parcel of the three-part Shasta-Whiskeytown-Trinity National Recreation Area, a forest preserve surrounding the three reservoirs. Lake Shasta is the largest of the three. Trinity Lake is also known as Clair Engle Lake, in honor of the local politician who helped make this ambitious reclamation project a reality. All three lakes are popular with fishermen, waterskiers, houseboat owners, and other recreational users.

🏛 Shasta Courthouse and Visitors' Center
Main St. 📞 *(530) 243-8194.* 🕐 *10am–5pm Wed–Sun.*

Mount Shasta ⓬

Road map B1. 🚉 *Dunsmuir.* 🚌 *Siskiyou.* 🚌 *Shasta.* **Visitors' Center** 📞 *(530) 926-4865.* 🕐 *May–Oct: Mon–Sat; Nov–Apr: Mon–Fri.* 🌐 *www.mtshastachamber.com*

MOUNT SHASTA reaches a height of 14,162 ft (4,317 m) and is the second highest of the Cascade Mountains, after Mount Rainier in Washington State. Visible more than 100 miles (160 km) away and usually covered with snow, the summit is a popular destination for mountaineers.

Mount Shasta, towering over the town of Shasta below

Tule Lake National Wildlife Refuges ⓭

Road map B1. 🚉 *Klamath Falls.* **Visitors' Center** 📞 *(530) 667-2231.*

SIX REFUGES on both sides of the California–Oregon border form one of the most popular bird-watching spots in the western United States.

Interior of the preserved Shasta Courthouse

Centering upon Tule Lake and the Lower Klamath River, much of the region has been set aside as wildlife refuges (*see pp420–21*), popular with bird-watchers. In the autumn the refuges attract hundreds of thousands of wildfowl as they make their migration south, from Canada to the Central Valley and beyond. Tule Lake is also the winter home to as many as 1,000 bald eagles, a comparatively rare species in California.

Lava Beds National Monument ⑭

Road map B1. ▦ *Klamath Falls.* **Visitors' Center** ▮ *(530) 667-2282.* ◯ *daily.*

THE LAVA BEDS National Monument spreads over 46,500 acres (18,800 ha) of the Modoc Plateau, the volcanic tableland of northeastern California, and preserves an eerie landscape of lava flows and cinder cones. Beneath the lava beds are more than 200 caves – cylindrical tunnels created by exposed lava turning to stone.

The greatest concentration of caves can be visited via the Cave Loop Road, 2 miles (3 km) south of the park's visitors' center. From here, a short trail leads down into Mushpot Cave, the only one with lights and a paved floor. The name derives from splatters of lava found near the entrance.

Other caves along the road are also named for their main feature: Crystal Cave contains sparkling crystals, and Catacombs Cave requires visitors to crawl through its twisting passages. To visit any of the caves, wear sturdy shoes, carry a flashlight, and be sure to check first with the visitors' center.

The park is also notable as the site of the Modoc War of 1872–3, the only major war between the US and the Native Americans in California. After being removed from the area to a reservation in Oregon, a group of Modoc Indians returned under the command of Chief Kientpoos, or "Captain Jack." For six months they evaded the US Cavalry, but

Captain Jack's Stronghold in Lava Beds National Monument

Captain Jack was eventually captured and hanged, and the rest were forced into a reservation in what is now Oklahoma. Captain Jack's Stronghold is along the park's north border.

Lassen Volcanic National Park ⑮

Road map B2. ▦ *Chester, Red Bluff.* **Visitors' Center** ▮ *(530) 595-4444.* ◯ *Jun–Sep: daily; Oct–May: Mon–Fri.*

PRIOR TO the eruption of Mount St. Helens in Washington in 1980, the 10,457-ft (3,187-m) high Lassen Peak was the last volcano to erupt on the mainland United States. In a series of nearly 300 eruptions between 1914 and 1917, Lassen Peak laid waste to 100,000 acres (40,500 ha) of the surrounding land. The area was set aside as Lassen Volcanic National Park in 1916.

The volcano is the southernmost in the Cascade Mountain range and is considered to be still active. Numerous areas on its flanks show clear signs of the geological processes. Bumpass Hell was named

after an early tour guide, Kendall Bumpass, who lost his leg in one of the boiling mudpots in 1865. This boardwalk trail leads past a series of steaming, sulfurous pools of boiling water, heated by molten rock deep underground. Bumpass Hell is one of the park's most interesting stops and is located along Hwy 89, 5 miles (8 km) from the Southwest Entrance Station.

In winter, Hwy 89 across the park is closed because of weather conditions. In summer, the road winds through the park, climbing more than 8,500 ft (2,590 m) high, up to Summit Lake. The road continues across to the Devastated Area, a bleak gray landscape of rough volcanic mudflows, ending at Manzanita Lake in the northwest corner of the park. Here the **Loomis Museum** displays a photographic record of Lassen Peak's many eruptions.

The park contains more than 150 miles (240 km) of hiking trails, including a very steep 2.5 mile (4 km) route up the side of Mount Lassen to the ashen gray summit.

🏛 **Loomis Museum**
Lassen Park Rd, North Entrance.
▮ *(530) 595-4444.* ◯ *late Jun–mid-Sep: daily.* ⬤ *Jul 4.*

Sulfur springs in Lassen Volcanic National Park

THE WINE COUNTRY

FAMOUS THROUGHOUT THE WORLD *for its superlative wines, the Wine Country interior has a temperate climate, miles of vine-covered hills, and spectacular architecture. To the west lie the dramatic, rocky landscapes of the Sonoma and Mendocino coastlines. Throughout the region, a wide choice of excellent food and, of course, premium wine is available, making this an ideal place for a relaxing retreat.*

California's wine industry was born in the small, crescent-shaped Sonoma Valley, when, in 1823, Franciscan fathers planted grape vines to produce sacramental wines. In 1857, the flamboyant Hungarian Count Agoston Haraszthy brought winemaking in California to a new level: using imported European grape varieties, he planted the state's first major vineyard at Sonoma's revered Buena Vista Winery *(see p449)*. Haraszthy made a name not only for himself (he is known as the "father of California wine") but also for this previously unrecognized wine-producing region.

Over the years, many wine producers have followed in the count's footsteps, most of them favoring the rich, fertile soil of the Napa Valley. Hundreds of wineries now stand side by side along the length of the valley floor. Most of them offer tours of their facilities and wine tastings. Many are also of architectural interest, including such gems as the Mission-style Robert Mondavi Winery and the white Mediterranean-style Sterling Vineyards, which is perched on a volcanic bluff. Nearby, the stunning modern winery of Clos Pegase is distinguished by rows of imposing russet- and earth-colored columns and towers.

Nestled at the northernmost edge of the Napa Valley is the small town of Calistoga, famous for its restorative mud baths, enormous geysers, and hot mineral-water tubs. West of the valley, the Russian River which is bordered by the Sonoma and Mendocino coastal areas flows into the Pacific Ocean. These wild stretches of shoreline provide perfect opportunities for bird- and whale-watching and beachcombing.

Goat Rock Beach at the mouth of the Russian River

◁ Mustard plants growing in a Napa Valley vineyard in the spring

Exploring the Wine Country

THE SHELTERED VALLEYS of the coastal ranges provide the best conditions for planting vines, particularly within the Russian River, Sonoma, and Napa valleys. To the west of these famous wine-producing areas, quaint coastal towns, such as Mendocino, Jenner, and Bodega Bay, are surrounded by pristine, secluded beaches and small rock pools. Inland, visitors can explore the ancient redwood groves on foot, horseback, or by train. For those who prefer to have a bird's-eye view of the region, trips are available in hot-air balloons that soar gracefully above the vineyards. A short drive away are several immense state historic parks, with dense forests and unique architecture. Nearby, a wide variety of watersports is offered at Clear Lake, California's largest freshwater lake, and Lake Berryessa, which is the second largest artificial lake in the state.

Gerstle Cove, site of a marine preserve at Salt Point

GETTING AROUND

The majority of visitors explore the Wine Country and the scenic areas along the Sonoma and Mendocino coasts by car. From San Francisco, Hwy 1 follows the coast; Hwy 101 runs south–north through the center of the region and into Humboldt County. Route 20 links Nevada City and the Wine Country, joining Hwy 101 north of Lake Mendocino. Public transportation services in the area are limited, although bus tours from San Francisco are available, and train tours of the Napa Valley *(see pp446–7)* and of the northern redwood forests *(see p443)* operate regularly. The closest international airports are in San Francisco and Oakland *(see pp598–9)*.

SEE ALSO

• *Where to Stay* pp531–3
• *Where to Eat* pp569–71

KEY

▤	Freeway
▬	Major road
▭	Minor road
▤	Scenic route
➳	River
☀	Viewpoint

Eureka

1 LEGGETT VALLEY

DOS RIG

101

FORT BRAGG

Noyo River

WIL

MENDOCINO 20
2 **COMPTCHE** UKIAH ROAD
3
VAN DAMME STATE PARK

Navarro River 128

1

MOUNTAIN VIEW ROAD

4 **POINT ARENA**
POINT ARENA LIGHTHOUSE

Garcia River

1

SALT POINT STATE PARK

FOR

HI

One of Napa Valley's many vineyards

SIGHTS AT A GLANCE

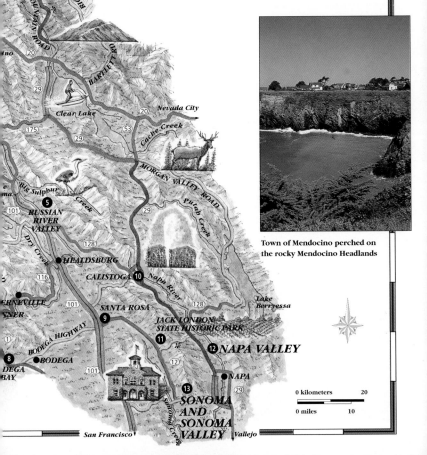

Town of Mendocino perched on
the rocky Mendocino Headlands

0 kilometers   20

0 miles   10

Leggett Valley ❶

Road map A2. 🚌 *to Leggett.*
ℹ️ *70400 Hwy 101.*

THIS LUSH, GREEN VALLEY, separated from the Pacific Ocean by the King Mountain Range, is famous in California for its majestic giant redwoods. In the 1930s a hole was cut in the trunk of one enormous redwood to allow motorists to drive through the tree.

Hikers come to Leggett Valley and the surrounding area to enjoy the atmospheric redwood forest trails (part of the forest here was used to film scenes for George Lucas's science-fiction epic, *Star Wars*). The local wildlife population includes raccoons and deer, and golden eagles can often be seen soaring above the trees, searching the forest floor for unsuspecting prey.

South Fork Eel River, which is rich in salmon and steelhead trout, attracts many birds, including herons. The river is also popular with anglers and, in summer, swimmers.

Mendocino ❷

Road map A3. 🏠 *1,200.* 🚌 ℹ️ *332 N Main St, Fort Bragg (707 961-6300; 800 726-2780).*

THE SETTLERS who founded this fishing village came to California from New England in 1852. They built their new homes to resemble as closely as possible those they had left behind on the East Coast, with pointed gables and decorative wooden trims. As a result, the Mendocino coastline is often referred to as "California's New England Coast."

Perched on a spectacular rocky promontory high above the Pacific Ocean, Mendocino has retained the picturesque charm of its days as a major fishing and logging center. Although tourism is now its main industry, the town remains virtually untarnished by commercialism. It is a thriving arts center and has a large number of resident artists and writers. Visitors can stroll around the many exclusive boutiques, bookshops, art galleries, and cafés. Those who prefer the attractions of nature can admire the beauty of the heather-covered bluffs, the migrating gray whales, and the stunning ocean vistas.

Giant ferns lining the beautiful Fern Canyon Trail in Van Damme State Park

Van Damme State Park ❸

Comptche Ukiah Rd. 📞 *(707) 937-5804.* 📠 *(707) 937-4016.* 🚌 *from Point Arena.* 🕐 *May–Sep: daily; Oct–Apr: Sat & Sun.* 💾 ♿

THIS BEAUTIFUL 2,200-acre (890-ha) preserve has some of California's most scenic forest trails, shaded by immense redwoods and giant ferns, and accompanied by meandering creeks. The coastal areas of the park are popular with abalone divers. For visitors who want to enjoy a hike or jog through gorgeous countryside, the lush Fern Canyon Trail is one of the best in the park, which also has several cycle trails.

Visitors also come to Van Damme to contemplate the peculiar Pygmy Forest, an eerie grove of old, stunted trees. Due to a combination of poor soil and bad drainage, these trees grow no taller than about 4 ft (1.2 m). The Pygmy Forest, 3 miles (5 km) north of the park, is accessible on foot or by car.

Point Arena Lighthouse ❹

Road map A3. 📞 *(707) 882-2777.* 🚌 *from Point Arena.* **Lighthouse and Museum** 🕐 *Jan–Nov: daily; Dec: Sat & Sun.* 💾 ♿ *museum only.* 🗗

ONE MILE (1.5 km) north of the little Point Arena fishing village stands this impressive 115-ft (35-m) lighthouse. Erected in 1870, the original brick building was destroyed in the great earthquake of 1906 *(see p20)*. It was replaced by the present reinforced concrete structure, produced in San Francisco by the Concrete Chimney Company.

A climb up the 145 steps to the top of the lighthouse provides a stunning view of the coastline – the effort is particularly worthwhile on fog-free

Mendocino overlooking the ocean from the bay's rocky headlands

days. Tours of the lighthouse, which are available all year round, give visitors a chance to see its huge original Fresnel lens close-up. Built in France, the lens measures more than 6 ft (1.8 m) in diameter, weighs more than 2 tons, and floats in a large pool of mercury.

The adjacent fog signal building, which dates from 1869, now houses a museum. Among the exhibits are several compressed-air foghorns and displays on the history of the lighthouse, including some fascinating old photographs.

Point Arena Lighthouse overlooking the Pacific Ocean

Russian River Valley ❺

from Healdsburg. 📋 16209 First St, Guerneville (707 869-9000).
W www.russianriverchamber.com

BISECTED BY the Russian River and its tributaries, the area known as the Russian River Valley is so vast that it contains several smaller valleys, some dominated by hillsides planted with grapevines and apple orchards, others by redwood groves, family farms, and sandy river beaches. About 60 wineries, many of which are open for wine tastings, are scattered throughout the valley.

At the hub of the valley is the small town of Healdsburg, where visitors often congregate around the splendid Spanish-style town square, with its shops, cafés, and restaurants.

Southwest of Healdsburg lies the tiny, friendly town of Guerneville, a summertime

THE SKUNK TRAIN

Since 1885, the Skunk Train has been running from Fort Bragg, a coastal logging town north of Mendocino, into the heart of the redwood groves. Thanks to the odoriferous mix of diesel and gasoline once used to fuel the locomotive, waiting passengers could always smell the train before they could see it, hence its name. Today, locomotive lovers can ride on one of the steam, diesel, or electric trains for a half- or full-day tour through the forests.

Skunk Train and its smoke cloud

haven for San Francisco Bay Area residents, particularly gay men and women. Every year in September, Guerneville plays host to the very popular Russian River Jazz Festival at Johnson's Beach. Johnson's is also a good place from which to take a canoe or rafting trip down the gentle Russian River, where turtles, river otters, and great blue herons are often sighted. Hikers and equestrians flock to Guerneville to visit the 805-acre (330-ha) **Armstrong Redwoods State Reserve**, which is the site of one of the few remaining old-growth redwood forests in California. Among the mighty redwoods in the park is a 308-ft (94-m) giant – a 1,400-year-old tree named Colonel Armstrong.

♣ Armstrong Redwoods State Preserve

17000 Armstrong Woods Rd, Guerneville. 📋 (707) 869-2015, 865-2391. ⏰ daily.

Salt Point State Park ❻

Hwy 1. 📋 (707) 847-3221, 847-3465. 🚌 from Santa Rosa. ⏰ daily.
🏖 ♿

WITHIN THIS FORESTED 6,000-acre (2,400-ha) seaside park are several rocky coves, frequented by abalone divers and surf fishers. Salt Point also includes Gerstle Cove Marine Reserve, where divers admire protected sea anemones, starfish, and various rock fish.

Numerous bridle paths and hiking trails wind through Salt Point's pines, redwoods, and flower-filled meadows. In April and May, the most popular park attraction is the route that leads through the 317-acre (130-ha) Kruse Rhododendron State Reserve, where rhododendrons with brilliant pink and purple blooms grow up to 30 ft (9 m) tall.

Gerstle Cove in Salt Point State Park

Cannon on display in front of the Russian Orthodox chapel at Fort Ross

Fort Ross State Historic Park **7**

Road map A3. **☏** *(707) 847-3286.* **🚌** *from Point Arena.* **◯** *sunrise– sunset daily.* **◯** *Jan 1, Thanksgiving, Dec 25.* 🚫 ♿

O N A WINDSWEPT headland, 12 miles (19 km) north of Jenner, stands the grand Fort Ross State Historic Park. A well-restored Russian trading outpost, the fort was founded in 1812 and was occupied until 1841 (the name "Ross" is a derivative of the Russian word "Rossyia", meaning Russia).

The Russians were the first European visitors to the region, serving as representatives of the Russian-American Company, which had been established in 1799. Although it was the presence of Russian fur hunters in the North Pacific that induced Spain to occupy Alta California in 1769, the Russians never tried to expand their territory in California. After 30 years of peaceful trading, they abandoned the fort.

Built in 1836, the original house of the fort's last manager, Alexander Rotchev, is still intact today, and several other buildings have been painstakingly reconstructed within the wooden palisade. The most impressive structure in Fort Ross is the Russian Orthodox chapel, which was constructed from local redwood in 1824.

A small visitors' center offers picnic facilities and maps and booklets about the fort. Every year, a living history day is held on the last Saturday of July. More than 200 costumed participants re-create life at the outpost in the 1800s.

Bodega Bay **8**

Hwy 1. **🏠** *1,300.* **🚌** **ℹ** *850 Hwy 1 (707 875-3422).*

I N 1963, THE COASTAL TOWN of Bodega Bay, with its white clapboard houses, appeared in Alfred Hitchcock's classic film, *The Birds*. In the tiny neighboring town of Bodega, visitors can still see the Potter Schoolhouse, now a private residence, which was featured in the film.

Bodega Head, the small peninsula sheltering Bodega **A harbor seal on Goat Rock Beach** Bay, is one of California's best whale-watching points. Other favorite Bodega Bay pastimes include golfing, bird-watching, digging for clams, and deep-sea fishing. In the evening, visitors can watch the fishing fleets unload their day's catch at Tides Wharf dock on Hwy 1.

The northern end of Bodega Bay marks the beginning of the Sonoma Coast State Beach, a 10-mile (16-km) stretch of ten beaches, separated by rocky bluffs. At the northernmost tip of this chain of beaches sits the charming little town of Jenner. Here, the wide Russian River spills into the Pacific Ocean, and hundreds of gray harbor seals bask in the sun and breed on Goat Rock Beach. The most rewarding time to watch the seals is during their "pupping season," which begins in March and lasts until late June.

Santa Rosa **9**

Road map A3. **🏠** *136,000.* **✈** *Sonoma County Airport, 6 miles (10 km) N of Santa Rosa.* **🚌** **ℹ** *9 4th St (707 577-8674; 800 404-7673).*

S ANTA ROSA, which is one of the fastest-growing cities in California, is best known for its past and present residents, most notably the horticulturist Luther Burbank (1849–1926). Burbank lived here for more than 50 years and became world famous for creating 800 new plant varieties including fruits, vegetables, and ornamental flowers.

Self-guided tours explore the one-acre (0.5-ha) site of the **Luther Burbank Home and Gardens**, which includes a rose garden, and an orchard. The Victorian garden features plants often found in domestic gardens in the 1880s.

Robert L Ripley (1893–1949) was also a Santa Rosa hero. An illustrator who collected peculiar artifacts, Ripley created the "Ripley's Believe It or Not!®" cartoon strip *(see p326)*. The **Robert L Ripley Memorial Museum** has unusual displays

Fishing boats at North Beach Jetty Marina in Bodega Bay

Spring flowers in bloom at Luther Burbank Home and Gardens

about the life of this former Santa Rosa native. A large collection of assorted Ripley memorabilia is also exhibited.

The late Charles Schulz, the creator of the beloved "Peanuts" series, was a resident of Santa Rosa. Admirers of Schulz's cartoon characters can visit **Snoopy's Gallery and Gift Shop**. The shop stocks the widest range of Snoopy, Charlie Brown, and "Peanuts" products in the world.

❧ Luther Burbank Home and Gardens
204 Santa Rosa Ave. ☎ (707) 524-5445. **Gardens** ☐ daily. **Home** ☐ Apr–Oct: Tue–Sun. ☑

⛫ Robert L Ripley Memorial Museum
492 Sonoma Ave. ☎ (707) 524-5233. ☐ Apr–Oct: Wed–Sun. ☒

⬛ Snoopy's Gallery and Gift Shop
1665 Steele Lane. ☎ (707) 546- 3385. ☐ 10am–6pm daily. ● Easter Sun.

Calistoga ⑩

Road map A3. 👥 4,715. 🚌
🛈 1458 Lincoln Ave (707 942-6333).

Visitors have enjoyed taking invigorating mineral or mud baths here since this little spa town was founded in the mid-19th century by the state's first millionaire, Sam Brannan (1819–89). Today, crowds are still drawn to Calistoga by its specialized spa treatments and good Wine Country cuisine. The town also has a range of pleasant accommodations and small boutiques selling everything from handmade soaps to European home furnishings.

Two miles (3 km) to the north of the town, the **Old Faithful Geyser** spouts jets of boiling mineral water 60 ft (18 m) into the sky approximately once every 40 minutes. To the west lies the **Petrified Forest**. Here hikers can see huge redwoods turned to stone by a volcanic eruption more than three million years ago (see p446).

Many visitors who prefer to hike among living redwoods travel east to the Robert Louis Stevenson State Park, where the author of *Treasure Island* and his wife, Fanny Osbourne, spent their honeymoon in 1880 (see p22). Those who climb the 5 miles (8 km) from the park to the summit of the 4,343-ft (1,325-m) Mount St. Helena, the Wine Country's highest peak, are rewarded by a breathtaking view of the vineyards below. To enjoy the bird's-eye view without making the rigorous ascent, it is worth taking a trip in a glider or hot-air balloon. These are available at the gliderport in nearby Calistoga.

⛰ Old Faithful Geyser
1299 Tubbs Lane. ☎ (707) 942-6463. ☐ daily. ☒

⛰ Petrified Forest
4100 Petrified Forest Rd. ☎ (707) 942-6667. ☐ daily. ● Thanksgiving, Dec 25. ☒ ♿ limited.

Jack London State Historic Park ⑪

London Ranch Rd, Glen Ellen. ☎ (707) 938-5216. **Park and Museum** ☐ daily. ● Jan 1, Thanksgiving, Dec 25. ☒ ♿ museum only. ☑

In the early 1900s, the world-famous author of *The Call of the Wild, The Sea Wolf,* and more than 50 other books (see p22) abandoned his hectic lifestyle to live in this tranquil 800-acre (325-ha) expanse of oaks, madrones, California buckeyes, and redwoods. London (1876–1916) aptly named this territory the Beauty Ranch, and it still contains his stables, vineyards, and the cottage where he wrote and where he died. Also here are the eerie ruins of London's dream home, the Wolf House, which was mysteriously destroyed by fire just before its completion. The park is an ideal place for a quiet picnic and a hike.

After London's death, his widow, Charmian Kittredge (1871–1955), built a magnificent home on the ranch, called the House of Happy Walls. The house is now a museum displaying London memorabilia. The author's writing desk and early copies of his work are exhibited, as well as his collection of South Pacific art objects.

Old Faithful Geyser spurting hot water into the sky

Napa Valley Tour ⓬

Statue at Clos Pegase

THE SLIVER OF LAND known as Napa Valley is 35 miles (56 km) long and lies at the heart of Northern California's wine industry. More than 250 wineries are scattered across its rolling hillsides and fertile valley floor, some dating from the early 19th century. Most of the wineries hug the scenic Silverado Trail and Hwy 29, two major arteries that run the length of the valley and through the towns of Yountville, Oakville, Rutherford, St. Helena, and Calistoga *(see p445)*. Many of Napa Valley's popular wineries offer visitors free tours of their facilities, while some charge a small wine-tasting fee.

Sterling Vineyards ⑦
An aerial tramway provide access to this large, white, Mediterranean-style winery, which is perched on a hill overlooking the valley and vineyards.

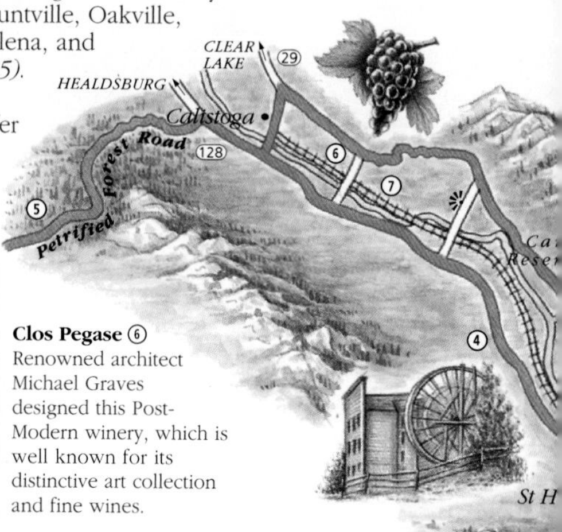

CLEAR LAKE
29
HEALDSBURG
Calistoga
Petrified Forest Road
128

Clos Pegase ⑥
Renowned architect Michael Graves designed this Post-Modern winery, which is well known for its distinctive art collection and fine wines.

Petrified Forest ⑤
This forest is the home of the largest petrified trees in the world *(see p445)*.

FOOD AND WINE IN THE NAPA VALLEY

In addition to a number of superior wines, the Wine Country is well known for its fresh produce and prestigious chefs. Produce stalls and farmers' markets line the valley roads, selling organic vegetables and fruit and freshly squeezed juices. Restaurants in most small towns serve excellent meals, prepared with the freshest ingredients. Classic Wine Country cuisine includes dishes such as Sonoma leg of lamb with fresh mint pesto, creamy risotto with artichoke hearts and sun-dried tomatoes, wild-mushroom sauté in herb-garlic phyllo pastry, and Sterling salmon sautéed and served with a Pinot Noir sauce.

Restaurant terrace at Domaine Chandon in Yountville

Bale Grist Waterwheel ④
Built in 1846, this waterwheel still grinds grain into meal and flour on weekends.

Robert Mondavi Winery ③
Beautiful sculptures and paintings are on display throughout this huge, Mission-style winery. Guided tours are available year round.

KEY

- Tour route
- Other roads
- Viewpoint

Napa Valley vineyard in the late-afternoon sunlight

TIPS FOR DRIVERS

Tour length: 40 miles (64 km), including the scenic Petrified Forest detour.

Stopping-off points: There are several bed-and-breakfast inns and hotels in the towns of St. Helena and Calistoga. For an excellent meal, visit Domaine Chandon or Mustards Grill in Yountville; Tra Vigne or Brava Terrace in St. Helena; or the Silverado Restaurant and Tavern in Calistoga (see also pp570–71).

Napa Valley Wine Train
Gourmet Wine Country cuisine and fine wines are served on this luxury train *(see p570)* as it makes a three-hour tour of the lush Napa Valley.

Rutherford Hill Winery ⑧
This contemporary winery has caves for aging wine. The caves are carved half a mile (0.8 km) into the hillsides.

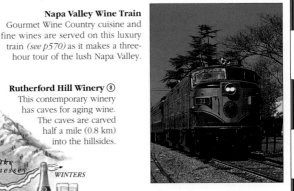

Mumm Napa Valley ⑨
Sparkling wines are made in the classic tradition at this winery, which is partly owned by French champagne producer GH Mumm.

Napa ①
Napa's streets are lined with restored buildings housing restaurants, stores, and art galleries.

Yountville ②
Founded in the mid-19th century by pioneer George Clavert Yount, this tiny town is now a popular spot from which to take a hot-air-balloon ride over the Wine Country.

0 kilometers 5

0 miles 2

WINTERS

Lake Hennessey

Silverado Trail

Conn Creek

Oakville

Napa River

Trancas St

VALLEJO

Sonoma and Sonoma Valley ⓭

N ESTLING IN THE NARROW, 17-mile (27-km) long
Sonoma Valley, cradled by the Mayacama
Mountains to the east and by the Sonoma
Mountains to the west, are 6,000 acres (2,400 ha)
of vineyards. At the foot of the valley lies the tiny
town of Sonoma with its 8-acre (3-ha) plaza, a
grass-covered town square designed in 1835 by
Mexican General Mariano Vallejo (1808–90).
In the early 1840s, American settlers arriving
in the area discovered that land ownership was
reserved for Mexican citizens. On June 14, 1846,
about 30 armed American farmers took General Vallejo
and his men prisoner, seized control of Sonoma, and
declared California an independent republic. The rebels'
flag was adorned with a red star and stripe and a crude
drawing of a grizzly bear. Although the republic was
abolished 25 days later, when the United States annexed
California *(see p43)*, the state legislature adopted the
Bear Flag design as the official California flag in 1911.

**Bear flag
monument**

Sonoma City Hall at the center o
the historic Sonoma Plaza

Exploring Sonoma

Sonoma's main attractions are
its internationally renowned
wineries and the attractive area
immediately surrounding the
Spanish-style **Sonoma Plaza**.
The well-shaded plaza is lined
with dozens of meticulously
preserved historical sites. Many
of the adobe buildings around
the square house wine shops,
charming boutiques, and chic
restaurants serving excellent
California and Wine Country

cuisine. At the very center of
the town's plaza stands the
Sonoma City Hall, a stone
Mission Revival building *(see
p27)* designed in 1908 by the
San Francisco architect AC
Lutgens. Close to the plaza's
northeast corner is the bronze
Bear Flag Monument, which
serves as a memorial to the
group of American settlers who
rebelled against the ruling
Mexican government in 1846.

🏠 Vasquez House

414 1st St East, El Paseo. ((707)
938-0510. ◯ Wed–Sun.
1:30–4:30pm. 🎫 🅿
This 1855 gabled house
belonged to Civil War hero
"Fighting Joe" Hooker, who
later sold it to settlers Pedro
and Catherine Vasquez. The
house is now the headquarte
of the Sonoma League for
Historic Preservation. Variou
historical exhibits and information on Sonoma walking
tours are available here.

🏠 Toscano Hotel

20 E Spain St. ((707) 938-1519. ◯
Sat–Mon 1–4pm. 🎫 🅿 obligatory
Located on the north side of
the plaza, the restored Toscar
Hotel is now a historic monument. The two-story wood-
frame building dates from the

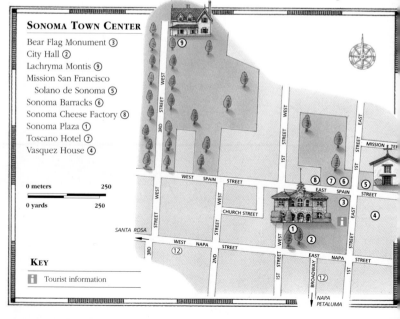

SONOMA TOWN CENTER

0 meters   250

0 yards   250

KEY

ℹ Tourist information

850s, when it was used as a
general store and library. It
was converted into a hotel for
old miners in 1886 and now
belongs to the state.

▮ Sonoma Cheese Factory
W Spain St. ((707) 996-1931.
daily. Jan 1, Thanksgiving,
Dec 25.
The famous Sonoma Jack
cheese has been produced in
the enormous vats in this factory since 1931. Visitors can
watch the production process
through a large observation
window. The finished mild,
white cheese can be purchased
in the factory shop.

▯ Lachryma Montis
W Spain & W 3rd Sts. ((707) 938-
9559. daily. Jan 1, Thanksgiving, Dec 25.
Visitors can glimpse the lavish
lifestyle of Mexican General
Vallejo by exploring Lachryma
Montis, his former home. This
yellow and white Gothic
Revival house was built of redwood in 1852. It features an
eclectic array of Vallejo memorabilia, which ranges from the
general's silver epaulettes and
a cattle brand to his favorite
books and photographs.
The name of the house is
Latin for "tears of the mountain," a reference to a mineral
spring on the property.

Lachryma Montis, once home to
Mexican General Mariano Vallejo

▯ Mission San Francisco Solano de Sonoma
E Spain St. ((707) 938-9560.
daily. Jan 1, Thanksgiving,
Dec 25.
Named after a Peruvian saint,
this beautifully restored old
mission (commonly called the
Sonoma Mission) was the last
of the historic chain of 21

Façade of the Mission San
Francisco Solano de Sonoma

Franciscan missions built in
California (see p42). Father
José Altimira of Spain founded
the mission in 1823 at a time
when California was under
Mexican rule. Today, all that
survives of the original building is the corridor of Father
Altimira's quarters. The present
adobe chapel was built by
General Vallejo in 1840 to be
used by the town's families
and soldiers.

> ### VISITORS' CHECKLIST
> **Road map** A3. 🏠 8,600.
> ✈ Sonoma County Airport,
> 6 miles (10 km) N of Santa Rosa.
> 🚌 90 Broadway & W Napa Sts,
> Sonoma Plaza. ℹ 453 1st St E
> (707 996-1090). 🎪 Valley of the
> Moon Vintage Festival (late Sep).

▯ Sonoma Barracks
E Spain St. ((707) 938-1519.
daily. Jan 1, Thanksgiving,
Dec 25.
Native American labor was
used to build this two-story
adobe structure between 1836
and 1840, when it served as
the headquarters for General
Vallejo and his troops. After the
1846 Bear Flag Revolt, the barracks became an outpost for
the United States Army for
about a decade. After being
purchased by the state in the
late 1950s, the building was
restored. It is now a California
Historical Landmark.

SONOMA VALLEY WINERIES

The arms of the
Sebastiani Vineyards

The Sonoma Valley has a rare perfect
combination of soil, sun, and rain for
growing superior wine grapes. In
1824, Father José Altimira planted
Sonoma's first grapevines, in order
to produce sacramental wine for
the masses held at the Mission San
Francisco Solano de Sonoma. When, in
1834, the ruling Mexican government
secularized the mission, General
Vallejo replanted grapevines on its land and sold the wine
he produced to San Francisco merchants. In 1857,
Hungarian Count Agoston Haraszthy (see p439) planted
the nation's first European varietals at Sonoma's Buena
Vista Winery, now the oldest premium winery in the state.
The Sonoma Valley encompasses the Sonoma Valley,
Carneros, and Sonoma Mountain wine-growing regions.
The climate varies slightly in each region, creating different
environments suitable for producing particular grape
varieties, including Cabernet Sauvignon and Chardonnay.
Today, Sonoma is home to more than 35 wineries, which
produce a total of 5.4 million cases of wine a year. Some of
the valley's most
notable wineries are
Sebastiani Vineyards,
Sonoma's largest
premium-variety
winery; Glen Ellen
Winery; Gundlach-
Bundschu Winery;
and Château St. Jean.
Most of Sonoma's
wineries offer picnic
areas and free wine
tastings and tours.

Vineyards in the Sonoma Valley

GOLD COUNTRY AND THE CENTRAL VALLEY

LOCATED AT THE GEOGRAPHICAL HEART *of California, the Gold Country is also central to the state's allure as the land of overnight success. Long before the gilded world of Hollywood took shape, this was a real life El Dorado, where a thick vein of solid gold, known as the Mother Lode, sat waiting to be discovered.*

The Gold Country is largely rural, despite being the birthplace of modern California with the Gold Rush of 1849 and the designation of Sacramento as state capital.

Before the miners arrived, this quiet region, located on the far fringes of the Spanish colonial empire, was sparsely populated by members of the Miwok and Maidu peoples. With the discovery of gold flakes in January 1848, however, the region turned into a lawless jamboree, and by 1852 an estimated 200,000 men from all over the world were working in the mines. But by 1860 most of the region had fallen silent again, as the mining boom went bust *(see pp44–5)*.

A few years after the Gold Rush, the region experienced another short-lived boom. The transcontinental railroad was constructed through the Sierra Nevada Mountains by low-paid laborers, many of whom were Chinese *(see pp46–7)*. In the early 20th century, the Central Valley became the heart of the state's thriving agricultural industry, which today exports fruit and vegetables worldwide.

Stretching for more than 100 miles (160 km) north to south, the region's landscape is ideal for leisurely hikes or afternoon picnics. The Gold Country also offers one of California's best scenic drives along Hwy 49. The route climbs up and down rocky ridges between pastoral ranch lands, lined with oak trees and crossed by fast-flowing rivers. Many of the picturesque towns it passes through, such as Sutter Creek, have survived unchanged since the Gold Rush.

Malakoff Diggins State Park, preserving the heyday of the Gold Rush

◁ **California State Capitol in Sacramento**

Exploring the Gold Country

THE GOLD COUNTRY ranges from flat delta flood plains to the rugged, river-carved foothills of the Sierra Nevada Mountains. At the heart of the region is Sacramento, the state capital and largest Gold Country city, which has the highest concentration of sights. But the real attraction of this area is in traveling along its many scenic routes. The rural landscape is dotted with small historic towns. Some are still thriving communities, while others are ghostly memorials to their past. The Central Valley, along I-5, is scattered with picturesque farming towns. Larger towns, such as Nevada City and Sutter Creek, make excellent bases for a Gold Country tour, and visitors are welcomed and well taken care of everywhere.

Impressive State Capitol building in Sacramento

Parrots Ferry Bridge over the picturesque New Melones Lake along Hwy 49 in Tuolumne County

SIGHTS AT A GLANCE

Replica dwelling in the Chaw'se Indian Grinding Rock State Park

SEE ALSO

- *Where to Stay* pp533–4
- *Where to Eat* pp571–2

GETTING AROUND

A car is essential for exploring the California Gold Country. Most sights are located along the Gold Rush Highway, Hwy 49. This makes the best and most scenic driving route as it undulates along the foothills through the most interesting Gold Country towns. Public transportation is severely limited, with only two long-distance bus services along the two main highways, I-80 and US 50, and a daily train service over the mountains from Sacramento. The area's main domestic airport is also in Sacramento, while the nearest international airport is San Francisco.

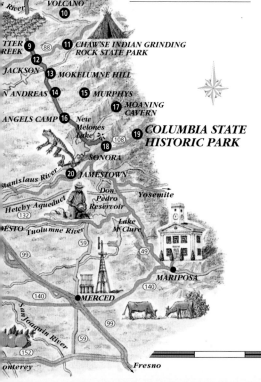

KEY

▬	Freeway
▬	Major road
▬	Minor road
▬	Scenic route
～	River
☀	Viewpoint

0 kilometers 25

0 miles 25

The man-made canyon created by hydraulic mining at Malakoff Diggins

Malakoff Diggins State Park ●

Road map B3. **C** (530) 265-2740. from Nevada City. ○ daily. ● buildings Oct–Apr:

As the original gold mining techniques became less rewarding in the late 1850s, miners turned to increasingly powerful and destructive ways of extracting the valuable ore. When the more easily recoverable surface deposits disappeared, the miners began to strip away the soil with powerful jets of pressurized water. Spraying more than 200,000 gal (115,000 liters) of water per hour, the jets washed away entire mountainsides in search of gold. The process was known as hydraulic mining. In 1884 the California legislature forbade the dumping of gravel into streams, but huge swathes of land had already been ruined and the rivers had been clogged up with debris (*see pp44–5*).

One of the largest of these hydraulic mining operations was at Malakoff Diggins, 27 miles (45 km) northeast of Hwy 49, in the mountains above Nevada City. The eroded hillsides created a canyon that now forms an eerily beautiful state park, with several preserved buildings from the 1870s mining town of North Bloomfield.

A nugget of gold set inside quartz crystal

Grass Valley ●

Road map B3. 9,000. **i** 248 Mill St (530 273-4667).

Long the largest and busiest town in the northern Gold Country, Grass Valley served the Empire Mine and other nearby hard rock gold mines.

In the 1870s and 1880s Grass Valley welcomed workers from the tin mines of Cornwall, England, who were affectionately known as "Cousin Jacks." Their expertise enabled the local mines to recover underground ore deposits and so remain in business after the rest of the area had fallen quiet (*see pp44–5*).

Grass Valley is also the location of one of California's best mining museums. The **North Star Mining Museum** is situated in the powerhouse of the former North Star Mine. Surrounding the museum's entrance are the giant Pelton wheels that greatly increased production in the region's underground mines. Displays inside the museum include a stamp mill (a giant pulverizer used to crush ore), a Cornish pump (used to filter out underground water), as well as various artifacts relating to the Cornish background of the local miners.

🏛 North Star Mining Museum

Mill St at Allison Ranch Rd. **C** (530) 273-4255. ○ May–Oct: daily. **Donation**.

Empire Mine State Historic Park ●

C (530) 273-8522. from Nevada City. ○ daily. ● Jan 1, Thanksgiving, Dec 25. Grounds & Empire Cottage.

One of the longest surviving and most lucrative gold mining operations in the state, the Empire Mine was in business until 1956. It has now been preserved by the state as a historic park. Starting with surface workings in the 1850s, the Empire Mine grew to include 365 miles (585 km) of underground tunnels, from which pure gold estimated at 5.8 million ounces (16.5 million grams) was recovered.

Head frames, which held the mine's elevator shafts and other mining equipment, are scattered over the park's 785 acres (318 ha), but for a real sense of how much money was made here you should visit Empire Cottage.

Designed by San Franciscan architect Willis Polk in 1897 for the mine's owner, William Bourn, the granite and red-brick exterior resembles an English manor house, while the redwood interior gives an air of casual affluence. The gardens next door to the cottage contain nearly 1,000 rose bushes and a large greenhouse.

More exhibits on the history of the Empire Mine and on hard-rock gold mining are on display in the visitors' center, along with samples of the precious metal.

Original stamp mill used to crush ore at the Empire Mine

Firehouse Number 1's façade, a Nevada City landmark

Nevada City 🕘

Road map B3. 🏯 2,855. 🚌 🚃
🛈 132 Main St (530 265-2692).

WITH VICTORIAN HOUSES and commercial buildings lining its steep streets, picturesque Nevada City deserves its reputation as "Queen of the Northern Mines." Located at the northern end of the Mother Lode gold fields, Nevada City thrived until gold mining peaked in the 1860s, then it faded into oblivion. Nearly a century later, the city was resurrected as a tourist destination, with galleries, restaurants, and inns re-creating Gold Rush themes.

Hwy 49 takes visitors arriving in Nevada City to the foot of Broad Street. Looking up the street, the large building on the left is the **National Hotel**. One of the oldest hotels in California, it first opened in the mid-1850s *(see p534)*.

A block east of the hotel is **Firehouse Number 1 Museum**, one of the region's most photographed façades. Dainty balconies and a white cupola decorate the exterior, and inside, a small museum displays local Maidu Indian artifacts, pioneer relics, including some relating to the tragic Donner Party *(see p470)*, and the altar from a Gold Rush Chinese temple. Antique mining devices are displayed in the park across the street, and several plaques attached to walls throughout the city commemorate events from its past.

Back on Broad Street, the arcaded brick façade marks the historic **Nevada Theater**, which has been in use as a performance venue since 1865. A block to the south is the **Miner's Foundry**, an old metalworks where the innovative Pelton wheel was first developed and produced. A block to the north is the Art Deco façade of the city's **County Courthouse**, one of the city's few 20th-century works of architecture.

🏛 Firehouse Number 1 Museum
214 Main St. 📞 *(530) 265-5468.*
🔲 *daily.* **Donation**.

Nevada Theater, used as a playhouse since 1865

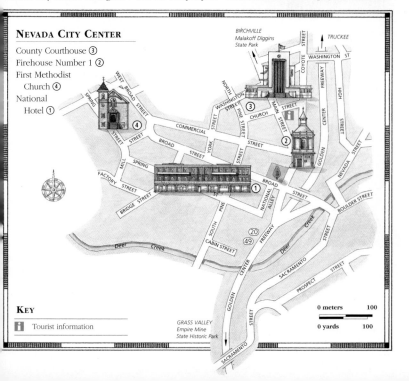

NEVADA CITY CENTER

County Courthouse ③
Firehouse Number 1 ②
First Methodist
   Church ④
National
   Hotel ①

BIRCHVILLE
Malakoff Diggins
State Park

TRUCKEE

COYOTE STREET
WASHINGTON ST

WEST BROAD STREET
SPRING STREET
NORTH WASHINGTON STREET
PINE STREET
CHURCH STREET
MAIN STREET
FREEWAY
HIGH STREET
CENTER STREET

COMMERCIAL STREET
BROAD STREET
YORK STREET
PINE STREET
BROAD STREET

FACTORY STREET
SPRING STREET
MILL STREET
BRIDGE STREET
SOUTH PINE STREET
CABIN STREET

NATIONAL ALLEY
FREEWAY
GOLDEN CENTER

NEVADA STREET
BOULDER STREET

Deer Creek
SACRAMENTO STREET
PROSPECT STREET

(20)
(49)

KEY

🛈 Tourist information

GRASS VALLEY
Empire Mine
State Historic Park

0 meters   100
0 yards   100

SACRAMENTO

Street-by-Street: Old Sacramento ❺

Californian railroad logo

COVERING SIX BLOCKS between the river and the modern city, Old Sacramento preserves many historic buildings within a precinct of shops, restaurants and museums. Some of the structures protected here were built to serve the gold miners of 1849 *(see pp44–5)*, but most date from the 1860s and 1870s, when Sacramento confirmed its position as the link between rural California and the commercial centers along the coast. The Pony Express and transcontinental railroad both had their western terminus here, with paddle-wheel riverboats providing the connection to San Francisco. A handful of museums trace the area's historic importance, and the riverfront location is ideal for walking and cycling.

Delta King Riverboat
One of the last Sacramento Delta riverboats still afloat, this moored paddle-wheel steamer is now a hotel and restaurant.

Old Schoolhouse
This one-room building is typical of a 19th-century California schoolhouse.

The former steamboat depot was the embarkation point for freight bound for San Francisco in the 1860s.

0 meters 5
0 yards 5

Theodore Judah Monument
This bas-relief commemorates Theodore Judah, the engineer who planned the transcontinental railroad (see pp46–7).

STAR SIGHTS

★ **BF Hastings Building**

★ **California State Railroad Museum**

KEY

– – – Suggested route

The Discovery Museum, housed in the city's former municipal buildings, contains memorabilia of Old Sacramento's 19th-century heyday.

★ California State Railroad Museum
Immaculately restored locomotives and train cars are part of this extensive collection.

Eagle Theatre
This is a reconstruction of the original theater, built in 1849 but ruined by a flood in 1850.

Visitors' Center

Pony Express Monument
This statue commemorates the 1,966-mile (3,163-km) mail run from Sacramento to St. Joseph, Missouri.

CA Military Museum

The old firehouse, built in 1853, was one of the first buildings to be restored.

★ BF Hastings Building
For a sense of what the legal system was like in California's early days, visit the restored chambers of the original Supreme Court, located above a general store.

Sacramento: California State Capitol

STANDING AT THE CENTER of a vast, landscaped park, the
California State Capitol is Sacramento's primary landmark and one of the state's handsomest buildings. It
was designed in 1860 by Miner F Butler in grand
Renaissance Revival style, with Corinthian porticos and a
tall central dome. The building was completed in 1874
after almost 15 years of construction and expenses
totaling $2.5 million. The Capitol was expanded in the
1950s and completely renovated and restored in the
1970s. The Governor of California operates from his
Capitol office, but the building also stands as a shining
example of the Golden State's proud past.

Along with the chambers of the state legislature, which
are open to visitors when they are in session, the Capitol
serves as a museum of the state's
political and cultural history.

Original 1860 statuary

★ Capitol Rotunda
The impressive rotunda was restored to its original 19th-century splendor in 1975. The copper ball on top of the dome is plated in gold.

Entrance

The Historic Offices
on the first floor contain a
few government offices
restored to their turn-of-the-
century appearance.

★ State Senate Chamber
The mezzanine gallery is open all year, but it is most interesting when the legislature is in session, making speeches and holding votes on issues of importance.

A portrait of George Washington, the first US president, occupies the focal point on the Chamber wall.

STAR FEATURES

★ Capitol Rotunda

★ State Senate Chamber

Crocker Art Museum

216 O St. ☎ (916) 264-5423. ◐
10am–5pm Tue–Sun (9pm Thu). ●
Jan 1, Jul 4, Thanksgiving, Dec 25. ✎
w www.crockerartmuseum.org

Founded in 1873, the Crocker Art Museum is the oldest public art museum west of the Mississippi. The collection includes Victorian painting and sculpture from Europe and the United States, but its real strength is the California art and photography, and the touring shows that the museum exhibits.

Another prime attraction is the Italianate Victorian building itself, designed by the architect Seth Babson. The gallery includes polychrome tile floors, elaborately carved woodwork, and a graceful central staircase. It was built in 1869 as a home for the brother of Charles Crocker, one of the "Big Four" transcontinental railroad barons (see pp456–7).

Foyer of the Crocker Art Gallery

Sutter's Fort

2701 L St. ☎ (916) 324-0539.
◐ daily. ● Jan 1, Thanksgiving,
Dec 25. ✎

Now somewhat marooned amid the suburban streets of the modern state capital, Sutter's Fort in its heyday was one of the most important and populous sites in early California history.

Established by John Sutter in 1839, the fort became the cultural and economic center of northern California in the years leading up to the Gold Rush. Apart from the 21 Spanish missions along the coast, Sutter's Fort was the only Anglo-European settlement in California. Throughout the 1840s, new immigrants following the rugged overland trails from the eastern states stopped here to avail themselves of the fort's blacksmith shop, grain mill, and its many other facilities.

Reconstructed 19th-century kitchen at Sutter's Fort

The three-story central building is all that survives of the original fort. The rest of the complex has been reconstructed to give a picture of frontier life. A courtyard, surrounded by 18-ft (5.5-m) walls, houses various historical exhibits along a self-guided audio tour. These include a prison, a bakery, and a blacksmith's. This is the one of the few official sites in California where the Mexican flag still flies.

California State Indian Museum

2618 K St. ☎ (916) 324-0539.
◐ daily. ● Jan 1, Thanksgiving,
Dec 25. ✎

This area of California was once occupied by the Maidu people. This small but fascinating museum, set in a park adjacent to Sutter's Fort, explores the different Native American cultures that existed in the state before the 16th-century arrival of the first Europeans (see pp40–41). Displays of handicrafts focus on the beautiful reed baskets that held both a practical and spiritual value to the Indians, and a series of dioramas recreate the look and feel of tribal reservations. Slide shows, tape recordings, and films document other aspects of tribal culture, from language to agricultural skills.

Special programs, generally held on weekends, celebrate the survival of ancient Native American ways of life into the present day.

JOHN SUTTER

The story of the early California entrepreneur John Sutter is a classic real-life rags to riches to rags adventure. Following bankruptcy in his native Switzerland, Sutter emigrated to California in 1839. Only a year after his arrival, he was granted a 50,000-acre (20,000-ha) tract of land by the Mexican government, which he patriotically named New Helvetia (New Switzerland). In 1843 Sutter went into debt once again in order to buy Fort Ross on the northern coast from its Russian owners (see p444). For the next five years his land and wealth made him virtual lord and master over most of northern California.

However, the discovery of gold flakes by his employee James Marshall at his mill in 1848 (see p454) spelled the end of his vast empire. Thousands of miners swarmed to the region and almost immediately took over his land. Sutter spent the rest of his life in Washington, DC, hoping for compensation from the US government, but he died almost penniless in 1880.

John Sutter (1802–80)

Reconstructed Sutter's Mill, where gold was first discovered

Marshall Gold Discovery State Park ❻

Road map B3. [phone] *(530) 622-3470.* [bus] *from Placerville.* [clock] *8am–5pm daily.* [closed] *Jan 1, Thanksgiving, Dec 25.*

COVERING SOME 250 acres (101 ha) along the banks of the American River, this peaceful state park protects and interprets the site where gold was first discovered in January 1848. James Marshall spotted shiny flakes in the water channel of a sawmill he and his fellow workmen were building for John Sutter *(see p459)*, and the rest is history.

Within a year, some 10,000 miners had turned Coloma into a thriving city, but with news of even richer deposits elsewhere the boom went bust as quickly as it began, and nowadays there is little sign of this busy era.

A full-scale reproduction of Sutter's Mill stands on the original site, and a statue of James Marshall can be found on a nearby hill to mark the spot where he is buried. The park's visitors' center includes the small **Gold Country Museum** with Native American artifacts, films, and other displays on the discovery of gold, as well as memorabilia relating to James Marshall.

🏛 Gold Country Museum
1273 High St, Auburn. [phone] *(530) 889-6500.* [clock] *Tue–Sun.* [closed] *Jan 1, Thanksgiving, Dec 25.*

Folsom ❼

Road map B3. [population] *46,000.* [bus] [info] *200 Wool St (916 985-2698).*

FOLSOM IS NOW a pleasant Sacramento suburb, despite being the site of the state penitentiary made famous by Johnny Cash's 1970s song "Folsom Prison Blues."

It played an important role as the last station on the Pony Express and transcontinental railroad. Folsom is now one of the few remaining transcontinental railroad sites, as documented in the local **Folsom History Museum**. Antique shops line the Wild West-style Sutter Street in the small downtown business district, set amid boxcars and other railroad memorabilia.

At the foot of Riley Street, behind Folsom Dam, there is also a large lake, which is a popular summer vacation spot with residents and visitors, for boating and fishing.

🏛 Folsom History Museum
823 Sutter St. [phone] *(916) 985-2707.* [clock] *Wed–Sun.* [closed] *public hols.* **Donation.**

Placerville ❽

Road map B3. [population] *15,000.* [bus] [info] *542 Main St (530 621-5885).*

DURING the Gold Rush, Placerville was a busy supply center for the surrounding mining camps. Still standing on one of the main routes traveling to and from Sacramento, Placerville has retained its importance as a transportation center, although the stagecoaches have long since given way to cars and trucks along US 50.

The downtown business district preserves a handful of historic structures and sites, but the best sense of Placerville's past comes from the **Placerville History Museum** on Main Street and the **El Dorado County Historical Museum**. The displays range from old mining equipment and a replica of a 19th-century general store to artifacts from the Chinese settlement and other local historical exhibits.

🏛 El Dorado County Historical Museum
104 Placerville Dr. [phone] *(530) 621-5865.* [clock] *Wed–Sun.* [closed] *public hols.* **Donation.**

Gold Rush general store in Placerville's El Dorado Museum

Sutter Creek ❾

Road map B3. [population] *2,000.* [bus] [info] *125 Peek St, Jackson (209 223-0350).*

NAMED AFTER John Sutter *(see p459)*, Sutter Creek is one of the prettiest Gold Country towns, full of antique shops and whitewashed country inns. It grew up around 1860 to service the Old Eureka Mine, which was owned by Hetty Green, reputedly the "Richest Woman in the World."

Leland Stanford, one of the "Big Four" railroad barons *(see pp46 – 7)*, made his fortune in Sutter Creek. He put $5,000 into the town's Lincoln Mine, which turned into a multimillion-dollar investment. He used the money to become a railroad magnate and then, governor of California.

An attractive drive in the region is along Sutter Creek Road to Volcano, past remains of former mining equipment.

Volcano ⓾

Road map B3. ⌘ *150.* 🚌
ℹ *125 Peek St, Jackson (209 223-0350).*

F OR A TASTE of the Gold Rush without the tourist trappings, visit Volcano, a picturesque ghost of a mining town containing a wealth of historic sights.

During the Gold Rush, the town had an unusual reputation for sophistication and culture, creating the state's first library and its first astronomical observatory. The old jail, stagecoach office, brewery, and a cannon dating from the Civil War are among the preserved buildings and artifacts on display around the four-block town. The most attractive Victorian building is the former **St. George Hotel**, covered with Virginia creeper.

Springtime visitors to the region should also follow the signs to Daffodil Hill, 3 miles (5 km) north of Volcano, when more than 300,000 naturalized daffodil bulbs come into full bloom on the hillside.

🏨 **St. George Hotel**
16104 Main St, off Volcano Rd. 📞
(209) 296-4458. ⬜ *mid-Feb–Dec: Wed–Sun.*

Chaw'se Indian Grinding Rock State Historic Park ⓫

🚌 *from Sacramento.* 🚉 *from Sacramento.* 🚌 *from Jackson.*
Jackson Visitors' Center ⬜ *daily.*
📞 *(209) 296-7488.*

T UCKED AWAY amid the oak trees in the hills above Jackson, this 136-acre (55-ha) park protects one of the largest and most complete Native American sites in the country. The area was once home to the Miwok people and the park is dedicated to their past and future. The aim of this comprehensive museum is to increase understanding of Native American life, centering on the Californian foothill peoples. Exhibits include an array of basketry, dance regalia, and ancient tools.

Hundreds of mortar holes form the main focus of the park. These limestone pockets were formed by generations of Miwok Indians grinding meal from acorns. There are also many rock carvings and replica Miwok dwellings, including a ceremonial roundhouse.

St. Sava's Serbian Orthodox Church outside Jackson

Jackson ⓬

Road map B3. ⌘ *3,500.* 🚌
ℹ *125 Peek St (209 223-0350).*

L OCATED at the crossroads of two main Gold Rush trails, Jackson was once a bustling gold mining community and has continued to thrive as a commercial center and lumber mill town since 1850.

The town center features a number of old Gold Rush buildings, but the most interesting stop is the **Amador County Museum**, located on a hill above the town. Here visitors can view working models of stamp mills *(see p454)* and a variety of other old mining equipment.

North of the town, in a small park off Hwy 49, are the massive tailing wheels from the Kennedy Mine, one of the deepest in the United States. Reaching 58 ft (18 m) in diameter, these wheels were used to dispose of leftover rocks after the gold had been extracted. St. Sava's Serbian Orthodox Church, built in 1894 with a delicate white steeple, is also situated within the park. It is a testament to one of the many cultures that contributed to the history of the Gold Country.

🏛 **Amador County Museum**
225 Church St, Jackson. 📞 *(209) 223-6386.* ⬜ *Wed–Sun.* ⬤ *public hols.* **Donation.**

Replica of a Miwok ceremonial roundhouse in Chaw'se State Park

Headstone on "Moke Hill"

Mokelumne Hill ⓭

Road map B3. 👥 *1,200.*
ℹ️ *1211 S Main St, Angels Camp (209 736-0049).*

BYPASSED by Highway 49, Mokelumne Hill is one of the most intriguing old Gold Country towns. A handful of old buildings, including the balconied Hotel Leger and the old Wells Fargo stagecoach station, form a one-block business district. But the sleepy ambience of "Moke Hill," as it is more commonly known, belies the town's unsavory and violent history.

Although much of the town has fallen into picturesque decay, during the Gold Rush era the hotels and saloons were packed with rowdy miners, whose drunken fights resulted in an average of one killing per week. Many of the victims ended up in the hilltop Protestant Cemetery – a short walk to the west of town. Here the multilingual headstones are now all that remain of the international population who came here in search of gold.

San Andreas ⓮

Road map B3. 👥 *1,500.*
ℹ️ *1211 S Main St, Angels Camp (209 736-0049).*

SAN ANDREAS is now a small, bustling city, home to the Calaveras County government. During the Gold Rush era,

however, it was a gritty mining camp, originally built by Mexicans who were later forcibly removed by white Americans after rich deposits of gold were found (*see pp44–5*). In 1883 the legendary outlaw Black Bart was captured here.

Very little now remains from the Gold Rush days, although San Andreas does house one of the Gold Country's best museums, the **Calaveras County Historical Museum**, in the old courthouse just north of Hwy 49. Along with exhibits tracing gold mining history from 1848 to the 1930s, the collection includes Miwok Indian artifacts and the courtroom where Black Bart was tried and convicted. His prison cell during the trial, situated behind the museum, is now surrounded by a pleasant, if somewhat incongruous, garden of indigenous plants and trees.

🏛 Calaveras County Historical Museum
30 N Main St. ☎ *(530) 233-6328.* ◯ *daily.* ⬤ *Jan 1, Thanksgiving, Dec 25.* 📷

Murphys ⓯

Road map B3. 👥 *2,000.*
ℹ️ *1211 S Main St, Angels Camp (209 736-0049).*

WITH MATURE sycamores, elms, and locust trees lining its quiet streets, Murphys is among the prettiest towns in the southern Gold Country. It offers a quiet break from the frantic tourism of many of

the other Mother Lode towns and sights in the area.

Having played host to such luminaries as Ulysses S Grant, Mark Twain, and Will Rogers, the restored Murphys Hotel, built in 1855, is now the town landmark. Across the street, the **Old-Timers' Museum** houses a quirky collection of Gold Rush memorabilia. The outside wall displays a series of humorous plaques detailing the town's history.

🏛 Old-Timers' Museum
450 Main St. ☎ *(209) 728-1160.* ◯ *Fri–Sun.* ⬤ *Jan 1, Thanksgiving, Dec 25.* 📷

Angels Camp ⓰

Road map B3. 👥 *3,000.*
ℹ️ *1211 S Main St (209 736-0049).*

ANGELS CAMP is a former gold mining town what was best known as the real-life location of Mark Twain's classic short story "The Celebrated Jumping Frog of Calaveras County" (*see pp22–3*). Today the town has grown into a commercial center for the surrounding area.

A few historic structures, including the Angels Hotel where Twain heard the story of the jumping frog, still line the steep streets of the compact downtown area, which comes alive every May for a popular reenactment of the frog-jumping competition.

Two huge 19th-century locomotives stand on Hwy 49 in front of the **Angels Camp Museum**, which contains a standard array of old mining

Picturesque main street of the gold mining town, Angels Camp

equipment. There is also a large collection of Indian artifacts and exhibits on Mark Twain and the jumping frog.

🏛 Angels Camp Museum
753 S Main St. **(** *(209) 736-2963.*
◯ *Apr–Nov: daily; Mar–Nov: daily, 10am–3pm; Jan–Feb: weekends only.*
● *Thanksgiving, Dec.* ⬚

Moaning Cavern ⓱

(*(209) 736-2708.* ◯ *daily.* ⬚

ONE OF THE largest limestone caverns in the area, Moaning Cavern took its name from the groaning sound emitted by the wind flowing out of the entrance. Unfortunately the sound was destroyed when the cavern was enlarged to improve public access.

Guided tours, lasting about an hour, focus on the large main "room," which is approximately 165 ft (50 m) high – tall enough to house the Statue of Liberty. Visitors can descend into the caves by way of a staircase or, if they dare, by rappelling down a rope.

A guided tour of Moaning Cavern

Sonora ⓲

Road map B3. ⬚ 5,000. ⬚
ℹ *55 W Stockton St (209 533-4420).*

OUTSTRIPPING Columbia *(see pp464–5)* for the seat of county government during the Gold Rush, Sonora is now the Tuolumne County seat and a busy commercial center and logging town. Its sedate main street shows little sign of the town's once-violent reputation during the second half of the 19th century.

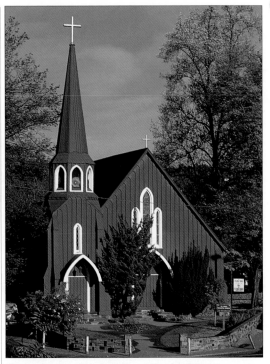

Nineteenth-century St. James Episcopal Church in Sonora

Many of its historic buildings have been preserved, including the St. James Episcopal Church, situated at the top of Washington Street. The town also has a number of interesting Victorian houses.

Sonora's old jail was built in 1857 and renovated after being destroyed by fire in 1866. It is now home to the **Tuolumne County Museum and History Center**. It houses a collection of Gold Rush artifacts, including gold nuggets and a number of 19th-century photographs.

🏛 Tuolumne County Museum and History Center
158 W Bradford St. **(** *(209) 532-1317.* ◯ *daily.* ● *Jan 1, Dec 25.*

BLACK BART

Famous for his politeness to his victims and his habit of leaving doggerel poetry at the scene of his crimes, the outlaw known affectionately as Black Bart has become one of the state's best-loved legends.

After holding up stagecoaches between 1877 and 1883, he was caught when the laundry mark on his handkerchief was traced to San Francisco. Black Bart turned out to be Charles Boles, a mining engineer.

After being tried and convicted in San Andreas, he spent five years in San Quentin prison. He disappeared from public view after his release in 1888.

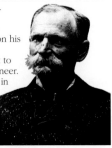

The outlaw Black Bart

Street-by-Street: Columbia State Historic Park ⓿

Stagecoach schedule sign

Aᴛ ᴛʜᴇ ʜᴇɪɢʜᴛ of the Gold Rush, Columbia was one of the largest and most important towns in the Gold Country. Most of California's mining camps were abandoned; they quickly disintegrated and disappeared after the gold ran out in the late 1850s. Unusually, Columbia remained active. It was proudly kept intact by its remaining residents until 1945, when the California government turned the entire town into a state historic park. A few of the buildings have been reconstructed, but the majority of them have been preserved in their original state.

The Chinese Herb Shop contains traditional medicines brought to the state by Chinese immigrants.

City Hotel

Johnson's Livery Stable
Several old-style wagons are housed here.

PACIFIC STREET

JACKSON STREET

MAIN STREET

COLUMBIA STR

BROADWAY

STATE STREET

Old jail

Museum

FULTON STREET

WASHINGTON STREET

★ Wells Fargo Express Office
This stagecoach office was the center of the town's transportation network.

Matelot Gulch Miners Supply
Visitors are sold pans of sand and gravel here so that they can try panning for gold themselves.

Palm Hotel on Main Street, Jamestown

★ **Columbia Schoolhouse**
*The building was last used
as a school in 1937, but in
1960 it was restored with
the help of funds raised by
California schoolchildren.*

```
0 meters                100

0 yards                 100
```

KEY

– – –   Suggested route

STAR SIGHTS

★ **Columbia
Schoolhouse**

★ **Wells Fargo
Express Office**

Jamestown ⑳

Road map B3. 2,300.
55 W Stockton St, Sonora (209
532-4212).

JAMESTOWN WAS home to the
largest gold mine in operation until 1993. The mine is still
visible south of the town along
Hwy 49. Some of the historic
town was destroyed by fire in
1966, but Main Street still has
many picturesque buildings.
**Railtown 1897 State
Historic Park**, north of downtown, preserves the steam
locomotives and historic carriages of the Sierra Railroad.
Rides are offered on weekends.

🏛 Railtown 1897 State
Historic Park
5th Ave & Reservoir Rd. (209)
984-3953. Jan 1, Thanksgiving,
Dec 25. **Donation**.

Stockton ㉑

Road map B3. 250,000.
46 W Fremont St (209 943-1987).

STOCKTON IS AN inland port
and a transportation hub
for Central Valley farms. It is
set on the eastern edge of the
delta at the confluence of the
Sacramento, American, and
San Joaquin Rivers.
Stockton's history is told at
the Haggin Museum, which
includes everything from
Native American crafts to 19th-
century storefronts and works
by Renoir. It also traces the
development by a local inventor of the Caterpillar track, later
adapted for use on army tanks.

🏛 Haggin Museum
1201 N Pershing Ave. (209) 462-
4116. ◯ Tue–Sun, 1.30–5pm.
Jan 1, Thanksgiving, Dec 25. **Donation**.

JOAQUIN MURIETA: THE CALIFORNIA BANDIT

Little documentary evidence exists about Joaquin Murieta,
the Gold Country criminal portrayed as everything from a
19th-century Gold Rush Robin Hood to a murderous outlaw.
His legend can be traced to the writer John Rollins Ridge,
who published a novel called *The Life and Adventures of
Joaquin Murieta, Celebrated
California Bandit* in 1854.
Ridge drew on the criminal
exploits of five outlaws, all
named Joaquin. The Gover-
nor of California offered a
$1,000 reward for the capture
of any of these men. In 1853
a man named Harry Love
delivered the head of one
Joaquin Murieta, which had
been pickled in a glass jar.
Ridge's novel was published
the following year, and the
Murieta legend was born.

THE HIGH SIERRAS

ORMING A TOWERING WALL *along the eastern side of central California, the densely forested Sierra Nevada mountains rise to over 14,000 ft (4,270 m) and include many of the most impressive peaks in the mainland United States. Known as the High Sierras, these rugged mountains make up one of the state's most popular recreation areas, preserved by a series of splendid national parks.*

The most popular High Sierras destination is Yosemite National Park, one of the world's most spectacular natural sights. Waterfalls, ranging from delicate cascades to raging torrents, drop steeply down the granite walls of this alpine valley. Rock-climbers, photographers, and sightseers come from all over the globe to experience the park first-hand. South of Yosemite, the Sequoia and Kings Canyon National Parks preserve more of the state's high country scenery, including groves of sequoia, the tallest living trees on earth.

To the north, Lake Tahoe has been a year-round recreational haven for over a century. It offers hiking, camping, and water sports on one of the bluest bodies of water in the US. In winter, the region becomes a skier's paradise, with many Olympic-class resorts.

East of the Sierra Nevada's granite spine lies a less-visited but equally compelling region. The ghost town of Bodie is preserved as it was when gold miners abandoned it in 1882. Nearby, Mono Lake is an eerie sight of limestone towers and alkaline water. The eastern slope of the High Sierras merits exploration, including the 14,500-ft (4,420-m) Mount Whitney, the highest peak on the US mainland, and the bristlecone pines of the White Mountains, some of which are more than 4,000 years old.

Bodie State Historic Park, a preserved ghost town to the east of the Sierras

◁ Imposing granite peak of Half Dome in Yosemite National Park

Exploring the High Sierras

THE HIGHEST PEAKS, the tallest trees, and some of the most impressive natural scenery in the United States are found in California's Sierra Nevada. This region includes one of the best-known wonders of the world, Yosemite National Park, as well as countless other remarkable examples of nature's prowess. North of Yosemite, the emerald waters of Lake Tahoe are set within an alpine valley at the highest point of the High Sierras, while to the south stand the immense groves of Sequoia and Kings Canyon National Parks.

Other than the resorts encircling Lake Tahoe, there are no real towns in the High Sierras. East of the mountains, however, near the shores of the eerily beautiful Mono Lake, the best ghost town in the state, Bodie, is immaculately preserved.

SIGHTS AT A GLANCE

HOW THE SIERRAS WERE MADE

The Sierras were formed 3 million years ago when a giant granite batholith (igneous rock), approximately 6 miles (10 km) deep, lifted up the earth's surface and tilted it from a tectonic "hinge" beneath California's Central Valley. The effects of this uplift are most clearly visible on the steep eastern slopes, typical of mountains on the earth's faults. The western slopes are more gradual, made up of sedimentary, volcanic, and metamorphic rock, mixed together over the epochs.

Granite peaks of the High Sierras

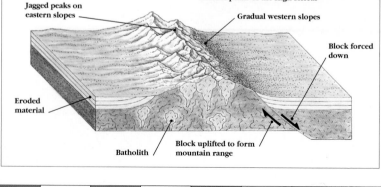

Jagged peaks on eastern slopes

Gradual western slopes

Block forced down

Eroded material

Batholith

Block uplifted to form mountain range

Yosemite Valley in Yosemite National Park

GETTING AROUND

There are no roads across the mountains for more than 150 miles (240 km) between Yosemite and Kings Canyon, so it is essential to plan your route well ahead. Most visitors approach the mountains from the west, on the highways climbing up from the San Joaquin Valley. The eastern face of the High Sierras, Bodie, and Mono Lake can all be reached via Hwy 395 through Owens Valley. Public transportation is limited, but there is a daily bus service from Merced to Yosemite National Park.

Delta Riverboat on Lake Tahoe

SEE ALSO

• *Where to Stay* pp535–6

• *Where to Eat* pp573–4

KEY

▨	Freeway
▨	Major road
▨	Minor road
▨	Scenic route
〜	River
⚜	Viewpoint

0 kilometers   25

0 miles   25

182

5 BODIE STATE
HISTORIC PARK
395

6 MONO LAKE

DEVIL'S POSTPILE
7 NATIONAL
MONUMENT

Lake
Crowley
6

BISHOP ●
S I E R R A
N A T I O N A L
F O R E S T

8 WHITE
MOUNTAINS
168
395

9 OWENS
VALLEY

Kings River

INDEPENDENCE ●
180

198

10 MOUNT
WHITNEY

Visalia

Kern River

11

SEQUOIA AND
KINGS CANYON
NATIONAL PARKS

FAIRVIEW
395

Kern River South Fork

J22
San
Bernadino

Lake
Isabella
ONYX

178

Bakersfield

LORAINE   Lancaster
Los Angeles

14

Los Angeles Aqueduct

Owens River

River

Donner Memorial State Park ❶

☎ *(530) 582-7892.* 🚊 *Truckee.* 🚌 *Truckee.*

Tʜɪꜱ ᴛʀᴀɴQᴜɪʟ 350-acre (140-ha) park, to the south of I-80, marks the site of one of the most tragic episodes of the United States frontier era.

In the winter of 1846–7 a group of 89 California-bound emigrants from Independence, Missouri, were trapped by heavy snowfall. Known as the Donner Party because two of the families shared that surname, the group was one of the many wagon trains bound for the West Coast from the Midwest, along the Oregon Trail. Halfway into their journey, the Donner families, and another family headed by James Reed, decided to leave the established trail and try a shortcut recommended by the contemporary adventurer Lansford Hastings. This turned out, however, to be a far more difficult route, and added three weeks to what in the best of circumstances was already an arduous journey. The Donner Party finally arrived at the eastern foot of the Sierra Nevada Mountains in October 1846, having lost the majority of their cattle and belongings.

After resting for a week they were caught by an early winter storm east of Truckee. A few members decided to struggle on foot across the snowy mountains to seek help from Sutter's Fort *(see p459)*, but the rest of the party, now trapped by the heavy snow and with insufficient supplies, were forced to resort to cannibalism in order to survive. By the time rescuers were able to reach them in mid-February 1847, 42 of the 89 pioneers had already died.

A statue of this heroic pioneering family, standing atop a 22-ft (6.7-m) pedestal indicating the depth of the snow they encountered, now marks the site. The park's **Emigrant Trail Museum** details the Donner Party's story, as well as describing the natural history of the High Sierras.

🏛 Emigrant Trail Museum

12593 Donner Pass Rd. ☎ *(530) 582-7892.* ◯ *daily.* ⬤ *Jan 1, Thanksgiving, Dec 25.*

Façade of the 19th-century Old Truckee Jail, now a museum

Truckee ❷

Road map B3. 🏂 *13,000.* 🚊 🚌 ℹ️ *10065 Donner Pass Road.* ☎ *(530) 587-2757.* ☎ *(530) 546-5253 winter weather hotline.*

Oɴᴇ ᴏꜰ ᴛʜᴇ ʜɪɢʜᴇꜱᴛ and coldest towns in California, Truckee is thought to have gotten its name when a native Paiute greeted the first white Americans with "Trokay," meaning "peace."

Truckee is situated along the main highway (I-80) and rail route across the Sierra Nevada Mountains. Its history as a transportation center goes back to 1863, when it was founded as a changeover point for railroad crews along the transcontinental railroad *(see pp46–7)*. The Southern Pacific Depot still serves rail and bus passengers as well as operating as a visitors' center.

Much of the town's Wild West character and history as a lumber center survives, especially along Commercial Row in the heart of town, where a line of old brick and wooden buildings faces the tracks. Many of these have now been converted into atmospheric shops, restaurants, and cafés.

Another evocative survivor of the town's past is the **Old Truckee Jail**, built in 1875. It is a small museum depicting the wilder side of frontier life.

Located only 25 miles (40 km) from Lake Tahoe, Truckee is also a popular historical base for winter skiers and summer hikers.

🏛 Old Truckee Jail

Jibboom & Spring Sts. ☎ *(530) 582-0893.* ◯ *May–Sep: Sat & Sun.* ⬤ *public hols.* ♿

SKIING AROUND LAKE TAHOE

The peaks surrounding Lake Tahoe, particularly on the California side, are famous for their ski resorts. The world-class Alpine Meadows and Squaw Valley are where the Winter Olympics were held in 1960. The largest ski area, Heavenly Valley, is above the city of South Lake Tahoe, with many more around the lake and at Donner Pass, west of Truckee, along I-80. There are also cross-country ski areas with groomed trails. The Lake Tahoe area receives more than 10 ft (3 m) of snow each winter and is the state's major center for winter recreation from November to March.

Skiing at Lake Tahoe's Alpine Meadows resort

A Tour of Lake Tahoe ❸

THE MOST BEAUTIFUL body of water in California, Lake Tahoe is 1,645 ft (501 m) at its deepest point and is surrounded by forested peaks. The area began to develop as a tourist resort after the construction of the first road in 1915 made it more accessible. Casinos opening on the Nevada border in the 1930s and the Winter Olympics in 1960 further increased its popularity.

View of Lake Tahoe from Heavenly Valley

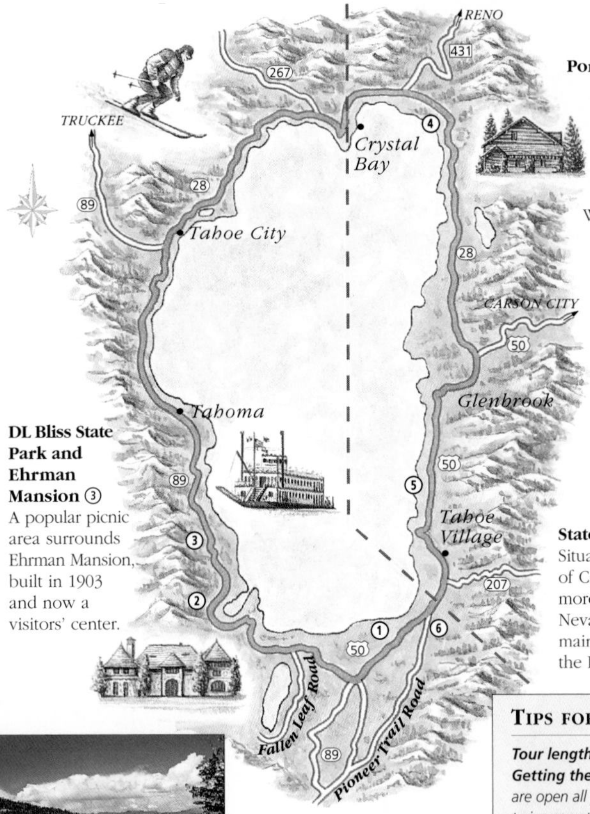

Ponderosa Ranch ④
Near the northeast shore of the lake, this summer-only amusement park is based on the cult 1960s Wild West TV show, *Bonanza*.

Cave Rock and Cave Rock Tunnel ⑤
Lake Tahoe's east shore is so rugged that part of the highway is tunneled through solid granite.

DL Bliss State Park and Ehrman Mansion ③
A popular picnic area surrounds Ehrman Mansion, built in 1903 and now a visitors' center.

Stateline ⑥
Situated on the border of California and the more liberal state of Nevada, Stateline is the main gambling town of the Lake Tahoe region.

Emerald Bay State Park and Vikingsholm ②
The beautiful inlet of Emerald Bay is the most photographed part of the lake. Vikingsholm, built as a summerhouse in the 1920s, is an incongruous reproduction of an old Nordic castle.

South Lake Tahoe ①
The largest town in the area, South Lake Tahoe caters for visitors to Nevada's casinos.

0 kilometers 10

0 miles 10

KEY

Tour route

Other roads

Viewpoint

TIPS FOR TRAVELERS

Tour length*: 65 miles (105 km).*
Getting there*: I-80 and US 50 are open all year round. Amtrak trains operate to Truckee. Greyhound buses and limited flights from San Francisco and Oakland serve South Lake Tahoe.*
When to go*: Peak tourist seasons are July, August, and winter, when the ski resorts are open. Spring and autumn are less crowded, but some facilities may be closed.*
Where to stay and eat*: For the best information, contact Lake Tahoe Visitors' Authority.*
Tourist information*: Lake Tahoe Visitors' Authority, South Lake Tahoe. ☎ (800) 288-2463.*

Yosemite National Park ❹

A WILDERNESS of evergreen forests, high meadows, and sheer granite walls, much of Yosemite National Park is accessible only to experienced hikers or horseback riders. The spectacular Yosemite Valley, a good base from which to explore the park, is easily reached by car and there are 200 additional miles (320 km) of paved roads providing access to more remote areas. Soaring cliffs, plunging waterfalls, gigantic trees, rugged canyons, mountains, and valleys all combine to lend Yosemite its incomparable beauty.

Yosemite Museum
The history of the Miwok and Paiute people is displayed here, along with works by Yosemite artists.

Lower Yosemite Falls
Yosemite Creek drops 2,425 ft (740 m), to form the highest waterfall in the US (see p474).

Ahwahnee Hotel
Rustic architecture, elegant décor, and beautiful views make this hotel one of the most renowned in the country (see p475).

Yosemite Chapel *(1879)*
This tiny wooden church is all that is left of Yosemite's 19th-century Old Village.

Valley Visitor Center

To Upper Yosemite Falls

Yosemite Creek

Yosemite Falls Trail

Yosemite Village

Sunnyside

Northside Drive

Yosemite Lodge

Merced River

Southside Drive

Sentinel Creek

Four-Mile Trail

Lower River

Staircase Falls

SENTINEL ROCK
7,038 ft (2,145 m)

Sentinel Falls

Sentinel Dome can be reached on foot from the valley floor. The trail continues to Glacier Point.

Mirror Meadow
Park rangers no longer interfere with nature by dredging the lake, so the water at the foot of Half Dome is now silting up and forming a meadow (see p475).

VISITORS' CHECKLIST

Road map C3. **i** *PO Box 577, Yosemite.* **(** (209) 372-0200. *from Merced.* *Yosemite Valley.* *from Merced.* *daily.* **w** www.nps.gov/yose

KEY

—	Major road
=	Minor road
- -	Paths and trails
- -	Shuttle bus
⊐⊏	Bike route
~	Rivers
P	Parking
⛽	Gas station
Δ	Camping
🏕	Picnic area
i	Tourist information
☆	Viewpoint

Washington Column

Half Dome
A formidable trail climbs to the top of this cliff, which juts above the valley floor (see p474).

Vernal Fall
The Merced River pours into its canyon over the 317-ft (97-m) lip of this fall.

NORTH PINES

WER NES Tenaya Creek

UPPER PINES

Merced River

0 meters   1000
0 yards   1000

Merced River
This beautiful river can be appreciated along both the Mist Trail and the Panorama Trail. Anglers enjoy fishing for brown trout in its waters.

Exploring Yosemite National Park

Some of the world's most beautiful mountain terrain is protected within the 1,170 sq miles (3,030 sq km) of Yosemite National Park. Hundreds of thousands of visitors descend upon the park each year to admire its breathtaking views, formed by millions of years of glacial activity. Each season offers a different experience, from the swelling waterfalls of spring to the rustic colors of autumn. The summer months are the most crowded, but during the snowbound winter months several roads are inaccessible. Bus tours and well-maintained cycle paths, hiking trails, and roads are all aimed at leading visitors from one awe-inspiring panoramic scene to another.

Upper Yosemite Falls, swollen with ice-melt in the spring

🏔 Half Dome
Eastern end of Yosemite Valley.
⭕ daily.

Standing nearly 1 mile (1.6 km) above the valley floor, the silhouette of Half Dome has become a symbol of Yosemite. Its curved back rises to a wave-like lip, before dropping vertically to the valley below.

Geologists believe that Half Dome is now three-quarters of its original size, rather than a true half. It is thought that as recently as 15,000 years ago, glacial ice floes moved through the valley from the Sierra crest, scything off rock and depositing it downstream.

The 8,840-ft (2,695 m) summit of Half Dome offers an unsurpassed view of the valley. Follow the 9-mile (14-km) trail from Happy Isles trailhead to reach the peak.

🏔 Yosemite Falls
North Yosemite Valley. ⭕ daily.

Yosemite Falls are the highest waterfalls in North America and tumble from a height of 2,425 ft (740 m) in two great leaps, Upper Yosemite and Lower Yosemite Falls. One of the most recognizable features of the park, the cascades are visible all over the valley.

The top of Upper Yosemite Falls, by far the longer and more elegant of the pair, can be reached via a strenuous 7-mile (11-km) round-trip trail. The Lower Falls are easier to visit, via a short trail that starts next to Yosemite Lodge and frames an unforgettable view of both falls.

As with all the park's waterfalls, Yosemite Falls are at their peak in May and June, when the winter snows melt and fill the creek to capacity. Conversely, by September the falls often dry up and disappear altogether, their presence marked only by a dark stain on the granite wall.

🏔 Vernal and Nevada Falls
Eastern end of Yosemite Valley.
⭕ daily.

A popular half-day hike in Yosemite National Park is the Mist Trail, which visits these two waterfalls.

The first fall visited on this 7-mile (11-km) round-trip is Vernal Fall, which plunges 320 ft (95 m) and spreads its spray across the trail. The trail then continues for 2 miles (3 km) to the top of Nevada Falls, which drops an impressive 595 ft (180 m). At the top of Nevada Falls the Mist Trail joins the John Muir Trail, which runs around the back of Half Dome all the way south to the summit of Mount Whitney (see p479).

Sheer drop of El Capitán

📷 Glacier Point

Glacier Point Rd. ☐ May–Oct: daily.

The great Yosemite panorama can be experienced from Glacier Point, which rests on a rocky ledge 3,215 ft (980 m) above the valley floor. Most of the waterfalls and other features of Yosemite Valley are visible from here, but the dominant feature is Half Dome. The panorama also includes much of the surrounding landscape, a beautiful area of alpine peaks and meadows.

Glacier Point can be reached only during the summer. The road is blocked by snow during winter at Badger Pass, which was developed in 1935 as California's first commercial ski resort. Another summer route is the Four-Mile Trail, which begins at the western side of the valley. Summer bus services also allow hikers to ride up to Glacier Point then hike down to the valley.

📷 Mariposa Grove

Visitors' Center Hwy 41, South Entrance. ☐ mid-May–Oct: daily.

At the southern end of Yosemite, this beautiful grove was one of the main reasons the park was established. More than 500 giant sequoia trees can be seen here, some of which are more than 3,000 years old, 250 ft (75 m) tall and more than 30 ft (9 m) in diameter at their base. A series of hiking trails winds through the grove, and open-air trams make a 5-mile (8-km) circuit along roads constructed during the early years of Yosemite tourism.

Tunnel View, looking across Yosemite Valley

📷 Tunnel View

Hwy 41 overlooking Yosemite Valley. ☐ daily.

One of the most photographed views of Yosemite can be had from this lookout on Hwy 41 at the western end of the valley. Despite the name, which is taken from the highway tunnel that leads to Glacier Point Road, the view is incredible, with El Capitán on the left, Bridalveil Fall on the right and Half Dome at the center.

📷 El Capitán

Northwestern end of Yosemite Valley. ☐ daily.

Standing guard at the western entrance to Yosemite Valley, the granite wall of El Capitán rises more than 4,500 ft (1,370 m) from the valley floor. The world's largest exposed rock, El Capitán is a magnet to rock-climbers, who spend days on its sheer face to reach the top. Less adventurous visitors congregate in the meadow below, watching the rock-climbers through binoculars.

Named by US soldiers, who in 1851 were the first white Americans to visit the valley, El Capitán is the Spanish phrase for "captain."

📷 Tuolumne Meadows

Hwy 120, Tioga Rd. ☐ Jun–Sep: daily.

In summer, when the snows have melted and the wildflowers are in full bloom, the best place to experience the striking beauty of the Yosemite landscape are these subalpine meadows along the Tuolumne River. Located 55 miles (88 km) from Yosemite valley via Tioga Pass Road, Tuolumne Meadows are also a base for hikers setting off to explore the area's many granite peaks and trails.

Black-tailed deer roaming Yosemite's meadows

🏨 Ahwahnee Hotel

Yosemite Valley. 📞 (209) 372-1407. ☐ daily. See **Where to Stay** p536.

A building that comes close to matching Yosemite's natural beauty, the Ahwahnee Hotel was built in 1927 at a cost of $1.5 million.

It was designed by Gilbert Stanley Underwood, who used giant granite boulders and massive wood timbers to create a rustic elegance that is in tune with its surroundings. The interior of the Ahwahnee Hotel also emulates the natural setting, decorated in a Native American style. A few Native American arts and crafts are on display in the lobbies. The hotel is also noted for its high-quality restaurant (see p574).

Giant sequoia trees in Mariposa Grove

Sierra Nevada, near Lone Pine ▷

Ghostly wooden buildings in Bodie State Historic Park

Bodie State Historic Park ❺

Road map C3. 🏔 10. 🚌 from Bridgeport. ℹ End of Hwy 270 (760 647-6445). ⭘ daily.

Hᴵɢʜ ᴜᴘ ɪɴ the foothills of the eastern Sierra Nevada, Bodie is the largest ghost town in California.

Now protected as a state historic park, Bodie was, during the second half of the 19th century, a bustling gold mining town, with a population that topped 8,000 in 1880. Named after the gold prospector Waterman S Bodey, who first discovered placer deposits (surface gold) here in 1859, Bodie boomed with the discovery of hard rock ore in the mid-1870s. Soon many different mines had been established in the area, but it all came to an end when the gold ran out in 1882. Later, a series of fires destroyed much of the town. Only the Standard Mine remained in business, but it closed in 1942 because of a wartime ban on mining.

The state acquired the entire town in 1962, and has maintained the 170 buildings in a condition of "arrested decay." The result is an evocative experience of empty streets lined by deserted wooden buildings. The Miners' Union Hall has been converted into a visitors' center and museum, with artifacts from Bodie's early days.

Mono Lake ❻

Road map C3. 🚍 (760) 647-3044. 🚉 Merced.

Oɴᴇ ᴏғ ᴛʜᴇ strangest looking places in the United States, and possibly one of the oldest lakes in the world, Mono Lake is a 60-sq mile (155-sq km) body of alkaline water at the eastern foot of the Sierra Nevada Mountains set between two volcanic islands. The lake has no natural outlet, but evaporation in the summer heat combined with water diversion to LA has caused it to shrink to one-fifth of its original size. The result is extremely brackish water, three times saltier than sea water. It has also exposed a number of contorted tufa spires. These were formed when calcium from underground springs came into contact with carbonates in the lake water, forming limestone. The tufa formations once sat under water, but the evaporation has left them arrayed along the lakeside.

In recent years, Mono Lake has also been the subject of a heated political and environmental debate, part of an ongoing battle over water rights. The City of Los Angeles purchased a large amount of land in the eastern Sierras and Owens Valley in 1905, and began diverting the streams and rivers through a system of aqueducts to LA in 1941. This has accelerated the lake's shrinkage and put local wildlife, the state's large seagull population, which breeds on the lake's islands, in danger (see pp192–3). In 1994 the California State Government ruled that LA must preserve the lake and its surrounding ecosystem at 6,392 ft (1,950 m) above sea level.

Tufa spires rising out of Mono Lake

Devil's Postpile National Monument 7

Road map C4. **(** *(760) 934-2289.* **⊞** *shuttle from Mammoth Mountain Inn.* **◯** *Jul–Sep: daily.* 🎨 ♿ ✓

O N THE WEST of the Sierra Nevada crest, but most easily accessible from the eastern resort of Mammoth Lakes, Devil's Postpile National Monument protects one of the most impressive geological formations in the state.

A wall of basalt columns, in varying geometrical shapes, predominantly pentagons and hexagons, cover a 545 sq yard (652 sq m) area. More than 60 ft (18 m) tall, they rise 7,560 ft (2,320 m) above sea level. The columns were formed around 100,000 years ago, when molten lava cooled and fractured. Set at the heart of an 800-acre (320-ha) park, they resemble a tiled floor seen from above. The monument is covered in snow most of the year and is only accessible in summer via a shuttle bus.

Rainbow Falls, 2 miles (3 km) from the Postpile, are named after the refraction of sunlight in their spray.

White Mountains 8

ℹ *798 N Main St, Bishop (760 873-2500).*

R ISING ALONG the eastern side of Owens Valley, the White Mountains, at 12,000 ft (3,660 m), are almost as high but far drier than the 13,000-ft (3,960-m) parallel range of Sierra Nevada. Lack of water has kept the peaks rugged and largely free of vegetation, but the few trees that do survive here, the bristlecone pines *(Pinus aristata)*, are among the oldest living things on earth.

These gnarled pine trees seem to thrive on the adverse conditions, which batter them into strange, contorted shapes. The species is found only on the lower slopes of the White Mountains and on a few of the mountains in neighboring Nevada. Extremely slow

Bristlecone pines on the slopes of the White Mountains

growing, they seldom reach more than 50 ft (15 m) in height, despite living for more than 4,000 years – 1,000 years longer than the oldest sequoia tree *(see pp480–81).*

Owens Valley 9

🚃 *Lone Pine.* ℹ *126 S Main St, Lone Pine (760 876-4444).*

O WENS VALLEY has more in common with Nevada than with the rest of California. It is sparsely populated but ruggedly beautiful, the valley being wedged between the White Mountains and the Sierra Nevada.

Once covered with farms and ranches, the land here was bought secretly in 1905 by agents working for the City of Los Angeles. Los Angeles needed to secure a water supply, and the aqueducts still drain the valley, destroying local agriculture.

In 1942 a detention camp was established at Manzanar for 10,000 Japanese-Americans, who were deemed a threat to national security and imprisoned for the duration of World War II. Exhibits on this and other aspects of Owens Valley can be seen at the **Eastern California Museum**, in the town of Independence.

🏛 Eastern California Museum

155 Grant St, Independence.
(*(760) 878-0364.* **◯** *Wed–Mon.* ⬤ *Jan 1, Easter, Thanksgiving, Dec 25.* **Donation.**

Mount Whitney 10

(*(760) 876-6200.* 🚃 *Merced.*

T HE HIGHEST PEAK on the US mainland, Mount Whitney rises to a height of 14,496 ft (4,420 m), forming a sheer wall above the town of Lone Pine. A steep 11-mile (18-km) trail leads from Whitney Portal Road to the summit, offering a panorama over the High Sierras. A permit is required to hike the trail. The mountain, named in honor of the geologist Josiah Whitney, was first climbed in 1873.

Mount Whitney borders the beautiful Sequoia National Park *(see pp480–81),* and the surrounding alpine meadows are ideal for backpacking in the summer months.

Owens Valley, backed by the White Mountains

Sequoia and Kings Canyon National Parks ⓫

Sequoia National Park sign

THESE TWIN national parks preserve lush forests, granite peaks, and glacier-carved canyons. Breathtaking scenery complements a habitat rich with wildlife. The parks embrace 34 separate groves of the giant sequoia tree, the earth's largest living species. America's deepest canyon, the south fork of the Kings River, cuts a depth of 8,200 ft (2,500 m) through Kings Canyon. Along the eastern boundary of Sequoia is Mount Whitney (see p479), the highest summit on the US mainland.

Roads serve the western side of the parks; the rest is accessible only to hikers or with rented pack-trains of horses or mules. Winter visitors can ski cross-country over both marked and unmarked trails.

Road "tunnel" formed by a felled giant sequoia in Sequoia National Park

Wilsonia •

180

Cedar Brook

Redwood Mountain Grove

Redwood Creek

North Fork Kaweah River

M465

BIG BALD

8,209 ft (2,50

SEQUOI
NATIONA
PARK

Yucca Creek

General Grant Tree
The third-largest sequoia is known as the "Nation's Christmas Tree."

KEY

▬▬	Major road
═══	Minor road
▪ ▪ ▪	Paths and trails
───	National Park boundary
∿∿	River
🎿	Skiing
🅰	Camping
🏕	Picnic area
ℹ	Tourist information
�	Viewpoint

Big Stumps
The sequoia's unyielding nature makes it uneconomical for lumber, as these tall stumps, left by loggers in the 1880s, prove.

VISITORS' CHECKLIST

Ash Mountain, Three Rivers.
Road map C4. 📞 *(559) 565-3341.* ◯ *daily.* 🚫 🅿️ ♿ *call ahead.* 🏠 🚻 *summer only.*
⏸️ ◻️ W *www.nps.gov/seki*

Moro Rock
A staircase carved into the rock takes visitors to the top of this granite monolith and affords a 360° view of the High Sierras and the Central Valley.

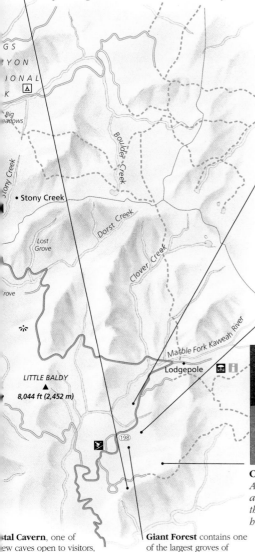

General Sherman's Tree
The world's largest living thing is 275 ft (84 m) tall, with a trunk measuring 36 ft (11 m) around its base. The tree still grows 0.4 inches (1 cm) every ten years.

Tharp's Log, a hollowed-out sequoia, was home to Hale Tharp, a 19th-century farmer who was introduced to the area by Native Americans.

Crescent Meadow
An array of sequoias border this area, which is more of a marsh than a meadow and too wet at its heart for the trees to survive.

...tal Cavern, one of
...ew caves open to visitors,
...led with stalagmites and stalactites.

Giant Forest contains one of the largest groves of living sequoias in the world.

0 kilometers   2

0 miles   2

NORTH CENTRAL CALIFORNIA

WITH A RUGGED SHORELINE *rising from the Pacific Ocean and dense forests covering coastal mountains, North Central California marks the visual transition between the north and south of the state. The landscape holds an embarrassment of riches, with golden beaches, splendid wilderness, and inland valleys that include some of the world's most productive agricultural regions.*

The natural beauty of the area, combined with a wealth of cultural history, makes this one of the state's most engaging regions. Native Americans lived along the coast and in the inland valleys for centuries prior to the arrival of Europeans in the 17th century. More than a century later the first European settlement was established at Monterey on June 3, 1770, marking the beginning of today's California. Monterey remained the capital of Upper California until the United States took formal control in 1848. The city still retains a unique character, with its many historic buildings now protected and restored.

North central California has also inspired some of the state's significant literature, from the poetry of Robinson Jeffers to the novels of Nobel prize-winner John Steinbeck. Many of the world's best photographers, including Ansel Adams and Edward Weston, have lived and worked here.

For all its culture and history, the region also abounds in recreational activities. Visitors can enjoy the historic amusement park at Santa Cruz, play golf on the world-famous courses at Pebble Beach, or simply walk around the many nature preserves, including the state's most beautiful stretch of coastline, Big Sur.

Writer John Steinbeck's house in Salinas

◁ **Bixby Creek Bridge on Coastal Hwy 1 at Big Sur**

Exploring North Central California

MONTEREY, the Spanish colonial capital of California, is at the heart of north central California and the best base from which to explore the region. The wealthy resorts of Pacific Grove and Carmel stand on a rugged peninsula just south of the town. Farther south is the wildest length of coastline in the state, Big Sur, where otters and whales can be spotted offshore. To the north is Santa Cruz, a lively beach town, backed by densely forested mountains. Inland, the Salinas and San Joaquin valleys give a taste of California's productive agricultural areas.

Pfeiffer Burns State Park at Big Sur

1 BIG BASIN REDWOODS STATE PARK

2 AÑO NUEVO STATE RESERVE

3 ROARING CAMP & BIG TREES NARROW GAUGE RAILWAY

4 SANTA CRUZ

San Francisco
San Jose

San Luis Reservoir

LOS BANO

5 SAN JUAN BAUTISTA

9 SALINAS

PACIFIC GROVE

6 MONTEREY

7 CARMEL MISSION

8 BIG SUR

SOLEDAD

10 PINNACLES NATIONAL MONUMENT

KING CITY

San Antonio Reservoir

San Obisp

San Benito River

Salinas River

San Antonio River

Looking out across Big Sur along Hwy 1

GETTING AROUND

Hwy 1, which runs along the coast south from Monterey to Big Sur, is one of the world's most beautiful drives and a must on any tour of California. A car, or a bicycle and strong legs, is the best way to get around, although there is a skeletal network of buses centering upon Monterey. Inland from the coast, Hwy 101 and I-5 run north–south through the predominantly agricultural region, but there are very few roads between the coast and inland valleys.

Sights at a Glance

Año Nuevo State Reserve **2**
Big Basin Redwoods State Park **1**
Big Sur pp498–9 **8**
Carmel Mission pp496–7 **7**
Fresno **11**
Hanford **12**
Monterey pp492–5 **6**
Pinnacles National Monument **10**
Roaring Camp and Big Trees Narrow Gauge Railroad **3**
Salinas **9**
San Juan Bautista **5**
Santa Cruz pp490–91 **4**

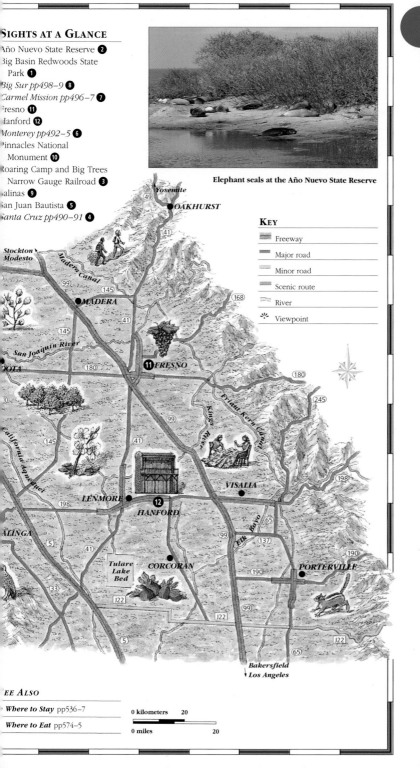

Elephant seals at the Año Nuevo State Reserve

Key

	Freeway
	Major road
	Minor road
	Scenic route
	River
☀	Viewpoint

Yosemite
49
OAKHURST

Stockton
Modesto
Madera Canal
99
145
MADERA
145
41
San Joaquin River
DOTA
180
11 FRESNO
180
245

California Aqueduct
145
Kings River
Friant Kern Canal
99
41
VISALIA
198
LEMORE
12
HANFORD
198
Elk Bayou
65
137

ALINGA
5
41
33
Tulare Lake Bed
CORCORAN
99
190
PORTERVILLE
190
J22
J22
5
99
65
J22

Bakersfield
↓ *Los Angeles*

0 kilometers   20

0 miles   20

The North Central Coastline

THE BEACHES of north central California are varied, from long, thin stretches to tiny coves at the foot of coastal bluffs. In summer, sun-worshipers and volleyball players congregate on the sands, and while the water is generally too cold for swimming, surfers don wet suits to brave the chilly waves. With almost no commercial developments along this stretch of coastline, these beaches are also ideal for leisurely walks, searching for driftwood or seashells. You may also catch a glimpse of the area's abundant wildlife, which ranges from shore birds and tidepool-dwellers to elephant seals and migrating gray whales.

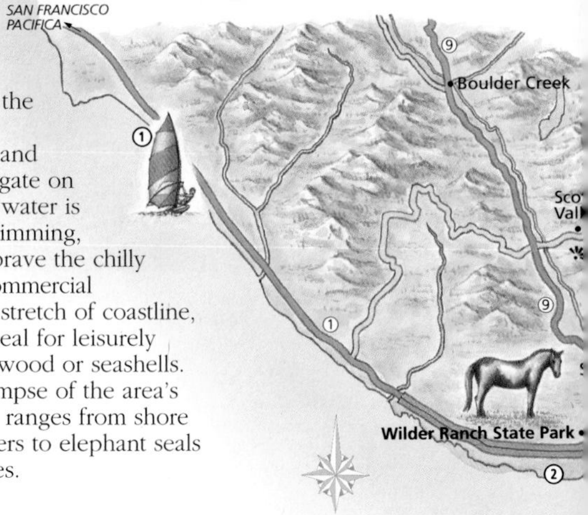
SAN FRANCISCO
PACIFICA
Boulder Creek
Wilder Ranch State Park

Moss Landing *is a colorful harbor and the home port for most of Monterey Bay's commercial fishing boats. It has many good seafood restaurants along its wharves.*

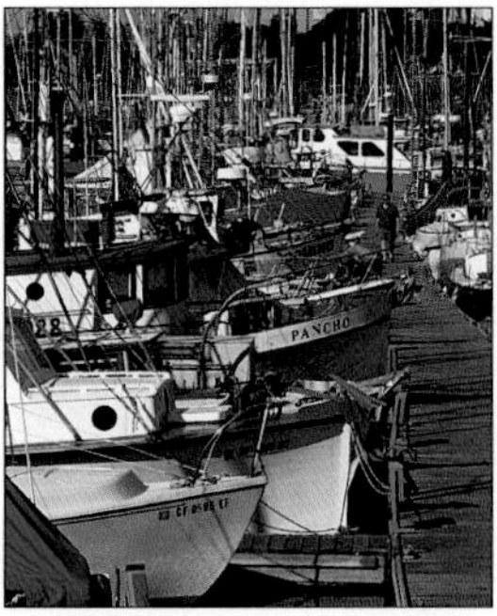

0 kilometers 5

0 miles 5

★ Santa Cruz Beach ③

🏄 🌊 🛟 ♿ 🚻

With free volleyball courts and barbecue pits backed by the popular Boardwalk Amusement Park *(see p490)*, this broad golden expanse is the area's most popular beach.

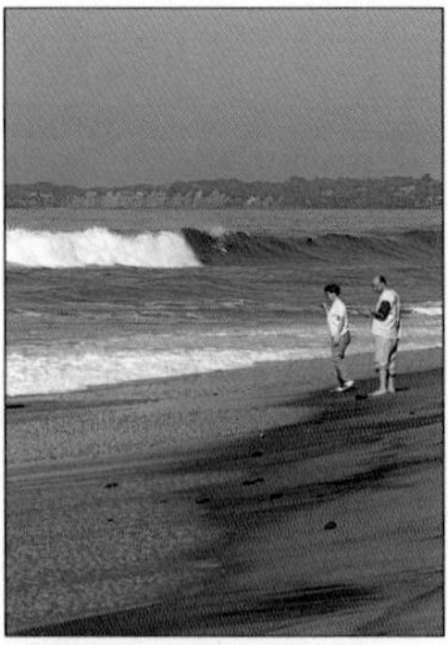

Waddell Creek Beach ①

🌊 🛟 ♿ 🚻

This golden strand of beach is part of the Big Basin Redwoods State Park *(see p488)* and is a favorite spot for picnickers, anglers, and windsurfers.

Lighthouse Field State Beach ②

🏄

This rugged 36 acres (14 ha) of shoreline is well suited to surfing or simply admiring the sculpted 40-ft (12-m) sandstone headlands. It is also a good place to spot sea otters, brown pelicans, and the occasional whale offshore.

Capitola Beach ④

🏄 🌊 🛟 ♿ 🚻

A wooden railway trestle bridges the small creek that meets the ocean at this sandy beach. Next to the beach is Capitola Wharf, with restaurants, shops, and observation decks. The Capitola Bluffs are an important paleontological site, and the prehistoric shells can be seen at low tide.

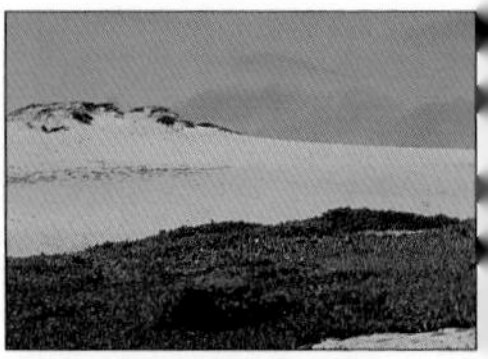

Marina State Beach ⑤

🏄 🌊 🛟 ♿ 🚻

Backed by sand dunes, this beach was once a part of a US Army base and is now part of a university campus.

KEY

- Freeway
- Major road
- Minor road
- River
- Viewpoint

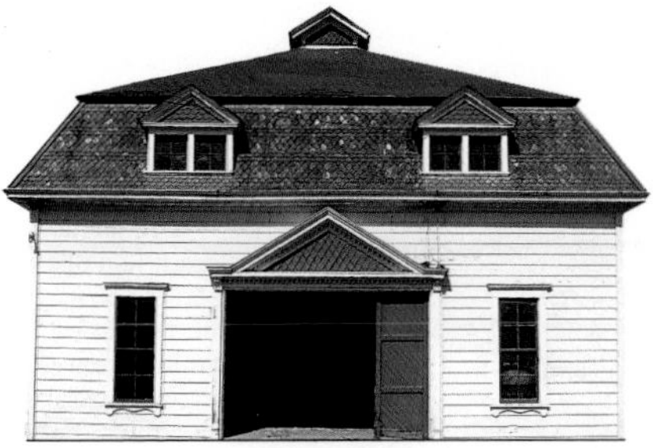

Wilder Ranch State Park, *at the northern edge of Santa Cruz, is a historic coastal dairy farm. Complete with ranch house and barns dating from the 1890s, it has been preserved as a state park.*

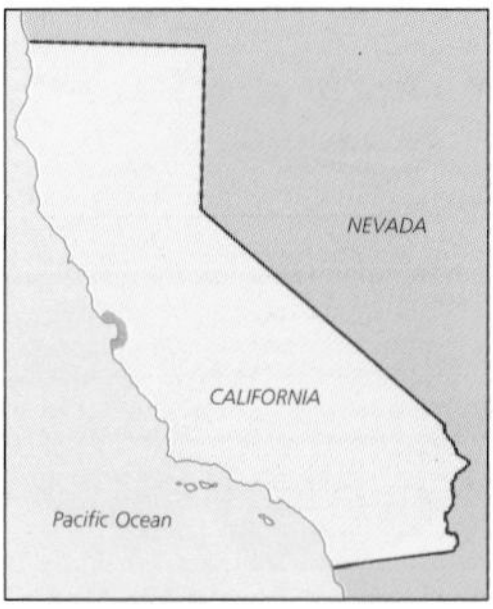
NEVADA
CALIFORNIA
Pacific Ocean

Locator Map

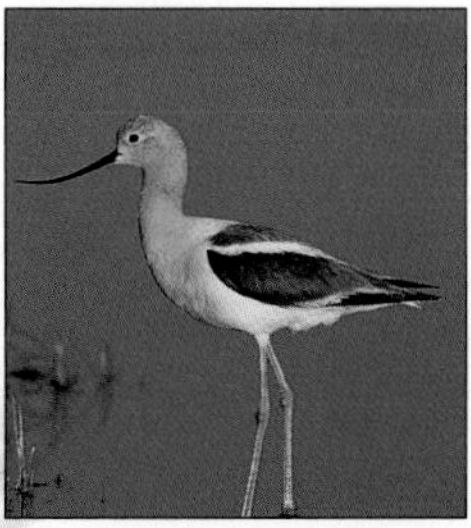

***Elkhorn Slough**, halfway along Monterey Bay, is one of the prime bird-watching areas along the North Central coastline.*

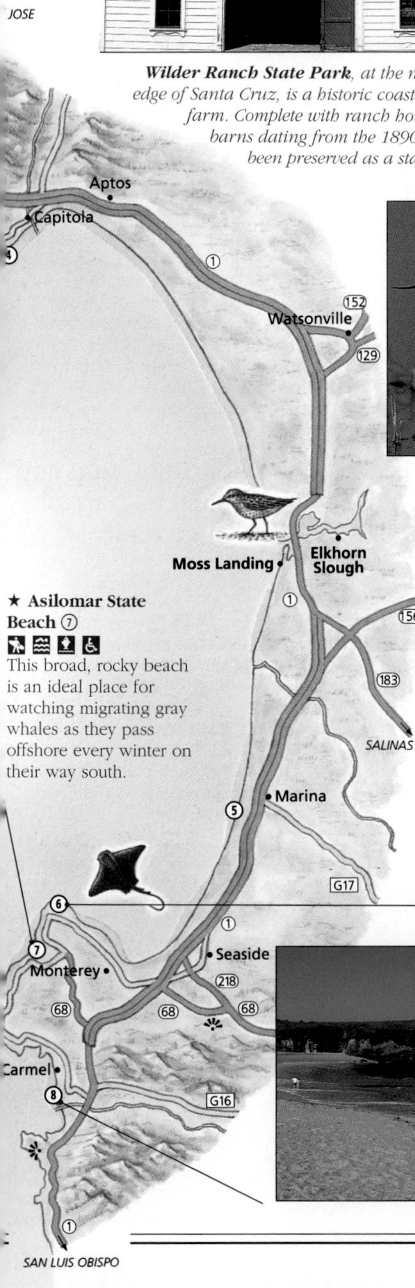
JOSE
Aptos
Capitola
Watsonville
152
129
1
Moss Landing
Elkhorn Slough
156
183
SALINAS
Marina
5
G17
6
7
Monterey
Seaside
218
68
Carmel
8
G16
SAN LUIS OBISPO

★ Asilomar State Beach [7]
🏄 🌊 🛟 ♿
This broad, rocky beach is an ideal place for watching migrating gray whales as they pass offshore every winter on their way south.

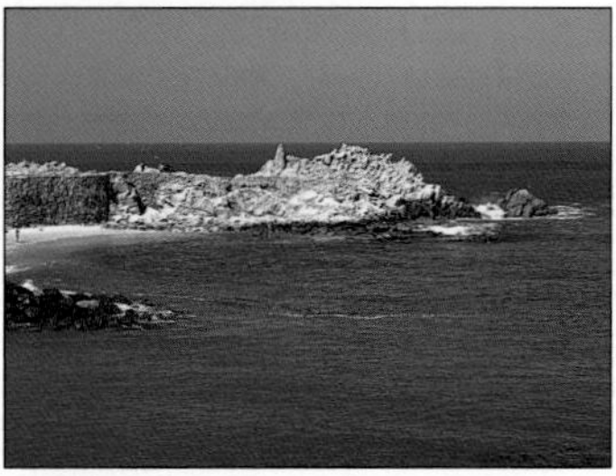

★ Lovers' Point [6]
🌊 ♿ 🚻
Originally called Lovers of Jesus Point, the headlands form a natural amphitheater that was used for religious revivals in the 1880s. It is one of the few sandy beaches on the northern Monterey Peninsula.

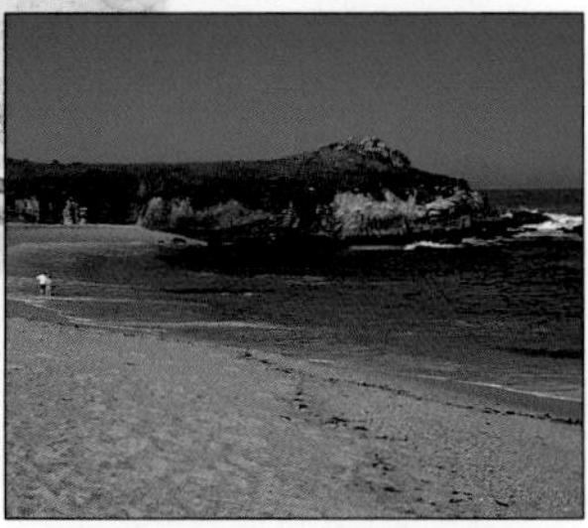

★ Carmel City Beach [8]
🏄 🌊 🛟 ♿ 🚻
Bright white sand and brilliant blue water are the distinguishing characteristics of this long beach, which sits at the foot of central Carmel's popular shopping and restaurant district *(see p494)*.

Elephant seals ashore at Año Nuevo State Reserve

Big Basin Redwoods State Park ❶

Santa Cruz, Boulder Creek Golf Course. **Visitors' Center** (831) 338-8860.

IN 1900 A GROUP of environ-mentalists formed the Sem-pervirens Club with the aim of preventing the logging of redwoods. This resulted in Big Basin Redwoods State Park, California's first state park, established in 1902. It covers 16,000 acres (6,475 ha) and protects the southernmost groves of the coastal redwood tree *(see p430)* and forests of Douglas fir and other conifers. It is also home to wildlife such as black-tailed deer and the mountain lion.

Trails lead through redwood groves to the park's many waterfalls, including the popular Berry Creek Falls. There are also more than 100 miles (160 km) of other routes, in-cluding the Skyline-to-Sea Trail, which drops down to the Pacific Ocean at Waddell Creek *(see pp486–7)*.

Exhibits detailing the park's history are on display inside the visitor center.

Año Nuevo State Reserve ❷

Road map B4. Santa Cruz, Waddell Creek. (831) 879-2025; 879-0227. daily.

THE AÑO NUEVO State Reserve, 60 miles, (96 km) north of Monterey, has as its main point of interest the breeding grounds of the Northern ele-phant seal, one of the world's most fascinating creatures. A short stretch of sandy beach and a small offshore island are populated each winter by hun-dreds of these giant mammals, which arrive here from all over the Pacific Ocean to mate and give birth.

Elephant seals were hunted almost to extinction in the 19th century because of their valuable oil-bearing blubber. A few survivors found refuge off the coast of Mexico and made their way back to Cali-fornia in the 1950s. The first pups were born at Año Nuevo in 1975. There are now some 120,000 elephant seals off the coast of California.

The seals are named after the dangling proboscis of the male, which can reach 20 ft (6 m) in length and weigh up-ward of 2 tons. Ungainly on land, elephant seals can per-form incredible feats in the sea – remaining under water for up to 20 minutes at a time and diving more than 4,000 ft (1,220 m) beneath the surface. Each December, the male seals arrive here and begin the battle for dominance, engaging in violent fights. Only a handful of the most powerful males are able to mate, but one male can father pups with as many as 50 different females in one season. After spending most of the year at sea, the females arrive in January to give birth to young conceived the pre-vious winter. Mating follows soon after, although concep-tion is delayed for up to four months while the female recovers from giving birth.

The name Año Nuevo ("New Year") was given to the island by explorer Sebastián Vizcaíno, who sailed past the area on January 1, 1603 *(see pp42–3)*. The park is open all year, but during the winter when the elephant seals are present, visitors are allowed only on guided tours. Tickets are avail-able through the California State Parks reservation service, DestiNet *(see p576)*.

Roaring Camp and Big Trees Narrow-Gauge Railroad ❸

(831) 335-4400. Santa Cruz. Jan–Mar: Sat & Sun. public hols. noon, 1:30pm, 3pm.
Santa Cruz Big Trees Railroad
(831) 335-4400. call ahead for times.

HIGH UP in the Santa Cruz Mountains, near the town of Felton, a pair of historic logging railroads have been kept in operation as the focus

Roaring Camp and Big Trees Railroad

Façade of Mission San Juan Bautista

of a family-orientated theme park devoted to the late 19th-century and early 20th-century lumber industry. Between December and March, a narrow-gauge train departs on a weekend 6-mile (10-km) round-trip through the adjacent forests of Henry Cowell Redwoods State Park. From April to November, the traditional-gauge Big Trees, Santa Cruz, and Pacific Railroad, sets off from Roaring Camp on an hour-long trip through the mountains and down to Santa Cruz. There is a three-hour stopover, during which passengers can enjoy the beach and Boardwalk Amusement Park before the return journey (see pp490–91). The trip can also be taken as a round-trip from Santa Cruz.

Santa Cruz ❹

See pp490–91.

San Juan Bautista ❺

Road map B4. 🏛 1,650.
🚌 from Hollister. 🚉 402 3rd St
(831) 623-2454.

F OR A QUICK INSIGHT into California's multifaceted history, there is no better place than San Juan Bautista. This small town has retained its rural character, despite being a mere 30 miles (48 km) from the heart of the high-tech Silicon Valley (see p412).

The main attraction of the town is Mission San Juan Bautista, which stands to the west of the central plaza. The largest of the missions built during Spanish colonial rule, it is also the only one to have aisles along the nave. Alfred Hitchcock used the mission's façade for the final scenes of his film *Vertigo*. The adjacent monastery has

El Camino Real sign

been converted into a museum of mission history, displaying mission artifacts and photographs of the town at various stages of development.

On the north side of the church there is a cemetery, next to which a faint trail marks the historic route of El Camino Real. This 650-mile (1,050-km) path linked the 21 California missions, all within a day's journey of their nearest mission (see pp42–3). By coincidence, this trail also follows the San Andreas Fault, the underlying source of all California's earthquakes (see pp20–21). A small seismograph on the edge of the town's plaza monitors tectonic activity along the fault line.

The east and south sides of the plaza are lined by three historic buildings, all of which have been preserved as part of San Juan Bautista State Historic Park. The Plaza Hotel incorporates part of the original barracks built in 1813. The town's stables now house antique carriages and stagecoaches, and Castro House was owned by Patrick Breen, a survivor of the tragic Donner Party (see p470).

THE LOMA PRIETA EARTHQUAKE

The powerful tremor that rocked San Francisco on October 17, 1989 had its epicenter beneath Loma Prieta, a hill between Santa Cruz and San Juan Bautista. Although the international media concentrated on the extensive damage caused in and around San Francisco, the worst damage occurred in Santa Cruz and the surrounding communities, where a number of homes and commercial buildings were destroyed. Approximately 40 businesses were forced to relocate to tentlike temporary buildings occupying three full blocks. The downtown district of Santa Cruz was a vast building site until the end of 1994. The majority of the damaged structures have now been repaired or replaced, but empty lots still remain where buildings once stood.

Destruction caused by the Loma Prieta earthquake

Santa Cruz ❹

PERCHED AT THE NORTHERN TIP of Monterey Bay, Santa Cruz is a composite of small-town California, with an agricultural rather than suburban feel. Its surrounding farmland forms a broad shelf between the bay and the densely forested Santa Cruz Mountains that rise to the east. These mountains separate Santa Cruz from the urban Silicon Valley *(see p412)* and, along with the scenic coastline, provide residents and visitors with an easy access to nature. The city's past is preserved in a replica 18th-century mission and in the excellent local history museum. The large University of California campus in the town, attracting students and professors from all over the world, also gives Santa Cruz a cosmopolitan and erudite character.

Exploring Santa Cruz

The downtown area, which centers on Pacific Avenue, is 875 yards (800 m) inland. Much of this area was badly damaged by the Loma Prieta earthquake *(see p489)*, but the city has recovered swiftly, with many good bookstores, art galleries, and cafés lining the streets. The historic core of the city, including the remains of the 1791 Mission Santa Cruz, is on a hill to the northeast of the town.

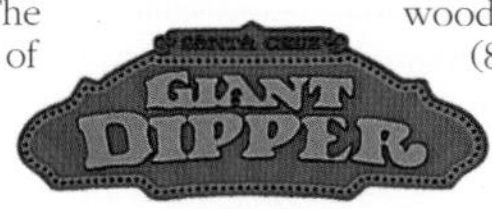

Detail of the Giant Dipper

The highlight of Santa Cruz is the waterfront, including the Boardwalk Amusement Park and scenic Cliff Drive that runs along the coast.

Santa Cruz Beach Boardwalk

400 Beach St. *(831) 423-5590.* *call ahead for opening times.*

The last surviving old-style amusement park on the West Coast, the Santa Cruz Beach Boardwalk offers a variety of attractions and games lined up along the beachfront. Visitors can wander freely, deciding which of the many exciting rides to try.

The main attraction is the Giant Dipper roller coaster, built in 1924 by Arthur Looff and now a National Historic Landmark. The car travels along the 1-mile (1.6-km) wooden track at 55 mph (88 km/h). The carousel nearby features horses and chariots handcarved by Looff's father, craftsman Charles Looff, in 1911. The ride is accompanied by a 100-year-old pipe organ. The park also has 27 more modern rides and an Art Deco dance hall.

Mission Santa Cruz

Emmet & High Sts. *(831) 426-5686.* *daily.* **Donation**.

On top of a hill overlooking the town, Mission Santa Cruz was founded on September 25, 1791 by Father Lasuén, as the 12th Franciscan mission in California. The buildings were completed three years later. The mission was never a

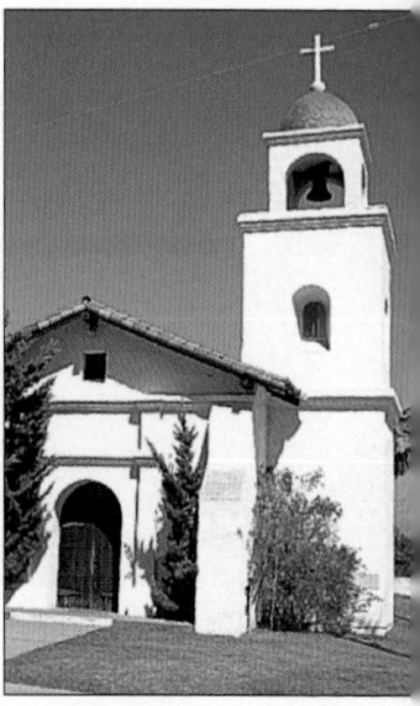
Reconstructed façade of Santa Cruz Mission

great success, however, due to earthquakes, poor weather, and its isolated location, all of which have eliminated any remains of the original structure. A park outlines the site, and a 1931 replica of the mission has been constructed. This houses a small museum that contains 18th-century relics and displays on mission history.

Museum of Art and History at the McPherson Center

705 Front St. *(831) 429-1964.* *Tue–Sun.* *Jan 1, Thanksgiving, Dec 25.*

www.santacruzmah.org

One positive development to arise out of the rubble of the 1989 Loma Prieta earthquake was this 20,000 sq ft (1,858 sq m) cultural center, which opened in 1993 to house the local art and history galleries. The Art Gallery shows works primarily by north central artists depicting the local landscape. The History Gallery includes a series of displays tracing the development of Santa Cruz County, from the pre-colonial and mission eras through to the present day.

Also in the History Gallery are exhibits detailing the region's agricultural and industrial heritage, with photographs of late 19th-century and early 20th-century farms and logging operations. The museum also incorporates the adjacent Octagon Gallery that was completed in 1882 as the County Hall of Records.

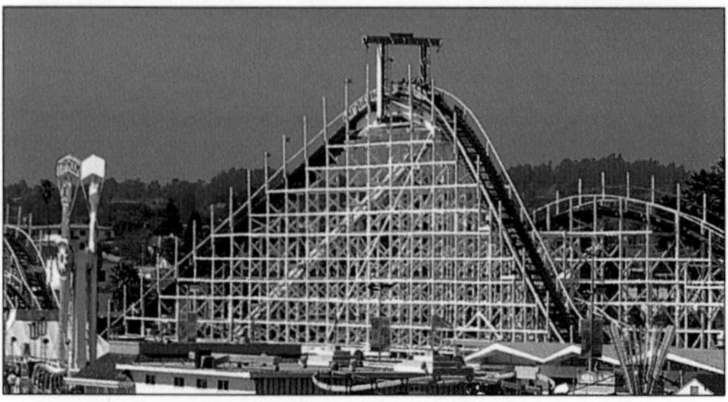
Giant Dipper roller coaster in the Boardwalk Amusement Park

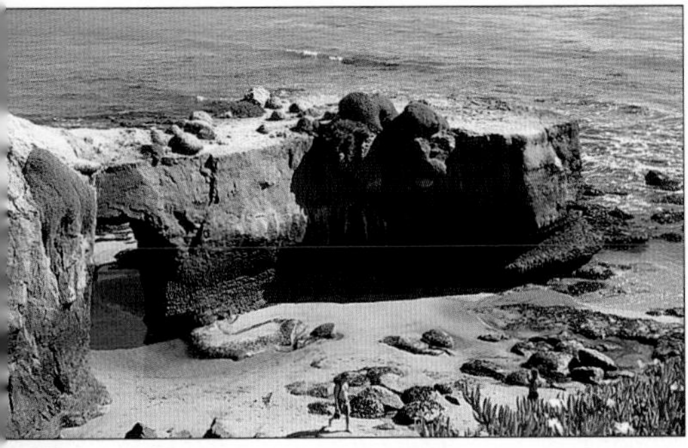

roded archway at the Natural Bridges State Beach

Natural Bridges State ;each

:531 W Cliff Dr. ☎ (831) 423-4609. ◯ daily. ♿ **Visitors' Center** *end of V Cliff Drive.* ◯ *daily.*

Vatural Bridges State Beach akes its name from the picuresque archways that were arved into the cliffs by the ocean waves. Two of the three original arches collapsed but one still remains, through which waves roll into a small sandy cove. The park also preserves a eucalyptus grove and a nature trail, showing all the stages in the life cycle of the beautiful monarch butterfly *(see p209).*

Santa Cruz Surfing Museum

Lighthouse Point, W Cliff Drive

☎ *(831) 420-6289.* ◯ *Wed–Mon.* ● *Jan 1, Thanksgiving, Dec 25.* **Donation**.

In a lighthouse overlooking the region's main surfing area, this museum has artifacts from every era of Santa Cruz surfing. The sport was brought to the state from Hawaii to promote tourism. It evolved into a truly Californian pursuit with the music of the Beach Boys in the 1960s *(see pp52–3)*. The surfboards range from the redwood planks of the 1930s to today's high-tech laminates.

Visitors' Checklist

Road map B4. 👥 *252,000.* ✈ *San Jose International Airport.* ✈ *Monterey Peninsula Airport.* 🚌 *920 Pacific Ave.* ℹ *701 Front St (831 425-1234).* 🎉 *Santa Cruz Fungus Fair (Jan); Clam Chowder Cook-Off (Feb).*

Mystery Spot

465 Mystery Spot Rd. ☎ *(831) 423-8897.* ◯ *daily.* ♿ [W] www.mysteryspot.com

Two miles (3 km) east of Santa Cruz, a redwood grove has been drawing visitors for decades due to various strange events. Balls roll uphill, parallel lines converge, and the laws of physics seem to be suspended. Part tourist trap, part genuine oddity, the Mystery Spot has to be seen.

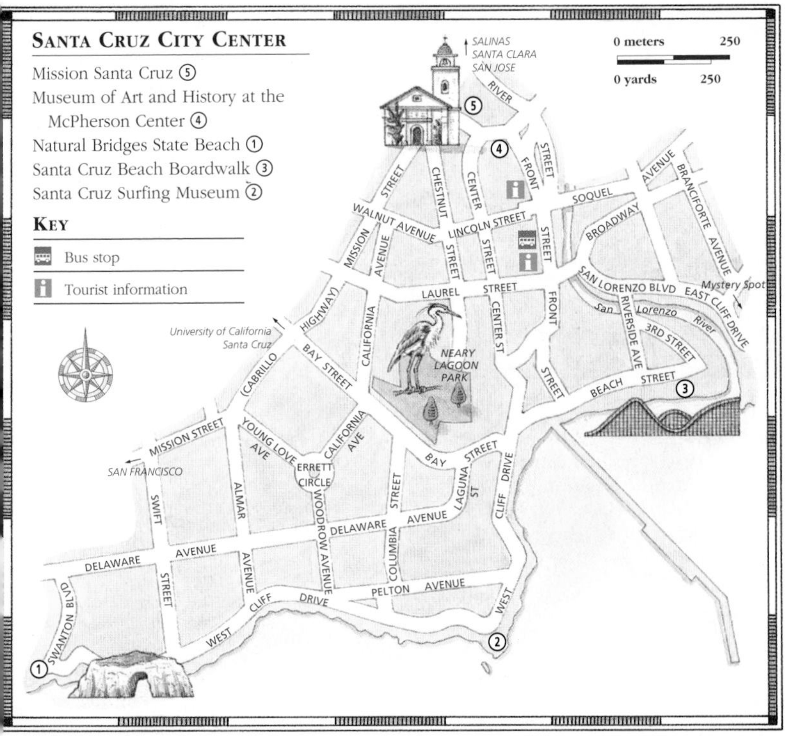
SANTA CRUZ CITY CENTER
Mission Santa Cruz 5
Museum of Art and History at the McPherson Center 4
Natural Bridges State Beach 1
Santa Cruz Beach Boardwalk 3
Santa Cruz Surfing Museum 2
KEY
Bus stop
Tourist information
0 meters 250
0 yards 250
SALINAS
SANTA CLARA
SAN JOSE
RIVER
FRONT STREET
SOQUEL
AVENUE
BRANCIFORTE AVENUE
BROADWAY
WALNUT AVENUE
LINCOLN STREET
MISSION
AVENUE
CHESTNUT STREET
CENTER STREET
LAUREL STREET
SAN LORENZO BLVD
EAST CLIFF DRIVE
Mystery Spot
San Lorenzo River
RIVERSIDE AVE
3RD STREET
BEACH STREET
HIGHWAY
CALIFORNIA
CENTER ST
NEARY LAGOON PARK
University of California Santa Cruz
BAY STREET
(CABRILLO
MISSION STREET
SAN FRANCISCO
YOUNG LOVE AVE
CALIFORNIA AVE
ERRETT CIRCLE
LAGUNA ST
CLIFF DRIVE
SWIFT
ALMAR
DELAWARE AVENUE
COLUMBIA STREET
WOODROW AVENUE
PELTON AVENUE
SWANTON BLVD
WEST CLIFF DRIVE
WEST

Street-by-Street: Monterey ❻

THE PORTUGUESE EXPLORER, Sebastián Vizcaíno, landed here in 1602 and named the bay after his patron, the Count of Monterrey. But it was not until the Spanish captain Gaspar de Portolá (1717–1784) and Father Serra *(see pp42–3)* landed here in 1770 and established a church and presidio that the garrison grew into a pueblo. Monterey served as the capital of California until 1848. After the Gold Rush *(see pp44–5)* the city lost its status to San Francisco and settled into the role of a hardworking fishing port, market town, and military base.

Today, visitors come to tour the historic sites, dine on seafood at Fisherman's Wharf, and attend the annual jazz festival.

California's First Theater
Built in 1847 as a boarding house, it became a theater in 1848. Victorian melodramas are still performed here every night.

★ Colton Hall
The California State Constitution was first signed here in 1849. The hall now houses a museum commemorating the event.

Larkin House
Thomas Larkin, an East Coast merchant, built this house in 1832. The architecture has become representative of Monterey style (see pp26–7).

The Sherman Quarters were General Sherman's military base from 1847–1849.

The Cooper-Molera Complex combines a garden, a carriage display and personal mementos of three generations of the Cooper family, who built the house between 1827 and 1900.

STAR SIGHTS
★ Colton Hall
★ Fisherman's Wharf

0 meters　　　100
0 yards　　　100

KEY

– – –　Suggested route

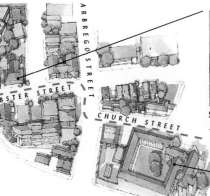

VISITORS' CHECKLIST

Road map B4. 🏠 *35,000.*
✈ *Monterey Peninsula Airport.*
🚌 *Tyler, Pearl & Munras Sts,*
(831) 899-2555. ℹ *401 Camino*
el Estero (831 648-5350).
🎉 *Monterey Blues Festival (Jul);*
Monterey Jazz Festival (Sep);
Laguna Seca Races (May–Oct).

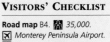

★ Fisherman's Wharf
Once the center of the fishing and whaling
industries, the area is now known for its
shops, seafood restaurants, and markets.

Custom House
This old government
building is preserved
as it was in the
1830s and '40s.

Old Whaling Station
Mementos of the Monterey whaling
industry are displayed in the house.
The paving outside the building
was made using whale bones.

Stevenson House
Robert Louis Stevenson lived here in
1879. The house is now a museum.

The Royal Presidio Chapel,
built in 1794, is the town's
oldest surviving building.

Exploring Monterey Peninsula

WRITERS AND ARTISTS have long extolled the spectacular coastline of the Monterey Peninsula. Its granite rocks have been cut into rugged coves and jutting points by the ocean. Forests of Monterey cypress and pine trees, wintering grounds of the monarch butterfly, cover the inland area. Otters and sea lions swim in the kelp forests beyond the shore. The peninsula is home to three main towns: Monterey, the capital of Spanish California (see pp492–3); the former religious retreat, Pacific Grove; and the picturesque village of Carmel-by-the-Sea.

Marine bird at the Monterey Bay Aquarium

Monterey Bay Aquarium

886 Cannery Row. **(** (831) 648-4888. ⭘ daily. ● Dec 25. 🖼 🔲 www.montereybayaquarium.org
Monterey Bay Aquarium is the largest aquarium in the US. More than 570 species and 350,000 specimens portray the rich marine environment of Monterey Bay. Among the exhibits are an enclosed kelp forest, a rock pool, and a display of live jellyfish. Visitors are allowed to touch the specimens, including sea stars and bat rays, relatives of sting rays.

A pool connected to the open bay attracts sea otters. The Outer Bay Wing has a huge tank in which the conditions of the ocean are re-created. It contains yellowfin tuna, ocean sunfish, green sea turtles, and barracuda. The Research Institute offers a chance for visitors to watch the marine scientists at work, and the Splash Zone is a hands-on aquarium/museum for kids.

Cannery Row

David Ave & Coastguard Pier.
((831) 649-6695. ⭘ daily.
This six-block harbor-front street, celebrated by John Steinbeck in his ribald novels *Cannery Row* and *Sweet Thursday (see p501)*, was once the site of more than 20 fish-packing plants that processed sardines from Monterey Bay. The canneries thrived from the early 20th century, reaching their greatest volume of production in the early 1940s. In 1945 the sardines suddenly disappeared, perhaps as a result of overfishing, and most of the canneries were abandoned, later to be demolished or burned down. The buildings that remain today house an eclectic collection of shops and restaurants. One notable historic building that remains, at No. 800, is the old laboratory of "Doc" Ricketts, noted marine biologist, beer drinker, and best friend of Steinbeck. The building is now a private club.

Street sign in Cannery Row

Pacific Grove

Forest & Central Aves. **(** (831) 373-3304. ⭘ daily. ● Jan 1, Thanksgiving, Dec 25.
This sedate town was founded in 1889 as a religious retreat, where alcohol, dancing, and even the Sunday newspaper were banned. Today it is best known for its wooden houses, many now converted into inns, its beautiful coastal parks, and the monarch butterflies that arrive between October and April (see p209). The annual return of the insects, which are protected by city ordinance, occasions a lively parade.

The Point Pinos Lighthouse was built in 1852 and is now the oldest operating lighthouse in California.

Carmel-by-the-Sea

San Carlos, 5th & 6th Sts. **(** (831) 624-1711. ⭘ Mon–Sat. ● Jan 1, Thanksgiving, Dec 25.
The varied array of homes in this picturesque village border the steep hillsides down to the ocean. City ordinances restricting streetlights, mail deliveries, and sidewalks gives the town its quaint atmosphere. Art galleries and shops abound along Ocean Avenue, and the town also sponsors an annual play-writing contest, a Bach Festival, and many art exhibitions.

Carmel River State Beach

Carmelo & Scenic Rds. **(** (831) 624-4909. ⭘ 7am–sunset, daily.
This 106-acre (43-ha) state park straddles the mouth of the Carmel River, containing a lagoon and wetland nature preserve for a bountiful population of native and migratory birds. Fishing is permitted on the beach, but swimming is discouraged because of dangerous currents and cold temperatures. The beach is a favorite picnic spot of Carmel residents.

Point Pinos Lighthouse at Pacific Grove

The 17-Mile Drive

SIGHTSEERS MAY TOUR the Monterey Peninsula via a toll road, the 17-Mile Drive. The road offers spectacular views of what the area has to offer, including crashing surf, coastal flora, and the Del Monte Forest. The extraordinary beauty of the region has also attracted many wealthy people to build imposing estates and mansions in the area. Most celebrated of all its attractions are the country clubs and championship golf courses.

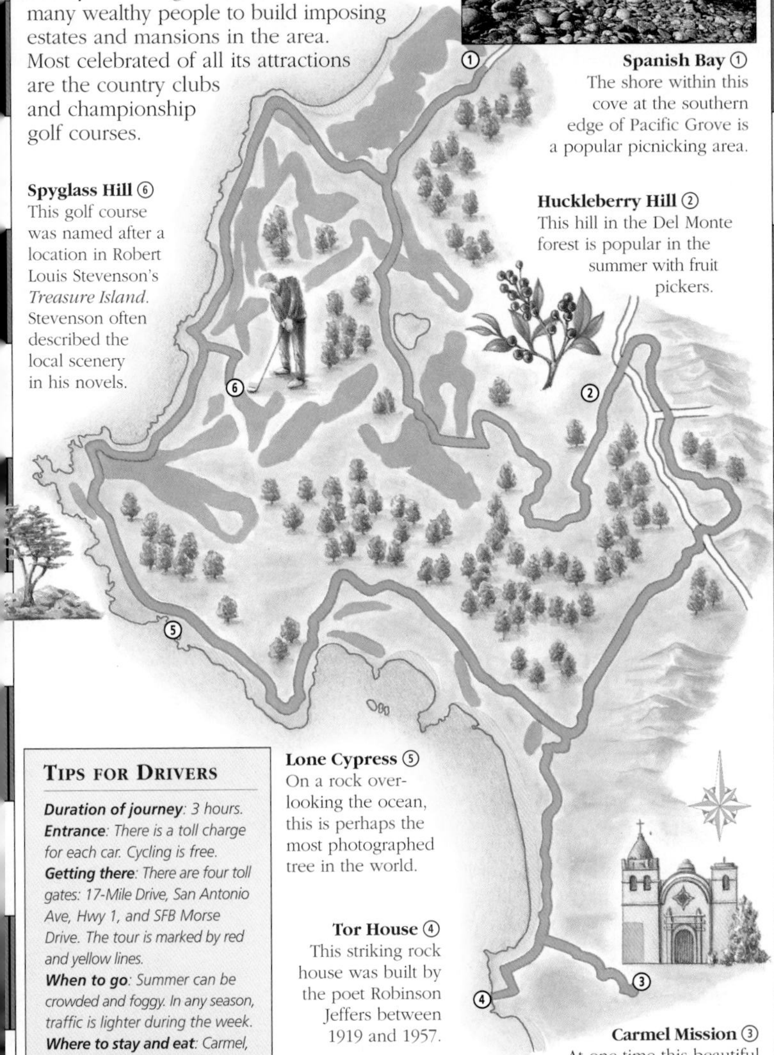

Spanish Bay [1]
The shore within this cove at the southern edge of Pacific Grove is a popular picnicking area.

Huckleberry Hill [2]
This hill in the Del Monte forest is popular in the summer with fruit pickers.

Spyglass Hill [6]
This golf course was named after a location in Robert Louis Stevenson's *Treasure Island*. Stevenson often described the local scenery in his novels.

Lone Cypress [5]
On a rock overlooking the ocean, this is perhaps the most photographed tree in the world.

Tor House [4]
This striking rock house was built by the poet Robinson Jeffers between 1919 and 1957.

Carmel Mission [3]
At one time this beautiful mission was the administrative center for northern California *(see pp496–7)*.

TIPS FOR DRIVERS

Duration of journey*: 3 hours.*
Entrance*: There is a toll charge for each car. Cycling is free.*
Getting there*: There are four toll gates: 17-Mile Drive, San Antonio Ave, Hwy 1, and SFB Morse Drive. The tour is marked by red and yellow lines.*
When to go*: Summer can be crowded and foggy. In any season, traffic is lighter during the week.*
Where to stay and eat*: Carmel, Monterey, and Pacific Grove have a wide selection of hotels and restaurants (see pp504–75).*
Visitor Information*: Monterey Peninsula Chamber of Commerce, 380 Alvarado St, Monterey.*
☎ *(831) 649-1770.*

KEY

- Tour route
- Other roads
- Golf courses

0 meters 500
0 yards 500

Carmel Mission ❼

Decorative wall plaque

FOUNDED IN 1770 by Father Junípero Serra (1713–84) and built of adobe brick by Native American laborers, Carmel Mission served as the administrative center for all the Northern California missions. Father Serra resided here until his death and is now buried at the foot of the altar. The mission was secularized and abandoned in 1834, quickly falling into disrepair. Restoration work began in 1924, carefully following the plans of the original mission, and replanting the gardens. The reconstructed living quarters detail 18th-century mission life. The mission still functions as a Catholic church.

The sarcophagus depicts Father Serra recumbent in death, surrounded by three mourning padres. It is among the finest of its type in the United States.

Kitchen
This restored room shows the kitchen as it was in missionary days, including the oven brought from Mexico. A section of the original adobe wall can be seen.

Bell tower

Dining room

Statue of Junípero Serra
Set within the beautiful front courtyard, a statue of Serra faces the mission church he founded.

★ Serra's Cell
Father Serra's simple way of life is evident in this sparse, restored cell. The wooden bed, chair, desk, and candlestick were the only pieces of furniture he possessed. He died here in 1784.

Façade and front courtyard of Carmel Mission

VISITORS' CHECKLIST

3080 Rio Rd, Carmel. **Road map** B4. (831) 624-3600. 9:30am–4:30pm Mon–Sat; 10:30am–4:30pm Sun. Thanksgiving, Dec 25. Sun: 7am, 8am, 9:30am, 11am, 12:30pm, 5:30pm.

Father Serra's burial place under the altar is marked with a plaque.

The Chapel Window is the only place where the original paintwork can still be seen.

The cemetery contains the graves of 18th-century missionaries.

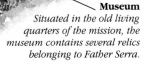

Museum
Situated in the old living quarters of the mission, the museum contains several relics belonging to Father Serra.

★ Main Altar
The Gothic arch of Carmel's altar, with its ornate decoration, is the only one of its kind among all the 21 Franciscan missions in California.

STAR FEATURES

★ Main Altar

★ Serra's Cell

Big Sur ⑧

IN THE LATE 18TH CENTURY, Spanish colonists at Carmel named this stretch of land *El Pais Grande del Sur*, the "big country to the south," and the coastline of Big Sur has been attracting hyperbole ever since. The novelist Robert Louis Stevenson called it "the greatest meeting of land and sea in the world," and the 100 miles (160 km) of breathtaking mountains, cliffs, and rocky coves still leave visitors grasping for adjectives.

The scenic Hwy 1 was constructed across this rugged landscape during the 1930s, but otherwise Big Sur has been preserved in its natural state. There are no large towns and very few signs of civilization in the area. Most of the shoreline is protected in a series of state parks that offer dense forests, broad rivers, and crashing surf, all easily accessible within a short walk of the road.

Crashing surf and rocky cliffs, typical of the Big Sur coastline

Point Lobos State Reserve
This is the habitat of the Monterey cypress, the only tree to survive the region's mixture of fog and salt spray. Its branches are shaped by the sea winds.

Point Sur Lighthouse
sits atop a volcanic cone. It was manned until 1974 but is now automated.

Nepenthe is a lovely resort hidden from the road by oak trees. It has long been frequented by Hollywood movie stars.

Bixby Creek Bridge
This photogenic arched bridge was built in 1932. For many years it was the world's largest single-arch span, at 260 ft (79 m) tall and 700 ft (213 m) long. Hwy 1 was named the state's first scenic highway here in 1966.

Andrew Molera State Park
Opened in 1972, this park includes 10 miles (16 km) of hiking trails and 2.5 miles (4 km) of quiet, sandy beach.

KEY

━━ Minor road

━━ Scenic route

- - - Hiking trails

── National park boundaries

〰 Rivers and lakes

🅰 Camping

🔆 Viewpoint

(map labels) GARRAPATTA STATE PARK ①
Little Sur
Coast Redwoods 🅰
Big Sur ●

VISITORS' CHECKLIST

Road map B4. 🚗 1,500.
🚌 Nepenthe Park. ℹ️ (831)
667-2100.

Julia Pfeiffer Burns State Park
A tunnel under Hwy 1, accessible only on foot, leads to the 100-ft (30-m) high bluff from which the McWay Creek waterfall spills into the Pacific Ocean.

The Esalen Institute was set up in the 1960s to hold New Age seminars. Its hot springs were first frequented by Native Americans and still attract visitors *(see p425).*

Ventana Wilderness
Part of the Los Padres National Forest, many of the steep ridges of this beautiful wilderness are accessible only to experienced hikers. Camp sites cover the lower reaches.

VENTANA
WILDERNESS

Tassajara Creek

LOS PADRES
NATIONAL FOREST

Big Creek

Lucia

Nacimiento Ferguson Rd

Plaskett

Los Burros Rd

Plaskett Creek

Jade Cove
This beautiful cove can be reached only by way of a steep path down the cliff face. The removal of jade is prohibited above the high tide level.

Antonio River

Lake San
Antonio

Nacimiento River

San Simeon Point is a natural harbor that was used by William Randolph Hearst to ship in materials for his estate, Hearst Castle™, on the inland hilltop *(see pp202–205).*

Alder Creek

Lake Nacimiento

| 0 kilometers | 10 |
| 0 miles | 10 |

San Simeon

Nobel prize-winning author John Steinbeck (1902–68)

Salinas ❾

Road map B4. 🏛 *128,343.* 🚉 🚌
ℹ️ *119 E Alisal St (831 424-7611).*

SITUATED AT THE north end of the predominantly agricultural Salinas Valley, which stretches for more than 50 miles (80 km) between San Francisco and San Luis Obispo, Salinas is the region's primary agricultural center. Vegetable-packing plants and canneries line the major highways and railroad tracks. The region is often referred to as the "salad bowl of the nation," its prime produce being lettuce, as well as tomatoes and garlic.

The town is perhaps best known, however, as the birthplace of the Nobel prize-winning author John Steinbeck, who set many of his natural-istic stories here and in the surrounding area. A selection of books, manuscripts, photo-graphs, and personal mem-orabilia relating to the author is on permanent display in a special room of the **John Steinbeck Library**. The library also supplies informa-tion on Steinbeck-related places to visit in the area and on the Steinbeck Festival, held in Salinas every August.

Hat in Three Stages of Land-ing, a large-scale, bright yellow steel sculpture of three cow-boy hats by the acclaimed Pop artist Claes Oldenberg, was erected in the town in the 1970s. It stands, appropriately, in front of the entrance to the California State Rodeo. Each Fourth of July one of the largest rodeos in the world is held here, bringing riders and their livestock from all over the United States, as well as various other entertainments.

🏛 **John Steinbeck Library**
350 Lincoln Ave. ☎ *(831) 758-7311.*
🕐 *Mon–Sat.* ⬤ *public hols.* ♿

Pinnacles National Monument ❿

Road map B4. ☎ *(831) 389-4485.*
🚉 *King City & Soledad.* 🕐 *daily.*
📷 ♿ *some trails.* ▶

HIGH IN THE HILLS above the Salinas Valley, 12 miles (20 km) east of the town of Soledad on US101, the Pin-nacles National Monument preserves 16,000 acres (6,500 ha) of a unique volcanic land-scape. A solid ridge of lava flows, eroded over millions of years into oddly contorted crags and spires, runs through the center of the park, in places forming cliffs more than 500 ft (150 m) tall. There are no roads across the park, but there are many carefully-maintained hiking trails.

One of the most popular and accessible spots in the park is the Balconies forma-tion, reached by a 1.5-mile (2.5 km) leisurely trail. Here beautiful red and gold cliffs rise high above the ground, attracting rock-climbers, photo-graphers, and bird-watchers. At the base of the cliffs, huge boulders caught between the narrow canyons have formed a series of dark talus caves. These were reputedly used in the past as hideouts by robbers and other outlaws.

The park is best visited in spring, when the temperature is cool and the wildflowers are in bloom. Mountain lions, coyotes, and eagles can occa-sionally also be sighted.

Volcanic crags of the Pinnacles National Monument

Fresno ⓫

Road map C4. 🏛 *411,600.*
✈ *Fresno Air Terminal.* 🚉 🚌
ℹ️ *2331 Fresno St (559 495-4800).*

FRESNO IS LOCATED at approxi-mately the geographical center of the state and is its eighth largest city. It is often referred to as the "Raisin Capital of the World" because of its abundant production of the dried fruit. Its central

Vegetable pickers and packers in the Salinas Valley

position makes a convenient base from which to make excursions to the High Sierras, Kings Canyon, Sequoia, and Yosemite National Parks *(see pp466–81)*.

🏛 Fresno Metropolitan Museum

1515 Van Ness 🄫 *(559) 441-1444.* ◯ *Tue–Sun.* 🈂
🆆 www.fresnomet.org

ENVIRONS: In Kearney Park, 7 miles (11 km) west of downtown Fresno, is **Kearney Mansion**. This elaborate French Renaissance-style house was erected in 1903 by Theodore Kearney, an agriculturalist who helped establish California's raisin industry. The house is now a period museum.

🏛 Kearney Mansion

7160 W. Kearney Blvd, Hwy 99. 🄫 *(559) 441-0862.* ◯ *Fri–Sun.* 🈂

Colonel Allen Allensworth, resident of Hanford

Hanford 🄓

Road map C4. 🄫 *40,000.* ▯ ▭
🄷 *200 Santa Fe Ave, Suite D (559) 582-0483).*

O NE OF MANY medium-sized farming communities in the area, Hanford is significant because of its diverse, multiethnic heritage. The China Alley neighborhood was once inhabited by one of the largest Chinese communities in California, many of whom worked on the construction of the transcontinental railroad *(see pp46–7)*. Located east of the town center, China Alley

Homegrown Fresno raisins

surrounds the historic **Taoist Temple**, built in 1893. The temple operated as a hostel for Chinese immigrants and a Chinese school as well as a religious shrine. Downtown Hanford, around Courthouse Square, has a beautiful antique carousel and a number of elegant buildings dating from the late 19th century, now converted into shops and restaurants.

🚏 Taoist Temple

China Alley. 🄫 *(559) 582-4508.* ◯ *by appointment only.* 🈂

ENVIRONS: The **Colonel Allensworth State Historic Park** is 30 miles (50 km) south of Hanford. Colonel Allen Allensworth believed his fellow African-Americans could combat racism by building their own future. He established a unique farming community in 1908 with a group of African-American families. Memorabilia of this independent community are now on display in the old farmhouses.

🏛 Colonel Allensworth State Historic Park

Off Hwy 99 on County Rd J22, Earlimart. 🄫 *(661) 849-3433 or 634-3795.* ◯ *daily.* 🈂

JOHN STEINBECK

One of California's most successful 20th-century writers, John Steinbeck (1902–68) was born in Salinas to an established family of farmers and ranchers. When he dropped out of Stanford University *(see p411)*, Steinbeck moved to the Monterey Peninsula in the late 1920s to write fiction. After several attempts he eventually gained a measure of success with the publication of the novella *Tortilla Flat* in 1935. Steinbeck then began a series of short stories and novels, the majority of them focusing on the people and places he knew well in the Salinas Valley and Monterey area. These included some of his greatest work: *Of Mice and Men* (1937), *Cannery Row* (1945), and *East of Eden* (1952).

His best-known work is *The Grapes of Wrath* (1939). The novel fictionalizes the mass westward migration that took place during the Depression of the 1930s, by documenting the struggles of the Joad family as they fled the dust bowl of Oklahoma for the greener pastures of California. It was an immediate bestseller and earned Steinbeck a Pulitzer Prize, although many Californians took its unhappy ending as an insult to their state, and even as Communist propaganda. Steinbeck reacted to this antipathy in 1943 by going to North Africa and becoming a war correspondent. On his return to the United States in 1945 he settled on Long Island, New York. In 1962, he was awarded the Nobel Prize for Literature. Steinbeck is the only American author to have received both the Pulitzer Prize and the Nobel Prize.

He died in New York City on December 20, 1968, but is buried in his hometown, in the Garden of Memories at No. 768 Abbott Street.

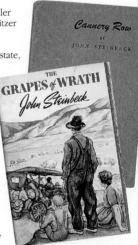

First editions of Steinbeck's most famous works, *Cannery Row* and *The Grapes of Wrath*

TRAVELERS'
NEEDS

WHERE TO STAY

RAMED BY RUGGED coastal mountains, lush wooded hills, sophisticated urban centers, and a long stretch of coastline, California is one of the premier vacation destinations in the world. Whether rustic lodges or five-star resorts suit your budget, there is a wealth of options for travelers to the state.

Top hotels can range from film-star luxury to high-tech business centers. Budget accommodations are widespread, from roadside motels to atmospheric inns that offer an insight into the state's history. All accommodations, are however, likely to

Doorman

offer double beds, bathrooms, and comfortable surroundings. A range of camping facilities is also available for those interested in the great outdoors.

Free magazines containing discount coupons for all sorts of accommodations are available from street distribution bins at freeway rest stops and at car rental centers. Many hotels also offer discounts on reservation during the off season, and it is worth booking ahead to negotiate the rate. The listings on pages 508–37 give full descriptions of quality accommodations throughout the state to suit all budgets.

HOTEL CLASSIFICATIONS

THE CALIFORNIA tourist industry is recognized for its quality lodgings. A guideline of value to travelers is the diamond rating system of the California State Automobile Association. Every lodging, from the most expensive four-diamond hotel to the budget one-diamond motel, is rated for service, cleanliness, and the range of facilities offered.

Another guideline is *Relais et Châteaux*, an established French organization that rates top holiday destinations worldwide. Only 26 properties in the United States have been invited to join the organization, and seven of these are located in California.

HOTELS

IN CALIFORNIA, hotels come in every shape and size. There are the historic showplaces such as the Sheraton Palace

in San Francisco (see p526), the Biltmore in Los Angeles, (see p509) and the Ahwahnee in Yosemite National Park (see p536). These were originally built to impress East Coast bankers and prove that the West Coast was worth their investment. There are also the trendy, visually stunning urban getaways such as the Triton Hotel in San Francisco (see p523) and the Mondrian in West Hollywood (see p513). There are hotels with fashion shops, with corporate conference centers, chandelier ballrooms, or landscaped gardens. There are also small hotels, called "boutique hotels," which have fewer than 100 rooms and the intimate ambience of a bed-and-breakfast.

No matter the size, you can always count on every hotel having a spacious foyer, a restaurant or café, a pool or exercise room, and a range of services such as laundry, ironing, and in-room video movies.

Lounge bar in the exclusive Beverly Wilshire Hotel (see p508)

If the hotel does not have its own exercise facility on-site, there is often an arrangement with a nearby health club that hotel guests can use for a fee of $8–$12 per day. No-smoking rooms are always available – many hotels have now set aside entire floors for nonsmokers only.

Rates for hotels range from an inexpensive $75 per night to a moderate $175. Rooms at upscale, well-located hotels can range from $175–$275. There are some luxury hotels in California, however, be it in Beverly Hills, Big Sur, or Napa Valley, that charge $185 for the smallest room off season, and in peak season can be as much as $500 a night.

Hotels are also subject to city and state taxes, which range from 11 percent in San

Biltmore Hotel in Los Angeles

Francisco to 14 percent in Los Angeles. Not included in room rates are additional charges for parking and heavy surcharges for outgoing telephone calls.

CORPORATE HOTELS

THESE CATER TO business travelers by offering weekly and monthly rates. There are also a number of all-suite hotels, with living rooms, in-room computers, and fax connections. Some even have on-site computer centers, providing ample work space for business travelers. Check the hotel listings on pages 508–37 to see where these services are available.

CHAIN HOTELS

YOU CAN COUNT on good service, moderate prices, and comfortable surroundings at a chain hotel. The popular chains in California include the **Westin**, **Hilton**, **Sheraton**, **Marriott**, **Ramada**, **Hyatt**, and **Holiday Inn**. Some of these chains operate more than one hotel in each city and designate one location as the flagship facility. All chain hotels listed on page 507 have Internet web sites, or you can call the hotel's toll-free number to ask about rates and availability.

Chateau Marmont on Sunset Boulevard *(see p513)*

TIPPING

THE HOTEL PORTER will often carry your bags to your room on arrival and load up your car on departing. A tip of $1–$2 per bag is fair for this service. If the hotel has valet parking, a tip of 15–20 percent of the parking charge should be given to the driver only when you leave. Room service also requires a 15–20 percent tip. A $2–$5 tip for maid service, especially after a long stay, is acceptable.

Sign over small chain hotel

RESORTS

WHETHER A RESORT has less than 100 rooms or close to 300, the cottages, villas, and grounds are always arranged to encourage privacy. Resorts have all the services of a hotel but are spread over larger grounds.

The key to a quality resort is the range of indoor and outdoor facilities that are offered, be it horseback riding, tennis courts, golf courses, Olympic-size swimming pools, yoga instruction, full-service health spa, or a four-star restaurant. A vacation at a resort is a destination in itself – the natural setting and range of on-site activities will more than hold your attention. Stays in resorts are expensive, but for both relaxation and sports they are worth every penny.

You may want to choose a resort based on location – wine country, oceanside, mountain hideaway, or urban retreat. California has many such hidden treasures, and some of the best are listed on pages 508–37.

San Diego Marriott Hotel, on San Diego Bay

Historic Mendocino Hotel *(see p532)*

MOTELS

Inexpensive roadside motels sprang up in California in the 1950s, as a product of an increasingly car-oriented lifestyle. Motels offer minimal facilities – double, queen, or king-size beds, television, telephone, tea and coffee, and bathroom facilities. There is always ample parking for cars, and many motels also have outdoor swimming pools – a necessity for travelers in California's summertime heat. Some have kitchen facilities, and most offer non-smoking rooms. Check with the motel to see if they allow pets.

There are a number of popular motel chains throughout the state that have a reputation for clean rooms and good service at inexpensive prices. These include **Best Western**, **Quality Inn**, **Motel 6**, and **Travelodge**. Rates range from $30–$65 a night.

HISTORIC INNS

Rich in regional history, these inns are often all that remain of late 19th-century buildings in many of California's small towns. As well as reflecting local history, some inns also have their own story to tell, having been, perhaps, a hunting and fishing lodge, a stern-wheeler riverboat, a Victorian mansion, or a hideaway for Hollywood movie stars in earlier times. Whatever their heritage, they all share a unique architecture and ambience. Many such inns, built during the era of railroad expansion in the West,

have achieved protected status and cannot be demolished or architecturally altered.

Similar to bed-and-breakfast hotels in atmosphere, historic inns are larger, with 20–100 rooms. Most serve complimentary continental breakfast and afternoon snacks of cakes or cookies. For more information, contact **California Historic Country Inns**.

Smaller lodgings, many also with a claim to historical significance, may have small, individual cabins with kitchen facilities for efficiency accommodations (self-catering). Rarely do these inns have on-site restaurants, cafés, or room service. The majority of them allow you to bring along pets, many have outdoor swimming pools, and larger ones may also have tennis courts. Check in advance whether smoking is allowed in the cabins – some inns in California now pride themselves on providing guests with a completely smoke-free environment.

BED-AND-BREAKFAST ACCOMMODATIONS

Most bed-and-breakfasts in California were originally private homes built many years ago and which retain the charm of a bygone era. In addition to breakfast, afternoon snacks or evening drinks may also be available. Prices range from $60–$175 a night. Ask whether the room has its own bathroom. There is often a two-night minimum stay, especially in peak season.

Libraries, living rooms, landscaped gardens, and swimming pools are common features of bed-and-breakfasts. The manager is often the owner and can provide details of local history and sights. See pages 508–37 for a range of bed-and-breakfasts or contact **Bed-and-Breakfast California**.

Casa Laguna Bed-and-Breakfast in Laguna Beach *(see p517)*

ROOMS IN PRIVATE HOMES

While many small inns and lodges may offer kitchen facilities, there is nothing like staying in a private home to get the real flavor of a specific city or town. There are two

Deetjen's Big Sur Inn *(see p536)*

Big Bear Log Cabin, near Lake Arrowhead

ways you can arrange this type of accommodation. The first is to rent an apartment or house from a real estate agency. Every city and town in the state has at least one, if not several, estate agencies that specialize in vacation rental property. These agencies will quote rental rates by the night, week, month, or even longer. Prices per week can range anywhere between $300–$3,000, depending on location and size of the rented property. You will have to pay a cleaning deposit, which is refundable when you leave. For the widest choice of properties, it is best to make reservations at least one month in advance. Contact any town's Chamber of Commerce for details of agencies.

Another option is to arrange a house exchange with a California resident. **Intervac US** is part of a worldwide home exchange network and publishes quarterly directories of people willing to exchange their homes for yours during vacations. Fees to obtain or be listed in this directory range from $65–$85 per year. The network does not match people up; arrangements are made by the individuals.

YOUTH HOSTELS

THIS IS THE least expensive accommodation option in California. Hostels offer clean, modern facilities, often in picturesque locations (including lighthouses, on national parkland, and mountain hideaways). They offer dormitory-style, single-sex sleeping arrangements, although some do have one or two private rooms available only to married couples. Most hostels also provide kitchen facilities.

Despite the name, youth hostels in the United States are not only for the young. There are also a number of Elder Hostels, catering to senior citizens who opt for budget travel. Contact **American Youth Hostels** for a full list of accommodations.

CAMPING, TRAILERS, AND RVS

CAMPERS are always welcome in California's national and state park system (see p576). There is also a large network of privately run camp sites with a range of facilities for trailers and RVs, such as electricity hook-up, water supply, disposal stations, picnic areas, and grocery stores.

Camping in Yosemite National Park (see pp472–5)

Choosing a Hotel

THE HOTELS in this guide have been selected across a wide price range for their excellent facilities and locations. Many also have a recommended restaurant. The chart lists the hotels by region, starting with Los Angeles; the color-coded thumb tabs indicate the regions covered on each page. For restaurant listings, see pp544–75.

	NUMBER OF ROOMS	RESTAURANT	CHILDREN'S FACILITIES	GARDEN/TERRACE	SWIMMING POOL
LOS ANGELES					
AIRPORT: *Los Angeles Airport Hilton and Towers* $$ 5711 W Century Blvd, CA 90045. **Road map** inset A. ☎ *(310) 410-4000; (800) 445-8667.* FAX *(310) 410-6250.* Located next to the airport, this huge hotel caters mostly to business travelers. Excellent facilities.	1100	●	■	●	■
AIRPORT: *Sheraton Los Angeles Airport Hotel* $$$ 6101 W Century Blvd, CA 90045. **Road map** inset A. ☎ *(310) 642-1111; (800) 445-7999.* FAX *(310) 645-1414.* This corporate chain hotel offers inexpensive weekend packages. Free airport shuttle every five minutes.	610	●	■		■
AIRPORT: *Wyndham Hotel at Los Angeles Airport* $$$ 6225 West Century Blvd, CA 90045. **Road map** inset A. ☎ *(310) 670-9000; (800) 327-8321.* FAX *(310) 670-7852.* A luxury business hotel next to the airport with comfortable, soundproof rooms. Service is excellent.	591	●	■		■
BEL AIR: *Lux Summit* $$$$ 11461 Sunset Blvd, CA 90049. **Road map** inset A. ☎ *(310) 476-6571; (800) 468-3541.* FAX *(310) 471-6310.* This resort-style hotel with spacious rooms is set in landscaped grounds; it offers tennis and a spa.	162	●		●	■
BEL AIR: *Hotel Bel-Air* W www.hotelbelair.com $$$$$ 701 Stone Canyon Rd, CA 90077. **Map** 4 A2. ☎ *(310) 472-1211; (800) 648-4097.* FAX *(310) 476-5890.* Some rooms have fireplaces at this glamorous resort-style hotel *(see p91)* with villas set in lush gardens.	92	●	■	●	■
BEVERLY HILLS: *Summit Hotel Rodeo Drive* $$$ 360 N Rodeo Drive, CA 90210. **Map** 5 F3. ☎ *(310) 273-0300; (800) 468-3541.* FAX *(310) 859-8730.* This hotel is nicely furnished, light and sunny. Guests can also use the amenities at the Summit Hotel Bel-Air.	86	●	■	●	■
BEVERLY HILLS: *Beverly Hilton* $$$$ 9876 Wilshire Blvd, CA 90210. **Map** 5 E4. ☎ *(310) 274-7777; (800) 445-8667.* FAX *(310) 285-1313.* This large corporate hotel has spacious rooms with views of LA. Many rooms have private patios.	581	●	■	●	■
BEVERLY HILLS: *Hotel Avalon* $$$$ 9400 W Olympic Blvd, CA 90212. **Map** 5 F4. ☎ *(310) 277-5221; (800) 535-4715.* FAX *(310) 277-4928.* This friendly 1940s Art Deco hotel near Rodeo Drive *(see p90)* is pleasantly furnished with large beds; double rooms have separate sitting areas.	44	●		●	■
BEVERLY HILLS: *Beverly Hills Hotel and Bungalows* $$$$$ 9641 Sunset Blvd, CA 90210. **Map** 5 D2. ☎ *(310) 276-2251; (800) 283-8885.* FAX *(310) 887-2887.* At this luxury complex set in tropical gardens *(see p91)*, some rooms have a kitchen and private terrace.	194	●	■	●	■
BEVERLY HILLS: *Peninsula Beverly Hills* $$$$$ 9882 South Santa Monica Blvd, CA 90212. **Map** 5 E4. ☎ *(310) 551-2888; (800) 462-7899.* FAX *(310) 788-2319.* Celebrities come to be pampered at this luxurious five-star hotel with rooms, suites, and villas.	196	●	■	●	■
BEVERLY HILLS: *Regent Beverly Wilshire* W www.regenthotels.com $$$$$ 9500 Wilshire Blvd, CA 90212. **Map** 5 F4. ☎ *(310) 275-5200; (800) 545-4000.* FAX *(310) 274-2851.* The palatial splendor of this famous hotel opposite Rodeo Drive attracts many celebrities *(see p87)*. The rooms – and baths – are enormous, and there are full spa facilities.	278	●	■	●	■
CENTURY CITY: *Century Plaza Hotel and Tower* $$$$ 2025 Ave of the Stars, CA 90067. **Map** 5 D5. ☎ *(310) 277-2000; (800) 228-3000.* FAX *(310) 5513355.* The service is friendly at this large, elegant hotel. Rooms in both of the buildings have panoramic views of the city.	1032	●	■	●	■

Price categories for a standard double room per night, inclusive of service charges and any additional taxes, such as local sales tax:
$ under $100
$$ $100–$150
$$$ $150–$200
$$$$ $200–$250
$$$$$ over $250

RESTAURANT
Hotel restaurant or dining room usually open to non-residents unless otherwise stated.

CHILDREN'S FACILITIES
Indicates cribs and/or a baby-sitting service available. A few hotels also provide children's portions and high chairs in the restaurant.

GARDEN/TERRACE
Hotels with a garden, courtyard, or terrace, often providing tables for eating outside.

SWIMMING POOL
Hotel with indoor or outdoor swimming pool.

	Price	NUMBER OF ROOMS	RESTAURANT	CHILDREN'S FACILITIES	GARDEN/TERRACE	SWIMMING POOL
CENTURY CITY: *Park Hyatt* 51 Ave of the Stars, CA 90067. **Map 5 E5.** ((310) 277-2777. FAX (310) 5-9240. A business hotel with good facilities and city views. Limousines can be provided for shopping or theater visits. 24 TV & P TV	$$$$$	367	●	■	●	■
DOWNTOWN: *Best Western Dragon Gate Inn* 8 N Hill St, CA 90012. **Map 11 F2.** ((213) 617-3077; (800) 528-1234. FAX (213) 0-3753. This comfortable, basic hotel in Chinatown attracts business travelers during the week and families on weekends. TV & P	$	52	●		●	
DOWNTOWN: *The Inn at 657* W www.patsysinn657.com 7 W 23rd St, CA 90007. **Road map** inset A. ((213) 741-2200; (800) 347-7512. These one- and two-bedroom suites have kitchens and private entrances that open onto garden or balcony areas. All are nonsmoking, and the price includes full breakfast and local telephone calls. TV P	$$	6			●	
DOWNTOWN: *Best Western, The Mayfair* 56 W 7th St, CA 90017. **Map 10 C4.** ((213) 484-9789; (800) 821-8682. ((213) 484-2769. This chic, friendly hotel has rooms, suites, and services well suited to the business traveler. 24 TV & P	$$	295	●			
DOWNTOWN: *Figueroa Hotel* 9 S Figueroa St, CA 90015. **Map 10 C5.** ((213) 627-8971; (800) 421-9092. ((213) 689-0305. This friendly hotel near the convention center was originally a YWCA. Rooms vary in size and are decorated in Spanish Colonial style. The exquisite garden has fruit trees and cacti. TV & P	$$	285	●	■	●	■
DOWNTOWN: *Holiday Inn LA Downtown* 0 S Garland Ave, CA 90017. **Map 10 B4.** ((213) 628-9900; (800) 628-5240. ((213) 628-1201. Half the rooms have king-size beds at this chain hotel one block west of the Financial District. TV & P TV	$$	205	●		●	■
DOWNTOWN: *Howard Johnson's Hotel* 19 Wilshire Blvd, CA 90057. **Map 10 A3.** ((213) 387-5311; (800) 446-4656. ((213) 380-8174. This beautiful Art Deco hotel is ten minutes from downtown. The 65 suites have kitchen facilities. TV & P	$$	200	●		●	■
DOWNTOWN: *Miyako Inn and Spa* 8 E 1st St, CA 90012. **Map 11 F4.** ((213) 617-2000; (800) 228-6596. FAX (213) 7-2700. This hotel in Little Tokyo has a karaoke lounge and separate spa facilities for men and women. The spacious rooms are furnished in traditional American style. Children under 12 stay free. 24 TV & P	$$	174	●			
DOWNTOWN: *Los Angeles Athletic Club* 1 W 7th St, CA 90014. **Map 11 D5.** ((213) 625-2211; (800) 421-8777. FAX (213) 9-1194. Built as a club in 1904, this hotel has luxurious Victorian-style rooms and racquetball courts. TV & P TV	$$$	72	●	■		■
DOWNTOWN: *Biltmore* 6 S Grand Ave, CA 90071. **Map 11 D4.** ((213) 624-1011; (800) 245-8673. ((213) 612-1545. The palatial splendor of the foyer extends to the large comfortable rooms and suites at this luxury hotel *(see p118)*. There is a spa and complimentary continental breakfast. 24 TV & P TV	$$$$$	690	●	■	●	■
DOWNTOWN: *Downtown Marriott* 3 S Figueroa St, CA 90012. **Map 11 D4.** ((213) 617-1133; (800) 228-9290. ((213) 613-0291. Convenient to Downtown Los Angeles sights, this luxury hotel offers every amenity. 24 TV & P TV	$$$$$	469	●	■	●	■
DOWNTOWN: *Hyatt Regency* 1 S Hope St, CA 90017. **Map 11 D4.** ((213) 683-1234; (800) 233-1234. FAX (213) 9-3230. Floor-to-ceiling windows give good views from the comfortable rooms of this four-star hotel in the Broadway Plaza. TV & P TV	$$$$$	485	●	■	●	■

For key to symbols see back flap

Price categories for a standard double room per night, inclusive of service charges and any additional taxes, such as local sales tax:
$ under $100
$$ $100–$150
$$$ $150–$200
$$$$ $200–$250
$$$$$ over $250

RESTAURANT
Hotel restaurant or dining room usually open to non-residents unless otherwise stated.

CHILDREN'S FACILITIES
Indicates cribs and/or a baby-sitting service available. A few hotels also provide children's portions and high chairs in the restaurant.

GARDEN/TERRACE
Hotels with a garden, courtyard, or terrace, often providing tables for eating outside.

SWIMMING POOL
Hotel with indoor or outdoor swimming pool.

	NUMBER OF ROOMS	RESTAURANT	CHILDREN'S FACILITIES	GARDEN/TERRACE	SWIMMING POOL
DOWNTOWN: *New Otani Hotel and Garden* $$$$ 120 S Los Angeles St, CA 90012. **Map 11 E4.** ☎ (213) 629-1200; (800) 273-2294. FAX (213) 622-0980. Some rooms are furnished in traditional Japanese style at this deluxe hotel; there is a sauna and health spa. 🏠 24 📺 ♿ 🅿 🌿	424	●	▪		
DOWNTOWN: *Westin Bonaventure Hotel and Suites* $$$$ 404 S Figueroa St, CA 90071. **Map 10 C5.** ☎ (213) 624-1000; (800) 228-3000. FAX (213) 612-4800. Rooms are large and comfortable at this immense newly remodeled hotel, made up of five glass towers built around a central atrium *(see p118)*. It has all the facilities of a luxury hotel. 🏠 24 📺 ♿ 🅿 🌿	1364	●		●	▪
DOWNTOWN: *Wyndham Checkers Hotel* $$$$ 535 Grand Ave, CA 90071. **Map 11 4D.** ☎ (213) 624-0000; (800) 996-3426. FAX (213) 626-9906. With four-star ratings, this hotel is extremely luxurious – there are even thermometers in the marble baths. It has a spa and also offers free limousine service around the area. 🏠 24 📺 ♿ 🅿 🍴 🌿	173	●		●	▪
GLENDALE: *Chariot Inn Motel* $$ 1118 E Colorado St, CA 91205. **Road map inset A.** ☎ (818) 507-9600; (800) 458-4080. FAX (818) 507-9774. The large rooms have queen or king-size beds; some have whirlpool baths. Continental breakfast is included. 🏠 📺 ♿ 🅿 🌿	30			●	▪
HALF MOON BAY: *Ritz-Carlton* W www.ritzcarlton.com $$$$$ 1 Miramontes Point Rd, CA 94019. ☎ (650) 712-7000; (800) 241-3333. FAX (650) 712-7070. Set atop an ocean bluff overlooking 50 miles (80 km) of coastline, this luxury hotel has five restaurants and a golf course. 🏠 📺 ♿ 🅿 🌿	261	●		●	▪
HOLLYWOOD: *Best Western Hollywood Plaza* $ 2011 N Highland Ave, CA 90068. **Map 2 B4.** ☎ (323) 851-1800; (800) 232-4353. FAX (323) 851-1836. This chain hotel, two blocks from Hollywood Boulevard, has comfortable rooms with refrigerators. 🏠 📺 ♿ 🅿 🌿	82	●		●	▪
HOLLYWOOD: *Hollywood Orchid Suites* $ 1753 Orchid Ave, CA 90028. **Map 2 B4.** ☎ (323) 874-9678; (800) 537-3052. FAX (323) 874-9931. This small hotel is a converted apartment building so the rooms are very spacious, and some have kitchens. 🏠 📺 ♿ 🅿 🌿	40			●	▪
HOLLYWOOD: *San Vincente Inn* W www.sanvincenteinn.com $ 845 N San Vincente Blvd, CA 90069. **Map 6 B1.** ☎ (310) 854-6915. This small but full-service hotel/motel is close to all the key sights in Hollywood, including Santa Monica Blvd. and Melrose Ave. Clothing optional. ♿ 🅿 🌿	26		▪	●	▪
HOLLYWOOD: *Ramada Inn* $$ 1160 N Vermont, CA 90029. **Road map inset A.** ☎ (323) 660-1788; (800) 272-6232. FAX (323) 660-8069. This well-run chain hotel near Universal Studios has suites and rooms with Internet, free continental breakfast, and a Jacuzzi. 🏠 📺 ♿ 🅿 🌿	98		▪		▪
HOLLYWOOD: *Beverly Garland's Holiday Inn* $$ 4222 Vineland Ave, CA 91602. **Road map inset A.** ☎ (818) 980-8000; (800) 238-3759. FAX (818) 766-0112. This hotel offers comfortable rooms with private balconies or patios, a spa, tennis courts, and laundry. 🏠 📺 ♿ 🅿 🌿	255	●		●	▪
HOLLYWOOD: *Hollywood Roosevelt Hotel* $$$ 7000 Hollywood Blvd, CA 90028. **Map 2 B4.** ☎ (323) 466-7000; (800) 950-7667. FAX (323) 462-8056. A beautiful old brick hotel recently restored to its original splendor. Often used for glamorous celebrity parties. 🏠 📺 ♿ 🅿 🌿	321	●	▪	●	▪
INGLEWOOD: *Los Angeles Adventura* $ 4200 W Century Blvd, CA 90304. **Road map inset A.** ☎ (310) 419-0999; (800) 852-0011. FAX (310) 412-9100. This friendly hotel, close to the airport, has large, comfortable rooms and offers free breakfast, afternoon tea, airport shuttle, and tours to Venice Beach, shops, casinos, and golf courses. 🏠 📺 🅿 🌿	150	●	▪	●	▪

LONG BEACH: *Inn of Long Beach* W www.innoflongbeach.com $
85 Atlantic Ave, CA 90802. **Road map** inset A. ((562) 435-3791; (800) 230-7500.
FAX (562) 456-7510. This pleasant, budget-priced motel with comfortable
rooms offers a spa and free continental breakfast. 🛏 TV 🕭 P 🖉   46

LONG BEACH: *Super 8 Motel* $
201 E Pacific Hwy, CA 90804. **Road map** inset A. ((562) 597-7701; (800) 800-8000.
FAX (562) 494-7373. This reliable budget motel has king-size beds. The half-
suites have kitchens. Rates include breakfast. 🛏 TV 🕭 P 🍴 🖉   49

LONG BEACH: *Best Western Golden Sails* $$
285 E Pacific Coast Hwy, CA 90803. **Road map** inset A. ((562) 596-1631; (800)
62-5333. FAX (562) 594-0623. This hotel overlooking the marina features whirl-
pool baths and free golf. Rates include breakfast and dinner. 🛏 TV P 🍴 🖉   172

LONG BEACH: *Lord Mayor's Inn* $$
35 Cedar Ave, CA 90802. **Road map** inset A. ((562) 436-0324. Set in a restored
Edwardian house, two 1908 cottages, and original horse barn, this
bed-and-breakfast inn is near downtown Long Beach. 🛏 P 🖉   13

LONG BEACH: *Hotel Queen Mary* $$$
126 Queen's Hwy, CA 90802. **Road map** inset A. ((562) 435-3511; (800) 437-
934. FAX (562) 437-4531. The famous ocean liner's first-class staterooms have
been updated and restored *(see p133)*. Breakfast is included. 🛏 TV 🕭 P 🖉   365

LONG BEACH: *Hyatt Regency* $$$
00 S Pine Ave, CA 90802. **Road map** inset A. ((562) 491-1234; (800) 233-
234. FAX (562) 983-1491. The rooms in this corporate hotel *(see p129)* have views
of Long Beach harbor. Weekend discounts available. 🛏 TV 🕭 P 🖉   522

LONG BEACH: *Renaissance Long Beach Hotel* $$$
11 E Ocean Blvd, CA 90802. **Road map** inset A. ((562) 437-5900; (800) 468-3571;
800) 228-9898. FAX (562) 499-2509. Some of the spacious rooms have ocean
views at this luxury hotel in the business district. 🛏 TV 🕭 P 🍴 🖉   374

MALIBU: *Casa Malibu Inn on the Beach* $$
2752 Pacific Coast Highway, CA 90265. **Road map** inset A. ((310) 456-2219; (800)
31-0858. FAX (310) 456-5418. This hotel is built on its own private beach.
Some rooms have balconies, fireplaces, VCRs, and kitchens. 🛏 TV P 🖉   21

MALIBU: *Malibu Beach Inn* $$$
2878 Pacific Coast Hwy, CA 90265. **Road map** inset A. ((310) 456-6444; (800)
62-5428. FAX (310) 456-1499. Each room has a balcony overlooking the beach
t this stylish luxury hotel with Mexican tiled floors. 🛏 24 TV 🕭 P 🖉   47

MARINA DEL REY: *Mansion Inn* $$
27 Washington Blvd, CA 90291. **Road map** inset A. ((310) 821-2557; (800) 828-
688. FAX (310) 827-0289. This hotel near the beach, on the border of Venice,
has country-style rooms and free continental breakfast. 🛏 TV 🕭 P 🖉   43

MARINA DEL REY: *Marina del Rey Hotel* $$
3534 Bali Way, CA 90292. **Road map** inset A. ((310) 301-1000; (800) 882-4000.
FAX (310) 301-8167. Most of the rooms and a gazebo at this resort-style hotel
overlook the marina. Free airport shuttles are provided. 🛏 TV 🕭 P 🖉   158

MONROVIA: *Holiday Inn* $$
24 W Huntington Drive, CA 91016. **Road map** inset A. ((626) 357-1900;
800) 465-4329. FAX (626) 359-1386. Close to shops and sights, this hotel has
spacious rooms and free morning coffee and muffins. 🛏 TV 🕭 P 🖉   170

NAPLES/SEAL BEACH: *Seal Beach Inn* $$$
12 5th St, CA 90740. **Road map** inset A. ((562) 493-2416; (800) 443-3292.
FAX (562) 799-0483. All rooms at this luxurious inn, one block from the beach,
re furnished with antiques. Breakfast is included. 🛏 TV 🕭 P 🖉   23

PASADENA: *Comfort Inn Eagle Rock* $
300 W Colorado Blvd, CA 90041. **Road map** inset A. ((323) 256-1199; (800) 221-
222. FAX (323) 255-7768. This basic inn near the Rose Bowl *(see p148)* offers con-
inental breakfast, a Jacuzzi, and a discount for senior citizens. 🛏 TV P 🖉   58

PASADENA: *Artist's Inn* $$
038 Magnolia St, CA 91030. **Road map** inset A. ((626) 799-5668. FAX (626) 799-
678. Each room in this bed-and-breakfast inn is furnished with a specific artist
n mind. The colorful Van Gogh Room is the most exciting. 🛏 TV 🕭 P 🖉   5

<table>
<tr><td colspan="2">

Price categories for a standard double room per night, inclusive of service charges and any additional taxes, such as local sales tax:
$ under $100
$$ $100–$150
$$$ $150–$200
$$$$ $200–$250
$$$$$ over $250

</td></tr>
</table>

RESTAURANT
Hotel restaurant or dining room usually open to non-residents unless otherwise stated.

CHILDREN'S FACILITIES
Indicates cribs and/or a baby-sitting service available. A few hotels also provide children's portions and high chairs in the restaurant.

GARDEN/TERRACE
Hotels with a garden, courtyard, or terrace, often providing tables for eating outside.

SWIMMING POOL
Hotel with indoor or outdoor swimming pool.

	NUMBER OF ROOMS	RESTAURANT	CHILDREN'S FACILITIES	GARDEN/TERRACE	SWIMMING POOL
PASADENA: *Pasadena Hotel* $$ 76 Fair Oaks Ave, CA 91103. **Road map** inset A. 📞 *(626) 568-8172; (800) 653-8886.* 📠 *(626) 793-6409.* All the rooms have VCRs, but the bathrooms are shared at this bed-and-breakfast inn in Old Pasadena *(see pp150–1).* The service is of a high standard, and the owners are very welcoming. 📺 ⬛	12	●			
PASADENA: *The Bissell House Bed and Breakfast* $$$ 201 Orange Grove Ave, CA 91030. **Road map** inset A. 📞 *(626) 441-3535.* 📠 *(626) 441-3671.* Built in 1887 on the famous "Millionaires' Row," the rooms have Victorian decor and claw-foot bathtubs. 🛏 📺 🅿 ⬛	4			●	
PASADENA: *Ritz Carlton Huntingdon Hotel* $$$$ 1401 S Oak Knoll Ave, CA 91106. **Road map** inset A. 📞 *(626) 568-3900; (800) 241-3333.* 📠 *(626) 568-3700.* Dating from 1907, this luxury hotel, set in a residential area, has elegant rooms. A wooden bridge between the two wings overlooks the Japanese gardens in the courtyard. 🛏 24 📺 ♿ 🅿 🍽 ⬛	383	●	■	●	■
SANTA MONICA: *Best Western Gateway Hotel* $$ 1920 Santa Monica Blvd, CA 90404. **Road map** inset A. 📞 *(310) 829-9100; (800) 528-1234.* 📠 *(310) 829-9211.* This downtown hotel is excellent value, with spacious rooms, free airport shuttle, and sun terraces. 🛏 📺 ♿ 🅿 🍽 ⬛	122	●			
SANTA MONICA: *Hotel Carmel by the Sea* $$ 201 Broadway, CA 90401. **Road map** inset A. 📞 *(310) 451-2469; (800) 445-8695.* 📠 *(310) 393-4180.* This 1920s hotel near the beach has spacious rooms and suites with ocean views. Children under 17 stay free. 🛏 📺 ♿ 🅿 ⬛	110				
SANTA MONICA: *Radisson Huntley Hotel* $$ 1111 2nd St, CA 90403. **Road map** inset A. 📞 *(310) 394-5454; (800) 333-3333.* 📠 *(310) 458-9776.* Just one block from the beach, this hotel has spacious rooms, good views, and facilities for business travelers. 🛏 📺 ♿ 🅿 ⬛	213	●	■		
SANTA MONICA: *Four Points Hotel* $$$ 530 W Pico Blvd, CA 90405. **Road map** inset A. 📞 *(310) 399-9344; (800) 465-4329.* 📠 *(310) 399-2504.* Five minutes from the beach, this new hotel has comfortable rooms, most with balconies. It offers a free airport shuttle, two Jacuzzis, and tours to local sights and Tijuana *(see p255).* 🛏 📺 ♿ 🅿 🍽 ⬛	314	●	■		■
SANTA MONICA: *Hotel California* $$$ 1670 Ocean Ave, CA 90401. **Road map** inset A. 📞 *(310) 393-2363.* 📠 *(310) 393-1063.* This small refurbished hotel on the beach has lovely ocean views from some rooms. All rooms are nonsmoking. 🛏 📺 ♿ 🅿 ⬛	20			●	
SANTA MONICA: *Miramar Sheraton Hotel* $$$ 101 Wilshire Blvd, CA 90401. **Road map** inset A. 📞 *(310) 576-7777; (800) 325-3535.* 📠 *(310) 458-7912.* This glamorous hotel built on the cliffs over-looking the ocean has a health center and many other amenities. Betty Grable was discovered here – singing in the lounge. 🛏 24 📺 ♿ 🅿 ⬛	302	●	■	●	■
SANTA MONICA: *Doubletree Guest Suites* $$$$ 1707 4th St, CA 90401. **Road map** inset A. 📞 *(310) 395-3332; (800) 424-2900.* 📠 *(310) 452-7399.* The large two-room suites at this luxury hotel near the beach have fabulous views. There is also a game room. 🛏 📺 ♿ 🅿 ⬛	253	●	■	●	■
SANTA MONICA: *The Georgian* $$$$ 1415 Ocean Ave, CA 90401. **Road map** inset A. 📞 *(310) 395-9945; (800) 538-8147.* 📠 *(310) 451-3374.* This four-diamond hotel with large rooms and suites, on the beach by Palisades Park, has been here since 1931. 🛏 📺 ♿ 🅿 ⬛	84	●	■	●	
SANTA MONICA: *Loews Santa Monica Beach Hotel* $$$$$ 1700 Ocean Ave, CA 90401. **Road map** inset A. 📞 *(310) 458-6700.* 📠 *(310) 458-6761.* An elegant four-star hotel on the beach, within walking distance of Santa Monica pier. The ocean views are wonderful. 🛏 24 📺 ♿ 🅿 ⬛	343	●	■		■

SANTA MONICA: *Shutters on the Beach* $$$$$ — 198 — ● ■ ● ■
1 Pico Blvd, CA 90405. **Road map** inset A. ((310) 458-0030; (800) 334-9000.
FAX (310) 458-4589. Luxury and glamour abound at this four-star hotel on the beach. Rooms are spacious and many have balconies. ⊞ 24 TV & P ♜ ☺

UNIVERSAL CITY: *Hilton Universal* $$$ — 453 — ● ■
555 Universal Terrace Parkway, CA 91608. **Road map** inset A. ((818) 506-2500; (800) 445-8667. FAX (818) 509-2058. A high-rise hotel overlooking Universal Studios. Rooms are spacious. Book ahead in summer. ⊞ 24 TV & P ♜ ☺

UNIVERSAL CITY: *Sheraton Universal* $$$$$ — 440 — ● ■
333 University Terrace Parkway, CA 91608. **Road map** inset A. ((818) 980-1212; (800) 325-3535. FAX (818) 985-4980. Free shuttles run to Universal Studios and City Walk from this busy, recently refurbished corporate hotel. ⊞ TV & P ♜ ☺

VAN NUYS: *Travelodge* $ — 74
6909 Sepulveda Blvd, CA 91405. **Road map** inset A. ((818) 787-5400; (800) 578-7878. FAX (818) 782-0239. Children under 12 stay free at this two-diamond motel in the San Fernando Valley with large rooms and breakfast. ⊞ TV P ☺

VENICE BEACH: *The Cadillac* $ — 41
8 Dudley Ave, CA 90291. **Road map** inset A. ((310) 399-8876. FAX (310) 399-4536. This gorgeous Art Deco hotel attracts a young, smart crowd. It is right on the beach, with a sauna, pool tables and sun terrace. ⊞ TV & P ♜ ☺

VENICE BEACH: *The Venice Beach House* $$ — 9 — ●
15 30th Ave, CA 90291. **Road map** inset A. ((310) 823-1966. FAX (310) 823-1842. This is a delightful bed-and-breakfast inn a short walk from the beach. The guest rooms are beautifully furnished with antiques. TV P ☺

WEST HOLLYWOOD: *Best Western Sunset Plaza Hotel* $$$ — 100 — ■ ● ■
8400 Sunset Blvd, CA 90069. **Map** 6 C1. ((323) 654-0750; (800) 421-3652. FAX (323) 650-6146. Ideally located on busy Sunset Boulevard, this elegant chain hotel has pleasant rooms and a secluded pool area. ⊞ TV P ☺

WEST HOLLYWOOD: *Hyatt Hotel* $$$ — 262 — ● ■ ● ■
8401 Sunset Blvd, CA 90069. **Map** 6 C1. ((323) 656-1234. FAX (323) 650-4169. This chain hotel, with a rooftop pool, is close to the House of Blues night-club (*see p459*). The rooms are modern and clean. ⊞ TV P ☺

WEST HOLLYWOOD: *Chateau Marmont* $$$$ — 62 — ● ■ ● ■
8221 Sunset Blvd, CA 90046. **Map** 1 B5. ((323) 656-1010; (800) 242-8328. FAX (323) 655-5311. Decorated in 1940s style (*see p100*), the Chateau's rooms, suites, and cottages are a haven for celebrities. ⊞ 24 TV & ☺

WEST HOLLYWOOD: *Mondrian Hotel* $$$$ — 224 — ● ■ ● ■
8440 Sunset Blvd, CA 90069. **Map** 6 C1. ((323) 650-8999; (800) 525-8029. FAX (323) 650-5215. Part of a small chain, this elegant hotel (*see p99*) is popular with musicians. Rooms have city views. ⊞ 24 TV & P ☺

WEST HOLLYWOOD: *Argyle Hotel* $$$$$ — 64 — ● ■ ● ■
8358 Sunset Blvd, CA 90069. **Map** 6 C1. ((323) 654-7100; (800) 225-2637. FAX (323) 654-1004. Originally built as apartments for film stars (*see p99*), the rooms here are Italian Art Deco in style. ⊞ 24 TV & P ☺

WESTWOOD: *Hilgard House Hotel* $ — 47
927 Hilgard Ave, CA 90024. **Map** 4 A4. ((310) 208-3945; (800) 826-3934. FAX (310) 208-1972. This busy hotel, close to UCLA, is decorated in old European style and offers breakfast and special business rates. ⊞ TV & P ☺

WESTWOOD: *Hotel del Capri* $$ — 81
10587 Wilshire Blvd, CA 90024. **Map** 4 B4. ((310) 474-3511; (800) 444-6835. FAX (310) 470-9999. A basic, modern hotel within walking distance of the UCLA campus and restaurants. Some rooms have kitchen facilities. TV P ☺

WESTWOOD: *Doubletree Hotel Westwood* $$$ — 295 — ● ■
10740 Wilshire Blvd, CA 90024. **Map** 4 B4. ((310) 475-8711; (800) 472-8556. FAX (310) 475-5220. The rooms in this hotel have Jacuzzis and Victorian-style decor. Facilities include a games room for children. ⊞ TV & P ♜ ☺

WESTWOOD: *Westwood Marquis Hotel and Gardens* $$$$$ — 258 — ● ■ ● ■
930 Hilgard Ave, CA 90024. **Map** 4 A4. ((310) 208-8765; (800) 323-7500. FAX (310) 824-0355. Rooms in this four-star hotel have every amenity. A buffet breakfast is included. ⊞ 24 TV & P ♜ ☺

<table>
<tr><td colspan="2">

Price categories for a standard double room per night, inclusive of service charges and any additional taxes, such as local sales tax:
$ under $100
$$ $100–$150
$$$ $150–$200
$$$$ $200–$250
$$$$$ over $250

</td></tr>
</table>

RESTAURANT Hotel restaurant or dining room usually open to non-residents unless otherwise stated. **CHILDREN'S FACILITIES** Indicates cribs and/or a baby-sitting service available. A few hotels also provide children's portions and high chairs in the restaurant. **GARDEN/TERRACE** Hotels with a garden, courtyard, or terrace, often providing tables for eating outside. **SWIMMING POOL** Hotel with indoor or outdoor swimming pool.	NUMBER OF ROOMS	RESTAURANT	CHILDREN'S FACILITIES	GARDEN/TERRACE	SWIMMING POOL

SOUTH CENTRAL CALIFORNIA

	Rooms	Rest.	Child.	Gard.	Pool
BAKERSFIELD: *Courtyard by Marriott* $ 3601 Marriott Drive, CA 93308. **Road map** C5. (*(661) 324-6660; (800) 321-2211.* FAX *(661) 324-1185.* The service is excellent at this modern chain hotel, which is well suited to business travelers. ▣ TV ⬧ P ▥ ▨	146	●	■	●	■
CAMBRIA: *Best Western Fireside Inn* $ 6700 Moonstone Beach Drive, CA 93428. **Road map** B5. (*(805) 927-8661; (800) 528-1234.* FAX *(805) 927-8584.* This basic waterfront hotel has large rooms, large beds, gas fireplaces, and continental breakfast. ▣ TV ⬧ P ▨	46		■		■
CAMBRIA: *Burton Drive Inn (Silvia's)* $$ 4022 Burton Drive, CA 93428. **Road map** B5. (*(805) 927-5125.* Run by a friendly English couple, this modern inn with large suites is on a bustling downtown street. Breakfast is served in your room. ▣ TV ⬧ P	8			●	
CAMBRIA: *Blue Whale Inn* $$ 6736 Moonstone Beach Drive, CA 93428. **Road map** B5. (*(805) 927-4647.* FAX *(805) 927-4647.* Built on a bluff overlooking the sea, every room in this top-rated bed-and-breakfast inn has an ocean view. You can observe seals and gray whales through a telescope. ▣ TV ⬧ P ▨	6			●	
MONTECITO: *Montecito Inn* $$$$ 1295 Coast Village Rd, CA 93108. **Road map** C5. (*(805) 969-7854; (800) 843-2017.* FAX *(805) 969-0623.* This Mediterranean-style hotel near the beach was built in 1928 by film star Charlie Chaplin. ▣ TV ⬧ P ▨	60	●	■		■
MONTECITO: *San Ysidro Ranch* $$$$$ 900 San Ysidro Lane, CA 93108. **Road map** C5. (*(805) 969-5046; (800) 368-6788.* FAX *(805) 565-1995.* Luxury cottages, each with a wood stove or fireplace, lie hidden from view in this stunning mountain resort. This is the perfect place to get away from it all. ▣ 24 TV ⬧ P ▨	42	●	■	●	■
MORRO BAY: *Blue Sail Inn* $ 851 Market Ave, CA 93442. **Road map** B5. (*(805) 772-7132; (800) 336-0707.* FAX *(805) 772-8406.* Even the best rooms with fireplaces are a bargain here. There is an observation deck for viewing ships at sea. ▣ TV ⬧ P ▨	48		■	●	■
MORRO BAY: *Embarcadero Inn* $$ 456 Embarcadero, CA 93442. **Road map** B5. (*(805) 772-2700; (800) 292-7625.* FAX *(805) 772-1060.* All rooms face the bay in this modern hotel; most have balconies and fireplaces. Continental breakfast is included. TV ⬧ P ▨	32		■	●	
MORRO BAY: *Inn at Morro Bay* $$$ 60 State Park Rd, CA 93442. **Road map** B5. (*(805) 772-5651; (800) 321-9566.* FAX *(805) 772-4779.* Built beside the bay, this hotel has deluxe country-style rooms with fireplaces and balconies. ▣ TV ⬧ P ▨	96	●	■		■
PASO ROBLES: *Paso Robles Inn* $$ 1103 Spring St, CA 93446. **Road Map** B5. (*(805) 238-2660.* FAX *(805) 238-4707.* This small, basic hotel, which has recently been refurbished, is ideally located halfway between Los Angeles and San Francisco. ▣ TV ⬧ P ▨	106	●		●	■
SAN LUIS OBISPO: *Lamplighter Inn* $ 1604 Monterey St, CA 93401. **Road map** B5. (*(805) 547-7777; (800) 547-7787.* FAX *(805) 547-7787.* Accommodations in this motel include a cottage that sleeps several and family suites, some with full kitchens. ▣ TV ⬧ P ▨	40				■
SAN LUIS OBISPO: *Garden Street Inn* $$ 1212 Garden St, CA 93401. **Road map** B5. (*(805) 545-9802.* Built in 1860, this restored Victorian house is furnished with original antiques. Some rooms have claw-foot bathtubs or fireplaces and Jacuzzis. ▣ ⬧ P ▨	13			●	

SAN LUIS OBISPO: *The Madonna Inn* $$$ — 109
100 Madonna Rd, CA 93405. **Road map** B5. (805) 543-3000; (800) 543-9666.
FAX (805) 543-1800. All the rooms have themes – for example, the Caveman Room is made entirely out of rock. Book in advance.

SANTA BARBARA: *Inn at the Harbor* $ — 43
433 W Montecito St, CA 93101. **Road map** C5. (805) 963-7851; (800) 626-1986.
FAX (805) 962-9428. Just two blocks from the beach, rooms in this rustic-style hotel are set around a lovely tropical-style courtyard.

SANTA BARBARA: *The Schooner Inn* $ — 96
533 State St, CA 93101. **Road map** C5. (805) 957-9300. FAX (805) 962-2412.
The original cage elevator is still the centerpiece of this hotel, built in 1926, five blocks from the beach. Breakfast is included.

SANTA BARBARA: *Glenborough Inn* $$ — 11
1327 Bath St, CA 93101. **Road map** C5. (805) 966-0589; (800) 962-0589.
FAX (805) 564-8610. This very romantic bed-and-breakfast inn is in three Victorian houses near Downtown. It has a hot tub.

SANTA BARBARA: *El Encanto Hotel and Garden Villas* $$$ — 84
1900 Lasuen Rd, CA 93103. **Road map** C5. (805) 687-5000; (800) 346-7039.
FAX (805) 687-3903. This grand old hotel in the hills has stunning ocean views. The rooms are in bungalows and cottages.

SANTA BARBARA: *Olive House* $$$ — 6
1604 Olive St, CA 93101. **Road map** C5. (805) 962-4902; (800) 786-6422.
FAX (805) 899-2754. In a quiet area, this beautifully restored 1904 house has rooms with lovely views; some have terraces and hot tubs.

SANTA BARBARA: *Tiffany Inn* $$$ — 7
1323 De La Vina St, CA 93101. **Road map** C5. (805) 963-2283; (800) 999-5672. FAX (805) 962-0994. Dating from 1898, this beautifully restored house has antiques and good views. Breakfast is included.

SANTA BARBARA: *Upham Hotel* $$$ — 50
1404 De La Vina, CA 93101. **Road map** C5. (805) 962-0058; (800) 727-0876.
FAX (805) 963-2825. This downtown landmark was built in 1871. The rooms have Victorian decor, and there is a good restaurant *(see p552)*.

SANTA BARBARA: *Four Seasons Biltmore* $$$$$ — 234
1260 Channel Drive, CA 93108. **Road map** C5. (805) 969-2261; (800) 332-3442. FAX (805) 565-8323. A luxury resort since the 1920s, the rooms, suites, and cottages are set in coastal gardens.

SANTA PAULA: *Fern Oaks Inn* $$ — 4
1025 Ojai Rd, CA 93060. **Road map** C5. (805) 525-7747. This stunning 1920s Mission Revival-style inn is set in idyllic landscaped gardens. The Casablanca Room has its own private sun porch.

SIMI VALLEY: *Simi Valley Travelodge* $ — 96
2550 Erringer Rd, CA 93065. **Road map** C5. (805) 584-6006; (800) 433-6030.
FAX (805) 527-5629. All rooms in this bargain hotel have cable TV and VCRs. There is also a sauna. Children under 17 stay free.

SIMI VALLEY: *Clarion Hotel* $$$ — 120
1775 Madera Rd, CA 93065. **Road map** C5. (805) 584-6300. FAX (805) 527-9969. The emphasis is on personal attention at this friendly hotel, which offers continental breakfast, special rates, and discounts.

SOLVANG: *Royal Copenhagen Motel* $ — 48
1579 Mission Drive, CA 93463. **Road map** C5. (805) 688-5561; (800) 624-6604.
FAX (805) 688-7029. Rooms in this motel resemble those in traditional Danish houses and overlook Solvang's Danish-style village square.

SOLVANG: *Storybook Inn* $$ — 9
409 1st St, CA 93463. **Road map** C5. (805) 688-1703; (800) 786-7925.
FAX (805) 688-0953. Rooms at this pretty bed-and-breakfast inn are named after Hans Christian Andersen stories. Breakfast is included.

SOLVANG: *Petersen Village Inn* $$$ — 40
1576 Mission Drive, CA 93463. **Road map** C5. (805) 688-3121; (800) 321-8985.
FAX (805) 688-5732. Canopied beds and antique furnishings add charm to this family-owned inn. A perfect place for a romantic getaway.

	Price categories / Facilities	NUMBER OF ROOMS	RESTAURANT	CHILDREN'S FACILITIES	GARDEN/TERRACE	SWIMMING POOL

Price categories for a standard double room per night, inclusive of service charges and any additional taxes, such as local sales tax:
- $ under $100
- $$ $100–$150
- $$$ $150–$200
- $$$$ $200–$250
- $$$$$ over $250

RESTAURANT
Hotel restaurant or dining room usually open to non-residents unless otherwise stated.

CHILDREN'S FACILITIES
Indicates cribs and/or a baby-sitting service available. A few hotels also provide children's portions and high chairs in the restaurant.

GARDEN/TERRACE
Hotels with a garden, courtyard, or terrace, often providing tables for eating outside.

SWIMMING POOL
Hotel with indoor or outdoor swimming pool.

ORANGE COUNTY

Hotel	No. of Rooms	Restaurant	Children's Facilities	Garden/Terrace	Swimming Pool
ANAHEIM: *Castle Inn and Suites* $ 1734 S Harbour Blvd, CA 92802. **Road map** D6. 📞 *(714) 774-8111; (800) 227-8530.* FAX *(714) 956-4736.* The bizarre castle-style exterior belies the comfortable but ordinary rooms. It is just opposite Disneyland *(see pp222–5).* 🛏 📺 ♿ P 🍴	200		■	●	■
ANAHEIM: *Crystal Suites Hotel* $ 1752 S Clementine St, CA 92802. **Road map** D6. 📞 *(714) 535-7773; (800) 992-0823.* FAX *(714) 776-9073.* Benefits here include breakfast, a free shuttle, and early entry to Disneyland. Children under three stay free. 🛏 📺 ♿ P 🍴	130		■	●	■
ANAHEIM: *Anaheim Marriott Hotel* $$$ 700 W Convention Way, CA 92802. **Road map** D6. 📞 *(714) 750-8000; (800) 228-9290.* FAX *(714) 750-9100.* This high-rise, child-friendly hotel near Disneyland has a video arcade, sauna, and laundry facilities. 🛏 📺 ♿ P 🍴	1033	●	■	●	■
ANAHEIM: *Disneyland Hotel* Ⓦ www.disneyland.com $$$$ 1150 W Cerritos, CA 92802. **Road Map** D6. 📞 *(714) 778-6600.* FAX *(714) 956-6597.* This large hotel with guest rooms or cottages is linked to Disneyland by monorail. The emphasis is on entertainment, with lots to see and do in the hotel, including six restaurants. 🛏 📺 ♿ P 🍴	1136	●	■	●	■
AVALON: *Hotel Metropole* $$$ Metropole Market Place, Crescent Ave, Catalina Island, CA 90704. **Road map** C6. 📞 *(310) 510-1884; (800) 541-8528.* FAX *(310) 510-2534.* This Mediterranean-style hotel on the beach offers spacious rooms and breakfast. 🛏 24 📺 ♿ 🍴	48		■	●	
AVALON: *Hotel Vista Del Mar* $$$ 417 Crescent Ave, Catalina Island, CA 90704. **Road map** C6. 📞 *(310) 510-1452; (800) 601-3836.* FAX *(310) 510-2917.* Rooms have refrigerators and fireplaces at this luxury hotel overlooking the bay. Breakfast is included. 🛏 📺 🍴	15		■	●	
COSTA MESA: *Sandpiper Motel* $ 1967 Newport Blvd, CA 92627. **Road map** D6. 📞 *(949) 645-9137; (800) 648-9137.* FAX *(949) 650-1702.* This super-value motel, close to Disneyland, has large, comfortable rooms, continental breakfast, and weekly rates. 🛏 📺 ♿ P 🍴	44				
COSTA MESA: *Wyndham Garden Hotel* $ 3350 Ave of the Arts, CA 92626. **Road map** D6. 📞 *(714) 751-5100; (800) 996-3426.* FAX *(949) 751-0129.* This comfortable hotel is close to beaches, jogging trails, Disneyland, and Orange County Airport. 🛏 📺 ♿ P 🍴	203	●	■	●	■
COSTA MESA: *Residence Inn* $$ 881 W Baker St, CA 92626. **Road map** D6. 📞 *(714) 241-8800; (800) 331-3131.* FAX *(714) 546-4308.* Suites here have private entrances, a balcony or patio, and a kitchen. Continental breakfast is included. 🛏 📺 ♿ P 🍴	144		■		■
COSTA MESA: *Country Side Inn and Suites* $$$ 325 Bristol St, CA 92626. **Road map** D6. 📞 *(714) 549-0300; (800) 322-9992.* FAX *(714) 662-0828.* Rooms in this European-style hotel have antiques and four-poster beds. Disneyland is nearby. 🛏 📺 ♿ P 🍴	300	●	■	●	■
DANA POINT: *Blue Lantern Inn* $$$ 34343 Street of the Blue Lantern, CA 92629. **Road map** D6. 📞 *(949) 661-1304; (800) 950-1236.* FAX *(949) 496-1483.* This romantic Victorian bed-and-breakfast inn is perched on a cliff overlooking the harbor. Rooms have fireplaces and Jacuzzis; some have terraces. Ask about package deals. 🛏 📺 ♿ P 🍴	29		■	●	
DANA POINT: *Ritz-Carlton Laguna Niguel* $$$$ 1 Ritz-Carlton Drive, CA 92629. **Road map** D6. 📞 *(949) 240-2000; (800) 241-3333.* FAX *(949) 240-0829.* A path leads to the ocean from this large luxury hotel. Rooms are tasteful and have coastal views. 🛏 24 📺 ♿ P 🍴	393	●	■	●	■

HUNTINGTON BEACH: *Quality Inn* $$
800 Pacific Coast Hwy, CA 92648. **Road map** D6. (*(714) 536-7500; (800) 228-5151.* FAX *(714) 536-6846.* This plain hotel near the beach offers fabulous sunset views, oceanfront suites, a rooftop spa, and breakfast. ⌂ TV & P
50

HUNTINGTON BEACH: *The Waterfront Hilton Beach Resort* $$$$
21100 Pacific Coast Hwy, CA 92648. **Road map** D6. (*(714) 845-8407; (800) 822-7873.* FAX *(714) 845-8424.* The spacious rooms at this four-diamond resort, opposite the beach, have balconies with ocean views. ⌂ TV & P
290

LAGUNA BEACH: *Casa Laguna Inn* $$
2510 S Coast Hwy, CA 92651. **Road Map** D6. (*(949) 494-2996; (800) 233-0449* FAX *(949) 494-5309.* Situated on the oceanfront, this is a Mission-style bed-and-breakfast inn. Rooms have private patios – there is even an aviary. ⌂ TV P
20

LAGUNA BEACH: *Hotel Laguna* $$
425 S Coast Hwy, CA 92651. **Road map** D6. (*(949) 494-1151; (800) 524-2927.* FAX *(949) 497-2163.* The town's oldest hotel, right on the beach, has smaller-than-average rooms but excellent service and great views. ⌂ TV & P
65

LAGUNA BEACH: *Surf and Sand Hotel* $$$$$
1555 S Coast Hwy, CA 92651. **Road map** D6. (*(949) 497-4477; (800) 524-8621.* FAX *(949) 494-2897.* The deluxe rooms, suites, and penthouses at this luxury hotel on the beach have whirlpool baths, balconies, and ocean views. There is also a superb restaurant. ⌂ TV & P
150

NEWPORT BEACH: *The Sutton Place Hotel* $$$
4500 MacArthur Blvd, CA 92660. **Road map** D6. (*(949) 476-2001; (800) 243-4141.* FAX *(949) 476-0153.* The emphasis is on luxury at this four-star hotel. Some rooms have balconies and ocean views. ⌂ 24 TV & P
435

NEWPORT BEACH: *Four Seasons Hotel* $$$$$
690 Newport Beach Center Drive, CA 92660. **Road map** D6. (*(949) 759-0808; (800) 332-3442.* FAX *(949) 760-8073; 759-0568.* You'll be treated like royalty at this luxurious five-diamond hotel. Some rooms have terraces and ocean views. There are tennis courts and golf courses nearby. ⌂ 24 TV & P
285

SUNSET BEACH: *Harbor Inn* $
16912 Pacific Coast Hwy, 90742. **Road map** D6. (*(562) 592-4770; (800) 546-4770.* FAX *(562) 592-3547.* This bed-and-breakfast inn near the beach has extra large rooms and discounts for longer stays. ⌂ TV & P
25

TWO HARBORS: *Banning House Lodge* $$
Two Harbors, Catalina Island, CA 90704. **Road map** C6. (*(310) 510-2800.* FAX *(310) 510-0244.* This intimate inn was built in 1910 as a hunting lodge. Rooms have antiques and wood floors; larger modern rooms in the out-buildings have big picture windows. Breakfast is included. ⌂ &
11

SAN DIEGO COUNTY

CARLSBAD: *Best Western Beach Terrace Inn* $$
2775 Ocean St, CA 92008. **Road map** D6. (*(760) 729-1078; (800) 433-5415.* FAX *(760) 729-1078.* Rooms here have kitchens, private terraces, and balconies overlooking the ocean. The beach is just minutes away. ⌂ TV
49

CARLSBAD: *Pelican Cove Inn* $$
320 Walnut Ave, CA 92008. **Road map** D6. (*(760) 434-5995; (888) 735-2683.* This delightful New England-style bed-and-breakfast inn has rooms with antiques, fireplaces, and private entrances. ⌂ TV & P
8

CORONADO: *Loew's Coronado Bay Resort* $$$$
4000 Coronado Bay Rd, CA 92118. **Road map** D6. (*(619) 424-4000; (800) 815-6397.* FAX *(619) 424-4400.* Rooms have bay views at this four-star resort set on a peninsula. There are tennis courts and a marina. ⌂ 24 TV & P
440

CORONADO: *Coronado Island Marriott Resort* $$$$$
2000 2nd St, CA 92118. **Road map** D6. (*(619) 435-3000; (800) 285-4660.* FAX *(619) 435-3032.* This luxury four-star hotel, built on the edge of the beach, has modern rooms and spa facilities. ⌂ 24 TV & P
300

CORONADO: *Hotel del Coronado* $$$$$
1500 Orange Ave, CA 92118. **Road map** D6. (*(619) 435-6611; (800) 468-3533.* FAX *(619) 522-8238.* This grand Victorian hotel *(see p245)* on the beach has been updated with modern annexes and a spa. ⌂ 24 TV & P
700

For key to symbols see back flap

Price categories for a standard double room per night, inclusive of service charges and any additional taxes, such as local sales tax:

$ under $100
$$ $100–$150
$$$ $150–$200
$$$$ $200–$250
$$$$$ over $250

RESTAURANT
Hotel restaurant or dining room usually open to non-residents unless otherwise stated.

CHILDREN'S FACILITIES
Indicates cribs and/or a baby-sitting service available. A few hotels also provide children's portions and high chairs in the restaurant.

GARDEN/TERRACE
Hotels with a garden, courtyard, or terrace, often providing tables for eating outside.

SWIMMING POOL
Hotel with indoor or outdoor swimming pool.

		NUMBER OF ROOMS	RESTAURANT	CHILDREN'S FACILITIES	GARDEN/TERRACE	SWIMMING POOL
DEL MAR: *Del Mar Hilton* 15575 Jimmy Durante Blvd, CA 92014. **Road map** D6. (*(858) 792-5200; (800) 445-8667.* FAX *(858) 792-9538.* Guests can play tennis, golf, or relax in the Jacuzzi at this Tudor-style hotel near the racetrack.	$	245	●			■
DEL MAR: *Clarion Carriage House Del Mar Inn* 720 Camino Del Mar, CA 92014. **Road map** D6. (*(858) 755-9765; (800) 451-4515.* FAX *(858) 792-8196.* A quiet hotel situated on bluffs overlooking the ocean. It has pretty rooms and English-style gardens.	$$	80		■	●	■
DEL MAR: *L'Auberge Del Mar Resort and Spa* 1540 Camino Del Mar, CA 92014. **Road map** D6. (*(858) 259-1515; (800) 553-1336.* FAX *(858) 755-4940.* Set on the beach, this New England-style hotel has elegant decor and sunset views, tennis, and a spa.	$$$	120	●	●	●	■
ENCINITAS: *Radisson Inn and Moonlight Beach* 85 Encinitas Blvd, CA 92024. **Road map** D6. (*(760) 942-7455; (800) 333-3333.* FAX *(760) 632-9481.* Rooms at this small hotel have balconies with either ocean or city views. Complimentary continental breakfast.	$$	89	●	■		■
JULIAN: *Julian Hotel* 2032 Main St, CA 92036. **Road map** D6. (*(760) 765-0201; (800) 734-5854.* This historic Victorian inn is the oldest operating hotel in California. Most rooms have open fireplaces. Full breakfast and afternoon tea are included.	$	15			●	
LA JOLLA: *Marriott San Diego/La Jolla* 4240 La Jolla Village Drive, CA 92037. **Road map** D6. (*(858) 587-1414; (800) 228-9290.* FAX *(858) 546-8518.* This high-rise hotel is 2 miles (3.2 km) from the beaches and near many downtown attractions.	$$	360	●	■		■
LA JOLLA: *Embassy Suites Hotel* 4550 La Jolla Village Drive, CA 92122. **Road map** D6. (*(858) 453-0400; (800) 362-2779.* FAX *(858) 453-4226.* This modern hotel with two-room suites is perfect for families. It offers breakfast and a game room.	$$$	335	●	■		■
LA JOLLA: *La Jolla Beach and Tennis Club* 2000 Spindrift Drive, CA 92037. **Road map** D6. (*(858) 454-7126; (800) 624-2582.* FAX *(858) 456-3805.* This small Mediterranean-style resort hotel has retained its 1920s charm. Some rooms have balconies. It has a private beach, tennis courts, a golf course, and croquet lawn.	$$$	90	●	■	●	■
LA JOLLA: *La Valencia Hotel* 1132 Prospect St, CA 92037. **Road map** D6. (*(858) 454-0771; (800) 451-0772.* FAX *(858) 456-3921.* This Spanish-style luxury hotel is located near the beach and the many local art galleries. The rooms are sumptuous and there is a wonderful hotel terrace.	$$$	100	●	■	●	■
LA JOLLA: *The Bed and Breakfast Inn at La Jolla* 7753 Draper Avenue, CA 92037. **Road map** D6. (*(858) 456-2066; (800) 582-2466.* FAX *(858) 456-1510.* The building, designed in 1913 by Irving Gill, has been named an Historic Site. Some of the elegantly furnished rooms have ocean views and two-person baths.	$$$	16			●	
RANCHO SANTA FE: *Rancho Valencia Resort* Box 9126, 5921 Valencia Circle, CA 92067. **Road map** D6. (*(858) 756-1123; (800) 548-3664.* FAX *(858) 756-0165.* This glamorous resort hotel is set in parkland, close to the beach and the racetrack. It has four golf courses, tennis courts, hiking trails, mountain bikes, and spa facilities.	$$$$$	43	●	■	●	■
SAN DIEGO: *Beach Cottages* 4255 Ocean Blvd, CA 92109. **Road map** D6. (*(858) 483-7440.* FAX *(858) 273-9365.* This family hotel on the beach offers cottages, suites, apartments, and rooms. Most of the rustic-style rooms have kitchens.	$	78		■	●	

SAN DIEGO: *Beach Haven Inn* — $ — 23
4740 Mission Blvd, CA 92109. **Road map** D6. ((858) 272-3812; (800) 831-6323.
FAX (858) 272-3532. This modern inn near the beach and Sea World *(see p250)* has family suites with kitchenettes and cable TV.

SAN DIEGO: *Blom House* — $ — 4
1372 Minden Drive, CA 92111. **Road map** D6. ((858) 467-0890; (800) 797-2566.
FAX (858) 467-0890. This friendly bed-and-breakfast inn has cozy rooms and a hot tub on the wooden terrace overlooking the city.

SAN DIEGO: *Holiday Inn Seaworld* — $ — 307
3350 Kemper St, CA 92110. **Road map** D6. ((619) 223-3395; (800) 219-8924. FAX (619) 224-9248. Features at this chain hotel include a sun terrace and sports bar. Rooms are large; some have balconies.

SAN DIEGO: *Hotel Circle Inn and Suites* — $ — 200
2201 Hotel Circle South, CA 92108. **Road map** D6. ((619) 291-2711; (800) 621-6341. FAX (619) 542-1227. This family-style motel, near all the sights, has a spa and sun terrace. Some of the suites have kitchens.

SAN DIEGO: *Wyndham Garden Hotel* — $ — 180
5975 Lusk Blvd, CA 92121. **Road map** D6. ((858) 558-1818; (800) 996-3426.
FAX (858) 558-0421. North of Downtown, this hotel is perfect for the business traveler on a budget. Buffet breakfast is included.

SAN DIEGO: *San Diego Mission Valley Hilton* — $$ — 350
901 Camino Del Rio South, CA 92108. **Road map** D6. ((619) 543-9000; (800) 733-2332. FAX (619) 296-9561. This modern 13-story hotel is close to Downtown. Rooms are comfortable and well equipped.

SAN DIEGO: *Heritage Park Bed and Breakfast Inn* — $$$ — 10
2470 Heritage Park Row, Old Town, CA 92110. **Road map** D6. ((619) 299-6832; (800) 995-2470. FAX (619) 299-9465. Rooms in these two Victorian houses are furnished in period style. Classic films are shown in the parlor.

SAN DIEGO: *Hyatt Regency* — $$$ — 875
1 Market Place, CA 92101. **Road map** D6. ((619) 232-1234; (800) 233-1234.
FAX (619) 233-6464. Views of the city and ocean are fabulous from the top of this modern hotel (the city's tallest building).

SAN DIEGO: *The Rancho Bernardo Inn* — $$$ — 287
17550 Bernardo Oaks Drive, CA 92128. **Road map** D6. ((858) 487-1611; (800) 542-6096. FAX (858) 675-8501. This four-star hacienda-style hotel offers golf, tennis, spa, or meal package deals, and seven outdoor Jacuzzis. Dine at the award-winning El Bizocho *(see p556)* restaurant.

SAN DIEGO: *US Grant Hotel* — $$$ — 280
326 Broadway, CA 92101. **Road map** D6. ((619) 232-3121; (800) 237-5029.
FAX (619) 232-3626. This four-diamond hotel downtown was built in 1910 by the son of Ulysses S. Grant, in honor of his father. It is furnished with reproduction antiques. Pets are welcome.

SAN DIEGO: *Marriott Hotel* — $$$$ — 1354
333 W Harbor Drive, CA 92101. **Road map** D6. ((619) 234-1500; (800) 228-9290.
FAX (619) 234-8678. A 25-story luxury hotel next to San Diego Bay with exceptional outdoor landscaping and facilities.

TIJUANA: *Grand Hotel Tijuana* — $$ — 423
4500 Blvd Agua Caliente, C.P. 22420. **Road map** D6. ((011-52-66) 81-70-00. FAX (011-52-66) 81-70-16. This is a large hotel complex with twin towers. Facilities include tennis courts and Jacuzzis.

THE INLAND EMPIRE AND LOW DESERT

BIG BEAR LAKE: *Grey Squirrel Resort* — $ — 17
39372 Big Bear Blvd (PO Box 1711), CA 92315. **Road map** D5. ((909) 866-4335. FAX (909) 866-6271. Charming one- to three-bedroom cottages with open fireplaces dot the mountain landscape at this year-round lake resort.

BIG BEAR LAKE: *Hillcrest Lodge* — $ — 12
40241 Big Bear Blvd (PO Box 3945), CA 92315. **Road map** D5. ((909) 866-7330; (800) 843-4449. FAX (909) 866-1171. Mountain ski slopes surround these motel rooms, cabins, and suites near Big Bear village *(see pp264–5)*. Rooms with Jacuzzis and open fireplaces are available.

						Number of Rooms	**Restaurant**	**Children's Facilities**	**Garden/Terrace**	**Swimming Pool**

Price categories for a standard double room per night, inclusive of service charges and any additional taxes, such as local sales tax:
$ under $100
$$ $100–$150
$$$ $150–$200
$$$$ $200–$250
$$$$$ over $250

Restaurant
Hotel restaurant or dining room usually open to non-residents unless otherwise stated.
Children's Facilities
Indicates cribs and/or a baby-sitting service available. A few hotels also provide children's portions and high chairs in the restaurant.
Garden/Terrace
Hotels with a garden, courtyard, or terrace, often providing tables for eating outside.
Swimming Pool
Hotel with indoor or outdoor swimming pool.

Hotel	Price	Rooms	Rest	Child	Gard	Pool
Big Bear Lake: *Apples Bed & Breakfast* 42430 Moonridge Rd, CA 92315. **Road map** D5. ((909) 866-0903. FAX (909) 866-6524. The rustic, Victorian-style rooms are named after varieties of apples at this luxury inn, surrounded by pine trees.	$$$	12	●	■	●	■
Big Bear Lake: *Windy Point Inn* 39015 N Shore Drive (PO Box 375), Fawnskin, CA 92333. **Road map** D5. ((909) 866-2746. FAX (909) 866-1593. This intimate, contemporary inn has award-winning architecture and spectacular views of the ski slopes. Rooms have open fireplaces. Midweek discounts are available.	$$$	3			●	
Borrego Springs: *Palms at Indian Head* 2220 Hoberg Rd, CA 92004. **Road map** D6. ((760) 767-7788; (800) 519-2624. FAX (760) 767-9717. A former playground hideaway for the Hollywood elite, this hotel lies at the foot of Indian Head Mountain, near hiking trails.	$$	10	●	■	●	■
Borrego Springs: *La Casa Del Zorro* 3845 Yaqui Pass Rd (PO Box 127), CA 92004. **Road map** D6. ((760) 767-5323; (800) 824-1884. FAX (760) 767-4782. A romantic, well-appointed oasis in the Anza-Borrego Desert State Park *(see p266)*. The lodgings range from large rooms to four-bedroom cottages, most with open fireplaces.	$$$	77	●	■	●	■
Desert Hot Springs: *Two Bunch Palms* 67425 Two Bunch Palms Trail, CA 92240. **Road map** D6. ((760) 329-8791; (800) 472-4334. FAX (760) 329-1317. Al Capone had a famous hideout here among the palms, mineral pools, and secluded bungalows of this glamorous resort. No one under 18 is allowed. It is closed in August.	$$$	45	●		●	■
Idyllwild: *Fern Valley Inn* 25240 Fern Valley Rd (PO Box 116), CA 92549-0116. **Road map** D6. ((909) 659-2205. FAX (909) 659-2630. Rooms in this charming Idyllwild getaway, set in expansive grounds, have hand-sewn quilts and antiques.	$	11			●	■
Idyllwild: *Idyllwild Inn* 54300 Village Center Drive (PO Box 515), CA 92549. **Road map** D6. ((909) 659-2552. Service is first rate at Idyllwild's oldest and largest inn, dating from 1904. There are miles of nearby hiking trails.	$	28		■	●	
Idyllwild: *Creekstone Inn* 54950 Pine Crest Ave (PO Box 1897), CA 92549. **Road map** D6. ((909) 659-3342; (800) 409-2127. Formerly a general store, this landmark bed-and-breakfast has pleasant, rustic-style rooms, many with fireplaces.	$$	9			●	
Indian Wells: *Indian Wells Resort Hotel* 76–661 Hwy 111, CA 92210. **Road map** D6. ((760) 345-6466; (800) 248-3220. FAX (760) 772-5083. Set at the base of the Santa Rosa Mountains, by the 11th tee of a golf course, rooms here have spectacular views and oriental touches; the two-room suites have large sunken baths.	$$$	152	●	■	●	■
Indian Wells: *Hyatt Grand Champions Resort* 44600 Indian Wells Lane, CA 92210. **Road map** D6. ((760) 341-1000. FAX (760) 568-2236. This luxurious resort is a golfer's paradise, with the use of two world-famous championship golf courses.	$$$$	336	●	■	●	■
Indio: *Best Western Indio Date Tree Hotel* 81909 Indio Blvd, CA 92201. **Road map** D6. ((760) 347-3421; (800) 292-5599. FAX (760) 347-3421. Popcorn is free at this hotel set in landscaped grounds with cacti and palms. Rates include continental breakfast.	$	120		■	●	■
Lake Arrowhead: *Eagle's Landing Bed & Breakfast* 27406 Cedarwood & Blue Jay 92317, Lake Arrowhead, CA 92352. **Road map** D5. ((909) 336-2642; (800) 835-5085. These hospitable lodgings have stained glass, high ceilings, enormous windows, and sweeping views.	$$	4			●	

PALM DESERT: *Shadow Mountain Resort and Racquet Club*　$$$　167
45–750 San Luis Rey, CA 92260. **Road map** D6. (*(760) 346-6123; (800) 472-3713.*
FAX *(760) 346-6518.* This friendly hotel also has condominiums and villas.
Amenities include Jacuzzis, saunas, and tennis courts. 📶 TV P 🏊

PALM DESERT: *Marriott Desert Springs Resort and Spa*　$$$$　844
74855 Country Club Drive, CA 92260. **Road map** D6. (*(760) 341-2211; (800)*
331-3112. FAX *(760) 341-1739.* Rooms have fabulous mountain views at this
enormous hotel, with two golf courses, tennis, and a spa. 📶 TV 🦽 P 🏊

PALM SPRINGS: *Desert Lodge*　$　51
1177 S Palm Canyon Drive, CA 92264. **Road map** D6. (*(760) 325-1356; (800)*
385-6343. FAX *(760) 325-7124.* This great bargain hotel has stunning mountain
views, a Jacuzzi, films, and home-baked continental breakfast. 📶 TV P 🏊

PALM SPRINGS: *Palm Springs Super 8 Lodge*　$　65
1900 N Palm Canyon Drive, CA 92262. **Road map** D6. (*(760) 322-3757; (800)*
800-8000. FAX *(760) 323-5290.* This quiet hotel near Downtown is a good
choice for budget travelers. Breakfast is included. 📶 TV 🦽 P 🏊

PALM SPRINGS: *Spa Hotel and Casino*　$$　230
100 N Indian Canyon Drive, CA 92262. **Road map** D6. (*(760) 325-1461; (800)*
854-1279. FAX *(760) 325-3344.* A natural hot mineral spring and 24-hour
casino are the highlights of this downtown hotel. 📶 24 TV 🦽 P 🏊

PALM SPRINGS: *Terra Cotta Inn*　$$　17
2388 E Racquet Club Rd, CA 92262. **Road map** D6. (*(760) 322-6057; (800) 786-*
6938. FAX *(760) 322-4169.* This clothing-optional hotel has tropical decor, a
Jacuzzi, spa treatments, video library, and free breakfast. 📶 TV 🦽 P 🏊

PALM SPRINGS: *Desert Shadows Inn*　$$$　74
1533 Chaparral Rd, CA 92262. **Road map** D6. (*(760) 325-6410; (800) 292-*
9298. FAX *(760) 327-7500.* This luxury nudist resort has tennis courts and
Jacuzzis. Some rooms have balconies and patios. 📶 TV 🦽 P 🎾 🏊

PALM SPRINGS: *Hyatt Regency*　$$$　192
285 N Palm Canyon Drive, CA 92262. **Road map** D6. (*(760) 322-9000; (800)*
233-1234. FAX *(760) 322-6009.* This luxury downtown hotel can arrange
golf and free tennis for guests at a nearby resort. 📶 TV 🦽 P 🎾 🏊

PALM SPRINGS: *Villa Royale*　$$$　33
1620 Indian Trail, CA 92264. **Road map** D6. (*(760) 327-2314.* FAX *(760) 322-3794.*
This perfect romantic getaway does not welcome children. Each room is
decorated in the style of a different European country. 📶 TV 🦽 P 🏊

PALM SPRINGS: *The Palm Springs Hilton Resort*　$$$$　260
400 E Tahquitz Canyon Way, CA 92262. **Road map** D6. (*(760) 320-6868; (800)*
522-6900. FAX *(760) 320-2126.* Near Downtown, this hotel's sports facilities
include tennis courts and access to local golf courses. 📶 TV 🦽 P 🎾 🏊

PALM SPRINGS: *Givenchy Hotel and Spa*　$$$$$　98
4200 E Palm Canyon Drive, CA 92264. **Road map** D6. (*(760) 770-5000; (800)*
276-5000. FAX *(760) 324-7280.* This hotel is the epitome of understated elegance. It has a golf course, tennis courts, and a spa. 📶 24 TV 🦽 P 🏊

RANCHO MIRAGE: *Ritz Carlton Rancho Mirage*　$$$　239
68900 Frank Sinatra Drive, CA 92270. **Road map** D6. (*(760) 321-8282; (800)*
241-3333. FAX *(760) 321-6928.* This modern resort-style hotel is on a plateau
in the mountains. Rooms are large. 📶 24 TV 🦽 P 🎾 🏊

RANCHO MIRAGE: *Rancho Las Palmas Marriott Resort*　$$$$　450
41000 Bob Hope Drive, CA 92270. **Road map** D6. (*(760) 568-2727; (800) 458-*
8786. FAX *(760) 568-5845.* This luxury resort is situated on three nine-hole
golf courses. Tennis and spa facilities are also available. 📶 TV 🦽 P 🏊

RIVERSIDE: *Historic Mission Inn*　$$　233
3649 Mission Inn Ave, CA 92501. **Road map** D6. (*(909) 784-0300.* FAX *(909)*
683-1342. Craftsmen built this elegant hotel in a variety of styles in 1888
(see p264). Some rooms have original furniture. 📶 TV 🦽 P 🏊

TWENTYNINE PALMS: *Tower Homestead Bed and Breakfast*　$　2
SE corner of Amboy Rd & Mojave Drive, CA 92277. **Road map** D5. (*(760) 367-*
0030. This 100-year-old house, near Joshua Tree National Park *(see pp268–9),*
has a luxurious outdoor spa. The huge rooms have open fireplaces. TV P 🏊

<table>
<tr><td colspan="2">

Price categories for a standard double room per night, inclusive of service charges and any additional taxes, such as local sales tax:

$ under $100
$$ $100–$150
$$$ $150–$200
$$$$ $200–$250
$$$$$ over $250

</td><td>

RESTAURANT
Hotel restaurant or dining room usually open to non-residents unless otherwise stated.

CHILDREN'S FACILITIES
Indicates cribs and/or a baby-sitting service available. A few hotels also provide children's portions and high chairs in the restaurant.

GARDEN/TERRACE
Hotels with a garden, courtyard, or terrace, often providing tables for eating outside.

SWIMMING POOL
Hotel with indoor or outdoor swimming pool.

</td><td>NUMBER OF ROOMS</td><td>RESTAURANT</td><td>CHILDREN'S FACILITIES</td><td>GARDEN/TERRACE</td><td>SWIMMING POOL</td></tr>
</table>

THE MOJAVE DESERT

	Rooms	Rest.	Child.	Gard.	Pool
BARSTOW: *Best Western Desert Villa Motel* $ 1984 E Main St, CA 92311. **Road map** D5. 📞 *(760) 256-1781.* **FAX** *(760) 256-9265.* The 18 mini-suites, 9 of which have an in-room whirlpool bath, make a perfect place for an extended stay in the desert. 🛏 📺 ♿ P 🍴	95	●	■		■
BARSTOW: *El Rancho Motor Court* $ 112 E Main St, CA 92311. **Road map** D5. 📞 *(760) 256-2401.* **FAX** *(760) 256-7421.* Built in 1947 entirely out of railroad ties, this newly refurbished motel is a "must stop" on California's historic Route 66. Elaborate murals depict the famed highway and its surrounding desert life. 🛏 📺 P 🍴	100		●	■	
BARSTOW: *Holiday Inn* $$ 1511 E Main St, CA 92311. **Road map** D5. 📞 *(760) 256-5673.* **FAX** *(760) 256-5917.* The rooms in this clean but basic chain hotel have queen-sized beds and some have whirlpool baths. Free morning newspapers. 🛏 📺 ♿ P 🍴	148	●	■		■
DEATH VALLEY: *Amargosa Hotel and Opera House* $ Death Valley Junction, CA 92328. **Road map** D4. 📞 *(760) 852-4441.* **FAX** *(760) 852-4138.* This 1920s hotel in an old mining town was refurbished by former ballerina Marta Becket, who performs cabaret shows in the small theater. Rooms are air-conditioned; food and drinks are sold. 🛏 P 🍴	14		■		
DEATH VALLEY: *Delight's Hot Spa* $ Tecopa Hot Springs Rd, Tecopa, CA 92389. **Road map** D4. 📞 *(760) 852-4343.* These clean cabins with kitchenettes retain the atmosphere of the 1940s. Healing mineral waters are found in four hot tubs. ♿ P	9				■
DEATH VALLEY: *Shoshone Inn* $ Junction of SR127 & SR178, Shoshone, CA 92384. **Road map** D4. 📞 *(760) 852-4335.* **FAX** *(760) 852-4250.* This simple 1950s brick motel is on the border of Death Valley Park *(see pp280–3)*. There are caves nearby. 🛏 📺 ♿ P 🍴	16	●		●	■
DEATH VALLEY: *Stove Pipe Wells Village* $ Stove Pipe Wells, CA 92328. **Road map** D4. 📞 *(760) 786-2387.* **FAX** *(760) 786-2389.* No telephones make this rustic all-year resort near the Death Valley Sand Dunes *(see p281)* a perfect desert escape. 🛏 📺 ♿ P 🍴	83	●	■		■
DEATH VALLEY: *Furnace Creek Ranch* $$$ 1 Main St (PO Box 1), CA 92328. **Road map** D4. 📞 *(760) 786-2345.* **FAX** *(760) 786-2514.* Children will enjoy the horseback riding at this California ranch with stunning scenery and many deluxe features. 🛏 📺 P 🍴	251	●	■	■	■
DEATH VALLEY: *Furnace Creek Inn* $$$$ 1 Main St, CA 92328. **Road map** D4. 📞 *(760) 786-2345.* **FAX** *(760) 786-2514.* This marvelous, historic resort is one of the most stylish places in the desert, with spring-fed pools, tennis, and golf. 🛏 24 📺 ♿ P 🍴	68	●	■	■	■
EAST MOJAVE: *Hotel Nipton* $ 107355 Nipton Rd (HCL Box #357), CA 92364. **Road map** E5. 📞 *(760) 856-2335.* **FAX** *(760) 856-2352.* This rustic turn-of-the-century hotel is in Nipton, a historic gold-mining town with a population of 40. ♿ P 🍴	4			●	
LAKE HAVASU: *Hidden Palms Allsuite Inn* $ 2100 Swanson Ave, AZ 86403. **Road map** E5. 📞 *(520) 855-7144; (800) 254-5611.* **FAX** *(520) 855-2620.* The one-bedroom suites can accommodate four adults at this quiet inn, close to Lake Havasu *(see p278)*. 🛏 📺 ♿ P 🍴	22		■		■
LAKE HAVASU: *London Bridge Resort* $$ 1477 Queens Bay, AZ 86403. **Road map** E5. 📞 *(520) 855-0888.* **FAX** *(520) 855-2414.* Enjoy fine views of London Bridge *(see p278)* from this resort, with live music in the lounge. There are rental boats and jet skis. 🛏 📺 ♿ P 🍴	150		■	●	■

San Francisco

Chinatown and Nob Hill: *Hotel Astoria* 510 Bush St, CA 94108. **Map 5 C4.** ☎ *(415) 434-8889; (800) 666-6696.* [FAX] *(415) 434-8919.* Conveniently situated between Chinatown and Union Square, this modest hotel has reasonably priced single rooms. 🚿 [TV] 💳	$	80		■		
Chinatown and Nob Hill: *Holiday Inn, Chinatown* 750 Kearny St, CA 94108. **Map 5 C3.** ☎ *(415) 433-6600; (800) 465-4329.* [FAX] *(415) 765-7891.* This chain hotel has a good location near Portsmouth Plaza, close to cable car lines. Children under 19 stay free. 🚿 [TV] ♿ [P] 💳	$$$	565	●	■		■
Chinatown and Nob Hill: *Huntington Hotel* 1075 California St, CA 94108. **Map 5 B4.** ☎ *(415) 474-5400; (800) 652-1539.* [FAX] *(415) 474-6227.* Built in 1922 as luxury apartments atop Nob Hill, the spacious rooms and suites have magnificent views. 🚿 [TV] ♿ *limited.* [P] 💳	$$$	140	●	■		
Chinatown and Nob Hill: *Mark Hopkins Inter-Continental* 999 California St, CA 94108. **Map 5 B4.** ☎ *(415) 392-3434; (800) 327-0200.* [FAX] *(415) 421-3302.* This landmark Nob Hill hotel is known for its striking Art Deco rooftop bar and its spectacular views. 🚿 [TV] ♿ [P] 💳	$$$	392	●	■		
Chinatown and Nob Hill: *The Ritz-Carlton, San Francisco* 600 Stockton St, CA 94108. **Map 5 C4.** ☎ *(415) 296-7465; (800) 241-3333.* [FAX] *(415) 291-0288.* Superb comfort and service are the hallmarks of this historic Beaux-Arts hotel near the top of Nob Hill. 🚿 [24] [TV] ♿ [P] 🍸 💳	$$$	336	●	■		■
Chinatown and Nob Hill: *Fairmont Hotel* 950 Mason St, CA 94108. **Map 5 B4.** ☎ *(415) 772-5000; (800) 527-4727.* [FAX] *(415) 781-3929.* Famous for its gorgeous foyer, this is the grandest hotel on Nob Hill. The panoramic views are unbeatable. 🚿 [24] [TV] ♿ [P] 💳	$$$$	596	●	■		
Chinatown and Nob Hill: *Hotel Triton* 342 Grant Ave, CA 94108. **Map 5 C4.** ☎ *(415) 394-0500; (800) 433-6611.* [FAX] *(415) 394-0555.* Small but stylish, this is the newest hip place to stay. You might even run into a rock star or two. 🚿 [TV] 💳	$$$$$	140	●			
Chinatown and Nob Hill: *Stouffer Renaissance Stanford Court* 905 California St, CA 94108. **Map 5 B4.** ☎ *(415) 989-3500; (800) 622-0957.* [FAX] *(415) 391-0513.* This luxurious Nob Hill retreat caters to busy executives, with opulent rooms and limousine service. 🚿 [24] [TV] ♿ [P] 💳	$$$$$	392	●	■		
Civic Center: *Alamo Square Inn* 719 Scott St, CA 94117. **Map 4 D5.** ☎ *(415) 922-2055; (800) 345-9888.* [FAX] *(415) 931-1304.* These two beautifully restored historic buildings overlook the square. Breakfast is included; no smoking allowed. 🚿 [TV] [P] 💳	$$	15		■		
Civic Center: *Edwardian Inn San Francisco* 1668 Market St, CA 94102. **Map 10 F1.** ☎ *(415) 864-1271.* [FAX] *(415) 861-8116.* This charming, small budget hotel is on a quiet stretch of Market Street, near public transportation and close to restaurants and nightclubs. 💳	$$	36				
Civic Center: *Phoenix Inn* 601 Eddy St, CA 94109. **Map 4 F4.** ☎ *(415) 776-1380; (800) 248-9466.* [FAX] *(415) 885-3109.* This classic 1950s motel has been called the "hippest hotel in town." Rooms on the first floor open on to the courtyard, second floor rooms have balconies. 🚿 [TV] ♿ [P] 💳	$$	44	●	■		■
Civic Center: *Archbishop's Mansion Inn* 1000 Fulton St, CA 94117. **Map 4 D5.** ☎ *(415) 563-7872; (800) 543-5820.* [FAX] *(415) 885-3193.* Inside this imposing 1904 building is an elaborate open staircase. The luxurious rooms are designed around operatic themes, and many have fireplaces with carved mantelpieces. 🚿 [TV] 💳	$$$	15		■		
Civic Center: *Best Western Carriage Inn* 140 7th St, CA 94103. **Map 11 A1.** ☎ *(415) 552-8600; (800) 444-5817.* [FAX] *(415) 863-2529.* There are spacious rooms, some with fireplaces. Transportation from train, bus stations, and Union Square is free. 🚿 [24] [TV] ♿ *limited.* [P] 💳	$$$$	48		■		
Downtown: *Aida Hotel* 1087 Market St, CA 94103. **Map 5 B5.** ☎ *(415) 863-4141; (800) 863-2432.* [FAX] *(415) 863-5151.* This hotel provides very basic accommodations in a bustling part of Downtown San Francisco. The decor is rather outdated, but the rooms are clean and comfortable. [TV] 💳	$	162				

Price categories for a standard double room per night, inclusive of service charges and any additional taxes, such as local sales tax:

$ under $100
$$ $100–$150
$$$ $150–$200
$$$$ $200–$250
$$$$$ over $250

RESTAURANT
Hotel restaurant or dining room usually open to non-residents unless otherwise stated.

CHILDREN'S FACILITIES
Indicates cribs and/or a baby-sitting service available. A few hotels also provide children's portions and high chairs in the restaurant.

GARDEN/TERRACE
Hotels with a garden, courtyard, or terrace, often providing tables for eating outside.

SWIMMING POOL
Hotel with indoor or outdoor swimming pool.

	Price	NUMBER OF ROOMS	RESTAURANT	CHILDREN'S FACILITIES	GARDEN/TERRACE	SWIMMING POOL
DOWNTOWN: *Golden Gate Hotel* 775 Bush St, CA 94108. **Map** 5 B4. ((415) 392-3702; (800) 835-1118. **FAX** (415) 392-6202. Small and charming family-run hotel on Nob Hill, near Union Square. European-style rooms are furnished with antiques. TV P	$	23				
DOWNTOWN: *Adelaide Inn* 5 Isadora Duncan Place (off Taylor St), CA 94102. **Map** 5 B5. ((415) 441-2261. **FAX** (415) 441-0161. This inn, in the tradition of a European *pension*, has simple rooms, shared bathrooms, and a quiet location. TV	$$	18				
DOWNTOWN: *Andrews Hotel* 624 Post St, CA 94109. **Map** 5 B5. ((415) 563-6877; (800) 926-3739. **FAX** (415) 928-6919. Rates include continental breakfast at this small, family-owned hotel near Union Square. Rooms are comfortable. TV	$$	48	●	■		
DOWNTOWN: *Chancellor Hotel* 433 Powell St, CA 94102. **Map** 5 B4. ((415) 362-2004; (800) 428-4748. **FAX** (415) 395-9476. This small hotel in the theater district dates from 1911 and has Edwardian-style beds, bathtubs, and shower fittings. TV P	$$	137	●			
DOWNTOWN: *Clarion Bedford Hotel* 761 Post St, CA 94109. **Map** 5 B5. ((415) 673-6040; (800) 227-5642. **FAX** (415) 563-6739. This 17-story hotel near Union Square has spectacular city views. The plain rooms have minibars and VCRs. TV *limited*.	$$	150	●	■		
DOWNTOWN: *Monticello Inn* 127 Ellis St, CA 94102. **Map** 5 B5. ((415) 392-8800; (800) 669-7777. **FAX** (415) 398-2650. Named after the home of Thomas Jefferson, this intimate hotel is furnished with colonial-style replica antiques. TV P	$$	90	●	■		
DOWNTOWN: *Sheehan Hotel* 620 Sutter St, CA 94102. **Map** 5 B4. ((415) 775-6500; (800) 848-1529. **FAX** (415) 775-3271. This former YWCA has the city's largest indoor pool. Rooms are plain, with fluorescent lighting, but the staff is friendly. TV P	$$	69		■		■
DOWNTOWN: *Crowne Plaza Union Square* 480 Sutter St, CA 94108. **Map** 5 B4. ((415) 398-8900; (888) 218-0808. **FAX** (415) 989-8823. On the Powell Street cable car line, this hotel boasts magnificent views of Nob Hill and Golden Gate Bridge. TV P	$$$	401	●	■		
DOWNTOWN: *Harbor Court Hotel* 165 Steuart St, CA 94105. **Map** 6 E4. ((415) 882-1300; (800) 346-0555. **FAX** (415) 882-1313. This is the only hotel in the city situated right on the waterfront. Rooms are small, but some have good views.	$$$	131	●			
DOWNTOWN: *Hotel Griffon* 155 Steuart St, CA 94105. **Map** 6 E4. ((415) 495-2100; (800) 321-2201. **FAX** (415) 495-3522. Some of the rooms in this elegant hotel have views of the Golden Gate Bridge. Popular with business travelers. TV P	$$$	62	●			
DOWNTOWN: *Kensington Park Hotel* 450 Post St, CA 94102. **Map** 5 B5. ((415) 788-6400; (800) 553-1900. **FAX** (415) 399-9484. Close to Union Square, this Spanish-Revival hotel has a beautiful lobby, spacious rooms, and continental breakfast. TV *limited*. P	$$$	86		■		
DOWNTOWN: *The Maxwell Hotel* 386 Geary St, CA 94102. **Map** 5 B5. ((415) 986-2000; (888) 734-6299. **FAX** (415) 397-2447. Situated at the heart of the city's Theater District (*see p310*), this older property is spacious and sunny and has good views. TV	$$$	152	●	■		

DOWNTOWN: *Hotel Rex* $$$ 94
562 Sutter St, CA 94102. **Map 5 B4.** [*(415) 433-4434; (800) 433-4434.* FAX *(415) 433-3695.* Recently refurbished, with European style and decor, this hotel has comfortable, quiet rooms and a helpful staff. TV limited.

DOWNTOWN: *San Francisco Marriott* $$$ 1500
55 4th St, CA 94103. **Map 5 C5.** [*(415) 896-1600; (800) 228-9290.* FAX *(415) 777-2799.* This futuristic-style, 39-story tower hotel is popular with convention groups. Children under 18 stay free. TV P

DOWNTOWN: *White Swan Inn* $$$ 26
845 Bush St, CA 94108. **Map 5 B4.** [*(415) 775-1755; (800) 999-9570.* FAX *(415) 775-5717.* Rooms in this small, country-style hotel are bright with floral prints and artificial fireplaces places. English breakfast is included. TV

DOWNTOWN: *York Hotel* $$$ 96
940 Sutter St, CA 94109. **Map 5 A4.** [*(415) 885-6800; (800) 808-9675.* FAX *(415) 885-2115.* There are comfortable, quiet rooms, and a small cabaret show in the bar. The staircase was in Hitchcock's *Vertigo.* TV limited.

DOWNTOWN: *Argent Hotel* $$$$ 667
50 3rd St, CA 94103. **Map 5 C5.** [*(415) 974-6400; (800) 434-7347.* FAX *(415) 543-8268.* Views from the floor-to-ceiling windows of this luxurious hotel are breathtaking. It has good weekend discounts. TV P

DOWNTOWN: *Campton Place Hotel* $$$$ 117
340 Stockton St, CA 94108. **Map 5 C4.** [*(415) 781-5555; (800) 235-4300.* FAX *(415) 955-5536.* This small, elegant hotel off Union Square offers plush rooms, good service, and sumptuous lobbies. 24 TV P

DOWNTOWN: *Grand Hyatt San Francisco* $$$$ 693
345 Stockton St, CA 94108. **Map 5 C4.** [*(415) 398-1234; (800) 233-1234.* FAX *(415) 391-1780.* Rooms in this 36-story tower on Union Square have good views and all the amenities of a large hotel chain. TV P

DOWNTOWN: *Parc Fifty Five* $$$$ 1009
55 Cyril Magnin Street, CA 94102. **Map 5 C5.** [*(415) 392-8000; (800) 650-7272.* FAX *(415) 421-5993.* This huge hotel is not very stylish for the price, but the special weekend offers make it worth considering. TV P

DOWNTOWN: *Prescott Hotel* $$$$ 166
545 Post St, CA 94102. **Map 5 B5.** [*(415) 563-0303; (800) 283-7322.* FAX *(415) 563-6831.* Business travelers predominate at this luxurious hotel, which is decorated like a gentlemen's club with dark wood walls. TV P

DOWNTOWN: *San Francisco Hilton* $$$$ 2044
333 O'Farrell St, CA 94102. **Map 5 B5.** [*(415) 771-1400; (800) 445-8667.* FAX *(415) 771-6807.* The city's largest hotel has excellent views from its 46-story tower. It has good service and numerous facilities. TV P

DOWNTOWN: *Sir Francis Drake Hotel* $$$$ 417
450 Powell St, CA 94102. **Map 5 B4.** [*(415) 392-7755; (800) 227-5480.* FAX *(415) 391-8719.* Now restored to its Art Deco splendor, this Union Square hotel is famous for its Beefeater doormen and rooftop bar. TV P

DOWNTOWN: *The Savoy Hotel* $$$$ 83
580 Geary St, CA 94102. **Map 5 B5.** [*(415) 441-2700; (800) 227-4223.* FAX *(415) 441-0124.* Elegance, helpful service, and feather beds with are the hallmarks here. Continental breakfast and afternoon tea are included. TV

DOWNTOWN: *Westin St. Francis* $$$$ 1189
335 Powell St, CA 94102. **Map 5 B4.** [*(415) 397-7000; (800) 228-3000.* FAX *(415) 774-0124.* The triple towers of this landmark hotel have defined Union Square's skyline since 1904. 24 TV P

DOWNTOWN: *Four Seasons Clift Hotel* $$$$$ 329
495 Geary St, CA 94102. **Map 5 B5.** [*(415) 775-4700; (800) 652-5438.* FAX *(415) 441-4621.* Well-appointed rooms, an old-fashioned ambience, and gracious service characterize this fine hotel. 24 TV P

DOWNTOWN: *Hotel Nikko* $$$$$ 521
222 Mason St, CA 94102. **Map 5 B5.** [*(415) 394-1111; (800) NIKKO-US.* FAX *(415) 394-1106.* This ultra-modern hotel caters to business travelers, especially Japanese, with top-notch services and facilities. 24 TV P

For key to symbols see back flap

Price categories for a standard double room per night, inclusive of service charges and any additional taxes, such as local sales tax:

$ under $100
$$ $100–$150
$$$ $150–$200
$$$$ $200–$250
$$$$$ over $250

RESTAURANT
Hotel restaurant or dining room usually open to non-residents unless otherwise stated.

CHILDREN'S FACILITIES
Indicates cribs and/or a baby-sitting service available. A few hotels also provide children's portions and high chairs in the restaurant.

GARDEN/TERRACE
Hotels with a garden, courtyard, or terrace, often providing tables for eating outside.

SWIMMING POOL
Hotel with indoor or outdoor swimming pool.

	NUMBER OF ROOMS	RESTAURANT	CHILDREN'S FACILITIES	GARDEN/TERRACE	SWIMMING POOL
DOWNTOWN: *Hyatt Regency San Francisco* $$$$$ 5 Embarcadero Center, CA 94111. **Map 6 D3.** ((415) 788-1234; (800) 233-1234. FAX (415) 398-2567. Built around a 15-story atrium lobby, this hotel is part of the prestigious Hyatt chain. It has recently been renovated and its rooms upgraded. ⏰ 24 TV & P 🌿	803	●	■		
DOWNTOWN: *Mandarin Oriental* $$$$$ 222 Sansome St, CA 94104. **Map 5 C4.** ((415) 885-0999; (800) 622-0404. FAX (415) 433-0289. This luxury hotel at the top of the 48-story First Interstate Center has magnificent views. ⏰ 24 TV & P 🌿	158	●	■		
DOWNTOWN: *Pan Pacific* $$$$$ 500 Post St, CA 94102. **Map 5 B5.** ((415) 771-8600; (800) 533-6465. FAX (415) 398-0267. The public areas are glamorous, the bedrooms elegant at this modern hotel with a 17-story atrium. ⏰ 24 TV & P 🌿	331	●	■		
DOWNTOWN: *Park Hyatt San Francisco* $$$$$ 333 Battery St, CA 94111. **Map 6 D3.** ((415) 392-1234; (800) 233-1234. FAX (415) 421-2433. Located next to the Embarcadero Center (*see p304*), this is the most luxurious Hyatt in San Francisco. The hotel offers week- end rates that provide particularly good value. ⏰ 24 TV & P 🌿	360	●	■		
DOWNTOWN: *Sheraton Palace Hotel* $$$$$ 2 New Montgomery St, CA 94105. **Map 5 C4.** ((415) 392-8600; (800) 325-3535. FAX (415) 543-0671. At the turn of the century the Palace was one of the world's most famous hotels and a favorite of visiting VIPs. Today its focal point is the glamorous Garden Court. ⏰ 24 TV & P 🌿	550	●	■	●	■
FISHERMAN'S WHARF: *San Remo Hotel* $ 2237 Mason St, CA 94133. **Map 5 B2.** ((415) 776-8688; (800) 352-REMO. FAX (415) 776-2811. The area's only budget hotel is known for its friendly atmosphere. It has shared bathrooms, except for the Honeymoon Suite. 🌿	62				
FISHERMAN'S WHARF: *Hyatt at Fisherman's Wharf* $$$ 555 North Point, CA 94133. **Map 5 A1.** ((415) 563-1234; (800) 233-1234. FAX (415) 749-6122. More family-orientated than the city's other Hyatts, it has good service and family discounts on a second room. ⏰ TV & 🔧 P 🌿	313	●	■		■
FISHERMAN'S WHARF: *Sheraton at Fisherman's Wharf* $$$ 2500 Mason St, CA 94133. **Map 5 B1.** ((415) 362-5500; (800) 325-3535. FAX (415) 956-5275. This family-oriented, tourist hotel is also popular with business people and has easy access to many attractions. ⏰ TV & P 🌿	525	●	■		■
FISHERMAN'S WHARF: *Suites at Fisherman's Wharf* $$$ 2655 Hyde St, CA 94109. **Map 5 A2.** ((415) 771-0200; (800) 227-3608. FAX (415) 346-8058. Efficiency (self-catering) suites are available at this pleasant hotel and are spacious enough to accommodate four people in comfort. ⏰ TV & limited. P 🌿	24		■		
FISHERMAN'S WHARF: *Tuscan Inn* $$$ 425 North Point St, CA 94133. **Map 5 B1.** ((415) 561-1100; (800) 648-4626. FAX (415) 561-1199. Children under 18 stay free at this spacious, stylish hotel with large rooms and local limousine service. ⏰ TV & P 🌿	221	●	■		
HAIGHT ASHBURY: *Beck's Motor Lodge* $$ 2222 Market St, CA 94114. **Map 10 E1.** ((415) 621-8212; (800) 227-4360. FAX (415) 241-0435. Handy for the Castro and Mission districts, this standard 1960s motel has a quiet location and low out-of-season rates. ⏰ TV P 🌿	57				
HAIGHT ASHBURY: *Red Victorian Bed and Breakfast* $$ 1665 Haight St, CA 94117. **Map 9 B1.** ((415) 864-1978. FAX (415) 863-3293. This unique hotel offers New Age accommodation in themed rooms such as the Flower Child Suite; no radios, TVs, or smoking. ⏰ 🌿	18				

HAIGHT ASHBURY: *Victorian Inn on the Park* $$ 12
301 Lyon St, CA 94117. **Map 9 C1.** ((415) 931-1830; (800) 435-1967. FAX (415) 931-1830. Housed in a mansion opposite Golden Gate Park, this stylish bed-and-breakfast hotel has Arts and Crafts reproduction furniture.

HAIGHT ASHBURY: *Stanyan Park Hotel* $$$ 36
750 Stanyan St, CA 94117. **Map 9 B2.** ((415) 751-1000. FAX (415) 668-5454. This comfortable hotel overlooking Golden Gate Park has antique furnishings and fireplaces. Breakfast is included. TV limited.

NORTH BEACH: *Washington Square Inn* $$ 15
1660 Stockton St, CA 94133. **Map 5 B2.** ((415) 981-4220; (800) 388-0220. FAX (415) 397-7242. Smoking is not allowed at this bed-and-breakfast hotel facing Washington Square Park. Children under five stay free. P

PACIFIC HEIGHTS: *Art Center Bed & Breakfast* $ 5
1902 Filbert St, CA 94123. **Map 4 E2.** ((415) 567-1526. This small, pretty New Orleans-style house is one of the Marina's oldest buildings and dates from 1857. One-, two- and three-room suites are available.

PACIFIC HEIGHTS: *Motel Capri* $ 46
2015 Greenwich St, CA 94123. **Map 4 D2.** ((415) 346-4667. FAX (415) 346-3256. This family-owned motel in a quiet residential street at the center of the Marina district is good for budget travelers. TV P

PACIFIC HEIGHTS: *Pacific Heights Inn* $ 40
1555 Union St, CA 94123. **Map 4 E2.** ((415) 776-3310; (800) 523-1801. FAX (415) 776-8176. This pleasant 1960s-era motel in a quiet street near public transportation and serves continental breakfast. TV limited. P

PACIFIC HEIGHTS: *Travel Lodge by the Bay* $ 36
1450 Lombard St, CA 94109. **Map 4 F2.** ((415) 673-0691. FAX (415) 673-3232. The standard motel rooms, in a 1950s ranch-style building, are rather noisy but handy for public transportation. TV P

PACIFIC HEIGHTS: *Bed and Breakfast Inn* $$ 11
4 Charlton Court, CA 94123. **Map 4 E3.** ((415) 921-9784. In a quiet cul-de-sac off Union Street, the city's oldest bed-and-breakfast hotel was once a Victorian farmhouse. Guests can use the library. limited. P

PACIFIC HEIGHTS: *Chateâu Tivoli* $$ 8
1057 Steiner St, CA 94115. **Map 11 A1.** ((415) 776-5462; (800) 228-1647. FAX (415) 776-0505. Guests are given a taste of 19th-century San Francisco in this friendly Victorian house furnished with authentic antiques.

PACIFIC HEIGHTS: *Holiday Inn, Golden Gateway* $$ 498
1500 Van Ness Ave, CA 94109. **Map 4 F4.** ((415) 441-4000; (800) HOLIDAY. FAX (415) 776-7155. Popular with groups, this 26-story modern tower is within easy access of the rest of the city. TV limited. P

PACIFIC HEIGHTS: *Marina Inn* $$ 40
3110 Octavia St, CA 94123. **Map 4 E2.** ((415) 928-1000; (800) 346-6118. FAX (415) 928-5909. The hotel has a good location, near Fort Mason and Union Street, but the traffic noise can be intrusive. TV limited.

PACIFIC HEIGHTS: *Edward II Inn and Suites* $$$ 39
3155 Scott St at Lombard, CA 94123. **Map 4 D2.** ((415) 922-3000; (800) 473-2846. FAX (415) 931-5784. Close to Yacht Harbor, this quiet, three-story 1949 house offers free breakfasts and afternoon sherry. TV P

PACIFIC HEIGHTS: *Majestic Hotel* $$$ 57
1500 Sutter St, CA 94109. **Map 4 E4.** ((415) 441-1100; (800) 869-8966. FAX (415) 673-7331. Most rooms in this ornate hotel have canopied beds, open fireplaces, and antiques. It is in a quiet area. 24 TV limited. P

PACIFIC HEIGHTS: *Miyako Hotel* $$$$ 218
1625 Post St, CA 94115. **Map 4 E4.** ((415) 921-4000; (800) 533-4567. FAX (415) 923-1064. Some rooms have steam baths or tatami mats in this stylish hotel in the Japan Center. Children under 12 stay free. TV P

PACIFIC HEIGHTS: *Sherman House* $$$$$ 14
2160 Green St, CA 94123. **Map 4 D3.** ((415) 563-3600; (800) 424-5777. FAX (415) 563-1882. Publicity-shy stars favor this quiet, luxuriously appointed small hotel. Rooms have antiques and woodburning fireplaces. TV

Price categories for a standard double room per night, inclusive of service charges and any additional taxes, such as local sales tax:
$ under $100
$$ $100–$150
$$$ $150–$200
$$$$ $200–$250
$$$$$ over $250

RESTAURANT
Hotel restaurant or dining room usually open to non-residents unless otherwise stated.

CHILDREN'S FACILITIES
Indicates cribs and/or a baby-sitting service available. A few hotels also provide children's portions and high chairs in the restaurant.

GARDEN/TERRACE
Hotels with a garden, courtyard, or terrace, often providing tables for eating outside.

SWIMMING POOL
Hotel with indoor or outdoor swimming pool.

THE BAY AREA

	NUMBER OF ROOMS	RESTAURANT	CHILDREN'S FACILITIES	GARDEN/TERRACE	SWIMMING POOL
BENICIA: *Captain Walsh House* $$ 235 E L St, CA 94510. **Road map** inset B 【 *(707) 747-5653*. FAX *(707) 747-6265*. This Gothic-style bed-and-breakfast inn near the ocean was named one of the top three in the US by *Better Homes & Gardens* magazine. 🛏 📺 ♿ 🅿 ✉	5			●	
BENICIA: *Union Hotel* $$ 401 1st St, CA 94510. **Road map** inset B. 【 *(707) 746-0100*. FAX *(707) 746-6458*. Some rooms here have views of the docks, while others enjoy a quiet garden setting. All are decorated with antiques. 🛏 📺 🅿 ✉	22	●		●	
BERKELEY: *Bancroft Hotel* $ 2680 Bancroft Way, CA 94704. **Road map** inset B. 【 *(510) 549-1000; (800) 549-1002*. FAX *(510) 549-1070*. This elegant 1920s Arts and Crafts hotel opposite the university was formerly a private women's club. Some of the spacious rooms have balconies with views of the hills and the bay. 🛏 📺 🅿 ✉	22		▨	●	
BERKELEY: *Gramma's Rose Garden Inn* $$ 2740 Telegraph Ave, CA 94705. **Road map** inset B. 【 *(510) 549-2145*. FAX *(510) 549-1085*. Some rooms in this gorgeous Victorian mansion have fireplaces and balconies. Full breakfast is included. 🛏 📺 ♿ 🅿 ✉	40	●	▨	●	
BERKELEY: *Hotel Durant* $$$ 2600 Durant Ave, CA 94704. **Road map** inset B. 【 *(510) 845-8981; (800) 238-7268*. FAX *(510) 486-8336*. This central hotel is large without being impersonal. Some of the spacious rooms have bay views. 🛏 📺 ♿ 🅿 ✉	140	●	▨		
BERKELEY: *Claremont Resort, Spa, and Tennis Club* $$$$ 41 Tunnel Road, Oakland, CA 94623. **Road Map** inset B. 【 *(510) 843-3000; (800) 843-7924*. FAX *(510) 549-8582*. With its Spanish Revival bell tower, this beautiful building at the foot of the Berkeley Hills is the area's grandest old hotel *(see p402)* and has wonderful views. 🛏 📺 ♿ 🅿 ✉	239	●	●	●	▨
BOLINAS: *Smiley's Schooner Saloon and Hotel* $ 41 Wharf Rd, CA 94924. **Road map** inset B. 【 *(415) 868-1311*. FAX *(415) 868-0502*. Straight out of a Hollywood Western, this hotel is directly above the bar. It is friendly and comfortable but noisy in the evenings. 🛏 🅿 ✉	5			●	
HALF MOON BAY: *Zaballa House* $$ 324 Main St, CA 94019. **Road map** inset B. 【 *(650) 726-9123*. Quaint, country-style accommodations are provided in a converted farmhouse, surrounded by lush gardens. Full breakfast is included. 🛏 🅿 ✉	9			●	
HALF MOON BAY: *Mill Rose Inn* $$$ 615 Mill St, CA 94019. **Road map** inset B. 【 *(650) 726-8750; (800) 900-7673*. FAX *(650) 726-3031*. Rooms at this bed-and-breakfast inn have VCRs, fireplaces, and midweek rates. No children under 10 allowed. 🛏 📺 🅿 ✉	6			●	
INVERNESS: *Manka's Inverness Lodge* $$ Corner of Argyle & Callendar, CA 94937. **Road map** A3. 【 *(415) 669-1034*. FAX *(415) 669-1598*. The cabins and rooms of this romantic, rustic retreat feature balconies, fireplaces and views of Tomales Bay. 🛏 📺 🅿 ✉	11	●	▨	●	
LAFAYETTE: *Lafayette Park Hotel* $$$ 3287 Mount Diablo Blvd, CA 94549. **Road map** inset B. 【 *(925) 283-3700; (800) 368-2468*. FAX *(925) 284-1621*. Just east of Berkeley, this hotel has an award-winning bar and restaurant, a whirlpool, and sauna. 🛏 📺 ♿ 🅿 ✉	139	●	▨	●	▨
MENLO PARK: *Mermaid Inn* $ 727 El Camino Real, CA 94025. **Road map** inset B. 【 *(650) 323-9481; (800) 237-4622*. FAX *(650) 323-0662*. This plain, modern family-owned hotel is near Palo Alto and convenient for Stanford University. 🛏 📺 ♿ 🅿 ✉	39		▨	●	

MENLO PARK: *Stanford Park Hotel* $$$$$ 162
100 El Camino Real, CA 94025. **Road map** inset B. ((650) 322-1234.
FAX (650) 322-0975. Many of these elegantly appointed rooms near Stanford University have fireplaces and separate sitting areas. 🛏 24 📺 🅿 ☺

MILL VALLEY: *Travelodge* $ 55
707 Redwood Hwy, CA 94941. **Road map** inset B. ((415) 383-0340; (800) 578-7878. FAX (415) 383-0312. Just west of Tiburon, this motel is close to Muir Woods and the city. Some rooms have Jacuzzis. 🛏 📺 ♿ 🅿 ☺

MOSS BEACH: *Seal Cove Inn* $$$ 10
221 Cypress Ave, CA 94038. **Road map** inset B. ((650) 728-7325; (800) 995-9987. FAX (650) 728-4116. Set on a hill overlooking the ocean, this charming inn has fireplaces in the rooms and a free video library. 🛏 📺 ♿ 🅿 ☺

MUIR BEACH: *The Pelican Inn* $$$ 7
10 Pacifica Way, CA 94965. **Road map** inset B. ((415) 383-6000. FAX (415) 383-3424. Roaring fireplaces, British beers, and gorgeous rooms, some with four-poster beds, are all within walking distance of Muir Woods. 🛏 ♿ 🅿 ☺

OAKLAND: *Waterfront Plaza Hotel* $$$$ 144
10 Washington St, CA 94607. **Road map** inset B. ((510) 836-3800. FAX (510) 832-5695. Many rooms have fireplaces and views across the bay at this well-appointed hotel at the edge of Jack London Square. 🛏 📺 🅿 ☺

PRINCETON-BY-THE-SEA: *Pillar Point Inn* $$$ 11
380 Capistrano Rd, CA 94018. **Road map** inset B. ((650) 728-7377. FAX (650) 728-8345. All the rooms at this romantic inn have ocean views, fireplaces, feather mattresses, and VCRs; business services available. 🛏 📺 ♿ 🅿 ☺

SAN JOSE: *Fairmont Hotel San Jose* $$$ 541
Fairmont Plaza, 170 S Market St, CA 95113. **Road map** inset B. ((408) 998-1900; (800) 527-4727. FAX (408) 287-1648. This rather impersonal luxury hotel has excellent business and leisure facilities. 🛏 24 📺 ♿ 🅿 🍴 ☺

SAN JOSE: *San Jose Hilton and Towers Hotel* $$$ 355
300 Almaden Blvd, CA 95110. **Road map** inset B. ((408) 287-2100; (800) 445-8667. FAX (408) 947-4489. This chain hotel is well equipped for the business traveler. Each floor has its own concierge. 🛏 📺 ♿ 🅿 ☺

SAN JOSE: *Hotel De Anza* $$$$$ 101
233 West Santa Clara St, CA 95113. **Road map** inset B. ((408) 286-1000; (800) 843-3700. FAX (408) 286-0500. The emphasis is on personal attention at this luxurious Art Deco hotel near the convention center. 🛏 📺 ♿ 🅿 ☺

SAN RAFAEL: *Panama Hotel* $ 15
4 Bayview, CA 94901. **Road map** inset B. ((415) 457-3993. FAX (415) 457-6240.
Each room at this hotel has its own distinct character, eclectically furnished with antique and second-hand furniture. 🛏 📺 ♿ 🅿 ☺

SAN RAFAEL: *Embassy Suites Hotel and Conference Center* $$ 228
101 McInnis Parkway, CA 94903. **Road map** inset B. ((415) 499-9222; (800) 362-2779. FAX (415) 499-9268. This large chain hotel has basic rooms, a business center and 24-hour access to leisure facilities. 🛏 📺 ♿ 🅿 🍴 ☺

SAUSALITO: *Hotel Alta Mira* $$ 30
125 Bulkley Ave (PO Box 706), CA 94966. **Road map** inset B. ((415) 332-1350.
FAX (415) 331-3862. Set on a hill with exceptional views of the bay, rooms here are comfortably furnished and the staff is welcoming. 🛏 🅿 ☺

SAUSALITO: *Casa Madrona Hotel* $$$ 32
801 Bridgeway, CA 94965. **Road map** inset B. ((415) 332-0502. FAX (415) 332-2537. Climbing up the hillside from the waterfront, this lovely hotel has distinctive rooms in an old house and adjacent cottages. 🛏 📺 🅿 ☺

SAUSALITO: *The Inn Above Tide* $$$ 30
30 El Portal, CA 94965. **Road map** inset B. ((415) 332-9535; (800) 893-8433.
FAX (415) 332-6714. Rooms at this relaxing harbor-front hotel have fireplaces and balconies over the bay; some have Jacuzzis. 🛏 24 📺 ♿ 🅿 ☺

WALNUT CREEK: *Marriott Hotel* $$ 337
2355 N Main St, CA 94596. **Road map** inset B. ((800) 228-9290.
FAX (925) 934-2000. This well-appointed hotel has a variety of conference facilities catering to business travelers. 🛏 📺 ♿ 🅿 ☺

Price categories for a standard double room per night, inclusive of service charges and any additional taxes, such as local sales tax:
$ under $100
$$ $100–$150
$$$ $150–$200
$$$$ $200–$250
$$$$$ over $250

Restaurant
Hotel restaurant or dining room usually open to non-residents unless otherwise stated.
Children's Facilities
Indicates cribs and/or a baby-sitting service available. A few hotels also provide children's portions and high chairs in the restaurant.
Garden/Terrace
Hotels with a garden, courtyard, or terrace, often providing tables for eating outside.
Swimming Pool
Hotel with indoor or outdoor swimming pool.

The North

	Number of Rooms	Restaurant	Children's Facilities	Garden/Terrace	Swimming Pool
Arcata: *Fairwinds Motel* $ 1674 G St, CA 95521. **Road map A2.** ☎ *(707) 822-4824.* This small, family-owned hotel, close to Arcata's Humboldt State University, provides reasonably priced but basic accommodations. 🛁 [TV] ♿ *limited.* [P] 💳	27		■		
Arcata: *Hotel Arcata* $$ 708 9th St, CA 95521. **Road map A2.** ☎ *(707) 826-0217.* [FAX] *(707) 826-1737.* This fully modernized hotel on the central square has a wide range of rooms, some of which have separate sitting areas. 🛁 [TV] 💳	32	●	■		
Crescent City: *Curley Redwood Lodge* $ 701 S Redwood Hwy, CA 95531. **Road map A1.** ☎ *(707) 464-2137.* [FAX] *(707) 464-1655.* Located just across the water from the harbor area, this rustic-style motel was constructed from a single redwood tree. 🛁 [TV] [P] 💳	36		■		
Dunsmuir: *Caboose Motel* $ 100 Railroad Park Rd, CA 96025. **Road map B2.** ☎ *(530) 235-4440.* [FAX] *(530) 235-4470.* The unusual rooms housed in renovated cabooses have a pleasant setting with stunning views of the nearby peaks. 🛁 [TV] [P] 💳	27	●	■	●	■
Eureka: *Best Western Humboldt Bay Inn* $ 232 W 5th St, CA 95501. **Road map A2.** ☎ *(707) 443-2234; (800) 521-6996.* [FAX] *(707) 443-3489.* Stunning redwood forests and beaches lie just a 15-minute drive away from this rather basic chain motel. 🛁 [TV] ♿ [P] 💳	114	●	■		■
Eureka: *Quality Inn* $ 1209 4th St, CA 95501. **Road map A2.** ☎ *(707) 443-1601.* [FAX] *(707) 444-8365.* Along with a prime location at the heart of Eureka's Old Town, this hotel offers spacious rooms and suites, plus a sauna. 🛁 [TV] [P] 💳	60	●	■		■
Eureka: *Eureka Inn* $$ 518 7th St, CA 95501. **Road map A2.** ☎ *(707) 442-6441.* [FAX] *(707) 442-0637.* Tudor-style architecture gives this large historic hotel an old-fashioned atmosphere. Top-quality facilities include a sauna and business services, as well as a good restaurant, the Rib Room *(see p569).* 🛁 [TV] [P] 💳	105	●	■		■
Eureka: *Carter House Country Inn* $$$ 301 L St, CA 95501. **Road map A2.** ☎ *(707) 444-8062; (800) 404-1390.* [FAX] *(707) 444-8067.* The rooms in this Victorian hotel in Old Town Eureka have contemporary furnishings. Close to forests and beaches. 🛁 [TV] ♿ [P] 💳	24	●		●	
Ferndale: *Gingerbread Mansion* $$ 400 Berding St, CA 95536. **Road map A2.** ☎ *(707) 786-4000; (800) 952-4136.* [FAX] *(707) 786-4381.* Surrounded by delightful gardens, this ornate inn dates from 1899. Rooms are luxuriously appointed, and a deluxe breakfast is included. 🛁 [P] 💳	11		■	●	
Garberville: *Humboldt House Inn* $ 701 Redwood Drive, CA 95542. **Road map A2.** ☎ *(707) 923-2771.* [FAX] *(707) 923-4259.* The most comfortable motel in redwood country has large rooms, most with balconies. Continental breakfast is included. 🛁 [TV] [P] 💳	76		■	●	■
Garberville: *Benbow Inn* $$$ 445 Lake Benbow Drive, CA 95542. **Road map A2.** ☎ *(707) 923-2124; (800) 355-3301.* [FAX] *(707) 923-2897.* Built in 1924, this landmark inn looks like an English country house amid the redwood groves. It has an opulent restaurant and sunny terrace; it is closed from January to March. 🛁 [TV] [P] 💳	55	●	■	●	■
McCloud: *McCloud Guest House* $$ 606 W Colombero Drive, CA 96057. **Road map B1.** ☎ *(530) 964-3160.* A lumber baron built this old mansion; rooms have window seats looking out over the forest. Guests can also use the antique billiards table. 🛁 [TV] [P] 💳	5	●		●	

MOUNT LASSEN: *Mineral Lodge* $ 20
O Box 160 Mineral, CA 96063. **Road map** B2. ((530) 595-4422. Popular
with hunters and hikers, this rustic lodge offers motel-style rooms, plus
a tavern and general store. It is on the southern fringes of Lassen
Volcanic National Park (see p437). 📶 TV P 🗐

MOUNT SHASTA: *Mount Shasta Ranch Bed and Breakfast* $ 8
1008 W A Barr Rd, CA 96067. **Road map** A2. ((530) 926-3870. This rustic retreat
has amazing views of Mount Shasta (see p436). Half the rooms are in the
spacious main house, the others are in the smaller carriage house with
shared bathrooms. A big country breakfast is included. TV P 🗐

MOUNT SHASTA: *Mountain Air Lodge* $ 38
121 S Mount Shasta Blvd, CA 96067. **Road map** A2. ((530) 926-3411; (800)
727-3704. This simple lodge-style hotel is in a wonderful mountain setting.
Ski slopes and water-sports facilities are just a short drive away. TV P 🗐

MOUNT SHASTA: *Strawberry Valley Inn* $ 15
1142 S Mount Shasta Blvd, CA 96067. **Road map** A2. ((530) 926-2052.
Popular with skiers, reservations are recommended at this quiet inn with
views of Mount Shasta. Each room has a different theme. 📶 TV & P 🗐

MOUNT SHASTA: *Tree House Inn* $ 95
111 Morgan Way, CA 96067. **Road map** A2. ((530) 926-3101. FAX (530) 926-
3542. Furniture and fixtures made of redwood add to the cozy ambience
of this modern motel. Some rooms have mountain views. 📶 TV P 🗐

SCOTIA: *Scotia Inn* $$ 11
100 Main Street, CA 95565. **Road map** A2. ((707) 764-5684. FAX (707) 764-1707.
Built for workers at Scotia's massive lumber mill (see p431), this beautiful
inn is a showcase of redwood craftsmanship. The renovated rooms feature
such period furnishings as canopy beds and claw-foot bathtubs. 📶 TV P 🗐

WEAVERVILLE: *Motel Trinity* $ 25
1112 Main St, CA 96093. **Road map** A2. ((530) 623-2129. FAX (530) 623-6007.
Accommodations in this small motel range from single rooms to two-
bedroom suites with kitchenettes. Some rooms have Jacuzzis. 📶 TV 🗐

WEAVERVILLE: *Victorian Inn* $ 61
1709 Main St, CA 96093. **Road map** A2. ((530) 623-4432.
Located at the edge of a historic mountain town (see p433), this medium-
sized motel offers spacious modern rooms. 📶 TV P 🗐

WEAVERVILLE: *Weaverville Hotel* $ 8
201 Main St, CA 96093. **Road map** A2. ((530) 623-3121. For a true taste of
old Weaverville, spend the night at this bargain-priced, old-fashioned hotel,
which occupies the upper floors of a historic building. 📶 TV P 🗐

WINE COUNTRY

BODEGA BAY: *Bodega Coast Inn* W www.bodegacoastinn.com $$$ 45
521 Hwy 1 (PO Box 55), CA 94923. **Road map** A3. ((707) 875-2217; (800) 346-
6999. FAX (707) 875-2964. This modern hotel, a stone's throw from the beach,
has a spa, spectacular views, and fireplaces in some rooms. 📶 TV & P 🗐

BOYES HOT SPRINGS: *Sonoma Mission Inn & Spa* $$$ 168
18140 Sonoma Hwy 12, CA 95476. **Road map** A3. ((707) 938-9000; (800) 862-
4945. FAX (707) 935-1205. Established in the mid-19th century, this inn has
luxurious rooms, many with fireplaces, and tennis courts. 📶 TV & P 🗐

CALISTOGA: *Calistoga Spa Hot Springs Resort Motel* $$ 57
1006 Washington St, CA 94515. **Road map** A3. ((707) 942-6269. This
friendly motel with mineral soaking pools and spa facilities (including
mud baths and massages) is perfect for families. 📶 TV & P 🍴 🗐

CALISTOGA: *Comfort Inn* $$ 55
1865 Lincoln Ave, CA 94515. **Road map** A3. ((707) 942-9400; (800) 228-5150.
FAX (707) 942-5262. This pleasant hotel has a mineral-water pool, as well
as a whirlpool, steam room, and sauna. 📶 TV & P 🗐

GEYSERVILLE: *Geyserville Inn* $$ 38
21714 Geyserville Ave, CA 95441. **Road map** A3. ((707) 857-4343; (877) 857-4343.
Surrounded by vineyards and more than 70 wineries, this inn offers a spa, an
outdoor events center, and complimentary Continental breakfasts. 📶 TV P 🗐

| | | **Price categories** for a standard double room per night, inclusive of service charges and any additional taxes, such as local sales tax:
$ under $100
$$ $100–$150
$$$ $150–$200
$$$$ $200–$250
$$$$$ over $250 | **RESTAURANT**
Hotel restaurant or dining room usually open to non-residents unless otherwise stated.
CHILDREN'S FACILITIES
Indicates cribs and/or a baby-sitting service available. A few hotels also provide children's portions and high chairs in the restaurant.
GARDEN/TERRACE
Hotels with a garden, courtyard, or terrace, often providing tables for eating outside.
SWIMMING POOL
Hotel with indoor or outdoor swimming pool. |

	NUMBER OF ROOMS	RESTAURANT	CHILDREN'S FACILITIES	GARDEN/TERRACE	SWIMMING POOL
GUALALA: *Whale Watch Inn* $$$ 535100 Hwy 1, CA 95445. **Road map** A3. ☎ *(707) 884-3667.* **FAX** *(707) 884-4815.* Perched on a bluff above the ocean, this hotel has spectacular views from every room. All rooms have fireplaces and balconies, some have whirlpool baths, and none have phones or TVs. Breakfast is included.	18			●	
HEALDSBURG: *Dry Creek Inn* $ 198 Dry Creek Rd, CA 95448. **Road map** A3. ☎ *(707) 433-0300; (800) 222-5784.* **FAX** *(707) 433-1129.* Part of the Best Western chain, this hotel has spacious rooms, a spa, and is convenient for the local wineries.	103		▦		
HEALDSBURG: *Camellia Inn* $$ 211 North St, CA 95448. **Road map** A3. ☎ *(707) 433-8182; (800) 727-8182.* **FAX** *(707) 433-8130.* This lovely, Italianate Victorian bed-and-breakfast inn has some rooms with fireplaces and whirlpool baths.	9		▦	●	▦
HEALDSBURG: *Madrona Manor* $$$ 1001 Westside Rd, CA 95448. **Road map** A3. ☎ *(707) 433-4231; (800) 258-4003.* **FAX** *(707) 433-0703.* This Victorian mansion is surrounded by vineyards and wineries. Some rooms have fireplaces and claw-foot bathtubs or Jacuzzis, as well as private terraces or balconies.	21	●	▦	●	▦
MENDOCINO: *Mendocino Hotel* $$ 45080 Main St (PO Box 587), CA 95460. **Road map** A3. ☎ *(707) 937-0511; (800) 548-0513.* **FAX** *(707) 937-0513.* This friendly Victorian hotel overlooking the dramatic coastline also has detached garden rooms.	51	●		●	
MENDOCINO: *MacCallum House* $$$ 45020 Albion St (PO Box 206), CA 95460. **Road map** A3. ☎ *(707) 937-0289; (800) 609-0492.* Not all rooms have private baths at this 19th-century inn. Ask for one of the annexes, many of which also have fireplaces.	21	●	▦	●	
NAPA: *The Chateau Hotel* $$ 4195 Solano Ave, CA 94558. **Road map** B3. ☎ *(707) 253-9300; (800) 253-6272.* **FAX** *(707) 253-0906.* This European-style hotel is geared toward business travelers, with comfortable rooms and a spa.	115		▦	●	▦
NAPA: *The Elm House* $$$ 800 California Blvd, CA 94559. **Road map** B3. ☎ *(707) 255-1831; (800) 788-4356.* **FAX** *(707) 255-8609.* Some rooms in this cozy bed-and-breakfast inn have fireplaces. Book early for summer visits. Close to wineries.	16		▦		
NAPA: *Silverado Country Club Resort* $$$$ 1600 Atlas Peak Rd, CA 94558. **Road map** B3. ☎ *(707) 257-0200; (800) 532-0500.* **FAX** *(707) 257-5400.* Luxurious guest bungalows surround an old mansion set in 1,200 acres (485 ha). Fabulous recreational facilities.	260	●	▦	●	▦
RUTHERFORD: *Rancho Caymus* $$$ 1140 Rutherford Rd (PO Box 78), CA 94573. **Road map** A3. ☎ *(707) 963-1777; (800) 845-1777.* **FAX** *(707) 963-5387.* This hacienda-style hotel, with beehive fireplaces and Mexican-tiled bathrooms, is built around a lovely courtyard. Some rooms have private balconies and Jacuzzis.	26		▦		
RUTHERFORD: *Auberge du Soleil* $$$$$ 180 Rutherford Hill Rd, CA 94573. **Road map** A3. ☎ *(707) 963-1211; (800) 348-5406.* **FAX** *(707) 963-8764.* The stylish cottages of this country inn and spa resort have fireplaces, bars, and exquisite views of the Napa Valley *(see pp446–7)*. There is also a notable sculpture garden.	50	●	▦	●	▦
ST. HELENA: *White Sulphur Springs Resort and Spa* $$ 3100 White Sulphur Springs Rd, CA 94574. **Road map** A3. ☎ *(707) 963-8588.* **FAX** *(707) 963-2890.* This rustic retreat has tiny log cabins and excellent spa facilities, including hot sulfur springs.	37	●	▦	●	▦

ST. HELENA: *Inn At Southbridge* $$$$ — 21
1020 Main St, CA 94574. **Road map** A3. ((707) 967-9400; (800) 520-6800.
FAX (707) 967-9486. This modern haven offers a welcome escape from
Wine Country chintz. All rooms have vaulted ceilings, fireplaces, and
French doors opening onto balconies.

ST. HELENA: *Meadowood Resort Hotel* $$$$$ — 99
900 Meadowood Lane, CA 94574. **Road map** A3. ((707) 963-3646; (800)
458-8080. FAX (707) 963-3532. Some of the lodges have stone fireplaces,
balconies, and terraces at this romantic retreat with golf courses, tennis
courts, spa facilities, and croquet lawns *(see p571)*.

SANTA ROSA: *Hotel La Rose* $$ — 49
308 Wilson St, CA 95401. **Road map** A3. ((707) 579-3200; (800) 527-6738.
FAX (707) 579-3247. Country-style décor and friendly service give this hotel in
Railroad Square the ambience of a bed-and-breakfast inn.

SONOMA: *Victorian Garden Inn* $$ — 5
316 E Napa St, CA 95476. **Road map** A3. ((707) 996 5339. FAX (707) 996 1689.
This peaceful Greek Revival farmhouse offers the perfect antidote to a
hectic tour of the region's wineries. Breakfast is included.

SONOMA: *Sonoma Valley Inn* $$$ — 75
550 2nd St, CA 95476. **Road map** A3. ((707) 938-9200; (800) 334-5784. FAX (707)
938-0935. This Mission-style hotel Downtown has rooms with balconies
over a courtyard, fireplaces, and continental breakfast.

YOUNTVILLE: *Napa Valley Lodge* $$$$$ — 55
2230 Madison St, CA 94599. **Road map** B3. ((707) 944-2468; (800) 368-2468.
FAX (707) 944-9362. Creature comforts at this hotel include a whirlpool
and sauna. Some rooms have fireplaces and balconies.

YOUNTVILLE: *Vintage Inn* $$$$$ — 80
6541 Washington St, CA 94599. **Road map** B3. ((707) 944-1112; (800) 351-1133.
FAX (707) 944-1617. Newly remodeled, this hotel is set in stunning gardens.
Bicycles and golfing facilities are available nearby.

GOLD COUNTRY AND THE CENTRAL VALLEY

AMADOR CITY: *Imperial Hotel* $$ — 7
14202 Hwy 49, CA 95601. **Road map** B3. ((209) 267-9172; (800) 242-5594.
FAX (209) 267-9249. This lovely 19th-century building near Sutter Creek has
been thoughtfully modernized. Breakfast is included.

AUBURN: *Best Western Golden Key* $ — 68
13450 Lincoln Way, CA 95603. **Road map** B3. ((530) 885-8611; (800) 528-1234.
FAX (530) 888-0319. Located a few miles northeast of Sacramento, this basic
hotel provides continental breakfast. Pets are allowed.

GRASS VALLEY: *Best Western Gold Country* $$ — 84
11972 Sutton Way, CA 95945. **Road map** B3. ((530) 273-1393; (800) 247-6590.
FAX (530) 273-4229. Complimentary continental breakfast is offered at this
basic hotel, which is surrounded by pines.

GRASS VALLEY: *Holbrooke Hotel and Restaurant* $$$ — 27
212 West Main St, CA 95945. **Road map** B3. ((530) 273-1353; (800) 933-7077.
FAX (530) 273-0434. Rooms in this downtown hotel – a California Historic
Landmark – are named after famous guests.

MURPHYS: *Murphys Historic Hotel and Lodge* $ — 35
457 Main St, CA 95247. **Road map** B3. ((209) 728-3444; (800) 532-7684. FAX (209)
728-1590. With bullet holes in the doorway and a fabulous Western bar, this
historic monument epitomizes California's Old Wild West. Modern rooms in a
separate wing have TV and private baths.

NEVADA CITY: *National Hotel* $ — 42
211 Broad St, CA 95959. **Road map** B3. ((530) 265-4551. FAX (530) 265-2445.
This historic building surrounded by pine trees has been a hotel since 1855.
All the rooms have Victorian furnishings.

NEVADA CITY: *The Parsonage Bed and Breakfast* $$ — 6
427 Broad St, CA 95959. **Road map** B3. ((530) 265-9478. FAX (530) 265-8147.
This family-run Victorian inn, furnished with antiques, is a peaceful and
romantic haven. A huge full breakfast is included.

Price categories for a standard double room per night, inclusive of service charges and any additional taxes, such as local sales tax:
- $ under $100
- $$ $100–$150
- $$$ $150–$200
- $$$$ $200–$250
- $$$$$ over $250

RESTAURANT
Hotel restaurant or dining room usually open to non-residents unless otherwise stated.

CHILDREN'S FACILITIES
Indicates cribs and/or a baby-sitting service available. A few hotels also provide children's portions and high chairs in the restaurant.

GARDEN/TERRACE
Hotels with a garden, courtyard, or terrace, often providing tables for eating outside.

SWIMMING POOL
Hotel with indoor or outdoor swimming pool.

	NUMBER OF ROOMS	RESTAURANT	CHILDREN'S FACILITIES	GARDEN/TERRACE	SWIMMING POOL
NEVADA CITY: *Emma Nevada House* $$$ 528 E Broad St, CA 95959. **Road map** B3. ((530) 265-4415; (800) 916-3662. FAX (530) 265-4416. This lovely Victorian bed-and-breakfast inn provides a perfect place to unwind. Some of the rooms have Jacuzzis. ☎ P ✉	6			●	
NEVADA CITY: *Grandmere's Inn* $$$ 449 Broad St, CA 95959. **Road map** B3. ((530) 265-4660. FAX (530) 265-4416. The finest hotel in town, this Colonial-style house is surrounded by terraced gardens. Breakfast includes freshly baked pastries and fruit. ☎ & P ✉	7		■	●	
SACRAMENTO: *River Boat Delta King Hotel* $$ 1000 Front St, CA 95814. **Road map** B3. ((530) 444-5464. FAX (530) 444-5314. This steam paddle boat (*see pp456–7*) has been restored to its original 1930s splendor and is furnished with antiques. It has large rooms and a deluxe continental breakfast is provided. ☎ TV & P 🍽 ✉	44	●	■		
SACRAMENTO: *Amber House* $$$ 1315 22nd St, CA 95816. **Road map** B3. ((916) 444-8085; (800) 755-6526. FAX (916) 552-6529. Thoughtful touches characterize this very special bed-and-breakfast inn. Some rooms have two-person Jacuzzis. ☎ TV P ✉	9			●	
SACRAMENTO: *Sheraton Hotel* $$$$ 1211 Point East Drive, Rancho Cordova, CA 95742. **Road map** B3. ((916) 638-1100; (800) 325-3535. FAX (916) 635-8356. This sophisticated modern hotel is perfect for the business traveler as well as the tourist. ☎ TV & P ✉	265	●	■	●	■
SACRAMENTO: *Sterling Hotel* $$$$ 1300 H St, CA 95814. **Road map** B3. ((916) 448-1300; (800) 365-7660. FAX (916) 448-8066. This luxurious hotel in a restored Victorian mansion is partly furnished with period, Art Deco, and oriental pieces. Rooms have Italian marble Jacuzzis, and continental breakfast is included. ☎ TV & P 🍽 ✉	16	●	■	●	
SOMERSET: *Fitzpatrick Winery and Lodge* $ 7740 Fairplay Rd, CA 95684. **Road map** B3. ((530) 620-3248; (800) 245-9166. FAX (530) 620-6838. Set in a vineyard in the Sierra foothills, this bed-and-breakfast inn has spectacular views. Some rooms have balconies, and there is an outdoor hot tub and evening wine tasting. ☎ & P ✉	5			●	
SONORA: *Lavender Hill* $$ 683 Barretta St, CA 95370. **Road map** B3. ((209) 532-9024; (800) 446-1333, ext. 290 (reservations). This 1900s Victorian home overlooks the old Gold Rush town of Sonora. There are year-round flower gardens. ☎ P ✉	4			●	
SONORA: *Sonora Days Inn & Café* $$ 160 South Washington St, CA 95370. **Road map** B3. ((209) 532-2400; (800) 580-4667. FAX (209) 536-1303. Housed in an 1890s Spanish-style building in old downtown Sonora; there is a motel annex at the back. ☎ TV & P ✉	64	●	■	●	■
SUTTER CREEK: *Gold Quartz Inn* $$ 15 Bryson Drive, CA 95685. **Road map** B3. ((209) 267-9155; (800) 752-8738. FAX (209) 267-9170. This pretty bed-and-breakfast inn has a romantic ambience. The back rooms overlook the rose garden, and some rooms have private porches. No children under ten allowed. ☎ TV & P ✉	24			●	
SUTTER CREEK: *Sutter Creek Inn* $$ 75 Main St, CA 95685. **Road map** B3. ((209) 267-5606. FAX (209) 267-9287. This English-style country inn has swinging beds that hang by chains from the ceiling. Some rooms have fireplaces and private patios. ☎ P ✉	17			●	
SUTTER CREEK: *Foxes* $$$ 77 Main St (PO Box 159), CA 95685. **Road map** B3. ((209) 267-5882. FAX (209) 267-0712. This friendly bed-and-breakfast inn has comfortable, antique-furnished rooms and a honeymoon suite. ☎ P ✉ 🛏	7			●	

The High Sierras

Bishop: *Best Western Bishop Holiday Spa Lodge* $ 1025 N Main St, CA 93514. **Road map C4.** ☎ *(760) 873-3543; (800) 576-3543.* [FAX] *(760) 872-4777.* Popular with outdoor recreation enthusiasts, this motel is a bargain, with refrigerators, microwave, and an indoor whirlpool. 🛁 [TV] [P] 💳	80		■		■
Bishop: *Creekside Inn* $$ 725 N Main St, CA 93514. **Road map C4.** ☎ *(760) 872-3044; (800) 273-3550.* [FAX] *(760) 872-1300.* This modern motel is set in spacious, attractively landscaped gardens along a natural creek. Some rooms have kitchen facilities. 🛁 [TV] [P] 💳	89		■	●	■
El Portal: *Cedar Lodge* $ 9966 State Hwy 140, CA 95318. **Road map C3.** ☎ *(209) 379-2612; (800) 321-5261.* [FAX] *(209) 379-2712.* At the western entrance to Yosemite National Park *(see pp472–5)*, rooms range from standard to large suites. 🛁 [TV] ♿ [P] 💳	206	●	■		■
Fish Camp: *Narrow Gauge Inn* $$ 48571 State Hwy 41, CA 93623. **Road map C4.** ☎ *(559) 683-7720.* [FAX] *(559) 683-2139.* This small, romantic inn offers old-fashioned hospitality and has an excellent restaurant *(see p573)*. It is closed during the winter. 🛁 [P] 💳	26	●	■	●	
Fish Camp: *Tenaya Lodge* $$$ 1122 State Hwy 41, CA 93623. **Road map C4.** ☎ *(559) 683-6555; (800) 635-5807.* [FAX] *(559) 683-8684.* Managed by the Marriott chain, this hotel has the best facilities around Yosemite, including a sauna and steam room. 🛁 [TV] [P] 🍸 💳	242	●	■	●	■
June Lake: *Boulder Lodge* $ June Lake (PO Box 68), CA 93529. **Road map C3.** ☎ *(760) 648-7533.* [FAX] *(760) 648-7330.* Surrounded by lakeside grounds, this peaceful, relaxing lodge offers standard rooms and deluxe two-bedroom cottages. 🛁 [TV] [P] 💳	60	●	■	●	■
Kings Canyon National Park: *Montecito Sequoia Lodge* $$ PO Box 858, Grant Grove, CA 93633. **Road map C4.** ☎ *(559) 565-3388.* [FAX] *(559) 565-3223.* Set amid groves of giant sequoias, this family-orientated lodge is open all year and offers standard rooms with bathrooms and rustic cabins without bathrooms. Boat rentals are available on the adjacent lake. [P] 💳	52	●	■	●	■
Kirkwood: *Kirkwood Resort* $$ Kirkwood (PO Box 1), CA 95646. **Road map C3.** ☎ *(209) 258-7000.* [FAX] *(209) 258-7400.* Located 30 miles (48 km) south of Lake Tahoe *(see pp470–71)*, this idyllic resort offers year-round recreation, from horseback riding to cross-country skiing. Most of the suites have kitchens and fireplaces. 🛁 [TV] [P] 💳	120	●	■	●	
Lee Vining: *Lake View Lodge* $ PO Box 345, CA 93541. **Road map C3.** ☎ *(760) 647-6543.* [FAX] *(760) 647-6325.* Set on the western shore of Mono Lake *(see p479)*, this motel makes an excellent base for exploring the area. Some rooms have kitchens. 🛁 [TV] [P] 💳	46		■	●	
Lone Pine: *Frontier Motel* $ 1008 S Main St, CA 93545. **Road map C4.** ☎ *(760) 876-5571.* [FAX] *(760) 876-5357.* Popular with fishermen and hikers, this motel offers continental breakfast and large rooms, many with whirlpool baths. 🛁 [TV] [P] 💳	73		■		■
Mammoth Lakes: *Austria Hof Lodge* $ 924 Canyon Blvd, CA 93546. **Road map C4.** ☎ *(760) 934-2764.* [FAX] *(760) 934-1880.* A short walk from the ski slopes of Mammoth Mountain, this charming hotel is especially popular on winter weekends. 🛁 [TV] [P] 💳	22	●	■		
Mammoth Lakes: *Shilo Inn* $$ 2963 Main St, CA 93546. **Road map C4.** ☎ *(760) 934-4500.* [FAX] *(760) 934-7594.* Guests are accommodated in large suites, with private bars and sitting rooms. Facilities include a sauna. 🛁 [TV] [P] 🍸 💳	71		■		■
South Lake Tahoe: *Timber Cove Inn* $$ 3411 Lake Tahoe Blvd, CA 96150. **Road map C3.** ☎ *(530) 541-6722.* [FAX] *(530) 541-7959.* Built on the shores of Lake Tahoe, this motel has its own beach. The rooms here, most of which have lovely views, are much more comfortable than those in many of the nearby motels. 🛁 [TV] [P] 💳	262	●	■	●	■
South Lake Tahoe: *Lake Tahoe Inn* $$$ 4110 Lake Tahoe Blvd, CA 96150. **Road map C3.** ☎ *(530) 541-2010.* [FAX] *(530) 542-1428.* There are pleasant, spacious grounds and some two-bedroom units for families in addition to the standard motel rooms. 🛁 [TV] [P] 💳	400	●	■	●	■

For key to symbols see back flap

Price categories for a standard double room per night, inclusive of service charges and any additional taxes, such as local sales tax:
$ under $100
$$ $100–$150
$$$ $150–$200
$$$$ $200–$250
$$$$$ over $250

RESTAURANT
Hotel restaurant or dining room usually open to non-residents unless otherwise stated.

CHILDREN'S FACILITIES
Indicates cribs and/or a baby-sitting service available. A few hotels also provide children's portions and high chairs in the restaurant.

GARDEN/TERRACE
Hotels with a garden, courtyard, or terrace, often providing tables for eating outside.

SWIMMING POOL
Hotel with indoor or outdoor swimming pool.

		NUMBER OF ROOMS	RESTAURANT	CHILDREN'S FACILITIES	GARDEN/TERRACE	SWIMMING POOL
SQUAW VALLEY: *Resort at Squaw Creek* 400 Squaw Creek Rd, CA 96146. **Road map** B3. (*(530) 583-6300; (800) 327-3353.* FAX *(530) 581-6632.* This luxurious resort lies at the foot of Squaw Mountain. It is popular with skiers in winter and golfers in summer.	$$$$	402	●	■	●	●
TAHOE CITY: *Tahoe City Travellodge* 455 North Lake Blvd, CA 96145. **Road map** B3. (*(530) 583-3766.* FAX *(530) 583-8045.* Services at this basic motel include free cable TV, dry sauna, outdoor Jacuzzi, and discounts at nearby restaurants.	$$	47		■		■
TAHOE CITY: *Chaney House* 4725 West Lake Blvd (PO Box 7852), CA 96145. **Road map** B3. (*(530) 525-7333.* FAX *(530) 525-4413.* Set in pine woods and surrounded by gardens, the house has a huge fireplace and its own private beach and pier.	$$$	4			●	
TRUCKEE: *Donner Lake Village Resort* Suite 101, 15695 Donner Pass Rd, CA 96161. **Road map** B3. (*(530) 587-6081; (800) 621-6664.* FAX *(530) 587-8782.* With its own beach and marina, this resort offers year-round recreation. It has some two-bedroom suites.	$$	64		■		
YOSEMITE NATIONAL PARK: *Wawona Hotel* State Hwy 41, CA 95389. **Road map** C3. (*(530) 252-4848.* FAX *(530) 456-0542.* This quaint old 1870 hotel is a cherished High Sierras landmark. Accommodations include a few rustic cottages, and there is golf, horseback riding, and tennis. Call six months ahead to reserve in summer.	$$	104	●	■	●	■
YOSEMITE NATIONAL PARK: *Yosemite Lodge* Yosemite Valley, CA 95389. **Road map** C3. (*(530) 252-4848.* FAX *(530) 456-0542.* Near Yosemite Falls *(see p474)*, you'll find the best selection of lodgings in the valley, with modern motel rooms and several rustic cabins.	$$	495	●	■	●	■
YOSEMITE NATIONAL PARK: *Ahwahnee Hotel* Yosemite Valley, CA 95389. **Road map** C3. (*(530) 252-4848.* FAX *(530) 456-0542.* With its unique mix of sophistication and rusticity, this is Yosemite's most stylish hotel *(see p475)*. Built in 1927, it features grand public areas and a fine restaurant *(see p574)*. Bicycles and horses can be rented.	$$$$	123	●	■	●	■

NORTH CENTRAL CALIFORNIA

		NUMBER OF ROOMS	RESTAURANT	CHILDREN'S FACILITIES	GARDEN/TERRACE	SWIMMING POOL
APTOS: *Best Western Seacliff Inn* 7500 Old Dominion Court, CA 95003. **Road map** B4. (*(831) 688-7300; (800) 367-2003.* FAX *(831) 685-3603.* This basic hotel is very close to the beach. The rooms are large and some have whirlpool baths.	$	140	●			●
APTOS: *Rio Sands Motel* 116 Aptos Beach Drive, CA 95003. **Road map** B4. (*(831) 688-3207; (800) 826-2077* FAX *(831) 688-6107.* All rooms have patios or balconies overlooking landscaped gardens. Some rooms have kitchen facilities.	$$	50			●	●
BIG SUR: *Big Sur River Inn* Hwy 1, Pheneger Creek, CA 93920. **Road map** B4. (*(831) 667-2700; (800) 548-3610.* FAX *(831) 667-2743.* The rooms at this rustic inn are basic and comfortable. The restaurant has live music on weekends.	$$	19	●	■	●	●
BIG SUR: *Deetjen's Big Sur Inn* Castro Canyon, CA 93920. **Road map** B4. (*(831) 667-2377.* This delightful hotel, in a rustic building with a good restaurant, has a loyal clientele. Children are allowed only in the two-room cottages.	$$	20	●		●	
BIG SUR: *Post Ranch Inn* PO Box 219, Hwy 1, CA 93920. **Road map** B4. (*(831) 667-2200; (800) 527-2200.* FAX *(831) 667-2824.* Buildings at this extraordinary resort with spa facilities include tree houses and earth shelters built into the hillside.	$$$$$	30	●		●	●

ᴀG Sᴜʀ: *The Ventana Inn* $$$$$ | 63
wy 1, CA 93920. **Road map** B4. **[** *(831) 624-4812; 667-2331; (800) 628-6500.*
[*(831) 667-2419.* Surrounded by forest, most rooms have fireplaces, and
me have ocean views. There are saunas and a library. 🖪 📺 ♿ Ᵽ 🥂

ᴀʀᴍᴇʟ: *Crystal Terrace Inn* $$$ | 16
815 Carpenter St, CA 93921. **Road map** B4. **[** *(831) 624-6400; (800) 600-4488.*
[*(831) 624-5111.* This quiet, romantic hotel near the town center is geared
ward couples. Some rooms have fireplaces and bars. 🖪 📺 ♿ Ᵽ 🥂

ᴀʀᴍᴇʟ: *Cypress Inn* $$$ | 34
ncoln & 7th Ave, CA 93921. **Road map** B4. **[** *(831) 624-3871; (800) 443-7443.*
[*(831) 624-8216.* Owned by the actress Doris Day, this inn encourages
ts, even in the public areas. Some rooms have Jacuzzis. 🖪 📺 ♿ Ᵽ 🥂

ᴀʀᴍᴇʟ: *La Playa Hotel* $$$ | 75
mino Real & 8th Ave, CA 93921. **Road map** B4. **[** *(831) 624-6476; (800) 582-*
00. **FAX** *(831) 624-7966.* This Spanish-style hotel also has five cottages with
eplaces and kitchenettes and is excellent for families. 🖪 📺 ♿ Ᵽ 🥂

ᴀʀᴍᴇʟ: *Los Laureles Lodge* $$$ | 28
3 W Carmel Valley Rd, Carmel Valley, CA 93924. **Road map** B4. **[** *(831) 659-2233;*
unique, rustic old hunting lodge with "Laura Ashley" decorations. A few
the rooms are wood-paneled converted horse stalls. 🖪 📺 Ᵽ 🥂

ᴀʀᴍᴇʟ: *Pine Inn* $$$ | 47
cean Ave & Monte Verde, CA 93921. **Road map** B4. **[** *(831) 624-3851; (800) 228-3851.*
[*(831) 624-3030.* Carmel's oldest hotel, dating from 1889, has cozy rooms
d a magnificent red lobby furnished with antiques. 🖪 📺 ♿ Ᵽ 🥂

ᴀʀᴍᴇʟ: *Carmel Valley Ranch* $$$$ | 100
Old Ranch Rd, CA 93923. **Road map** B4. **[** *(831) 625-9500; (800) 422-7635.*
[*(831) 624-2858.* Some rooms have fireplaces and Jacuzzis at this
xurious modern hotel and golf club. 🖪 📺 ♿ Ᵽ 🥂

ᴀʀᴍᴇʟ: *Quail Lodge* $$$$ | 100
05 Valley Greens Drive, CA 93923. **Road map** B4. **[** *(831) 624-1581; (800)*
8-9516. **FAX** *(831) 624-3726.* This complex is the height of luxury, with a
olf course, hiking trails, and even a pet-sitting service. 🖪 📺 ♿ Ᵽ 🥂

ᴀʀᴍᴇʟ: *Highlands Inn and Restaurant* $$$$$ | 142
cific Coast Hwy 1, CA 93923. **Road map** B4. **[** *(831) 624-3801; (800) 682-4811.*
[*(831) 626-1574.* This rustic hotel, set in woodland on a bluff overlooking
e coast, has beautiful views. Some rooms have Jacuzzis. 🖪 📺 ♿ Ᵽ 🥂

ᴏɴᴛᴇʀᴇʏ: *Casa Munras Garden Hotel* $$$ | 152
0 Munras Ave, CA 93940. **Road map** B4. **[** *(831) 375-2411; (800) 222-2446.*
[*(831) 375-1365.* Within walking distance of all the sights, this hotel has
loyal clientele. Some comfortable rooms have fireplaces. 🖪 📺 ♿ Ᵽ 🥂

ᴏɴᴛᴇʀᴇʏ: *Monterey Plaza Hotel* $$$$ | 285
0 Cannery Row, CA 93940. **Road map** B4. **[** *(831) 646-1700; (800) 334-3999.*
[*(831) 646-5937.* Some rooms have balconies with views over Monterey
ay. The hotel is near all the town sights. 🖪 🕐24 📺 ♿ Ᵽ 🥂

ᴏɴᴛᴇʀᴇʏ: *Old Monterey Inn* $$$$ | 10
0 Martin St, CA 93940. **Road map** B4. **[** *(831) 375-8284; (800) 350-2344.*
[*(831) 375-6730.* Guests are pampered at this Tudor-style manor set in English-
yle gardens. Rooms have fireplaces and Jacuzzis. Adults only. 🖪 ♿ Ᵽ 🥂

ᴀᴄɪꜰɪᴄ Gʀᴏᴠᴇ: *The Martine Inn* $$$$ | 20
5 Ocean View Blvd, CA 93950. **Road map** B4. **[** *(831) 373-3388; (800) 852-*
88. **FAX** *(831) 373-3896.* This Mediterranean-style inn has an 1890s billiard
ble and old MGs on display. Some rooms have fireplaces. 🖪 ♿ Ᵽ 🥂

ᴀɴᴛᴀ Cʀᴜᴢ: *Sunset Inn* $$ | 32
24 Mission St, CA 95060. **Road map** B4. **[** *(831) 423-7500.* This completely
novated, pleasant hotel has microwaves and refrigerators in all rooms.
ose to excellent restaurants and all corporate businesses. 🖪 📺 ♿ Ᵽ 🥂

ᴀɴᴛᴀ Cʀᴜᴢ: *Babbling Brook Inn* $$$ | 12
25 Laurel St, CA 95060. **Road map** B4. **[** *(831) 427-2437; (800) 866-1131.*
[*(831) 427-2457.* Rooms have fireplaces, Jacuzzis, or balconies at this
erfect romantic retreat. Breakfast is included. 🖪 📺 ♿ Ᵽ 🥂

For key to symbols see back flap

WHERE TO EAT

O F ALL THE STATES IN THE US, California has perhaps the widest variety of places to eat. "California cuisine" – light food prepared in a range of international styles using locally grown ingredients – was pioneered by chefs such as Jeremiah Towers, Wolfgang Puck, and Alice Waters and is now internationally recognized. There is an ample number of Italian and French restaurants, but many other international cuisines are also available.

California diner sign

In every town you can eat Japanes sushi, Thai noodles, Chinese dim sur Mexican burritos, Middle Easter falafel, or Indian tandoori. Whi ethnic cooking reflects th state's many cultures, there also no shortage of that cla sic all-American meal: han burger, French fries, and col The restaurants listed on pag 544–75 have been selected fo their variety, service, and goo value. Some typical meals served i California are shown on pages 540–4

CALIFORNIA EATING PATTERNS

S OME SAY AMERICANS make the best breakfast in the world, and this is evident in California. From diners to top restaurants, the breakfast menu is vast. Omelettes with fries and toast, pancakes or waffles topped with fruit and syrup, and eggs, bacon, or sausage served with toast or a muffin are popular options. Less filling choices are coffee with a bagel or pastry, or cereal topped with raisins or bananas. Breakfast is served from 6:30am to 11am. Brunch extends the breakfast menu with grilled meats. It is always available on Sundays, and in selected restaurants on Saturdays, from 9am to 2pm.

California lunch is light – soup and salad or a sandwich. Dinner is the main meal of the day for Americans. Many restaurants make dinner a special occasion by setting out candles and tablecloths, and presenting the chef's specialties as creatively as possible. Dinner is served from 5:30pm to 10:30pm.

PRICES AND TIPPING

E ATING OUT in California is very reasonable. A snack in a café should cost no more than $5 per person. A main meal in a diner will set you back up to $15. A three-course meal in a good restaurant, excluding wine, will cost $25–$30, but gourmet meals can begin at $40. Fixed-price menus are rare, but lunch menus are much cheaper and are generally very similar to the dinner menu.

Tipping should be based on service: if satisfactory, leave 15 percent; if superlative, leave

Rex Restaurant in the Oviatt Building, LA *(see p545)*

20 percent. Make sure the tip is calculated on the net cost of the meal and does not include the tax. Restaurant tax i California is up to 8.5 percent

FAST FOOD

A UBIQUITOUS FEATURE of the California landscape, fas food outlets are rarely more than five minutes away. They offer filling, inexpensiv food, which stretche the travel budget for families. Chain-owned diners include Denny's, Sizzlers, and Marie Callendar's While the seating areas are large and the selections on th menu are extensive, the food is prepared in bulk and may therefore be a little bland.

Planet Hollywood *(see p546)*

HEALTHY EATING

A NUMBER OF restaurants in California now follow the American Heart Association's guidelines for reducing cholesterol and dietary fat. A red heart beside a dish denotes an AHA-approved "Healthy Heart meal, low in calories and cholesterol. If a restaurant doe not offer such meals, you can ask your waiter to omit certain ingredients where appropriate Vegetarian cuisine is not a strong feature in California restaurants, but they all offer salads and many of them will make up meat-free meals for customers if requested.

COFFEE HOUSES, TEA HOUSES, AND CAFÉS

COFFEE HOUSES exist all over California. At "internet" coffee houses, patrons plug into computers as they eat and drink. Other coffee houses are attached to bookstores, where customers can drink and read. Coffee houses do not offer a full menu, but specialize in drinks (coffees, sodas, juices, and wine) and cakes.

Tea houses are also popular, particularly in LA, for their elegant and subdued atmosphere.

Cafés usually have only one or two tables for outside dining, but the atmosphere inside is usually informal and long stays are encouraged.

El Paseo Restaurant, Santa Barbara *(see p552)*

Ratto's Italian delicatessen in Oakland

PICNICS AND TAKEOUTS

DELICATESSENS and super-markets with deli counters stock cold meats, cheeses, pickles, and salads. They will also make up fresh sandwiches to your personal order to take-out and enjoy in one of the parks or open areas that abound in California.

You can also order takeouts from any restaurant, although the prices for this are the same as eating in the restaurant itself.

MICROBREWERY BARS

IN THE WORLD of beer, micro-breweries are big news. In every city there is a healthy number of on-site brewmasters with bars serving a selection of national and international beers, but also brewing their own specials, such as Anchor Steam in San Francisco and Karl Straus Amber Lager in San Diego *(see pp542–3)*. If a beer proves successful locally, it can then go on to earn national and sometimes international recognition.

A variety of snack foods is also served at microbrewery bars to soak up the beer.

SMOKING

CALIFORNIA is an antismoking state, and the California State Legislature has banned smoking in all restaurants and public places unless there is a separate air circulation system. Some restaurants with outdoor tables may have a separate section reserved for smokers, and sometimes the bar area will allow smokers in a separate section. Cigars are rarely allowed.

Elegant and leisurely Craviotto's Café in Santa Barbara

WHEELCHAIR ACCESS

ALL NEW RESTAURANTS in California, and old restaurants undergoing renovation, must make their site accessible to wheelchair users. This means that there should be no steps into the restaurant or to the tables, and that there should be wide bathroom doors.

CHILDREN'S FACILITIES

MOST RESTAURANTS are children-friendly and offer a children's menu and high chairs or booster seats. However, in the quieter, upscale restaurants, parents are expected to keep children seated at the table, and take noisy or upset children outside until they calm down.

DRESS CODES

WITH CALIFORNIA'S leisurely lifestyle, many gourmet restaurants do not require men to wear jackets and ties or women to wear dresses, although jeans, shorts, sneakers, and T-shirts are definitely not allowed.

BOOKING AHEAD

IT IS ALWAYS best to make a reservation in advance to avoid disappointment. City restaurants, in particular, are often very busy, and established or fashionable spots are sometimes booked up more than a month in advance. If you make a reservation that you later cannot keep, call the restaurant and cancel.

What to Eat in California

Food in California reflects the ethnic diversity of the state's population – Chinese and Italian dishes are popular, and there is a strong emphasis on Mexican-style cuisine. Because of similarities in climate, California cooking is also very influenced by Mediterranean cuisine. Traditional Provençal or Italian recipes are given a California twist, often with the addition of an exciting new ingredient, resulting in exotic, colorful salads

Flavored olive oil

and innovative pasta dishes. California is rich in natural resources. Fresh, seasonal fruit and vegetables, grown year-round in the many fertile valleys, are a hallmark of California cuisine. The long coastline means that there is also an abundance of seafood, as well as freshwater fish from the state's rivers and lakes.

Waffles
Topped with fruit and whipped cream, waffles are often part of a full breakfast in California.

Bagels

Focaccia

Bread
Distinctive breads are used for sandwiches or served with soup or salads.

Sourdough bread

Deli Sandwiches
In most delicatessens, customers choose from various fillings to create substantial sandwiches.

Guacamole (avocado and garlic dip)

Salsa (chunky tomato, onion, and chili sauce)

Taco (filled and folded tortilla)

Burger and Fries
American burgers are usually made of beef and served with cheese, relish, and onion rings.

Arroz (rice), flavored with tomato

Burritos (steamed and rolled tortilla, with various fillings)

Nachos (crisp fried corn chips, often with a spicy flavor)

Frijoles (black or *pinto* beans)

MEXICAN FOOD
Spicy Mexican food, which is available all over the state, always includes a salsa, rice and beans, and steamed, fried, or baked flour or corn tortillas (thin pancakes).

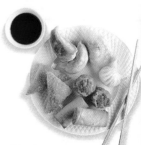

Dim Sum
A Chinese specialty, these little dumplings are stuffed with fish, meat, or vegetables.

Ahi Tuna
Wafer-thin slices of Ahi tuna are served rare with a pepper sauce. Vegetables add color.

Spaghetti Vongole
This Italian dish of pasta and steamed clams is offered at many oceanfront restaurants.

Lobster and Vegetables
Lobster is one of the many seafood delicacies popular along the region's coastline.

California Pizza
California pizzas have imaginative toppings, such as grilled vegetables, meat, or fish.

Zucchini (courgette)

Red pepper

Grilled polenta

Eggplant (aubergine)

Grilled Vegetables Mediterranean Style
Vegetables are marinated in olive oil, garlic, and herbs, and then grilled until they are soft and tender. They are often served with fried polenta (cooked cornmeal).

Salad in Tortilla
This California-style salad is beautifully presented in a crisp tortilla shell.

Fruit Dessert
Fresh fruit is often served as a dessert, sometimes with a passion fruit or other sauce.

Cantaloupe melon

Dates

Peaches

Cherries

Strawberries

Apricots

Pineapple

CALIFORNIA FRUIT
Much of the fruit available in California is grown in the state's sunny, fertile valleys and makes a refreshing breakfast, dessert, or snack.

Limes

Figs

Kumquats

What to Drink in California

Beer label

CALIFORNIANS ARE devoted to the consumption of beverages, partly because they tend to do so much outdoor exercise in the heat and partly as a social activity. Soft drinks, or "sodas," play the largest role in the state's beverage culture, although alcohol is also important. Many restaurants tempt weekend customers with champagne brunches. Beer can be enjoyed on the beach or while watching a game of baseball. Wine, particularly local California wine (see pp422–3), is popular with dinner.

Sign in the Napa Valley wine-producing region in Northern California

Tequila bottle **Colorful Sunset Strip** **Strawberry Daiquiri**

SOFT DRINKS

CALIFORNIANS ARE generally very health-conscious, and they consume a lot of fruit juice. Staff at juice stalls in shopping centers or on the street will squeeze juice from almost any kind of fruit, or a mixture of fruit and vegetables, while you wait. Also available on the street, as well as in most hotel lobbies, are machines supplying soft drinks and free cold water and crushed ice. Most fast-food outlets offer a range of soft drinks in three sizes, although the same products can usually be purchased much less expensively from supermarkets.

Iced cola

The most popular nonalcoholic drink in the state remains the all-American cola. However, health awareness has led to a growth in the consumption of diet and caffeine-free versions of colas and other carbonated soft drinks.

Sports-loving Californians often carry flexible thermos flasks filled with drinks chilled overnight in the refrigerator.

Freshly squeezed strawberry juice

COCKTAILS

SIPPING COCKTAILS beside the ocean at sunset is part of the popular image of the "California dream." The margarita cocktail still ranks as the firm favorite throughout the state. Served in ever-wider glasses, margaritas are a blend of tequila, lime juice, and an orange-flavored liqueur, with the rim of the glass dipped in salt.

The Sunset Strip, named after the infamous section of Sunset Boulevard (see pp98–103), consists of equal parts of gin, rum, triple sec, vodka, pineapple juice, and lemonade.

Margarita with slice of lime

Another cocktail popular in the state is the piña colada. This is a blend of fresh pineapple, cream of coconut, and equal parts of papaya juice, lime mix, orange juice, and pineapple juice. A shot of rum is added, and the finished drink is served over ice in tall, elegant glasses.

TEA AND COFFEE

PEOPLE IN CALIFORNIA consume large quantities of "designer" coffee. Café latte, café au lait, cappuccino, frappuccino (iced coffee), and flavored brews, such as almond and mocha, are on hand at coffee houses and street stalls. Tea is also becoming increasingly popular, and imported teas come in every imaginable flavor.

Cappuccino

Café latte

Frappuccino **Lemon tea**

WINE

GRAPE VINES THRIVE IN the mild climate of Northern California, where cooling fogs help the fruit to reach perfection. The main red wine varieties grown in the region are Cabernet Sauvignon, Pinot Noir, Merlot, and Zinfandel (see pp422–3). White wines are also classified by grape variety, with Chardonnay by far the most popular of recent years. Grown throughout the West Coast region, this prestige grape produces wines varying in character from dry, light, lemon, and vanilla-scented to the more headstrong and oaky.

California has acquired an international reputation for excellent champagne-style wines at the right price, reflected in the fact that the finest French producers have huge investments in the state. Moët & Chandon and Mumm, among others, have set up wineries in the Napa Valley and elsewhere.

Wine is much cheaper in supermarkets or liquor stores than in restaurants. State law allows customers to take their own bottles into restaurants, where the corkage fee is generally $5–10.

Sparkling Cuvée Napa by Mumm

Rosé or blush wine

Napa Chardonnay

Cabernet Sauvignon

WATER

A VARIETY OF mineral waters is produced in the state, the best of which comes from the spa town of Calistoga in the Napa Valley (see p445). Many mineral waters are flavored with fresh fruit and most are carbonated. Most public places, including office buildings, have water dispensers. California tap water is fresh, clean, and safe to drink.

Calistoga mineral water

ALCOHOLIC DRINKS

Alcohol cannot be purchased or consumed in California by anyone under the age of 21. It is not uncommon for shops and bars to refuse service or admittance to anyone not carrying documents proving that they are at least 21 years old. Licensing hours, however, are relaxed; those old enough to drink legally can buy or consume alcohol from 6am until 2am, seven days a week.

Busy bar in Santa Barbara

BEER

BEERS OF EVERY variety – foreign, American, even homemade – have become highly desirable. The recent resurgence in small breweries across the United States can be credited to the success of San Francisco's Anchor Brewery, whose Steam Beer, Liberty Ale, and other products show that American beer need not be bland and tasteless. Other excellent local brews to look out for include Mendocino County's rich Boont Amber and Red Tail Ale.

Copying the self-brewing concept that began in Canada, many Californians are now opening do-it-yourself breweries. Experts are on hand to assist with malting, boiling, carbonating, hopping, fermenting, and bottling. A personal-label brew takes two to six weeks to ferment. Microbrewery beers, brewed on the premises of a bar (see p539), are also extremely popular.

Anchor Steam Beer **Red Tail Ale** **Liberty Ale**

Choosing a Restaurant

THE RESTAURANTS in this guide have been selected across a wide range of price categories for their exceptional food, good value, and interesting location. They are listed here by region, starting with Los Angeles. The thumb tabs on the pages use the same color-coding as the corresponding regional chapter in the main section of the guide.

Los Angeles

	Outdoor Eating	Vegetarian Specialties	Bar Area/Cocktail Bar	Fixed-Price Menu	Children's Facilities
Bel Air: *Bel-Air Hotel Restaurant* $$$$$ 701 Stone Canyon Rd, CA 90077. **Map** 4 A2. ☎ *(310) 472-1211.* At this award-winning restaurant, you can dine in the elegant dining room, the library-like lounge, or on the lovely terrace that overlooks gardens and a lake with swans. The cuisine is California-French. ♿ 👔 *D.* 🎵 🍷 💳	■	●	■		■
Beverly Hills: *Factor's Famous Deli* $ 9420 W Pico Blvd, CA 90035. **Map** 5 F5. ☎ *(310) 278-9175.* The portions are enormous at this genuine Jewish deli, so you may want to split a sandwich between two. The service is brisk but friendly. ● *Sun.* ♿ 💳		●			■
Beverly Hills: *Koo Koo Roo* $ 262 S Beverly Drive, CA 90212. **Map** 5 F4. ☎ *(310) 274-3121.* This restaurant chain sells healthy fast food all over LA – delicious turkey sandwiches, flame-grilled skinless chicken, salads, and homemade breads. ♿ 💳					■
Beverly Hills: *Nate 'n' Al's Deli* $ 414 N Beverly Drive, CA 90210. **Map** 5 F3. ☎ *(310) 274-0101.* Everyone comes here for fabulous sandwiches, deli items, and dinners (roast turkey or chicken with mashed potatoes and gravy). Breakfast is served all day. ♿ 💳					■
Beverly Hills: *Barney Greengrass* $$ Barney's New York, 9570 Wilshire Blvd, CA 90212. **Map** 5 F4. ☎ *(310) 777-5877.* This is one of the hippest places to eat lunch, with a wonderful view and delicious upscale deli fare. It's also great for tea and desserts. ♿ 💳	■	●	■		■
Beverly Hills: *Benihana of Tokyo* $$ 38 N La Cienega Blvd, CA 90211. **Map** 6 C4. ☎ *(323) 655-7311.* A chef prepares the food at your table – vegetables, chicken, seafood, and beef – at this Japanese steakhouse. The spectacle is fun and the food is good. It gets very busy so book ahead. ● *Sat & Sun L.* ♿ 💳			■		■
Beverly Hills: *Café Rodeo* $$ 360 N Rodeo Drive, CA 90210. **Map** 5 F3. ☎ *(310) 273-0300.* This busy, newly remodeled restaurant offers snacks, salads, and drinks served outside on sidewalk tables for good people-watching. ♿ 💳	■	●	■		■
Beverly Hills: *Jackson's Farm of Beverly Hills* $$$ 439 N Beverly Drive, CA 90210. **Map** 5 F3. ☎ *(310) 273-5578.* This open and airy restaurant is excellent for salads, cheese platters, sandwiches, and pastas, with a wonderful selection of breads and desserts. ♿ 💳	■	●			■
Beverly Hills: *Lawry's Prime Rib* $$$ 100 N La Cienega Blvd, CA 90211. **Map** 6 C4. ☎ *(310) 652-2827.* This is the place to go in LA for prime rib. Enormous, succulent portions of beef are carved at the table and served with Yorkshire pudding. ● *L.* ♿ 💳			■		■
Beverly Hills: *McCormick & Schmick's The Fish House* $$$ 206 N Rodeo Drive,CA 90210. **Map** 5 F3. ☎ *(310) 859-0434.* This excellent restaurant serves up to 30 varieties of fresh fish, including a huge selection of oysters. The large menu also offers pastas, meat, and poultry. ♿ 💳	■	●	■		
Beverly Hills: *Kate Mantilini* $$$$ 9109 Wilshire Blvd, CA 90210. **Map** 5 F4. ☎ *(310) 278-3699.* California cuisine is offered at this spacious, airy restaurant. Sample the fabulous white chili (made with chicken and white beans). ♿ 🍴 💳		●	■		■
Beverly Hills: *Matsuhisa* $$$$ 129 N La Cienega Blvd, CA 90211. **Map** 6 C4. ☎ *(310) 659-9639.* This outstanding Japanese seafood restaurant serves exotic dishes, such as hot sea urchin or green-lipped mussels. Reservations are necessary. 💳		●		●	■

Price categories for a three-course meal for one, including a half bottle of house wine, sales tax, and service:
$ under $25
$$ $25–$35
$$$ $35–$50
$$$$ $50–$70
$$$$$ over $70

OUTDOOR EATING
Some tables on a patio or terrace.

VEGETARIAN SPECIALTIES
One menu always includes a selection of vegetarian dishes.

BAR AREA/COCKTAIL BAR
There is a bar area or cocktail bar within the restaurant.

FIXED-PRICE MENU
A good-value fixed-price menu offered at lunch, dinner or both, usually with three courses.

CHILDREN'S FACILITIES
Small portions and/or high chairs available on request.

	OUTDOOR EATING	VEGETARIAN SPECIALTIES	BAR AREA/COCKTAIL BAR	FIXED-PRICE MENU	CHILDREN'S FACILITIES
BEVERLY HILLS: Piazza Rodeo $$$ 208 Rodeo Drive, CA 90210. **Map 5 F3.** (310) 275-2428. The fabulous pasta dishes are recommended at this busy Italian restaurant. For lighter fare, there is also a good selection of antipasti, salads, and sandwiches.	■	●	■		■
BEVERLY HILLS: Dining Room, Regent Beverly Wilshire Hotel $$$$$ 9500 Wilshire Blvd, CA 90212. **Map 5 F3.** (310) 275-5200. This extremely elegant hotel supper club *(see p508)* attracts an upscale older crowd with its European old world ambience. The paella is extraordinary.		●	■	●	
BEVERLY HILLS: Mr. Chow $$$$$ 344 N Camden Dr, CA 90210. **Map 5 F3.** (310) 278-9911. Celebrities come to this stylish restaurant for delicious Peking-style cuisine. Favorites include drunken fish and gamblers' duck. ● *Sat & Sun L.*		●	■		
BURBANK: Smoke House $$ 4420 Lakeside Dr, CA 91505. **Road map inset A.** (818) 845-3731. Tasty all-American fare, a real "meat-and-potatoes" place. Located across the street from Warner Bros. and Disney Studios, this is a great restaurant for grownups and kids.					
CENTURY CITY: Johnny Rocket's. $ 10250 Santa Monica Blvd, CA 90067. **Map 5 D4.** (310) 788-9020. Kids of all ages love this new chain restaurant, with its 1950s ambiance of a real soda fountain. Burgers, shakes, and fries are tops on the menu, and they also serve the best veggie burgers in town.		●			■
CENTURY CITY: La Cachette $$$$ 10506 South Santa Monica Blvd, CA 90025. **Map 4 C5.** (310) 470-4992. This very chic restaurant, one of LA's best, serves French-Mediterranean cuisine. The spacious surroundings are light and airy.		●	■		■
DOWNTOWN: Patinette at Moca $ 250 S Grand Ave, CA 90012. **Map 11 D4.** (213) 626-1178. This café-style restaurant in the courtyard of the Museum of Contemporary Art *(see p121)* serves great salads and sandwiches. ● *Mon, Tue & Wed D, Fri & Sat D.*	■	●			■
DOWNTOWN: Checkers $$$ 535 S Grand Ave, CA 90071. **Map 11 D4.** (213) 624-0000. Furnished with marble and antiques, this intimate hotel restaurant *(see p510)* has an award-winning menu featuring eclectic California cuisine.		●	■		
DOWNTOWN: Sonora Café $$$ 180 S La Brea, CA 90036. **Map 7 F3.** (323) 857-1800. Wonderful Mexican-influenced southwestern staples are on offer at this candlelit restaurant. Favorites include fabulous *quesadillas* (Mexican stuffed flat pies) filled with goat cheese, brie, and smoked bacon. ● *Sat & Sun L.*	■	●	■		
DOWNTOWN: Bernard's $$$$ Biltmore Hotel, 506 S Grand, CA 90012. **Map 11 D4.** (213) 612-1580. This elegant restaurant features fixed-price and *à la carte* menus and special wine dinners and lunches. They have a good selection of fish dishes as well as steak and lamb specialties. ● *Sun, Mon D, Sat L.*		●	■	●	■
DOWNTOWN: Cicada $$$$ 617 S Olive St, CA 90014. **Map 11 D4.** (213) 488-9488. The contemporary Italian cuisine packs in the customers at this beautiful Art Deco restaurant in the Oviatt Hotel. ● *Sun, Mon–Wed L, Sat L.*		●	■	●	
DOWNTOWN: Water Grill $$$$ 544 S Grand Ave, CA 90017. **Map 11 D4.** (213) 891-0900. This restaurant has an oyster bar and serves delicious seafood, from crab cakes to Santa Barbara prawns. They also have a live lobster and crab tank.		●	■		■

For key to symbols see back flap

Price categories for a three-
course meal for one,
including a half bottle of
house wine, sales tax, and
service:
$ under $25
$$ $25–$35
$$$ $35–$50
$$$$ $50–$70
$$$$$ over $70

OUTDOOR EATING
Some tables on a patio or terrace.
VEGETARIAN SPECIALTIES
One menu always includes a selection of vegetarian dishes.
BAR AREA/COCKTAIL BAR
There is a bar area or cocktail bar within the restaurant.
FIXED-PRICE MENU
A good-value fixed-price menu offered at lunch, dinner
or both, usually with three courses.
CHILDREN'S FACILITIES
Small portions and/or high chairs available on request.

	OUTDOOR EATING	VEGETARIAN SPECIALTIES	BAR AREA/COCKTAIL BAR	FIXED-PRICE MENU	CHILDREN'S FACILITIES

GLENDALE: *Damon's Steak House* $$
317 North Brand Blvd, Glendale, CA 91203. **Road map** inset A. [(818) 956-9056. The
tropical décor, paradoxically mixed with a 1930s vibe, belies this popular
restaurant's traditional American fare. & ♥ ☻
| | ● | ■ | ● | ■ |

HOLLYWOOD: *Canter's Deli* $
419 N Fairfax Ave, CA 90036. **Map** 7 D2. [(323) 651-2030. The hip crowd
ends up at this wonderful 24-hour deli between 2am and 4am
for the huge, delicious sandwiches and diner-style meals. & ☻
| | ● | ■ | | ■ |

HOLLYWOOD: *Cha Cha Cha* $
656 N Virgil Ave, CA 90004. **Map** 9 F1. [(323) 664-7723.
Paella and jerk chicken are especially good at this contemporary Carib-
bean restaurant. The spicy sauces can be served on the side. & ♫ ☻
| | ● | | | |

HOLLYWOOD: *Hollywood Hills Coffee Shop* $
6145 Franklin Ave, CA 90028. **Map** 2 C4. [(323) 467-7678. Inside the Best
Western Hollywood Hills Hotel, this friendly restaurant serves classic American
diner food with the added bonus of plenty of star-sightings. & ☻
| | ● | | | ■ |

HOLLYWOOD: *Kokomo Café* $
Farmer's Market, 6333 W 3rd St, CA 90036. **Map** 7 D3. [(323) 933-0773.
This café is a great place to eat breakfast and lunch and as a result is
often packed with hungry customers. Try the applewood-smoked chicken
breast sandwiches or the delicious turkey burgers. ● D. & ☻
| ■ | ● | | | ■ |

HOLLYWOOD: *Mario's Peruvian* $
5786 Melrose Ave, CA 90038. **Map** 8 B1. [(323) 466-4181. This uninspired-
looking place serves wonderful Peruvian dishes including a delicious
fish stew and fish marinated in lemon juice (served cold). Arrive early;
it gets busy. Alcohol is not served, but you can bring your own. & ☻
| | ● | | | ■ |

HOLLYWOOD: *Souplantation* $
Beverly Center, 8491 W 3rd St, CA 90048. **Map** 6 C3. [(323) 655-0381.
This all-you-can-eat restaurant chain is a real bargain. Serve yourself
from the buffet bars with a huge selection of soups, salads, baked
goods, fruit, and yogurt. Children under five eat for only $1.49. & ☻
| ■ | ● | | | ■ |

HOLLYWOOD: *The Gumbo Pot* $
Farmer's Market, 6333 W 3rd St, CA 90036. **Map** 7 D3. [(323) 933-0358. Try
gumbo stew and enormous Po'Boys (foot-long sandwiches) at this Cajun
fast-food bar, with occasional live Cajun bands. ● D. & ♫ ☻
| ■ | ● | | | |

HOLLYWOOD: *Hollywood Canteen* $$
1006 N Seward St, CA 90038. **Map** 2 C5. [(323) 465-0961. American cuisine
with Italian influences is served at this lovely 1940s-style restaurant. New
York steaks and marinated salmon are good. ● Sun, Mon–Sat L. & ♫ ☻
| ■ | ● | ■ | | |

HOLLYWOOD: *Shin* $$
1972 Hillhurst Ave, CA 90027. **Road map** inset A. [(323) 664-1891. The salmon
tempura at this minimalist Japanese restaurant is wonderful, as is the
sushi and sashimi (raw fish). Order the bento box to taste a little bit
of everything. ● Sun, Mon–Sat L. & ☻
| | ● | | | |

HOLLYWOOD: *The Clay Pit* $$
145 S Barrington, CA 90049. **Map** 4 A5. [(310) 476-4700. This nice, new
restaurant in the Brentwood section is worth the trip for excellent
northern Indian cuisine. Reservations are recommended. & ☻
| ■ | ● | | ● | ■ |

HOLLYWOOD: *Ca'brea* $$$
346 S La Brea Ave, CA90036. **Map** 7 F3. [(323) 938-2863. The surroundings
are stylish, and the atmosphere is warm at this busy restaurant serving
hearty northern Italian cuisine. Try the tasty lentil soup. ● Sun. & ☻
| | ● | ■ | | |

HOLLYWOOD: *Campanile* $$$$
624 S La Brea Ave, CA 90036. **Map 7 F4.** ☎ *(323) 938 1447.* The cuisine is California-Mediterranean at this stylish restaurant. Smoking is allowed at the bar where there are 70 grappas offered. ● *Sun D.* ♿ 🍷 💳

HOLLYWOOD: *Mandalay* $$$$
611 N La Brea Ave, CA 90036. **Map 7 F3.** ☎ *(323) 933-0717.* This choice French-Vietnamese restaurant has an eclectic menu that includes sushi, dumplings, and traditional Vietnamese dishes such as spicy beef salad. ● *L.* ♿ 👔 ♫ 💳

LONG BEACH: *M Bar & Grill* $$
213A Pine Ave at Broadway St, CA 90802. **Road map** inset A. ☎ *(562) 435-2525.* A fusion of Mediterranean and Latin flavors highlights the cuisine at this trendy café with rotating art exhibits and good live bands. ● *Sat & Sun L.* ♿ ♫ 💳

LONG BEACH: *Parker's Lighthouse* $$
435 Shoreline Village Drive, CA 90802. **Road map** inset A. ☎ *(562) 432-6500.* Nautical themes prevail in this converted lighthouse serving excellent seafood. The mesquite-grilled fresh fish is memorable. ♿ 💳

LONG BEACH: *Shenandoah Café* $$
4722 E 2nd St, CA 90803. **Road map** inset A. ☎ *(562) 434-3469.* Homemade apple fritters and hickory-smoked ribs are favorites at this quaint café serving Southern-style food. Try the Sunday brunch. ● *Sat L.* ♿ 💳

LONG BEACH: *Sir Winston's Restaurant* $$$
Queen Mary Seaport, 1126 Queen's Hwy, CA 90801. **Road map** inset A. ☎ *(562) 435-3511.* Majestic dark-wood decor sets the tone for romantic formal dining aboard the Queen Mary. The cuisine is continental. ● *L.* 👔 🍷 ♫ 💳

MALIBU: *Beau Rivage* $$$
26025 Pacific Coast Hwy, CA 90265. **Road map** inset A. ☎ *(310) 456-5733.* The Mediterranean romantic/California cuisine sets the stage for a great evening. Breathtaking sunsets and fantastic Sunday brunch. ♿ ♫ 🍷 💳

MALIBU: *Gladstone's 4 Fish* $$$
17300 Pacific Coast Hwy, CA 90272. **Road map** inset A. ☎ *(310) 454-3474.* This oceanside seafood restaurant is great fun for families. Portions are huge, but you can take home the leftovers in an aluminum foil sculpture. ♿ 💳

MALIBU: *Saddle Peak Lodge* $$$$
419 Cold Canyon Road, CA 91302. **Road map** inset A. ☎ *(818) 222-3888.* A stylish crowd frequents this restaurant hidden away in the Santa Monica Mountains. It is the best place in LA for game. ● *Mon, Tue.* ♿ 🍷 💳

MARINA DEL REY: *Alejo's* $
4002 Lincoln Blvd, CA 90292. **Road map** inset A. ☎ *(310) 822-0095.* Bring your own alcohol to this fabulous restaurant serving good cheap Italian food on Formica-top tables. There are always lines to get in. ● *Sat & Sun L.* 💳

MARINA DEL REY: *Killer Shrimp* $
523 Washington St, CA 90292. **Road map** inset A. ☎ *(310) 578-2293.* Nothing except shrimp in divine sauces is on offer at this stylish chain restaurant, and it never fails to attract customers in droves. 💳

MARINA DEL REY: *The Cheesecake Factory* $
4142 Via Marina, CA 90292. **Road map** inset A. ☎ *(310) 306-3344.* People line up to get into this local chain restaurant. The menu ranges from Asian to French to Italian – and features more than 30 varieties of cheesecake! ♿ 💳

PASADENA: *Gordon Biersch Brewery* $$$
41 Hugus Alley, CA 91103. **Road map** inset A. ☎ *(626) 449-0052.* A mostly young singles crowd frequents this upscale chain restaurant with its own brewery. The beer is really good, as are the burgers, pasta, and fish. ♿ 💳

PASADENA: *Parkway Grill* $$$
510 S Arroyo Pkwy, CA 91105. **Road map** inset A. ☎ *(626) 795-1001.* This restaurant serving California cuisine is one of the region's best. The dining room is like a garden, with trees and flowers. ● *Sat L.* ♿ 🍷 ♫ 💳

PASADENA: *Shiro* $$$
1505 Mission St, CA 91030. **Road map** inset A. ☎ *(626) 799-4774.* Voted the top restaurant in LA in 1996 by the Zagat's survey, this very popular restaurant serves excellent French-Japanese cuisine. ● *Mon, Tue–Sun L.* ♿ 💳

Campanile		●	■		■
Mandalay		●	■		■
M Bar & Grill	■	●			■
Parker's Lighthouse	■	●	■	●	■
Shenandoah Café		●			■
Sir Winston's Restaurant		●	■	●	■
Beau Rivage	■	●	■		
Gladstone's 4 Fish	■	●	■		■
Saddle Peak Lodge	■	●	■		
Alejo's		●			
Killer Shrimp	■				
The Cheesecake Factory		●	■		■
Gordon Biersch Brewery	■	●	■		■
Parkway Grill		●	■		■
Shiro					

Price categories for a three-course meal for one, including a half bottle of house wine, sales tax, and service:

$ under $25
$$ $25–$35
$$$ $35–$50
$$$$ $50–$70
$$$$$ over $70

OUTDOOR EATING
Some tables on a patio or terrace.

VEGETARIAN SPECIALTIES
One menu always includes a selection of vegetarian dishes.

BAR AREA/COCKTAIL BAR
There is a bar area or cocktail bar within the restaurant.

FIXED-PRICE MENU
A good-value fixed-price menu offered at lunch, dinner or both, usually with three courses.

CHILDREN'S FACILITIES
Small portions and/or high chairs available on request.

	OUTDOOR EATING	VEGETARIAN SPECIALTIES	BAR AREA/COCKTAIL BAR	FIXED-PRICE MENU	CHILDREN'S FACILITIES
PASADENA: *Yujean Kang's* — $$$		●		●	
67 N Raymond Ave, CA 91103. **Road map** inset A. ☎ *(626) 585-0855.* Presentation is everything at this very elegant Chinese restaurant, which is always busy. Try the "lobster with strange flavors." Lunch is a bargain. ● *Tue.* ⚫ ⚫					
SAN PEDRO: *22nd Street Landing* — $$$	■	●	●		■
141A W 22nd St, CA 90731. **Road map** inset A. ☎ *(310) 548-4400.* This large seafood restaurant on San Pedro harbor has nautical-style decor and is always busy and bustling. Try the seafood cassoulet baked in filo pastry. ⚫ ⚫ ⚫					
SANTA MONICA: *Broadway Bar & Grill* — $$	■	●	●		
1460 Third Street Promenade, CA 90401. **Road map** inset A. ☎ *(310) 393-4211.* Business is brisk at this stylish bar and grill serving continental food, notably grilled fish and steaks, with an extensive wine list. ⚫ ⚫ ⚫					
SANTA MONICA: *Schatzi on Main* — $$	■	●	●		■
3110 Main St, CA 90405. **Road map** inset A. ☎ *(310) 399-4800.* Hollywood star Arnold Schwarzenegger owns this pleasant restaurant serving Austrian specialties and healthy California cuisine. There is a Sunday champagne brunch. ⚫ ⚫					
SANTA MONICA: *Ocean Avenue Seafood* — $$$	■	●	●		■
1401 Ocean Ave, CA 90401. **Road map** inset A. ☎ *(310) 394-5669.* This very busy restaurant has an oyster bar and a relaxed atmosphere. Go there for the flakiest, tenderest Chilean sea bass marinaded in saki sauce. ⚫ ⚫					
SANTA MONICA: *Buffalo Club* — $$$$	■	●	■		
1520 Olympic Blvd, CA 90404. **Road map** inset A. ☎ *(310) 450-8600.* Consistently voted among the top ten restaurants in LA, the food here is delicious – American cuisine at its most imaginative. The shrimp and lobster dumplings with spicy black bean sauce are fabulous. ● *Sun & Mon, Tue–Sat L.* ⚫ ⚫ ⚫					
SANTA MONICA: *Café Delfini* — $$$$		●			
147 W Channel Rd, CA 90402. **Road map** inset A. ☎ *(310) 459-8823.* This intimate and romantic restaurant serves delicious Italian dishes, including hand-made gnocchi (only on Thursdays). Reservations are advised. ● *L.* ⚫ ⚫					
SANTA MONICA: *Drago* — $$$$		●	●		■
2628 Wilshire Blvd, CA 90403. **Road map** inset A. ☎ *(310) 828-1585.* Wonderful Sicilian dishes are served in this lovely, sleek restaurant. Try the risotto with pheasant and morel mushroom ragout. ● *Sat & Sun L.* ⚫ ⚫ ⚫					
SANTA MONICA: *Chinois on Main* — $$$$$			■		■
2709 Main St, CA 90405. **Road map** inset A. ☎ *(310) 392-9025.* Wolfgang Puck's establishment is another of LA's top ten, presenting a mixture of Chinese, Japanese, and California cuisine. Dishes such as the sizzling sea scallops with potato strings are truly special. ● *Sat–Tue L.* ⚫ ⚫ ⚫					
SANTA MONICA: *Michael's* — $$$$$	■	●	■	●	■
1147 3rd St, CA 90403. **Road map** inset A. ☎ *(310) 451-0843.* People dress up to go to this award-winning restaurant serving American cuisine in 1930s surroundings, with original works by notable painters. Special dishes include salmon with caviar and chives. ● *Sun & Mon, Sat L.* ⚫ ⚫ ⚫					
SANTA MONICA: *Valentino* — $$$$$	■	●	■		■
3115 Pico Blvd, CA 90405. **Road map** inset A. ☎ *(310) 829-4313.* Voted the best Italian cuisine in LA, this northern Italian restaurant also has one of the city's best wine lists. Everything is made on the premises, from the bread and pasta to the desserts and sorbets. ● *Sun, Mon–Thu L, Sat L.* ⚫ ⚫ ⚫					
STUDIO CITY: *Pinot Bistro* — $$$	■	●	■		■
12969 Ventura Blvd, CA 91604. **Road map** inset A. ☎ *(818) 990-0500.* This French bistro is a little bit of Paris in LA. The cozy room provides the perfect setting for the wonderful cuisine. ● *Sat & Sun L.* ⚫ ⚫ ⚫ ⚫					

STUDIO CITY: *La Loggia* $$$$
11814 Ventura Blvd, CA 91604. **Road map** inset A. [(818) 985-9222. This northern
Italian restaurant is very busy and very small – but famous for its homemade
spaghetti with river shrimp, scallops, and calamari. ● Sun, Sat L. & ▮ ▮

UNIVERSAL CITY: *BB King's Blues Club* $$$
1000 Universal Center Drive, CA 91608. **Road map** inset A. [(818) 622-5464.
There is a gospel brunch on Sundays, at this Southern restaurant serving
fried chicken with biscuits and gravy, and Cajun catfish. ● L. & ♬ ▮

VENICE: *Café 50s Diner* $
838 Lincoln Blvd, CA 90291. **Road map** inset A. [(310) 399 1955. This tiny 50s café
serves typical diner food – sandwiches, salads, hamburgers, and milkshakes
– and "blue plate special" dinners, such as pot roast, in the evenings. & ▮

VENICE: *Jody Maroni's Sausage Kingdom* ☑ www.maroni.com $
2011 Ocean Front Walk, CA 90291. **Road map** inset A. [(310) 348-1500. A sausage
sandwich on an onion roll with onions and peppers is a favorite at
this casual walk-up sausage stand on the boardwalk (no seating). &

VENICE: *The Rose Café & Market* $
220 Rose Ave, CA 90291. **Road map** inset A. [(310) 399-0711. This casual café
at the corner with Main Street serves tasty standards such as burgers and
chicken. The Chinese chicken salad is very good. ● Sun D. & ♬ ▮

VENICE: *Hama Sushi* $$
213 Windward Ave, CA 90291. **Road map** inset A. [(310) 396-8783. A very
social singles crowd makes for a long wait, but there is delicious sushi and
other authentic Japanese dishes, plus great sakes and imported beers. & ▮

VENICE: *Hal's* $$$
1349 Abbot Kinney Blvd, CA 90291. **Road map** inset A. [(310) 396-3105.
This friendly, busy, hip bistro serves classic American food and pastas
in light, airy surroundings with contemporary art on the walls. ♬ ▮

WEST HOLLYWOOD: *Astroburger* $
7475 Santa Monica Blvd, CA 90046. **Map 7 E1.** [(323) 874-8041. Great
American food: burgers, fries, onion rings, and a good choice of
vegetarian dishes. They stay open until 3am for late revelers. &

WEST HOLLYWOOD: *Cajun Bistro* $
8301 Sunset Blvd, CA 90069. **Map 6 C1.** [(323) 656-6388. The best jambalaya
this side of New Orleans. Good Cajun food such as the blackened red fish,
gumbos, fried and broiled meats, and big salads are specialties. & ▮

WEST HOLLYWOOD: *Marix* $
1108 N Flores St, CA 90069. **Road map** inset A. [(323) 656-8800. Fabulous
Mexican food is served in this noisy, laid-back restaurant that is pop-
ular with the gay crowd. It also has a huge selection of Margaritas. & ▮

WEST HOLLYWOOD: *The Rainbow Bar and Grill* $
9015 Sunset Blvd, CA 90069. **Map 6 A1.** [(310) 278-4232. This high-energy
hang-out for the entertainment industry *(see p98)* features continental cuisine
with Italian flair. It is also a nightclub in the evenings. ● Sat & Sun. & ▮ ▮

WEST HOLLYWOOD: *Cyrano* $$
8840 Beverly Blvd, CA 90210. **Map 6 B2.** [(310) 271-4193. The California-
French/Mediterranean-style cuisine at this restaurant includes lamb and
seafood and the best chocolate souffle in town. & ▮ ▮

WEST HOLLYWOOD: *Jones Hollywood* $$
7205 Santa Monica Blvd, CA 90046. **Map 2 A5.** [(323) 850-1727. Try the New
York steaks, seared and grilled in the woodburning pizza oven, at this
busy restaurant serving California-Italian fare. ● Sat & Sun L. & ▮

WEST HOLLYWOOD: *Georgia* $$$
7250 Melrose Ave, CA 90046. **Map 7 F2.** [(323) 933-8420. The food is superb
at this upscale soul food restaurant. Try the meatloaf or Southern fried
chicken. Corn bread and fried green tomatoes served on the side. & ♬ ▮

WEST HOLLYWOOD: *L'Arancino* $$$
8908 Beverly Blvd, CA 90048. **Map 6 A2.** [(310) 858-5777. Southern Italian
food is the order of the day here. Try the calamari and the rice croquett.
The atmosphere is cute and bright. & ▮

For key to symbols see back flap

Price categories for a three-course meal for one, including a half bottle of house wine, sales tax, and service:
$ under $25
$$ $25–$35
$$$ $35–$50
$$$$ $50–$70
$$$$$ over $70

OUTDOOR EATING Some tables on a patio or terrace.
VEGETARIAN SPECIALTIES One menu always includes a selection of vegetarian dishes.
BAR AREA/COCKTAIL BAR There is a bar area or cocktail bar within the restaurant.
FIXED-PRICE MENU A good-value fixed-price menu offered at lunch, dinner or both, usually with three courses.
CHILDREN'S FACILITIES Small portions and/or high chairs available on request.

Restaurant	OUTDOOR EATING	VEGETARIAN SPECIALTIES	BAR AREA/COCKTAIL BAR	FIXED-PRICE MENU	CHILDREN'S FACILITIES
WEST HOLLYWOOD: Pane e Vino $$$ 8265 Beverly Blvd, CA 90048. **Map 6 C1.** (323) 651-4600. This busy Italian restaurant serves pasta, risottos, and fish. The walls are decorated with a heavenly fresco. Get there early if you want a seat outside. Sun L.	■	●	■		■
WEST HOLLYWOOD: Talesai $$$ 9043 Sunset Blvd, CA 90069. **Map 6 A1.** (310) 275-9724. This Thai restaurant is friendly, and the food is delicious. The steamed duck, deep fried and served with a ginger soybean sauce, is spectacular. Sun, Sat L.		●	■	●	
WEST HOLLYWOOD: Carafe $$$$ 8284 Melrose Ave, CA 90046. **Map 6 C1.** (323) 655-8880. Mirrors and carved rosewood provide an elegant and romantic setting for the fine French cuisine. The crab cakes are really good. They also serve venison and rabbit. Open for lunch Fridays only. Mon.		●		●	
WEST HOLLYWOOD: Citrus $$$$ 6703 Melrose Ave, CA 90038. **Map 8 A1.** (323) 857-0034. This award-winning restaurant dishes up French-California cuisine on its covered patio. It gets busy so make sure you book ahead. Sun	■		■	●	
WEST HOLLYWOOD: House of Blues $$$$ 8430 Sunset Blvd, CA 90069. **Map 6 C1.** (323) 848-5100. Housed in a huge Southern-style tin shack (see p99), this trendy restaurant turns out fabulous soul food dishes such as chicken and sausage gumbo.		●	●		■
WEST HOLLYWOOD: Le Dome $$$$ 8720 Sunset Blvd, CA 90069. **Map 6 C1.** (310) 659-6919. Portions are huge at this popular restaurant serving continental cuisine. The *filet mignon* with three-peppercorn sauce is excellent. Sun.	■	●	■		
WEST HOLLYWOOD: fenix at the Argyle $$$$$ Argyle Hotel, 8358 Sunset Blvd, CA 90069. **Map 6 C1.** (323) 848-6677. The French-California cuisine at this hotel restaurant (see p99) is served in elegantly stark surroundings. Book a week ahead. Mon–Sat L.		●	■	●	■
WEST HOLLYWOOD: L'Orangerie $$$$$ 903 N La Cienega Blvd, CA 90069. **Map 6 C1.** (310) 652-9770. This five-diamond French restaurant is extremely elegant and always busy. The stunning specials include fillet of John Dory with roasted figs. Mon.	■	●	■	●	
WEST HOLLYWOOD: Patina $$$$$ 5955 Melrose Ave, CA 90038. **Map 8 B2.** (323) 467-1108. This truly fabulous restaurant serving French-California cuisine is considered by many to be one of the best eating establishments in Los Angeles. Try the delicious peppered tuna with Chinese vegetables.		●	■	●	
WESTWOOD/WEST LA: John O'Groats $ 10516 W Pico Blvd, CA 90064. **Road map** inset A. (310) 204-0692. For years, this place was open only for breakfast and lunch. Now a good selection of classic American dinner dishes have been added. You can bring your own wine or beer. The John O'Groats is very popular with families. Sun–Wed D.		●			■
WESTWOOD/WEST LA: Bombay Café $$ 12021 W Pico Blvd, CA 90025. **Road map** inset A. (310) 473-3388. One of the best Indian restaurants in LA, this place serves homecooked dishes from the owner's native city. It gets very busy. Mon		●			■
WESTWOOD: La Bruschetta $$$ 1621 Westwood Blvd, CA 90024. **Road map** inset A. (310) 477-1052. This friendly, award-winning restaurant serves Italian cuisine featuring homemade pasta and regional dishes from all over Italy. Sun.		●			

SOUTH CENTRAL

BAKERSFIELD: *Wool Growers* $$
620 E 19th St, CA 93305. **Road map** C5. (*(661) 327-9584.* This restaurant serves French Basque cuisine as well as American standards. Everything comes with salad and French fries. Perfect for children. ● *Sun.* & 🍴

CAMBRIA: *The Brambles* $$$
4005 Burton Drive, CA 93428. **Road map** B5. (*(805) 927-4716.* This lovely restaurant near Hearst Castle *(see pp202–5)* serves international dishes as well as steaks. The menu is cheaper from 4–6pm. ● *Mon–Sat L.* & 🍴

GOLETA: *The Good Earth Restaurant and Bakery* $
5955 Calle Real, CA 93117. **Road map** B5. (*(805) 683-6101.* The emphasis is on healthy food at this restaurant, 9 miles (14 km) outside Santa Barbara, including a wonderful vegetarian lasagna. Families are welcome. Eat indoors or outside among the apple trees on the brick patio. & 🍴

LOS OLIVOS: *Los Olivos Café* $
2879 Grand Ave, CA 93441. **Road map** C5. (*(805) 688-7265.* This charming Mediterranean-style bistro serves pizzas, pastas, and salads along with good local wine. They also make up picnic baskets for wine tours. & 🍷 🍴

MONTECITO: *Montecito Café* $$$
1295 Coast Village Rd, CA 93108. **Road map** B5. (*(805) 969-3392.* This restaurant, housed in a hotel originally owned by Charlie Chaplin, serves good American food, such as grilled *filet mignon* with forest mushroom sauce. It gets busy, so you may wait for a table. & 🍷 🍴

MONTECITO: *Ristorante Piatti* $$$
516 San Ysidro Rd, CA 93108. **Road map** B5. (*(805) 969-7520.* This popular Italian restaurant serves a fine selection of traditional dishes, including fresh seafood, veal, pasta, and pizzas. & 🍴

MONTECITO: *Stonehouse* $$$$
San Ysidro Ranch, 900 San Ysidro Lane, CA 93108. **Road map** B5. (*(805) 969-4100.* There are mountain views from the terrace of this restaurant. Diners enjoy southwestern American cuisine, such as crispy Pacific oysters with spinach. Three fixed-price menus are available. & 🍷 🍴

MORRO BAY: *Windows on the Water* $$$$
699 Embarcadero, CA 93442. **Road map** B5. (*(805) 772-0677.* Great views overlooking the ocean, this restaurant serves French-California cuisine. Dishes include seafood ravioli with tomato sauce.. & 🍷 🍴

OJAI: *Wheeler Hot Springs Spa and Restaurant* $$$
16825 Maricopa Hwy, CA 93024. **Road map** C5. (*(805) 646-8131.* This hip resort is worth a detour from Santa Barbara. Enjoy a massage or hot tub before a delicious modern continental meal. ● *Mon–Wed.* & 🎵 🍴

PISMO BEACH: *Spyglass Inn Restaurant* $$$
2703 Spyglass Drive, CA 93449. **Road map** B5. (*(805) 773-1222.* Every table in this clifftop restaurant has spectacular ocean views. Steak and seafood, particularly crab and lobster, are specialties. & 🍷 🎵 🍴

SAN LUIS OBISPO: *Tio Alberto's* $
1131 Broad St, CA 93401. **Road map** B5. (*(805) 546-9646.* The specialty is *carne asada* (grilled beef) at this old-style Mexican restaurant, which is popular with the locals and open until 4am. No alcohol is served or allowed. & 🍴

SAN LUIS OBISPO: *Buona Tavola* $$
1037 Monterey St, CA 93401. **Road map** C5. (*(805) 545-8000.* This tiny stylish restaurant serves northern Italian cuisine. The bread, dressings, pasta, and desserts are all made on the premises. Great wine list ● *Sat & Sun L.* & 🍴

SAN LUIS OBISPO: *Café Roma* $$
1020 Railroad Ave, CA 93401. **Road map** B5. (*(805) 541-6800.* The Tuscan decor of this Italian restaurant reflects its cuisine. There is a selection of pastas, pizzas, and flavored olive oils. ● *Mon; Sat & Sun L.* & 🍷 🍴

SANTA BARBARA: *Be Bop Burgers* $
111 State St, CA 93101. **Road map** C5. (*(805) 966-1956.* This 1950s-style diner has a classic car indoors and a DJ on weekends. It serves burgers, sandwiches, milkshakes, and ice-cream sundaes. No alcohol. & 🍴

For key to symbols see back flap

Price categories for a three-course meal for one, including a half bottle of house wine, sales tax, and service:
$ under $25
$$ $25–$35
$$$ $35–$50
$$$$ $50–$70
$$$$$ over $70

OUTDOOR EATING
Some tables on a patio or terrace.
VEGETARIAN SPECIALTIES
One menu always includes a selection of vegetarian dishes.
BAR AREA/COCKTAIL BAR
There is a bar area or cocktail bar within the restaurant.
FIXED-PRICE MENU
A good-value fixed-price menu offered at lunch, dinner or both, usually with three courses.
CHILDREN'S FACILITIES
Small portions and/or high chairs available on request.

Restaurant	Outdoor Eating	Vegetarian Specialties	Bar Area/Cocktail Bar	Fixed-Price Menu	Children's Facilities
SANTA BARBARA: *La Super-Rica Taco* ($) 622 N Milpas St, CA 93103. **Road map** C5. ((805) 963-4940. Super-chef Julia Child recommends this wonderful Mexican *taqueria*. Specials vary daily and include *tamales* and *enchiladas* as well as vegetarian dishes. 🚹	■	●			■
SANTA BARBARA: *El Paseo* ($$) 10 El Paseo, CA 93101. **Road map** C5. ((805) 962-6050. This historic hacienda offers a taste of the real Mexico, with pork, fish, and shrimp dishes and 90 kinds of tequila. Drinks are served in handmade glassware. 🚹🎵🌿	■	●	■		■
SANTA BARBARA: *Louie's at the Upham* ($$) 1404 de la Vina St, CA 93101. **Road map** C5. ((805) 963-7003. Set in the oldest hotel in town *(see p515)*, this restaurant is very romantic. The food is California-continental, featuring fish and pasta. ● *Sat & Sun L.* 🚹🌿	■	●	■		■
SANTA BARBARA: *Something's Fishy* ($$) 502 State St, CA 93101. **Road map** C5. ((805) 966-6607. The crowd is mixed at this lively Japanese restaurant. Sit at the all-you-can-eat sushi bar or have a Benihana-style dinner cooked and served at your table. 🚹🌿			■		■
SANTA BARBARA: *The Harbor Restaurant & Longboards Grill* ($$) 210 Stearns Wharf, CA 93101. **Road map** C5. ((805) 963-3311. Built on a pier, every seat has an ocean view. Longboards serves fish and chips, pizzas, and buffalo wings, and there is a huge patio. The Harbor is more upscale, specializing in fresh fish, seafood, and prime rib. 🚹🌿	■	●	■		■
SANTA BARBARA: *Piranha* ($$) 714 State St, CA 93101. **Road map** C5. ((805) 965-2980. It can get very busy at this lively restaurant. The style is modern but cozy. Delicious treats include grilled salmon with shiso leaf and pesto sauce, peppercorn-coated Ahi tuna, as well as fabulous sushi. ● *Mon, Tue–Sun L.* 🚹🌿	■	●	■	●	■
SANTA BARBARA: *Cold Spring Tavern* ($$$) 5995 Stagecoach Rd, CA 93105. **Road map** C5. ((805) 967-0066. This small restaurant is housed in an old stagecoach stop. The Old West decor reflects the rustic California food, with an emphasis on game. 🚹🎵🌿		●	■	●	■
SANTA BARBARA: *Downey's* ($$$) 1305 State St, CA93101. **Road map** C5. ((805) 966-5006. The regional American cuisine here has won the Distinguished Restaurants of North America award. Their dessert of fresh raspberries with white chocolate mousse in puff pastry deserves world fame. ● *Mon, Tue–Sun L.* 🚹🍷🌿				●	
SANTA BARBARA: *Paradise Café* ($$$) 702 Anacapa St, Ca 93101. **Road map** C5. ((805) 962-4416. All meals come with either soup, salad, or vegetables at this "scene" café, which gets very busy. The chocolate mousse pie with espresso topping is famous. 🚹🌿	■	●	■	●	■
SANTA BARBARA: *The Wine Cask* ($$$) 813 Anacapa St, CA 93101. **Road map** C5. ((805) 966-9463. Mediterranean cuisine is offered here and one of the best wine lists in the US. Eat inside under the decoratively painted ceiling or in the courtyard. ● *L.* 🚹🍷🌿	■	●	■		■
SANTA BARBARA: *La Marina, Four Seasons Biltmore Hotel* ($$$$) 1260 Channel Drive, CA 93108. **Road map** C5. ((805) 969-2261. The ocean views from this hotel restaurant *(see p515)* are breathtaking. Try the ahi wrapped in phyllo with wasabi potatoes or the angel hair pasta with garlic prawns. ● *L.* 🚹🍷🌿		●	■	●	■
SANTA BARBARA: *The Patio at the Four Seasons Biltmore Hotel* ($$$$$) 1260 Channel Drive, CA 93108. **Road map** C5. ((805) 969-2261. This elegant hotel restaurant *(see p515)* serves California-style cuisine in a dining room with ocean views. The evening buffet is a great bargain. 🚹🍷🌿	■	●	■	●	■

SANTA BARBARA: *Citronelle* [$][$][$][$][$]
901 E Cabrillo Blvd, CA 93103. **Road map** C5. ☎ *(805) 963-0111.* Good French-California cuisine is served here against fine views of the ocean. A classical guitarist plays on Sundays, Mondays, and Tuesdays. ♿ ♫ 🍸 💳

– ● ■ ● ■

SHELL BEACH: *McLintok's* [$][$][$]
750 Mattie Rd, Shell Beach, CA 93449. **Road map** B5. ☎ *(805) 773-1892.* Come here for a great American barbeque in upbeat, Western-style surroundings. Steaks and chicken are grilled over an oak fire. ● *Mon–Sat L.* ♿ ♫ 💳

– ● ■ – ■

SHELL BEACH: *Sea Cliffs Restaurant* [$][$][$]
2757 Shell Beach Rd, CA 93449. **Road map** B5. ☎ *(805) 773-3555.* Sunday brunch is exceptional at this relaxed resort restaurant with gorgeous ocean views. The cuisine is Mediterranean. Book ahead. ♿ ♫ ♿

■ ● ■ – ■

ORANGE COUNTY

ANAHEIM: *Goofy's Kitchen* [$]
Disneyland Hotel, 1150 W Cerritos, CA 92803. **Road map** D6. ☎ *(714) 778-6600.* Children love this buffet hotel restaurant *(see p516)*, where they can eat simple food with favorite Disney characters. ● *Mon–Fri L.* ♿ 💳

■ ● ■ ● ■

ANAHEIM: *Mandarin Gourmet* [$][$]
1500 Adams Ave, CA 92626. **Road map** D6. ☎ *(714) 540-1937.* This Chinese restaurant has a comprehensive menu, and standards such as chicken chow mein are delicious. The service is friendly, even when busy. ♿

– ● ■ ● ■

ANAHEIM: *Mr. Stox* [$][$][$][$]
1105 E Katella Ave, CA 92805. **Road map** D6. ☎ *(714) 634-2994.* This smart restaurant serves an eclectic continental-style cuisine. Salads, fish, pasta, and meat dishes are imaginatively presented. The *crème brûlée* is one of the best in Orange County. ● *Sat & Sun L.* ♿ ♫ 🍸 💳

■ ● ■ ● ■

AVALON: *Ristorante Villa Portofino* [$][$]
Hotel Villa Portofino, Avalon, Catalina Island, CA 90704. **Road map** D6. ☎ *(310) 510-0508.* The Italian dishes are homemade at this elegant restaurant with lovely views. ● *Jan–mid-Feb: daily; mid-Feb–Dec: Mon & Tue, Wed–Sun L.* ♿ 🍸 💳

– ● ■ – ■

CORONA DEL MAR: *The Five Crowns* [$][$][$][$]
3801 E Coast Hwy, CA 92965. **Road map** D6. ☎ *(949) 760-0331.* This pub-style restaurant has brocade furnishings, antiques, and a continental menu.The wine list features over 800 selections. Try the Sunday brunch. ● *Mon–Sat L.* ♿ 🍸 💳

■ ● ■ – ■

CORONA DEL MAR: *Oyster's* [$][$][$][$][$]
2515 E Coast Hwy, CA 92625. **Road map** D6. ☎ *(949) 675-7411.* This local nightspot is popular for its live jazz and its delicious food, so reserve ahead. The tempura Ahi tuna appetizer is spectacular. ● *L.* ♿ ♫ 🍸 💳

– ● ■ – ■

COSTA MESA: *Wolfgang Puck Café* [$][$][$]
South Coast Plaza, 3333 Bristol Ave, CA 92626. **Road map** D6. ☎ *(714) 546-9653.* Celebrity chef Wolfgang Puck's café is a less expensive version of his other restaurants. Great pizzas, salads, and pasta dishes are offered. ♿ 💳

■ ● – – ■

COSTA MESA: *Armani Café* [$][$][$][$][$]
South Coast Plaza, 3333 Bristol St, CA 92626. **Road map** D6. ☎ *(714) 754-0300.* Armani-clad waiters dish up Italian sandwiches, pizzas, salads, and pasta dishes in trendy surroundings next door to the Armani boutique. The *Portelli alla Piacentina* pasta is a recipe from Armani's grandmother. ♿ 💳

■ ● ■ – ■

FULLERTON: *The Cellar* [$][$][$][$]
305 N Harbor Blvd, CA 92632. **Road map** D6. ☎ *(714) 525-5682.* This fine French restaurant has a wine list with over 1,200 selections. Early diners can order the budget fixed-price menu. ● *daily L.* 🍸 💳

– ● ■ ● –

GARDEN GROVE: *Pinnacle Peak* [$]
9100 Trask Ave, CA92844. **Road map** D6. ☎ *(714) 892-7311.* This steakhouse serves open-grill beef at decent prices. Picnic-bench seating gives an "Old West" atmosphere. No bar, but a good selection of American beers. ♿ 💳

– – – – ■

IRVINE: *Bistango* [$][$]
19100 Von Karmen Ave, CA 92612. **Road map** D6. ☎ *(949) 752-5222.* The steaks and lamb dishes are excellent at this dramatic, artsy atrium restaurant. It's always crowded because the food is reliably good, so call ahead for reservations. ♿ ♫ 💳

■ ● ■ ● –

Price categories for a three-course meal for one, including a half bottle of house wine, sales tax, and service:
$ under $25
$$ $25–$35
$$$ $35–$50
$$$$ $50–$70
$$$$$ over $70

OUTDOOR EATING
Some tables on a patio or terrace.
VEGETARIAN SPECIALTIES
One menu always includes a selection of vegetarian dishes.
BAR AREA/COCKTAIL BAR
There is a bar area or cocktail bar within the restaurant.
FIXED-PRICE MENU
A good-value fixed-price menu offered at lunch, dinner or both, usually with three courses.
CHILDREN'S FACILITIES
Small portions and/or high chairs available on request.

IRVINE: *Il Fornao* $$
18051 Von Karman Ave, CA 92715. **Road map** D6. ☎ *(949) 261-1444.* Part of a chain, this Italian restaurant serves a good selection of pizzas and pasta dishes. Fresh-baked Italian breads are available to take out. ♿ ✉

IRVINE: *The Chanteclair* $$$$
18912 MacArthur Blvd, CA 92714. **Road map** D6. ☎ *(949) 752-8001.* French cuisine is served at this lovely, antique-filled restaurant. The salmon with orange soy sauce is outstanding. ● *Sun, Sat L.* ♿ ♥ ✉

LAGUNA BEACH: *Café Zinc* $
350 Ocean Ave, CA 92651. **Road map** D6. ☎ *(949) 494-6302.* Locals come here for breakfast or just for coffee. The soups and sandwiches are very good, as are the desserts. It's great for a budget lunch. ● *D.* ♿

LAGUNA BEACH: *Las Brisas* $$$
361 Cliff Drive, CA 92652. **Road map** D6. ☎ *(949) 497-5434.* This Mexican restaurant is always crowded because of its stunning clifftop view. The menu features fresh seafood, beef, and salads. This is an ideal place to go for margaritas at sunset or a champagne brunch on Sundays. ♿ ✉

LAGUNA BEACH: *Splashes* $$$
Surf and Sand Hotel, 1555 South Coast Hwy, CA 92651. **Road map** D6.
☎ *(949) 497-4477.* The Mediterranean-style cuisine and the stunning view of the ocean, with waves crashing nearby, are superb at this hotel restaurant *(see p517)*. Go at sunset to really appreciate it. ♿ ♥ ✉

LAGUNA NIGUEL: *The Lounge at the Ritz Carlton Hotel* $$$$$
Ritz Carlton Hotel, 1 Ritz Carlton Drive, CA 92629. **Road map** D6.
☎ *(949) 240-2000.* One of three hotel restaurants, the Lounge has a splendid view of the ocean. It serves appetizers, pasta, club sandwiches, and seafood, as well as traditional English high tea. ♿ ♫ ♥ ✉

NEWPORT BEACH: *The Ritz* $$$
880 Newport Center Drive, CA 92660. **Road map** D6. ☎ *(949) 720-1800.* The continental-style cuisine has won several food and wine awards. On Sundays there is a budget fixed-price dinner menu. ● *Sat & Sun L.* ♿ ♫ ♥ ✉

NEWPORT BEACH: *John Dominis* $$$$
2901 W Coast Hwy, CA 92663. **Road map** D6. ☎ *(714) 650-5112.* This popular continental-style seafood restaurant has harbor views and live Hawaiian music on Sundays. ● *Mon–Sat L.* ♿ ♫ ♥ ✉

ORANGE: *The Hobbit* $$$$$
2932 Chapman Ave, CA 92669. **Road map** D6. ☎ *(714) 997-1972.* The fixed-price, seven-course dinner here starts with champagne and hors d'oeuvres while you choose from the famous wine cellar. The continental menu changes daily. Book months ahead. ● *Mon, Tue–Sun L.* ♥ ✉

SANTA ANA: *Topaz* $$
Bowers Museum, 2002 N Main St, CA 92706. **Road map** D6. ☎ *(714) 835-2002.* This museum restaurant *(see p229)* serves sandwiches, salads, and a children's menu at $1 per plate. ● *Sun & Mon, Tue D.* ♿ ♫ ✉

SUNSET BEACH: *Harbor House Café* $
16341 Pacific Coast Hwy (Anderson St), CA90742. **Road map** D6. ☎ *(562) 592-5404.* This 24-hour diner on the beach serves enormous plates of classic American food. Breakfast here will set you up for the day. ♿ ✉

TUSTIN: *Zov's Bistro* $$
17440 E 17th St, CA92680. **Road map** D6. ☎ *(714) 838-8855.* This popular bistro serves delicious Mediterranean dishes such as lamb burger on a ciabatta bun with yogurt mint dressing. ● *Sun, Mon–Tue L.* ♿ ✉

Restaurant	Outdoor Eating	Vegetarian Specialties	Bar Area/Cocktail Bar	Fixed-Price Menu	Children's Facilities
Il Fornao	■	●	■		■
The Chanteclair	■	●	■	●	■
Café Zinc	■	●			■
Las Brisas	■	●	■		■
Splashes	■	●	■		■
The Lounge at the Ritz Carlton Hotel		●			
The Ritz		●	■	●	■
John Dominis			■	●	■
The Hobbit		●	■	●	
Topaz	■	●	■		■
Harbor House Café		●			■
Zov's Bistro		●			■

TWO HARBORS: *Doug's Harbor Reef Restaurant* $$$$$
Two Harbors, Catalina Island, CA 90704. **Road map** C6. *(310) 510-2800.*
Boats dock here for the fresh fish, baby back ribs, and chicken. There is weekend dancing at the outdoor bar. ● *Jun–Nov: L; Dec–May: daily.*

YORBA LINDA: *El Torito* $$$$
22699 Oakcrest Circle, CA 92887. **Road map** D6. *(714) 921-2335.* Generous portions of authentic Mexican cuisine are served at this quality chain restaurant. It also offers Sunday brunch and happy-hour specials.

SAN DIEGO COUNTY

CORONADO: *Poehe's* $$$$$
1201 1st St, Old Ferry Landing Plaza. **Road map** D6. *(619) 437-4474.*
There are lovely views of Downtown San Diego from this restaurant, which serves creative Polynesian cuisine. The setting is very Hawaiian, with waterfalls and tropical plants every place you look.

CORONADO: *The Brigantine* $$$$$
1333 Orange Ave, CA 92118. **Road map** D6. *(619) 435-4166.*
Specializing in steak and seafood, this restaurant has wonderful views of San Diego Bay. The marinated swordfish is excellent. ● *Sat & Sun. L*

CORONADO: *Prince of Wales Grill* $$$$$$
1500 Orange Ave, CA 92118. **Road map** D6. *(619) 522-8818.* Set in the elegant Hotel del Coronado *(see p245),* this Art Deco restaurant retains its 1930s decor. The cuisine is classic American. ● *L.*

DEL MAR: *The Dining Room at L'Auberge* $$$$$$
1540 Camino Del Mar, CA 92014. **Road map** D6. *(858) 259-1515.* American standards and pasta dishes are served in this resort restaurant *(see p518).* As a treat, eat outside on the patio overlooking the waterfall garden.

LA JOLLA: *Alfonso's of La Jolla* $$
1251 Prospect St, CA 90237. **Road map** D6. *(858) 454-2232.* This family-friendly restaurant serves imaginative Mexican food as well as authentic standards. The bar, open until 2am, can be very lively. ● *Sun D.*

LA JOLLA: *The French Pastry Shop Café and Restaurant* $$$$
5550 La Jolla Blvd, CA 92037. **Road map** D6. *(858) 454-9094.* This San Diego favorite has been operating for 15 years. It serves fresh bread, pastries, *crêpes* (savory and sweet), and pasta. ● *Mon D, Sat.*

LA JOLLA: *George's at the Cove* $$$$$
1250 Prospect St, CA 92037. **Road map** D6. *(858) 454-4244.* This restaurant serves fresh seafood in light sauces, as well as lamb, steak, and chicken dishes. The chocolate soufflé is a fitting end to the evening.

LA JOLLA: *Marine Room* $$$$$$$
2000 Spindrift Drive, CA 92037. **Road map** D6. *(858) 459-7222.* At this elegant beach restaurant, California cuisine is given a French twist – dishes include *filet mignon* with wild mushroom sauce. The cheesecake with bittersweet chocolate shavings is superb.

LA JOLLA: *Top O' The Cove* $$$$$$$
1216 Prospect St, CA 92037. **Road map** D6. *(858) 454-7779.*
Fabulous coastal views, celebrity customers, and delicious food guarantee the success of this famous restaurant. The cuisine is contemporary French with a Pacific Rim influence. Dress up.

PACIFIC BEACH: *Nick's At The Beach* $$$$
809 Thomas St, CA 92109. **Road map** D6. *(619) 270-1730.* This beach café serves American standards such as meatloaf and crab cakes from its seasonal menu. Don't leave without trying the orange *crème brûlée.*

SAN DIEGO: *Big Kitchen* $$
3003 Grape St, CA 92102. **Road map** D6. *(619) 234-5789.* The best breakfast in town and rumored to be where Whoopi Goldberg washed dishes. The staff is good-humored, the place is kid-friendly, and it's very, very popular. ● *D.*

SAN DIEGO: *Hob Nob Hill* $$
2271 1st Ave, CA 92101. **Road map** D6. *(619) 239-8176.* This 1940s diner is the place to go for breakfast – buttermilk pancakes, pecan waffles, and coffee cake are served up in authentic surroundings. ● *Sat.*

For key to symbols see back flap

Price categories for a three-course meal for one, including a half bottle of house wine, sales tax, and service:
$ under $25
$$ $25–$35
$$$ $35–$50
$$$$ $50–$70
$$$$$ over $70

OUTDOOR EATING
Some tables on a patio or terrace.
VEGETARIAN SPECIALTIES
One menu always includes a selection of vegetarian dishes.
BAR AREA/COCKTAIL BAR
There is a bar area or cocktail bar within the restaurant.
FIXED-PRICE MENU
A good-value fixed-price menu offered at lunch, dinner or both, usually with three courses.
CHILDREN'S FACILITIES
Small portions and/or high chairs available on request.

	Price	OUTDOOR EATING	VEGETARIAN SPECIALTIES	BAR AREA/COCKTAIL BAR	FIXED-PRICE MENU	CHILDREN'S FACILITIES
SAN DIEGO: *Mandarin China*	$		●		●	■
SAN DIEGO: *Anthony's Fish Grotto*	$$	■	●	■		■
SAN DIEGO: *Bali Ha'i*	$$	■				■
SAN DIEGO: *Karl Strauss' Old Columbia Brewery and Grill*	$$		●	■		■
SAN DIEGO: *Bayou Bar and Grill*	$$$	■		■		
SAN DIEGO: *Buffalo Joe's*	$$$		●	■	●	■
SAN DIEGO: *Café Pacifica*	$$$	■	●	■		■
SAN DIEGO: *Fifth and Hawthorn*	$$$		●	■		
SAN DIEGO: *Fio's*	$$$	■	●			
SAN DIEGO: *Grant Grill*	$$$	■	●	■		
SAN DIEGO: *Harbor House*	$$$	■	●	■		
SAN DIEGO: *El Bizcocho*	$$$$		●	■		■

SAN DIEGO: *Mandarin China* $
4110 W Point Loma Blvd, CA 92110. **Road map** D6. **(** *(619) 222-6688.* Known for its *dim sum*, this restaurant serves Mandarin, Szechuan, and Cantonese cuisine. Book in advance or eat takeout overlooking the ocean.

SAN DIEGO: *Anthony's Fish Grotto* $$
1360 N Harbor Drive, CA 92101. **Road map** D6. **(** *(619) 232-5103.* Try the seafood appetizer bar at this casual restaurant. Lobster and king crab combinations are the specialties here. For dessert try banana flambé or French wedding cake. ● *Mon.*

SAN DIEGO: *Bali Ha'i* $$
2230 Shelter Island Drive, CA 92106. **Road map** D6. **(** *(619) 222-1181.* Set on a man-made island, this round Polynesian restaurant offers diners stunning views of San Diego Bay. The food is Cantonese-Polynesian, featuring "Chicken of the Gods" in a sweet and sour sauce. ● *Sat L.*

SAN DIEGO: *Karl Strauss' Old Columbia Brewery and Grill* $$
1157 Columbia St, CA 92101. **Road map** D6. **(** *(619) 234-2739.* This bar and restaurant serves American food and home-brewed beers, with no additives or preservatives. It can be very busy on weekends.

SAN DIEGO: *Bayou Bar and Grill* $$$
329 Market St, CA 92101. **Road map** D6. **(** *(619) 696-8747.* The seafood at this Cajun-Creole restaurant is flown in fresh from Louisiana every day. Try the delicious Mardi Gras pasta (with crayfish, shrimp, sherry, creole spices, and cream sauce). The atmosphere is always festive.

SAN DIEGO: *Buffalo Joe's* $$$
600 5th Ave, CA 92101. **Road map** D6. **(** *(619) 236-1616.* This American restaurant serves mostly barbecued ribs, as well as alligator, buffalo, and chicken specials. The portions are enormous.

SAN DIEGO: *Café Pacifica* $$$
2414 San Diego Ave, Old Town, CA 92110. **Road map** D6. **(** *(619) 291-6666.* Twinkling tree lights enhance the atmosphere at this romantic seafood restaurant. There is also a pretheater menu. ● *Sat & Sun L.*

SAN DIEGO: *Fifth and Hawthorn* $$$
5th Ave & Hawthorn St, CA 92101. **Road map** D6. **(** *(619) 544-0940.* This small, cozy restaurant, popular with locals, has a fine selection of seafood as well as classic dishes such as *filet mignon*. New menus daily.

SAN DIEGO: *Fio's* $$$
801 5th Ave, CA 92101. **Road map** D6. **(** *(619) 234-3467.* This modern Italian restaurant serves a selection of pasta and pizzas. Candlelit tables and live piano music add to the atmosphere. ● *Sat & Sun L.*

SAN DIEGO: *Grant Grill* $$$
326 Broadway, CA 92101. **Road map** D6. **(** *(619) 239-6806.* This continental-style restaurant is most famous for its seafood but also serves prime rib and rack of lamb. Live jazz is played in the lounge.

SAN DIEGO: *Harbor House* $$$
831 W Harbor Drive, CA 92101. **Road map** D6. **(** *(619) 232-1141.* Located on the boardwalk with a beautiful view of the ocean, this restaurant serves seafood with contemporary California flare. There is an oyster bar.

SAN DIEGO: *El Bizcocho* $$$$
17550 Bernardo Oaks Drive, CA 92128. **Road map** D6. **(** *(858) 487-1611.* This elegant French-California restaurant, set in the Rancho Bernardo Inn *(see p519)*, has views of the golf course and mountains. Try the roast Long Island duck or the Colorado rack of lamb.

SAN DIEGO: *Dobson's* $$$$
56 Broadway Circle, CA 92101. **Road map** D6. ((619) 231-6771. This award-winning restaurant is famous for its mussel bisque with puff pastry top. A divine *crème brûlée* is always on the menu. ● *Sun, Sat L.* ⎿ ▣

SAN DIEGO: *Old Trieste* $$$$
3335 Morana Blvd, CA 92110. **Road map** D6. ((619) 276-1841. Hearty Italian cuisine is the order of the day at this candlelit restaurant. The walnut cake has been a specialty for years. ● *Sun & Mon, Sat L.* ⎿ ♟ ▣

SAN DIEGO: *Wine Seller & Brasserie* $$$$
9550 Waples St, #115, CA 92121. **Road map** D6. ((858) 450-9557. This small brasserie serves French-influenced California cuisine. On Saturday they have special "tasting" lunches – three tastings of wine with three courses. Book well in advance. ● *Sun L, Mon, Tue–Fri L.* ⎿ ♟ ▣

SAN DIEGO: *Humphrey's* $$$$$
2241 Shelter Island Drive, CA 92106. **Road map** D6. ((619) 224-3577. Named after Humphrey Bogart and decorated in the style of his film *Casablanca*, this seafood restaurant serves lobster fresh from the tank. ⎿ ♫ ♟ ▣

SAN DIEGO: *Mister A's* $$$$$
2250 5th Ave, Ca 92103. **Road map** D6. ((619) 239-1377. This restaurant, on the 12th floor of the Financial Center, has fabulous views of down-town. The continental-style cuisine includes such dishes as mock turtle soup, baked oysters, and a selection of pasta. ● *Sat L.* ⎿ ♫ ♟ ▣

RANCHO SANTA FE: *Mille Fleures* $$$$$
6009 Paseo Delicias, CA 92067. **Road map** D6. ((858) 756-3085. Dress up to go to what some consider to be the best restaurant in the country. Country French cuisine, extensive wine list. ● *Sun & Mon, Tue–Sat L.* ♫ ♟ ▣

THE INLAND EMPIRE AND LOW DESERT

BIG BEAR LAKE: *Madlon's* $$
829 W Big Bear Blvd, Big Bear City, CA 92314. **Road map** D5. ((909) 585-3762. This English cottage-style restaurant is a favorite with locals. The varied menu has something for everyone; service is excellent. ⎿ ♟ ▣

BORREGO SPRINGS: *Borrego Springs Country Club* $
1112 Tilting "T" Drive, CA 92004. **Road map** D6. ((760) 767-3057. Classic American cuisine is served in an ornate, yet informal, setting. Sunday brunch and happy hour (4–6pm) at the bar are both very popular. ⎿ ▣

BORREGO SPRINGS: *Pablito's of the Desert* $
590 Palm Canyon Drive, CA 92004. **Road map** D6. ((760) 767-5753.
Excellent Mexican cuisine is served in an Old West setting in this resort restaurant. Reservations are recommended for dinner. ● *Mon–Thu D.* ⎿ ♫ ▣

IDYLLWILD: *Jan's Red Kettle* $
54220 North Circle Drive, CA 92549. **Road map** D6. ((909) 659-4063.
Open for breakfast and lunch, many Idyllwild residents start their day here. The food is excellent, plentiful, and well priced. ● *D.* ⎿ ▣

IDYLLWILD: *Gastrognome* $$
54381 Ridgeview Drive, CA 92549. **Road map** D6. ((909) 659-5055. Set against a mountain backdrop, this restaurant features American cuisine in a French-country setting. Try the deep-fried sage leaves. ⎿ ♟ ▣

LA QUINTA: *La Quinta Cliffhouse* $$$
78250 Hwy 111 (Washington St), CA 92253. **Road map** D6. ((760) 360-5991. Perched on top of a mountain, it is worth eating here for the views alone. The menu is also impressive with a daily fresh-fish special. ⎿ ▣

LA QUINTA: *La Quinta Grill* $$$$
78045 Calle Cadiz, CA 92253. **Road map** D6. ((760) 564-4443. This restaurant has mountain views, a cozy cocktail bar, and good basic California cuisine with a super grill. ♟ ▣

PALM DESERT: *Louise's Pantry* $
44491 Towncenter Way, CA 92260. **Road map** D6. ((760) 346-9320. The expanded dining room in this 1940s-style diner serves such American standards as corn bread, pies, roast leg of lamb with gravy, and a delicious homemade meatloaf with mashed potatoes. No alcohol is served. ▣

<table>
<tr><td colspan="5">

Price categories for a three-course meal for one, including a half bottle of house wine, sales tax, and service:

$ under $25
$$ $25–$35
$$$ $35–$50
$$$$ $50–$70
$$$$$ over $70

</td><td colspan="6">

OUTDOOR EATING
Some tables on a patio or terrace.
VEGETARIAN SPECIALTIES
One menu always includes a selection of vegetarian dishes.
BAR AREA/COCKTAIL BAR
There is a bar area or cocktail bar within the restaurant.
FIXED-PRICE MENU
A good-value fixed-price menu offered at lunch, dinner or both, usually with three courses.
CHILDREN'S FACILITIES
Small portions and/or high chairs available on request.

</td></tr>
</table>

		OUTDOOR EATING	VEGETARIAN SPECIALTIES	BAR AREA/COCKTAIL BAR	FIXED-PRICE MENU	CHILDREN'S FACILITIES

PALM DESERT: *Cuistot* $$$$
73111 El Paseo, CA 92260. Road map D6. (*(760) 340-1000*. This elegant French-California restaurant offers three or four fish specials every night. The exotic floating islands dessert is delicious. ● *Sun L, Mon.* ⑇ 🍷 🖴

| | | | ● | ■ | | ■ |

PALM DESERT: *Tuscany Ristorante* $$$$
Marriott's Desert Springs Resort and Spa, Country Club Drive, CA 92260. Road map D6. (*(760) 341-1725*. This Italian-style hotel restaurant *(see p521)* serves excellent pasta dishes and specials such as veal. The twilight dinner specials (5:30–6:30pm) are a real bargain. ● *L.* ⑇ 🍷 🖴

| | | | ● | ■ | ● | ■ |

PALM SPRINGS: *Billy Reeds* $$
1800 N Palm Canyon Drive, CA 92262. Road map D6. (*(760) 325-1946*. This restaurant gets very busy, particularly on weekends when there is live jazz. The food is pure American, and breakfasts are very good. ⑇ 🎵 🖴

| | | | ● | ■ | | |

PALM SPRINGS: *Cedar Creek Inn* $$
1555 S Palm Canyon Drive, CA 92264. Road map D6. (*(760) 325-7300*. Superb salads and sandwiches are served all day and main courses are served from 4:30pm. Service is friendly and efficient. ⑇ 🎵 🖴

| | | ■ | ● | ■ | ● | ■ |

PALM SPRINGS: *Flower Drum* $$
424 S Indian Canyon Drive, CA 92262. Road map D6. (*(760) 323-3020*. Five chefs serve five regional styles of Chinese cooking. There is a stream running through the center of the restaurant filled with fish and, from Wednesday to Saturday, there are Chinese classical dancers. ● *L.* ⑇ 🖴

| | | | ● | ■ | | ■ |

PALM SPRINGS: *John Henry's Café* $$
1785 E Tahquitz Canyon Way, CA 92262. Road map D6. (*(760) 327-7667*. It is as difficult to get into this wonderful restaurant as it is to find it. Enormous portions of meat, fish, and pasta are always served, and the specials change daily. Book well in advance. ● *Sun, Mon–Sat L.* ⑇ 🖴

| | | ■ | ● | | | |

PALM SPRINGS: *Lord Fletcher Inn* $$
70385 Hwy 111 (Country Club Drive), CA 92270. Road map D6. (*(760) 328-1161*. The food here is British-American, such as prime rib steak with Yorkshire pudding. But the atmosphere is purely British, with Toby jugs and royal portraits. ● *Jul & Aug: daily; Sep–Jun: Sun & Mon, Tue–Sat L.* ⑇ 🖴

| | | | | ■ | ● | |

PALM SPRINGS: *Riccio's* $$
2155 N Palm Canyon Drive, CA 92262. Road map D6. (*(760) 325-2369*. This smart restaurant serves traditional Italian cuisine. The wine list features Italian reds, dessert wines, and ports. ● *Sat & Sun L.* ⑇ 🎵 🍷 🖴

| | | | ● | ■ | | ■ |

PALM SPRINGS: *Lyon's English Grille* $$$
233 E Palm Canyon Drive, CA 92264. Road map D6. (*(760) 327-1551*. Lyon's has an extensive British menu, featuring steak-and-kidney pie, and beef Wellington. All meals come with salad or vegetables. ● *L.* ⑇ 🎵 🖴

| | | | ● | ■ | | ■ |

PALM SPRINGS: *Europa* $$$$
1620 Indian Trail, CA 92264. Road map D6. (*(760) 327-2314*. One of the loveliest restaurants in Palm Springs, this is part of the Villa Royale Inn *(see p521)*. The cuisine is northern Italian. ● *Mon, Tue–Sun L.* ⑇ 🍷 🖴

| | | ■ | ● | ■ | ● | |

PALM SPRINGS: *Le Vallauris* $$$$
385 W Tahquitz Canyon Way, CA 92262. Road map D6. (*(760) 325-5059*. Classic French cuisine is served in this popular, ornately decorated restaurant. Reservations are absolutely necessary. ⑇ 🍷 🖴

| | | ■ | ● | ■ | | |

RANCHO MIRAGE: *Cactus Corral* $
67501 Hwy 111, Cathedral City, CA 92234. Road map D6. (*(760) 321-8558*. Great barbecues and live country-and-western music await you at this American country-style restaurant and club. ● *Mon, Tue.* ⑇ 🎵 🖴

| | | | ● | ■ | ● | ■ |

RANCHO MIRAGE: *Ritz-Carlton Rancho Mirage Hotel* $$$$$
68900 Frank Sinatra Drive, CA 92270. **Road map** D6. *(760) 321-8282.*
The main dining room at this elegant hotel *(see p521)* serves French cuisine.
A jazz band provides ambience. ● *Mon, Tue, Wed–Sun L.*

REDLANDS: *Joe Greensleeves* $$$
222 North Orange St, CA 92373. **Road map** D6. *(909) 792-6969.* Game
dishes (venison and wild boar) are the specialty of this restaurant.
Seafood and Canadian salmon are also offered. ● *Mon.*

RIVERSIDE: *Mario's Place* $$$
1725 Spruce St, CA 92507. **Road map** D6. *(909) 684-7755.* Chef Leone
Palagi seamlessly fuses French and Italian cuisine with pasta, meat, and
fish dishes. There is live music several nights a week. ● *Sun.*

THE MOJAVE DESERT

BAKER: *The Mad Greek's Diner* $
Hwy 127 & I-15 intersection, CA 92309. **Road map** D5. *(760) 733-4354.* This
restaurant is a corner of Greece set in the tiny town of Baker. Specialties
are *gyros* (sliced roast lamb), *shish kebab* (meat cooked on skewers), and
tabbouleh (a bulgur wheat salad). American food is also available.

BARSTOW: *Cactus Kitchen* $
1511 E Main St, CA 92311. **Road map** D5. *(760) 256-8806.* American food
is offered at this café set in a large Holiday Inn. After a hearty meal,
the popular Calico Ghost Town *(see p275)* is just minutes away.

BARSTOW: *Idle Spurs Steak House* $$
690 Old Hwy 58, CA 92311. **Road map** D5. *(760) 256-8888.* This is a Western-
style steakhouse where the meat is thickly sliced and the atmosphere
is friendly. The prime rib is tender and delicious. ● *Sat & Sun L.*

DEATH VALLEY: *Wrangler Steakhouse* $$
Furnace Creek Ranch, CA 92328. **Road map** D4. *(760) 786-2345 (ext. 250).*
This classic steak house offers steaks, chops, chicken, and seafood in a
Southwestern setting. There is also a well-stocked salad bar.

DEATH VALLEY: *Inn Dining Room* $$$
Furnace Creek Inn, CA 92328. **Road map** D4. *(760) 786-2345 (ext. 253).*
There are wonderful mountain views from this popular Continental res-
taurant set in the Furnace Creek Inn *(see p522)*. ● *Mon.*

LAKE HAVASU: *Krystal's Fine Dining* $$
460 El Camino Way, AZ 86403. **Road map** E5. *(520) 453-2999.* This family-
friendly, unpretentious restaurant offers steak, seafood, and chicken
dishes. There is also a large selection of desserts and cheesecakes.

LAKE HAVASU: *London Arms Pub and Restaurant* $$
422 English Village, AZ 86403. **Road map** E5. *(520) 855-8782.* Fish and
chips are the house specialty at this English restaurant. Desserts such
as bread pudding and English trifle complete the atmosphere. English
beers are on tap, and there is a happy hour from 4–6pm daily.

LAKE HAVASU: *Shugrue's Restaurant* $$
1425 McCulloch Blvd, AZ 86403. **Road map** E5. *(520) 453-1400.* This
family restaurant, with a view of London Bridge *(see p278)*, serves
seafood and steaks. The library setting is quiet and relaxing, and the
bakery on the premises makes desserts and dinner rolls.

LAS VEGAS: *Battista's Hole in the Wall* $
4041 Audrie Lane, NV 89109 **Road map** E4. *(702) 732-1424.* A strolling
accordion player sets the scene at this old-fashioned Italian spot. The
price includes all the wine you can drink. Book ahead.

LAS VEGAS: *Stratosphere Tower Revolving Restaurant* $$$
Stratosphere Tower Hotel, 2000 South Las Vegas Blvd, NV 89104. **Road
map** E4. *(702) 380-7777.* Dress up for the adults-only formal dining
room. The continental cuisine features meats and seafood.

LAS VEGAS: *Andre's* $$$$$
401 S 6th St, NV 89101. **Road map** E4. *(702) 385-5016.*
This upscale French restaurant is set in an old house, decorated with
tapestries and lace. Call the day before to request special orders. ● *L.*

Price categories for a three-course meal for one, including a half bottle of house wine, sales tax, and service:

$ under $25
$$ $25–$35
$$$ $35–$50
$$$$ $50–$70
$$$$$ over $70

Outdoor Eating
Some tables on a patio or terrace.

Vegetarian Specialties
One menu always includes a selection of vegetarian dishes.

Bar Area/Cocktail Bar
There is a bar area or cocktail bar within the restaurant.

Fixed-Price Menu
A good-value fixed-price menu offered at lunch, dinner or both, usually with three courses.

Children's Facilities
Small portions and/or high chairs available on request.

SAN FRANCISCO

	Price	Outdoor Eating	Vegetarian Specialties	Bar Area/Cocktail Bar	Fixed-Price Menu	Children's Facilities
CHINATOWN AND NOB HILL: Cordon Bleu	$					
CHINATOWN AND NOB HILL: Kan's	$		●	■		●
CHINATOWN AND NOB HILL: Pot Sticker	$		●		●	■
CHINATOWN AND NOB HILL: Swan Oyster Depot	$			■		
CHINATOWN AND NOB HILL: Tokyo Express Restaurant	$		●	■		■
CHINATOWN AND NOB HILL: Empress of China	$$		●	■		
CHINATOWN AND NOB HILL: Fornou's Oven	$$$			■		■
CHINATOWN AND NOB HILL: Big Four Restaurant	$$$$		●	■		■
CHINATOWN AND NOB HILL: Tommy Toy's	$$$$		●			■
CHINATOWN AND NOB HILL: Masa's	$$$$$			■		
CHINATOWN AND NOB HILL: The Dining Room	$$$$$		●	■	●	■
CIVIC CENTER: Mifune	$		●			■

CHINATOWN AND NOB HILL: Cordon Bleu $
1574 California St., CA 94109. **Map** 5 A4. *(415) 673-5637.* This tiny hole-in-the-wall restaurant serves good Vietnamese food at low prices. The menu is short but includes a wonderful "five-spice" roast chicken. ● *Sun L, Mon.*

CHINATOWN AND NOB HILL: Kan's $
708 Grant Ave, CA 94108. **Map** 5 C4. *(415) 362-5267.*
This traditional Chinese restaurant, located in the heart of Chinatown, is famous for its Peking duck and honey walnut shrimp.

CHINATOWN AND NOB HILL: Pot Sticker $
150 Waverly Pl, CA 94109. **Map** 5 C4. *(415) 397-9985.* This popular northern Chinese restaurant is located in one of Chinatown's more attractive side streets. It is best known for its dumplings and its budget menus.

CHINATOWN AND NOB HILL: Swan Oyster Depot $
1517 Polk St, CA 94109. **Map** 4 F3. *(415) 673-1101.* If you crave fresh oysters and a glass of Anchor Steam beer, go to Swan, the oldest oyster bar in the city. The friendly bar staff will advise on the best varieties. ● *Sun.*

CHINATOWN AND NOB HILL: Tokyo Express Restaurant $
660 Sacramento St, CA 94108. **Map** 5 C4. *(415) 956-3040.* High-quality Japanese food is available at this budget-priced sushi bar. Great seafood and tasty soba noodles and an assortment of Japanese beers. ● *Sun L, Mon, Sat L.*

CHINATOWN AND NOB HILL: Empress of China $$
838 Grant Ave, CA 94108. **Map** 5 C3. *(415) 434-1345.* This is a good place to come for authentic Chinese food in the center of Chinatown. The Peking duck is excellent. Call ahead to reserve – it can be busy.

CHINATOWN AND NOB HILL: Fornou's Oven $$$
905 California St, Stanford Court Hotel, CA 94108. **Map** 5 C3. *(415) 989-1910.* The name comes from the large Portuguese tile oven in the center of this Mediterranean-style restaurant. The rack of lamb is wonderful.

CHINATOWN AND NOB HILL: Big Four Restaurant $$$$
1075 California St, CA 94108. **Map** 5 B4. *(415) 771-1140.* Next to the foyer of the Huntington Hotel *(see p523)*, the formal setting includes memorabilia relating to the "Big Four" railroad barons *(see pp46–7)*. The food is excellent but not very adventurous. *limited.*

CHINATOWN AND NOB HILL: Tommy Toy's $$$$
655 Montgomery St, CA 94111. **Map** 5 C3. *(415) 397-4888.* Tapestries and antique mirrors adorn San Francisco's only four-star Chinese restaurant, where diners eat by lamplight. French nouvelle cuisine is fused with traditional Chinese cooking. ● *Sat & Sun L.*

CHINATOWN AND NOB HILL: Masa's $$$$$
648 Bush St, CA 94108. **Map** 5 B4. *(415) 989-7154.* Masa's serves nouvelle cuisine to an exceptionally high standard. The wines are also world-class and the desserts excellent. ● *Sun, Mon.*

CHINATOWN AND NOB HILL: The Dining Room $$$$$
600 Stockton St, CA 94108. **Map** 5 C4. *(415) 296-7465.* Located in the Ritz Carlton Hotel *(see p523)* the excellent California cuisine here is prepared with a French flourish. ● *Sun, Mon–Sat L.*

CIVIC CENTER: Mifune $
Japan Center, 1737 Post St, CA 94115. **Map** 4 E4. *(415) 922-0337.* Mifune is a long-standing favorite for noodle soup. The Japanese noodles are made daily on the premises, with a choice of more than 20 toppings. *limited.*

CIVIC CENTER: *Sanppo* $
Japan Center, 1702 Post St, CA 94115. **Map 4 E4.** ((415) 346-3486. A range of traditional dishes is served in this popular restaurant. The atmosphere is welcoming and the food is inexpensive and reliable. ● *Sun L, Mon.*

CIVIC CENTER: *Indigo* $$
687 McAllister St, CA 94102. **Map 4 F5.** ((415) 673-9353. Fresh local ingredients are served with Californian flair in this popular restaurant. Friendly staff welcome you into a sumptuous décor of velvet and cherrywood . ● *Sun L, Mon.*

CIVIC CENTER: *Maharani* $$
1122 Post St, CA 94112. **Map 5 A5.** ((415) 775-1988. This is perhaps one of the better Indian restaurants in the city. Settle down on the cushions in the Fantasy Room and enjoy the succulent tandooris and curries. ● *L.*

CIVIC CENTER: *Puccini & Pinetti* $$
129 Ellis St, CA 94109. **Map 4 D5.** ((415) 392-5500. This busy Italian restaurant is the perfect place to collapse after a hard day's shopping. The choice of entrées is huge, from the usual pizza or pasta to the more adventurous.

CIVIC CENTER: *Stars Café* $$
500 Van Ness Ave, CA 94102. **Map 4 F5.** ((415) 861-4344. This bright café is a spin-off of Stars. The California-style dishes include crab cakes and handmade pasta pillows.

CIVIC CENTER: *Zuni Café* $$$
1658 Market St, CA 94102. **Map 10 F1.** ((415) 552-2522. Some of the city's freshest seafood is available here, with as many as ten different kinds of oysters. The smokey pizzas are also good. ● *Mon.* limited.

CIVIC CENTER: *Acquerello* $$$$
1722 Sacramento St, CA 94109. **Map 5 A4.** ((415) 567-5432. The beautiful décor matches the sophisticated menu. The specialties and the menu change regularly. ● *Sun, Mon.*

CIVIC CENTER: *Hayes Street Grill* $$$$
320 Hayes St, CA 94102. **Map 4 F5.** ((415) 863-5545. This is an unpretentious place serving the freshest of fish, grilled, steamed, or sautéed. The restaurant is popular with politicians and operagoers. ● *Sat & Sun L.*

CIVIC CENTER: *Postrio* $$$$
545 Post St, CA 94102. **Map 5 B5.** ((415) 776-7825. A mix of Mediterranean and Californian-Asian dishes are on the menu of Wolfgang Puck's restaurant. Pizzas and drinks are available at the bar.

CIVIC CENTER: *Stars* $$$$$
555 Golden Gate Ave, CA 94102. **Map 4 F5.** ((415) 861-7287. This bustling restaurant claims to have the longest bar in San Francisco. The food is American bistro-style with fabulous desserts. ● *Sat & Sun L.*

DOWNTOWN: *Delancey Street Restaurant* $
600 Embarcadero, CA 94107. **Map 6 E5.** ((415) 512-5179. Delancey Street Restaurant serves a variety of American dishes as well as more eclectic ethnic fare. From the patio the Bay Bridge looms high overhead. ● *Mon.*

DOWNTOWN: *House of Nan King* $
919 Kearny St, CA 94133. **Map 5 C3.** ((415) 421-1429. Many consider this the best budget Chinese restaurant in the country. There is an extensive, Shanghai menu of braised meats and vegetable dishes. ● *Sun L.*

DOWNTOWN: *Café Bastille* $$
22 Belden Place (north of Bush St between Kearny St and Montgomery St), CA 94104. **Map 5 C4.** ((415) 986-5673. This small café offers traditional bistro food and a range of beer and wine. At night there is live jazz. ● *Sun.*

DOWNTOWN: *Café de la Presse* $$
352 Grant Ave, CA 94108. **Map 5 C4.** ((415) 249-0900. All the ingredients of classic French cooking are to be found in this good-value restaurant. The bar is popular with locals.

DOWNTOWN: *Eddie Rickenbacker's* $$
133 Second St, CA 94105. **Map 6 D5.** ((415) 543-3498. Known for its straightforward American grill fare, the chef's are venturing into Cal-Mex cuisine The decor holds lots of World War I memorabilia. ● *Sun.*

Price categories for a three-course meal for one, including a half bottle of house wine, sales tax, and service:
$ⓢ under $25
$ⓢⓢ $25–$35
$ⓢⓢⓢ $35–$50
$ⓢⓢⓢⓢ $50–$70
$ⓢⓢⓢⓢⓢ over $70

OUTDOOR EATING
Some tables on a patio or terrace.
VEGETARIAN SPECIALTIES
One menu always includes a selection of vegetarian dishes.
BAR AREA/COCKTAIL BAR
There is a bar area or cocktail bar within the restaurant.
FIXED-PRICE MENU
A good-value fixed-price menu offered at lunch, dinner or both, usually with three courses.
CHILDREN'S FACILITIES
Small portions and/or high chairs available on request.

	OUTDOOR EATING	VEGETARIAN SPECIALTIES	BAR AREA/COCKTAIL BAR	FIXED-PRICE MENU	CHILDREN'S FACILITIES
DOWNTOWN: *Hana Zen* $ⓢⓢ 115 Cyril Magnin St, CA 94102. **Map** 5 B5. [(415) 421-2101. This is the best and most authentic *yakitori* restaurant in the city. The food combines zesty charcoal-grilled meats, chicken, and vegetables with Japanese delicacy and visual presentation. ● *L.* & 🖼		●			
DOWNTOWN: *Harbor Village Restaurant* $ⓢⓢ 4 Embarcadero Center, lobby level, CA 94111. **Map** 6 D3. [(415) 781-8833. Traditional Cantonese fare and innovative contemporary dishes are served here, to a largely expatriate Chinese clientele. & 🖼		●			
DOWNTOWN: *Litsu* $ⓢⓢ 550 Geary St, CA 94114. **Map** 5 B5. [(415) 441-4442. Litsu is a new restaurant with reasonable prices and a good Fusion Asian/California menu. There is limited seating, so call ahead for reservations. ● *L.* & 🖼		●			
DOWNTOWN: *Sam's Grill and Seafood Restaurant* $ⓢⓢ 374 Bush St, CA 94104. **Map** 5 C4. [(415) 421-0594. One of San Francisco's oldest and best seafood restaurants. The famously grumpy waiters deal efficiently with the crowds at lunchtime. ● *Sat & Sun.* & *limited.* 🖼		●	■		■
DOWNTOWN: *Splendido* $ⓢⓢ 4 Embarcadero Center, CA 94111. **Map** 6 D3. [(415) 986-3222. Splendido is a huge restaurant with a good view of San Francisco Bay. It serves a range of Mediterranean-based foods including *tapas* (starters) and pizzas. & 🖼		●	■		■
DOWNTOWN: *Yank Sing* $ⓢⓢ 427 Battery, CA 94111. **Map** 6 D3. [(415) 957-9300. There are more than 100 different varieties of *dim sum (see p540)* here, which are chosen from passing trolleys. Prices are only about $3 to $4 a plate. ● *D.* & 🖼		●			■
DOWNTOWN: *Carnelian Room* Ⓦ www.carnelianroom.com $ⓢⓢⓢ Bank of America, 555 California St, CA 94104. **Map** 6 D3. [(415) 433-7500. Fine California cuisine can be enjoyed here on the 52nd floor, while looking out on a panoramic view of the city. ● *Mon–Sat L.* & 🍷 🛈		●	■		
DOWNTOWN: *Il Fornaio* $ⓢⓢⓢ 1265 Battery St, CA 94111. **Map** 5 C2. [(415) 986-0100. Il Fornaio is a stylish but unpretentious trattoria, best known for its home-baked breads and pizzas. The menu also offers well-prepared pasta and grilled meats, and a spicy dish of sausage and polenta. Desserts are excellent. & 🖼	■	●			■
DOWNTOWN: *Kuleto's* $ⓢⓢⓢ 221 Powell St, CA 94109. **Map** 5 B5. [(415) 397-7720. Although it is always crowded, it is worth the wait to eat here. Theatergoers often fill up on preshow appetizers at the bar, which are as good as the main meals. & *limited.* 🖼		●	■		
DOWNTOWN: *Kyo-ya* $ⓢⓢⓢ 2 New Montgomery St, CA 94105. **Map** 5 C4. [(415) 546-5090. The luxurious Kyo-ya, in the Sheraton Palace Hotel *(see p526)* has a number of traditional Japanese dishes that are rarely seen on American menus, as well as sushi and other more familiar meals. ● *Sun, Sat L.* & 🖼		●			■
DOWNTOWN: *MacArthur Park* $ⓢⓢⓢ 607 Front St, CA 94111. **Map** 6 D3. [(415) 398-5700. Grilled meats are the specialty here, especially the delicious oak-smoked baby back ribs, grilled fish, and steaks. The atmosphere is comfortable and casual. ● *Sun L.* & 🖼		●			■
DOWNTOWN: *Palio D'Asti* $ⓢⓢⓢ 640 Sacramento St, CA 94111. **Map** 5 C4. [(415) 395-9800. This restaurant caters to business people and is popular at lunchtimes. The menu features high quality Italian favorites, such as antipasti, pizzas, and pastas. ● *Sun, Sat L.* & 🖼	●	■		■	

DOWNTOWN: *Perry's Sports Bar and Grill* $$$
185 Sutter St, CA 94111. **Map** 5 C4. ☎ *(415) 989-6895*. Perry's is a popular after-work stop for office workers. There is an attractive bar, and live music is played on weekday nights. ● *Sun L.* 🕭 *limited.* 🎵 🖾

DOWNTOWN: *Sanraku* $$$
101 Fourth St, CA 94103. **Map** 5 C5. ☎ *(415) 369-6000*. This stylish Japanese restaurant serves fresh sushi, teriyaki, and a wide assortment of vegetarian dishes. Fine imported sake and Japanese beers are available. 🕭 🖾

DOWNTOWN: *St. Francis Café* $$$
335 Powell St, CA 94102. **Map** 5 B4. ☎ *(415) 774-0329*. The St. Francis in the Westin St. Francis Hotel *(see p526)* has an elegant, peaceful wood-paneled dining room and excellent food. ● *L.* 🕭 🍷 🖾

DOWNTOWN: *Tadich Grill* $$$
240 California St, CA 94111. **Map** 6 D4. ☎ *(415) 391-2373*. Tadich Grill opened during the Gold Rush *(see pp44–5)* and is the longest-established restaurant in California, serving superb seafood. ● *Sun.* 🕭 🖾

DOWNTOWN: *Aqua* $$$$
252 California St, CA 94111. **Map** 5 D4. ☎ *(415) 956-9662*. Fish-lovers will enjoy this sophisticated seafood restaurant. Try the Dungeness crab, followed by smoked swordfish wrapped in prosciutto. ● *Sun, Sat L.* 🕭 🖾

DOWNTOWN: *Bix* $$$$
56 Gold St, CA 94133. **Map** 5 C3. ☎ *(415) 433-6300*. This beautiful restaurant re-creates a 1920s supper club, with a sophisticated, almost decadent atmosphere. The food is contemporary American. ● *Sat & Sun L.* 🕭 🎵 🖾

DOWNTOWN: *Boulevard* $$$$
1 Mission St, CA 94105. **Map** 6 E4. ☎ *(415) 543-6084*. Traditional dishes such as roast meats and mashed potatoes are enlivened by chef Nancy Oakes with unusual sauces and a theatrical presentation. ● *Sat & Sun L.* 🕭 🖾

DOWNTOWN: *John's Grill* $$$$
63 Ellis St, CA 94102. **Map** 5 C5. ☎ *(415) 986-0069*. Writer Dashiell Hammett made this place famous when he used it as a setting in *The Maltese Falcon* in 1930. It serves old-fashioned American fare. ● *Sun L.* 🕭 *limited.* 🖾

DOWNTOWN: *Silks* $$$$
222 Sansome St, CA 94104. **Map** 5 C4. ☎ *(415) 986-2020*. California-Asian cuisine is the specialty at Silks, in the Mandarin Oriental Hotel *(see p525)*. Try the spiced jumbo shrimp, grilled on a skewer. Book ahead. 🕭 🍷 🖾

DOWNTOWN: *Campton Place* $$$$$
340 Stockton St, CA 94108. **Map** 5 C4. ☎ *(415) 955-5555*. Set in the Campton Place Hotel *(see p525)*, this may be the best restaurant in the city. The food is notable for its sophisticated preparation. 🕭 🍷 🖾

DOWNTOWN: *Cypress Club* $$$$$
500 Jackson St, CA 94133. **Map** 5 C3. ☎ *(415) 296-8555*. There is no more attractive combination of good food, great style, and indefinably San Franciscan "buzz" than in this popular Jackson Square haunt. ● *L.* 🕭 🖾

DOWNTOWN: *Fleur de Lys* $$$$$
777 Sutter St, CA 94109. **Map** 5 B4. ☎ *(415) 673-7779*. This is one of the city's most expensive and highly regarded restaurants. The food is excellent, with a wide range of carefully presented dishes. ● *Sun, Mon–Sat L.* 🕭 🖾

FISHERMAN'S WHARF: *Pompei's Grotto* $
340 Jefferson St, CA 94133. **Map** 5 A1. ☎ *(415) 776-9265*. The locals flock to this Italian-style seafood restaurant, which has operated here since the 1940s. Specialties include wonderful fresh Dungeness crab. 🕭 🖾

FISHERMAN'S WHARF: *Scoma's* $$
Pier 47, Fisherman's Wharf, CA 94133. **Map** 5 A1. ☎ *(415) 771-4383*. Fresh fish is delivered daily straight to this seafood restaurant located on the pier. The shellfish sauté, with four types of shellfish, is delicious. 🕭 🍷 🖾

FISHERMAN'S WHARF: *A. Sabella's* $$$
2766 Taylor St, CA 94133. **Map** 5 A1. ☎ *(415) 771-4416*. This elegant Italian restaurant has lovely views of the ocean. It serves exquisite seafood, such as "pirate salad," containing lobster, crab, and shrimp. 🕭 🍷 🎵 🖾

<table>
<tr><td rowspan="2">

Price categories for a three-course meal for one, including a half bottle of house wine, sales tax, and service:

$ under $25
$$ $25–$35
$$$ $35–$50
$$$$ $50–$70
$$$$$ over $70
</td><td colspan="5">

OUTDOOR EATING
Some tables on a patio or terrace.

VEGETARIAN SPECIALTIES
One menu always includes a selection of vegetarian dishes.

BAR AREA/COCKTAIL BAR
There is a bar area or cocktail bar within the restaurant.

FIXED-PRICE MENU
A good-value fixed-price menu offered at lunch, dinner or both, usually with three courses.

CHILDREN'S FACILITIES
Small portions and/or high chairs available on request.
</td></tr>
</table>

	OUTDOOR EATING	VEGETARIAN SPECIALTIES	BAR AREA/COCKTAIL BAR	FIXED-PRICE MENU	CHILDREN'S FACILITIES
FISHERMAN'S WHARF: *Fog City Diner* $$$ 1300 Battery St, CA 94111. **Map** 5 C2. 📞 *(415) 982-2000*. A range of burgers, ribs, chops, and chicken dishes is offered here. Situated near the waterfront, with a good bar, it is often crowded but well worth a visit. 🔵	■	●	■		
FISHERMAN'S WHARF: *Alioto's* $$$$ Pier 45, CA 94122. **Map** 5 A1. 📞 *(415) 673-0183*. Fresh seafood has been served here by the Alioto family since 1930. Fine views of Golden Gate Bridge. 🔵 🎵		●	■		■
FISHERMAN'S WHARF: *Greens* $$$$ Building A, Fort Mason Center, CA 94123. **Map** 4 E1. 📞 *(415) 771-6222*. This is the most highly regarded vegetarian restaurant on the West Coast. It is famous for its fixed-price Saturday dinners. There is a simpler mid-week menu, which includes unusual vegetable stews. ⬤ *Sun D, Mon L.* 🔵		●		●	■
GOLDEN GATE PARK AND THE PRESIDIO: *PJ's Oysterbed* $ 737 Irving St, CA 94122. **Map** 8 F3. 📞 *(415) 566-7775*. It is worth a short detour to visit this seafood specialist, a block south of Golden Gate Park. Choose from the range of char-grilled fish and other dishes. 🔵					
GOLDEN GATE PARK AND THE PRESIDIO: *New Eritrea Restaurant* $$ 907 Irving St, CA 94122. **Map** 8 F3. 📞 *(415) 681-1288*. This family-owned Eritrean and Ethiopian restaurant has the best all-you-can-eat weekday buffet lunch in the city. Specials include chicken, lamb, or beef stews, Injera bread, and spicy condiments. The full bar offers African and other imported beers. 🔵		●	■		
GOLDEN GATE PARK AND THE PRESIDIO: *Pacific Café* $$ 7000 Geary Blvd, CA 94121. **Map** 7 C1. 📞 *(415) 387-7091*. Seafood has been served here for many years, and the café is the best value in San Francisco. There is free wine while you wait for a table. ⬤ *L.* 🔵 *limited.* 🔵					■
GOLDEN GATE PARK AND THE PRESIDIO: *Straits Café* $$ 3300 Geary Blvd, CA 94118. **Map** 3 B5. 📞 *(415) 668-1783*. A mouthwatering array of Cantonese, Indonesian, and Indian cuisine is offered here. Try *kway paita* – a pastry filled with a shrimp and vegetable mixture. 🔵		●			
HAIGHT ASHBURY: *Cha Cha Cha* $ 1801 Haight St, CA 94133. **Map** 9 B1. 📞 *(415) 386-5758*. You will have to wait for a table at this very popular *tapas* bar. The menu changes daily and mixes Caribbean, Cajun, and Mexican influences. Cha Cha Cha is notable for its crazy decor and its individualistic Haight Street clientele. 🔵			■		
HAIGHT ASHBURY: *Indian Oven* $ 233 Fillmore St, CA 94117. **Map** 10 E1. 📞 *(415) 626-1628*. Traditional Indian cuisine has been updated with California panache here. The vegetarian dishes are impressive and vary according to the seasons. 🔵		●			
NORTH BEACH: *Brandy Ho's* $ 450 Broadway, CA 94133. **Map** 5 C3. 📞 *(415) 362-6268*. The Hunan food here is very good, although the modern decor is rather brash. The smoked meats are delicious, but not for the faint-hearted. 🔵 *limited.* 🔵		●			
NORTH BEACH: *Il Pollaio* $ 555 Columbus Ave, CA 94133. **Map** 5 B2. 📞 *(415) 362-7727*. This friendly, family-run restaurant specializes in chicken that is marinated, then grilled to perfection. Complementing the poultry are fresh salads, good soups, and inexpensive Italian table wines. ⬤ *Sun.* 🔵					■
NORTH BEACH: *Little Joe's & Baby Joe's* $ 523 Broadway, CA 94133. **Map** 5 C3. 📞 *(415) 433-4343*. Little Joe's is one of the best cheap Italian eating places in San Francisco. It is very lively, and the food is good. The garlic squid is particularly popular. 🔵 *limited.* 🔵		●			■

NORTH BEACH: *Caffè Macaroni* $()$
59 Columbus Ave, CA 94111. **Map** 5 C3. (*(415) 956-9737.* The food at Caffè Macaroni is always reliable, with very good daily special menus and reasonable prices. The portions are extremely generous. ● *Sat & Sun L.*		●			
NORTH BEACH: *Capp's Corner* $()$
1600 Powell St, CA 94133. **Map** 5 B2. (*(415) 989-2589.* This good-value North Beach institution is popular with families. It offers a wide range of Italian-American dishes from a set menu. ● *Sat & Sun L.* & *limited.*		●		●	■
NORTH BEACH: *Helmand* $()$
430 Broadway, CA 94133. **Map** 5 C3. (*(415) 362-0641.* Afghan food is served in this small restaurant. Main dishes come with vegetables, rice, or sautéed barley and lentils. The prices are reasonable. ● *Sat & Sun L.*					■
NORTH BEACH: *Little City Antipasti Bar* $()$
673 Union St, CA 94133. **Map** 5 B2. (*(415) 434-2900.* Little City serves California versions of Mediterranean *tapas* in a stylish, often crowded room. Order a series of small appetizers rather than a main dish. &		●			
NORTH BEACH: *Stinking Rose: A Garlic Restaurant* $()$
325 Columbus Ave, CA 94133. **Map** 5 C3. (*(415) 781-7673.* This busy North Beach restaurant serves every dish strongly flavored with garlic. The decor is rustic, with terra-cotta walls and marble tables. & *limited.*		●	■	●	■
NORTH BEACH: *Café Jacqueline* $()()$
1454 Grant Ave, CA 94133. **Map** 5 C2. (*(415) 981-5565.* This romantic French café features airy soufflés with a choice of different ingredients such as garlic or prosciutto. Each soufflé serves two. ● *Mon, Tue, Wed–Sun L.* &		●			
NORTH BEACH: *Julius' Castle* $()()$
1541 Montgomery St, CA 94133. **Map** 5 B2. (*(415) 392-2222.* Italian and French cuisine is served in a romantic setting with views of Telegraph Hill. ● *L.*	■	●	■		
NORTH BEACH: *Moose's* $()()$
1652 Stockton St, CA 94133. **Map** 5 B2. (*(415) 989-7800.* This large, noisy North Beach restaurant is frequented by politicians and media people. The food is reliably good, and the setting is sunny. ● *Mon.* &		●			■
PACIFIC HEIGHTS: *Golden Turtle* $()$
2211 Van Ness Ave, CA 94109. **Map** 4 F3. (*(415) 441-4419.* A selection of traditional Vietnamese dishes is available here, including three types of crab. The atmosphere is casual. ● *Mon, Tue–Sun L.* &		●			■
PACIFIC HEIGHTS: *Tortola* $()$
3640 Sacramento St, CA 94118. **Map** 3 B4. (*(415) 929-8181.* This casual local chain serves tasty Cal-Mex variations on burritos, tacos, and enchiladas, including signature items like the tamales special.			■		
PACIFIC HEIGHTS: *Café Marimba* $()$
2317 Chestnut St, CA 94123. **Map** 3 C2. (*(415) 776-1506.* The brightly painted café in the Marina district makes a perfect backdrop for the innovative southern Mexican specialties served here. ● *Mon.* &		●			
PACIFIC HEIGHTS: *Scott's Seafood Grill* $()$
2400 Lombard St, CA 94123. **Map** 4 D4. (*(415) 981-0622.* The fish is wonderfully fresh at this cheerful seafood restaurant housed in a Victorian building. Changing exhibitions of local artists' work are held here. &			■		
PACIFIC HEIGHTS: *Balboa Café* $()()$
3199 Fillmore St, CA 94123. **Map** 4 D2. (*(415) 921-3944.* This café serves excellent all-American food at good prices. It is housed in a white timber-framed shed that looks like a dive in a 1940s gangster film. &		●	■		
PACIFIC HEIGHTS: *Elite Café* $()()$
2049 Fillmore St, CA 94115. **Map** 4 D4. (*(415) 346-8668.* This busy, moderately priced restaurant has long been a neighborhood favorite. The bar is lively, and the seating consists of old wooden booths. ● *Mon–Sat L.* &			■		■
PACIFIC HEIGHTS: *Plump Jack Café* $()()$
3127 Fillmore St, CA 94123. **Map** 4 D2. (*(415) 563-4755.* Known for its well-priced and extensive wine list, Plump Jack offers California-Mediterranean cuisine. The place is trendy and tiny, so make reservations. ● *Sun.*		●			■

For key to symbols see back flap

<table>
<tr><td colspan="2">

Price categories for a three-course meal for one, including a half bottle of house wine, sales tax, and service:

$ under $25
$$ $25–$35
$$$ $35–$50
$$$$ $50–$70
$$$$$ over $70

</td><td>

OUTDOOR EATING
Some tables on a patio or terrace.
VEGETARIAN SPECIALTIES
One menu always includes a selection of vegetarian dishes.
BAR AREA/COCKTAIL BAR
There is a bar area or cocktail bar within the restaurant.
FIXED-PRICE MENU
A good-value fixed-price menu offered at lunch, dinner or both, usually with three courses.
CHILDREN'S FACILITIES
Small portions and/or high chairs available on request.

</td></tr>
</table>

		OUTDOOR EATING	VEGETARIAN SPECIALTIES	BAR AREA/COCKTAIL BAR	FIXED-PRICE MENU	CHILDREN'S FACILITIES
PACIFIC HEIGHTS: *Prego* 2000 Union St, CA 94123. **Map 4 D2.** ☎ *(415) 563-3305.* A wide range of well-prepared food is offered here and presented with flair. The appetizing antipasti dishes are some of the best in town. ♿ *limited.* 📷	$$$		●			
PACIFIC HEIGHTS: *Harris'* 2100 Van Ness Ave, CA 94109. **Map 4 F3.** ☎ *(415) 673-1888.* This award-winning restaurant specializes in steaks and prime ribs. The decor is old San Francisco-style, with booths and wooden floors. ♿ 🍷 🎵 📷	$$$$		●	■		
THE MISSION DISTRICT: *El Nuevo Frutilandia* 3077 24th St, CA 94110. **Map 10 F4.** ☎ *(415) 648-2958.* The authentic Cuban and Puerto Rican specialties here are complemented by a casual Caribbean atmosphere. Tropical fruitshakes are on the menu. ● *Mon.* 📷	$		●			■
THE MISSION DISTRICT: *Mission Villa Restaurant* 2391 Mission St, CA 94110. **Map 10 F3.** ☎ *(415) 826-0454.* This historic Mexican restaurant opened in 1906 and is decorated with antiques. All the traditional Mexican dishes are served with rice and beans. ♿	$		●		●	■
THE MISSION DISTRICT: *Ti Couz* 3108 16th St, CA 94110. **Map 10 F2.** ☎ *(415) 252-7373.* Savory crêpes filled with meats, vegetables, or cheese and sweet crêpes topped with chocolate and other sauces are specialties. It is inexpensive and always crowded. ♿ 📷	$		●			■
THE MISSION DISTRICT: *The Original Cuba Restaurant* 2886 16th St, CA 94110. **Map 10 F2.** ☎ *(415) 255-0946.* Diners from all over the city come here for traditional Cuban food, although the location is a little on the rough side. The three-course set lunches are an excellent value, but the gourmet dinners are the real attraction. ● *Thu.* ♿	$$				●	■

THE BAY AREA

		OUTDOOR EATING	VEGETARIAN SPECIALTIES	BAR AREA/COCKTAIL BAR	FIXED-PRICE MENU	CHILDREN'S FACILITIES
BERKELEY: *Bette's Ocean View Diner* 1807 4th St, CA 94710. **Road map inset B.** ☎ *(510) 644-3230.* Located at the center of Berkeley's popular shopping district, this 1940s-style diner has great American food. Be prepared to wait for a table. ● *D.* 📷	$		●			■
BERKELEY: *Plearn Thai* 2050 University Ave, CA 94704. **Road map inset B.** ☎ *(510) 841-2148.* There are so many Thai restaurants in the East Bay that they must be really good to succeed. People line up here for delicious, cheap food. ♿ 📷	$		●			■
BERKELEY: *Cambodiana's* 2156 University Ave, CA 94704. **Road map inset B.** ☎ *(510) 843-4630.* This restaurant is well worth a visit for its superb French-Cambodian cooking, with delights such as quail in lemon-and-ginger sauce. ● *Sat & Sun L.* ♿ 📷	$$		●			■
BERKELEY: *Ginger Island* 1820 4th St, CA 94710. **Road map inset B.** ☎ *(510) 644-0444.* This busy, noisy restaurant in the trendy Fourth Street section of Berkeley serves good Asian-influenced American food in sunny surroundings. ♿ 📷	$$	■	●	■		■
BERKELEY: *Chez Panisse Restaurant* 1517 Shattuck Ave, CA 94709. **Road map inset B.** ☎ *(510) 548-5525.* Founder chef Alice Waters is credited with having invented California cuisine here. One of the country's top restaurants, it is expensive, but upstairs is a café with a budget menu. ● *Sun.* ♿ 🍷 📷	$$$$$		●	■	●	
BOLINAS: *Bolinas Bakery and Café* 20 Wharf Rd, CA 94924. **Road map inset B.** ☎ *(415) 868-0211.* This is basic hippie fare. Sample the microbrewed beers and wine, homemade quiches, pizzas, soups, and probably the best cheesecake in the world. ♿ 📷	$	■	●			

BOLINAS: *Café Carumba*   ⓢ
46 Wharf Rd, CA 94294. **Road map** inset B. 【 *(415) 868-9984.* This tiny Mexican restaurant is very popular and known for its tasty, spicy specials and a wide selection of beers. Friendly, slightly disorganized, and busy. ● *Mon, Tue D.* ⚫

BURLINGAME: *Kuleto's Trattoria*   ⓢⓢⓢ
1095 Rollins Rd, CA 94010. **Road map** inset B. 【 *(650) 342-4922.* Centered around an open kitchen with a woodburning pizza oven, this lively restaurant serves fine Italian food in a family atmosphere. ● *Sat L.* ⚫ 🌐

HALF MOON BAY: *San Benito House*   ⓢⓢ
356 Main St, CA 94019. **Road map** inset B. 【 *(650) 726-3425.* This lovely restaurant serves Mediterranean food in a tiny dining room. The deli is open every day from 11am–3pm. ● *Mon–Wed, Thu–Sat L.* ⚫ 🌐

LAFAYETTE: *Postino*   ⓢⓢⓢ
3565 Mount Diablo Blvd, CA 94549. **Road map** Inset B. 【 *(925) 284-3565.* The rustic decor of this restaurant reflects its Mediterranean cuisine: fresh seafood, oven-roasted meats, and a choice of pasta. ⚫ 🌐

LARKSPUR: *Lark Creek Inn*   ⓢⓢⓢ
234 Magnolia Ave, CA 94939. **Road map** inset B. 【 *(415) 924-7766.* This well-known restaurant serves chef-owner Bradley Ogden's award-winning American country-style cuisine. ● *Sun D, Sat L.* ⚫ 🍷 🌐

MILL VALLEY: *Samurai*   ⓢ
425 Miller Ave, CA 94941. **Road map** inset B. 【 *(415) 381-3680.* Fried tempura, succulent seafood, and absolutely fresh sushi rule at this crowded Mill Valley Japanese restaurant. ● *Sun, Mon–Sat L.* ⚫ 🌐

MILL VALLEY: *D'Angelo Restaurant*   ⓢⓢ
22 Miller Ave, CA 94941. **Road map** inset B. 【 *(415) 388-2000.* The simple Italian cuisine served in a spacious dining room attracts a mixed crowd, from young Marin County teenagers to film directors and rock stars. ⚫ 🌐

MILL VALLEY: *Buckeye Roadhouse*   ⓢⓢⓢ
15 Shoreline Hwy, CA 94941. **Road map** inset B. 【 *(415) 331-2600.* This road-side restaurant may look like part of a steakhouse chain but, once inside, expect a roaring fire and good, simple American cooking. ⚫ 🌐

MILL VALLEY: *Frantoio*   ⓢⓢⓢ
152 Shoreline Hwy, CA 94941. **Road map** inset B. 【 *(415) 289-5777.* Named after the on-site olive press, this restaurant makes its own extra-virgin olive oil – a main ingredient in its Mediterranean cuisine. ⚫ 🌐

OAKLAND: *Rockridge Café*   ⓢ
5492 College Ave, CA 94618. **Road map** inset B. 【 *(510) 653-1567.* For a hearty breakfast or a fine hamburger, look no farther than this popular neighborhood haunt, which is styled like a 1940s diner. 🌐

OAKLAND: *Milano*   ⓢⓢ
3425 Grand Ave, CA 94610. **Road map** inset B. 【 *(510) 763-0300.* This stylish restaurant has a loyal following of regulars who come here to enjoy huge helpings of northern Italian cuisine. ● *Sat & Sun L.* ⚫ 🌐

OAKLAND: *Bay Wolf*   ⓢⓢⓢⓢ
3853 Piedmont Ave, CA 94611. **Road map** inset B. 【 *(510) 655-6004.* The menu at this elegant establishment changes every two weeks. The American-Mediterranean cuisine is deservedly acclaimed. ● *Sat & Sun L.* 🌐

ORINDA: *Siam Orchid Thai*   ⓢ
23-H Orinda Way, CA 94563. **Road map** inset B. 【 *(925) 253-1975.* In a small village 4 miles (6 km) east of Berkeley, this pleasant restaurant offers Thai staples at bargain prices. The staff is very friendly. ● *Sat & Sun L.* ⚫ 🌐

PALO ALTO: *Gordon Biersch*   ⓢⓢ
640 Emerson St, CA 94301. **Road map** inset B. 【 *(650) 323-7723.* The Gordon Biersch brewery restaurant is characterized by good California cuisine, stylish decor, and a choice of beers brewed on the premises. ⚫ 🌐

PESCADERO: *Duarte's Tavern*   ⓢⓢ
202 Stage Rd, CA 94060. **Road map** inset B. 【 *(650) 879-0464.* In business for over a century, and still run by the same family, this landmark restaurant serves hearty seafood and great homemade pies. 🌐

Price categories for a three-course meal for one, including a half bottle of house wine, sales tax, and service:
$ under $25
$$ $25–$35
$$$ $35–$50
$$$$ $50–$70
$$$$$ over $70

OUTDOOR EATING
Some tables on a patio or terrace.
VEGETARIAN SPECIALTIES
One menu always includes a selection of vegetarian dishes.
BAR AREA/COCKTAIL BAR
There is a bar area or cocktail bar within the restaurant.
FIXED-PRICE MENU
A good-value fixed-price menu offered at lunch, dinner or both, usually with three courses.
CHILDREN'S FACILITIES
Small portions and/or high chairs available on request.

		Price	OUTDOOR EATING	VEGETARIAN SPECIALTIES	BAR AREA/COCKTAIL BAR	FIXED-PRICE MENU	CHILDREN'S FACILITIES
POINT REYES STATION: *Station House Café* 11180 Main St, CA 94956. **Road map** A3. (*(415) 663-1515.* This modest restaurant is a casual gourmet treat. You should not miss the barbecued oysters when they are in season.		$$		●	■	●	
SAN JOSE: *Tied House Café and Brewery* 65 N San Pedro St, CA 95112. **Road map** B4. (*(408) 295-2739.* Best known for its beers, which are made on the premises, this lively, airy restaurant features especially good seafood dishes. ● Sun L.		$$		●			■
SAN JOSE: *Emile's* 545 South 2nd St, CA 95112. **Road map** B4. (*(408) 289-1960.* This restaurant is famous for its classic continental cuisine, award-winning wine list, and elegant surroundings. ● Sun & Mon, Tue–Thu L, Sat L.		$$$$		●	■	●	
SAUSALITO: *Christophe* 1919 Bridgeway, CA 94965. **Road map** A1. (*(415) 332-9244.* This small French bistro has good food, wonderful atmosphere, and a very nice wine list. Perfect for a romantic hideaway.		$$$		●		●	
TIBURON: *Guaymas* 5 Main St, CA 94920. **Road map** A3. (*(415) 435-6300.* This restaurant serves authentic Mexican regional cooking. Its views of San Francisco can be enjoyed from the terrace on a sunny day or a clear night.		$$	■	●	■		
TIBURON: *Sam's Anchor Café* 27 Main St, CA 94920. **Road map** A3. (*(415) 435-4527.* Thanks to its location on the docks of San Francisco Bay, this casual restaurant and cocktail bar draws a lively crowd, especially on summer weekends.		$$	■		■		■
WALNUT CREEK: *Spiedini* 101 Ygnacio Valley Blvd, CA 94596. **Road map** B3. (*(925) 939-2100.* Located near John Muir National Historic Site *(see p398)*, this fashionable northern Italian restaurant serves meat and poultry spit-roasted over a wood fire, homemade pasta, pizzas, and charcoal-grilled fish. ● Sat & Sun L.		$$	■	●			

THE NORTH

		Price	OUTDOOR EATING	VEGETARIAN SPECIALTIES	BAR AREA/COCKTAIL BAR	FIXED-PRICE MENU	CHILDREN'S FACILITIES
ARCATA: *Crosswinds Vegan Restaurant* 860 10th St. **Road map** B2. (*(707) 826-2133.* On Saturday and Sunday, diners enjoy a free glass of champagne at this homey restaurant. Food is American-style, adapted for the vegan diet. ● Mon, Tue–Sun D. (Sun).		$		●		●	■
ARCATA: *TJ's Classic Café* 1057 H St, CA 95521. **Road map** B2. (*(707) 822-4650.* Typical American breakfasts and lunches are offered in this rustic restaurant. They specialize in skillet dishes, served still sizzling in the hot pan at your table. ● D.		$		●		●	■
CRESCENT CITY: *Ship Ashore* 12370 Hwy 101 North, CA 95531. **Road map** A1. (*(707) 487-3141.* Housed alongside a permanently dry-docked ship, this popular family restaurant serves up generous portions of fresh seafood.		$$			■		■
EUREKA: *Samoa Cookhouse* 59 Cookhouse Lane, CA 95501. **Road map** A2. (*(707) 442-1659.* For a taste of the North Coast woods as they used to be, nothing beats this century-old dining hall, which still serves mountains of good food *(see p430)*.		$				●	■
EUREKA: *Hotel Carter Restaurant* 301 L St, CA 95501. **Road map** A2. (*(707) 444-8062.* This stylish haunt serves adventurous, well-prepared dishes, such as pork tenderloin with homemade apple chutney. ● L.		$$$		●		●	

EUREKA: *Rib Room* $$$
518 7th St, CA 95501. **Road map** A2. (707) 442-6441. This deluxe restaurant is housed in the landmark Eureka Inn *(see p530)*. Attentive service and excellent food make this a memorable experience. L.

GARBERVILLE: *Woodrose Café* $
911 Redwood Drive, CA 95442. **Road map** A2. (707) 923-3191. Located in the heart of redwood country, this friendly café serves healthy food such as tofu burgers and vegetable soups. Sat & Sun, Mon–Fri D.

LEWISTON: *Hitching Post Café* $
Turnpike & Deadwood Rds, CA 96052. **Road map** A2. (530) 778-3486. This classic American coffee shop serves huge portions of home-style food. The roast chicken is excellent, as are the fresh pies.

MOUNT SHASTA: *Lily's* $$
1013 S Mount Shasta Blvd, CA 96067. **Road map** B1. (530) 926-3372. A little bit of everything is on the menu at this very popular restaurant, from eggs Benedict and breakfast burritos to classic meat, poultry, seafood, and pasta dinners. Reservations are recommended.

MOUNT SHASTA: *Michael's* $$
313 N Mount Shasta Blvd, CA 96067. **Road map** B1. (530) 926-5288. Delicious sandwiches, light lunches, and Italian dinners have made this restaurant in the Mount Shasta area a favorite for many years. Sun.

ORICK: *Rolf's Park Café* $$
Hwy 101 at Davidson Rd, CA 95555. **Road map** A1. (707) 488-3841. With portions to match the scale of the mighty redwood trees, this German-run café serves hearty breakfasts and a range of Bavarian specialties.

REDDING: *Jack's Grill* $$
1743 California St, CA 96002. **Road map** B2. (530) 241-9705. Jack's is a 1930s bar that serves great food, specializing in hearty beef dinners. Be aware that the lines are long, and they don't take reservations. Sun, Mon–Sat L.

REDWAY: *Mateel Café* $
3342 Redwood Drive, CA 95560. **Road map** A2. (707) 923-2030. Doubling as a regional cultural center, this café has salads and pizzas for lunch and a range of international dishes for dinner. Sun, Mon D.

SUSANVILLE: *St. Francis Café* $$
830 Main St, CA 96130. **Road map** B2. (530) 257-4820. Every Friday and Saturday night, this lively restaurant draws a crowd from miles around to enjoy the prime rib and Basque soups. Sun L.

TRINIDAD: *Larrupin' Café* $$
1658 Patrick's Point Drive, CA 95570. **Road map** A2. (707) 677-0230. This little restaurant, 20 miles (32 km) north of Arcata, overlooks the Pacific Ocean and serves fresh seafood. Tue, Wed–Sun L.

UKIAH: *Ukiah Brewing Company* $$
102 State St, CA 95482. **Road map** A3. (707) 468-5898. A big step above the usual brew pub, the Ukiah Brewing Company offers hot curries, burgers, excellent vegetarian specials, and an amazing list of beers brewed in-house. All food, wine, and beer is totally organic. Sun seasonally.

WEAVERVILLE: *La Grange Café* $$
315 N Main St, CA 96093. **Road map** A2. (530) 623-5325. Adventurous, California health food is offered here at moderate prices, including organic salads and a wide range of vegetarian dishes. Sun.

WINE COUNTRY

BOONVILLE: *Boonville Hotel* $$$
Hwy 128 by Lambert Lane, CA 95415. **Road map** A3. (707) 895-2210. Food aficionados flock to sample chef John Schmidt's California cuisine with Mexican and Italian influences. Tue, Wed–Mon L.

CALISTOGA: *All Seasons Café* $$
1400 Lincoln Ave, CA 94515. **Road map** A3. (707) 942-9111. The menu in this popular restaurant changes regularly and is designed to accompany the award-winning wine list. A wine shop and tasting area is situated at the back of the restaurant. Thu.

	OUTDOOR EATING	VEGETARIAN SPECIALTIES	BAR AREA/COCKTAIL BAR	FIXED-PRICE MENU	CHILDREN'S FACILITIES

Price categories for a three-course meal for one, including a half bottle of house wine, sales tax, and service:
- $ under $25
- $$ $25–$35
- $$$ $35–$50
- $$$$ $50–$70
- $$$$$ over $70

OUTDOOR EATING
Some tables on a patio or terrace.

VEGETARIAN SPECIALTIES
One menu always includes a selection of vegetarian dishes.

BAR AREA/COCKTAIL BAR
There is a bar area or cocktail bar within the restaurant.

FIXED-PRICE MENU
A good-value fixed-price menu offered at lunch, dinner or both, usually with three courses.

CHILDREN'S FACILITIES
Small portions and/or high chairs available on request.

CALISTOGA: Catahoula and Wappo Bar and Bistro $$$
1457 Lincoln Ave, CA 94515. Road map A3. (707) 942-2275. American cuisine inspired by the Deep South is on offer at this contemporary restaurant. Delicious panfried catfish is one of the specialties. ● Tue.

FORESTVILLE: Russian River Vineyards Restaurant $$$
5700 Gravenstein Hwy North, CA 95436. Road map A3. (707) 887-1562. Located in the Russian River Valley in 23 acres (9 ha) of organically farmed grapes, this idyllic restaurant serves old Greek family recipes mixed with continental cuisine. ● Mon & Tue.

NAPA: Downtown Joe's Restaurant and Brewery $
902 Main St, CA 94558. Road map B3. (707) 258-2337. This busy microbrewery is great for American breakfasts, burgers, salads, and pizzas. They have live bands in the bar in the evenings.

NAPA: La Boucane $$$
1778 2nd St, CA 94559. Road map B3. (707) 253-1177. Classic French cuisine is served in a beautifully restored Victorian dining room. All main dishes are accompanied by soup or salad. The wine list is the produce of some of California's top vineyards. ● Jan; L.

NAPA: Napa Valley Wine Train www.winetrain.com $$$$
1275 McKinstry St, CA 94559. Road map B3. (800) 427-4124. Gourmet California cuisine is served on this luxury diesel train (see p447), as you enjoy the views of the beautiful Wine Country. ● Mon & Tue D.

RUTHERFORD: Auberge du Soleil $$$$
180 Rutherford Hill Rd, CA 94573. Road map A3. (707) 967-3111. Fireplaces and high beamed ceilings lend a rustic stylishness to this dining room. The views from the terrace are the best in the Napa Valley.

ST. HELENA: Trilogy $$
1234 Main St, CA 94574. Road map A3. (707) 963-5507. Owned and run by a husband-and-wife team, this small restaurant serves light French dishes with California flair and is renowned for its Zinfandel wines. ● Mon–Sat L.

ST. HELENA: Brava Terrace $$$
3010 N St Helena Hwy, North St, CA 95470. Road map A3. (707) 963-9300. This stylish restaurant attracts a mixed crowd who come here to enjoy French- and Italian-influenced California cuisine. Don't leave without buying a bottle of their lemon-infused olive oil. ● Nov–Apr: Wed.

ST. HELENA: Meadowood Restaurant $$$
900 Meadowood Lane, CA 94574. Road map A3. (707) 963-3646. Exquisite Provençale cuisine, beautiful presentation, and exceptional service are the key features of this elegant restaurant, which is part of the Meadowood Resort Hotel (see p533). ● Mon–Sat L.

ST. HELENA: Showley's $$$
1327 Railroad Ave, CA 94574. Road map A3. (707) 963-1200. This restaurant provides excellent Provençale cuisine with Italian influences. On Friday evenings, there is live jazz. ● Mon L.

ST. HELENA: Tra Vigne $$$
1050 Charter Oak, CA 94574. Road map A3. (707) 963-4444. This popular Italian restaurant has its own bakery, where bread and pasta are made outdoors in the vine-covered courtyard.

ST. HELENA: Wine Spectator Greystone Restaurant $$$
2555 St Helena Hwy, CA 94574. Road map A3. (707) 967-1010. Part of the Culinary Institute of America, the chefs here are all culinary students. The cuisine is Mediterranean-influenced. ● public hols, Tue.

SANTA ROSA: *Lisa Hemenway's Bistro* $$$
714 Village Court Mall, Farmer's Lane, CA 95401. **Road map** A3. ☎ *(707) 526-5111*.
A regular visitor to Thailand, chef-owner Lisa Hemenway serves Far Eastern-
inspired California cuisine in her restaurant. Reservations needed. ⓹ ☷ ✆

SANTA ROSA: *Mixx-An American Bistro* $$$
135 Fourth St, CA 95401. **Road map** A3. ☎ *(707) 573-1344*. This 1940s-style
restaurant has matching background jazz music. It is known for the
nicest ambience in Santa Rosa. ● *Sat & Sun L.* ⓹ ✆

SONOMA: *Ristorante Piatti* $$
405 1st St West, CA 94576. **Road map** A3. ☎ *(707) 996-2351*. This bustling Italian
bistro is part of a small California chain. The risotto of the day is always
delicious, as are the signature pizzas, pasta dishes, and chicken. ⓹ ✆

YOUNTVILLE: *The Diner* $
6476 Washington St, CA 94599. **Road map** B3. ☎ *(707) 944-2626*. The
menu at this well-established diner mixes American- and Mexican-
influenced dishes. Don't leave without trying the homemade fresh
seafood sausage, served with polenta and wilted greens. ● *Mon.* ⓹

YOUNTVILLE: *Mustards Grill* $$$
7399 St Helena Hwy, CA 94558. **Road map** B3. ☎ *(707) 944-2424*. The
emphasis is on California cuisine at this popular roadside restaurant. The wine list is extensive. Book well in advance. ⓹ ☷ ✆

YOUNTVILLE: *Napa Valley Grille* $$$
6795 Washington St, Hwy 29 at Madison, CA 94599. **Road map** B3. ☎ *(707)
944-8686*. The chef at this popular roadside restaurant, Bob Hurley, serves
delicious Wine Country cuisine, using fresh local ingredients. ⓹ ☷ ✆

YOUNTVILLE: *Brix* $$$$
7377 St. Helena Hwy, CA 94558. **Road map** B3. ☎ *(707) 944-2749*. Brix boasts a
classically trained chef and a menu of Californian and French cuisine with
a strong Asian influence. Sample the award-winning wine list of rare local
vintages whilst taking in the view of vineyards and mountains. ⓹ ♫ ☷ ✆

YOUNTVILLE: *Domaine Chandon* $$$$
1 California Drive, CA 94599. **Road map** B3. ☎ *(707) 944-2892*. Set in one of
the Napa Valley's most famous wineries, this elegant French restaurant has
views of the surrounding vineyards. ● *Oct–Apr: L.* ☷ ☷ ♫ *(Mon pm).* ✆

YOUNTVILLE: *The French Laundry* $$$$$
6640 Washington St, CA 94599. **Road map** B3. ☎ *(707) 944-2380*. You have
to book one month in advance for a place at this excellent restaurant. It
serves American cuisine, with an impressive selection of half bottles of rare
wines. The fixed-price menus are bargains. ● *Sun L, Mon, Tue L.* ⓹ ☷ ✆

GOLD COUNTRY AND THE CENTRAL VALLEY

AMADOR CITY: *Imperial Hotel and Restaurant* $$$
14202 Hwy 49, CA 95601. **Road map** B3. ☎ *(209) 267-9172*. French windows
overlook the flower-filled patio at this hotel restaurant *(see p533)*. All
dishes on the menu can be ordered as a light meal. ● *L.* ⓹ ✆

CHICO: *Sierra Nevada Brewing Company Restaurant and Tap Room* $$
1075 E 20th St, CA 95928. **Road map** B2. ☎ *(530) 345-2739*. The beer
brewed on the premises is one of the most popular in California.
The food is good standard pub fare. ● *Sun D, Mon, Fri & Sat L.* ⓹ ✆

GRASS VALLEY: *Scheidel's Old European Restaurant* $$
10100 Alta Sierra Drive, CA 95949. **Road map** B3. ☎ *(530) 273-5553*. An old-
fashioned German-style restaurant, serving traditional Bavarian cuisine.
The atmosphere is pleasantly informal. ● *Mon & Tue, Wed–Sun L.* ⓹ ✆

GRASS VALLEY: *Holbrooke Hotel and Restaurant* $$$
212 West Main St, CA 95945. **Road map** B3. ☎ *(530) 273-1353*. This
spacious hotel restaurant *(see p533)* fills up at weekends. Live music
can be heard from the oldest saloon bar in California next door. ⓹ ♫ ✆

JAMESTOWN: *Bella Union* $$$
18242 Main St, CA 95327. **Road map** B3. ☎ *(209) 984-2421*. Housed in an
historic building, Bella Union offers alligator fried in breadcrumbs,
and stuffed pheasant served with couscous. ● *Mon, Tue L.* ⓹ ✆

	Outdoor Eating	Vegetarian Specialities	Bar Area/Cocktail Bar	Fixed-Price Menu	Children's Facilities

Price categories for a three-course meal for one, including a half bottle of house wine, sales tax, and service:

$ under $25
$$ $25–$35
$$$ $35–$50
$$$$ $50–$70
$$$$$ over $70

Outdoor Eating
Some tables on a patio or terrace.

Vegetarian Specialities
One menu always includes a selection of vegetarian dishes.

Bar Area/Cocktail Bar
There is a bar area or cocktail bar within the restaurant.

Fixed-Price Menu
A good-value fixed-price menu offered at lunch, dinner or both, usually with three courses.

Children's Facilities
Small portions and/or high chairs available on request.

Restaurant	Price	Outdoor Eating	Vegetarian Specialities	Bar Area/Cocktail Bar	Fixed-Price Menu	Children's Facilities
Nevada City: *Citronée* 320 Broad St, CA 95959. **Road map** B3. (530) 265-5697. A classic mix of California and Mediterranean cuisine is served here. Most of the fresh vegetables used are grown in the proprietor's own garden. ● *Sun.*	$		●			
Nevada City: *Country Rose Café* 300 Commercial St, CA 95959. **Road map** B3. (530) 265-6248. This busy bistro-style café, housed in an 1860s brick building, specializes in French country cuisine, such as sautéed chicken breast. A classical guitarist often plays at weekends. Reservations are recommended.	$$	■	●			■
Sacramento: *Aldo's* 2914 Passatiempo Lane, CA 95814. **Road map** B3. (916) 483-5031. A variety of French and California cuisine, with a delicious dessert menu, is available at this popular, reasonably priced restaurant.	$		●			
Sacramento: *El Taquito Rico* 6223 Franklin Blvd, CA 95824. **Road map** B3. (916) 392-5290. Steak *fajitas* served with rice, beans, fried potatoes, salad, and tortillas is a popular choice at this little Mexican restaurant. ● *Mon D.*	$	■	●			■
Sacramento: *Fat City Bar & Café* 1001 Front St, CA 95814. **Road map** B3. (916) 446-6768. Situated in a 19th-century building in the heart of Old Sacramento *(see pp456–7)*, the restaurant serves substantial American fare. Ideal for children.	$		●	■		
Sacramento: *Capitol Grill* 2730 N St, CA 95816. **Road map** B3. (916) 736-0744. Old political memorabilia covers the walls of this Sacramento restaurant. The varied menu features contemporary American cuisine. Book ahead.	$$		●	■		
Sacramento: *Paragary's* 1401 28th St, CA 95618. **Road map** B3. (916) 457-5737. The decor here is New York bistro-style. Italian specialties include a wide range of pizzas and rosemary noodles with seared chicken, cheddar, and garlic. The restaurant is popular with locals, particularly families with children.	$$		●	■		■
Sacramento: *Pilot House Restaurant* 1000 Front St, CA 95814. **Road map** B3. (916) 441-4440. Housed in a refurbished 1930s steam paddleboat *(see p534)*, this hotel restaurant has river views and serves American standards such as prime rib and grilled salmon. The Sunday champagne buffet brunch is extremely popular.	$$	■	●			■
Sacramento: *Sterling Hotel* 1300 H St, CA 95814. **Road map** B3. (916) 442-0451. This intimate hotel restaurant *(see p534)* serves French-California cuisine with good vegetarian choices such as Anaheim chili pepper stuffed with three cheeses. Meat eaters are equally well catered to. Book in advance.	$$$	■	●	■		
Sacramento: *The Firehouse* 1112 2nd St, CA 95814. **Road map** B3. (916) 442-4772. The original fire pole still stands in this converted fire station, built in the 1850s. Dishes include glazed duck and *filet mignon*. ● *Sun, Mon D, Sat L.*	$$$	■	●	■	●	■
Sonora: *Wilma's Café* 275 S Washington St, CA 95370. **Road map** B3. (209) 532-9957. This cheerful diner serves classic American cuisine such as steaks, burgers, barbecued ribs, and homemade fruit pies in substantial portions.	$		●			■
Sonora: *Banny's Café* 83 S Stewart St, Suite 100, CA 95370. **Road map** B3. (209) 533-4709. An eclectic mixture of California, Italian, Mediterranean, and Thai cuisine is served from the seasonal menu at this pleasant café. ● *Sun.*	$$		●	■		

THE HIGH SIERRAS

BIG PINE: *Rossi's* $
100 N Main St, CA 93513. **Road map** C4. [(760) 938-2254. This large, family-run restaurant serves a variety of Italian-American dinners. The walls are covered with photographs tracing the history of the Owens Valley. ▯ 🖼

BISHOP: *Firehouse Grill* $$
2206 N Sierra Hwy, CA 93514. **Road map** C4. [(760) 873-4888. Continental-style grilled fare is available at this restaurant. The decor is elegant and old-fashioned. Popular with tourists and business people. ♿ ▯ 🖼

BISHOP: *Whiskey Creek* $$
524 N Main St, CA 93514. **Road map** C4. [(760) 873-7174. An extensive menu of traditional American meat and fish dishes is available at this spacious, rustic restaurant. The soups and salads are delicious. 🖼

FISH CAMP: *Narrow Gauge Inn* $$$
48571 State Hwy 41, CA 93623. **Road map** C4. [(559) 683-6446. Part of the Narrow Gauge Inn hotel (see p535), this small restaurant serves some of the best food in the High Sierras. The setting is romantic, with oil lamps on the tables and a large fireplace. ● Nov–Apr: L. 🖼

MAMMOTH LAKES: *Anything Goes* $
645 Old Mammoth Rd, CA 93546. **Road map** C4. [(530) 934-2424. Before a day's skiing, have a delicious breakfast of fresh scones and pastries. Evening meals range from Italian to Southeast Asian fare. ● Tue D, Wed.

MAMMOTH LAKES: *Whiskey Creek Restaurant* $$
Minaret & Old Main Sts, CA 93541. **Road map** C4. [(530) 934-2555. Barbecued ribs, prime rib steaks, and seafood are among the specialties at this attractive American restaurant. ● L; Mon. ♿ ▯ 🖼

MAMMOTH LAKES: *Restaurant at Convict Lake* $$$
Convict Lake, CA 93546. **Road map** C4. [(530) 934-3803. The ambience is rustic at this comfortable High Sierras lodge. Dinners feature local trout, plus well-prepared beef, lamb, and seafood dishes. ● L. 🖼

NORTH LAKE TAHOE: *Bridgetender Tavern and Grill* $
50 Westlake Blvd, CA 93 96145. **Road map** C3. [(530) 583-3342. This water-front tavern is next to Fanny Bridge, a popular spot for watching fish. The Bridgetender is known for its exceptional hamburgers. ♿ 🖼

NORTH LAKE TAHOE: *Soule Domain* $$$
9983 Cove St, King's Beach, CA 96143. **Road map** C3. [(530) 546-7529. This rustic log cabin restaurant is casual but elegant. The California cuisine includes dishes such as *filet mignon* with burgundy butter sauce, shiitake mushrooms, Gorgonzola, and brandy. ● Mon–Sun L. ♿ 🖼

SOUTH LAKE TAHOE: *Carlos Murphy's* $
3678 Lake Tahoe Blvd, CA 95731. **Road map** C3. [(530) 542-1741. Huge portions of traditional Mexican-American food and inexpensive cock-tails are the main attractions of this popular, casual restaurant. 🖼

SOUTH LAKE TAHOE: *Evans American Gourmet Café* $$$
536 Emerald Bay Rd, CA 95731. **Road map** C3. [(530) 542-1990. Tahoe's best California cuisine is on offer at this stylish, semiformal restaurant. Come here to enjoy the great desserts and award-winning wine list. The café is very small, so book in advance. ● Sun, Mon–Sat L. ♿ ▯ ▯ 🖼

STATELINE: *Sage Room* $$$
Hwy 50, NV 89449. **Road map** C3. [(775) 588-2411. Housed in the venerable Harvey's casino resort, this gourmet restaurant boasts Tahoe's finest beef dishes, as well as wild boar and venison. ● L. 🖼

TAHOE CITY: *Tahoe House* $$
625 W Lake Blvd, CA 96145. **Road map** B3. [(530) 583-1377. Dinner consists of Swiss specialties, such as *ramschnitzel* (veal scallop). The European-style bakery, open all day, produces bread, cakes, and sandwiches. ▯ 🖼

TAHOE CITY: *Christy Hill* $$$
115 Grove St, CA 96145. **Road map** B3. [(530) 583-8551. Stylish surroundings set the stage for a stylish feast from a daily changing menu of the freshest ingredients available. ● Mon, Tue–Sun L. ▯ 🖼

For key to symbols see back flap

Price categories for a three-course meal for one, including a half bottle of house wine, sales tax, and service:
$ under $25
$$ $25–$35
$$$ $35–$50
$$$$ $50–$70
$$$$$ over $70

OUTDOOR EATING
Some tables on a patio or terrace.

VEGETARIAN SPECIALTIES
One menu always includes a selection of vegetarian dishes.

BAR AREA/COCKTAIL BAR
There is a bar area or cocktail bar within the restaurant.

FIXED-PRICE MENU
A good-value fixed-price menu offered at lunch, dinner or both, usually with three courses.

CHILDREN'S FACILITIES
Small portions and/or high chairs available on request.

	Outdoor Eating	Vegetarian Specialties	Bar Area/Cocktail Bar	Fixed-Price Menu	Children's Facilities
TAHOE CITY: *Sierra Vista* $$$ 700 N Lake Blvd, CA 96145. **Road map** B3. ((530) 583-0233. An eclectic menu of California cuisine makes this restaurant one of the best. Ask to sit on the porch or on the lovely wooden terrace overlooking Lake Tahoe.	●		●	●	●
TAHOE VISTA: *Le Petit Pier* $$$ 7238 N Lake Blvd, CA 96148. **Road map** B3. ((530) 546-4464. French-style cuisine is served at this romantic restaurant beside Lake Tahoe. Maine lobster and tenderloin of lamb are among the dishes offered. ● *Tue.*		●	●	●	
TRUCKEE: *Pianeta* $$$ 10096 Commercial Rd, CA 95734. **Road map** B3. ((530) 587-4694. In the heart of Truckee lies this fine little Italian restaurant. Romantic decor matches rustic Italian cuisine. ● *Tue, Wed–Mon L.*					●
YOSEMITE NATIONAL PARK: *Wawona Dining Room* $$$ State Hwy 41, CA 95389. **Road map** C3. ((559) 252-4848. American cuisine is served in the comfortable dining room of a 19th-century hotel (*see p536*). Although the food is unremarkable, the ambience is relaxing. ● *Nov–Mar.*		●	●		●
YOSEMITE NATIONAL PARK: *Ahwahnee Dining Room* $$$$ Yosemite Valley, CA 95389. **Road map** C3. ((559) 252-4848. The soaring ceiling of this beautiful hotel dining room (*see p536*) makes up for rather bland food. Steaks and other simple dishes are a safe bet.			●		

NORTH CENTRAL CALIFORNIA

	Outdoor Eating	Vegetarian Specialties	Bar Area/Cocktail Bar	Fixed-Price Menu	Children's Facilities
APTOS: *Chez Renée* $$$ 9051 Soquel Drive, CA 95003. **Road map** B4. ((831) 688-5566. This restaurant, nestled in a redwood grove, has won awards for its California cuisine with French and Italian influences. Fixed-price dinner menus are available on Sundays. ● *Sun L, Mon & Tue.*	●	●	●	●	
BIG SUR: *Nepenthe* $$ Hwy 1, CA 93920. **Road map** B4. ((831) 667-2345. Originally a honeymoon retreat for Orson Welles and Rita Hayworth, this restaurant – on a clear day – has a view of a 35-mile (56-km) stretch of coastline. The emphasis is on basic American cuisine; desserts and breads are homemade.	●	●	●		●
BIG SUR: *Deetjen's* $$$ Castro Canyon, CA 93920. **Road map** B4. ((831) 667-2378. This hotel restaurant (*see p536*) is set in rustic surroundings. It is famous for its breakfasts and its French-California dinner menu. ● *L.*	●	●			
BIG SUR: *Sierra Mar* $$$$ Hwy 1, CA 93920. **Road map** B4. ((831) 667-2800. Part of the Post Ranch Inn (*see p537*), the restaurant is stylish and has fabulous ocean views. The cuisine is exquisite, and everything is available *à la carte*.		●	●	●	
CARMEL: *Ridge Restaurant* $$$ 200 Punta del Monte, Carmel Valley, CA 93924. **Road map** B4. ((831) 659-0170. Part of the Robles del Rio Lodge hotel (*see p537*), excellent French-California cuisine is served in a lovely dining room with a fireplace.		●	●		●
CARMEL: *The French Poodle* $$$ Junipero & 5th Ave, CA 93921. **Road map** B4. ((831) 624-8643. This intimate restaurant was selected as one of the best French restaurants in the US by the International Restaurant Rating Bureau. ● *Sun, Mon–Sat L.*		●			
CARMEL: *The Terrace Grill, La Playa Hotel* $$$ 8th Ave/Camino Real, CA 93920. **Road map** B4. ((831) 624-6476. California cuisine is served in the dining room of this hotel (*see p537*), overlooking beautiful gardens and the ocean. The early-bird menu is a bargain.	●	●	●	●	●

CARMEL: *Hog's Breath Inn* $)$)$)$
San Carlos/5th, CA 93921. **Road map** B4. (831) 625-1044. This Clint
Eastwood-owned restaurant serves cowboy fare (prime rib, steaks,
and hamburgers) in publike surroundings. ● *Fri & Sat L.*

CARMEL: *The Covey at Quail Lodge* $)$)$)$
8205 Valley Greens Drive, Carmel Valley, CA 93923. **Road map** B4. (831)
624-1581. This hotel restaurant *(see p537)* has won several awards for its
California cuisine and wine. ● *L.*

CARMEL: *Anton and Michel* $)$)$)$)$
Mission & 7th Sts, CA 93921. **Road map** B4. (831) 624-2406. This
elegant Carmel restaurant serves international cuisine. Famous
dishes include the *Châteaubriand* and rack of lamb.

CASTROVILLE: *The Franco Restaurant* $
10639 Merrit St, CA 95012. **Road map** B4. (831) 633-2090. Housed in
a 1930s Art Deco building, Franco's serves diner food, including
enormous hamburgers, amid Marilyn Monroe memorabilia.

HANFORD: *Imperial Dynasty* $)$
2 China Alley, CA 93230. **Road map** C4. (559) 582-0196. This family-owned
restaurant serves continental and American staples, including prime rib,
seafood, and steak, in oriental surroundings. ● *Mon, Tue–Sun L.*

MONTEREY: *Thai Hut* $
580 Broadway, CA 93955. **Road map** B4. (831) 899-1191. Diners come
here to enjoy delicious Thai food. On Mondays, Wednesdays, and Fridays
a very reasonable all-you-can-eat lunch buffet is offered. ● *Sun L.*

MONTEREY: *Domenica's on the Wharf* $)$)$
50 Fisherman's Wharf, CA 93940. **Road map** B4. (831) 372-3655. Enjoy fine
dining in relaxed surroundings overlooking the wharf. The menu features
seafood and mesquite barbecues. There is also an oyster bar.

MONTEREY: *Tarpy's Roadhouse* W www.tarpys.com $)$)$
2999 Monterey-Salinas Hwy, CA 93940. **Road map** B4. (831) 647-1444.
Basic American food, from cheeseburgers and T-bone steaks to
game and fresh seafood, is served in an old ranch house.

MONTEREY: *Fresh Cream* $)$)$)$
99 Pacific St, Suite 100C, Heritage Harbor, CA 93940. **Road map** B4. (831)
375-9798. This award-winning restaurant, with its harbor views, offers
some of the best French food in Northern California. ● *L.*

PACIFIC GROVE: *Fandango* $)$)$)$
223 17th St, CA 93950. **Road map** B4. (831) 372-3456.
The menu here is varied, featuring Mediterranean food from pasta to
lobster. One room is warmed by an open mesquite grill.

SANTA CRUZ: *Santa Cruz Brewing Company and Restaurant* $
516 Front St, CA 95060. **Road map** B4. (831) 429-8838. Warm and casual,
with lots of wooden decor, this hamburger/grill "pub" attracts a mixed
crowd who are here mostly for the homemade beer.

SANTA CRUZ: *The Crêpe Place* $
1134 Soquel Ave, CA 95062. **Road map** B4. (831) 429-6994. The
decor at this restaurant is as eclectic as its menu. Choose from a
wide selection of *crêpes* or invent your own. ● *Fri & Sat D.*

SANTA CRUZ: *Whole Earth Restaurant* $
Redwood Building, University of California, CA 95064. **Road map** B4. (831)
426-8255. The decor at this campus restaurant is rustic, and the food ranges
from Mexican to Asian and European. ● *university holidays, Sat & Sun D.*

SANTA CRUZ: *Gabriella's* $)$)$
910 Cedar St, CA 95060. **Road map** B4. (831) 457-1677. This popular
restaurant serves Italian cuisine with an emphasis on organic vegetables,
seafood, and pasta. The wine list features mostly local wines.

SEASIDE: *El Migueleño* $
1066 Broadway, CA 93955. **Road map** B4. (831) 899-2199. This Salvadoran
restaurant serves Mexican and Salvadoran food. The house special is
Playa Azul, a dish composed of seven different kinds of seafood.

For key to symbols see back flap

SPECIAL INTEREST VACATIONS AND ACTIVITIES IN CALIFORNIA

CALIFORNIA is practically synonymous with the great outdoors. The state has protected its landscape so that future generations can visit places of beauty. The deserts, redwood forests, alpine meadows, granite mountains, lakes, and white beaches all welcome visitors. California

Whitewater rafting on the Merced River *(see p578)*

has a culture rich with physical activity, and wilderness is never far from any city. Golfers are well provided for around the Monterey Peninsula *(see p495)* and winter skiers flock to Lake Tahoe *(see p471)*. For details of main events in the sports calendar, see pages 32–5.

Tahquitz Golf Course, Palm Springs

SPECIAL INTEREST VACATIONS

DETAILS OF special interest vacations are available from the **California Office of Tourism**. One of the most popular of these are tours of California's missions along El Camino Real *(see pp42–3)*.

Writers who make California their home often give readings at local writers' workshops. The best of these are the **Santa Barbara Writers' Conference** and the **Squaw Valley Community of Writers**.

Artists can take advantage of the state's various craft centers. Nationally renowned artists hold painting courses at the **Crescent Harbor Art Gallery** in Crescent City and at the **Mendocino Arts Center**.

Institutes such as **Great Chefs** at the Robert Mondavi Winery *(see p447)* and **Tante Marie's Cooking School** provide accommodations, cooking classes, shopping tours, visits to the Wine Country, and fine meals during week-long intensive courses in the summer.

CAMPING

CALIFORNIA has always valued its wilderness: Yosemite Valley *(see pp472–5)* and the Mariposa Grove of giant redwoods were protected parkland as early as 1864. Today there are more than 250 places classified as either state parks, wilderness areas, historic sites, or recreation areas.

At every site, there are hiking trails and parking lots. Many also provide bathrooms and camp sites. All state and federal parks allow day-use visitors, charging a small parking fee. For camping, reserve a site with **State Park Reservations** or **Yosemite Reservations**. Most camp sites accept reservations eight weeks in advance.

Camping trips into the state's desert are organized by **Desert Survivors**. They include environmental information.

HIKING

DAY HIKES and longer trips in the country are popular with both residents and visitors. There are more than 1 million miles (1.6 million km) of trails in California, the longest being the Pacific Crest Trail. The 2,640-mile (4,245-km) route stretches from Canada to Mexico. One of its highlights is the 200-mile (320-km) John Muir Trail, from Yosemite's high country to Mount Whitney *(see pp472–9)*. The **Sierra Club** organizes guided outings and provides detailed maps.

Hiking along the John Muir Trail at Mount Whitney

HORSEBACK RIDING

EQUESTRIANS will find a wide variety of riding trails in California, across all types of landscape – pine-covered mountains, lush meadows, chaparral hills, and dry valleys. Many state and national parks allow horses and pack mules on their trails.

Traditional cowboy life can still be found at privately owned ranches, such as **Spanish Springs Ranch** in Ravendale. These are working ranches, and guests can ride with the ranch hands and herd animals, or simply ride for pleasure on their extensive network of trails. **El Alisal Guest Ranch and Resort** holds annual roundups and cattle drives.

Horseback riding in Ventura County

MOUNTAIN BIKING

MANY STATE PARKS allow cyclists on their hiking trails. One spectacular trail for cyclists begins at High Camp in Squaw Valley, Lake Tahoe (*see p471*). A 2,000-ft (610-m) ascent via an aerial tram is followed by a heart-stopping downhill ride to Shirley Lake. Contact the **Bicycle Trails Council** to find out where mountain bikes are welcome.

Outfitters such as **Backroads** also lead groups of cyclists on tours of the state's abundant rolling countryside, often with stops for leisurely gourmet lunches. Transport vans accompany the cyclists, carrying heavy equipment and camping gear for week-long trips. Popular destinations

Mountain biking in Marin County

include the Napa Valley (*see pp446–7*) and the country lanes of Sonoma, Monterey, and Santa Barbara Counties.

BEACHES

BEACHES along California's 900-mile (1,450-km) coastline vary considerably. Some have rough waves and rocky beaches, ideal for rock pool exploration and quiet reflection. Others have the white sand, arching waves, and warm water that attract the surfers of California legend.

Whether you want to surf or simply watch the golden boys of summer, the best beaches include the Leo Carrillo State Beach in Orange County (*see pp220–21*), Windansea Beach in La Jolla (*see pp238–9*), and Corona del Mar in Newport Beach (*see pp220–21*). The **Club Ed Surf School** offers a 7-day surfing camp for beginners to the sport held between April and October.

Many spots along the coast are good diving areas, including Scripps Shoreline Underwater Preserve in La Jolla (*see p239*), the coves of Laguna Beach (*see p221*), and Monterey Bay (*see p495*). Equipment can be rented from the **Aquarius Dive Shop**. The **Underwater Schools of America** in Oceanside also offers diving lessons for beginners.

Natural Bridges State Park in Santa Cruz (*see pp490–91*) and Pfeiffer State Beach in Big Sur (*see pp498–9*) are good sites for rock pool exploration, where the ocean has eroded the rock in unusual formations. Torrey Pines State Beach (*see p238*) offers forests and dramatic white-capped swells. Pismo Beach is famous for its sand dunes, surfing, and clam digging (*see p198*).

Southern California's water is warm enough for swimming from April to November. In the sea north of San Francisco a wet suit should be worn at all times of the year.

Golden beaches of La Jolla cove

WHITEWATER RAFTING AND KAYAKING

WHITEWATER RAFTING is like a thrilling roller coaster ride combined with stunning scenic views. Specialty outfitters such as **Mariah Wilderness Expeditions**, **Outdoor Unlimited**, and **Whitewater Voyages** provide rafts, paddles, and life jackets. They take groups of six to eight people, accompanied by a guide, down a tributary of one of California's major rivers. Trips may last one day only or include an overnight stay.

The rafting season lasts from April to September. Trips are graded by their level of difficulty: Classes I and II are relatively safe, with a few exciting twists and turns. Beginners wanting a safe but slightly more exciting ride should book a trip on a Class III river. Only experienced rafters should go on a Class IV, or higher, trip.

Most organizations that offer river rafting also provide kayak and canoe trips. For more information, contact **Friends of the River** or the **American River Touring Association**.

Waterskiing in San Diego

WATER SPORTS

THE LAKES and beaches in California offer a variety of activities. Houseboats are available to rent for a slow cruise through the maze of inlets in the Sacramento Delta. Speedboats are available at Lake Tahoe *(see p471)*, Lake Shasta *(see p436)*, and the man-made lakes that are part of the state recreation system.

One of the newest sports is parasailing. With water skis and a parachute, participants are harnessed to a speedboat and launched into the air for an exhilarating ride. It's a safe sport, but life jackets should be worn. Contact **Parasailing Catalina** for details.

Rafting at Yosemite National Park *(see pp472–5)*

BIRD-WATCHING

CALIFORNIA'S coastline and rivers are feeding grounds for migrating birds. In autumn, ducks, geese, and other shorebirds leave Canada to winter in South America, stopping in California along the way. The Point Reyes National Seashore *(see pp396–7)* supports at least 45 percent of US bird species. More than 425 species have been sighted here.

Just south of San Diego, the **Tijuana Slough National Estuarine Research Reserve** hosts 400 species, best seen in spring and autumn.

Bird-watching in La Jolla *(see p251)*

FISHING

CALIFORNIA is an angler's paradise. From the end of April through to the middle of November, anglers head to the rivers and streams of the Sierra Nevada Mountains for trout fishing. Bass fishing in California's multitude of lakes and reservoirs is plentiful throughout the year. During the autumn and winter months, schools of salmon and steelhead make their way upriver, with especially good fishing in the Klamath, American, Eel, and Sacramento rivers. Sturgeon and striped bass can also readily be caught in the Sacramento River Delta.

Almost every coastal city in the state offers charter boats for deep-sea ocean fishing. In Northern California, the summer months are particularly good for halibut and ocean salmon, but throughout the Pacific, from autumn to early spring, 40–50-lb (18–23-kg) hauls of cod and rock fish are not unusual. In the warmer waters off Southern California, blue fin, yellow fin, and

Fishing on Lake Molena in San Diego

skipjack tuna, as well as barracuda are particularly plentiful during the summer. To rent a charter boat for fishing contact **Helgren's Sportfishing Trips**, **Hot Pursuit Sport Fishing**, or **Anchor Charters**.

To find out which fish are in season, contact the **State Department of Fish and Game**. Fly fishing, another popular California sport, is available from **Mammoth Lakes Fishing Services** in the eastern Sierras.

ROCK CLIMBING AND CAVING

Rock climbing combines the dexterity of gymnastics with the grace of dance, as individuals scale vertical rock walls using only their hands and high-friction shoes.

Rock climbing at Joshua Tree National Park

The sport can be practiced throughout the year in rock-climbing gyms in major cities. Other places to learn how to rock climb or simply to watch others in action are the Joshua Tree National Park (see pp268–9), the alpine village of Idyllwild, near Palm Springs (see p266), and Squaw Valley in Lake Tahoe (see p471). Contact the **American Mountain Guides Association** or **Mission Cliffs Climbing School** for information.

Spelunkers (cave explorers) should head for the Pinnacles National Monument (see p501) or Lassen Volcanic National Park (see p437), where volcanoes have created unusual caves and rock formations.

HANG GLIDING

If you've ever wanted to ride the thermal air currents at speeds of 25–50 mph (40–80 km/h), this is the sport for you. A hang glider is a kite-shaped, plastic-covered light metal frame. The harnessed rider hangs onto a triangular control bar, jumps from the top of a cliff or hill, and, supported by air currents, glides to the ground. For beginners, flights can be made in tandem with a qualified pilot, equipped with a safety parachute.

The main hang-gliding areas, for both participants and spectators, are

Fort Funston off the Bay Area coastline (see pp396–7), **Torrey Pines Glider Port** in San Diego, or Vista Point in Palm Desert (see p264). If you want to learn the sport, they will recommend instructors. They also sell and rent gliding equipment.

GARDENS

The warm, sunny climate of California has inspired numerous skilled and amateur gardeners to experiment with horticulture. The result is a rich variety of arboretums, botanical gardens, city parks, and private estates all over the state that are now open to the public.

Huntington Library Art Collections and Botanical Gardens are Henry Huntington's idealistic monument to art and culture. Work began on the gardens in 1904. They cover three-quarters of the 200-acre (80-ha) estate and are among the finest of their kind in California (see pp154–7).

The **Descanso Gardens** in La Cañada offer 4 acres (1.6 ha) of roses, an impressive 30-acre (12-ha) grove of live oaks, and a protected forest of camellia trees. William Bourn's landscaped grounds and elegant estate of Filoli in the Bay Area town of Woodside (see p411) and **Villa Montalvo Arboretum** in Saratoga are both carefully tended so that their flowers are in bloom all year long. Weekend jazz concerts are held at Saratoga during the summer months, adding to the cultured environment.

Hot air ballooning over California's landscape

HOT AIR BALLOONING

H OT AIR BALLOONING is a popular excursion in the Napa Valley *(see pp446–7)*, Monterey *(see pp494–5)*, and Temecula County. The rides are taken at sunrise or sunset when there is the least wind and are quiet and gentle, offering incomparable panoramic views of the countryside. Outfitters such as **Adventures Aloft** and **Napa Valley Balloons** provide private and group outings, which are then followed by a picnic.

WHALE WATCHING

F ROM DECEMBER through to April, gray whales journey 7,000 miles (11,260 km) along the California coast, having left Alaska's Bering Strait for the warmer climate of Mexico's Baja Peninsula. Ocean cruises offer views of these impressive mammals. Humpback, killer whales, pilot, and blue whales also frequent the coast between San Francisco and Monterey in late summer. Charter operators such as **Shearwater Journeys** provide a glimpse of the gray whales, as well as the dolphins and porpoises that accompany them on their trips. For more information, contact **Oceanic Society Expeditions**.

HOT SPRINGS

A LONG SOAK in a hot spring (a bubbling tributary of an underground river, heated by the earth) is said to be very good for one's health. Calistoga in Northern California *(see p445)* has numerous spas, offering everything from heated pools with mineral water to mud baths, steam baths, and massages. Contact the **Calistoga Chamber of Commerce** for a full list of area resorts.

ISLAND HOPPING

F IVE VOLCANIC ISLANDS off the coast of Southern California make up the Channel Islands National Park *(see p214)*. This stark nature preserve is ideal for hiking, viewing wildlife, and exploring rock pools. It is also an excellent spot to see whales and dolphins, as well as many species of shore birds. Ferries depart from Ventura and Santa Barbara harbors. Reserve your trip with **Island Packers**.

The Wrigley Memorial Garden on Catalina Island is accessible by ferry from San Pedro, Long Beach, Redondo Beach, and Balboa. It is more developed than the Channel Islands National Park, with shops, restaurants, and accommodations. Developed as a summer resort in the 1920s by chewing-gum magnate William Wrigley, Jr, the island offers trails for cycling, hiking, and opportunities for diving and snorkeling *(see pp232–3)*.

Farther north, **Angel Island**, in San Francisco Bay, is a 740-acre (300-ha) marine sanctuary, reached by ferry from Fisherman's Wharf. Extensive hiking trails, picnic areas, and camp sites are available to visitors. Gray whales and a wide range of shore birds can be observed.

Two Harbors at Ismus Cove on Catalina Island

DIRECTORY

SPECIAL INTEREST VACATIONS

California Office of Tourism
PO Box 9278,
Van Nuys, CA 91409.
 (800) 862-2543.

Great Chefs
PO Box 106,
Oakville, CA 94562.
 (707) 944-2866.

Mendocino Arts Center
PO Box 765,
Mendocino, CA 95460.
 (707) 937-5818.

Crescent Harbor Art Gallery
200 Marine Way,
Crescent City, CA 95531.
 (707) 464-9133.

Santa Barbara Writers' Conference
PO Box 304,
Carpinteria, CA 93014.
 (805) 684-2250.

Squaw Valley Community of Writers
PO Box 2352,
Olympic Valley, CA 96146.
 (530) 583-5200; (530) 274-8551.

Tante Marie's Cooking School
271 Francisco St,
San Francisco, CA 94133.
 (415) 788-6699.
 www.tantemaries.com

CAMPING

Desert Survivors
PO Box 20991,
Oakland, CA 94620-0991.
 (510) 769-1706.

Sequoia National Park Reservations
 (888) 252-5757.
 www.visitsequoia.com

State Park Reservations
 (800) 444-7275.
 www.cal–parks.ca.gov

Yosemite Reservations
 (559) 252-4848.
www.yosemitepark.com

HIKING

Sierra Club
730 Polk St,
San Francisco,
CA 94109.
 (415) 977-5500.

HORSEBACK RIDING

El Alisal Guest Ranch and Resort
1054 Alisal Rd,
Solvang, CA 93463.
 (805) 688-6411.

Spanish Springs Ranch
PO Box 270,
Ravendale, CA 96123.
 (800) 560-1900.

MOUNTAIN BIKING

Backroads
801 Cedar St,
Berkeley, CA 94710.
 (510) 527-1555.

Bicycle Trails Council
PO Box 494,
Fairfax, CA 94978.
 (415) 456-7512.

BEACHES

Aquarius Dive Shop
32 Cannery Row,
Monterey, CA 93940.
 (831) 375-6605.

Club Ed Surf School
5 Isabel Drive,
Santa Cruz,
CA 95060.
 (831) 459-9283.

Underwater Schools of America
707 Oceanside Blvd,
Oceanside, CA 92054.
 (760) 722-7826.

WHITEWATER RAFTING AND KAYAKING

American River Touring Association
24000 Casa Loma Rd,
Groveland, CA 95321.
 (209) 962-7873.

Outdoor Unlimited
Box 0234A,
San Francisco, CA 94117.
 (415) 476-2078.

Whitewater Voyages
PO Box 20400,
El Sobrante, CA 94820.
 (510) 222-5994.
 www. whitewatervoyages.com

WATER SPORTS

Parasailing Catalina
PO Box 2275,
Avalon, CA 90704.
 (310) 510-1777.

BIRD-WATCHING

Tijuana Slough National Estuarine Research Reserve
301 Caspian Way,
Imperial Beach, CA 91932.
 (619) 575-3613.

FISHING

Anchor Charters
Noyo Harbor,
Fort Bragg, CA 95437.
 (707) 964-4550.

Hot Pursuit Sport Fishing
Fisherman's Wharf,
San Francisco, CA 94133.
 (415) 567-7610.

Mammoth Lakes Fishing Services
PO Box 353,
Mammoth Lakes,
CA 93546.
 (760) 934-1990

State Department of Fish and Game
1416 9th St, 12th Floor,
Sacramento, CA 95814.
 (916) 653-7664.

ROCK CLIMBING AND CAVING

American Mountain Guides Association
PO Box 2128, Estes Park,
Colorado 80517.
 (970) 586-0571.

Mission Cliffs
2295 Harrison St,
San Francisco, CA 94116.
 (415) 550-0515.
 www.mission-cliffs.com

HANG GLIDING

Torrey Pines Glider Port
2800 Torrey Pines Scenic Drive, La Jolla, CA 92037.
 (858) 452-9858.

GARDENS

Descanso Gardens
1418 Descanso Drive,
La Canada-Flintridge,
CA 91011.
 (818) 952-4400.

Villa Montalvo Arboretum
15400 Montalvo Rd,
Saratoga, CA 95071.
 (408) 741-3421.

HOT AIR BALLOONING

Adventures Aloft
6525 Washington St,
Yountville, CA 94599.
 (707) 944-4408.

Napa Valley Balloons
6795 Washington St,
Yountville, CA 94599.
 (707) 253-2224.

WHALE WATCHING

Oceanic Society Expeditions
Fort Mason Center,
San Francisco, CA 94123.
 (415) 441-1106.

Shearwater Journeys
PO Box 190,
Hollister, CA 95024.
 (831) 637-8527.

HOT SPRINGS

Calistoga Chamber of Commerce
1458 Lincoln Ave, No. 9,
Calistoga, CA 94515.
 (707) 942-6333.

ISLAND HOPPING

Angel Island Ferry
 (415) 435-2131

Island Packers
1867 Spinnaker Drive,
Ventura, CA 93001.
 (805) 642-1393.

SHOPPING IN CALIFORNIA

ALIFORNIA is a manufacturing giant and a major player in the global economy. It is the largest producer of children's clothing in the US, and is equally famous for its sportswear and swimwear. Produce from the San Joaquin Valley, including fruit, nuts, and vegetables, feeds the nation. Aside from the shopping districts of LA *(see pp166–7)* and San Francisco *(see*

Antique Dealers' Association sign

pp376–9), the state's smaller towns and countryside offer a wide range of merchandise and local produce. Roadside food stands, wineries, antique shops, and crafts by local artisans are some of the attractions of California's backroads. Prices tend to be cheaper than in the cities, and in some places, such as flea markets, you will be expected to barter and negotiate.

Window-shopping along Ocean Avenue, Carmel *(see p494)*

SHOPPING HOURS

SINCE THE LOCAL population tends to view shopping as a recreational activity, most major stores in California are open for business seven days a week. Typical business hours are 10am – 6pm, Monday to Saturday, and noon–5pm on Sundays. In smaller communities, stores may be closed on Sunday or Monday. Opening hours for these stores are sometimes 11am–7pm.

HOW TO PAY

MOST STORES accept credit cards, including MasterCard, American Express and Visa, and traveler's checks. Paying by traveler's checks requires some form of identification, such as a passport or driver's license. Few stores will accept checks drawn on foreign banks. Cash is the best way to pay for any small purchases *(see pp594–5)*.

SALES TAX

SALES TAX (VAT) in California ranges from 7.25 to 8.5 percent. All items except groceries and prescription drugs are taxed. In general, tax is not included in the advertised price but is added separately at the cash register.

RIGHTS AND REFUNDS

MERCHANTS are not required by law to give a cash refund or credit for returned goods, although most do so. All stores will refund the cost of a defective item, if it is not marked "flawed" or "sold as is." Inspect the item before you buy it and keep all receipts. If an item is faulty, go back to the store with the receipt and original packaging. Many stores will refund your money up to 30 days after purchase.

SHIPPING PACKAGES

FOR A CHARGE, most stores ship goods worldwide, or send your items home by Federal Express or US Express Mail Service *(see pp596–7)*. You will be asked to fill out a form giving a short description of the goods and stating their monetary value. Keep receipts of the transaction in case the items should get lost in transit.

WHERE TO SHOP

A NUMBER OF COASTAL towns noted for their locally owned shops can be found along Hwy 1 or US 101. These include Santa Barbara *(see pp210–11)*, Big Sur *(see pp498–9)*, Carmel *(see p494)*, Santa Cruz *(see pp490–91)*, and Sausalito *(see pp398–9)*.

On Hwy 99 and other roads that cross the San Joaquin Valley, many farms sell locally grown fruit and vegetables. Palm Springs *(see pp264–5)* is known for its fashion shops. Antique dealers are plentiful in towns in the Sierra foothills, such as Sutter Creek *(see p460)*.

FASHION

CALIFORNIA is known for its casual clothing – the dress-down Friday business look was invented here. However, the East Coast also looks to California for the very best of cutting-edge fashion.

Seventy percent of all swimwear designed in the US is designed here, by names such as

San Franciscan original, The Gap

Catalina and **California Wave**. Sixty-five percent of the country's younger female fashion is also produced here.

Children's wear is a specialty of the state. **Sara's Prints**, **Traci Lynn**, and **Levi Strauss** are some of the best.

Other local heroes include designer Nicholas Graham of **Joe Boxer Inc**, who turned men's boxer shorts into art statements, and **Jessica McClintock Inc**, known for her ballgowns and bridal wear. **The Gap**, now an international retail giant, originated in San Francisco in 1969 and was the first store to mass-market denim jeans.

FLEA MARKETS

FLEA MARKETS (also called swap meets) are held on weekends, usually on Sundays. Vendors set up booths within a vast parking lot, football stadium, or even in the grounds of one of the famous missions. Just about everything imaginable is for sale. It is often possible to find a one-of-a-kind treasure at a good price, but don't accept the quoted price – bargaining is *de rigueur*. Be sure to bring cash with you because most vendors will not accept credit cards or traveler's checks.

Notable flea markets include the **Berkeley Flea Market**, the **San Jose Flea Market**, the **Rose Bowl Flea Market** in Pasadena, and **San Juan Bautista Peddlars Fair**. Flea markets may charge a nominal entrance fee of 75 cents or $1.

Browsers at an open-air flea market in Sausalito

Cover of a vintage Hollywood magazine from the 1950s

POP CULTURE ANTIQUES

MEMORABILIA stores are a California specialty. Sun Valley's **The Game Doc** sells a variety of old games for all ages. **Hello Central** sells all kinds of antique telephones, from early models to the 1940s black rotary dial telephones. **Hillcrest Vintage Paper Collectables** and **Sarah Stocking Fine Vintage Posters** specialize in old movie posters. A range of Hollywood memorabilia is easily found in LA *(see pp166 – 7)*. Other stores, such as **Camperos Collectables** in Sutter Creek, also sell such items.

OUTLET CENTERS

ONE OF THE STATE'S most popular retail trends is factory outlet malls. These sell off-season or surplus goods, such as clothing and household items, directly to consumers at prices lower than those in department stores.

Outlet centers usually have around 20 shops, but the **Factory Stores of America at Nut Tree** has more than 100 stores. Other popular centers include the **American Tin Cannery Factory Outlets** in Monterey, **Napa Factory Stores**, **Desert Hills Factory Stores**, **Palm Springs Square**, **Pismo Beach Outlet Center**, and the **San Diego Factory Outlet Center**. For special outlet center tours contact **Shopper Stopper Tours**.

SIZE CHART

For Australian sizes follow the British and American conversions.

Children's clothing

American	2–3	4–5	6–6x	7–8	10	12	14	16 (size)
British	2–3	4–5	6–7	8–9	10–11	12	14	14+ (years)
Continental	2–3	4–5	6–7	8–9	10–11	12	14	14+ (years)

Children's shoes

American	7½	8½	9½	10½	11½	12½	13½	1½	2½
British	7	8	9	10	11	12	13	1	2
Continental	24	25½	27	28	29	30	32	33	34

Women's dresses, coats and skirts

American	4	6	8	10	12	14	16	18
British	6	8	10	12	14	16	18	20
Continental	38	40	42	44	46	48	50	52

Women's blouses and sweaters

American	6	8	10	12	14	16	18
British	30	32	34	36	38	40	42
Continental	40	42	44	46	48	50	52

Women's shoes

American	5	6	7	8	9	10	11
British	3	4	5	6	7	8	9
Continental	36	37	38	39	40	41	44

Men's suits

American	34	36	38	40	42	44	46	48
British	34	36	38	40	42	44	46	48
Continental	44	46	48	50	52	54	56	58

Men's shirts

American	14	15	15½	16	16½	17	17½	18
British	14	15	15½	16	16½	17	17½	18
Continental	36	38	39	41	42	43	44	45

Men's shoes

American	7	7½	8	8½	9½	10½	11	11½
British	6	7	7½	8	9	10	11	12
Continental	39	40	41	42	43	44	45	46

Antique shops in Temecula, near Palm Springs

BOOKS, MUSIC, AND CRAFTS

BOOKSTORES, whether part of a large chain or independent, are a feature of even the smallest California town.

The best selection of music is generally available only in major cities, in chains such as **Tower Records**, **Virgin Megastore**, and **Wherehouse**. If a town has a university, head toward the student district where new and used record stores thrive.

Native American and Mexican arts and crafts are available throughout California. Contact the **American Indian Contemporary Arts Center** and the Mexican Museum *(see p255)* for more information.

ANTIQUES

CALIFORNIA'S small towns are awash with traditional antiques such as fine gold and silver jewelry, Native American Indian artifacts, textiles, antique clothing, Bakelite jewelry, and period furniture dating back to the 18th and 19th centuries.

The West Coast is the port of entry to the US for many Pacific Rim countries and, as a result, many antique porcelain sculptures from Japan and China, and antique Asian furniture are available. Twentieth-century collectables include Arts and Crafts and Art Deco furniture, clothing, posters, prewar tin toys, blown glass, and pottery.

Antique dealers often rent space together in one large mall, barn, or warehouse building that is open to the public. The largest antique mall is **Antique Plaza**, just east of Sacramento. Almost 300 dealers trade here. There is also a café serving coffee and sandwiches.

FOOD

MANY OF CALIFORNIA'S farms, particularly in Sonoma or Fresno counties, sell their produce to visitors on self-guided farm trails. In Sonoma, contact the **Sonoma County Farm Trails** or the **Sonoma Valley Chamber of Commerce**. The Fresno County Blossom Trail is a 62-mile (100-km) trail passing through groves, orchards, and vineyards. It begins at **Simonian Farms**, which sells local fruits, honey, and mustards. Contact the **Fresno County Farm Bureau** for information.

California has a number of unique food shops scattered around the state. In Napa's Anderson Valley, the **Apple Farm** is a year-round fruit

Fresh local produce at a farmers' market

stand selling locally grown apples and pears. Also in Napa, the **Jimtown Store** sells local jams, honey, olives, mustards, vinegars, and salad dressings. On Hwy 152, east of Gilroy, **Casa de Fruta**, which began as a simple cherry stand in the 1940s, has grown into a vast complex with a fruit stand, coffee shop (Casa de Coffee), restaurant (Casa de Burger), and gift shop (Casa de Gift).

Harris Ranch, almost midway between LA and San Francisco on I-5, is a vast complex set amid a working cattle ranch. The Spanish-style hacienda has a gift shop featuring Harris Ranch produce and fresh meat, as well as a restaurant, coffee shop, and overnight lodging.

Italian Marketplace at the Viansa Winery

WINERIES

IN ADDITION TO the fine wine of Napa and Sonoma counties, wineries are known for the shops located inside their tasting rooms. A range of merchandise related to wine is for sale. For a list of California's wineries, contact the **Wine Institute of San Francisco**.

The Italian Marketplace at the **Viansa Winery** sells Italian cheeses and breads, cookbooks, and kitchenware. The **Sebastiani Vineyards** sell a variety of wine-related souvenirs. The gift shop in the **Sterling Vineyards** offers silk scarves, silver jewelry, and regional history books.

The **Hakusan Sake Garden** serves *sake* in a picturesque Japanese garden and sells it in their on-site shop.

DIRECTORY

FASHION

The Original Levi Strauss
1155 Battery,
San Francisco,
CA 94111.
☎ (415) 501-6000.

California Wave
1247 E 58th Place,
Los Angeles, CA 90001.
☎ (323) 233-0077.

Catalina
6040 Bandini Blvd,
City of Commerce,
CA 90040.
☎ (323) 726-1262.

The Gap
1 Harrison St,
San Francisco,
CA 94105.
☎ (650) 952-4400.

Jessica McClintock Inc
1400 16th St,
San Francisco, CA 94103.
☎ (415) 495-3030.

Joe Boxer Inc
1265 Folsom St,
San Francisco, CA 94103.
☎ (415) 431-5719.

Sara's Prints
3018-A Alvarado St,
San Leandro, CA 94577.
☎ (510) 352-6060.

Traci Lynn
655 E 30th St,
Los Angeles, CA 90011.
☎ (323) 235-2181.

FLEA MARKETS

Berkeley Flea Market
1837 Ashby Ave,
Berkeley, CA 94703.
☎ (510) 644-0744.

Pasadena's Rose Bowl
1001 Rose Bowl Drive,
Pasadena, CA 91103.
☎ (626) 577-3100.

San Jose Flea Market
1590 Berryessa Road,
San Jose,
CA 95133.
☎ (408) 453-1110.

San Juan Bautista Peddlars Fair
Mission San Juan Bautista,
San Juan Bautista,
CA 95023.
☎ (831) 623-2454.

POP CULTURE ANTIQUES

Camperos Collectables
PO Box 1629,
Sutter Creek,
CA 95685.
☎ (209) 245-3725.

The Game Doc
8000 Wheatland Ave,
Sun Valley, CA 91352.
☎ (818) 504-0440.

Hello Central
2463 Ladera Court,
San Luis Obispo,
CA 93401.
☎ (805) 541-9123.

Hillcrest Vintage Paper Collectables
3412 W MacArthur Blvd,
Unit G, Santa Ana,
CA 92704.
☎ (714) 751-4030.

Sarah Stocking Fine Vintage Posters
472 Jackson St,
San Francisco, CA 94111.
☎ (415) 984-0700.

OUTLET CENTERS

American Tin Cannery Factory Outlets
125 Ocean View Blvd,
Monterey, CA 93942.
☎ (831) 372-1442.

Desert Hills Factory Stores
48400 Seminole Rd,
Cabazon, CA 92230.
☎ (909) 849-5018.

Factory Stores of America at Nut Tree
321-2 Nut Tree Rd,
Vacaville, CA 95687.
☎ (707) 447-5755.

Napa Factory Stores
629 Factory Stores Drive,
Napa, CA 94558.
☎ (707) 226-9876.

Palm Springs Square
Palm Springs,
CA 92173.
☎ (760) 320-7444.

Pismo Beach Outlet Center
Pismo Beach,
CA 93449.
☎ (805) 773-4661

San Diego Factory Outlet Center
4498 Camino de la Plaza,
San Ysidro,
CA 92173.
☎ (619) 690-2999.

Shopper Stopper Tours
PO Box 535,
Sebastopol,
CA 95473.
☎ (707) 829-1597.

BOOKS, MUSIC, AND CRAFTS

American Indian Contemporary Arts Center
23 Grant Ave, 6th fl,
San Francisco,
CA 94108.
☎ (415) 989-7003.

Tower Records
2500 Del Monte St,
Sacramento,
CA 95691.
☎ (916) 373-2500.

Virgin Megastore
8000 W Sunset Blvd,
Hollywood,
CA 90046.
☎ (323) 650-8666.

Wherehouse
19701 Hamilton Ave,
Torrance, CA 90502.
☎ (800) 776-8290.

ANTIQUES

Antique Plaza
11395 Folsom Blvd,
Rancho Cordova,
CA 95742.
☎ (916) 852-8517.

FOOD

Apple Farm
18501 Greenwood Rd,
Philo, CA 95466.
☎ (707) 895-2333.

Casa de Fruta
10031 Pacheco Pass Hwy,
Hollister, CA 95023.
☎ (831) 637-0051.

Fresno County Farm Bureau
1274 West Hedges,
Fresno, CA 93728.
☎ (559) 237-0263.

Harris Ranch
24505 West Dorris Ave,
Coalinga, CA 93210.
☎ (557) 935-0717.

Jimtown Store
6706 Hwy 128,
Healdsburg,
CA 95448.
☎ (707) 433-1212.

Simonian Farm
2629 S Clovis Ave,
Fresno, CA 93725.
☎ (559) 237-2294.

Sonoma County Farm Trails
PO Box 6032,
Santa Rosa, CA 95606.
☎ (707) 571-8288.

Sonoma Valley Chamber of Commerce
651-A Broadway,
Sonoma, CA 95476.
☎ (707) 996-1033.

WINERIES

Hakusan Sake Garden
1 Executive Way,
Napa, CA 94558.
☎ (707) 258-6160.

Sebastiani Vineyards
389 Fourth St East,
Sonoma, CA 95476.
☎ (707) 938-5532.

Sterling Vineyards
1111 Dunaweal Loane,
Calistoga, CA 94515.
☎ (707) 942-3300.

Viansa Winery
25200 Arnold Drive,
Sonoma, CA 95476.
☎ (707) 935-4700.

Wine Institute of San Francisco
425 Market St,
Suite 1000,
San Francisco, CA 94105.
☎ (415) 512-0151.

SURVIVAL
GUIDE

PRACTICAL INFORMATION

CALIFORNIA IS A VIBRANT and diverse vacation destination. The spirit of the state can be felt in the busy cities of San Francisco, LA, and San Diego as much as in the quiet wilderness of the Sierra Nevada Mountains; and all over the state the needs of visitors are generally well tended. Even so, it is advisable to plan ahead, especially outside the main cities. Most places have visitors' centers providing local information for the

UNITED STATES POSTAL SERVICE®
United States Postal
Service logo

surrounding areas. The Survival Guide that follows contains valuable information that will help in every aspect of a visit. Personal Security and Health (pp592–3) outlines some recommended precautions. Banking and Currency (pp594–5) answers the essential financial questions faced by visitors. There are also sections on how to use the California telephone system and the US postal service (pp596–7).

Skiing on the slopes of Alpine Meadows in Lake Tahoe (see p470)

WHEN TO GO

TOURIST SEASON, from mid-April to September, sees a rush of visitors to the state's major tourist destinations. The winter months are also very popular with visitors, either for the warm climate of the south or the ski slopes of Lake Tahoe. During the quieter off-season it is sometimes possible to visit many of the tourist attractions at lower admission prices and without the usual crowds.

ADMISSION CHARGES

MAJOR MUSEUMS, theme parks, art galleries, and other tourist attractions generally charge an admission fee. Entry fees range from $5 to $8, with discounts for the disabled (see p590), students, senior citizens, and children. Smaller tourist attractions are

either free or request a small donation. At most larger institutions entrance is free on one day a month (telephone for details). Free guided tours, demonstrations, and lectures are frequently offered.

OPENING HOURS

MOST BUSINESSES are open on weekdays from 9am to 5pm and do not close for lunch. Many are also open on Sundays. In addition, some groceries, drugstores, and gas stations in the larger towns and cities are open 24 hours a day.

Most museums are closed on Mondays and/or Tuesdays and on major public holidays, but occasionally stay open until early evening.

Many Californians eat early in the evenings, and restaurants often have their last sitting at about 10pm. Most bars are open until 2am, particularly on Fridays and Saturdays.

TOURIST INFORMATION

ADVANCE INFORMATION can be obtained from the **California Division of Tourism** or the nearest US Consulate. Maps, guides, event listings, and discount passes for public transportation and tourist attractions are available at local Visitors' and Convention Bureaus. These offices are usually open from Monday to Friday, 9am to 5:30pm.

This guide provides the address and telephone number of the tourist information office in each town or city.

SIGHTSEEING TIPS

TO AVOID the crowds, visit the region's major sights in the morning and leave unstructured visits and tours until after lunch. Visit a group of sights in the same vicinity on the same day to save time and transportation costs. In general sights are more

Spanish colonial façade of the San Diego Museum of Art (see p247)

crowded on weekends. Rush hours are Monday to Friday, 7am to 9am and 4pm to 6:30pm, when transportation and city streets are crowded.

VISAS

V ISITORS HOLDING an EU or Canadian passport and planning to stay less than 90 days do not require a visa. However, it is necessary to fill out a visa waiver form at the airport check-in desk or on the airplane. Visitors from all other parts of the world need a valid passport and a non-immigrant visitor's visa. This can be obtained from a US Embassy or Consulate.

TAX AND TIPPING

T HE CALIFORNIA State Government levies a 7.25 percent general sales and use tax. In major cities, an additional 1–1.25 percent tax is added to all bought items except those for out-of-state delivery and food for preparation (see p582).

Visitor Information Center in Hallidie Plaza, San Francisco

There are no sales tax charges on hotel rooms, but a 12–14 percent transient occupancy tax is generally incurred.

In restaurants, it is normal to tip 15–20 percent of the total bill. Allow for a tip of 15 percent for taxi drivers, bar staff, and hairdressers. Porters at hotels and airports expect $1–1.50 per bag. It is also usual to leave hotel chambermaids $1–2 for each day of your stay.

SMOKING

I T IS ILLEGAL to smoke in any public building throughout the entire state of California. Ask about smoking policies when reserving a restaurant or hotel room. Remember that in California smoking is banned in restaurants, bars, and in all public places unless there is a separate air-circulation system.

TOURIST INFORMATION

STATEWIDE

California Division of Tourism
801 K St, Suite 1800,
Sacramento,
CA 58814.
((916) 322-2881.
FAX (916) 322-3402.

SAN FRANCISCO

San Francisco
Lower Level of Hallidie
Plaza,
Powell and Market Sts.
((415) 391-2000,
(415) 974-6900.

THE NORTH

Redding
777 Auditorium Drive.
(800) 874-7562.

Eureka
2112 Broadway.
((707) 442-3781,
(800) 356-6381.

WINE COUNTRY

Mendocino County
239 S Main St,
Willits.
((707) 459-7910.

Napa Valley
1310 Napa Town Center.
((707) 226-7459.

GOLD COUNTRY

Sacramento
1421 K St.
((916) 264-7777.

Tuolumne County
55 W Stockton St,
PO Box 4020, Sonora.
((209) 533-4420,
(800) 446-1333.

HIGH SIERRAS

Tahoe North
950 N Lake Blvd, Suite 3,
Tahoe City.
((800) 824-6348.

Bishop
690 N Main St.
((760) 873-8405.

NORTH CENTRAL

Fresno City and County
808 M St.
((559) 233-0836.

Monterey County
380 Alvarado St.
((831) 649-1770.

LOS ANGELES

Downtown Los Angeles
685 S Figueroa St.
((213) 689-8822.

Hollywood
6541 Hollywood Blvd.
((213) 689-8822.

SOUTH CENTRAL

Santa Barbara
510 State St, Suite 1.
((805) 966-9222,
(800) 927-4688.

San Luis Obispo County
1041 Chorro St.
((805) 541-8000,
(800) 634-1414.

ORANGE COUNTY

Anaheim/Orange County
800 W Katella Ave.
((714) 758-0222.

SAN DIEGO

San Diego
11 Horton Plaza.
((619) 236-1212.

Escondido
720 N Broadway.
((760) 745-2125.

PALM SPRINGS

Riverside
3443 Orange St.
((909) 787-7950.

Palm Springs
69 Hwy 111, Suite 201,
Rancho Mirage.
((760) 770-9000.

MOJAVE DESERT

Death Valley
118 Hwy 127,
Shoshone.
((760) 852-4524.

Selection of newspapers available in California

Street distribution bin for newspapers

local visitors' center. These should give all the up-to-date information on local entertainment and festivals, and details of popular bars and restaurants. In the major cities there is a variety of listings sources, including the *Bay Guardian* in San Francisco, *LA Weekly* and *Los Angeles Reader,* and the *San Diego Reader.*

NEWSPAPERS, TELEVISION, AND RADIO

IT IS POSSIBLE to buy the *New York Times* and the *Wall Street Journal* throughout most of California, and the *Los Angeles Times* is read all over the state. There is a selection of local daily papers available, many of which can be purchased from street distribution bins or in bookshops.

Television in California is similar to that all over the US. Much of it is supplied by cable or satellite systems. Most hotel rooms have a television, and bars frequently have screens showing sports. There is a wide selection of national and local channels, most of them showing sitcoms, magazine programs, children's cartoons, and talk shows. There are also Spanish and Asian foreign-language channels and news and music channels. Most newspapers cover program times, and hotel rooms often supply local television schedules.

Similarly, there are numerous commercial radio stations. They cover many subject matters, languages, and music styles. Listings of stations can be found in the local newspapers mentioned above.

ENTERTAINMENT LISTINGS

MOST SIZABLE communities have free newspapers that can be found in street distribution bins or at the

DISABLED TRAVELERS

CALIFORNIA LAW requires that every public building is accessible to travelers with disabilities. Disabled people also receive privileges such as free parking and admission reductions to many national and state parks. It is advisable to notify sights and hotels in advance, so that they can prepare for special needs. The Society for the Advancement of Travel for the Handicapped (SATH) uses a blue H sign to symbolize special facilities in restaurants, hotels, and tourist sights. For information contact the **Disability Rights, Education, and Defense Fund**. Travel for the disabled can be arranged by the **California Relay Service**.

International Student ID Card

Parking bay for the disabled

GAY AND LESBIAN TRAVELERS

CALIFORNIA's large gay community is mainly focused in the major cities, particularly in the Castro District of San Francisco *(see p350)*, Hillcrest in San Diego, and the West Hollywood area of LA *(see pp96–115)*. Free newspapers and magazines that contain gay listings include *The Edge* in Los Angeles; *Frontier,* which covers the whole of Southern California; and the many magazines in San Francisco, such as *Gay Times.* Listings of gay events in San Francisco and the Bay Area can also be obtained from the **Out and About** telephone newsletter. The **Gay Switchboard** is a referral service in the Bay Area that provides both crisis support and listings.

STUDENT TRAVELERS

THERE ARE FEW reductions for students in California. The ISIC (International Student Identity Card) is rarely accepted, and it is advisable for the young to carry a passport for entry into bars, as the under-21 ban is strictly enforced. The **Student Travel Association** has two offices in the Bay Area and three in LA. There are many youth hostels in the state. For handbooks, listings, and advance information contact **Hosteling International-American Youth Hostels**.

Hitchhiking should be avoided. Check noticeboards at hostels or universities for safe car-sharing opportunities.

CONSULATES

MOST COUNTRIES have consulates in both San Francisco and Los Angeles. They are usually open from 9am to 5pm, Monday to Friday. Although they are not expressly concerned with visitors' problems, it is very important to contact them in times of emergency. Consulates will not lend money, but they can help with lost passports and give advice on legal matters in emergencies. The address of the nearest office in each city can be found in the local telephone directory.

ELECTRICAL APPLIANCES

IN THE UNITED STATES all electrical current flows at a standard 110–120 volts AC (alternating current). To operate 220-volt appliances requires a voltage converter and an adapter plug with two flat parallel prongs to fit US outlets. The same applies to battery pack rechargers. Many hotels have hair dryers mounted on the bathroom wall and special plugs for electric shavers that carry 110- or 220-volt current.

Standard plug

CONVERSION CHART

Bear in mind that 1 US pint (0.5 liter) is a smaller measure than 1 UK pint (0.6 liter).

US Standard to Metric
1 inch = 2.54 centimeters
1 foot = 30 centimeters
1 mile = 1.6 kilometers
1 ounce = 28 grams
1 pound = 454 grams
1 US quart = 0.947 liter
1 US gallon = 3.8 liters

Metric to US Standard
1 centimeter = 0.4 inch
1 meter = 3 feet 3 inches
1 kilometer = 0.6 miles
1 gram = 0.04 ounce
1 kilogram = 2.2 pounds
1 liter = 1.1 US quarts

RELIGIOUS ORGANIZATIONS

CALIFORNIA, and particularly Northern California, has the reputation of attracting unconventional forms of worship (*see pp424–5*). Sects, cults, and alternative religions seem to thrive in the state as much as the more conventional churches and temples.
   The Catholic Church has the largest following, with nearly a quarter of its number of Hispanic origin. Los Angeles has the second largest Jewish community in the US, and there are many beautiful synagogues. Hindu temples, Islamic mosques, and a range of more unusual shrines abound throughout the state. Details of places for every type of worshiper can be found in the telephone book under "Churches."

Self-realization church, an alternative place of worship

CALIFORNIA TIME

California is in the Pacific Time Zone. Daylight Saving Time begins on the last Sunday in April (at 2am) when clocks are set ahead one hour. It ends on the last Sunday in October (at 2am) when clocks are set back one hour.

City and Country	Hours + or - PT	City and Country	Hours + or - PT
Athens (Greece)	+10	Moscow (Russia)	+11
Auckland (New Zealand)	+20	New York (US)	+3
Beijing (China)	+16	Paris (France)	+9
Berlin (Germany)	+9	Perth (Australia)	+16
Chicago (US)	+2	Sydney (Australia)	+18
Kowloon (Hong Kong)	+16	Tokyo (Japan)	+17
London (UK)	+8	Toronto (Canada)	+3
Madrid (Spain)	+9	Washington, DC (US)	+3

Personal Security and Health

Bear warning sign in Northern California

Like most major cities, the cities of California have some dangerous neighborhoods. Check with friends or hotel staff which parts of town are considered unwise to visit, either alone or at night. San Francisco is considered one of the safest large cities in the US; unfortunately, problems are more visible in some areas of LA. When traveling in the countryside, always take a good local map, particularly in the deserts and the mountains. It is important to take the advice of the local authorities seriously and in cases of all outdoor pursuits, normal safety procedures should be observed.

GUIDELINES ON SAFETY

The notorious gangs of California, particularly in Los Angeles, are rarely seen outside their own areas and are not necessarily interested in visitors. Visitors are more likely to be the target of theft or car crime. Police officers regularly patrol most of the tourist areas, but it is still advisable to prepare the day's itinerary in advance and to use common sense. Do not allow strangers into your hotel room or give them details of where you are staying.

Lock any valuables away in the hotel safe – do not carry them around with you. Most hotels will not guarantee the security of any belongings kept in your room.

Road safety for pedestrians is also observed by law: jaywalking, or crossing the road anywhere except at an intersection, can result in a fine.

San Francisco police officer

LOST PROPERTY

Although the chances of retrieving property lost in the street are very slim, telephone the **Police Non-Emergency Line**. It is important to report all lost or stolen items to the police. If you want to make an insurance claim on your return home, you will need to obtain a copy of the police report to send to the insurance company. In case of loss, it is useful to have a list of serial numbers and a photocopy of all documents kept separately as proof of possession.

If your passport is lost or stolen, get in contact with your embassy or consulate immediately *(see p591)*. For lost or stolen traveler's checks or credit cards, you should contact the nearest issuing company's office *(see p593)*.

TRAVEL INSURANCE

Travel insurance is not compulsory, but strongly recommended. You should take out coverage for emergency medical and dental care while also insuring your personal property. It is also advisable to buy insurance coverage for lost or stolen baggage and travel documents, accidental death or injury, trip cancellation, and legal advice.

SAFETY OUTDOORS

The Pacific Ocean is rarely warm, even in summer. The ocean can also be rough, more suited to surfers than swimmers, with a strong undertow. On the beach, thefts can occur, so always look after your valuables. Take full suntanning precautions.

It is important to prepare equipment before hiking in the wilderness. Notify someone of your plans before setting off. Leave the countryside as you found it, and be wary of the occasionally dangerous wildlife in many of the parks. As firewood is scarce and forest fires can start quickly, check with the park ranger whether camp fires are allowed.

National park ranger

Local maps are available from the Chamber of Commerce in the nearest town. **The Sierra Club** can advise about excursions. Rock climbing and mountaineering are becoming increasingly popular in California. In many parks there are services for climbers *(see p579)*. Contact local ranger services for

Patrol motorcycle

Police car

Ambulance

Fire engine

DIRECTORY

CRISIS INFORMATION

All Emergencies
 911 and alert police, fire, or medical services.

Crime Victims' Hotline
 (800) 842-8467.

Police Non-Emergency Line
San Francisco
 (415) 553-0123.
Los Angeles
 (213) 625-3311.

Travelers' Aid Society
San Diego
 (619) 295-8393.

LOST OR STOLEN CREDIT CARDS AND CHECKS

American Express
 (800) 233-5432.

Diners Club
 (800) 234-6377.

MasterCard
 (800) 826-2181.

VISA
 (800) 336-8472.

OUTDOOR RECREATION

California State Department of Parks and Recreation
PO Box 942896,
Sacramento, CA 94296-0001.
 (916) 653-6995.

National Park Service
Western Region Information Service,
Fort Mason, Bldg 201,
San Francisco, CA 94123.
 (415) 556-0560.

The Sierra Club
730 Polk St,
San Francisco, CA 94109.
 (415) 977-5500.

EARTHQUAKE INFORMATION

The US Geological Survey
Earth Science Information Centers,
345 Middlefield Rd,
Menlo Park, CA 94025.
 (650) 329-4390

advice on instructors, specific equipment required, and current weather conditions.

Be careful in the desert. At lower levels, it is usually hot and dry; at high elevations, temperatures often drop below freezing at night. Carry extra gas and water. If your car overheats, do not leave it to go for help. Turn it off; check to see if the radiator hoses are broken. If they're not, fill the overflow tank with water and restart the car. For further information contact the Death Valley Visitors' Center (see p280).

MEDICAL MATTERS

To visit a doctor's office, hospital, or pharmacy in the US, it is important to have medical insurance. Even with medical coverage you may have to pay for the services, then claim reimbursement from your insurance company. If you take medication, bring a back-up prescription with you.

EMERGENCIES

For emergencies that require medical, police, or fire services, call 911. Hospital casualty departments are

called emergency rooms; city-owned hospitals, found in the Blue Pages of the telephone book, are often crowded. Private hospitals can be found in the Yellow Pages of the telephone book. Hotels will often call a doctor or dentist to visit you in your room. The national organization **Travellers' Aid Society** can also provide assistance in many kinds of emergency.

EARTHQUAKES

The expectation and fear of earthquakes should not get in the way of everyday activities. You may experience a tremor, but the most important thing is not to panic. Precautions are important, such as keeping shoes and a flashlight by the bed when asleep, in case of power cuts or broken glass. Most injuries occur from falling material. If inside, stand in a doorway or crouch under a table. In a car, decrease speed, pull to the side of the road, and stop. When outside, avoid being near trees, power lines, or bridges. For further information on earthquake precautions, contact **The United States Geological Survey**.

Banking and Currency

SAN FRANCISCO AND LA are major West Coast financial centers – the fine buildings in their financial districts are reflective of their prestige. For the convenience of residents and visitors alike, there are numerous automated teller machines (ATMs) that operate 24 hours a day. In smaller towns, some banks may not exchange foreign currency or traveler's checks, so it is best to note the bank opening times in advance. Credit cards are very useful, and many situations, such as booking hotels or renting a car, require them as a form of security.

Bank in San Francisco

for a credit card imprint on check-in. The majority of car rental companies often penalize patrons without credit cards by asking for a large cash deposit. Hospitals will accept most credit cards in payment.

BANKING

BANK OPENING times vary throughout the state. They are generally open between 10am and 3pm. Banking hours within major cities may be longer: some open as early as 7:30am and close at 6pm, and are often open on Saturday mornings. Credit Unions serve only their own members, so look for banks that offer services to the general public. Always ask about commissions before making a transaction. US dollar traveler's checks can usually be cashed with a recognized form of photographic identification, such as a passport or an ISIC card. Foreign currency exchange is available in main branches of the larger banks.

CREDIT CARDS

AMERICAN EXPRESS, Diners Club, JCB, MasterCard (Access), and VISA are widely accepted throughout California. As well as the convenience of not carrying cash on your person, credit cards also occasionally offer insurance on bought merchandise or other benefits. They can be used all over the state to book hotel rooms or rent a car *(see p602)*. Most hotels will ask

AUTOMATED TELLER MACHINES

AUTOMATED teller machines (ATMs) can be found in most bank foyers or on the outside wall near the bank's entrance. They are in operation day and night, so that cash can be accessed outside normal banking hours. US currency, usually in $20 notes, can be withdrawn electronically from your bank or credit card account within seconds. Ask your own bank which ATM system your card can access in California and how much each transaction will cost. The more popular systems are **Cirrus** and **Plus**. ATMs also accept various US bank cards, in addition to MasterCard (Access), VISA, and other credit cards.

Robberies can occur at ATMs, so it is advisable to use them in the daytime or when there are plenty of people nearby. Withdrawals from ATMs may provide a better foreign currency exchange rate than cash transactions.

Foreign currency exchange sign

TRAVELER'S CHECKS

TRAVELER'S CHECKS issued by American Express and Thomas Cook in US dollars are accepted at most hotels, restaurants, and shops without a fee. It is necessary to show a passport as identification. If you lose your checks, contact **Thomas Cook Refund Assistance** or the **American Express Helpline**.

Foreign currency traveler's checks may be cashed at a large bank or at major hotels. Rates of exchange are printed in the newspapers and posted up at banks where exchange services are offered. Personal checks drawn on foreign banks are rarely accepted.

CURRENCY EXCHANGE

FEES AND COMMISSIONS are charged at currency exchanges. They are usually open on weekdays from 9am to 5pm. The best-known firms are **Thomas Cook Currency Services** and **American Express Travel Service**. Both of these companies have offices throughout California. Alternatively, try a city's main branch of a major bank or look in the Yellow Pages of the telephone directory.

Automated teller machine (ATM)

Coins

American coins come in 1-dollar, 50-, 25-, 10-, 5-, and 1-cent pieces (actual size shown). The new goldtone $1 coins are in circulation, as are the State quarters, which feature an historical scene on one side. Each coin has a popular name: 1-cent pieces are called pennies, 5-cent pieces are nickels, 10-cent pieces are dimes and 25-cent pieces are quarters.

**25-cent coin
(a quarter)**

**10-cent coin
(a dime)**

**5-cent coin
(a nickel)**

**1-cent coin
(a penny)**

Bank Notes

Units of currency in the United States are dollars and cents. There are 100 cents in a dollar. Notes (bills) come in $1, $5, $10, $20, $50, and $100s. $2 bills are rarely circulated. All bills are the same color, so check the amount carefully. The new $5, $10, $20, and $50 bills are now in circulation; the pictures and numbers are larger.

**1-dollar coin
(a buck)**

DIRECTORY

FINANCIAL SERVICES

Thomas Cook Currency Services
75 Geary St, San Francisco.
Map 5 C4.
[*(415) 362-3452.*

Thomas Cook Refund Assistance
[*(800) 223-7373.*

American Express Travel Service
455 Market St, San Francisco.
Map 6 D4.
[*(415) 536-2600.*

Hilton Center,
901 W 7th St, Los Angeles.
Map 10 C4.
[*(213) 627-4800.*

American Express Helpline
[*(800) 221-7282.*

Cirrus
[*(800) 424-7787.*

Plus
[*(800) 843-7587.*

1- dollar bill ($1)

5- dollar bill ($5)

10- dollar bill ($50)

20- dollar bill ($20)

50- dollar bill ($50)

100- dollar bill ($100)

Using California's Telephones

PUBLIC TELEPHONES can be found on many street corners, in hotels, restaurants, bars, theaters and department stores. Most are either coin-operated, using 5-, 10-, and 25-cent pieces, or take phonecards. There are now several, however, that take credit cards.

PUBLIC TELEPHONES

MODERN pay phones have a hand receiver and a 12-button key pad. Pacific Bell (PacBell) operates the majority of public pay phones. These are marked by a blue and white receiver sign with a bell in a circle. They are mounted on walls, posts, or in a booth. Some independent companies also operate pay phones, but generally these are not as reliable, and can be more expensive. All charges must be indicated by law. Telephone directories are supplied at most public phones. If there are any complaints about a service, call the operator by dialing 0, the phone company's business office, or the **California Public Utilities Commission**.

PAY PHONE CHARGES

THE COST of a local call within the same area code varies with the length of the call, but it is usually a minimum of 50 cents. After three minutes the operator may interrupt the call to request more money. When calling a number outside the town or city you are in but within the same area code, a recorded message will tell you how much more money to add. Long-distance calls are to numbers with a different area code. These can be

Souvenir phonecards

expensive, but will be less so when dialed direct, without the help of the operator.

Local and long-distance calls are cheaper between 6pm and 8am weekdays and on weekends. Hotels charge all calls at premium rate. Telephone numbers that begin with 800, 888, or 877 are free. To make a collect call, you will need to contact the operator.

Phonecards are available from post offices, drugstores, or convenience stores. They are issued by major telephone companies such as AT&T. The cards are convenient if you need to make a call and do not have the correct change; they can be used on any phone by calling the free number on the back of the card and quoting its PIN (personal identification number). The PIN can also be used to receive instructions in your preferred language. To re-charge the card, call the recharge number on the back and quote both the PIN and your credit card number.

FAX SERVICE

WORLDWIDE FAX SERVICES are readily available in post offices, hotels, and copying-service shops. Fax charges

Airport fax machine

USING A COIN-OPERATED PHONE

1 Lift the receiver and listen for the dial tone.

2 Insert the required coin or coins. The coin drops as soon as you insert it.

3 Dial or press the number.a

Coins
Make sure you have plenty of these coins available.

5 cents

10 cents

25 cents

4 If you want to cancel the call before it is answered, or if the call does not connect, press the coin release lever and take your coins from the coin return.

5 If the call is answered and you talk longer than three minutes, the operator will interrupt and tell you how much more money to deposit. Payphones do not give change.

are usually based on the time of day of the transmission, the destination, and the number of pages faxed. Incoming faxes can also be received and will be charged by the page. Look under *Facsimile Transmission Services* in the Yellow Pages of the telephone directory for further details. For telegrams, telexes, faxes, and electronic mail, you can also contact **Western Union**.

REACHING THE RIGHT NUMBER

• Direct-dial call outside the local area code, but within the US and Canada: dial **1**.
• International direct-dial call: dial **011** followed by country code (UK: **44**; Australia: **61**; New Zealand: **64**), then the city or area code (omit the first 0) and then the local number.
• International call via the operator: dial **01**, followed by the country code, then the city code (without the first 0), and then the local number.
• International directory inquiries: dial **00**.
• International operator assistance: dial **01**.
• A **1- 800, 866, 888,** or **877** prefix indicates a free call.
• Local directory inquiries: dial **411**.
• There have been changes to some California area codes over the last few years. If you experience difficulties reaching any number, call directory inquiries.
• **For emergency police, fire, or ambulance services, dial 911.**

USEFUL NUMBERS

California Public Utilities Commission
((800) 649-7570.

Western Union
((800) 325-6000.

Directory Inquires within the US
(1- (area code) 555-1212.

Sending a Letter

APART FROM POST OFFICES, letters can be sent from hotel reception desks or mailed in letter slots in office reception areas and at air, rail, and bus terminals. Street mailboxes are painted either blue, or red, white, and blue. Weekend mail delivery is limited. Stamps can be purchased at post offices, hotel reception desks, or from vending machines in convenience stores and supermarkets. Check international and domestic postal rates.

POSTAL SERVICE

ALL DOMESTIC MAIL is first class and will usually arrive within 1 to 5 days. Letters without the zip (or postal) code will take longer. International airmail to New Zealand, Australia, Canada, Ireland, and the United Kingdom takes 5–10 working days. Packages sent overseas by surface parcel rate may take 4–6 weeks for delivery. The federal post office offers two special services. Priority Mail promises delivery faster than first class mail. The more expensive Express Mail delivers next day within the United States, and within 72 hours to many international destinations. Private express mail can be arranged through the delivery services listed in the Yellow Pages of the telephone directory. The two main international express mail companies are **DHL** and **Federal Express**.

US commemorative stamps

GENERAL DELIVERY

LARGER CITY post offices have a general delivery service where letters sent c/o General Delivery will be held for 30 days before being returned to the sender.
The zip code of the post office and the address of the sender should be clearly marked. The recipient's last name should be underlined so that the letter is filed correctly at the receiving office.

US mail van

San Francisco
c/o General Delivery,
Civic Center, 101 Hyde St,
San Francisco, CA 94142.

Los Angeles
c/o General Delivery,
Los Angeles Main Post Office,
900 N Alameda,
Los Angeles, CA 90086.

San Diego
c/o General Delivery,
San Diego Main Post Office,
San Diego, CA 92110.

POSTAL SERVICES

DHL
((800) 225-5345.

Federal Express
((800) 463-3339.

United States Postal Service
((800) 275-8777.

Standard US mailbox

TRAVEL INFORMATION

S AN FRANCISCO AND LA are the two main gateways for visitors traveling to California by air. You can also get there by car, Amtrak train, long-distance bus, or by ocean liner. Despite continuing problems with traffic congestion and environmental pollution, Californians remain devoted to driving.

A passenger jet

Large, comfortable cars, cheap gas, and a comprehensive network of roads make this an efficient and pleasurable way to tour the state. Public transportation is a viable and inexpensive option in the major cities, where historic cable cars and ferries work alongside modern buses and mass transit systems.

Airport arrivals board

TRAVELING BY AIR

A IR TRAVEL is an integral part of the American lifestyle, and California is no exception. Airports are efficiently designed, with computerized ticketing systems. Competition between airlines has led to a high level of service.

Frequent and reliable connections are offered all over the state. Los Angeles (LAX) and San Francisco (SFO) are the two main airports used by visitors to California. International flights also land at San Diego (SAN), Oakland (OAK), and San Jose (SJC). The state has more than 30 airports handling domestic flights. The major domestic airports include Sacramento and Palm Springs, as well as Santa Barbara, John Wayne/ Orange County, and Fresno.

AIR FARES

F ARE STRUCTURES are complex, with a variety of passes and bonus systems offered by the numerous airlines flying to and within California. Prices also vary according to season, with the most expensive tickets coinciding with summer months and the holiday periods, such as Christmas and Thanksgiving *(see p35)*. It is always cheaper to travel to or from California on weekdays rather than on weekends. The lowest regular offer

is the APEX (Advanced Purchase Excursion Fare), which should be purchased two to three weeks before departure and is nonrefundable. A reputable travel agent will be able to supply details on all the latest offers and promotions. They will also be able to point out the advantages

and restrictions that accompany the fares and routes available, and tell you whether a visa is required to enter the US.

Most travelers from Europe choose nonstop flights to California, but fares are often cheaper if you fly via another American "hub" city such as Newark or Houston. The

The Encounters Restaurant, Los Angeles Airport

AIRPORT	INFORMATION
Los Angeles (LAX)	(*(310) 646-5252*
San Francisco (SFO)	(*(650) 761-0800*
Oakland (OAK)	(*(510) 577-4000*
San Diego (SAN)	(*(619) 231-2100*
San Jose (SJC)	(*(408) 277-4759*
Sacramento (SMF)	(*(916) 929-5411*
Palm Springs (PSP)	(*(760) 323-8161*

volume of passengers flying, particularly in peak season, is so high that it is best to book as early as possible. If you are touring, a fly-drive package booked before you leave will generally be cheaper than making car rental arrangements in California *(see p602).*

AT THE AIRPORT

WITH A VAST number of passengers arriving and departing at one time, huge international airports such as Los Angeles and San Francisco can seem bewildering to the jet-lagged, first-time visitor. Lines at immigration and customs points are inevitable at peak times. Dispose of any fresh fruit you may be carrying (a strictly enforced customs regulation) and plan transportation from the airport to your destination in advance.

All the major airports have multilingual information booths for the newly arrived. These help with inquiries about the airport and also give information on the various forms of transportation into the city. Car rental desks *(see p602),* currency exchange facilities *(see pp594–5),* and shuttle bus services can also be found in the airports.

Most car rental companies supply a shuttle bus to the car pick-up points, usually located on the outskirts of the airport. Shuttle buses can also be chartered for a door-to-door service to and from the airport

Baggage check-in desk

and a specific city address. One-way fares vary in price, depending on the distance covered. Journey times given below also vary, according to the number of passengers and their required stops.

All airports have facilities for assisting disabled passengers, although it is advisable to prearrange this through your airline. Smoking is not permitted in any of California's airport terminals.

Rental car shuttle

Door-to-door shuttle bus

CUSTOMS AND DUTY FREE

VISITORS ARRIVING in the US by air and sea are issued with customs declaration forms that must be filled in completely. Adult nonresidents are permitted to bring in a limited amount of duty-free items. These include 0.2 gals (1 liter) of alcoholic beverages (beer, wine, or spirits), 200 cigarettes, 50 cigars (but not Cuban) or 4.4 lbs (2 kg) of smoking tobacco, and $100 worth of gifts for other people.

AIRLINE CARRIERS (US CONTACT NUMBERS)

All Nippon Airlines
[(800) 235-9262.
w www.ana.co.jp
American [(800) 433-7300 w www.aa.com
British Airways
[(800) 247-9297.
w www.britishairways.com
Continental [(800) 525-0280. w www.continental.com
Delta [(800) 221 - 1212.
w www.delta–air.com
Southwest [(800) 435-9792. w www.southwest.com
United [(800) 241-6522.
w www.ual.com
USAirways [(800) 428-4322. w www.usairways.com
TWA [(800) 221-2000
w www.twa.com
Virgin Atlantic
[(800) 862-8621.
w www.virgin–atlantic.com

DISTANCE FROM CITY	TAXI FARE TO CITY	SHUTTLE BUS
15 miles (24 km) from Downtown	approx $26.50 to Downtown approx $22 to Beverly Hills	30 mins to Downtown
14 miles (22 km) from city center	approx $35 to Downtown	25 mins to city center
8 miles (12 km) from city center	approx $25-28 to Oakland	20 mins to city center
3 miles (5 km) from city center	approx $10-12 to San Diego	10-15 mins to city center
8 miles (12 km) from city center	approx $8-10 to San Jose	15 mins to city center
12 miles (19 km) from city center	approx $25 to Sacramento	20 mins to city center
2 miles (3 km) from city center	approx $15 to Palm Springs	20 mins to city center

Getting Around California

Authorized taxi license

ALTHOUGH OFTEN more time-consuming, traveling by train, bus, and ferry can be an inexpensive and rewarding way of getting around California. Within the major cities of San Francisco *(see pp380–83)*, Los Angeles *(see pp168–9)*, and San Diego *(see pp256–7)*, there are adequate public transportation networks, offering buses, trams, Metro trains, ferries, and cable cars. They are very busy during the rush hour periods. Taxis and shuttle buses are also useful in the cities. The network of Amtrak railroad lines and connecting bus services serves the state's most populous areas and offers some scenic journeys. It is also possible to travel within the state by bus.

Taxi cabs in San Francisco

Coaster train ticket machine

TRAVELING BY RAIL

THE USE OF RAILROADS in the US is dwindling, yet there are still connections between major cities. **Amtrak** runs direct, long-distance routes from LA to Chicago, Seattle, Albuquerque, and San Antonio, but no longer offers a direct service to the East Coast.

In California, the rail network is divided into three sections: the San Diegan (linking Santa Barbara and San Diego), the Capitol (between San Jose and Sacramento), and the San Joaquin (connecting Emeryville and Bakersfield). A bus service heads out in many directions from stops along these lines. Local commuter lines include **Caltrain** (linking San Jose and San Francisco); the Coast Starlight Connection (between San Luis Obispo and Santa Barbara); LA Metrolink; and the Coaster (connecting San Diego and Oceanside).

LONG-DISTANCE BUSES

THE NETWORK of bus routes operated by **Greyhound Lines** reaches all parts of the US. In California, services include scenic coastal connections as well as frequent express routes linking major cities such as San Francisco, Sacramento, San Jose, LA, and San Diego. Guided tours provide a leisurely way of sightseeing. Several companies offer short package trips in deluxe buses visiting sights such as Hearst Castle *(see pp202–5)*, Yosemite National Park *(see pp472–5)*, and Monterey *(see pp492–5)*. Information about these services can be found in the Yellow Pages of the telephone book.

For travelers with more time to spare and who wish to get a real feel for the state, the alternative-minded **Green Tortoise** offers leisurely journeys between the major cities of the Pacific Coast. Passengers can break their trip to camp, prepare meals, and explore the countryside.

TAXIS

TAXIS (often called "cabs") can usually be found outside main transportation terminals and major hotels. Elsewhere it is best to order one by telephone – numbers can be found in the Yellow Pages of the telephone directory. Never stand in a street at night expecting one to pass.

Not all drivers know their way around, so it will help to have your destination marked on a map if it is off the beaten track. All taxi fares are metered according to the distance traveled. Some taxis take credit cards, but it is best to inquire in advance. A tip of 15 percent is generally expected.

SHUTTLE VANS

CHEAPER THAN taxis and quicker than buses, shuttle vans are a secure and reliable way of traveling within and around California's cities. They provide an efficient travel network, especially between hotels and airports.

Greyhound bus parked along a California highway

When calculating your trip time, bear in mind that other passengers will be picked up and dropped off en route. Competition between shuttle bus companies has led to a high standard of service. Their details can be found in the telephone directory. Call several companies to obtain the best quote before booking a long journey. Bus drivers will expect a tip of at least $1.

BOATS AND FERRIES

Express boat services provide a fast link from Los Angeles to Santa Catalina Island (see pp232–3), while others sail more leisurely across San Francisco Bay (see pp288–9). Most ferries carry foot passengers and bicycles, but not motor vehicles.

Despite the building of new bridges, several commuter ferries survive to offer their customers a breezy alternative to the smog of the rush hour traffic. Routes, such as those connecting Oakland, Sausalito, and Tiburon with San Francisco, and the San Diego–Coronado ferry, provide a pleasant and reasonably priced way to enjoy a city. To find out about ferry timetables, prices, and locations in San Francisco and the Bay Area see page 383, and in San Diego see page 257.

see pp232–3 ... see pp288–9 ... see page 383 ... see page 257.

DIRECTORY

TRAIN INFORMATION

Amtrak (800) 872-7245.
W www.amtrak.com
Caltrain
(800) 660-4287.
W www.transitinfo.org

BUS AND COACH INFORMATION

Greyhound Lines
(800) 231-2222.
W www.greyhound.com
The Green Tortoise
494 Broadway, San Francisco,
CA 94133. (415) 956-7500.
W www.greentortoise.com

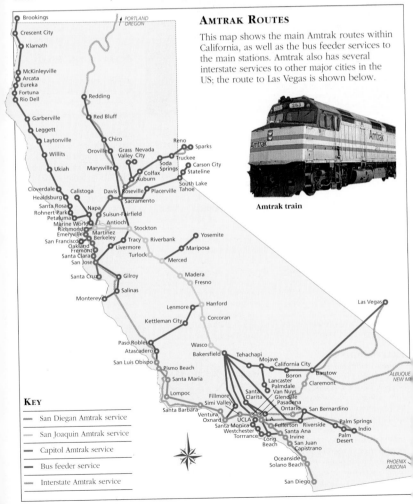

AMTRAK ROUTES

This map shows the main Amtrak routes within California, as well as the bus feeder services to the main stations. Amtrak also has several interstate services to other major cities in the US; the route to Las Vegas is shown below.

Amtrak train

KEY

— San Diegan Amtrak service
— San Joaquin Amtrak service
— Capitol Amtrak service
— Bus feeder service
— Interstate Amtrak service

Traveling by Car

Driving is an essential part of the California way of life, and for both residents and visitors it is the most convenient way to travel around the state. Roads are well maintained so that they are able to cope with the great volume of rush hour traffic that pours in and out of the main cities every weekday. The state has an efficient network of major roads linking the cities and towns. In remote areas, such as in the deserts and mountains, it is sometimes necessary to use a four-wheel-drive vehicle.

Traffic on the Harbor Freeway, Los Angeles

RENTING A CAR

It is best to arrange a fly-drive package before leaving for California. Take note of exactly what is included in the deal, and find out whether any extra payments may arise when the car is returned. These additions – which can include optional fuel purchase, extended insurance cover, collision damage waiver, delivery or drop-off charges, and rental tax (a daily city vehicle rental tax) – can double the original prepaid fee. It is particularly important to find out exactly what is included in the insurance policy offered by the rental company. Drivers should remember that in California, where litigation is an everyday occurrence, it is sensible to be fully insured.

To rent a car, the driver must be over 25 and have a US or internationally valid driver's license. A major credit card is also important, if not vital, as a guarantee. Some companies may rent to younger drivers or accept a cash deposit in lieu of a credit card number, but expect higher charges in return. Taking a rented car across the border into Mexico is not permitted without prior arrangement. The gas tank should be full when you return the vehicle, and you should allow sufficient time to process and check your final bill.

Car rental is generally least expensive at airports *(see p599)*, but call the free numbers advertised by rental companies to find out about discounts.

Rental cars generally have automatic transmission. If necessary, spend some time getting familiar with this system. Some companies supply cars with manual transmission ("stick-shift") on request. Classic cars, Harley-Davidson motorcycles, and RVs (motor homes) can also be rented from specialty companies.

RULES OF THE ROAD

Californians drive on the right. Seat belts are compulsory for both driver and passengers. In the US, speed limits are individually set by each state. In California, the maximum speed limit is generally 65 mph (104 km/h) but on selected freeways, 70 mph (110 km/h) limits have now been introduced. In cities, the speed limits are restricted as marked. These controls are rigorously enforced by the Highway Patrol. Drunk driving is a serious offense and carries very heavy penalties.

Highways are known as Freeways or Interstates. Bicycles are not permitted on these roads. In rush hours, carpool or diamond lanes, which can only be used by cars carrying more than one passenger, come into force on

TRAFFIC SIGNS

A range of different signs offer warnings and instructions for drivers. Speed limits may vary every few miles, depending on the conditions of the road and the amount of traffic, and should be adhered to. In more remote areas, drivers must be wary of wildlife that may occasionally stray onto the roads. Disregarding traffic signs will result in fines from the Highway Patrol.

Wildlife warning
ELK CROSSING NEXT 2 MILES

Traffic flows in a single direction

Entry prohibited **Maximum speed**

Give way to all vehicles **Stop at intersection**

Time elapsed shown here

Insert coins here

Turn handle to register coins

Curbing wheels in San Francisco – the curb acts as a block

PREVENT RUNAWAYS
CURB WHEELS
PARK IN GEAR
SET BRAKE

PARK AT 90 DEGREES

Curbside parking signs in San Francisco to prevent cars rolling downhill

some roads. It is permissible to turn right on red at traffic lights if there is nothing coming the other way. The first vehicle to reach a stop sign junction has the right of way.

The **Automobile Association of America** (AAA) offers maps, emergency road service, and discounts at many hotels and restaurants. The AAA is linked with many automobile clubs abroad, so inquire ahead whether they will honor your membership. If not, the annual fee is about $60.

AAA sign

GASOLINE

Gas, or gasoline, is either unleaded or diesel quality. It is sold in gallons rather than liters. Inexpensive by European standards, the price includes a small gasoline tax. Gas stations are not as widespread as many visitors expect, so be sure to fill up the tank before driving into the mountains, desert, or through other remote areas. Many gas stations have pump attendants. Some pumps take credit cards, and in self-service stations it is common to pay for your gas prior to putting it into the car.

PARKING

Parking in California cities is strictly controlled and can be expensive. Valet parking is obligatory if you pull up outside many hotels and restaurants. Hand the keys to the attendant and pay on departure. Most parking meters accept quarters, but some systems require dollars to be "posted" into the slot relating to the parking space. Parking lots have their own set prices. Parking is free outside at shopping malls or, if parking inside, you can have your ticket validated at any store where you've made a purchase to reduce the parking fee.

Parking restrictions are indicated by curb colors. If the curb is painted red, parking is prohibited; yellow indicates a loading zone; green allows parking for up to ten minutes; white five minutes only during business hours. Blue curbs are for disabled parking only. If parking on the steep hills in San Francisco, you must curb your wheels into the road if facing uphill and toward the curb if facing downhill. If your vehicle is booted or towed, contact the local **Police Department Towed Vehicle Information Center**.

General Index

Acknowledgments

DORLING KINDERSLEY would like to thank the following people whose contributions and assistance have made the preparation of this book possible.

MAIN CONTRIBUTORS

Jamie Jensen grew up in LA and now lives in Northern California. He contributed to San Francisco in the DK Guides series, and his most recent book is *Road Trip USA: Cross-Country Adventures on America's Two-Lane Highways.*
Ellen Payne is Managing Editor of *Los Angeles Magazine* and has worked on numerous travel publications.
J Kingston Pierce is a Seattle writer specializing in West Coast history. He is a contributing editor of *San Francisco Focus* and *Seattle* magazines and his book credits include *San Francisco, You're History!*
Rebecca Poole Forée is Editor-in-Chief at Foghorn Press, San Francisco. She has written many travel books, including *Northern California Best Places.*
Nigel Tisdall is the author of several travel guides. He has contributed to *France, Seville and Andalusia* and *Portugal* in the DK series.
Stanley Young lives in LA. He has written several books including *The Missions of California* and *Paradise Found: The Beautiful Retreats and Sanctuaries of California and the Southwest.*

CONTRIBUTORS AND CONSULTANTS

Virginia Butterfield, Dawn Douglas, Rebecca Renner, Tessa Souter, Shirley Streshinsky, Barbara Tannenbaum, Michael Webb, John Wilcock.

ADDITIONAL PHOTOGRAPHY

Steve Gorton, Gary Grimaud, Kirk Irwin, Neil Lukas, Neil Mersh, Erhard Pfeiffer.

ADDITIONAL ILLUSTRATORS

James A Allington, Arcana Studios, Hugh Dixon, Richard Draper, Dean Entwhistle, Eugene Fleury, Chris Forsey, Andrew Green, Steve Gyapay, Toni Hargreaves, Philip Hockey, John Lawrence, Nick Lipscombe, Mel Pickering, Sallie Alane Reason, Peter Ross, Simon Roulston, John See, Tristan Spaargaren, Ed Stuart, Paul Williams.

CARTOGRAPHY

Lovell Johns Ltd, Oxford, UK; ERA-Maptec Ltd, Dublin, Ireland. Street Finder Maps based upon digital data, adapted with permission from original survey by ETAK INC 1984–1994.
MAP CO-ORDINATORS Emily Green, David Pugh

DESIGN AND EDITORIAL

Dorling Kindersley Limited
MANAGING EDITORS Vivien Crump, Helen Partington
DEPUTY ART DIRECTOR Gillian Allan
DEPUTY EDITORIAL DIRECTOR Douglas Amrine
SENIOR EDITOR Fay Franklin
Peter Bennett, Hilary Bird for indexing, Sophie Boyak, Joanna Craig, Cullen Curtiss, Donna Dailey, Stephanie Driver, Michael Ellis, William Gordon, Emily Green, Paul Hines, Thomas A Knight, Ciaran McIntyre, Annie McQuitty, Sam Merrell, Ellen Root, Ingrid Vienings, Marek Walisiewicz.

SPECIAL ASSISTANCE

Marianne Babel, Wells Fargo History Museum, San Francisco; Liz Badras, LA Convention and Visitors' Bureau; Craig Bates, Yosemite Museum; Joyce Bimbo, Hearst Castle, San Simeon; Elizabeth A Borsting and Ron Smith, the *Queen Mary*, Long Beach; Jean Bruce-Poole, El Pueblo de Los Angeles National Monument; Carolyn Cassady; Covent Garden Stamp Shop; Marcia Eymann and Joy Tahan, Oakland Museum of California; Donna Galassi; Mary Jean S Gamble, Salinas Public Library; Mary Haas, California Palace of the Legion of Honor; Nancy Masten, Photophile; Miguel Millar, US National Weather Service, Monterey; Warren Morse, LA County Metropolitan Transportation Authority; Anne North, San Diego Visitors' and Convention Bureau; Donald Schmidt, San Diego Zoo; Vito Sgromo, Sacramento State Capitol Museum; Dawn Stranne and Helen Chang, San Francisco Visitors' and Convention Bureau; Cherise Sun and Richard Ogar, Bancroft Library; Gaynell V Wald, Mission San Juan Capistrano; Chris Wirth, Wine Institute, San Francisco; Cynthia J Wornham and Lori Star, the J Paul Getty Trust.

PHOTOGRAPHY PERMISSIONS

Dorling Kindersley would like to thank the following for their assistance and kind permission to photograph at their establishments:
Balboa Park, San Diego; Columbia State Historic Park; Disney Enterprises, Inc.; J Paul Getty Museum, LA; Hearst Castle, San Simeon; Huntington Library, San Marino; Knotts Berry Farm, Buena Park; Los Angeles Children's Museum; Los Angeles County Museum of Art; Museum of Contemporary Art, LA; Museum of Miniatures, LA; Museum of Television and Radio, LA; Museum of Tolerance, LA; Norton Simon Museum, Pasadena; Petersen Automotive Museum, LA; *Queen Mary*, Long Beach; Sacramento State Capitol; San Diego Aerospace Museum; San Diego Automotive Museum; San Diego Museum of Art; San Diego Wild Animal Park; San Diego Zoological Society; Santa Barbara Mission; Southwest Museum, LA; John Steinbeck Library, Salinas; Tao House, Danville; Timken Museum of Art, San Diego; Universal Studios, LA; University of California, Berkeley; University of California, LA; University of Southern California, LA; Wells Fargo History Room, San Francisco; Winchester Mystery House, San Jose; and all other churches, missions, museums, parks, wineries, hotels, restaurants, and sights too numerous to thank individually.

PICTURE CREDITS

t = top; tl = top left; tc = top center; tr = top right; cla = center left above; ca = center above; cra = center right above; cl = center left; c = center; cr = center right; clb = center left below; cb = center below; crb = center right below; bl = bottom left; b = bottom; bc = bottom center; br = bottom right; bla = bottom left above; bca = bottom center above; bra = bottom right above; blb = bottom left below; bcb = bottom center below; brb = bottom right below; d = detail.

Works of art have been reproduced with the permission of the following copyright holders: © AGAGP, Pans and DACS, London 1997: 302tl; © Alan bowness, Hepworth Estate, *Figure for Landscape*, bronze 1960: 247b; By permission of Dara Birnbaum: 308cl; *Creativity Explored* © 1993, Creativity Explored. All rights reserved. 297t; © DACS, London 1997: 308c; Museum of Contemporary Art, LA, Robert Rauschenberg Coca-Cola Plan (1958), The Panza Collection: 121c; © Disney Enterprises, Inc 222c, 222c, 223, 224t, 224b, 225t, 225b; *8 Immortals (Bok-sen) & 3 Wisdoms* © 1979, Josie Grant. All rights reserved. 297br; By permission of the Estate of Philip Guston: 295cr; © Man Ray Trust/ADAGP, Paris and DACS, London 1997: 309cra; © Eduardo Paolozzi 1997 All rights reserved DACS: 50–51c; Succession Picasso/DACS 1997: 152t; *Untitled* © 1978, Michael Rios. All rights reserved. 296tr; By permission of the University of California, Berkeley: *Within*, 1969, by Alexander Lieberman, gift of the artist, University Art Museum: 405t.
Dorling Kindersley would like to thank the following individuals, companies and picture libraries for permission to reproduce their photographs: Ace Photo Agency: T&J Florian 480tl, 480tr, 481b; David Kerwin 13t; Cash Mauritius 598b; Vladimir Pcholkin 96; Laszlo Willinger 159t; Zephyr Pictures/James Blank 18b; Action-Plus Photographers: Chris van Lennep/Keith Maloy 188–9c; Neale Haynes 189br; Allsport: 158tr Stephen Dunn 53br; Apple Computer Inc: 52tr; Aquarius Library: 98cla, 102cr, 103t; *Gone with the Wind*, MGM 102b, *The Jazz Singer*, Warner Bros 103crb; *Jurassic Park*, Spielberg/Universal 145c; Arcaid: Richard Bryant 27c, 69cra; Architectural Association: J Stirling 69tr; Art Directors Photo Library: 67cra, Craig Aurness 151cr; Spencer Grant 255b; Gene Autry Western Heritage Museum: 147c.
Bancroft Library, University of California, Berkeley: 40tr, 42crb, 42b, 45tl, 465b, 501c; Barnaby's Picture Library: 15c, 49t, 50clb, *Giant*, Warner Bros 51br; 52ca, 52br, 53cla, 496cla; BFI Stills, Posters and Designs: *Mantrap*, Paramount Studios 48–9c; *The War of the Worlds*, Paramount Studios 109b; Bison Archives: Marc Wanamaker 64bl, *The Sting*, Universal Studios 65cl; Marilyn Blaisdell Collection: 47t; Bridgeman Art Library, London: Scottish National Portrait Gallery, Edinburgh 22tr; Kunsthistorisches Museum, Vienna 42c; Britstock IFA: 29c, Bernd Ducke 51bl. California Academy of Sciences: 294b, 360tl, 360c, 360b, 361t; Trevor Hill 361cra; Caroline Kopp 357b; Dong Lin 360tr, 360bc, 361bl; California State Railroad Museum: 46cla, 46clb, 47cra, 456tl; California Western Railroad: 443t; J Allan Cash: 490t; Carolyn Cassady: 23c, 330b; Center for the Arts Galleries: 295br, 312t; Center for the Arts Theater/Margaret Jenkins Dance Company: 313t; Cephas Picture Library: Bruce Fleming 584c; R&K Muschenetz 201t; Mick Rock 446bl, 447c; Ted Stefanski 438; Colorific: J Aaronson 53b; Black Star/Alan Copeland 52cb; David Burnett 53clb; Chuck Nacke 33t; Alon Reiniger 34t, 34cr; Visages/Peter Lessing 16c; Patrick Ward 168b; Corbis: Beebe Photography/ Morton 30tr; Bettmann/UPI 22c, 51crb, 53clb, 425cr; Steve Jay Crise 593t; Jim Corwin 483; Darrell Gulin 421tr;

Conway/W Perry 60c; Robert Holmes 193b, 376cr; 507b, 580t; Macduff Everton 425b; David Muench 192t, 479b; Neal Preston 114cr; Tony Roberts 362-363; Michael T. Sedam 341br; Everett, *The Maltese Falcon*, Warner Bros 23bl; Galen Rowell/Mountain Light Photography Inc 469b; Reuters NewMedia Inc. 373b; Joseph Sohm; CromoSohm Inc. 10b.
Crocker Art Museum: 459c; Imogen Cunningham Trust: *Two Callas*, 1925, Imogen Cunningham © (1970, 1997) The Imogen Cunningham Trust, 25t. Del Mar Thoroughbred Club: 238cb; © 2001 The Disneyland Resort® Inc. All Rights Reserved 222c, 222b, 223b, 225b; Embarcadero Center: 302tr; Mary Evans Picture Library: 9 (inset), 19bl, 44tr, 47crb, 49b, 50t, 55 (inset), 424t; Exploratorium: 294t. Eyewire Collection/Getty Images: 34cb; The Fine Arts Museums of San Francisco: *Sailboat on the Seine*, c.1874, by Claude Monet, gift of Bruno and Sadie Adrian, 294cla; High chest, gift of Mr & Mrs Robert A Magowan, 356tr; *Old Woman*, c.1618 –9, Georges de La Tour, Roscoe & Margaret Oakes Collection, 75.2.10, 364t; *Virgin and Child*, c.1460, Dieric Bouts Workshop Roscoe & Margaret Oakes Collection, 75.2.14, 364c; *The Tribute Money*, c.1612, Peter Paul Rubens, purchased with funds from various donors, 44.11, 365t; *The Impresario*, c.1877, Edgar Degas, gift of Mr & Mrs Louis A Benoist, 1956.72, 365cra; *Water Lilies*, c.1914 –7, Claude Monet, Mildred Anna Williams Collection, 1973.3, 365cb; *The Thinker*, c.1880, cast c.1904, Auguste Rodin, gift of Alma de Bretteville Spreckels, 1924.18.1, 365b; The Flight Collection: Erik Simonsen 598t; Fort Mason Museums: Museo ItaloAmericano: *Muto*, 1985, Mimmo Paladino, etching, gift of Pasquale Iannetti, 295tl; *Meta III*, 1985, Italo Scanga, oil and lacquer on wood, gift of Alan Shepp, 341bl; Mexican Museum: *Indios Verdes No 4*, 1980, Manuel Neri, mixed media/paper, 341br.
Collection of the J Paul Getty Museum, Malibu, California: Joseph Nollekens, *Venus* (1773), marble, 124 cm, 56c; Pierre-Auguste Renoir, *La Promenade* (1870), oil on canvas, 81.3 x 65 cm, 66c; Vincent Van Gogh, *Irises* (1889), oil on canvas, 71 x 93 cm, 78t; *Hispano-Moresque Deep Dish* (Valencia, mid-15th century), tin-glazed and lustered earthenware, 10.8 x 49.5 cm, 78b; Attr. André-Charles Boulle, Cabinet on Stand (c.1675–80), veneered oak with gilt bronze mounts , 230 x 151 x 66.7 cm, 79t; Peter Paul Rubens, *Korean Man* (c.1617), black chalk with touches of red chalk in the face, 38.4 x 23.5 cm, 79cra; Claude Monet, *Wheatstacks, Snow Effect, Morning* (1891), oil on canvas, 79crb; Rembrandt, *The Abduction of Europa* (1632), oil on a single oak panel, 79b; Jean-François Millet, *Man with a Hoe* (1860–2), oil on canvas, 80 x 99cm, 80t; Carleton E Watkins, *Cape Horn, Columbia River, Oregon* (negative 1867, print 1881–3), albumen, 40.5 x 52.3 cm, 80b; Sèvres Porcelain Manufactory, Basket (1756), soft paste porcelain, gilding, 22 x 20.1 x 18 cm, 81t; Footed Bowl (Venice, c.1500–50), free-blown calcedonio glass, 12.5 x 19.5 cm, 81c; Gospels (Helmarshausen, c.1120–40), tempera colours, gold and silver on vellum bound between paper boards covered with brown calf, 22.8 x

16.4 cm, 81b; Golden Gate Bridge Highway and Transportation District: 51t, 370tl, 370c, 370b, 370–1t, 371cl, 371cb; Charles M Hiller 51tl; Golden Gate National Recreation Area, National Park Service: 329blb, 329bc; Ronald Grant Archive: 48tl, 98cr, 101cl, 103cl, 583t; Capitol 188tr; LA Story, Warner Bros 16t; Rebel Without A Cause, Warner Bros 64cra; The Last Action Hero Columbia Pictures 64crb; E.T., The Extra-Terrestrial, Spielberg/ Universal Studios, 65br; Gidget, Columbia Pictures 188c. Robert Harding Picture Library: 186t, 193c, 288c, 584t; Bildagentur/Schuster 188b; FPG 20cl, 48cla, 49clb, 51cra; Jon Gardey 481t; Tony Gervis 467; Michael J Howell 19tr; Dave Jacobs 421b, 481c; Robert Landau 69crb; Westlight/Bill Ross 10b, 146tr,/Steve Smith 19br 29t; Hearst Castle/Hearst San Simeon State Historical Monument: Z Baron 202br; John Blades 202tr, 202clb, 203b, 204c, 205c; V Garagliano 202bc; Ken Raveill 202ca, 203t, 203cra, 204b; Amber Wisdom 203crb; Phoebe Hearst Museum of Anthropology: 41crb; Robert Holmes Phtography: Markham Johnson 295bl; Hulton Getty: 53cr, 101t; Huntington Library: 25b, 156b; Madonna and Child, Roger van der Weyden 67crb; Breakfast in Bed, Mary Cassatt 154c; Gutenberg Bible 155t; Blue Boy, Thomas Gainsborough 155crb; Diana the Huntress, Houdon 156t; The Wife of Bath from The Canterbury Tales, Chaucer (Ellesmere MS), 156c; Hutchison Library: Robert Francis 279t; B Regent 166cl. Image Bank: David Hamilton 19tl; Marvin E Newman 314; Charles C Place 441t; 192clb; Paul Slaughter 496tl; Weinberg-Clark 422tl; Image Works: Lisa Law 424–5c; Impact: Mike McQueen 193t; Kirk Irwin: 16b, 187t, 208c, 208b, 281b, 429, 586–7. Catherine Karnow: 190br; Katz Pictures: Lamoine 166cr; SABA/Steve Starr 21tl, /Lara Jo Regan 65bl; Robert E Kennedy Library: Special Collections, California Polytechnic State University 205t; Knott's Berry Farm: 226-227c, 226br, 227br; Kobal Collection: Sabrina, © 1995 Paramount/Brian Hamill 65tr; LA Story, Guild Film Distribution 65cla, The Big Sleep, Warner Bros 75b; The Wild One, Columbia Pictures 190bl. LA Convention and Visitors' Bureau: Michele & Tom Grimm 169; LA County Museum of art: La Trahison des Images (Ceci n'est pas une pipe), René Magritte, purchased with funds provided by the Mr & Mrs William Preston Harrison Collection, 66t; In the Woods at Giverny: Blanche Hoschedé at Her Easel with Suzanne Hoschedé Reading, Claude Monet, Mr & Mrs George Gard De Sylva Collection 110t; Mother About to Wash Her Sleepy Child, Mary Cassatt, Mrs Fred Hathaway Bixby Bequest 110cla; Flower Day, Diego Rivera, LA County Fund 110c; Mulholland Drive: The Road to the Studio, David Hockney, purchased with funds provided by the F Patrick Burnes Bequest 111t; Plate, purchased with funds provided by the Art Museum Council 111cr; Standing Warrior (The King), The Proctor Stafford Collection, purchased with funds provided by Mr and Mrs Allen C Balch 112tl; Magdalen with the Smoking Flame, Georges de La Tour, gift of The Ahmanson Foundation 112tr; Monument to Honoré de Balzac, Auguste Rodin, gift of B Gerald Cantor; 112c; The Cotton

Pickers, Winslow Homer, Acquisition made possible by museum trustees 112b; Pair of Officials, China, 618–907, Gift of Leon Lidow 113t; Dunes, Oceano, Edward Weston, © 1981 Center for Creative Photography, Arizona Board of Regents 113b; LA Department of Water and Power: 48clb, 192b; LA Dodgers Inc: 148b; Jack London Collection: California State Parks 22b. Magnes Museum Permanent Collections: 19th-century blue velvet embroidery brocade robe, 403t; Magnum Photos: Michael Nichols 53tl; Marine World Africa USA: Charlotte Fiorito 288tr; Andrew McKinney Photography: 43cl, 290tl, 290tr, 291cr, 292tr, 293tr, 293br, 297cr, 297bc, 303crb, 321t, 336c, 359b, 371bl, 398t; Metropolitan Transit Development Board, San Diego: Stephen Simpson 256cla; Metropolitan Water District of Southern California: 192c; Robert Mondavi Winery: 446br; John Muir National Historic Site: National Park Service 398b; Museum of Television and Radio: Grant Mudford 86t. The Names Project: AIDS Memorial Quilt © 1988 Matt Herron 53tr; The National Motor Museum, Beaulieu: 191bl; Peter Newark's American Pictures: 43br, 44br, 191tl, 293crb; Peter Newark's Western Americana: 44cla, 44bl, 44–5c, 185 (inset), 243br, 285 (inset), 417 (inset), 503 (inset), 587 (inset); NHPA: Joe Blossom 77tr; Rich Kirchner 35t, 444c; Stephen Krasemann 487cra; P McDonald 232b; David Middleton 420t, 432t; Kevin Schafer 420b; John Shaw 209b, 220b, 269t, 420cl, 475c; Roger Tidman 231b; New York Public Library: I N Phelps Stokes Collection, Miriam and Ira D Wallach Division of Art, Prints and Photographs, The New York Public Library, Astor, Lenox and Tilden Foundations 44clb; The Norton Simon Foundation, Pasadena: Still Life with Lemons, Oranges and a Rose, Francisco de Zurbaran (1633) 152b; Buddha Enthroned, Kashmir, India (8th century) 153b; Woman with a Book, Pablo Picasso (1832), Estate of Robert Ellis Simon, 1969, 152t; Saints Paul and Frediano, Filippino Lippi (1483) 153t; Self-Portrait, Rembrandt van Rijn (c.1636–38) 152c; The Little Fourteen-Year-Old Dancer, Edgar Degas (1878–81) 153bc. Courtesy of the Oakland Museum of California: Yosemite Valley, Albert Bierstadt (1868) 8–9; Figure on a Porch, Richard Diebenkorn (1959) 24cl; Afternoon in Piedmont, Xavier Tizoc Martinez (c.1911) 24br; California Venus, Rupert Schmid (c.1895) 25c; The Oakland Museum History Department: 20bl, 39b, 40cla, 40–1cb (2), 41cla, 43cr, 45ca, 45crb, 46tl, 48tr, 49cb, 52cla, 52bl, 369br, 408tl, 408tr, 408b, 409t, 425t; The Oakland Museum Kahn Collection 459b; The Oakland Tribune Collection, Gift of Alameda Newspaper Group 50b, 424cl, 424b; Oxford Scientific Films: Daniel J Cox 421ca; Michael Fogden 480c; Stan Osolinski 421cr. Pasadena Convention and Visitors' Bureau: 150b; Richard Pfeiffer: 21tr, 26t, 26b, 27b, 59bl, 68t, 69tl, 84, 85, 86b, 87c, 116, 118cl, 128cla, 128b,129t, 129c, 129b, 136, 137, 145t, 539b; Photo Network: Mary Messenger 584b; Phyllis Picardi 191br; Woodard 32b; Photophile: 30b, 57t, 186c, 234; Jose Carrillo 33b; Scott Crain 14c; Arthur Fox 578t; Mark Gibson 583b;

Jim Gray 187b; Michael Hall 64tr, 162t; Matt Lindsay 17b, 33c, 256b, 257b, 600c; Sal Maimone 123bl, 167, 186b, 242br, 418b, 506c; LLT Rhodes 42tl; PHOTO TREK INC: M J Wickham 418cb; PICTOR INTERNATIONAL–LONDON: 54–5, 58t, 58bl, 58br, 190tr, 226bl; 276–7, 282b, 289tl, 450, 482, 497t; PICTORIAL PRESS LTD: J Cummings 53cra, 349b; PICTURES COLOUR LIBRARY: 18t, 35bl, 70, 119t; Leo de Wys 577c; POPPERFOTO: 500t. PRESIDIO OF SAN FRANCISCO: NPS staff photos 367tl, 367cra, 367br; RETNA PICTURES LTD: LGI Photo Agency/Marco Shark 23br; Steve Granite 65t; REX FEATURES: 350b; RIVERSIDE MUNICIPAL MUSEUM: Chris Moser 40cr. SALINAS PUBLIC LIBRARY: Courtesy of the Steinbeck Archives, 23t, 501b; SAN FRANCISCO ART INSTITUTE: D Wakely 296c (d), 331t; SAN FRANCISCO CABLE CAR MUSEUM: 293tl, 293bl; SAN FRANCISCO CONVENTION AND VISITORS' BUREAU: 35br, Mark Gibson 292c; Courtesy of Brown, Zukov & Associates 372t; SAN FRANCISCO MUSEUM OF MODERN ART: *Back View*, 1977, Philip Guston, oil on canvas, gift of the artist, 295cr; *Zip-Light*, 1990, Sigmar Willnauer, leather, polyester, zipper, SFMOMA purchase, 308tl; *Aerial Gyrations*, 1953, Charles Sheeler, oil on canvas, Mrs Manfred Bransten Special Fund purchase, 308tr; *Les Valeurs Personnelles*, 1952, by Rene Magritte, purchased through a gift of Phyllis Wattis 308tr; No. 14, 1960 by Mark Rothko 308c; *Nearly Hit*, 1928, Paul Klee, oil on board, Albert M Bender Bequest Fund purchase 308c; PM Magazine, 1982, Dara Birnbaum, video installation, Accessions Committee Fund and purchased by a gift of Rena Bransten, 308b; *Melodious Double Stops*, 1980, Richard Shaw, porcelain with decal overglaze, purchased with funds from the National Endowment for the Arts and Frank O Hamilton, Byron Meyer and Mrs Peter Schlesinger, 309tl; *Untitled (Elsa Schiaparelli)* c.1933, by Man Ray, gelatin silver print, The Helen Crocker Family Funds Purchase, 309cra; *The Nest*, 1994, by Louis Bourgeois, steel; Points of Departure: Connecting with Contemporary Art, March 23-August 7, 2001 309cra; *The Flower Carrier*, 1935, by Diego Rivera, oil and tempera on masonite, Albert M Bender Collection, gift of Albert M Bender in memory of Caroline Walter, 309crb; *Country Dog Gentlemen*, 1972, by Roy De Forest, polymer on canvas, gift of the Hamilton-Wells Collection, 309b; *Orange Sweater*, 1955, by Elmer Bischoff, oil on canvas, gift of Mr and Mrs Mark Schorer, 313cr; SAN FRANCISCO PUBLIC LIBRARY HISTORY ROOM: 50cla, 329bla, 359c; SAN MATEO COUNTY HISTORICAL ASSOCIATION: 396t; SANTA BARBARA MISSION ARCHIVE LIBRARY: 42cl, 43tl; SANTA BARBARA MUSEUM OF ART: *The Ripened Wheat*, Jules Bastien-Lepage (1884),

Museum purchase with funds provided by Suzette and Eugene Davidson and the Davidson Endowment Fund 210cl; SCIENCE PHOTO LIBRARY: NASA 274c; George Bernard 412b; Simon Fraser 14t; David Parker 20t; Peter Menzel 20cr, 489b; SONOMA VALLEY VISITORS' BUREAU: Bob Nixon 449b; SOUTHWEST MUSEUM: ID CT.122, Photo by Don Meyer (491.G.-802) 67tr; SPECTRUM COLOUR LIBRARY: 2–3, 190tl, 255tl, 456tr, 493t, 576b; D&J Heaton 334, 538t; STANFORD UNIVERSITY ARCHIVES: Department of Special Collections, 47b; STEVENSON HOUSE COLLECTION, MONTEREY STATE HISTORIC PARK: Sharon Fong 492t, 493cr, 493b TONY STONE IMAGES: 34b, 397crb, 418t, 468; Jerry Alexander 447t; Glen Allison 354; Ken Biggs 32t, 59tl, 168c; James Blank 139; David Carriere 578r; Jim Corwin 300; Chad Ehlers 59tr; Johan Elzenga 270, 273, 280t, 282t; David R Frazier 426; Roy Giles, 324cla; Lorentz Gullachsen 15t; Gavin Hellier 478t; John Lamb 322; D C Lowe 471t; David Madison 577t; David Maisel 288b; Ed Pritchard 284–5; A&L Sinibaldi 15br, 419cr; Alan Smith 205b; Larry Ulrich 427; John Warden 434–5; LEVI STRAUSS & CO: 333cr, 333b; TIM STREET-PORTER: 28b, 29b, 68bl. TATE GALLERY LONDON: *It's a Psychological Fact that Pleasure helps your Disposition*, 1948, Eduardo Paolozzi 50–1c; TELEGRAPH COLOUR LIBRARY: 11, 14b; EDWARD THOMAS PHOTOGRAPHY: 28t. TRAVELPIX: Robert Holmes 600tr; ULSTER MUSEUM, BELFAST: By kind permission of the Trustees 41cl; © 2000 UNIVERSAL STUDIOS INC 143b, 144tl, 144cr, 145tr, 145bl; © 2001 UNIVERSAL STUDIOS INC 144cl; © 1999 UNIVERSAL STUDIOS INC All Rights Resrved 144br; BY COURTESY OF THE US POSTAL SERVICE: 588t; Stamp Designs © 1995, 307c, 597t. WELLS FARGO BANK: 45bl, 302b, 304b, 463b; WORLD PICTURES: 12, 13b, 17t, 30c, 64tl, 132–3, 143c, 165, 166b, 189t, 216, 394, 582c, 601. YOSEMITE MUSEUM: National Park Service 40tl, 40cra, Craig & Jennifer Bates 40cl; Michael Dixon 40clb; YOSEMITE NATIONAL PARK RESEARCH LIBRARY: 47ca. ZEFA PICTURES: 1, 35c, 422cla, 476–7; Damm 602t; BILL ZELDIS PHOTOGRAPHY: 38; ZEUM: 312clb; ZOOLOGICAL SOCIETY OF SAN DIEGO: 249b. Jacket: All images special photography except ROBERT HARDING PICTURE LIBRARY: Adrian Nevil front 1; PICTURES COLOUR LIBRARY: front t; TONY STONE IMAGES: front cra. All other images © Dorling Kindersley. See www.DKimages.com for more information.

JACKET

Front - DK PICTURE LIBRARY: Trevor Hill cb; Neil Lukas clb; Neil Setchfield bl; GETTY IMAGES: Richard Price main image. Back - DK PICTURE LIBRARY: Max Alexander t; WORLD PICTURES: Stuart Pearce b. Spine - GETTY IMAGES: Richard Price.

Road Map of California

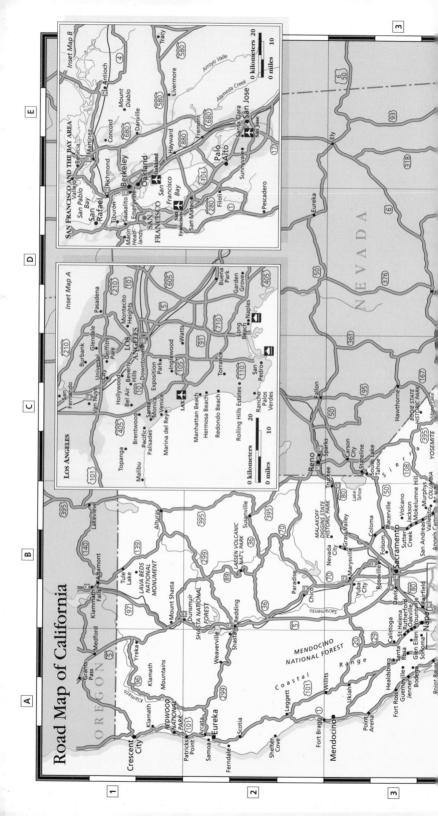

Inset Map A

LOS ANGELES

0 kilometers 10 20
0 miles 10

Inset Map B

SAN FRANCISCO AND THE BAY AREA

0 kilometers 10 20
0 miles 10